DAVE MARSH

AND

JAMES BERNARD

A FIRESIDE BOOK
PUBLISHED BY
SIMON & SCHUSTER
New York   London   Toronto
Sydney   Tokyo   Singapore

The New Book of Rock Lists

FIRESIDE
Rockefeller Center
1230 Avenue of the Americas
New York, New York 10020

Copyright © 1981 by Duke and Duchess Ventures, Inc., and Heaven
Research, Inc.

Revised edition Copyright © 1994 Duke & Duchess Ventures, Inc., and
James Bernard.

First Fireside Edition 1994

FIRESIDE and colophon are registered trademarks of
Simon & Schuster Inc.

Designed by Hyun Joo Kim
Manufactured in the United States of America

1   3   5   7   9   10   8   6   4   2

Library of Congress Cataloging-in-Publication Data is available.

ISBN 0-671-78700-4

Song Lyric Credits:
"Brown Eyed Girl" by Van Morrison, © 1967 Web IV Music Co.
"Don't Pass Me By" by Ringo Starr, © 1968 Nida Music Publishing Co.
"Double Shot of My Baby's Love" by Vetter & Smith, © 1966 Windsong
   Music Co.
"Greenback Dollar" by Fred Fisher, © 1963 Davon Music Co.
"Hold On, I'm Comin' " by David Porter & Isaac Hayes, © 1966 East
   Memphis Music Corp. and Cotillion Music Inc.
"I Hear Voices" by Screamin' Jay Hawkins, © 1962 Rightsong Music Co.
"Locomotive Breath" by Ian Anderson, © 1971 Chrysalis Music Corp.
"Mamacita" by Clint Ballard, Jr., & Larry Kusik, © 1975 Bourne Co.
"Miracles" by Marty Balin, © 1968 Diamond Music Co.
"Money" by Roger Waters, © 1973 Hampshire House Publishing Corp.
"The Out Crowd" by A. Resnick & D. Young, © 1965 T. M. Music Inc.
"Rhapsody in the Rain" by Christie & Herbert, © 1966 Rambed Music
   Publishing Co.
"Walk on the Wild Side" by Lou Reed, © 1972 Oakfield Avenue Music Co.
"(Angels Wanna) Wear My Red Shoes" by Elvis Costello, © 1977 Street
   Music Co.
"You Look Good in Blue" by Jimmy Destri, © 1976 Jiru Music Co./Monster
   Island Music Co.
"Glass Onion" by Paul McCartney and John Lennon, © 1968 Maclen Music
   Co.
"The Ten Commandments of Love" Words & Music by M. Paul, © 1958,
   1981 Arc Music Corp., New York. Used by Permission.

TO CURTIS MAYFIELD
Hero, inspiration, teller of the *whole* tale

"Shall I tell it like it is?
Ain't none o' your business.
Yes it is.
So let me use the so-called right of my opinion."

—*The Young Mod's Forgotten Story*

Acknowledgments

There are many people whose contributions to *The New Book of Rock Lists* were invaluable. Minya Oh stayed with this project from the beginning and to call her an intern would be an insult. Her clutch plays in the way of research and tireless brainstorming always seemed to come at the right time. We'd also like to thank Reginald C. Dennis of *The Source* for allowing us to tap into his encyclopedic knowledge of hip-hop. Under the leadership of David Mills, the staff of *Uncut Funk* explore the outer limits of P-Funkdom in several places throughout the book. Larry Flick offered up a fascinating set of lists pertaining to dance music. *Billboard* is lucky to have him. *RIP*'s Katherine Turman was helpful for her metal-related input, and Brian Keizer's twin obsessions with both the Rolling Stones and postpunk culture made an indelible mark on these pages. Greil Marcus, Steve Leeds, the inestimable Lee Ballinger, Phyllis Pollack, and especially Steve Propes all came through brilliantly in the clutch with expertise ranging from the influence of Bob Dylan to the ways in which record collectors rip each other off. We thank them for the loan of everything from their experience in the record-plugging mills and the bar bands to the high seas off Vietnam and the battle against Tipper and her clan. And, last but not least, we have to give a shout out to the lads from Lawrenceville (Kansas)— Danny Alexander and David Cantwell, along with Billy Chin, Doris Saltkill, and James McGraw—whose collective knowledge of arcane band names will probably get them arrested one day. Sandy Choron, our agent, lives up to that old gospel-soul message: "Stand By Me." She does this through thick and thin. David Dunton, our editor, not only figured out which keyboardists we almost forgot but made an arduous task a good deal more fun. We thank them both for their assistance, support, and belief in what we're up to. Only Barbara Carr and Jennifer Fleming put up with more, for which we thank them even when we're making them grit their teeth.

Contents

Ridiculous Debut Singles • The 10 Most Disappointing Debut Albums • Famous Turn-Downs • Performers Discovered by John Hammond • Performers Discovered by Sam Phillips • Run-D.M.C.'s Famous Firsts

CHAPTER EIGHT: CRITICISM
Discredited Rock Theories • Frank Zappa's Favorite Rock Critics • The Least Promising Interview Openers Cameron Crowe Has Encountered • From the Page to the Stage—And Back: Performers and Producers Who Have Also Been Critics and Journalists • "When I Get My Picture on the Cover of the *Rolling Stone*": Most Frequent Appearances on the Magazine's Cover • Most Appearances on the Cover of *16 Magazine* • 28 Songs About the Beatles • We Can Work It Out: Musical Comments on the Beatles' Breakup • Bob Dylan's 25 Greatest Hits • Reginald C. Dennis's Favorite Songs of All Time • Critics' Pets: Artists Critics Believe Can Do No Wrong • Sez Who?: Bands and Singers Critics Love to Hate • What About Us? Musicmakers Critics Mistakenly Ignore

CHAPTER NINE: ART
Most Beautiful Record Labels • 75 Great Album Cover Designs • You Can't Judge A Record by Its Cover: 10 Great Sleeves You Wouldn't Want to Open • Pedro Bell's Favorite Album Covers of All Time (in Alphabetical Order) • Lester Bangs Selects the Worst LP Covers of All Time by Major Rock Artists • Arty Rockers • Faces on the Cover of *Sgt. Pepper's Lonely Hearts Club Band* • Peter Wolf Lists His Favorite Rock and Roll Artists • Famous Musicians Who Have Appeared on U.S. Postage Stamps • "Hey, Mate, Pass Me the Brush": The Dreaded British Art School Connection • Art School Groups • Who Made Who? Artists and the Bands that Helped to Make Their Names • 15 Great Psychedelic Poster Artists • Devo's Favorite Modern Conveniences • Best Rock Photographers

CHAPTER TEN: FILM
Best Rock and Rap Movies • Worst Rock and Rap Movies • Best Unreleased Rock Films • Who Cares What Picture We See? The 15 Best Songs About the Movies • 40 Songs Based on Film Titles • Beyond *The Big Chill:* The 25 Best Movie Soundtracks • Best Film Appearances by Rock and Rap Performers • Worst Film Appearances by Rock and Rap Performers • Performers Who Appeared at Woodstock But Not in the Movie • Rock Performers Who Appear in The Rolling Stones' "Rock and Roll Circus"

CHAPTER ELEVEN: BROADCASTING
Can't Live Without It? The Best Songs About Radio • Radio DJs Who Became Performers • Fabled British Pirate Radio Stations • L.A.'s Top 100 Radio Hits, 1956–1979 • KNAC's Top 75 Songs •

Nothin' On? 20 Songs About TV • 20 Great TV Themes Based on Rock, Country, and Soul • The 20 Best Rock TV Shows • The 10 Worst Rock TV Shows • Performers Who Made Their TV Debuts on *American Bandstand* • Eight Is Enough: Rock'n'Rap Cartoon Shows • Alice Cooper's 10 Favorite TV Shows • Musical Guests on *Saturday Night Live*, 1976–92 • Doing the Bartman: A Dozen Rockers Do *The Simpsons* • Reginald C. Dennis selects the Harshest Disses on Video • 10 Best Things About MTV • 10 Worst Things About MTV • Millicent Shelton Picks the 12 Best Music Videos • Katherine Turman Picks the 10 Best Metal Videos • MTV's First 5 Veejays • 12 Key Figures in the Founding of MTV, 1981–82

CHAPTER TWELVE: LITERATURE
Biblical Characters Who Appeared in Bob Dylan's Songs *Before* He Became a Christian • Rock and Rap Music Based on Literature, Fairy Tales, Nursery Rhymes, and Comix • Most Profound Rock Lyrics—Sorta . . . • What You Talkin' 'Bout? Outrageous House Song Titles or Lyrics • Harshest Disses on Wax • The Rock and Roll Library: Best Rock Books • Is There A CD in the Cliff's Notes? Best Pop Music Fiction, selected by Greil Marcus • The *Real* Rock Bottom Remainders: Worst Rock Books • And Then I Wrote . . . 25 Musicians Who Are Also Authors • Author! Author! Rockers Who Should Write Books • Buckle Down! Rockers Who Should *Read* Books • Loosen Up! Rockers Who Should Read Fewer Books • "We Play Music as Well as Metallica Writes Novels": The Rock Bottom Remainders • Truman Capote's 10 Favorite Rock Performers • Best Liner Notes • Worst Liner Notes • Mike Callahan's "Rock and Roll Soap Opera": 20 Tragic Tales • Every Day I Sing the Book

CHAPTER THIRTEEN: FASHION
Stylin' and Profilin': The Rock 'n' Rap Wardrobe • *The Source* Magazine's Hip-Hop Fashion Do's and Don'ts • Music Stars Who Have Made Mr. Blackwell's Worst-Dressed List • Music Stars Who Have Made Mr. Blackwell's "Fabulous Fashion Independents" List • Rockers with Items in the Hard Rock Café • 20 Groups Known for Their Costumes • Fashion Accessories for the Serious Funkadelic Clone • 25 Known for Their Hats • Back in Black • Five with Famous Leather Jackets • Did It Hurt? Cool Tattoos • Best Hair • Known for Their Long Hair • Bald (by Choice or by Nature) • Four Eyes • Best Groomed • 15 Tall Ones • 18 Short Ones • Best Rap Songs About Butts

CHAPTER FOURTEEN: HISTORY
Rock and Roll Celebrates Itself: Great Songs About the Birth, Death, Power, and Endurance of Rock and Roll • Rappers Celebrate Themselves • Broadway and Tin Pan Alley Standards that Have Been Converted to Rock and R&B • Rick Whitesell's Prehistoric

Chapter Twenty-one: LIFE—REAL AND SURREAL

CHAPTER TWENTY-TWO: POLITICS

Enemies List • Fake Friends • Rap Haters • Tragedy, the Intelligent Hoodlum, Lists the 10 Best Rap Songs that Dis the Government and Politicians • Tragedy, the Intelligent Hoodlum, Lists the 10 Best Rap Songs that Dis the Police • Shot Down in Flames: 5 Songs About Police that Never Came Out Due to the "Cop Killer" Controversy • Greatest Fifties Protest Songs • Greatest Sixties Protest Songs • Greatest Seventies Protest Songs • Greatest Eighties Protest Songs • Greatest Nineties Protest Songs • Apocalypse Now: Songs of Nuclear Anxiety • Musicians United for Safe Energy: Performers at the MUSE Concerts for a Non-Nuclear Future, Madison Square Garden, September 19–24, 1979 • The Antiwar Top 40 • Lee Ballinger Picks the 10 Best Antiwar Records • Performers Whose Careers Were Damaged by Their Politics • The Staff of *Uncut Funk* Picks the Most Significant Overt Political Statements by the P-Funk Mob • Right-Wingers • Riding a Stairway to Perdition: Records Accused of Satanic Backmasking • The Most Diabolical Song of All Time: Great Versions of "Stagger Lee" (aka "Stackolee," "Stack-A-Lee," etc: The Bad-Man Ballad of the Century) • 25 Famous Censorship Cases • Phyllis Pollack Picks the 10 Best Songs that Dis Tipper Gore • Best Songs to Pass the Censor • The Most Controversial Record Covers • Controversial Advertising Campaigns • Tipper Gore's Favorite Records

CHAPTER TWENTY-THREE: DRUGS, DEATH, AND ROCK 'N' RAP

25 Pieces of Evidence Proving that Paul McCartney Is Dead • Death Songs • Songs About Suicide • Three Dozen Musical Murders • 10 Bob Dylan Songs About Death and Dying • 10 Bruce Springsteen Songs About Death and Dying • The Johnny Ace Memorial Lists • Most Spectacular Deaths • Rock and Roll Heaven: A List of Probable Inductees • Rock and Roll Hell: A List of Probable Inductees • Ted Bundy's Top 5: Best Songs About Mass Murderers • King Heroin • White-Line Fever • Reefer Madness • Have a Drink On Us • Antidrug Top 15 • White Light, White Heat: Former Heroin Users • Down on Drugs • Drugs Prescribed to Elvis by His Pal, Dr. Nick • Top Songs About Selling Crack

CHAPTER TWENTY-FOUR: BORN TO BE WILD

Nick Cohn Picks Rock's "The Good, The Baaad and the Ugly" of The Fifties, Sixties, and Seventies • Paul Burlison Lists the 5 Wildest Rock and Roll Cats of the 1950s • Jim Morrison's Arrest Record • Slammer Blues • In the County It's a Party 'Cause You Know Everybody: Artists Who've Done Time • Famous Busts • Jailbait • Performers Who Reached Stardom Before Turning 18 • 10 Famous Bubblegum Groups • Post-Punk Teendom's Greatest Hits • We Got the Beat: The Greatest Songs About Masturbation • 20 Punk

Introduction

When Cornwallis surrendered to Washington at Yorktown, the British band played "The World Turned Upside Down." We never listened to that song as we assembled *The New Book of Rock Lists*, but that's a good description of what we found.

Quite accidentally, *The Book of Rock Lists* appeared on the cusp of the most important changes popular music had seen since the advent of rock 'n' roll. By 1981, the rotting corpse of punk and the fading ghosts of disco had begun providing the compost from which alternative rock and the hip-hop culture bloomed. The socially moribund seventies gave way to ten years of social activism, which took every form from teary-eyed charity to steely-gazed militance. The old hippie-derived dishabille in which the principle stylistic distinction between country-rockers and (American) punks came down to the selection of Sta-prest blue jeans versus torn black Levis erupted in a rare (for the U.S.) fashion riot. Virtually subterranean streams born in the previous period—P-Funk's psychedelic R&B and Kiss's glamorized metal, especially—now loomed as centerpoints of an entire aesthetic.

Three years after the original *Book of Rock Lists* appeared, in the summer of 1984, pop radio exploded into one last brilliant summer of glory, which incorporated Madonna, Prince, Bruce, "Girls Just Want to Have Fun," what seems to have been the last heyday of British pop, and eeentsy hip-hop intrusions. Meantime, pop radio, long the dominant disseminator of the music we boldly call "ours," found itself displaced by the new monster called MTV and its various offshoots and imitators. (All hail The Box!) Since then, no coherent picture of the whole pop world has been possible. If you're capable of *conceiving* of such a picture, you're marked as a remnant of the old order.

So *The New Book of Rock Lists* quite cheerfully and gladly presents an incoherent picture, in which the biases of the authors (and our collaborators) dictate what's important as well as what's invisible. What we've established is a vast playground, located in a community with deep roots and a hopeful future, with elastic boundaries and grouchy antagonisms (intended and otherwise). It's the playground of a polyglot community, which refuses to recognize hip-hop, rock 'n' roll, heavy metal, grunge, "alternative," punk, and the rest as anything other than the colors of the various gangs that play there.

What we love best about the place is the racket just short of a riot that these various gangs make as they clang into one another.

In our version of this playground, *nobody* is excluded—although everybody entering the gates risks being ridiculed, parodied, mocked, and generally dissed. In some ways, that might be considered our community's major sport. This is our—and your—chance to play.

Which just means that trivia—even trivia—takes the shape of its time. If in the course of reading what we've compiled, you happen to find some of these lists enlightening, or even educational, as well as entertaining, don't blame us, just take some pride in yourself for being smart enough to notice what we've tried to keep well hidden.

—Dave Marsh and James Bernard

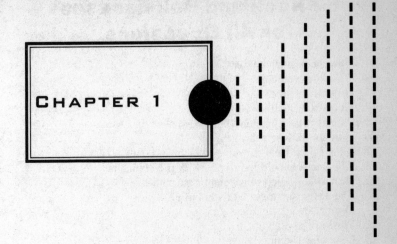

CHAPTER 1

Wisdom

Irv Zuckerman's List of 50 Rock and Roll Excuses for All Occasions

1. The check is in the mail
2. He's in a meeting.
3. He's out to lunch.
4. He's got two calls waiting.
5. I'll call you on Monday.
6. Hold on for just a second.
7. I'll get right back to you.
8. The check should have been with the contracts.
9. He was supposed to get right back to me.
10. I've never met a girl like you before.
11. Didn't you get my message?
12. I lost my pass.
13. Of course I remember you.
14. We'll make it up to you next time.
15. Your name's on the list.
16. The mail must really be screwed up.
17. If only the album had come out sooner.
18. There's been a ton of shows in the market.
19. The record company is totally supporting this.
20. We're definitely buying strong support for the tour.
21. There's none in town.
22. It wasn't in the deal.
23. It's a last-minute town.
24. It's the best album they ever made.
25. That's what everyone's paying.
26. Didn't you get the new rider?
27. They're going into ARBs.[1]
28. They're just coming out of ARBs.
29. They said we're getting the bullet back next week.
30. He said it's in heavy rotation.
31. Of course you'll get a completed contract before the gig.
32. Of course they'll do interviews.
33. Our set never runs over.
34. There are T-shirts for everyone.
35. These jackets run really small.
36. The hall sounds a lot better when the kids are inside.
37. It sounds great out front.
38. You should see 'em live.
39. They said they don't have much equipment.
40. But they're huge in England.

41. It's an easy load-in.
42. They sound much better with the new singer.
43. They never do sound checks.
44. There's plenty of power.
45. He swore he'd bring back the limo in five minutes.
46. Nobody reads the reviews anyway.
47. We're losing on the sound and lights.
48. There's no place open this late.
49. They always do it this way.
50. It's a union rule.

Irv Zuckerman is the leading concert promoter in St. Louis and Kansas City. He has also been involved in personal management, most notably with Head East. This list originally appeared as an advertisement in Performance Magazine *and was compiled by Zuckerman, Steve Schankman, and Steve Litman.*

---

[1] ARB is a radio rating service, similar to television's Nielsen ratings. During weeks when the rating samples are taken, radio stations pull all kinds of stunts and rarely risk playing unheard music; these weeks are commonly known as ARBs.

Cub Koda's 10 Rules of Rock and Roll

1. The best gig in the world is a packed bar on a Friday night. Reason: Everybody gets paid and everybody wants to get laid. Any band that can't go over on a Friday night should be shot.
2. Rock and roll operates on the beat of the Geedus. Put the money in the Cubmaster's hand and the Cub will rock (that is, no Geedus, no rockus).
3. There is a difference between rock and rock and roll; beware of inferior imitations (avoid contact with any musician who doesn't know how to play Chuck Berry music).
4. Junk food will keep you alive on the road: Eat at White Castle and Krystal's as often as possible.
5. When you're out of Schmuzz, you're out of buzz, a day without Schmuzz is like a day without rock and roll.
6. Don't believe everything written about you. (Especially avoid fat, cigar-chewing record execs who keep telling you you're a genius: These guys never pay up.)
7. When you've got it to spend, everybody's your friend: If you're gonna blow all your money, at least leave a beautiful corpse.
8. Rock and roll musicians are the Men of the Great Indoors; avoid sunlight whenever possible and develop your moon tan.

9. Never give a roadie anything of value. (I have a large box of toothpicks in my kitchen cupboard that used to be a Les Paul.)
10. In the world of rock and roll, some gigs go fantastically, some are total crap. My best advice to young rock and rollers who find themselves in a crappy situation is to stare at the ceiling and scream at the top of their lungs, "Please, Reverend Jim, more Kool-Aid!"

Singer, guitarist, and songwriter Cub Koda made his mark on the rock and roll charts with Brownsville Station, most notably with "Smokin' in the Boy's Room." A consummate record collector and author of the column "The Vinyl Junkie" in Goldmine *magazine, he has recorded several fine solo albums, including two containing nothing but tunes by his boyhood (and adulthood) idols,* Cub Plays Chuck *and* Cub Plays Bo.

Robert Hunter's 10 Commandments of Rock and Roll

1. Suck up to the top cats.
2. Do not express independent opinions.
3. Do not work for common interests, only factional interests.
4. If there's nothing to complain about, dig up some old gripe.
5. Do not respect property or persons other than band property or personnel.
6. Make devastating judgments about persons and situations without adequate information.
7. Discourage and confound personal, technical, and/or creative projects.
8. Single out absent persons for intense criticism.
9. Remember that anything you don't understand is trying to fuck with you.
10. Destroy yourself physically and mentally and insist that all true brothers do likewise as an expression of unity.

Robert Hunter is a longtime lyricist for the Grateful Dead and has made several solo recordings.

15 Quotations from Chairman Townshend

1. "People say, 'You've gotta go on, man, otherwise all those kids, they'll be finished, they'll have nothing to live for.' That's rock and roll!"
2. "Rock and roll is all that counts, I'll tell you, in ten years, you'll know. 'Cause ten years are past and we know."
3. "I think the thing really is that there's a certain honor attached to it because of the fact that rock has said: 'We will do it right. You've done it all wrong. We will do it right. We will show you that not only can we write a song like "My Generation," where we write off the Establishment, where we write off the politicians, where we write off the group, but we write off the whole lot of you! We'll get it right.' "
4. "I am not a leader. Neither yours nor anyone else's. I am a rock musician, a mirror. You see yourself when you see the Who."
5. "Pop has become solemn, irrelevant, and boring. What it needs now is more noise, more size, more sex, more violence, more gimmickry, more vulgarity. Above all, it desperately needs a new messiah who will take things right back to the glamour, power, and insanity of the Elvis Presley age."
6. "I wrote the lines of 'My Generation' without thinking, hurrying them—scribbling them on a piece of paper in the back of a car. For years I've had to live by them, waiting for the day when someone says, 'I thought you said you hoped you'd die when you got old. Well, now you are old. What now?' Of course, most people are too polite to say that sort of thing to a dying pop star. I say it often to myself."
7. "I realized that the only way I was ever going to fit into society and have a role was with the guitar."
8. "Let's face it, you can't worship a guy for destroying an instrument in the name of rock."
9. "I think that without having the stage and the guitar—the weapon of the guitar—I don't think I would have gone on."
10. "I smash guitars because I like them."
11. "I think you should keep on playing rock for as long as you have an axe to grind, and if you haven't got an axe to grind, you should go into cabaret."
12. "Rock is art and a million other things as well: It's an indescribable form of communication and entertainment combined, and it's a two-way thing with very complex but real feedback processes."
13. "Sometimes I really do believe that we're the only rock band

on the face of this planet that knows what rock and roll is all about."

14. "Quite simply, I feel that The Stones are the world's best rock and roll band."

15. "Audiences are very much like the kids at Tommy's Holiday Camp. They want something without working for it."

Pete Townshend has been rock's Supreme Pontiff (or at least Pontificator, no matter what Bono thinks) since writing "My Generation" in 1965. These are only the cream of his many critical pronouncements and outlines of rock philosophy. His particular blend of wit 'n' wisdom now adorns the Broadway stage nightly, in the Tony-winning shape of The Who's "Tommy."

Outside Is America, Listening to Bono Prattle

"We've been telling him to shut up for ages, but he finally needed to pay someone to tell him"—Adam Curry on sending U2's lead singer to the doctor, 1983.

1. "People can see through pretend—if a band can't do it for real, then people shouldn't go see them. Emotion is everything."

2. "I think the chances of succeeding . . . success are pretty slim. I mean, surviving success with a sense of humor, for instance."

3. "As a lyric writer, I'm more interested in people than politics, and more interested in why people should want to hit each over the head with a broken bottle rather than where they do it."

4. "The lyrics are like a puzzle to me, because on *October*, I didn't know what I was saying a lot of the time."

5. "I'm really not into movements, myself. I'm into a movement of one."

6. "If you want to be on this stage, then you must do what I'm doing!"

7. "We feel as close to the people back there as the ones up here."

8. "I never considered myself a pop star."

9. "We make big music and we can make it in these big places, these tin boxes."

10. "I'm almost a liability to the group because I'm so open. I haven't yet learned how to hold the cards close to my chest. But we really don't take ourselves too seriously, *really*. The music's serious."

11. "People are interested in bridges. I guess I've always been interested in what goes on beneath bridges."

12. "Hey! Let's party. Remember, we're a real serious political group."
13. "You know, not everyone can go off and be Batman and Robin, and right the wrongs."
14. "Let us turn to the sixties and let the music lead the way to justice."
15. "I could go on stage, unzip my pants, and hang my dick out and people would think it was some statement or something."
16. "Without [U2], I wouldn't know where I'd be as a person—I think I'd make a pretty shit bank manager!"
17. To Bob Dylan: "I said, 'Those songs are gonna last forever, Bob.' And he said, 'Your songs are gonna last forever too—the only thing is, no one's gonna be able to play them.' "
18. "I feel we *must* bite the hand that feeds us, even if it's making us fat."
19. "I wouldn't take on the job of making people aware of reality. I'd take on the job of making *myself* aware of reality. Being in a rock and roll band certainly removes you from reality, so it's a full-time job."
20. "People think I've got all the answers when in fact I've just got a whole list of questions."

Source Outside Is America: U2 in the U.S., *Carter Alan (Faber and Faber, 1992).*

"I Am Woman, Hear Me Bleat"
Julianna Hatfield, the World's Least Liberated Female Rocker, Explains the Facts of Life

1. "I have these weird latent misogynist tendencies. A lot of women put themselves in the position where they can play the dependent or the weak person. I think that women should try to be in good shape. Women should be as strong as they can be, because they're naturally weaker."
2. "How many girls other than Bonnie Raitt can play a guitar solo? I can't, you know. I haven't seen any female guitar players that are really anything special."
3. "I want to try something that hasn't been done before. I want to play guitar and sing in a trio. I want it to be heavy and hard."
4. "I'm not a joiner at all. But, in music, it's like you either have to be a feminist or a rock chick; you can't just be an individualist."
5. "I'm like that [obsessed over finding a boyfriend], too, sometimes, and I hate it. I feel that it's my female nature, and I wish

it weren't like that. That's why I try not to get down on girls. They can't help it."

6. "I'm not really worried about exposing too much of myself in the songs, because I change a lot and I change really fast. My point of view changes every few months, so if I expose a lot of myself at one time it won't matter because I'm not gonna feel the same way later."

7. "I can't stand auditioning people. It's so depressing 'cause most people suck. And, um, most people are losers."

8. "No, I don't regret [saying I'm a virgin]. I just try and move on after I do something stupid."

Julianna Hatfield is an inexplicably (or, after this, maybe all too explicably) critically adored singer-songwriter. She actually said all this shit in famous magazines.

Growin' Up
Bruce Springsteen Remembers
a New Jersey Boyhood

1. "When I was growing up, there were two things that were un-popular in my house. One was me, and the other was my gui-tar."

2. "In the third grade a nun stuffed me in a garbage can under her desk because she said that's where I belonged. I also had the distinction of being the only altar boy knocked down by a priest during Mass."

3. "The student body at college tried to get me expelled because I was just too weird for them, I guess."

4. "I didn't even make it to class clown. I had nowhere near that amount of notoriety. I didn't have the flair to be a complete jerk. It was like I didn't exist."

5. "I never got into being discouraged because I never got into hoping . . . I got used to failing. Once you do that, the rest is easy."

6. "They wouldn't let me in the bars because I wouldn't play Top Forty. You should know the New Jersey shore bars, the people who smile at me today wouldn't let me in the places then."

7. "Some of those club owners were crazy. There was one guy, pulled out a gun one night and shot an amplifier. Can you see it? Smoke curling up to the ceiling. Absolutely quiet. And he says, 'I told you to turn it down.' "

8. "When I was eighteen and playing in this bar in California, people would come up to us and say, 'Hey, I really dig you

guys. Where ya from?' And I'd say New Jersey and they'd just go, 'Yech! Ech!' "

9. "Until I realized that rock music was my connection to the rest of the human race, I felt like I was dying, for some reason, and I didn't really know why."

10. "My first guitar was one of the most beautiful sights I'd ever seen in my life. It was a magic scene. There it is. The Guitar. It was real and it stood for something. 'Now you're real.' I had found a way to do everything I wanted to do."

Quotations from Chairman Elvis

1. "I get lonesome sometimes. I get lonesome right in the middle of a crowd."
2. "Rhythm is something you either have or don't have, but when you have it, you have it all over."
3. "I was thinking about a Presley used-car lot."
4. "I know practically every religious song that's ever been written."
5. "When music starts, I gotta move."
6. "Rock and roll music, if you like it, if you feel it, you can't help but move to it. That's what happens to me. I can't help it."
7. "I want to entertain people. That's my whole life—to my last breath."
8. "I wanted to be a singer because I didn't want to sweat."
9. "I don't know anything about music. In my line, you don't have to."
10. "I hope I haven't bored you."

Chrissie Hynde's Advice to Chick Rockers

1. Don't moan about being a chick, refer to feminism or complain about sexist discrimination. We've all been thrown down stairs and fucked about, but no one wants to hear a whining female. Write a loosely disguised song about it instead and clean up ($).
2. Never pretend you know more than you do. If you don't know chord names, refer to the dots. Don't go near the desk unless you plan on becoming an engineer.
3. Make the other band members look and sound good. Bring out the best in them; that's your job. Oh, and you better sound good, too.

4. Do not insist on working with "females"; that's just more b.s. Get the best man for the job. If it happens to be a woman, great —you'll have someone to go to department stores on tour with instead of making one of the road crew go with you.
5. Try not to have a sexual relationship with the band. It always ends in tears.
6. Don't think that sticking your boobs out and trying to look fuckable will help. Remember you're in a rock and roll band. It's not "fuck me," it's "fuck you!"
7. Don't try to compete with the guys; it won't impress anybody. Remember, one of the reasons they like you is because you don't offer yet more competition to the already existing male egos.
8. If you sing, don't "belt" or "screech." No one wants to hear that shit; it sounds "hysterical."
9. Shave your legs, for chrissakes!
10. Don't take advice from people like me. Do your own thing always.

Chrissie Hynde is the Pretenders.

Source: Sire Records press release, May 1994

Blonde Anthology
Madonna on Madonna

1. "If I weren't as talented as I am ambitious, I would be a gross monstrosity."
2. "Manipulating people, that's what I'm good at."
3. "Coming from a big family had something to do with it. There's that competitiveness that you have when there's a whole bunch of you and you want your parents' attention, and you don't want the hand-me-down clothes, you wanna stand out, you wanna be treated special."
4. "I had a very middle-, lower-middle class sort of upbringing, but I identify with people who've had, at some point in their lives, to struggle to survive. It adds another color to your character."
5. "From when I was very young, I just knew that being a girl and being charming in a feminine sort of way could get me a lot of things, and I milked it for everything I could."
6. "When I was a little girl, I wished I were black. All my girl-friends were black."
7. "You know how religion is, guys get to do everything. They get

to be altar boys. They get to stay out late. Take their shirts off in the summer. They get to pee standing up. They get to fuck a lot of girls and not worry about being pregnant. Although that doesn't have anything to do with being religious."

8. "The angriest time in my life—I'd have to say that was in my teen years."
9. "Ever since I was small I wanted to be the girl who stole everybody's heart."
10. "I act out of instinct just like an animal."
11. "I never had any money and I never had any help, and probably having to deal with all that and having to struggle to survive has made me as tough as I am."
12. "I know exactly what I want. If that makes me a bitch, okay!"
13. "I always said I wanted to be famous. I just love all the glamour and the attention."
14. "I used to go out with graffiti writers, but I really lost the zest for writing my name everywhere. Now I have suitors that do it for me."
15. "I don't want people to forget my name. I want everyone to know it. I want everything there is in life and love. I want to reach everyone."
16. "I've always known this was going to happen to me. My success was something that was meant to be."
17. "I wouldn't have turned out the way I was if I didn't have all those good old-fashioned values to rebel against."
18. "It seems like when you're twenty there's more of an opportunity for you to behave childishly and get away with it. When you're thirty, you have to really grow up and get responsible."
19. "It's a great feeling to be powerful. I've been striving for it all my life. I think it's just a quest of every human being—power."
20. "I feel that most gay men are so much more in touch with a certain kind of sensitivity that heterosexual men aren't allowed to be in touch with—their feminine side. Straight men need to be emasculated. . . . Every straight guy should have a man's tongue in his mouth at least once."

Source: Madonna: Blonde Ambition, *by Mark Bego (Harmony Books, 1992).*

Mouthin' Off
Wisdom from the Hip-Hop Nation

1. "There's a ten- to eleven-year block of nonmusicians. That's why all these kids grab samples from the seventies and sixties.

In those days, there were real musicians. What's gonna happen when we get to the year 2000 and people reach back to the music of the eighties and nineties? It will just be the music of the sixties and seventies."—Dr. Dre

2. "In my songs, I don't really speak out about shit that's going on. Okay, so my record's nasty. But come on. I'm surrounded by negativity. If I go make a positive record, it might flop. So here's what I do: I use me something negative to make enough money to do something positive. For this new single I got coming out, I'm gonna give that money away. Might set up a fund to start new businesses."—AMG

3. "We've gotten into a fantasy studio gangsta phase now. There's no integrity to sell a record. If I said, 'Put doo-doo on your head and it would sell records,' they'd do it tomorrow with doo-doo on their heads."—Ced Gee of Ultramagnetic MC's

4. "I think if it wasn't for rap, I'd be in jail or something. I think I'd a murdered something."—Tragedy

5. "I love that hip-hop has become international. I love it when I go to France and hear French hip-hooop groups. I love when I go to England and hear British hip-hop groups. I love to go see hip-hop groups all through Africa. Hip-hop has taken a lot of brothers and sisters who might be doing negative things and have gotten into the rap world to see other people's way of life."—Afrika Bambaataa

6. "There's no such thing as rap music. Rap is a rhyming lyrical form over any kind of music. So long as there's different types of music, rap will always be around. Besides, there will always be people that can't sing."—Fresh Prince

7. "If people paid closer attention in English class when they were talking about literature, if they knew what a good poem or a good short story was, they'd know what a good rap song was."—Mista Lawnge, Black Sheep

8. "Real rap comes from the soul and the mind, from the inner self."—Chuck D

9. "Look at me! I don't have no parents. I was doing all kinds of wrong shit, and I changed my life. I meet girls every day who say they can't get off welfare. Yes, they can. You can get a baby-sitter and get your ass in school. You have the same capacity to understand and learn everything that Donald Trump does."—Ice-T

10. "Rap is like the polio vaccine. At first no one believed in it. Then once they knew it worked, everyone wanted it."—Grand-master Flash

11. "If I roll up in a fat Benz, fat chain on, clothes that are made for me and shit, already these kids are like, 'Yo. This looks too complicated. I can't get to this.' So they don't want to really mess with you. But you come out there with your sweats, your

hat on, your T-shirt, talking junk on the court like everybody else, then it's like, boom! They can talk to you."—Parrish Smith

12. "I think it's sort of outrageous, just a little bit, the way lyrics are now. You never heard James Brown say, 'Ah! Fuck that!' " — Roxanne Shanté

13. "I could never feel lonely because I love me. I think I'm dope, personally. I don't think there's nobody fresher than me. I am my fan. I'm on my own dick."—KRS-One

14. "Rap wasn't made for Middle America. But that's not necessarily saying you have to be from the ghetto or the city to understand it. If you're focused and you have enough awareness of yourself and you have enough interest in different cultures and also in words and music, it's open to everybody."—Pete Nice

15. "Rap's taking over the world. Literally. I don't mean just bumping all other music out of the box. But taking over to the point where everybody in the fucking world, from kids to grownups, will like rap."—Tim Dog

16. "As long as you remain black, you're still gonna be a nigga."—Eazy E

17. "The only thing that is makin' it really difficult for rap music right now is the fact that you can make a video and have a bullshit song come across as good. If there wasn't videos and video shows, there would be a lot of out-of-work motherfuckers, and maybe me too."—L.L. Cool J

18. "The best thing about being a famous rapper is going on stage and saying the same thing night after night and getting paid $8,000, $10,000, or $5,000 each time. And it's so fuckin' easy. My royalty checks alone will make you break your face smiling." —Too Short

19. "On this album, *Ain't No Other*, all I wanted to do was please the audience. I have no messages because I've learned that sometimes people don't take too kindly to rappers preaching to them, so I gave people what they want: fat-ass beats, fat-ass lyrics, and no substance at all."—MC Lyte

20. "Say what you want, but if you get your ass kicked, don't get mad. Suffer the penalties."—Chuck D

Rock and Roll Reflections

1. "Rock and roll motivates. It's the big, gigantic motivator, at least it was for me."—Bruce Springsteen

2. "It's the music that kept us all intact . . . kept us from going crazy. You should have two radios in case one gets broken."—Lou Reed

3. "So, what is it about this rock and roll? Well, it's the thing that shakes you out of your marriage. It's the thing that disarranges your kidneys. It's what kills your liver. It's what sells McDonald's. It's a gathering place."—Iggy Pop

4. "Let's face it, rock and roll is bigger than all of us."—Alan Freed

5. "One nation under a groove."—George Clinton

6. "One title is worth a million lyrics."—Mike Watt, The Minutemen

7. "We like this kind of music. Jazz is strictly for the stay-at-homes."—Buddy Holly

8. "It's not music, it's a disease."—Mitch Miller

9. "We like to look sixteen and bored shitless."—David Johansen, New York Dolls

10. "If I could find a white man who had the Negro sound and Negro feel, I could make a billion dollars."—Sam Phillips, discoverer of Elvis

11. "There's limits on what you can do, if you want to keep your job. You never know who you're going to offend or when the PMRC is gonna come knocking on your door."—Ice-T

12. "Rock and roll is an asylum for emotional imbeciles."—Richard Neville

13. "I'll be damned if it isn't everything we can give or there's no point in existing."—Axl Rose

14. "I want to tell the world how the guy in the filling station feels." —John D. Loudermilk, composer of "Tobacco Road" and other garage rock anthems

15. "Rock and roll is simply an attitude. You don't have to play the greatest guitar."—Johnny Thunders

16. "Three chords and an attitude."—The Rock Bottom Remainders (actually, Stephen King)

17. "Rap is the CNN of young black America."—Chuck D, Public Enemy

18. "The Mersey Sound is the voice of 80,000 crumbling houses and 30,000 people on the dole."—*The Daily Worker*, 1963

19. "Don't forget, the penis is mightier than the sword." —Screamin' Jay Hawkins

20. "Rock and roll meant fucking originally—which I don't think is a bad idea. Let's bring it back again."—Waylon Jennings

21. "Pop music is sex, and you have to hit them in the face with it."—Andrew Loog Oldham, producer/manager of The Rolling Stones

22. "I use a microphone like a plumber uses a tool."—Schoolly D

23. "It's better than fighting."—Wilko Johnson

24. "It's just entertainment, and the kids who like to identify their youthful high spirits with a solid beat are thus possibly avoiding other pursuits that could be harmful to them."—Bill Haley

25. "People . . . didn't think of me as a songwriter, so when I started coming up with songs, they'd look at me like: 'Who *really* wrote that?' I don't know what they must have thought—that I had someone back in the garage who was writing them for me?"—Michael Jackson

26. "The first album was the first time that headphones meant anything to me. What I heard coming back to me over the cans while I was singing was better than any chick in the land."—Robert Plant

27. "I'm only interested in heavy metal when it's me who's playing it. I suppose it's a bit like smelling your own farts."—John Entwistle, The Who

28. "I hate that term 'heavy metal.' "—Angus Young, AC/DC

29. "This is not just dance music. It's about knowing yourself and knowing who is against you and who is trying to bring you down."—Ice Cube

30. "Rock and roll is a means of pulling the white man down to the level of the Negro. It is part of a plot to undermine the morals of the youth of our nation."—Secretary of the North Alabama White Citizens Council, circa 1956

31. "Millions of Americans were buying *Purple Rain* with no idea what to expect."—Tipper Gore, who evidently missed the movie

32. "I do feel angry, though, when they play all that backward surf music and talk about the *harm* our music did these kids, 'cause I think it was the best thing they had."—K. K. Downing, Judas Priest

33. "I fight authority. Authority always wins."—John Mellencamp

34. "Everyone I know is so sick of all that punk violence and pessimism. Anyway, the truth is that it's much harder to write a pop song that everyone can relate to than some anthem of hate for a few punks."—Boy George

35. "When I die, bury me on my stomach and let the world kiss my ass."—L.L. Cool J

36. "Elvis left us our kind of groundbreaking guide to what to do after forty—and now I'm sayin', Goddamn, please, Rollin' Stones, don't mess up, somebody gotta keep on, man."—Billy Gibbons, ZZ Top

37. "It's better to burn out than to fade away."—Neil Young

38. "I'd rather kill myself . . . I'm not going to be around to witness my artistic decline."—Elvis Costello, who was wrong

39. "It has no beginning and no end, for it is the very pulse of life itself."—Larry ("Bony Moronie") Williams

40. "Ever get the feeling you've just been had?"—Johnny Rotten

Norman Petty's Instructions to the Crickets

Producer Norman Petty gave Buddy Holly and the Crickets the following advice as they set out on their first tour away from their West Texas home. We discovered it in the booklet accompanying The Complete Buddy Holly Story, *the first rock and roll box set. Much of what Petty suggests still seems relevant thirty-five years later.*

1. Be at the Amarillo air terminal by at least 6:30 to check reservations and check baggage.
2. Take enough cash to pay for excess weight and meals between flights. (He recommended thirty or forty dollars in cash, the rest in traveler's checks—Ed.)
3. Be sure to take all available identification for each member of the group.
4. Sign only engagement contracts and nothing more.
5. Take extra sets of guitar strings, drumsticks, heads, etc.
6. Take out floater insurance for the entire group with everyone's name on the contract.
7. Be sure to pack record with clothes to take on trip.
8. Take all available clean underwear . . . and other articles for use on the trip.
9. When you get to New York . . . take a cab directly to the Edison Hotel and check in there.
10. Get at least two dozen Dramamine tablets . . . and take one tablet at least fifteen minutes before departure.
11. Make out trip insurance to your parents.
12. Take at least twenty-five feet of extension cord.
13. Take small shine kit.
14. Toilet articles of your choice.
15. Get telephone credit card and carry with you.
16. Take a small Bible with you and READ IT!
17. Get hotel credit cards or at least make applications for them.
18. Be sure to get and keep receipts for all money spent.
19. Be sure to send money to Clovis for bank account.

Malcolm McLaren's 10 Lessons of Rock Success

1. Manufacture your group.
2. Establish the name.

3. Sell the Swindle.
4. Do not play. Do not give the game away.
5. Steal as much money as possible from the record company of your choice.
6. Become the world's greatest tourist attraction.
7. Cultivate hatred. It is your greatest asset.
8. Diversify business.
9. Take civilization to the barbarians.
10. Who killed Bambi?

Malcolm McLaren, manager of the Sex Pistols, is star of the posthumously released movie about the band, The Great Rock'n'Roll Band Swindle. *The picture elaborately presents McLaren's rules of promotional acumen, ostensibly those he used for the allegedly talentless Pistols.*

Popular Rap Rumors, as Told by Reginald C. Dennis

1. Vanilla Ice is coming back hard.
2. Ice-T is a real gang-banger.
3. Big Daddy Kane has AIDS.
4. Too Short is dead.
5. Snoop Doggy Dogg is dead.
6. N.W.A. breakup was a hoax to ensure success of reunion album.
7. EPMD breakup was a hoax to ensure success of reunion album.
8. KRS-1 hunted down and murdered the man responsible for Scott La Rock's death.
9. Kool Moe Dee is currently an NYC bicycle messenger.
10. M.C. Hammer donated a helicopter and ten squad cars to the Oakland police department.

Slogans—Unforgettable and Regrettable

1. "Tomorrow's sound today."—Philles Records, 1962
2. "The sound of young America."—Motown Records, 1963
3. "If it's a hit, it's a Miracle."—Miracle Records (Motown subsidiary), 1964
4. "We love you Beatles, oh yes we do."—Beatlemaniacs, 1964
5. "Kill ugly radio."—The Mothers of Invention, 1967
6. "Disco sucks."—Rock and Rollers, 1975 to 1978

7. "Kill for peace."—The Fugs, 1967
8. "Music, love, and flowers."—The Monterey International Pop Festival, 1967
9. "The man can't bust our music."—CBS Records, 1968
10. "Kick out the jams, motherfuckers."—The MC5, 1968
11. "Three days of peace and music."—The Woodstock Festival, 1969
12. "The revolutionaries are on CBS."—CBS Records, 1969
13. "On Warner/Reprise, where they belong."—Warner Bros. Records, 1969–71
14. "Happy Xmas, war is over if you want it."—John Lennon and Yoko Ono, 1971
15. "I saw rock and roll future and its name is Bruce Springsteen." —Jon Landau, 1974
16. "Free your mind and your ass will follow."—George Clinton, 1978
17. "The only band that matters."—Clash fans, 1978
18. "I want my MTV."—The entire musical universe, ca. 1981
19. "No sleep 'til Hammersmith."—Motorhead, 1981
20. "Girls just want to have fun."—Cyndi Lauper, 1984
21. "I can't live without my radio."—L.L. Cool J, 1985
22. "Fight for your right to party."—The Beastie Boys, 1986
23. "I still haven't found what I'm looking for."—U2 and its fans, 1987
24. "Don't believe the hype."—Public Enemy, 1988
25. "Corporate rock still sucks."—SST Records, late eighties
26. "Fuck the police!"—N.W.A, 1988; The citizens of Los Angeles, 1992
27. "Me so horny."—2 Live Crew, 1989
28. "Parental guidance—explicit lyrics."—Tipper Gore and her asshole buddies, 1990
29. "Are you down with O.P.P.?"—Naughty by Nature and everybody else in America, 1991
30. "Free your mind and your butt will follow."—En Vogue, 1992

Reginald C. Dennis's 10 Ways to Tell if a Rapper's Career Is on the Way Out

1. Achieves massive crossover appeal and financial success.
2. Embarks on a college lecture tour.
3. Appears on *Nightline*.
4. Has a 90 percent Caucasian concert audience.
5. Has become a religious fanatic, a race leader, and/or a prophet.

6. Has begun work on his fourth album.
7. Says that he is "coming back hard" on the next album.
8. Has taken a three-year hiatus between records.
9. Has just celebrated his thirty-fifth birthday but dresses and acts as if he is a sixteen-year-old.
10. Has become the darling of MTV.

Reginald C. Dennis is the music editor of The Source.

Scott Pellegrino's 21 Rockers, Rappers, and Poppers Who'd Lose to Beavis and Butt-head in a Meeting of the Minds

1. Sebastian Bach
2. Marky Mark
3. James Hetfield
4. Steve Albini
5. Joey Lawrence
6. Harry Connick, Jr.
7. Billy Ray Cyrus
8. Dr. Dre
9. Belinda Carlisle
10. Jon Bon Jovi
11. Shabba Ranks
12. Grace Slick
13. Joe Satriani
14. George Harrison
15. Sammy Hagar
16. Anyone who ever again says, "Throw your hands in the air and wave 'em like you just don't care."
17. Charlie Daniels
18. Eric Clapton
19. Run-D.M.C.
20. Michael Bolton
21. Fresh Prince

Scott Pellegrino is a native New Yorker who specializes in media provocation, in which capacity he has gotten in the face of everyone from Bill Clinton and Bob Grant to Pete Townshend and, frequently, Dave Marsh.

Shuddafuccup!

1. Bono
2. Barney
3. Tipper Gore
4. Albert Goldman
5. Little Richard (Hey, *you* started it)
6. Everyone at MTV except Beavis, Butt-head, and Gilbert Gottfried
7. Madonna's critics
8. Madonna
9. Wynton Marsalis
10. Antimusic men of God . . . and politics

11. Dave Marsh
12. Pete Townshend
13. Andrew Lloyd Webber
14. Timothy White
15. Quincy Jones
16. G. E. Smith and his Talking Guitar
17. Biz Markie
18. *Rolling Stone*
19. *Spin*
20. Michelle Shocked
21. KRS-One
22. Donald Wildmon
23. Jon Bon Jovi
24. Pauly Shore
25. Mike Love
26. Bob DeMoss
27. All Judds
28. Ike Turner
29. Tina Turner
30. James Hetfield
31. Juliana Hatfield
32. Just about every radio personality in America
33. Bob Dylan
34. Mick Jagger
35. Big Daddy Kane
36. L.L. Cool J
37. Sinead O'Connor
38. Billy Crystal
39. Paul Schaffer
40. James Brown
41. Lou Reed
42. Robert Christgau
43. The California Raisins
44. Dr. James Dobson
45. Luther Campbell
46. The Rock Bottom Remainders
47. Chrissie Hynde
48. Ray Davies
49. All nonartists at Rock and Roll Hall of Fame induction dinners
50. Danny Goldberg
51. Cyndi Crawford
52. Robert James Waller
53. Steve Albini
54. The American Federation of Musicians
55. The American Federation of Radio and Television Artists
56. The Rhythm and Blues Foundation until everybody gets paid
57. The National Music Foundation until somebody gets housed
58. Paul Simon (either or preferably both)
59. Marky Mark
60. Fresh Prince
61. Jesse Jackson
62. Michael Jackson
63. LaToya Jackson
64. Katherine Jackson
65. Joe Jackson (Michael's father and the third-rate Brit jazzbo-rocker)
66. Any other Jackson tempted to talk about Michael
67. Terry Rakolta
68. Danny Partridge
69. The Brady Bunch
70. Record biz lobbyists
71. Prince or Christopher or whatever the fuck he thinks his name is
72. Chuck Eddy
73. Weird Al Yankovic
74. Easy-E
75. Courtney Love
76. Neil Young (look where his "insight" got Kurt Cobain)
77. Raffi
78. Cher
79. Dionne Warwick and the Psychic Hot-Line along with her
80. Steve Vai
81. Stephen Davis

82. George Michael
83. Boy George
84. George Harrison
85. All other ex-Beatles
    including Pete Best
86. Yoko Ono Lennon
87. Linda Eastman
    McCartney
88. Billy Ray Cyrus
89. Billy Crystal
90. Peter Noone
91. Isaac Hayes

92. Barry White
93. Joe Carducci
94. Bruce Willis
95. Arsenio Hall
96. Michael Stipe
97. George Clinton
98. Bruce Springsteen
99. Everyone involved in
    making this list
100. Kenny G (We've never
    heard him say a word but
    just in case . . .)

The idea for this list and some of the choices were stolen from Kristen Carr, who was herself stolen from us on January 3, 1993. She had intended to make her stepfather, Dave Marsh, number one on this list but he is neither that proud nor that humble. Her list would undoubtedly have been far hipper. Thanks also to Scott Pellegrino, Sheldon Bull, Karen Hall, Al Kooper, Joyce McRae-Moore, Barbara Nellis, and Greil Marcus (but please see item 99).

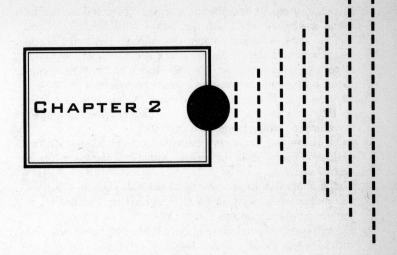

Money

Shake Your Moneymaker

1. $1 billion: Amount Sam Phillips estimated he could make if he found a white singer "with the Negro sound and the Negro feel" in 1954. Also, the amount that Michael Jackson, a Negro singer who occasionally displays the Caucasian sound and feel, allegedly could earn from his 1991 deal with Sony Entertainment. Both numbers overstate the case considerably.
2. $270 million: The amount U2 supposedly stands to earn from its 1993 contract with PolyGram International. Don't count on this chicken coming home to roost, either.
3. $230 million: Sid Bernstein's estimated gross for a single Beatles reunion concert, 1980. At least as realistic as the estimates in items 1 and 2.
4. $200 million: Estimated value of Elvis Presley estate, 1993.
5. $80 million: Amount paid by Capitol-EMI to The Beatles in settlement of back royalties claim, 1990.
6. $70 million: Estimated value of Boyz II Men's seven-album deal with Motown, 1993.
7. $60 million: Estimated value of Madonna's Sire Records contract, 1992.
8. $45 million: Amount The Rolling Stones nabbed from Virgin Records for three albums plus rights to their seventeen-album post-1971 catalogue.
9. $30 million: Estimated value of Sire Records' president Seymour Stein's contract with Time-Warner.
10. $25 million: Amount of life insurance policy for Elton John taken out by MCA Records, 1975.
11. $10 million: Alleged value of Elvis Presley's estate, 1977.
12. $1 million: Cost of recording Fleetwood Mac's *Tusk*, 1970–80.
13. $110,000: Advance paid by Atlantic Records to Led Zeppelin, 1969.
14. $100,000: Cost of recording The Beatles' *Sgt. Pepper's Lonely Hearts Club Band*, 1967.
15. $75,000: Initial advance paid to The Who by Polydor Records, 1965.
16. $35,000: Advance paid Elvis Presley on signing with RCA Records, 1956 (an additional $5,000 was paid to Sam Phillips for Presley's Sun Records contract).
17. $12,000: Recording cost of *The Ramones*, 1976.
18. $3,200: Lorne Michael's final bid to The Beatles to perform on *Saturday Night Life*, 1978.
19. 1,400 English pounds (roughly $3,000 U.S.): Damage done by The Who and entourage to the Bonaventure Hotel in Montreal, 1973.
20. $2,500: Bail bond posted by Bill Graham for release of Roger

Daltrey and Pete Townshend, when they were thrown in jail after kicking a policeman offstage during their concert at Fillmore East, 1969.

21. $2,400: Paid to The Beatles for their *Ed Sullivan Show* appearance, February 9, 1964.
22. $50: Paid to Bob Dylan for performing on harmonica on a Harry Belafonte album, 1960.
23. $20 (U.S. equivalent): Price of a CD in Europe and Japan, 1990s.
24. $15.98: List price of U.S. CD, 1990s.
25. $3.98: List price of LP, mid-1960s.
26. Nine cents: Current legally mandated maximum price per disc songwriter and publisher receive for a recording under the so-called force licensing provision of the Copyright Act.
27. Two cents: Legally mandated maximum amount songwriter and publisher received per recording per disc under the Copyright Act from 1908 through 1976.

Sitting on Top of the World . . .

Because they made the Forbes *annual listing of the 40 highest-earning entertainers (*Forbes *ranks performers by the amount it estimates they have grossed in the preceding two years).*

(Rank/listing/two-year total income, in millions.)

1987

3	Bruce Springsteen	$56
7	Madonna	$47
8	Whitney Houston	$44
9	Michael Jackson	$43
11	U2	$37
12	ZZ Top	$31
14	Bon Jovi	$29
16	Kenny Rogers	$26
17	Van Halen	$25
18	Wayne Newton	$24
19	Neil Diamond	$24
20	Prince	$23
21	Billy Joel	$23
24	Paul McCartney	$18
28	Willie Nelson	$17
37	Julio Iglesias	$13
38	Phil Collins	$12
39	Barbra Streisand	$11

1988

1	Michael Jackson	$97
7	Bruce Springsteen	$61
9	Madonna	$46
11	U2	$42
13	George Michael	$38
16	Bon Jovi	$34
17	Whitney Houston	$30
19	Pink Floyd	$29
20	Julio Iglesias	$28
22	Kenny Rogers	$26
24	Tina Turner	$25
26	Van Halen	$25
28	Sting	$24
29	Prince	$24
31	John Mellencamp	$23
32	The Grateful Dead	$23
35	Wayne Newton	$21
37	Billy Joel	$18
40	Frank Sinatra	$16

1989

1	Michael Jackson	$125
7	Pink Floyd	$56
8	The Rolling Stones	$55
10	George Michael	$47
11	Julio Iglesias	$46
15	Madonna	$43
18	Bruce Springsteen	$40
19	Bon Jovi	$40
20	Prince	$36
21	U2	$33
22	The Who	$32
23	Def Leppard	$30
24	Van Halen	$27
28	Frank Sinatra	$26
29	The Grateful Dead	$25
31	Guns N' Roses	$24
32	Kenny Rogers	$23
35	Aerosmith	$21
36	Rod Stewart	$21

1990

2	Michael Jackson	$100
3	The Rolling Stones	$88
5	New Kids on the Block	$78

8	Madonna	$62
14	Paul McCartney	$45
15	Julio Iglesias	$44
17	The Who	$35
19	Bon Jovi	$35
20	Prince	$35
22	Billy Joel	$32
23	Aerosmith	$31
24	Pink Floyd	$30
25	The Grateful Dead	$30
26	Janet Jackson	$30
28	Frank Sinatra	$27
30	U2	$25
33	Paula Abdul	$18
39	George Michael	$18
40	Guns N' Roses	$17

1991

1	New Kids on the Block	$115
4	Madonna	$63
5	Michael Jackson	$60
8	The Rolling Stones	$55
11	Paul McCartney	$49
12	Julio Iglesias	$45
13	Janet Jackson	$43
18	Aerosmith	$34
19	M.C. Hammer	$33
20	The Grateful Dead	$33
22	Billy Joel	$31
25	Frank Sinatra	$27
28	Guns N' Roses	$25
31	Prince	$25
33	Paula Abdul	$24
37	Xuxa*	$19
40	Vanilla Ice	$18

1992

4	New Kids on the Block	$62
6	Michael Jackson	$51
8	Madonna	$48
9	Julio Iglesias	$48
10	Guns N' Roses	$47
12	Prince	$45
13	Garth Brooks	$44
16	U2	$36
20	The Grateful Dead	$31

25	ZZ Top	$29
27	Hammer	$28
33	The Rolling Stones	$25
38	Frank Sinatra	$23
40	Janet Jackson	$22

1993

4	Guns N' Roses	$53
5	Prince	$49
8	U2	$47
9	Garth Brooks	$47
12	Michael Jackson	$42
13	Julio Iglesias	$40
15	Madonna	$37
16	Eric Clapton	$33
17	The Grateful Dead	$33
22	Billy Ray Cyrus	$29
27	Neil Diamond	$28
28	Xuxa*	$37
33	Paul McCartney	$24
40	Jimmy Buffet	$20

---

* Xuxa is a Brazilian children's singer, TV host and, for reasons few Americans will ever grasp, blonde bombshell.

Career Opportunities
40 Songs About Working

1. "Allentown," Billy Joel
2. "Back on the Chain Gang," Pretenders
3. "Big Boss Man," Jimmy Reed
4. "Black Land Farmer," Frankie Miller
5. "Blue Collar," Bachman-Turner Overdrive
6. "Blue Money," Van Morrison
7. "Car Wash," Rose Royce
8. "Chain Gang," Sam Cooke
9. "Don't Look Now (It Ain't You Or Me)," Creedence Clearwater Revival
10. "Factory," Bruce Springsteen
11. "Feel Like a Number," Bob Seger
12. "Five O'Clock World," The Vogues
13. "Found a Job," Talking Heads
14. "Friday on My Mind," The Easybeats
15. "Get a Job," The Silhouettes

16. "Got a Job," The Miracles
17. "Handy Man," Jimmy Jones (also Del Shannon, James Taylor)
18. "A Hard Day's Night," The Beatles
19. "If We Make It Through December," Merle Haggard
20. "The Load Out," Jackson Browne
21. "Luxury," The Rolling Stones
22. "Maggie's Farm," Bob Dylan
23. "Manic Monday," The Bangles
24. "Money for Nothing," Dire Straits
25. "My Town," The Michael Stanley Band
26. "Night Shift," Bob Marley and the Wailers
27. "9 to 5," Dolly Parton
28. "One Piece at a Time," Johnny Cash
29. "Patches," Clarence Carter
30. "Rain on the Scarecrow, John Cougar Mellencamp
31. "Six Days on the Road," Dave Dudley
32. "Sixteen Tons," Tenessee Ernie Ford
33. "Summertime Blues," Eddie Cochran
34. "Take This Job and Shove It," Johnny Paycheck
35. "Welcome to the Working Week," Elvis Costello
36. "Workin' at the Car Wash Blues," Jim Croce
37. "Workin' for the Man," Roy Orbison
38. "Working for the Weekend," Loverboy
39. "Working in the Coal Mine," Lee Dorsey
40. "Working on the Highway," Bruce Springsteen

Really Big Record Deals

In the past decade, one prominent symbol of the changes in music industry stature is the intense scrutiny given music business dealings. As a result, rather than having to base this list on wild guesses based on our own experience, we can use the wild guesses made by tabloid journalists and legit business reporters. This frees us to spend more time offering analysis of the relative intelligence of such deals and, since we are not of the opinion that all money spent on artists is squandered, to assess them a lot more sensibly than those saddled with the viewpoint that only the likes of Lawrence Tisch, Aiko Morita, and Lew Wasserman should be enriched by artistic endeavor.

1. CBS RECORDS—Price when sold to Sony Entertainment, 1988, $2 billion. At the time, the deal seemed to many observers insane. Since then, with small-fry labels with thin artist rosters (A&M, Island, Virgin) going for $400 million and up, Sony looks to have made the deal of the century. After all, it acquired the premier recording company of the past twenty-five years, a massive back catalogue, and what is widely regarded as the supreme international music marketing company. Superstars like Michael Jackson, Barbra Streisand, and Bruce Springsteen lend the label much prestige, it continues to score heavily in R&B, metal, and country, and the only question is whether it can continue to develop rock stars to match more lightweight successes like Michael Bolton and the New Kids on the Block. In the mid-nineties, the jury's out on the company's future but by now, Sony's probably earned back enough money to fully justify the deal.

2. MICHAEL JACKSON—Reported value, 1991, $1 billion. Probable actual guaranteed value, $100 million, plus or minus a substantial signing bonus. In addition to record royalties of about three dollars per CD, grants Jackson profit participation of about 50 percent, after he earns back an enormous guarantee (in the neighborhood of $10 million per album). Michael's deal with Sony Entertainment also provides him with a record production and film production company, neither of which he shows much sign of putting into use.

3. GEFFEN RECORDS—Estimated price when sold to MCA, 1990, $400 million. But within a few months, MCA sold out to Japan-based Matsushita Electronics. As MCA's biggest individual stockholder, owner David Geffen more than doubled his money, making him the first rock 'n' roll billionaire. Although Geffen's amazing success with its initial Guns N' Roses album wasn't repeated with the followup, MCA's attempt to join the Sony and Time-Warner record groups as a major player was greatly enhanced by acquiring an artist roster that included Guns N' Roses, Nirvana, Peter Gabriel, Tesla, and a host more.

4. U2—Reported value, 1993, $220 million to $270 million; the former figure probably comes closer to the mark. U2 already owned a significant proportion of Island Records before it was sold for about $400 million to PolyGram International in 1991. The success of *Achtung Baby* (1992) made them perhaps the premier rock band in the world at the time and gave them leverage for this renegotiation. But, as with all these deals, they must continue to sell records at high levels to reach the top figure. The actual guarantees might be as little as one-quarter of the reported value. On the other hand, as with all of these deals, there was probably substantial upfront bonus money involved.

5. PRINCE—Reported value, 1992, $100 million. Actual value only marginally less *if* Prince sells records—since signing, he's announced retirement from recording, as well as a specious name change—and continues to make films and to produce successful recordings with others. He's done both in the past but many observers doubt that he can continue, or really wants to. By late '93, the bad blood between the artist and Warner Brothers Records resulted in his avowed "retirement."

6. THE ROLLING STONES—Reported value, 1992, $45 million. Actual value may even be in that neighborhood. The Stones have to sell records, though, something they're never been nearly as good at as they are at selling concert tickets. (Their average album probably sells about 2 million or fewer copies worldwide.) Virgin paid a heavy premium for both this deal and Janet Jackson's because owner Richard Branson was in the process of selling off his company, to EMI, and needed a superstar artist roster to up the price. Virgin's mettle, as much as that of the Stones, is probably being tested here.

7. JANET JACKSON—Reported value, 1991, $40 million. Actual value probably in that neighborhood, especially since her first record for Virgin Records, *janet* (1993), sold wildly and spent many weeks at number one, even as she relaunched her acting career with John Singleton's *Poetic Justice.* On this one, Virgin seems to have met the test.

8. MADONNA—Reported value, 1992, $30 million to $70 million; the lower figure more likely fits, even though Madonna's deal came packaged with film and book deals. Warner deals (Madonna's Sire label is part of Warner Records) that are *re*negotiations with their own artists tend to carry lower royalty and advance figures than renegotiated deals with other major record labels. Even so, *if* Madonna hasn't peaked, and if she can sort out her movie deal (or if her record label ever comes up with an enduring star), she could outstrip the estimates on this one.

9. AEROSMITH—Reported value, 1991, $25 million. Actual value probably the same. Maybe the most controversial of all the megamillion-dollar superstar pacts of the early eighties, because Aerosmith is an aging hard rock group that signed with Sony while still owing its current label, Geffen Records, at least one more album. But that album, *Get a Grip,* turned out to be a hit at least as substantial as their other recent discs, the group members have rehabilitated themselves after years of chemical abuse, and their audience base remains both loyal and younger than you'd expect. The Stones deal, for one, seems far riskier, especially since both Aerosmith and Sony have the bulk of the band's back catalogue to exploit if new hits are over the horizon.

10. BARBRA STREISAND—Estimated value, 1992, $20 million. This may not seem like so much but name another singer with traditional Broadway material and phrasing you'd pay 25 percent as much for. And this is one of the more straightforward, no-bullshit deals—Sony did *not* buy into Streisand's substantial movie career here, although it probably didn't hurt its cinematic relations with her by making it.

Really Dumb Record Deals

1. ELVIS PRESLEY'S FUTURE ROYALTIES SOLD TO RCA VICTOR, 1973

Of all the mismanagement Colonel Tom Parker rendered unto Elvis during their quarter-century together, his negotiations with RCA rank at the top. His second RCA contract did not even contain a provision allowing the artist to audit the record company's royalty statements, a gross invitation to larceny. But Parker outstripped all competitors in March 1973, when he sold Elvis's entire record catalogue to RCA outright. There were more than seven hundred chart records in that catalogue, yet RCA paid only $8.9 million ($5.4 million plus $500,000 per year for the next seven years), a deal that was profitable long before Elvis's death made it obscenely so. Chances are that the Presley estate had sufficient leverage to force RCA to renegotiate the deal in the eighties. Nevertheless, it's hard to imagine a more one-sided transaction.

2. SUN RECORDS' SALE OF ELVIS PRESLEY TO RCA VICTOR, 1955

Sam Phillips sold Presley's Sun contract for $35,000 flat. He retained no percentage of Elvis's future royalties, although it wasn't unusual for producers to maintain such an interest in their discoveries. Admittedly, thirty-five grand constituted a relative fortune at the time, but it pales in comparison to what even a small slice of Elvis's future surely must have been worth. Anyway, Phillips sold Elvis, it's said, because he believed Carl Perkins had it in him to be bigger—history's most severe case of underestimating the value of charisma.

3. THE SEX PISTOLS WITH A&M RECORDS, 1976

The Pistols and EMI had already come to their parting of the ways, but at least that one made a certain censorious sense: EMI thought it was signing the next teen sensation and deep-sixed the deal when it turned out that it had actually purchased the right to release records by specialists in anarchist outrage. EMI was just being EMI—a multinational electronics and military manufacturer that had no use for its consumer products division if it proved any more disreputable than the Beatles. A&M, on the other hand, prided itself on being a bastion of Los Angeles hipsterism, an independently owned label whose roster featured the likes of Peter Frampton, former Yes keyboardist Rick Wakeman, pre-Islamic Cat Stevens, and Joe Cocker (even if its biggest success stories were the unchic Carpenters and owner Herb Alpert's Tijuana Brass). Of course, if they were so hip, they should have noticed that the Pistols hated all that long before they signed them to a 75,000-pound (about $150,000) advance. Or at least, they ought to have heard "God Save the Queen," the record they found too antimonarchist to put out in the year of Queen Elizabeth II's Silver Jubilee. As it was, the label panicked, and only a week after signing, the Pistols were cut loose with nothing to show for the association but a fatter bankroll. The band went on to sell millions of records worldwide. A&M suffered an image loss, undoubtedly considerably lessened by its acquisition of the Police, who not only sold far more records than the Pistols but sometimes even acted fairly polite about it.

4. MILLI VANILLI, ARISTA RECORDS AND THE GRAMMIES, 1989

When Arista Records signed Milli Vanilli (whose name means "positive energy" in Turkish), the act already had scored several European hits, success immediately repeated in the United States with four number-one singles and one number two. Arista probably never gave any thought to whether Vanilli's Rob Pilatus and Fabrice Morvan (Rob and Fab to their fans) made the actual noises on their record. Nor did it seem to cross the minds of the voters of the National Academy of Recording Arts and Sciences, who, in their distinctly finite wisdom, awarded Milli Vanilli a Grammy as best new artists of the year. Only after Rob and Fab entered into a lawsuit with their German producer was it revealed that their records were put-up jobs: Rob and Fab did not sing on them. In a surge of self-righteousness, amidst some nastily homophobic bashings from the press, the Grammy was withdrawn, Arista denied all suspicion but settled a class action suit out of court (which entitled disgruntled Milli Vanilli buyers to coupons to putatively more authentic Arista albums), and Rob and Fab engulfed themselves in a series of press conferences and statements that only made matters worse. As none other than George Clinton pointed out, lip-synching and dubbing in other voices are venerable practices within the codes of dance music, but it made no matter. *Nobody* came out of this one without something ugly attached to their shoe soles.

5. GAMBLE AND HUFF WITH ATLANTIC, 1971

When Kenneth Gamble and Leon Huff were getting started as record producers, their closest relationship was with Atlantic, for which they produced Archie Bell and the Drells, among others. But when Gamble and Huff created Philadelphia International Records in 1971, Atlantic passed on their distribution deal, claiming it was too expensive (probably meaning that Gamble and Huff not only wanted to get paid but to own their own masters). Philadelphia International went on to become one of the major successes of the decade, a goldmine for CBS. Which just about makes up for . . .

6. STAX/VOLT WITH CBS, 1973

Stax had been distributed by Atlantic almost from the company's beginning in the early sixties. But in 1973, Clive Davis, desperate to fulfill a corporate mandate to shore up CBS's weak position in black music, lured Stax away from Atlantic for several million dollars, as big as bucks went in those days. (Davis had been warned against making such an acquistion by the famous Harvard Business School study of the black record market that CBS had commissioned.) Unfortunately for Clive, the tide in black pop taste was turning. Stax was in ruinous financial condition and its tenure with CBS distribution was a complete bust.

7. THE ROLLING STONES WITH CBS, 1985

The dumbness of this pact doesn't have to do with its high price. True, at $28 million, CBS Records chief Walter Yetnikoff clearly overpaid for the Stones, who may be the World's Greatest Rock Band but hadn't had a big hit since the late seventies and failed to garner one during their five-year tenure here. Yetnikoff's more important miscalculation had to do with also negotiating a separate solo contract with Mick Jagger. Like a lot of folks, Yetnikoff must have imagined that Mick meant more than his band. But not only did Jagger's first two solo albums bomb critically and commercially, his commitment to making them inflamed his relationship with Keith Richards—and that relationship is what's really at the heart of the Stones. Offended, Keith went off to make his own solo album, and for a time, it seemed like the end of the band. It wasn't, but the often-public dissension had a lot to do with why the Stones stumbled into the nineties as a shell of their old selves (which may mean that their 1992 agreement with Virgin Records—not incidentally, the home base for *Keith's* solo work—which guarantees the band about $45 million, will come in somewhere near the top of this list in this book's next life).

8. NEIL YOUNG WITH GEFFEN RECORDS, 1982—88

Neil Young spent the first decade of his solo career quite happily working with Reprise Records, an affiliation he (and Frank Sinatra, alone among the artist roster) retained even after the entire Reprise catalogue was transferred to its Warner Brothers parent. But in 1982, Young switched labels, signing with David Geffen's self-titled new company. There, he proceeded to make a series of albums that continued the eccentricities of his Reprise work, drifting from electronic noise-rock to country to rockabilly to folk-rock quite randomly. By the fifth year of their agreement, Geffen's disappointment in Young's failure to produce a commercial record— or even a consistent bundle of eccentricities that it might profitably market on a smaller scale—caused the company to wax wroth. Young proved as intractable as ever (which should hardly have come as a surprise to David Geffen, who had been his manager in the early seventies). So Geffen Records sued Young, accusing him of not even trying to produce marketable records—which, in his annoyance at what he rightly perceived as artistic interference, he might actually have been, though who could tell given his precedents? Anyway, the suit was finally settled out of court and Young moved back to Reprise. The black eye went to Geffen, its image as an artist-friendly environment considerably damaged by perceived mal-treatment of one of the across-the-board icons of eighties rock.

9. DELANEY AND BONNIE WITH COLUMBIA RECORDS, 1972

When Delaney and Bonnie decided they wanted out of their contract with Atlantic, to which they'd turned after making one record for Stax and one for Elektra, they chose Columbia—and Clive Davis—as their next option. Or target. In his autobiography, *Clive: Inside the Record Business*, Davis says that he signed the group to a contract for seven years and $600,000; then an enormous sum. Davis doesn't mention the hefty override paid to Atlantic for the group. To make matters worse, Delaney and Bonnie broke up almost immediately and never made an album for Columbia, and their solo careers amounted to less than a whisper each.

10. BRUCE SPRINGSTEEN WITH LAUREL CANYON PRODUCTIONS, 1972

There are many instances of artists too hastily signing contracts they'd live to regret: Creedence Clearwater Revival, Billy Joel, and Run-D.M.C. are only the most obvious examples of desperation for a shot at the big time and lack of a good lawyer overwhelming common sense and caution. But Springsteen's deal with Laurel Canyon—Mike Appel and his partner, Jim Cretecos—takes the cake. Allegedly signed on the hood of a car in the parking lot of a Jersey rock club, the deal gave Laurel Canyon the right to record Springsteen, market his records, and, together with side agreements, to publish his songs and manage his career. The contract specified that whenever these rights were in conflict, the managers were entitled to act in their own best interest, not his. To top it all off, although Laurel Canyon signed Springsteen for only five albums, it committed him to Columbia for ten. The result wasn't only a predictable mire of mismanagement but one of the most elongated lawsuits in music biz history, keeping Springsteen from recording a followup to his *Born to Run* breakthrough for nearly three years.

Joyce McRae-Moore Lists 10 Reasons Why Your Record Royalties Haven't Been Paid

1. It's in the mail, really it is.
2. We didn't know your address. Of course, we made no effort to find your address.
3. How do you spell your name?
4. Oh, we wrote off the debt years ago for IRS purposes. But

you're more than $100,000 in the red, so we didn't see any reason to mail a statement to you.
5. It's Tuesday, why are you asking?
6. Oh, do we owe you money? We don't owe you money, do we?
7. So sue us!
8. Well, you see, the master really came from this bankrupt company, and according to them, you still owed them money, so we don't owe you money, because you owed them money and they no longer exist but boy, is this a great reason not to pay you anything and make 100 percent profit.
9. It's standard industry practice. We pay no one else. What makes you think you're special?
10. There must have been a clerical error.

Joyce McRae-Moore, who has represented many artists, including Jackie Wilson, the Jackson family, and Shirley Caesar, currently manages Sam Moore and sits on the board of the Rhythm and Blues Foundation. Over the past twenty-odd years, she has heard variations on each of these themes on several occasions.

Annual Record, Tape, and CD Sales (in Millions of Dollars)

These figures are somewhat deceptive, because the Recording Industry Association of America (RIAA), which began compiling them in 1921, calculates sales volume on the basis of list price, but until recently records, tapes, and CDs were almost never sold at more than about 80 percent of that mythical figure. Nonetheless, because RIAA figures don't account for the enormous amount of money spent on concert tickets and other music-related purchases, the proportions are fairly correct for the music business as a whole. It's also worth noting that the more than $4 billion gross depicted in 1978 is a spectacular illusion, since that year proved to be more disastrous than prosperous because of a vast upsurge in the number of unsold records and tapes returned to producers. The 1979 total, then, indicates some return to sanity, at least as far as manufacturers' shipping and returns policies are concerned.

YEAR	RECORDS	TAPES	COMPACT DISCS	TOTAL
1921	$ 105.6	—	—	$ 105.6
1930	$ 46.2	—	—	$ 46.2
1940	$ 48.4	—	—	$ 48.4
1945[1]	$ 109.0	—	—	$ 109.0
1950	$ 189.0	—	—	$ 189.0
1954[2]	$ 213.0	—	—	$ 213.0
1955	$ 277.0	—	—	$ 277.0

Year				
1956[3]	$ 377.0	—	—	$ 377.0
1957	$ 460.0	—	—	$ 460.0
1958	$ 511.0	—	—	$ 511.0
1959	$ 603.0	—	—	$ 603.0
1960	$ 600.0	—	—	$ 600.0
1961	$ 640.0	—	—	$ 640.0
1962	$ 687.0	—	—	$ 687.0
1963	$ 698.0	—	—	$ 698.0
1964[4]	$ 758.0	—	—	$ 758.0
1965	$ 862.0	—	—	$ 862.0
1967[5]	$1,051.0	$ 122.0	—	$1,173.0
1968	$1,124.0	$ 234.0	—	$1,358.0
1969	$1,170.0	$ 416.0	—	$1,586.0
1970	$1,182.0	$ 478.0	—	$1,660.0
1971	$1,251.0	$ 493.0	—	$1,744.0
1972	$1,383.0	$ 541.0	—	$1,924.0
1973	$1,436.0	$ 580.6	—	$2,016.6
1974	$1,550.0	$ 650.2	—	$2,200.2
1975	$1,696.0	$ 692.0	—	$2,388.0
1976	$1,908.0	$ 829.0	—	$2,737.0
1977	$2,440.2	$1,060.6	—	$3,500.8
1978	$2,733.6	$1,397.8	—	$4,131.4
1979	$2,136.0	$ 604.6	—	$2,740.6
1980	$2,290.3	$ 776.4	—	$3,066.7
1981	$2,341.7	$1,062.8	—	$3,404.5
1982	$1,925.1	$1,384.5	—	$3,309.6
1983[6]	$1,689.0	$1,810.9	$ 17.2	$3,517.1
1984	$1,548.8	$2,383.9	$ 103.3	$4,036.0
1985	$1,280.5	$2,411.5	$ 389.5	$4,081.5
1986	$ 983.0	$2,499.5	$ 930.1	$4,412.6
1987	$ 793.1	$2,959.7	$1,593.6	$5,346.4
1988	$ 532.2	$3,385.1	$2,089.9	$6,007.2
1989	$ 220.3	$3,345.8	$2,587.7	$6,153.8
1990	$ 86.5	$3,472.4	$3,451.6	$7,010.5
1991	$ 29.4	$3,019.6	$4,337.7	$7,386.7
1992[7]	$ 13.5	$3,116.3	$5,326.5	$8,456.3

[1] After the Depression, sales volume finally catches up to the 1921 level.
[2] Beginning of rock and roll era.
[3] Elvis's first big year.
[4] The Beatles arrive in America.
[5] This is the first year in which the RIAA separates tape sales from album volume—just as cassettes and eight-track tapes begin to catch on. By the end of the seventies, record sales volume would triple (partly through price increases), but tape volume would increase by ten times, with far fewer price increases to account for the dramatic surge.
[6] Oh, oh! Here comes the CD!
[7] The CD's list price increases two bucks.

This Magic Mogul
Music Execs Really Worth Their Percentages

1. **BERRY GORDY, JR.**—Founder of Motown Records. The most musically talented executive in the history of the record business—wrote, produced, and played piano on massive hits. Son of family prominent in Detroit's black middle class, Gordy nevertheless found himself working on the assembly line at a Ford plant after his initial musical venture—a jazz record store—went bust on the hipster premises of his own taste. Never came close to making such a miscalculation of what his audience wanted again. Wrote an impressive series of hits for Jackie Wilson, including his all-time great "Lonely Teardrops," made some hits for Marv Johnson that he leased to other labels, then decided it would be easier to get paid if he just set up his own record business. Tamla/Motown began in 1959, had its first hits with Barrett Strong and the Miracles in 1960 and by the following year had burst onto the record-buying consciousness with a distinct sound, a miles-deep artist roster, and some of the finest session band and production talent ever assembled. By the mid-sixties, Motown and Gordy were the most successful black business and businessman in the United States. Although it petered out in the early seventies, after they'd left Detroit for Los Angeles, from the debut of "Money" through the heyday of the Jackson 5 and on into the postpsychedelic soul period of Stevie Wonder and Rick James, Motown remained not only the finest black-owned record label that America ever saw, but probably the highest-quality musical institution that the nation has ever produced. All who were present agree that the success stemmed directly from the involvement of the owner.

2. **DAVID GEFFEN**—King of the hill on dollars alone, and the only rock 'n' roll *billionaire*, thanks to his 1991 deal selling Geffen Records to MCA/Matsushita. Geffen began as a William Morris agent but soon turned personal manager (Laura Nyro, Crosby, Stills, and Nash, Joni Mitchell), then started Asylum Records to promote Jackson Browne. After Asylum became the hottest singer-songwriter label, he sold it to Warner Communications for $7 million ("the biggest number I could think of"), dropped out of rock to run Warner Films, then retired altogether when faced with a cancer scare. That resolved, he formed the Geffen label in 1980 (originally stocking it with warhorses John Lennon, Asia, Elton John, Donna Summer, Mitchell, Neil Young) based on his famous personal nurturing of artists. When new blood was required, he turned the company's artistic decisions over to his A&R staff, regarded at the time as a radical move, and let them come up with Peter Gabriel, Guns N' Roses, Nirvana, Tesla, and several more. Probably the most influential nonperformer in contemporary showbiz, Geffen has advised,

at one time or another, everyone from Michael Jackson, Madonna, and Cher to Bill Clinton.

3. ALLEN GRUBMAN—Attorney to the stars, deal-making equivalent of Hollywood's Michael Ovitz, though not nearly so imperious. Grubman started out by finishing last in his class at Brooklyn College Law School (or so he boasts), wound up representing Springsteen, Sting, Michael Jackson, Madonna, Billy Joel (till Joel sued him), many if not most of the industry's highest-powered executives, and other names too numerous to mention, not to mention negotiating contracts for such irregular clients as Bob Dylan. Grubman's greatest liability may be his law degree—if he simply presented himself as an agent (which is mainly how he operates), the so-called "conflicts of interest" in his close associations with music execs would count less than the measurable advances he's secured in artists' royalty rates, advance structures, and general control of their own work. In the eighties and nineties, nobody but nobody in the music industry has been more influential than Allen Grubman, whether the task was finding a record deal, renegotiating one, selling a company, or finessing through an executive employment contract.

4. AHMET ERTEGUN—Founder of Atlantic Records, songwriter (though some of his credits have recently been called into question), and another whose career advice has on occasion amounted to a kind of management for artists ranging from Ray Charles through Mick Jagger, not to mention executives like David Geffen. Suffice to say that, in his autobiography, Clive Davis envies only one other record exec: Ahmet. An aristocratic Turk who may still see himself as slumming even after a half-century of day-to-day record warring, he'd be legendary if all he had done was found (with Herb Abramson and his more jazz-oriented brother, Nesuhi) the foremost R&B label of the 1950s. But Ertegun kept his company prosperous and creative well into the seventies, and never less than prosperous since then.

5. SAM PHILLIPS—Founder of Sun Records, discovered or first recorded (with assistance from such as Ike Turner and Marion Keisker) Elvis, Jerry Lee Lewis, Howlin' Wolf, Carl Perkins, Johnny Cash, Roy Orbison, Charlie Rich. Grew up poor on an Alabama farm, became a disc jockey in the forties, made records on the side, went full-time in the early fifties and scored with the likes of Big Rufus Thomas and Little Junior Parker, before Keisker pulled his coat to Elvis and weirdos from all over the South began beating a rockabilly path to his door. Made only $40,000 from selling Elvis's contracts (he got $35k for the artist contract and record masters, another 5 G's for song publishing) but parlayed it into a fortune, not by recording that stellar roster so much as by investing in that other Memphis juggernaut of the 1950s—Holiday Inn. Phillips now owns several radio stations, including WLVS, in Memphis, whose call letters tell the tale.

6. CLIVE DAVIS—The greatest trainer of executive talent the record industry has ever seen, and despite his schlock-defining taste, one of its outstanding talent spotters. Davis graduated Harvard Law, joined CBS and got assigned to the record division, where he clambered to a position as heir to legendary Goddard Leiberson, whose suavity he never approached. Davis's mandate was to immerse the CBS Records division in the rock culture it had previously rejected, and he did this with great panache, beginning with his signing of Janis Joplin after the Monterey Pop Festival in 1967. He led the company through 1972, acquiring the artists who were the linchpins of its success in the ensuing decade: Springsteen, Billy Joel, Neil Diamond, the Jacksons including Michael Jackson, and Pink Floyd. Fired for charging the expenses of his son's high-profile showbiz bar mitzvah to the company (in essence, ousted in a nasty corporate purge), Davis took some time off, wrote one of the industry's more memorable memoirs *(Clive: Inside the Record Business)*, then secured financing from Columbia Pictures and started Arista Records. There, he's developed such stars as Whitney Houston, Barry Manilow, and Patti Smith, and fostered the careers of a host of upper-management types (notably Columbia Records prez Don Ienner), which continues a knack of executive talent scouting he'd also displayed at CBS, and meddled endlessly as "executive producer" of far too many albums. Prides himself on being able to pick songs that will hit, but his interference is one reason Arista has never developed a rock—as opposed to middle-of-the-road pop—star of long-range consequence. Nevertheless, a formidable force for more than three decades.

7. FRANK BARSALONA—Founded Premier Talent, the most important hard rock concert booking agency from the Who to U2, Grand Funk Railroad to Bruce Springsteen. Originally an agent at GAC (after brief career as a preadolescent country yodeler), Barsalona founded Premier in 1965 when he espied an opening for an all rock 'n' roll agency, an opening that existed mainly because the big-league bookers held the music in contempt. Starting out with a motley roster that included the likes of Mitch Ryder and Little Anthony and the Imperials, Premier soon found its niche with the burgeoning British rock 'n' roll scene, which Barsalona correctly understood was the music that had the greatest long-range career potential. Premier rep'd the Stones, The Who, Hendrix, Traffic, the Yardbirds, and a host of others: When the scene shifted back toward the United States, it handled J. Geils, Lynyrd Skynyrd, Springsteen, Van Halen, and Tom Petty. Although the company means less in the postmodern period, Barsalona's shrewd career advice (he has served several performers as a surrogate manager), management of oft-volatile relations between artists and promoters, nurturing of both executive and musical talent help Premier maintain its prestige.

8. JIMMY IOVINE—No other contemporary record exec has Iovine's breadth of experience or his eclecticism of taste, or for that matter, his feel for artistic need. Began as a tape operator at New York's Record Planet fresh out of high school, graduated to engineering in time to work on John Lennon's *Rock and Roll*, Springsteen's *Born to Run* and *Darkness on the Edge of Town*. Graduated to production by wangling Patti Smith "Because the Night," went on to produce Tom Petty, U2, Dire Straits, Bob Seger, and many more. A&M Records virtually turned over its prestigious Los Angeles studio to Iovine in the late eighties. He wound up founding Interscope Records with Chicago department store heir Ted Field. They scored a variety of relatively minor hits before coming up with the sensation of 1993 in Dr. Dre and *The Chronic*. Fast-talking, always on the phone, somehow always available to artists. He'll almost certainly wind up running one of the major labels someday.

9. RICK RUBIN—King of contemporary outrage. Began his record business out of a New York University dorm; formed Def Jam Records with acquaintance Russell Simmons while still there. He brought the Beastie Boys, Public Enemy, and L.L. Cool J to Def Jam. Rubin left soon after the Beasties cracked the company's—and hip-hop's—future wide open. Moved to California and set up Def American (now just American), a label whose roster includes Slayer, Andrew Dice Clay, the Black Crowes, the Jayhawks, and Johnny Cash. Hasn't stuck with hip-hop but Rubin's certainly the funkiest white record producer of his era. Witness his work in 1992 with Mick Jagger, who under Rubin's direction finally sounds like a true honky funkateer and not just a wannabe.

10. BILL GRAHAM—So he was a bully who wound up mainly being the big cheese in San Francisco (and even there, found himself outranked by the likes of Herb Caen and Francis Ford Coppola). Graham *did* run the Fillmores to a faretheewell, he was an able and loyal manager to Carlos Santana, and for all his greed and pettiness, he did establish some kind of standard for showmanship and at least nominal community service. As a refugee Jew who saw some of the harshest civilian sides of World War II, then served in Korea with an otherwise all-black unit, Graham may even have had some excuses for the extremity of his personal behavior.

11. LUTHER CAMPBELL—Neither respected nor respectable. This child of the Miami ghetto has built the area's biggest black-owned business, and not only with his and 2 Live Crew's silly dirty-mouth rap but with additional hip-hop success, such as H-Town and Fresh Kid Ice. Luther makes certain to give back to his community, where he is both a major player and a controversial political player: One reason the political shit came down on him so hard was that the Luke label (then known as Skyywalker) made a record praising Janet Reno, in her race to become Dade County prosecutor. It was her opponent, Jack Thompson, who sicced the cops on 2 Live Crew for obscenity. He's never backed down, and has the dough, the hot cars, and the hot women to show why that strategy pays off.

12. CLIFF BURNSTEIN AND PETER MENSCH—Kings of the hill among heavy metal managers. Beginning their career with Iron Maiden, they now handle Metallica and many other major metallists. This may seem a minor accomplishment but they've brought credibility, professionalism, and a measure of vision to an area of the industry long dominated by sleaze.

13. MAURICE STARR—The only black entrepreneur in American history to make a fortune selling a *white* act to a *white* audience. Starr had his hooks in New Edition but they slipped away. He vowed his next teen-R&B property never would, and for as long as they were hot, the New Kids on the Block never did. He may market schlock but he's also broken one of America's ugliest molds.

14. PETER GRANT—A hard boy from London's East End (where he worked as a bouncer and as a movie extra) who went on to manage the late Yardbirds, then guided Led Zeppelin's lucrative career, and those of such Zep acolytes as Bad Company. If he was as much a bully as his great nemesis, Bill Graham, this gargantuan (three hundred pounds and more) always made sure his gang got paid.

15. JOHN HAMMOND, SR.—Makes the list on pure integrity and musical giftedness. The most famous talent scout in history, Hammond rediscovered Bessie Smith in the thirties, unleashed a horde of jazz greats (Benny Goodman, Charlie Christian, Count Basie, Teddy Wilson, up to and including George Benson), tried to make sense of it all with the great Carnegie Hall "From Spirituals to Swing" concert, and signed Bob Dylan and Aretha Franklin to their first record contracts. His impact on rock 'n' roll goes beyond Dylan and Aretha, though, to include Bruce Springsteen, Stevie Ray Vaughan, and even Leonard Cohen, all of whom were signed by CBS Records at his behest. Born a Vanderbilt, he outlived the family fortune, mainly because he did not take percentages of the talent he discovered, instead working on straight salary for his various employers (mainly Columbia Records but also Mercury and Vanguard). A noble figure with a strict political conscience—he helped the Scottsboro Boys win their media case, but resigned from the NAACP national board over the war in Vietnam—Hammond stands as the nonpareil music industry figure who was in it for love of the music above all. Needless to say, he's rarely mentioned these days.

Most Overrated Bizzers

1. COLONEL TOM PARKER—Oh yeah, a *real* genius. Shackled Elvis to the interests of Hill and Range music publishers, assuring him of a steady supply of second-rate material; signed him to William Morris and Hal Roach, who turned him into the cinematic equivalent of Wonder Bread; allowed RCA to package him with the grace and acuity of a package of defective pencils; interacted so well with Elvis personally that the man drugged and drank himself to death twenty years before his time; sold Presley's personal appearances to Vegas hotels and concert promoter Jerry Weintraub at a fraction of their true value; made side deals for merchandising and the like in which the Colonel wound up making more money than his star; finally dealt off Elvis's record royalties to RCA for a fragment of their worth and with no thought to the future; generally behaved like a small-time carny hustler rather than the big-league adviser Elvis deserved. And he did all this for a 50 percent commission, only two and a half times what a professional manager would have charged. Of course, you could also make the case that, since the Colonel consistently received far less than Elvis's true worth for all their endeavors, he only ended up raking in what a merely competent manager would have made. Whatta wizard! Whatta crud!

2. BRIAN EPSTEIN—Another overmatched manager. True, the Beatles wound up rich—but how much richer might they have been, if they'd had a personal manager who understood, for instance, how to renegotiate their contract during their bombshell success? Even if you give Epstein credit for hustling "his boys" into those collarless suits that made them palatable to Ed Sullivan and his adult audience, the publishing deal that Lennon and McCartney wound up signing with Northern Songs alone precludes an image of Epstein as the genius in "A Cellarful of Noise." It's also worth noting that, while talent surrounded the Beatles in abundance, not one of the other acts Epstein acquired for his management company amounted to more than Gerry and the Pacemakers. At least his acolyte, Robert Stigwood, found long-lasting second-raters in the Bee Gees. Like their idol Elvis, the Beatles' long-lived fame came more in spite of than because of their manager.

3. BILL GRAHAM—True, Graham pioneered the electric concert bill at the Fillmore East, and true, he brought great flair to all of his promotions. But those great sixties blues-meets-rock-meets-jazz bills came from an open-minded audience as much as any promoter—and all those blues and jazz players worked cheap. Furthermore, Graham's flair always came at the expense of his artists and their listeners. This was literally the case with his infamously elaborate backstage areas, with their lavish flowers, basketball courts, and such, which always, come settlement time, wound up being paid for out of the act's end of the gate, even at Live Aid (which cost about ten times more to produce in Philadelphia than in London for just that reason). And it was certainly figuratively true when Graham grandstanded on issues of "principle" that most often wound up displaying a bully's sense of fair play and a glory hound's attitude to community spirit. (Who can forget him edging slowly, carefully onto the stage at the end of the Live Aid broadcast, ostensibly to correct a problem—one that would have been either ignored or handled by a guitar roadie at any other show—but really to get his picture on the screen?) Besides that, give or take a Stones tour every other year, after 1971, when he pronounced rock a dying institution and closed Fillmore East in New York, Graham's principal clout came as the most potent promoter in San Francisco, not even one of the top ten markets in the United States. Given that Graham still passed himself off as the Hurok of rock when his clout extended no further than the East Bay, he's just about the definition of "overrated."

4. RUSSELL SIMMONS—Shoulda been one of the greats, because the impact of Run-D.M.C., L.L. Cool J, and Public Enemy, not to mention the Beastie Boys, gave him mid-eighties stature as the great hip-hop entrepreneur. But by the mid-nineties, he'd managed to parlay all that into nothing more substantial or charismatic than a label and management roster consisting of those stars in a radically faded state and no newcomer with as much charisma as a Beasties' B-side.

5. CHARLES KOPPELMAN—This great showman epitomizes the idea of "failed upward." In the sixties, the cigar-chomping music publisher's claim to fame was the Lovin' Spoonful, an act that fell apart at the peak of its fame partly in frustration over its inability to get paid fairly. In the seventies, he presided as Columbia Records' head of A&R at its nadir—Koppelman's the bright man who heard the seeds of *Born to Run* and suggested Bruce Springsteen record in Nashville with session pros. In the eighties, he did manage to hoodwink CBS into selling him its valuable music publishing properties at a deep discount, which he turned into a great fortune by selling them at a greater piece of their true value to EMI. Koppelman then founded SBK Records, known for such schlock as Vanilla Ice and Wilson Phillips and absolutely nothing more enduring, before being made head of EMI's U.S. music empire, which quickly sank in rank just as it was closing on a place as a genuine competitor to the Sony and Warner groups.

6. RUSS SOLOMON—The head of the Tower Records chain has grey hair down past his shoulders, which has deceived some into thinking of him as a hipster. But he's really as uncool as any other shopkeeper in the biz. His stores are miracles—miles of aisles crammed with product organized so haphazardly that shopping in them induces headaches. Furthermore, Tower led the campaigns to add the parental warning sticker, which got more than one act arrested, and to keep the ecologically insane CD "long box," a piece of cardboard scrap the rest of us were expected to endure so that Russ wouldn't have to pay to refixture his shops.

7. MALCOLM MCLAREN—Sure, he gave the Sex Pistols their ideology. But he also lent them a basic disrespect for the quality of their own music that ensured their premature burial, and it's hard to see how that's any kind of *business* triumph. Since then, while McLaren has occasionally pounced upon something interesting (notably with "Double Dutch," his premature hip-hop record), he's treated all of it as a scam, with results far more minuscule than they need have been. Last time out, this putative wizard came up with a rock version of *Madame Butterfly*, something that wouldn't have impressed anybody as original back in the hippie daze he's wont to bash.

8. WHOEVER THE HELL'S BEEN RUNNING RCA VICTOR FOR THE PAST FORTY YEARS—These guys started out with *Elvis Presley*, and what have they got to show for it? Bruce Hornsby and the Jefferson Starship catalogue?

9. DON KIRSCHNER—If this badly toupeed stiff had lacked the chutzpah to front his own TV show for a few campy years, would anyone remember him at all, let alone as the mannequin-maker who cast the Monkees?

10. CLIVE DAVIS—But only by himself. If Davis managed to eschew his periodic forays into media overexposure, where he shoots off his yap with pompous piety, more people would recognize what is, despite the crappiness of Manilow and Whitney Houston's schlocky, Clive-driven song selection, perhaps the most impressive executive career of the record industry's post-Beatles period.

Steve Propes Selects the Rarest 45s that Are Really Worth the Price

1. "Rocket 88," Jackie Brenston and the Delta Cats (Chess 1458), ca. 1954, $9,300—Rock and roll's, and Ike Turner's, first, from Memphis by way of Clarksdale, Mississippi. Only two copies of this 45 pressing are known to exist. One recently sold at auction for the above amount.
2. "Golden Teardrops," The Flamingos (Chance 1145), 1953 red vinyl, $3,000; black vinyl, $1,000—Doo-wop's best group, the all-time finest.
3. "It Ain't the Meat (It's the Motion)," The Swallows (King

4501), 1953 green vinyl, $1,000; black vinyl, $400—Even more racy than "Sixty Minute Man."

4. "That's All Right," Elvis Presley (Sun 210), 1954, $750—Elvis's debut disc, featuring a song taken from a 1940s blues. It's every bit as good as rock and roll's most famous career.

5. "Nitey Night," The Majestics (Marlin 802), 1956, $500—From this Miami doo-wop group came Sam Moore of Sam and Dave, though he's loath to admit it. Great talking doo-wop blues.

6. "My Saddest Hour," The Five Keys (Aladdin 3214), 1953, $500 —Doo-wop's second-best group, their finest.

7. "Gloria," The Cadillacs (Josie 765), 1954, $250—National anthem of doo-wop by the Cadillacs from New York, long before they became a novelty act. Song has a long and confused pedigree, starting with the writing and production talents of L.A.'s Leon Rene, no matter what the Josie label claimed.

8. "All That Wine Is Gone," Big Jay McNeely with Three Dots and a Dash (Imperial 5115), 1951, $200—Debut recording sessions for L.A.'s doo-wop godfather, Jesse Belvin (he wrote "Earth Angel" and "Goodnight My Love," among others). This rocking number with Big Jay's honking tenor sax was atypical Belvin, but it's great regardless.

9. "Come to Me," Marv Johnson (Tamla 101), 1959, $150; reissue on United Artists, $10—Debut disc of the Motown empire. A hit on United Artists.

10. "My Diary," Rosa Lee Brooks (Revis 1013), 1962, $100—A session for a tiny Los Angeles label, this doo-wop-styled vocal ballad used the uncredited guitar backing of Jimi Hendrix, supposedly his debut session. Also backing Brooks was her girl group, the Rosalettes.

Steve Propes Selects Fool's Gold
10 Worthless Expensive Records (In Order of Worthlessness)

1. "(Do) The Screw," The Crystals (Philles 111), $200—Though a few copies of this exist, as do many more bootlegs, it was never officially released, which accounts for its value. Basically, it's a girl group chant with a male voicing intoning the title.

2. "Keep A Lovin' Me," The Everly Brothers (Columbia 21496), $100—The first record by rock and roll's most celebrated duet came out two years before they cut their deal with Cadence Records. It's average country music at best, no excitement.

3. "Barbie," Kenny and the Cadets (Randy 422), ca. 1962, $150—Wimpy ode to a Barbie doll by a Kenny Doll, recorded with their mom by the guys who would become the Beach Boys.

4. "My Bonnie," Tony Sheridan and the Beat Boys (Decca 31382), 1962, $3,000; on MGM, $20—Proves why Sheridan only made one Beatles record, but doesn't explain why he appeared even on that one. Later reissued onto the charts by MGM, so anyone can hear the musical disaster cheaply. Ten commercial copies known to exist, more on Decca's pink promotional label, which is worth a lowly $500.

5. "Oh Maria," Joe Alexander and the Cubans (Ballad 1008), 1955, $100—The highly regarded first performance by Chuck Berry, known here as backing guitarist Chuck Berryl. Those who revere this have never heard the music—a weak calypso with passive guitar strumming. Known to exist only on 78 rpm.

6. "Box Top," Ike Turner with Carlson Oliver and Little Ann (Tune Town 501), 1959, $150—Little Ann turns out to be Annie Mae Bullock, later to be known as Tina Turner. This is Tina's debut disc. It's nothing short of a takeoff on Billy and Lillie's Philly-based calypso sound, a la "La Dee Dah" and "Lucky Lady Bug," records that Dick Clark seemed to play every four minutes. "Box Top" might have been easy to ignore even if he had gone that far with it.

7. "Stormy Weather," The Five Sharps (Jubilee 5104), 1951, $3,000—Doo-wop's holy grail, or at least its rarest record. Weak, almost sleepy harmony, proving this must have been a vanity recording for this early group. It's certainly not valuable because of the excellence of the performance. In fact, the record's best feature is its rain sound effects. A fire caused the master tape to be lost forever, so when demand started growing in 1964, Jubilee did the obvious thing—after all, even most collectors had never heard it. So they brought in a white, Italian-American harmony group they dubbed the Five Sharps. That group's "Stormy Weather" (Jubilee 5478) *and* the competing version by the Five Sharks (Times Squares 35) sound better than the legendary original. (Note: In the 1970s, two original 78s finally were located. One fetched well over $3,000; the other was cracked, then legally reissued on Bim Bam Boom Records, then bootlegged on a . . . lessee, a fourth generation 45 . . . I think. That's the one I have. Worth: 50 cents.)

8. "Korea Blues," Fats Domino (Imperial 5099), 1950, $500—Mournful blues by Fats, completely obscured by Dave Bartholomew's squawking trumpet, allegedly playing taps (RIP). Talk about two radio stations being played simultaneously.

9. "Big Boy," The Jackson Five (Steeltown 681), ca. 1968, $100—Michael Jackson's legendary disc debut proves why some people never grew up. Pressed at least twice, once on a crude-looking

orange label that looks as if it comes from Jamaica, though it actually came from Gary (which is more valuable, worth perhaps $200), the second distributed by Atlantic, which might occasionally wonder why it didn't pick up this group's option. *That* had lasting value.

10. "Shop Around," The Miracles (Tamla 54034), 1960, $100— This one came out twice, in a well-known story: After it had been released for a few minutes, Berry Gordy pulled it back after hearing it on the radio. The group redid it in an overnight session and came out with a really commercial sound, their first chart smash, reaching number two in *Billboard*. This first try was really a rehearsal, it was okay, but they really didn't have it yet. So it got pulled. Discerning the difference between the rare original issue and the better-known second try hit is like trying to determine a series of pure numbers, but here goes: The rare wax has the number 45-H55518A-2 in the dead wax, while the hit version has 45-LI in that space.

Steve Propes Selects the 15 Most Valuable Christmas 45s and the 5 Most Valuable Christmas LPs

45s

1. "Hey Santa Claus," The Moonglows, 1954 (red vinyl 45 is a bootleg) — $800
2. "It's Christmas Time," The Five Keys, 1951 — $750
3. "Blue Christmas," Elvis Presley, 1957 (RCA Victor 0808 promo 45 rpm only; RCA Victor 0720, the 1964 reissue with picture sleeve, valued at $50) — $750
4. "Lonely Christmas," The Orioles, 1950 (Jubilee 5017 on 45 rpm only, Jubilee 5001 from 1949 issued only on 78 rpm) — $500
5. "Rock N Rollin Santa Claus," The Hepsters, 1955 — $400
6. "Love for Christmas," The Ebonaires, 1955 — $300
7. "The Beatles Christmas Records," 1963 (U.K. only release on flexi-disc) — $250
8. "Cool Cool Christmas," The Sabres, 1955 — $200
9. "Season's Greetings from The Beatles," 1964 (sound card—paper; released in United Kingdom as "Another Beatles Christmas Record") — $200

10. "Let Christmas Ring," The Coolbreezers, 1958 $150
11. "The Beatles Third Christmas Record," 1965 $125
    (released by Beatles U.S.A. Limited Fan Club)
12. "Everywhere It's Christmas," The Beatles, 1966 $125
    (vinyl-coated postcard)
13. "Christmastime (Is Here Again)," The Beatles, $125
    1967
14. "Santa Claus Boogie," The Voices, 1955 $80
15. "Beatles 1968 Christmas Record," 1968 (7-inch $80
    flexi-disc)

LPs

1. *Elvis Presley Christmas Album*, 1957 (original press- $500
    ing only)
2. *The Beatles Christmas Album*, 1970 $100
3. *A Christmas Gift to You from Phil Spector*, 1963 $80
    (original Philles pressing only)
4. *"Twas the Night Before Christmas,"* Huey "Piano" $75
    Smith, 1962
5. *Charles Brown Sings Christmas Songs,* 1961 (original $50
    King issue #775 only)

Steve Propes's 21 Reasons Why I Collect 45s
(None of These Has Ever Been on CD or LP)[1]

1. "Have Love Will Travel," Richard Berry and the Pharoahs—His original "Louie Louie" appears on an obscure Flip LP, then an Earth Angel import album, but not Flip's original version of this song, which has been performed by everybody from the Sonics to Springsteen.
2. "He's a Rebel," Debby Boone—The original flip side of her godawful "You Light Up My Life," this version of the Crystals' classic isn't bad.
3. "He's a Rebel," Vikki Carr—The original (pre-Crystals) version.
4. "The Shadow Knows," The Charlatans—Dan Hicks's first single, and the debut of the seminal San Francisco band
5. "My Baby," Ray Charles—His very first side for ABC-Paramount.
6. "At the Discoteque," Chubby Checker—One of his final discs for Parkway Records; according to some, it inspired the term "disco."
7. "Git It," The Crystals—Or any of the other Phil Spector B-

sides, all of which have been characterized as "throwaways" . . . which, granted, most of them should have been.

8. "Rockin' Chair," Fats Domino—Many of his early sides didn't make the box set, although many may have been issued in Europe.

9. "Get You in the Mood," The Eagles—The flip of their first hit, 1972's "Take It Easy."

10. "Ooh Looka There Ain't She Pretty," Bill Haley and the Comets.

11. "Thou Shalt not Steal," John D. Loudermilk—The original of Dick and Dee Dee's massive hit, recorded by its composer.

12. "Heart Darling Angel," The Orlons—Great female doo-wop, their first disc.

13. "Tough Enough," Johnny Otis—And various other singles from his Dig label. Though many of these were issued on LP by England's Ace reissue company, strangely, this one, Otis's final Dig release, was not.

14. "Honky Tonky," The Queen—A 1958 pseudonym for Dinah Washington, who was doing rock 'n' roll by covering the Drifters, of which her ordinary pop-jazz admirers would never have approved.

15. "Jimmy's Boogie," Jimmy Reed—The bluesman's second release, from 1953.

16. "Orbit," Paul Revere and the Raiders—Their very first, a killer surf-style instrumental with space sound effects.

17. "Stoned," The Rolling Stones—Their first U.S. single, censored or at least controversial because of its title. The record's hardly corrupting, being an instrumental.

18. "Pink Cadillac," Bruce Springsteen—And his many other non-LP/CD B-sides.

19. "Fine and Mellow," Rufus Thomas—The original flip of his hit, "The Dog," not on any package including Atlantic's *Complete Stax/Volt Singles*.

20. "The New Breed," Jackie Wilson—Missed by every repackager, including the ones who assembled his box set.

21. "Salt Lick," ZZ Top—Their first on London.

Author's Note: Five years ago, this would have been a much longer list. But with recent box sets and other reissues booming, obscure 45-only releases by Elton John, Led Zeppelin ("Hey, Hey What Can I Do"), Bo Diddley ("I'm Bad"), the Police, Prince B-sides, Jimi Hendrix ("Johnny B. Goode") and the Isley Brothers ("I'm Gonna Knock on Your Door") have finally been compiled. In other cases, European companies have reissued obscurities by Chuck Berry ("That's My Desire" and "Lonely Schooldays"), Brenda Lee ("Bigelow 6-200"), and Johnny Otis ("Mumblin' Mosie"). But that's OK because the non-CD flip side tradition continues thanks to Aerosmith ("Don't

Stop"), the Black Crowes ("Darling of the Underground Press"), the Red Hot Chili Peppers ("Nobody Wired Like Me"), and R.E.M. ("The Lion Sleeps Tonight").

---

[1] At time of publication.

Steve Propes Lists a Dozen Hoaxes (and Dispels a Few Rumors)

RECORDS THAT DON'T (OR MIGHT NOT) EXIST BUT WOULD BE WORTH PLENTY IF THEY DID

1. "Cross Cut Blues Saw," Binghampton Blues Boys (XL 901), date unknown—Title appeared in *Blues Records 1942–1966* by Mike Leadbitter but was deleted from the updated *Blues Records 1943–1976,* published in 1987. The title first appeared on unspecified blues want lists (like those from the United Kingdom). The song is real enough: Albert King hit with a 1966 version. XL also existed, as a Memphis-based label. But the disc has never turned up except on paper.

2. "So Long," Little Jimmy Brown (NRC), 1955—This one is mentioned in *James Brown: The Godfather of Soul* as his first release. I've never seen one on disc or even on a list, want, sale, or otherwise. Have you?

3. "Shake It Sally," Freddy Cannon and the Belmonts (label unknown), ca. 1981/2—Mentioned by Bo Diddley as a session he worked on. Again, too little is known to make a decision, so I called Freddy. "It was put in a movie called *The Junkman* overseas," he told me. "It was made by the guy who made *Gone in 40 Seconds.* Me and the Belmonts were in it. Probably 1981 or 1982. Japan seems to be running this movie a lot. Bo just played on that cut. I had him come to the studio, this record had the Bo Diddley feel, he had a stereo guitar at the time." Unlikely that it ever made it to a record.

4. "That's What You'll Get," The Castiles (no label), 1966—Springsteen's first group. This exists on a demo, now in the Asbury Park Springsteen museum. But despite reports to the contrary, it never saw any kind of release.

5. "Too Much," Bernard Hardison (Republic 7111), 1954—Hardison is indeed a known blues vocalist and Republic a known label. Song supposedly the original of Elvis's hit, but where is a copy of it? This one more-than-likely, though.

6. "Such a Pain Inside," The Heart Throbs (Harbor), 1955—A

true hoax, created by a prominent promoter during the doo-wop revival of the early 1960s, in order to make collectors' mouths water.

7. "T.G.'s Voodoo Lounge," The Joy Buzzers (Motown 1061), 1964—Created by Don Waller for his *Motown Story* book in 1985, as a way of checking against uncredited use of data, I guess. He merely found an unused Motown catalogue number just begging to be used.

8. "My Rockin' Baby," Chris Montez (label unknown), date unknown—Montez, Ritchie Valens's protégé, had rocking hits ("Let's Dance") and middle-of-the-road hits ("Call Me"). This supposedly is his first record, except no one knows what label, year, or anything else. That "no one" includes Montez.

9. "Bosom Divine," Jesse Presley with Jo-Jo Fineaus and His Hattiesburg Hepcats (Furniture Frolic 107)—Part of writer Nick Tosches's discography in *Unsung Heroes of Rock and Roll*. Represented as Elvis's elusive twin brother, who also recorded as Esau Smith in 1955.

10. "True Fine Mama" b/w "Any Way the Wind Blows," The Soul Giants (Danni 103), 1964—This was the Pomona group that hooked up with Frank Zappa when he created the Mothers of Invention on Mother's Day, 1964. Singer Ray Collins had backed Little Julian Herrera and the Tigers on the original "True Fine Mama," while the flip was a Zappa original, a song later used on his Ruben and the Jets project. I've never seen a copy but rumors persist in Zappadom.

11. "Let's Rock," Barrett Strong (Tamla 54022), 1959—A recent creation, its provenance made more enticing by the fact that Strong hit in 1959 with "Money," the first Tamla record, though the hit version appeared on Anna. Mention has been made of "Let's Rock" in the liner notes to Motown's *Hitsville U.S.A.* singles compilation box set. Presto! Label photos began to surface with a cover story that it was found in cracked condition in the collection of a Detroit deejay, who sold it for $200 with the buyer turning it over for $2,500.

12. Buddy Holly MCA Canada albums—In the 1970s, when the resurgence of interest in Holly and his music began to take hold, an advertisement appeared for a new Canadian edition of his work on MCA. Problem is, the album by the title advertised did not exist. Suddenly, this became a most wanted title, one no one could get. Was it ever even a test pressing? Readers please advise.

13. "Annie Had a Miscarriage," The Midnighters—Hank Ballard's vocal group not only had a 1954 hit with "Work with Me Annie," they created a sensation and a cottage industry, considering all the releases—followups, cover records, answer records, the works—that emanated: "Annie's Answer," "Annie Met

Henry," "Annie Kicked the Bucket," "Annie Pulled a Humbug," and even a few hits, including the Midnighters' own
"Annie Had a Baby," and Etta James's "Roll with Me Henry,"
bleached into the national charts by Georgia Gibbs under the
pseudonym "The Wallflower." (Henry, of course, was in each
instance Mr. Ballard.) "Annie Had a Miscarriage" *should* have
but didn't exist; it's the product of a collector's overactive imagination. Too bad.

While we're on the subject, some collectors covet Ballard's
original version of "The Twist" by the Midnighters (Federal
12345), supposedly his last on that label before Syd Nathan
transferred him to the big sister label, King. Again, no such
luck. The Federal catalogue number was assigned to another
release, so the only known catalogue assignment for "The
Twist" is in fact King 5171, by Hank Ballard and the Midnighters from early 1959. Two versions of the disc exist, the original
and one with a dubbed-in saxophone sounding like a continuous
fart, stinking up the whole works. Which brings us to . . .

14. "The Jet" and "Samson and Delilah" b/w "Those Dancin' Di-
nosaurs," Chubby Checker (Parkway 808)—Both these titles
have appeared in various label listings, discographies, and price
guides, but I don't know anyone who owns an original 45. "The
Jet" does exist on LP. Most likely, Checker's followup to "The
Class" was his remake of Ballard's "The Twist."

NOW, CONSIDER THESE . . .

15. *Wipe Out*, The Impacts (Delfi 1234), 1963—*Wipe Out*, a surf
instrumental LP, had reasonable sales back in 1963, the same
year an instrumental single with the same title by the Surfaris
hit number two nationally, propelled by its crazed drum solo. It
became a rock and roll standard, in some circles, a legend. Time
passed. In 1987 or 1988, the original *Wipe Out* album, the Impacts one, was reissued (Ocean 8701), this time with the tune
"Wipe Out" sounding very much like the Surfaris hit (something not so evident on the original Delfi version). Was this a
trick of engineering or had some obscure tapes been located?
Reportedly, there was some legal maneuvering over who had
the original "Wipe Out," but we're record fans, not lawyers (and
we don't want to talk to any), so this story has no conclusion.

16. Little Willie John's Capital Records session—Never in release.
John was signed to King at the time. But this record's no rumor.
It does exist, as recorded with producer H. B. Barnum on February 28, 1966, and Capital or EMI or whatever their name is
these days ought to get on the case and put it out.

Steve Propes cowrote What Was the First Rock and Roll Record *with
Jim Dawson, and* Merry Christmas, Baby: Christmas Music from

Bing to Sting *with Dave Marsh. He presents a great deal of rock's hidden history in his forthcoming* The Secret History of Rock and Roll: The First One Hundred Years, *an exhaustive compendium of thousands of rock and roll oddities.*

Battle of the Big-Buck Books
The Most Valuable LPs According to Price Guides

The record-collecting world uses two basic price guidebooks, Jerry Osborne's Official Price Guide to Records *and* Goldmine's Price Guide to Collectible Record Albums, *edited by Neal Umphred. (*Goldmine *is the best-known record collector's magazine, Osborne edits another,* DISCoveries*). Umphred provides a list of "The 100 Most Valuable U.S. Albums." Osborne doesn't offer such lists. Since opinions vary as to the usefulness and accuracy of each book, it seemed logical to compare them, using the top 25 entries from Umphred's book as a starting point. Because the books evaluate records so differently, and because picayune differences too subtle to bother with here can make a big difference, we've used Osborne's highest price for point of comparison. It makes little difference anyway, since the chance of running across the rare version of* Freewheelin' *at the neighborhood garage sale has never been much less infinitesimal than the prospect of locating a Picasso in the same fashion. But, unless you are the kind of collector who takes such chances seriously, the comparison is fun— and instructive, about the nature of value, among other things.*

ALBUM	UMPHRED PRICE	OSBORNE PRICE
1. *The Freewheelin' Bob Dylan*	$20,000	$2,000–$3,000

This is the famous Dylan album with four tracks—"Talkin' John Birch Society Blues," "Gamblin' Willie's Dead Man's Hand,," "Rocks and Gravel," and "Let Me Die in My Footsteps"—that were pulled and replaced at the last minute when CBS Records got political cold feet. Umphred says that a *mono* copy would be worth $10,000; Osborne never mentions the stereo version.

2. *The Beatles and Frank Ifield On Stage*	$9,000	$2,000–$3,000

The books also differ on the characteristics—including title!—of the most valuable version.

3. *Introducing the Beatles*	$8,000	$800–$1,200
4. *Hear the Beatles Tell All*	$8,000	$50–$60

5. *Yesterday and* $7,500 $5,000–$10,000
   Today

The Beatles album, with original butcher cover, in stereo.

6. *12 X 5* $7,500 $50–$75

Umphred's price is for a rare release on blue vinyl, which does not appear in Osborne's tenth-edition book.

7. *River Deep,* $7,500 $1,000–$2,000
   Mountain High

Their album on Phil Spector's Philles label. Both books agree that it would be well-nigh impossible to find one with a cover, as Spector dumped the LP when the single flopped, so only a few pressings exist.

8. *Billy Ward and* $7,500 $1,000–$2,000
   His Dominoes

9. *Hey Jude/The* $6,000   not listed
   Beatles Again

Umphred cites an alternative cover prototype for the album, bearing *The Beatles Again* as the title. Osborne never mentions it.

10. *Blood on the* $5,000 $25–$35
    Tracks

Original test pressings with alternative takes of four songs cited by Umphred. Osborne estimates the value of any promotional copy of the album (which a test pressing would be) at no more than the above, does not mention the altered songs.

11. *The Black Album* $5,000 $1,000–$2,000

Prince's unreleased erotic masterwork.

12. *Rhythm and Blues* $4,500   not listed
    Party

"Copies of this album in collection condition are so rare that delineating a price for condition is ludicrous. There are probably fewer than ten copies known to exist," according to the *Goldmine* Guide. Osborne is just more . . . hopeful?

13. *The Midnighters:* $4,500 $1,500–$2,000
    Their Greatest
    Hits

14. *Boyd Bennett* $4,000 $800–$1,200

15. *Diamond Dogs* $4,000 $500–$750

David Bowie's album with dog genitals depicted on the cover.

16. *Mood Music* $4,000 $400–$500

Charles Brown's great album on Aladdin. The more valuable version is on red vinyl.

17. *Rockin' the Boogie* $4,000 $500–$1,000

Amos Milburn album, on red vinyl.

18. *Mule Skinner* $3,500 $800–$1,200
    Blues

The Fendermen's album, named after their only hit.

19. *Poetry for the* $3,500   not listed
    Beat Generation
Jack Kerouac reads poetry. Osborne uninterested?
20. *Out of the Bachs* $3,000   not listed
Goldmine calls this "recently unearthed punk-psych gem" "minor
key, haunting and melodic . . . like an American Zombies if they
were in a garage/psych mood." Osborne seems less captivated by
this kind of disc in general or maybe he went to print before its
"unearthing." (What would a record that had been "earthed" sound
like when you dug it up?)
21. *Johnny Burnett &* $3,000 $1,000–$2,000
    the Rock 'n' Roll
    Trio
The original non-Elvis rockabilly LP.
22. *Damon* $3,000   not listed
Osborne doesn't bother with what Umphred calls "this privately
pressed psych album."
23. *Party After Hours* $3,000 $500–$1,000
This time, they can't even agree on who made the damn thing.
Umphred lists Amos Milburn, Wynonie Harris, and Crown Prince
Waterford, Osborne claims they're joined by Velma Nelson. Either
way, it's R&B again.
24. *Through the Past* $3,000 $8–$10
    Darkly
Umphred values this so highly in a picture disc version that Osborne
never mentions.
25. *A Hard Day's* $2,500 $75–$100
    Night
Osborne doesn't list the promo version that Umphred values most
highly; his highest price is for the Capitol Record Club issue.

*Editor's Note: Strictly speaking, these aren't Umphred's top 25 albums—
he lists several different versions of each of the Beatles albums in between.
Even doing it our way, though, the twenty-fifth album would have been
Frank Sinatra's Sinatra-Jobim, which we've skipped because we're uninterested.*

CHAPTER 3

Record
Companies

12 Problems Artists Have with Record Companies

1. Getting paid.
2. Royalties withheld as a "provision for returns."
3. "Favors" and perks (even video shoots) that wind up being charged against royalties.
4. Verbal agreements that end with the words "trust me."
5. Loss of interest after initial signing period.
6. Insistence on using record company support services for tour merchandising, song publishing, and the like.
7. Lack of tour support.
8. Getting someone to listen to demos or come to shows.
9. Needing to have the "right" lawyer or manager to receive attention and promotion.
10. Counterfeiting within the record company.
11. Publishing swindles as a condition of release from bad contracts.
12. Interference with the actual content of albums—censoring lyrics, insistence on involvement in song selection, or selection of producers, for instance.

Rapper's Top 11 Complaints About Their Record Companies (Compiled by Bill Stephney)

1. Record company won't consider ammunition as a nonrecoupable marketing expense.
2. Record company waiting room not large enough to accommodate group's seventeen extra "associates."
3. Constant battle with publicity department over exposing to the black press that artist's personal manager, lawyer, and accountant aren't white—just *extremely* light-skinned.
4. Bootleggers on the street are backed by an evil triumvirate of the Ku Klux Klan, Korean nationals, and the hip-hop artist's record company.
5. Record company's A&R exec has no hip-hop credibility and is a sellout because he knows how to read.
6. Record company does not have enough biracial female staff members available for video shoots.
7. Record company forgot to tell Arsenio that group wants to perform a mock drive-by on the studio audience.

8. Video promotional tour does not include booking on all-nude public access channel.
9. Artist informs record company that if they don't get that Beatles' sample cleared, they might have to fuck up Ringo.
10. Record company refuses to replace office water cooler with malt liquor vending machine.

AND LAST BUT NOT LEAST . . .
11. "How come my record isn't on the radio?"

A veteran of both Rush Management and the Bomb Squad, Bill Stephney is the President of StepSun Music Entertainment.

The 10 Most Innovative Record Companies

1. SUN—Invented rock and roll as we know it. Founded in the early fifties by Memphis talent scout and recording studio owner Sam Phillips, Sun nurtured as much talent as any label in history: Rufus Thomas, Carl Perkins, the Prisonaires, Jerry Lee Lewis, Charlie Rich, Johnny Cash, Billy Lee Riley, and biggest and best of all, Elvis Presley.

2. ATLANTIC—Proved that an independent company could compete on an equal footing with the majors. Formed in the late forties by two young Turkish aristocrats, Ahmet and Nesuhi Ertegun, and their dentist partner, Herb Abramson, Atlantic created a very appealing style of rhythm and blues, culminating in recordings by the Drifters (featuring Clyde McPhatter), the Coasters, and Ray Charles, all of which helped bring authentic black voices into the American musical mainstream. Without the capital resources of the major labels, Atlantic made its stand and continued to grow with a mixture of soul and British rock acts through the late sixties, when it was sold to Warner Brothers.

3. MOTOWN—Obliterated the marketing distinctions between pop and soul. Former Detroit record-store owner Berry Gordy, Jr., created a veritable hit-making machine that spewed dozens of unforgettable smashes by such stars as Smokey Robinson and the Miracles, Diana Ross and the Supremes, Marvin Gaye, the Four Tops, Stevie Wonder, Martha Reeves and the Vandellas, and the Temptations. These artists split their appeal between black and white teenage audiences, living up to the label's motto: "The sound of young America."

4. AMERICAN (FORMERLY PRECEDED BY DEF)—This guy's either insane or ingenious. Owner (and star producer) Rick

Rubin has made a career of going to extremes. Anyone who can make stars of speed metalists Slayer, pop rapper Sir Mix-A-Lot, master of the dirty limerick Andrew Dice Clay, and Rolling Stones fans the Black Crowes while managing to woo Johnny Cash cannot be stable. Rich, but not stable.

 5. DEF JAM—Founders Russell Simmons and Rick Rubin (who subsequently left to found Def American) served up black anger and ghetto attitudes without dilution or apology. Then they popularized it, taking hard-core hip-hop to the suburbs. With the most enviable roster in hip-hop—including L.L. Cool J, Public Enemy, Slick Rick, and dozens more—Def Jam remains the premier rap label, despite an early-nineties cool spell.

 6. STIFF—Proved that an independent company did not have to compete on an equal basis with the majors. By the mid-seventies, when Jake Riviera and Dave Robinson, a pair of minor-league English music businessmen, gathered their forces (Nick Lowe, Elvis Costello, Ian Dury) to form Stiff, the majors had backed independent labels into a corner, driving up artist prices and marketing costs to a point where it was all but unimaginable for canny entrepreneurs without great capital resources to survive. Stiff stood these equations on their head by creating an environment that determinedly opposed such strategies, attracting marginal but profitable renegades.

 7. ROUGH TRADE—With such acts as the Slits, the Smiths, the Delta Five, the Young Marble Giants, and others, Rough Trade, an English consortium of groups and support personnel, was the first successful collective in rock business.

 8. UPTOWN—Uptown expanded the hip-hop universe beyond the b-boy. Realizing that b-girls want romance and thirtysomethings crave sweet melodies as well as hard beats, founder Andre Harrell built an empire on the likes of "the overweight lover" Heavy D and hip-hop diva Mary J. Blige, playing to the black radio crowd like no other label formed since before Michael Jackson sang in public.

 9. RHINO RECORDS—Before Rhino, reissues were either too obscure or too poorly packaged; record companies treated them like a chore. But Rhino founders Richard Foos and Harold Bronson made them fun—and profitable. With collections like *The Best of Louie Louie* and *Golden Throats 1* (sample cut: William Shatner crooning "Lucy in the Sky with Diamonds"), the company created a market for quality cheese. When they won a Grammy for their *Jack Kerouac* collection, they proved that they could nurture and preserve as well as poke fun. And now that Atlantic Records has entrusted them with the treasures in their vault, Rhino's future belongs to documenting America's rich musical history.

 10. SUB POP—Perhaps cofounders Jonathan Poneman and Bruce Pavitt were simply in the right place at the right time. But it took a certain genius to foresee in 1986 that Seattle (of all places) would eventually birth the nineties' most vibrant rock scene. With a vague sense of something-on-the-horizon, these fervent regionalists happily volunteered their label as its midwife, releasing important (if not immediately lucrative) albums by Nirvana, Mudhoney, Soundgarden, Tad, and L7. And then the Lollapalooza generation was born.

Record Companies that Turned Down the Beatles

1. Decca
2. Pye
3. Columbia
4. HMV
5. EMI

The Beatles were turned down by Norrie Paramor, EMI's chief A&R man, who preferred the sterling sounds of Cliff Richard as the company's rock 'n' roll contribution. They were signed by George Martin, an A&R man with Parlophone, until that point, regarded as a backwater label. Parlophone, ironically, was an EMI subsidiary, and Beatles records were released on EMI worldwide, including that company's U.S. subsidiary, Capitol.

Sun Records 20 Greatest Hits

1. "Whole Lot of Shakin' Going On," Jerry Lee Lewis, 1957
2. "Mystery Train," Elvis, Scotty and Bill, 1955
3. "Good Rockin' Tonight," Elvis, Scotty and Bill, 1954
4. "Blue Suede Shoes," Carl Perkins, 1956
5. "Milkcow Blues Boogie," Elvis Presley, 1955
6. "Red Hot," Billy Riley and the Little Green Men, 1957
7. "Lonely Weekends," Charlie Rich, 1960
8. "Dixie Fried," Carl Perkins, 1956
9. "Great Balls of Fire," Jerry Lee Lewis, 1957
10. "Flyin' Saucers Rock & Roll," Billy Riley and the Little Green Men, 1957
11. "That's All Right," Elvis Presley, 1954
12. "Just Walkin' in the Rain," The Prisonaires, 1954
13. "Mystery Train," Little Junior's Blues Flames, 1953
14. "Ooby Dooby," Roy Orbison and the Teen Kings, 1956
15. "High School Confidential," Jerry Lee Lewis, 1958
16. "Who Will the Next Fool Be," Charlie Rich, 1960
17. "I Walk the Line," Johnny Cash, 1956
18. "When It Rains It Pours," Billy "The Kid" Emerson, 1955
19. "Breathless," Jerry Lee Lewis, 1958
20. "Devil Doll," Roy Orbison and the Roses, 1960

Motown's Top 40

1. "I Heard It Through the Grapevine," Marvin Gaye, 1968
2. "Reach Out I'll Be There," The Four Tops, 1966
3. "Do You Love Me," The Contours, 1962
4. "Heat Wave," Martha and the Vandellas, 1963
5. "What's Going On," Marvin Gaye, 1971
6. "Since I Lost My Baby," The Temptations, 1965
7. "Ain't No Mountain High Enough," Marvin Gaye and Tammi Terrell, 1967
8. "I Want You Back," The Jackson 5, 1970
9. "Bernadette," The Four Tops, 1967
10. "You Keep Me Hangin' On," The Supremes, 1966
11. "Uptight," Stevie Wonder, 1966
12. "Let's Get It On," Marvin Gaye, 1965
13. "My Girl," The Temptations, 1965
14. "Stop! In the Name of Love," The Supremes, 1965
15. "The Tracks of My Tears," Smokey Robinson and the Miracles, 1965
16. "Superstition," Stevie Wonder, 1973
17. "Money," Barrett Strong, 1960
18. "Shotgun," Jr. Walker and the All Stars, 1965
19. "I Can't Help Myself," The Four Tops, 1965
20. "It Takes Two," Marvin Gaye and Kim Weston, 1967
21. "Fingertips—Pt. 2," Little Stevie Wonder, 1963
22. "Ain't That Peculiar," Marvin Gaye, 1965
23. "Ooo Baby Baby," The Miracles, 1965
24. "What Becomes of the Brokenhearted," Jimmy Ruffin, 1966
25. "This Old Heart of Mine," The Isley Brothers, 1966
26. "If I Were Your Woman," Gladys Knight and the Pips, 1971
27. "Papa Was a Rolling Stone," The Temptations, 1972
28. "Dancing in the Street," Martha and the Vandellas, 1964
29. "Super Freak," Rick James, 1981
30. "The Way You Do the Things You Do," The Temptations, 1964
31. "Signed, Sealed, Delivered, I'm Yours," Stevie Wonder, 1970
32. "My Guy," Mary Wells, 1964
33. "Every Little Bit Hurts," Brenda Holloway, 1964
34. "I Second That Emotion," Smokey Robinson and the Miracles, 1967
35. "Leavin' Here," Eddie Holland, 1964
36. "The Love I Saw in You Was Just a Mirage," Smokey Robinson and the Miracles, 1967
37. "Got to Be There," The Jackson 5, 1971
38. "I Wish It Would Rain," The Temptations, 1968
39. "ABC," The Jackson 5, 1970

40. "The Hunter Gets Captured by the Game," The Marvelettes, 1967

The 25 Greatest Stax/Volt Hits

1. "Hold On, I'm Comin'," Sam and Dave, 1966
2. "Knock on Wood," Eddie Floyd, 1966
3. "(Sittin' On) the Dock of the Bay," Otis Redding, 1968
4. "In the Midnight Hour," Wilson Pickett, 1965
5. "I've Been Loving You Too Long," Otis Redding, 1963
6. "When Something Is Wrong with My Baby," Sam and Dave, 1967
7. "Green Onions," Booker T. and the MGs, 1962
8. "Everybody Loves a Winner," William Bell, 1967
9. "634-5789," Wilson Pickett, 1966
10. "Who's Making Love," Johnnie Taylor, 1968
11. "Time Is Tight," Booker T. and the MGs, 1962
12. "These Arms of Mine," Otis Redding, 1963
13. "Private Number," Judy Clay and William Bell, 1968
14. "Tramp," Otis Redding and Carla Thomas, 1967
15. "Respect Yourself," The Staple Singers, 1971
16. "Your Good Thing (Is About to End)," Mable John, 1966
17. "Mr. Pitiful," Otis Redding, 1965
18. "Walking the Dog," Rufus Thomas, 1963
19. "Born Under a Bad Sign," Albert King, 1967
20. "You Don't Miss Your Water," William Bell, 1962
21. "Last Night," The Mar-Keys, 1961
22. "Raise Your Hand," Eddie Floyd, 1967
23. "You Don't Know Like I Know," Sam and Dave, 1966
24. "Fa-Fa-Fa-Fa-Fa," Otis Redding, 1966
25. "In the Rain," The Dramatics, 1972

Note: Wilson Pickett recorded "In the Midnight Hour" and "634-5789" at Stax Studios, using the house musicians, but the Atlantic label issued these records.

Sugarhill's Greatest Hits

1. "The Message," Grand Master Flash and the Furious Five
2. "White Lines (Don't Do It)," Grandmaster Melle Mel
3. "Rapper's Delight," The Sugarhill Gang
4. "That's the Joint," Funky Four + 1
5. "Apache," The Sugarhill Gang

6. "The Adventures of Grand Master Flash on Wheels of Steel," Grand Master Flash and the Furious Five
7. "Spoon'nin Rap," Spoonie Gee
8. "Yes We Can-Can," Treacherous Three
9. "We Want to Rock," Crash Crew
10. "Funk You Up," Sequence

Tommy Boy's Greatest Hits

1. "O.P.P.," Naughty by Nature
2. "Planet Rock," Afrika Bambaataa and Soulsonic Force
3. "Looking for the Perfect Beat," Afrika Bambaataa and Soulsonic Force
4. "The Payoff Mix" (Mastermix of G.L.O.B.E. and Whiz Kid's "Play That Beat Mr. D.J."), Double Dee and Steinski
5. "Danger Zone," Planet Patrol
6. "No Sell Out," Malcolm X and Keith LeBlanc
7. "Doowutchyalike," Digital Underground
8. "Me Myself and I," De La Soul
9. "Tender Love," Force M.D.s
10. "Ladies First," Queen Latifah
11. "The Humpty Dance," Digital Underground
12. "Play at Your Own Risk," Planet Patrol

Rhino Records 20 Greatest Hits

1. *The Best of Louie Louie, Vol. 1* and *Vol. 2*
2. *Santa's Got a Brand New Bag,* James Brown
3. *Queen of Soul—The Atlantic Recordings,* Aretha Franklin (box set)
4. *Mr. Excitement,* Jackie Wilson (box set)
5. *Jubilation!: Great Gospel Performances Vol. 1–3*
6. *Sweat 'n' Soul,* Sam and Dave
7. *Anthology (1962–1974),* The Righteous Brothers
8. *For The Lonely: A Roy Orbison Anthology (1956–1965)*
9. *The Best of Cool Yule*
10. *Soul Shots: A Collection of '60s Soul Classics, Vol. 1–4*
11. *The Isley Brothers Story, Vol. 1* and *Vol. 2*
12. *The British Invasion, Vols. 1–4* (box set)
13. *Street Jams Electric Funk Part 1–4; Hip-Hop From the Top Part 1–4*

14. *Didn't It Blow Your Mind!: Soul Hits of the '70s*, Vol. 1–15
15. *20th Anniversary Collection—The Greatest Novelty Records of All Time*, Dr. Demento
16. *Beat the Boots!* Frank Zappa (box set)
17. *Treacherous: A History of the Neville Brothers (1955–85)*
18. *The Disco Years*, Vol. 1–5
19. *Live (1965)*, Ernest Tubb
20. *Troubadours of the Folk Era*, Vol. 1–3 (box set)

The 12 Greatest Artist- and Producer-Owned Record Labels

1. Apple, The Beatles (Jackie Lomax, Badfinger, Billy Preston, Doris Troy, among others)
2. Philles, Phil Spector (The Crystals, The Ronettes, The Righteous Brothers, Darlene Love, Ike and Tina Turner)
3. A&M, Herb Alpert with Jerry Moss (Janet Jackson, Joe Cocker, The Police, Sting, The Carpenters, Cat Stevens, and numerous others up to and including Peter Frampton and the Brothers Johnson)
4. Philadelphia International, Kenneth Gamble and Huff (Teddy Pendergrass, Harold Melvin and the Blue Notes, The O'Jays, MFSB, McFadden and Whitehead, and a raft of others)
5. Sugar Hill, Sylvia Robinson (The rap label, featuring Grandmaster Flash, The Treacherous Three, The Funky Four, and other ferocious crews)
6. Def American, Rick Rubin (Black Crowes, Sir Mix-A-Lot, Andrew Dice Clay, Slayer, Johnny Cash, and other crimes against nature)
7. Uptown, Andrew Harrell (Mary J. Blige, Jodeci, Heavy D and the Boyz, et al.)
8. Bang, Bert Berns, Ahmet Ertegun, Nesuhi Ertegun, Jerry Wexler (Van Morrison, Neil Diamond, The McCoys, The Strangeloves)
9. Luke, Luther Campbell (2 Live Crew, Luther Campbell, H-Town, Professor Griff, and more)
10. SST, Greg Ginn (Ground-breaking American postpunk by, among others, The Minutemen, Black Flag, Negativland, Meat Puppets, Screaming Trees, Husker Dü, Sonic Youth)
11. Red Bird and Blue Cat, Jerry Leiber, Mike Stoller, George Goldner (The Shangri-Las, The Dixie Cups, The Ad Libs, The Trade Winds)
12. Invictus/Hot Wax, Holland-Dozier-Holland (Parliament, Chairmen of the Board, Freda Payne, Eighth Day, Laura Lee)

25 Artists Who Were On Apple Records

1. Badfinger (The Iveys)
2. The Beatles
3. The Black Dyke Mills Band
4. Brute Force
5. The Elastic Oz Band
6. Elephant's Memory
7. George Harrison
8. Chris Hodge
9. Mary Hopkin
10. Hot Chocolate
11. John Lennon
12. Jackie Lomax
13. Paul McCartney
14. The Modern Jazz Quartet
15. David Peel
16. Billy Preston
17. Rada Krishna Temple
18. Ronnie Spector
19. Ringo Starr
20. The Sundown Playboys
21. John Tavener
22. James Taylor
23. Trash
24. Doris Troy
25. Lon and Derek Van Eaton

Great Chicago Blues Labels

1, 2, AND 3. ARISTOCRAT, CHESS, CHECKER—These labels were owned by the Chess Brothers, Leonard and Phil. Aristocrat, their original, featured Muddy Waters, who moved with them to Chess, where he joined Howlin' Wolf as the label's initial big sellers. Checker was the logical spinoff; its biggest star in the blues (prerock) years was Little Walter, the singer and harpist who'd started his Checker career in Muddy's band.

4. J.O.B.—Co-owned by singer-pianist St. Louis Jimmy, J.O.B.'s most celebrated records were made by the great J. B. Lenoir. The label lasted only briefly during the fifties; its masters were bought up by Chess and have been lost in confusion since that label's subsequent demise.

5. CHANCE—The original label of J. B. Hutto and his various Hawks also recorded Sunnyland Slim, John Lee Hooker, and for a time Little Walter.

6, 7. STATES, UNITED—Junior Wells first cut "Hoodoo Man" for States, Robert Nighthawk was sister label United's most imaginative performer.

8. PARROT—Both John Brim, Jimmy Reed's sometime sidekick, and J. B. Lenoir recorded for this label, which had nothing to do with the London Records subsidiary for which Savoy Brown and Tom Jones would later cut.

9. VEE-JAY—Primarily a soul label, Vee-Jay made its blues reputation with the seminal Jimmy Reed boogies and Billy Boy Arnold's marvelous "I Wish You Would."

10. COBRA—This was the leading label for West Side blues players of the fifties, particularly Otis Rush.

11. ARTISTIC—Buddy Guy got his start here.

12. CHIEF—Magic Sam's best early work was recorded for Chief, as well as Junior Wells's and the late Earl Hooker's.

13. DELMARK—Run out of Bob Koester's Jazz Record Mart shop, this label cut as much jazz (including the avant-gardists in the Association for the Advancement of Creative Music or AACM) as blues but the excellence of both its new recordings (some of the finest stuff by Magic Sam, for instance) and its steady reissuing of classics (by Sleepy John Estes and Junior Wells, for example) make it a landmark among collectors.

14. ALLIGATOR—Initially, Bruce Iglauer's shoestring company, which he began in order to contemporarize what his ex-bosses at Delmark were doing, did a magnificent job of documenting the late seventies and early eighties Chicago scene, including such ace artists as Hound Dog Taylor, Lonnie Brooks, and Son Seals. Later on, it fell into sonically and musically conservative habits, but that's something we have to bitch about only because companies today fold less rarely than those of yesteryear—in the old days, Alligator wouldn't have survived long enough to sink so deep into the doldrums.

CHAPTER 4

Promotion

They'd Like to Teach the World to Sing . . . A Case of Coke Commercial Makers

In the eighties and nineties, Pepsi dominated the Cola Wars, at least as they applied to music endorsements. But in the sixties and seventies, long before "Unh hunh" became a marketing tool instead of a gospelized grunt, only one soft drink actively recruited rockers, and it wasn't the one that tried to name a Generation after itself. As an exemplar of that more innocent time, here are twenty-four of the finest artists who succumbed to singing "Things go better with . . ." (Incidentally, the first fifteen are all in the Rock and Roll Hall of Fame.)

1. The Beach Boys
2. James Brown
3. Ray Charles
4. The Coasters
5. The Drifters
6. The Four Seasons
7. The Four Tops
8. Aretha Franklin
9. Marvin Gaye
10. The Impressions
11. Roy Orbison
12. Otis Redding
13. The Supremes
14. The Temptations
15. The Everly Brothers
16. Ashford and Simpson
17. The Bee Gees
18. The Chi-Lites
19. Gladys Knight and the Pips
20. The Pointer Sisters
21. Sister Sledge
22. The Troggs
23. Conway Twitty
24. Vanilla Fudge

They Got the Right One, Baby?

These folks have made the choice of a new generation, or at least that's what Pepsi has paid them to say.

1. David Bowie
2. Charo
3. Ray Charles
4. Vic Damone
5. Gloria Estefan
6. Glenn Frey
7. Hammer
8. Michael Jackson
9. The Jackson 5
10. Madonna
11. Robert Palmer
12. Lionel Ritchie
13. Tiny Tim
14. Tina Turner
15. Young MC

Famous Last Words
Stars Who've Sworn Never to Do Commercials

Back when the first edition of this book was published, it was so rare for rockers to do advertisements, it seemed kinda cute and we had trouble filling out the list of "Artists Who Made Commercials." (It had only eight entries.) But first the Rolling Stones toured for Jovan Musk Oil perfume, and then The Who for Miller beer, and, as the saying goes, apres le Who, le deluge. So in this edition, we've got a list of those who've declined to sell their songs to the highest bidder:

1. **BRUCE SPRINGSTEEN**—Reportedly turned down a $10 million *opening* offer from Chrysler, as well as numerous sums from everybody else in Corporate America back when he was rock and roll's Great White Hope of the eighties.

2. **NEIL YOUNG**—Made the hilarious "This Note's for You" video, blasting superstars who shill, only to have it (temporarily) banned by MTV because it featured too many name brand products (which MTV bans from videos lest advertisers find a cheaper way of exposing their products on the channel).

3. **CHUCK D AND PUBLIC ENEMY**—Just as Ice Cube was making his heavy-duty pitch for St. Ides Malt Liquor, Chuck D discovered PE's music used in one of the brew's commercials. Smelling its extra alcoholic content as an invitation to self-genocide, PE sued and the commercials came off the air. Put Cube in a tight spot, too, and the resulting dialogue must have made *somebody* think.

4. **JOAN JETT**—She ranks way up on the list because, as a marginal record-seller and concert artist, keeping to her principles costs her more than the others. But she *does* love rock 'n' roll and not selling her songs proves it.

4. **BOB DYLAN**—Lucrative as the offers must be, there has never been a Dylan song used in a commercial or advertisement. (Ooops! Times have changed—and Dylan just sold "The Times They Are A-Changin' " to Cooper and Lybrandt, an accounting firm.)

6. **JOURNEY**—Did one tour with corporate sponsorship, hated the interference and the inference, and not only never did another (which might not have been such a big deal, since the band soon broke up) but spoke out about how bad it sucked.

7. **PRINCE**—Although it's not clear exactly which sponsors could *use* "Purple Rain" or "1999," some wine cooler must certainly have tried to pry "Let's Go Crazy" loose.

8. **JOHN MELLENCAMP**—A hard-ass here, as everywhere.

9. **AEROSMITH**—For all their foibles, this is one area where

they've remained whistle-clean and proud of it. Setting a good example, despite their best instincts.

10. JANET JACKSON—Given her family background and TV training, it's amazing that this nineties superstar hasn't given it up to a corporate concern. Of course, given those very things, she's the most likely on this list to renege. (Most likely—but not the first.)

Steve Leeds Offers 82 Reasons Why Radio Stations Won't Play Your Record

1. It's not for us (or our sound).
2. No room.
3. No label support.
4. We want to give the record the best shot, so will have to wait until we have more room.
5. No local sales.
6. No national action.
7. We're considering.
8. We're watching and waiting.
9. It's the wrong image.
10. It's not modal.
11. We need another copy.
12. Poor reaction when we featured it.
13. The jocks don't like it.
14. No phone reaction.
15. We played the import.
16. We're gonna wait and see what the competition does.
17. We'll wait for the single.
18. The record's not in the stores yet.
19. We need approval from headquarters.
20. The program director doesn't like it.
21. It was vetoed in the music meeting.
22. It's too hard.
23. It's too soft.
24. It's too wimpy.
25. It's not as good as the last record.
26. It needs to be relistened to.
27. It's too disco.
28. It's too pop.
29. We didn't get the copromotion of the live date.
30. Trade chart numbers don't merit air play.
31. It sounds like everything else.
32. It's not a good record.
33. I don't like it.
34. It's warped (or broken).
35. There's a scratch in the vinyl on that track.
36. The wrong LP was in the jacket.
37. We're saving room for scheduled new releases.
38. Going into the book (station's ARB rating period).
39. We're already playing too many women.
40. We don't have the album yet.
41. No tip-sheet advertising.

42. Nothing hits me.
43. Don't like the mix.
44. Not enough guitar.
45. Too many strings.
46. Overproduced.
47. Underproduced.
48. Don't like the album cover.
49. This particular cut is not consistent with the rest of the album.
50. Our listeners won't be able to relate.
51. It's too rhythm oriented.
52. We need more copies for each jock.
53. We can't play too many singers.
54. That music only works in certain markets.
55. Our competition's call letters appeared in the background of their music video.
56. We're waiting for the full-length release; we don't play tracks.
57. We don't play rap.
58. It's too techno.
59. We're waiting for the remix.
60. I haven't listened to it yet.
61. It's already receiving airplay across the street.
62. Our audience isn't familiar with this act or song.
63. It's boring.
64. We've never played their previous stuff.
65. It's too dancey.
66. We're testing it this week.
67. We're playing too many of your releases.
68. Where's the MTV airplay?
69. There's no request activity.
70. The audience research was bad.
71. It's not our demographic.
72. It's a male record.
73. It's a female record.
74. We didn't get the [advertising] time buy.
75. It's too long; we need an edit.
76. The group is over-exposed.
77. They sucked live.
78. Their name is offensive.
79. We played their last record and nothing happened.
80. The last time we had the band on the air they were real jerks.
81. They're not popular in this market.
82. It's not on [fill in call letters] yet.

Steve Leeds is a radio and video promotion executive in New York City. He has been an executive at MTV and Atlantic Records, and an independent FM promotion man. He also programmed the innovative music video TV station U68, in Newark, New Jersey.

Top 10 Excuses that Urban Stations Give for Not Playing Rap as Told by Sincere

1. It offends my target audience.
2. This type of music doesn't need my support to sell. It sells all right by itself.
3. I don't think it will last. It's just a fad.
4. Rap music is degrading to women and my mother listens to the station.
5. The consultants (or the management) won't let me play any rap.
6. The artist doesn't fit the image that the station is trying to project.
7. The sales department can't sell to that demographic.
8. The pop station is already playing it, so I don't need to play it.
9. The record has to be Top 20 before I can play it.
10. I just don't like it.

Sincere is the Senior National Director of Rap Promotions for the PolyGram Label Group.

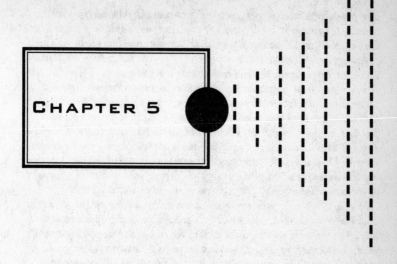

CHAPTER 5

Production

Best Producers

The producer's role in rock and roll has changed immensely in the past decade. It still covers a vast array of functions, none of them definitive, all having to do with "getting the job done" in the recording studio. Today's producers range from people who impose styles, like Teddy Riley and Jimmy Jam and Terry Lewis, to those who impose ways of conceiving music, like Brian Eno, from men who are essentially soundcraftsmen of the highest order, like Mutt Lange, to those who seem to get by mainly by showing up (examples too numerous and embarrassing to mention present themselves, but how much different from Thriller *does the actual soundscape of Michael Jackson's* Bad *sound to you, and how much of the difference is an improvement?). Originally, the producer had complete responsibility for selection and arrangement of material, though the best producers always responded to the artistic imperative. The old style of record production perhaps peaked with Phil Spector, a producer more famous than almost any of the artists with whom he worked. The producer's stature reached its peak in the late seventies and early eighties, when picking the producer became a top priority in the record-making process. In black music and dance music, particularly, the producer now becomes the dominant figure in the record-making process, although this is far less true with hip-hop, with its general intermingling of roles. While it remains hard to define what a producer does, these twenty men—there has yet to be a prominent female record producer—define what a producer can do.*

1. SAM PHILLIPS

As much as any single nonperformer, Sam Phillips deserves credit as a father of modern rock and roll and R&B, the whole complex of music that spewed out of the fifties and carries forward to today. In 1954–55, he spent the better part of a year working at his Sun Records Studio in Memphis with Elvis Presley, guitarist Scotty Moore, and bassist Bill Black, creating the breakthrough that allowed black style to fully penetrate the pop mind. In earlier work with Little Junior Parker, Howlin' Wolf, Rufus Thomas, and many others, Phillips helped lay the foundations of black rhythm's emergence; in later sessions with Jerry Lee Lewis, Roy Orbison, Johnny Cash, and Carl Perkins, Phillips helped capture a sound that defined one edge of rock. Four decades later, the ambience of these recordings remains shimmering, overflowing with life—as mortal and imperishable as the souls of the men who made it. Definitive work: Elvis Presley, *The Sun Sessions.*

2. PHIL SPECTOR

"Tomorrow's sound today," the slogan of his Philles label, actually held up pretty well—Spector's dense "Wall of Sound," which melded forty instruments into a single unified yet detailed blare, taking R&B to the edge of pop and pop to the brink, heralded the density of today's hip-hop and metal. Those massed gangs of guitars, strings, and percussion, even more than Spector's high-hormonal teen romanticism, are what link Brian Wilson, Bruce Springsteen, and, whether they know it or not, Mutt Lange and Dr. Dre. Essential recordings: Collected on *Back to Mono (1958–1969)*, a four-CD compilation of Spector's work that begins with his apprenticeship with Jerry Leiber and Mike Stoller, covers all the key hits, and omits only John Lennon's solo LPs among his greatest productions.

3. BRIAN HOLLAND AND LAMONT DOZIER

At Motown, the first black-owned company to capitalize on the rise of the rock and soul sensiblity, Holland-Dozier reigned supreme: Their productions with the Supremes, the Four Tops, Marvin Gaye, Smokey Robinson, and the rest grafted Sun Records' clarity, Spectorian grandeur, and gospel power and grace to a remarkable set of songs (written by the duo with Brian's lyricist brother, Eddie) and singers. If the Supremes began as nothing more than a frothier confection along the lines of Spector's Ronettes, it was Spector who defined the greatness of Holland-Dozier's masterpiece, "Reach Out (I'll Be There)," when he described it as "a black man singing Bob Dylan." In summary, that's *visionary* soul music. Later, the vision would play itself out on Holland-Dozier-Holland's own Invictus/Hot Wax labels, where they worked with the likes of the Chairmen of the Board, Freda Payne, Laura Lee, and 8th Day. There, they also became the first to give George Clinton's Parliament the freedom to rock a groove. Essential recordings: The best of the Supremes and the Four Tops; it's worth seeking out the original singles, because those were the hottest masters and no others quite capture their vitality.

4. LEE "SCRATCH" PERRY

Perry defined the roiling, boiling turbulence of vintage reggae, epitomized by Junior Murvin's "Police and Thieves." His brief collaboration with the Clash gave him white rock prominence but it was his perfection of "dub," reggae with steamroller bass lines and only the ghost of a vocal track, that made him internationally influential —for dub laid the essential sonic groundwork for eighties and nineties dance music. Essential recording: *Lee "Scratch" Perry and Friends*, a three-LP set (put together by England's Trojan Records in 1989) that includes some of his finest dub, contrasted with original vocal versions by the likes of the Heptones and the Diamonds.

5. JERRY LEIBER AND MIKE STOLLER

Best known for their songwriting (which produced key hits for Elvis, among others), Leiber and Stoller pioneered elaborate productions of pop songs with their three-minute "playlets" with The Coasters. The first of these was 1953's "Riot in Cell Block #9" by the Robins, the Coasters' predecessors. Working with engineer Abe "Bunny" Robyn, Leiber and Stoller had defined the art of rock 'n' roll concept records three years before they split Los Angeles for

New York. Their recordings with the Coasters, the Ben E. King version of the Drifters, King's early solo records, and later, on their own Red Bird label with girl groups, soul singers, and studio rockers leave an unshakable legacy that long outlasted its fifties and sixties environs. Their training of Phil Spector, whose entire production strategy is based on their work, only adds to their significance. Essential recording: *There's A Riot Goin' on: The Rock 'n' Roll Classics of Leiber & Stoller*.

6. THE BEATLES AND GEORGE MARTIN

They'd be landmark figures if they'd *only* created *Sgt. Pepper's Lonely Hearts Club Band*, which remains an inexhaustible source of production style and subtlety. (Doubters should ask themselves what *else* the Posies and P.M. Dawn have in common.) Add to it such rock-baroque masterworks as *Revolver, The White Album*, and *Abbey Road*, and you have a body of work that's formidable simply for what it sounds like, much less for what it says. Then add in the early singles, which can rock a house as hard today as when they were first created. Essential recording: You don't have to be a sentimentalist sap to see all of the Beatles' recordings as essential, but in a pinch, you could probably get by with *Meet the Beatles, Revolver, Sgt. Pepper's*, and *Abbey Road*.

7. KENNETH GAMBLE AND LEON HUFF

In the seventies, Philadelphia's Sigma Sound Studios became Mecca for the remnants of soul music. Gamble and Huff's Philadelphia International elevated unknowns like Teddy Pendergrass to superstardom, renovated journeymen like the O'Jays into enduring celebrities, and even turned out the last great R&B-based instrumental hit in MFSB's "TSOP." You could even argue that their links to predecessors like Holland-Dozier and Spector are deepened by the neo-girl-group hits of the Three Degrees. That Philly International—which featured all manner of producers, writers, arrangers, and singers operating under the firm guidance of Gamble and Huff—managed to make music of such character against the faceless impulse of the Eurodisco explosion counts as a kind of latter-day miracle. But it was the kind of miracle for which Gamble and Huff had worked hard, woodshedding through the late sixties by making hits with Jerry Butler, Archie Bell and the Drells, and the Intruders, among others. Essential recording: *Philadelphia Classics*, a 1977 LP, covers some major hits but you need the Butler *Ice* albums, and at least "best of" 's by Harold Melvin and the Bluenotes, the O'Jays and, most important, the O'Jays.

8. ROBERT JOHN "MUTT" LANGE

Premier sonic architect of the eighties, Lang, South African–born and an engineer by training, crafted the devastating crunch of AC/DC's *Back in Black* and Def Leppard's *Hysteria*, came up with the definitive postsoul hit in Billy Ocean's "Get Out of My Car," and even perfected wimp balladry with "Everything I Do (I Do It for

You)" by Bryan Adams. Each of these records is astonishingly clean and massively powerful, the reflection of Lange's obsession with detail and his refusal to ever let that obsession interfere with a record's fundamental spirit. Essential recording: the above.

9. ISAAC HAYES AND DAVID PORTER

Like Holland and Dozier and Leiber and Stoller, Hayes and Porter may be best known as songwriters, which has somewhat overshadowed their Stax productions, which rank as the greatest in Southern soul. That's saying something, considering that Stax itself encompassed talents like Otis Redding, Eddie Floyd, Jim Stewart, Steve Cropper, Al Jackson, and Don Davis. If Redding's records epitomized the earthiness of Stax, it's Hayes and Porter's that show off its adult sophistication, and not even Floyd's discs had more raw power. The culmination of this grandiloquent excitement came with their inestimable series of hits and LPs with Sam and Dave. Later, as a performer, Hayes helped usher in the postsoul era, notably with *Hot Buttered Soul*, an album as expansive and influential as *What's Going On, Superfly* and *There's a Riot Going On*. Essential recordings: Sam and Dave's *Sweat 'n' Soul (1965–1971)* and Hayes's *Hot Buttered Soul*.

10. RICK RUBIN

Rubin's straightfoward, bare-knuckles approach to the mixing boards has revolutionized pop music. On L.L. Cool J's debut album, he pushed the punch and smack of the drum track even further into the listener's face than Run-D.M.C. had just months earlier, helping to set the sonic stage for the fury of later rap. He next took three punks from the Lower East Side and armed them with Zeppelinesque crunch, turning the Beastie Boys into the multiplatinum heroes of every white frathouse in America (before they defected from the ranks of serious rappers to become punks once again). Then he put Run-D.M.C. in the studio with Aerosmith, ushering in the rap-rock alliance. He preserved Slayer's buzzsaw sound, gave the Cult muscle, and locked the Red Hot Chili Peppers in an abandoned mansion until the veteran punk-funk outfit wrote their first ballad, "Under the Bridge," their breakthrough hit. He made Mick Jagger sound as if he cares and convinced Johnny Cash to do a rock record. And he did all this before he turned thirty. Essential recordings: *Radio*, L.L. Cool J; "Walk This Way," Run-D.M.C.; *Licensed to Ill*, the Beastie Boys; *Wandering Spirit*, Mick Jagger.

11. BERNARD EDWARDS AND NILE ROGERS

The hits that Edwards and Rogers made with Chic, a studio group in which they also performed, alone qualify them as the foremost American disco producers. Their ability to adapt rock licks to dance production put them a good five years ahead of their time, a fact borne out by later productions of artists like David Bowie. Edwards and Rogers discovered engineer Bob Clearmountain, whose mixes gave them the hottest sound in the world (until everybody else discovered them), the precision of their arrangements can be breathtaking, especially given the utter absence of clutter (virtually alone among disco-era rhythm record-makers), and Edwards ranks among the most adept bassists ever to cut a track.

12. GLYN JOHNS

The king of British engineer-producers (the mold from which Mutt Lange was struck with Roy Thomas Baker [Queen, the Cars] as missing link), Johns worked with giants: the Beatles (as engineer only), the Stones and the Who. Certainly, his greatest work came on *Who's Next*, for which he received production credit, but he may have done almost as much for *Beggars Banquet*, for which he didn't. His sound was the hardest and most sophisticated hard rock of its period. He went on to work with considerably softer performers, notably the Eagles on their first two albums and Joan Armatrading on a whole series of memorable LPs. Essential recording: *Who's Next*.

13. DR. DRE

Dr. Dre brought musical sensiblities to hard-core rap, a genre that generally detests melody and traditional song structure. N.W.A's *Straight Outta Compton* was not only musical but visual. Listening to the record, you could close your eyes and see southern Cali's mean streets even if you'd never been there. *The Chronic*, Dre's first solo album, stayed in the Top Ten on the pop charts because it combined the gangster attitude with songs that have choruses to hum along to. Along with his undeniable talent, Dre has one of the best track records in pop: Every album that he has produced has earned either a gold or platinum award, from forgettable cheerleader-types J.J. Fad, to original hip-hop diva Michel'le, and *No One Can Do It Better*, the D.O.C.'s astonishing debut album. Essential recordings: *Straight Outta Compton*, N.W.A; *The Chronic*, Dr. Dre.

14. PRINCE

His work on his own records—tight, sparse, irresistibly danceable —established the Minneapolis funk-rock sound, and alone justifies his spot on this list. On outside projects, Prince is never quite as far-reaching. Nevertheless, the simplicity of his work on the Time albums show that his catchy funk can stand on its own without his signature quirkiness. And his work with Mavis Staples betrays his rich, emotional connection to the gospel church. Anyway, anyone who can make Vanity (or, better yet, Apollonia) interesting or give Sheena Easton an edge has gotta be a genius in our book. Essential recordings: *Dirty Mind*, *Sign of the Times*, Prince; *What Time Is It?* The Time.

15. ARTHUR BAKER

Baker's productions with Afrika Bambaataa and Soulsonic Force, "Planet Rock" and "Searching for the Perfect Beat," helped define hip-hop, electronifying the basic rap approach and marking it as the

most innovative development in black popular music in a generation. His work with U.K. avant-gardists New Order resulted in
"Confusion," the most danceable Britfunk ever made and one which
the rest of the sceptered isle still seems trying to catch up to. Later,
he "remixed"—which meant recasting, and in effect, re-producing
—mid-eighties hits like Cyndi Lauper's "Girls Just Want to Have
Fun," Springsteen's "Born in the U.S.A.," and Diana Ross's
"Swept Away." Baker also played a crucial role in popularizing
house music, whose dense beats and bluesy take on electro-funk
stem from just one more search for that perfect beat. Essential recording: *Tommy Boy's Greatest Hits,* which includes the Bambaataa
tracks and his work with the hip-hop studio group Planet Patrol. Also
worth seeking out are the Lauper and Springsteen remixes (he did
several for Bruce), "I.O.U." by Freez, and *Tina B.,* a post-girl-group
funk record.

16. GIORGIO MORODER

The king of Eurodisco, best-known for making Donna Summer
Queen of Disco. Sure Moroder, and key collaborators Pete Bellotte,
Harold Faltermayer, and Keith Forsey, worked to a formula. But
that formula gave rise to some tremendously exciting records: big,
bold, with the fattest beats of their day, and worthy of the boogie on
which that rigid beat insisted. Furthermore, by successfully making
English-language hits in Munich, the Italian Moroder heralded the
coming internationalization of pop. Essential recording: Donna
Summer's albums *Bad Girl, On the Radio* (a greatest hits compilation), and, for rockers mostly, *The Wanderer,* their last work together.

17. JIMMY JAM AND TERRY LEWIS

Currently held in highest regard for their series of best-selling
albums by Janet Jackson, but the Jam/Lewis exploits have deeper
roots. They'd already been deployed in the Time, a band that was
far more than the Prince's puppets it was portrayed as being. After
that band broke up in 1984, Jam and Lewis immediately produced a
series of hot singles for the S.O.S. Band, collected in the album *On
the Rise,* plus one-shots like Cherrelle's "I Didn't Mean to Turn You
On," Human League's huge hit "Human," and remixes for George
Michael. They also produced for singer Alexander O'Neal what are
arguably the finest neosoul albums of the late eighties/early nineties.
These never crossed over but they served as a kind of warmup for
their work with Michael's famous sister. With Jackson, with whom
they seem to work in the truest production collaboration dance music
has seen since Donna Summer dumped Giorgio Moroder, they've
displayed the usual funkateer propensity for expropriating every influence they've laid their ears on (although not until 1993's *janet* did
they begin sampling much), fusing it with a garage rock sense of
how to create an unforgettably trashy moment. Essential recording:
Jackson's *Control, Rhythm Nation,* and *janet.*

18. THE BOMB SQUAD

They were great while they lasted. After cutting their teeth on Public Enemy's first album, Hank and Keith Shocklee, Bill Stephney, and Eric "Vietnam" Sadler masterminded perhaps the most ambitioius album of the eighties, P.E.'s *It Takes a Nation of Millions to Hold Us Back*. Chuck D's baritone rode its swirling wall of sound like a bucking bronco. They did the same for Ice Cube's *AmeriKKKa's Most Wanted*, but the team wandered in different directions by the time it sleepwalked through P.E.'s *Fear of a Black Planet*. Having fizzled, the Bomb Squad never recovered. However, the power of *Nation* and *AmeriKKKa* alone easily dwarfs the entire oeuvres of lesser producers. Essential recordings: *It Takes a Nation of Millions to Hold Us Back*, Public Enemy; "You Can't Fade Me," Ice Cube. Even though the Bomb Squad still exists in name, the original members have gone their separate ways and, with them, the Squad's fire.

19. TEDDY RILEY

Riley invented New Jack Swing, which is like R&B with a hip-hop attitude, influencing scores of imitators (a situation that led Riley to flee New York City's tight quarters for Virginian breathing room). Essential recording: *The Future*, Guy; "Rump Shaker," Wrecks N Effect.

20. BRIAN ENO

Eno brought avant-garde ambient music to the pop mainstream with his work with the Talking Heads and U2. The Roxy Music founder subverted traditional pop melodies in favor of atmospheric mysticism, creating sweeping emotional landscapes full of ambiguity. Seal and R.E.M. are only two of the numerous pop stars who should forward half their royalty checks to him. Essential recordings: *Remain in Light*, Talking Heads; *The Unforgettable Fire*, U2.

Reginald C. Dennis Picks the Greatest Hip-Hop Producers

1. DR. DRE

The man behind N.W.A, the D.O.C., and Snoop Doggy Dogg, Dre's high-end synthesized compositions refined the "gangsta" sound into an art.

2. MARLEY MARL

A decade-long career proves his ability to change with the times. His music has been the foundation for artists like Roxanne Shanté, Biz Markie, MC Shan, and Big Daddy Kane. He was the driving force behind L.L. Cool J's 1990 comeback.

3. LARGE PROFESSOR

A large record collection and an ear for the rugged East Coast funk have made him an underground favorite.

4. PETE ROCK

He is considered the king of the soulful horn loop and old-style R&B arrangements.

5. PRINCE PAUL

His studio wizardry brought De La Soul to the forefront. Not afraid to break new ground, he has become the master of the unorthodox audio sample.

6. SHOCK G

A spiritual descendant of George Clinton. His work with Digital Underground demonstrates a knack for making beats for both street and pop audiences.

7. THE BOMB SQUAD

The originators of the abrasive Public Enemy sound. The inventors of hip-hop's industrial noise.

8. DJ PREMIER

This half of the GangStarr duo brought the rap-jazz collaboration to new heights. Pioneered the use of soft piano lines and the acoustic bass sounds.

Bill Stephney's Top 20 Recordings of All Time

1. "Good Times," Chic
2. "Sucker M.C.'s" Run-D.M.C.
3. *It Takes A Nation of Millions to Hold Us Back*, Public Enemy
4. "Heartbeat," Taana Gardner
5. *Led Zeppelin*, Led Zeppelin
6. "Make It Funky," James Brown
7. "Love T.K.O.," Teddy Pendergrass
8. *Straight Outta Compton*, N.W.A
9. *Gratitude*, Earth, Wind and Fire
10. *Raising Hell*, Run-D.M.C.
11. "Dance to the Drummer's Beat," Herman Kelly
12. "Set It Off," Stafe
13. *Zenyatta Mondatta*, The Police
14. "Don't Look Any Further," Dennis Edwards with Siedah Garrett
15. "I Know You, I Live You," Chaka Khan
16. *Licensed to Ill*, The Beastie Boys
17. "Raw," Big Daddy Kane

18. "Super Sperm," Captain Skyy
19. *Songs in the Key of Life*, Stevie Wonder
20. "Mr. Magic," Grover Washington, Jr.

As a founding member of the Bomb Squad, Bill Stephney was one of the principal architects of the first two Public Enemy albums as well as Ice Cube's AmeriKKKa's Most Wanted. Currently, he is the president of StepSun Music Entertainment.

Tom Dowd Explains How to Know a Great Record (Not!)

10. Nothing sounds like you thought it did (a sign that you're getting older).
9. Digital is here to stay. People adjusted to going from kerosene lamps to gas light and now halogens. Your ears adjust quickly. It's your listening habit that's slow to change.
8. If it was originally recorded in mono, nothing can make it "true" stereo.
7. Do not try to equate taste to technology.
6. If the drum part sounds the same throughout the entire album, just imagine how long it took to train the drummer to play that way.
5. If your "old" cassette copy of the album sounds like the "new" CD version, something's wrong!
4. With the volume up all the way and your speakers on the floor, if your neighbors don't complain, then you need to add some bass.
3. Remember there's only one side to a CD so do not expect to be awakened at the halfway mark.
2. When all the vocals and solos sound the same, it may be the only key/chords they can play in.
1. Even if you can make an old 45-rpm record fit in your CD drawer, it won't sound very good.

Tom Dowd pioneered engineering excellence in rock and R&B recordings at Atlantic Records in the 1950s and 1960s, working with producers Jerry Leiber and Mike Stoller, Ahmet Ertegun and Jerry Wexler, and Neshui Ertegun, and doing some of the first stereo recordings of nonclassical music. At the end of the sixties, he began producing and since has worked with a staggering array of stars including Aretha Franklin, Rod Stewart, Lynyrd Skynyrd, the Rascals, Derek and the Dominoes, the Allman Brothers Band,

Eric Clapton, and Dr. John. Many of these artists made their biggest hits with Dowd at the production helm.

Great Engineers, Compiled by Peter Bochan

1. ALAN LOMAX
For his field recordings with Woody Guthrie, Muddy Waters, and Leadbelly, among others.

2. LES PAUL
Pioneer of the electric solid-body guitar also initiated multitrack recording, flanging, sound-on-sound, variable recording speeds, close miking, delay echo—and on and on!

3. SAM C. PHILLIPS
For his work with Elvis and the slapback sound of Sun Records.

4. TOM DOWD
Mr. Atlantic R&B. Pioneer of stereo in rock and rhythm and blues recordings.

5. BUNNY ROBYN
L.A.'s version of Dowd—the cat who actually cut the tape for Leiber and Stoller's early recordings, as well as the bulk of the rest of Hollywood-style R&B and doo-wop.

6. LARRY LEVINE
The mastermind at the master control board for Phil Spector and Brian Wilson's Beach Boys.

7. GLYN JOHNS
Sonic auteur of the Stones *Let It Bleed*, control room mastermind for the Beatles, Stones, Who, Led Zeppelin, the early Eagles, and Joan Armatrading.

8. BOB CLEARMOUNTAIN
Remixer extraordinaire, sometime producer, cut his spurs with Chic, has since worked with Springsteen, the Stones, Bryan Adams, INXS, and a host of others.

9. GEOFF EMERICK
Engineered the Beatles' *Abbey Road* (named for his workplace) and the best of Pink Floyd, among much else.

10. ROGER NICHOLS
His work satisfied Steely Dan's Donald Fagen, Walter Becker, and Gary Katz. It would be hard to praise its meticulousness any more grandiosely.

11. JOHN "JELLYBEAN" BENITZ

12. STEPHEN BRAY

13. SHEP PETTIBONE
These three comprise the Madonna School of Sound.

14. EDDIE KRAMER

Jimi Hendrix's techno partner. Also worked with the Stones and Zep.

15. JASON ROBERTS AND D. J. MUGGS

Cypress Hill's sonic doctors.

16. HUGH PADGHAM

The one part of the Police that Sting carried forward; also works with XTC.

17. DON WAS

His own productions of Bonnie Raitt, Brian Wilson, and Was (Not Was).

18. TODD RUNDGREN

Most notably, the records he's made by himself, true solo discs that offer an exceptionally high sonic standard. Also Grand Funk Railroad, Patti Smith, Hall and Oates, more.

19. DANIEL LANOIS

Another who makes his own fine-sounding records, but Lanois is better-known for the records he's made with U2, Bob Dylan, and Robbie Robertson.

20. TYRELL (COMPUTER WIZ)

The man who makes P.M. Dawn sound so luxuriously laid-back.

21. SCOTT LITT

Much postpunk rock, notably R.E.M.

22. ROY HALEE

His best work has been done with Simon and Garfunkel and more recently, Paul Simon, which means he's made fine music all over the world.

23. RICHARD DASHUT

Lindsey Buckingham's indispensable partner, both solo and at the helm of Fleetwood Mac.

24. TEDDY RILEY

25. JIMMY JAM

Kings of New Jack Swing (Guy, Michael Jackson, Janet Jackson, Babyface, Alexander O'Neal, and others).

Peter Bochan has been a radio producer and air personality for more than twenty years, making his home base at WBAI. National Public Radio airs his "Short Cuts" as annual year-end specials, which, like his BAI program, All Mixed Up, raise aural montage to new heights.

Hey DJ
A Half-Dozen Great Dance Remixers

After more than a decade, remixers are still viewed as also-rans and wannabes in "serious" production circles. They are perceived as studio step-

children, lacking the depth and attention span to helm an entire project from scratch. Nothing could be further from the truth. All of the folks listed below have actually made a successful transition into production. Remixers are the doctors who nurse weak and ailing original recordings to hip club stature and increased sales success. They work on the fly, with limited budgets, small fees, and minimal mainstream recognition. An ever-evolving art form, re-mixing has quickly grown from merely rearrranging pre-existing tracks to re-producing and often rewriting songs.

1. ARTHUR BAKER

The king of all mastermixers. This legendary dude almost single-handedly paved the road that an army of remixers now effortlessly prances down. It would be easier to name an artist whose work he has not tinkered with than to list his top credits. Rockers still gag on the memory of Baker bringing Bruce Springsteen and Fleetwood Mac into the clubs with "Dancing in the Dark" and "Big Love," respectively.

2. SHEP PETTIBONE

Long before he became world-renowned as the man who cowrote and produced "Vogue" with Madonna, Pettibone ruled dance floors with a string of hits that included the bulk of the delicious Salsoul Records catalogue and the timeless "I Like It" by Phyllis Nelson. Now in remix retirement, Pettibone has become the production choice of such postdisco songbirds as Taylor Dane, Cathy Dennis, and Chynna Phillips.

3. DAVID MORALES

Morales is still rightly revered as the man with the golden groove touch. His genius work on gems like "What Is This Thing Called Love" by Alexander O'Neal and "Finally" by CeCe Peniston solidifies his supreme power in house music circles. However, his forays into R&B and reggae styles via recent collaborations with Maxi Priest, Shabba Ranks, and Sly & Robbie support the belief that there is more to Morales than meets the eye.

4. STEVE "SILK" HURLEY

The mere mention of his name triggers swirls of hypnotic sax loops and hard, clickin' beats in any fan of Chicago house. That town's most successful son first tickled punters' fancies on a national level with his 1991 remix of "Strike It Up" by Black Box. From there, the floodgates swung open, and he held the world captive with his knack for respecting the tune, while kickin' the beats. Even the wildly territorial Michael Jackson bowed to Hurley's talent, allowing him to radically revamp two hits from the singer's *Dangerous* opus, "Remember the Time" and "Jam."

5. TODD TERRY

The undisputed king of sampling. Terry won initial attention by building tracks from snippets of records by others. Since then, he has developed quite a head for creating his own melodies, though his raw beat intensity and cheeky street humor remain at the center of each record he graces. One of the primary architects of the current underground New York sound, Terry is working many a nerve by credibly venturing into the urban/hip-hop arena. Investigate his work on Janet Jackson's "If" for proof of his continued growth.

6. ROBERT CLIVILLES AND DAVID COLE

Perhaps the perfect pair of dance music. DJ Clivilles has a flair for knockin' rugged beats, while musician Cole has a virtually flawless ear for hooks and melody. Together, they have infiltrated Top 40 radio like few others, injecting pillowy, retro-minded dance sensibilities into pop. Reach back to their late eighties association with Vendetta Records and their classic recordings with Seduction for a few thrills.

Reginald C. Dennis Picks the Greatest Hip-Hop Remixers

1. Marley Marl
2. Pete Rock
3. Large Professor
4. The BeatNuts
5. The Bomb Squad
6. DJ Quik
7. A Tribe Called Quest
8. Dr. Dre

Bob Clearmountain's Favorite Producers and Their Best Albums

1. Todd Rundgren, *A Wizard, A True Star,* Todd Rundgren
2. Nick Lowe, *Armed Forces,* Elvis Costello
3. Roger Bechirian, *Stateless,* Lene Lovich
4. Roy Thomas Baker, *A Night At The Opera,* Queen
5. David Gilmour, Roger Waters, James Guthrie and Bob Ezrin, *The Wall,* Pink Floyd
6. Robert John ("Mutt") Lange, *The Fine Art Of Surfacing,* The Boomtown Rats
7. Jimmy Miller, *Let It Bleed* and *Sticky Fingers,* The Rolling Stones
8. David Bowie and Tony Visconti, *Scary Monsters,* David Bowie
9. Jimmy Iovine, *Damn the Torpedoes,* Tom Petty and the Heartbreakers
10. George Martin, *Meet the Beatles*

Having gone from enfant terrible *to virtual* eminence grise *among re-mixers and engineers, Bob Clearmountain, who's worked with everybody from Chic and the Rolling Stones to Bruce Springsteen and Bryan Adams, has also produced several artists himself.*

Bill Stephney's Favorite Producers of All Time

1. James Brown: Any recording by him up to 1975
2. Marley Marl: "The Bridge," MC Shan; "Nobody Beats the Biz," Biz Markie
3. Stevie Wonder
4. George Martin and The Beatles
5. Prince: "Sign O' the Times"; "Love Bizarre," Sheila E
6. Dr. Dre and D.J. Yella: "F—— Tha Police" and "Real Niggaz Don't Die," N.W.A; "Nicety," Michel'le
7. Kenny Gamble and Leon Huff: Philadelphia International Records, Teddy Pendergrass, MFSB, O'Jays
8. Rick Rubin: His work for Def Jam Recordings, especially "Fight For Your Right to Party"
9. Jimmy Jam and Terry Lewis: "Get It Up," The Time; "Encore," Cheryl Lynn
10. Malcolm McLaren: Bow Wow Wow, The Sex Pistols, and other historical hoaxes
11. Norman Whitfield: "Papa Was a Rolling Stone," "Ball of Confusion," and "I Heard It Through the Grapevine"
12. Larry Smith, Davy D and Russell Simmons: "Action," Alyson Williams; "Sucker M.C.'s" Run-D.M.C.
13. Maurice White and Charles Stepney: Earth, Wind and Fire's early years
14. Niles Rodgers and Bernard Edwards: "Good Times," Chic; and, yes, "He's the Greatest Dancer," Sister Sledge
15. Teddy Riley: "Groove Me" and "I Like," Guy; "My Prerogative," Bobby Brown

HONORABLE MENTION
1. George Clinton
2. Led Zeppelin
3. The Original Bomb Squad (Carl Ryder, Flavor Flav, Eric Sadler, Bill Stephney, Hank Shocklee, Keith Shocklee)
4. Todd Terry
5. Steely and Clevie

Bill Stephney was a founding member of the Bomb Squad. He is currently the president of StepSun Music Entertainment.

Games Beatles Play

1. **"BABY, YOU'RE A RICH MAN," 1967**
Rumor has it that at the end of this song, the Beatles sing, "Baby, you're a rich fag Jew," perhaps a slur on their manager, Brian Epstein, who was certainly Jewish, definitely wealthy, and probably gay.

2. **"GIRL," 1965**
The background singers repeat the syllable *tit*.

3. **"I AM THE WALRUS," 1967**
John Lennon included cryptic chanting and a portion of Shakespeare's *King Lear* at the end of the song.

4. **"I'M ONLY SLEEPING," 1966**
The guitar solo was recorded straight, then overdubbed into the tape backward.

5. **"I FEEL FINE," 1964**
Lennon claimed that at the beginning of this song, he plays the first deliberately recorded guitar feedback in history.

6. **"NORWEGIAN WOOD," 1965**
George Harrison debuts the sitar as a rock and roll instrument.

7. **"PAPERBACK WRITER," 1966**
The backing voices sing "Frere Jacques."

8. **"RAIN," 1966**
Lennon used the vocal track for the last verse backward.

9. **"STRAWBERRY FIELDS FOREVER," 1967**
Lennon says "cranberry sauce"; millions believe he says "I buried Paul."

10. **"YELLOW SUBMARINE," 1966**
At the end of the section where the strange spoken voice repeats the lyrics, Ringo seems to sing "slubmarine."

Rock Bands that Emerged from Session Work

1. **AREA CODE 615**
This short-lived group, led by Charlie McCoy, featured the cream of Nashville's country session players.

2. **ATLANTA RHYTHM SECTION**
ARS was formed from a variety of Georgia sessionmen, several of whom had aided producer Buddy Buie in creating the Classic IV's great sixties hit, "Spooky." On their own, they scored with "Imaginary Lover" and others.

3. BAREFOOT JERRY

Formed by veteran Nashville guitarist Wayne Moss, whose credits includes *Blonde on Blonde*. Other band members—Jim Colvard, Russ Hicks, Si Edwards, Terry Dearmore, and Warren Hartman—are also well-respected Nashville session players.

4. BOOKER T. AND THE MGS

The only one of these bands in the Rock and Roll Hall of Fame, and they made it on pure merit. Besides providing the essential instrumental energy behind Otis Redding, Sam and Dave, Wilson Pickett, and other Memphis-bred stars, the MGs—Booker T. Jones, Steve Cropper, Duck Dunn (who replaced original bassist Lewis Steinberg), and the immortal drummer Al Jackson—achieved stardom in their own right with a series of hits beginning with "Green Onions."

5. DELANEY AND BONNIE AND FRIENDS, MAD DOGS AND ENGLISHMEN, AND DEREK AND THE DOMINOES

In 1968, top Los Angeles session guitarist Delaney Bramlett and his wife, singer Bonnie, decided to form a band of their own. The group they assembled included such other top Hollywood studio names as Leon Russell, Jim Price, Bobby Whitlock, Bobby Keys, Carl Radle, and Jim Keltner. Unfortunately, while these performers were well known for their musicianship, they were somewhat less notorious for their loyalty—the essence of session work involves flowing where the long green runs heaviest. Soon after the group opened for Blind Faith on its American tour and was joined by Eric Clapton on a European tour of its own, Whitlock and Radle left to help Clapton start Derek and the Dominoes. Not long after that, Russell took several of the others to help form Joe Cocker's big band, Mad Dogs and Englishmen, while the Bramletts, left high and dry, disintegrated musically as well as maritally.

6. FULL FORCE

Working behind UTFO, they kicked off a craze with "Roxanne, Roxanne," still *the* classic street-level rap, then perfected the act backing Lisa Lisa and Cult Jam with "I Wonder if I Take You Home," "All Cried Out," and more. "All Cried Out" gave Bow Legged Lou (Lucien George), and his brothers Paul Anthony and Brian "B-Fine," cousins Curtis Bedreau, Gerald Charles, and Junior "Shy Shy" Clark the confidence to dabble in their own highly conceptualized (and often very funny) funk, including the 1988 hit "All in My Mind."

7. JO MAMA

Various permutations of Los Angeles session aces from the generation after the Delaney and Bonnie bunch, Jo Mama mostly featured stalwart guitarist Danny Kortchmar, later a key collaborator with both Don Henley and Jon Bon Jovi.

8. KING CURTIS AND THE KING PINS

Curtis, of course, was the greatest of the New York sax session players, emerging after Sam "The Man" Taylor established the mold and exploding it with a series of great tenor breaks on records by the likes of the Coasters. Curtis's first solo group called itself the Noble Knights (who scored with "Soul Twist"), but it was as the King Pins that they they blew minds while touring behind Aretha Franklin and hit with "Memphis Soul Stew."

9. MFSB

Gamble and Huff's Philly soul owed a lot to the sound of the unheralded sessioneers who played on hits by the Three Degrees, the O'Jays, McFadden and Whitehead, and Teddy Pendergrass's Harold Melvin and the Bluenotes. MFSB landed a number one on its own with 1974's "T.S.O.P. (The Sound of Philadelphia)."

10. THE MEMPHIS HORNS

All veterans of Memphis recording sessions, Wayne Jackson, Andrew Love, Jack Hale, and James Mitchell went on to record several albums, charting a few R&B sides for RCA.

11. THE METERS

The finest instrumental combo to emerge from rock-era New Orleans formed in 1966 behind Art Neville (yes, one of those Nevilles), Joseph "Zigaboo" Modliste, Leo Nocentelli, and George Porter. Their primordial funk gave them a couple of 1969 hits, "Sophisticated Cissy" and "Cissy Strut," and led them to a 1975 tour opening for the Rolling Stones.

12. THE MUSCLE SHOALS HORNS

Less acclaimed than the Muscle Shoals Rhythm Section, the Horns made several well-received funk albums. Band members include Harrison Calloway, Harvey Thompson, and Charles Rose.

13. RONIN

Linda Ronstadt's band, led by guitarist Waddy Wachtel, made only one album, a self-titled Rolling Stones–style melange that is better than the aimless funk made by the Section and Stuff, if not necessarily as hot as the straight rock of Jo Mama and the Atlanta Rhythm Section.

14. THE SECTION

The musicians who brought you the unmistakable sounds of southern California rock bring you their own jazz-rock offerings. Russ Kunkel, Leland Sklar, Danny Kortchmar, and Craig Doerge recorded with James Taylor, Jackson Browne, Carly Simon, Nicolette Larson, and others of similar ilk.

15. PAUL SHAFFER AND THE WORLD'S MOST DANGEROUS BAND

Though they never recorded as such (well, Shaffer made a loungelike solo set), they acted as the musical conscience of David Letterman's *Late Night* and Shaffer used cohorts like Will Lee, David

Sanborn, and Sid McGinness to entertain the crowds annually at the first half-dozen Rock and Roll Hall of Fame dinners. Those four were the core—other members came and went.

16. STUFF

The seventies New York equivalent of the Section, Stuff became better known not so much for its rather desultory albums but through its stint as *Saturday Night Live*'s house band. In the daytime, Richard Tee, Cornell Dupree, Eric Gale, Gordon Edwards, and Christopher Parker also toured with Paul Simon, whose most famous pre-*Graceland* records are the hallmark of their backup sound.

17. TACKHEAD

Led by supersonic bassist Doug Wimbish (now a member of Living Colour), these guys represented both the expansiveness of eighties studio craft and its ultimate dead end: With the rise of machines, super-session playing became not so much less esteemed as less essential. Their own albums offer sometimes exciting avant-funk-rock.

18. TOTO

Jeff Porcaro, David Paich, Steve Lukather, David Huntgate, Steve Porcaro, and Bobby Kimball—several of whom are sons of Los Angeles session musicians and arrangers from the fifties and sixties—wound up laying way too far back on most of their own recordings, which is odd since Jeff Porcaro ranks as the most driving drummer since his mentor Hal Blaine. Their best hits, "Hold the Line" and "Rosanna," have that definitive early eighties Hollywood pop flavor—slick as it is smooth.

Billy Preston Lists His 10 Most Memorable Sessions

1. "Let It Be," The Beatles (George Martin)
2. "Get Back," The Beatles
3. "That's the Way God Planned It," Bill Preston (George Harrison, producer)
4. "Stoney End," Barbra Streisand (Richard Perry, producer)
5. *Goat's Head Soup*, The Rolling Stones (Jimmy Miller, producer)
6. *Black and Blue*, The Rolling Stones (the Glimmer Twins, producers)
7. *Aretha Franklin Live at Fillmore West* (Jerry Wexler, Arif Mardin, Tom Dowd, producers)
8. "My Sweet Lord," George Harrison (George Harrison, Phil Spector, producers)
9. "I Wrote a Simple Song," Billy Preston (Quincy Jones, producer)

10. "Let's Go Get Stoned," Ray Charles (Ray Charles, Joe Adams, producers)

Billy Preston has been a touring and recording sideman for more than twenty years, appearing as vocalist and keyboardist with Little Richard, the Beatles, and the Rolling Stones. He also recorded a string of late seventies hit records, including "Outta Space" and "Will It Go 'Round in Circles."

Arrangements by John Paul Jones

Before joining Led Zeppelin, John Paul Jones was one of the leading session bassists and arrangers on the British rock scene.

1. "Sunshine Superman," Donovan
2. "Mellow Yellow," Donovan
3. "Hurdy Gurdy Man," Donovan; features Jimmy Page on lead guitar—the first time Page and John Bonham played together
4. "She's a Rainbow," The Rolling Stones
5. "Little Games," The Yardbirds
6. *Their Satanic Majesties Request*, The Rolling Stones—a substantial part of the considerable orchestration

Jimmy Page as Sessionman

Before forming Led Zeppelin and joining the Yardbirds, Jimmy Page was one of the hottest guitar players on the London recording scene.

1. **"YOU REALLY GOT ME," THE KINKS**
   Page definitely played on these and perhaps other tracks from the first Kinks album. Whether it is Page or Kinks guitarist Dave Davies who plays the ground-breaking fuzz-tone solo on the single is a matter of much dispute, though. Ray Davies says Page's instrument on the track was actually tambourine, at the insistence of producer Shel Talmy (the same person who brought him into the Who's session).
2. **"BALD HEADED WOMAN," THE WHO**
   Page plays rhythm guitar, doubling Pete Townshend.
3. **"WITH A LITTLE HELP FROM MY FRIENDS," JOE COCKER**
   Page plays lead guitar.

4. **"GLORIA" AND "HERE COMES THE NIGHT," THEM**
Page plays second guitar on both.

5. **"HURDY GURDY MAN," DONOVAN**
This international hit also features drummer John Bonham and bassist John Paul Jones—in other words, all the instrumentalists in Led Zeppelin

6. **"DIAMONDS," JET HARRIS AND TONY MEEHAN**
According to Stephen Davis's *Hammer of the Gods*, this English hit by two former members of Cliff Richard and the Shadows was Page's first professional session.

7. **"I SEE A MAN DOWNSTAIRS" AND "LITTLE GIRL," SONNY BOY WILLIAMSON**
Page plays lead guitar on a session arranged by the Yardbirds' first manager, Giorgio Gomelsky, long before Jimmy joined the 'Birds.

Songs on which Phil Spector Performs

1. **"TO KNOW HIM IS TO LOVE HIM," THE TEDDY BEARS**
Spector was a singing member of the group. He also produced and wrote the song, taking the title from the inscription on his father's grave.

2. **"I REALLY DO" / "I KNOW WHY," "MR. ROBIN" / "MY HEART STOOD STILL," THE SPECTORS THREE**
Spector put together this studio group after the demise of the Teddy Bears; he was producing now but still singing.

3. **"ON BROADWAY," THE DRIFTERS**
Plays the guitar solo. Spector played on several singles by the Coasters, Ben E. King, and the Drifters, according to *Collecting Phil Spector* by John J. Fitzpatrick and James E. Fogerty, but this is by far his most memorable moment with any of them.

4. **"PLAY WITH FIRE," "LITTLE BY LITTLE," THE ROLLING STONES**
Spector plays guitar on "Play with Fire" and maracas on "Little by Little."

5. **"MY SWEET LORD," GEORGE HARRISON**
Sings background vocals, probably did not advise on melodic similarity to old Chiffons' hits.

6. **"OH YOKO," JOHN LENNON**
Spector sings background vocals (credited as part of the "J&P Duo") on this track from *Imagine*, which also hit as a single.

In addition, Spector may have played on any number of his own tracks, especially the earlier ones.

Norman Petty Lists 5 Special Buddy Holly Records

"All recordings we made of Buddy Holly are favorites of mine, each very different in musical content as well as providing fond memories of things that took place in the studio at the time each recording was made," said Petty in reply to Rick Whitesell's question for the first edition. "It would be very difficult to select only five recordings as 'the favorites,' but the following list would comprise special recordings that stand out in my mind."

1. "PEGGY SUE"

The sound experimentation is interesting and rather advanced considering the recording-studio experience at that time. It resulted in a meeting of minds between the engineer and recording artist, producing very successful results for all concerned.

2. "EVERYDAY"

Here again, absolute freedom in choosing musical instruments, as well as sound experimentation, produced very pleasing results, and that freedom is reflected in the easygoing, nice sound from the artist.

3. "EARLY IN THE MORNING"

This was one of the first times we ventured into the "big" sound of other musicians and arrangers. Dick Jacobs did a fantastic arrangement, and his direction of the orchestra shows that he and the artist really felt what each was trying to do. It was great fun and interesting to be in a New York control room—in much different surroundings than I have been used to working in.

4. "TRUE LOVE WAYS"

Again in New York, under the expert direction of Dick Jacobs, this recording became a fine example of the "extremes" we felt we could take with the artist. The song was not written for Buddy, but was to be shown to artists known for recording ballads. It was not until later that he decided to record it. Vi Petty was the first artist to record the song, followed by Jimmy Gilmer, Peter and Gordon, and others; there are many good recordings of the song, but the only big sales figures were from the ones made by Peter and Gordon and, lately, Mickey Gilley.

5. "LOVE IS STRANGE"

This is one of the most interesting recordings, in my mind, for it was completely restructured and rerecorded after the demise of Buddy Holly. Several edits were made; instruments were retuned; musicians attempted to match the varying tempos and pitches on the artist's original mono recording, which was never released. (Other interesting things that took place during the completion of this "built" recording will be described in a forthcoming book.)

Norman Petty helped invent rock and roll by working as producer at his studios in Clovis, New Mexico, with such artists as Buddy Holly, Roy Orbison, Buddy Knox, and Jimmy Bowen. He died in 1984, without completing the book referred to above.

10 of the Earliest Rock and Roll Hits Recorded in Stereo

1. "Don't Let Go," Roy Hamilton, January 1958
2. "(I Don't Wanna) Hang Up My Rock and Roll Shoes," Chuck Willis, April 1958
3. "What Am I Living For," Chuck Willis, May 1958
4. "Yakety Yak," The Coasters, May 1958
5. "Born Too Late," The Poni-Tails, July 1958
6. "Chariot Rock," The Champs, August 1958
7. "Summertime, Summertime," The Jamies, August 1958
8. "It's All in the Game," Tommy Edwards, August 1958
9. "I Wish," The Platters, September 1958
10. "It's Only Make Believe," Conway Twitty, September 1958

Les Paul Lists the Most Important Technological Innovations in Recorded Music

1. Solid-body electric guitar
2. Echo
3. Flanging
4. Phase-shifting
5. Electromagnetic pickup
6. Reverb
7. Time delay
8. Sound-on-sound

Les Paul is, of course, either the inventor or one of the most important figures in innovating all of these devices. He is a unique character, with a wry wit and nonstop mind. He's a guitarist par excellence, even fifty years into his career, and his milestones in the field of recording and electronics are many. Most folks still remember him as the guy who did "How High the Moon" with Mary Ford, though.

Songs that Made Feedback Famous

1. "Juke," Little Walter, 1952
2. "Train Kept a-Rollin'," Johnny Burnette and the Rock and Roll Trio, 1958
3. "Anyway, Anyhow, Anywhere," The Who, 1965
4. "My Generation," The Who, 1965
5. "I Feel Fine," The Beatles, 1965
6. "Train Kept a-Rollin'," The Yardbirds, 1966
7. "Purple Haze," The Jimi Hendrix Experience, 1967
8. "Sister Ray," The Velvet Underground, 1968
9. "Weasels Ripped My Flesh," The Mothers of Invention, 1970
10. "Born in the U.S.A.," Bruce Springsteen

Performers Whose Music Was Propelled Upward by Rick Rubin

Whether he's turning knobs at the mixing boards or making calls from the back of a club (or the back of his white Rolls), Rubin's magic ears have rarely failed him, the acts lucky enough to work with him, or just about anybody who makes a habit of visiting record stores. Here's a sampling.

1. L.L. Cool J
2. Public Enemy
3. The Beastie Boys
4. Run-D.M.C.
5. The Cult
6. Slayer
7. Andrew Dice Clay
8. Sir Mix-A-Lot
9. The Black Crowes
10. The Red Hot Chili Peppers
11. Mick Jagger

Songs that Made Scratching Famous

1. "Grandmaster Flash on the Wheels of Steel," Grandmaster Flash & the Furious Five
2. "It's Yours," Jazzy Jay & T-La Rock
3. "One For the Treble," Davey DMX
4. "Rockit," Herbie Hancock
5. "AJ Scratch," Kurtis Blow

Not So Fast
25 Records with False Endings

1. "All by Myself," Eric Carmen
2. "Bernadette," The Four Tops
3. "The Best Part of Breaking Up," The Ronettes
4. "Born in the U.S.A.," Bruce Springsteen
5. "Born to Run," Bruce Springsteen
6. "Breathless," Jerry Lee Lewis (of course, maybe he just ran out of breath)
7. "Cold Sweat," James Brown
8. "Do You Love Me," The Contours
9. "Do You Wanna Dance," Bobby Freeman
10. "Good Lovin'," The Young Rascals
11. "Good Vibrations," The Beach Boys
12. "I Got You Babe," Sonny and Cher
13. "I've Got You Under My Skin," The Four Seasons
14. "I Need Your Loving," Don Gardner and Dee Dee Ford
15. "In the Still of the Night," The Five Satins
16. "Jump," Van Halen
17. "Keep on Dancing," The Gentrys
18. "Lady Madonna," The Beatles
19. "Last Night," The Mar-Keys
20. "Let Me," Paul Revere and the Raiders
21. "Light My Fire," The Doors
22. "The Little Girl I Once Knew," The Beach Boys
23. "Lookin' Out My Back Door," Creedence Clearwater Revival
24. "Monday Monday," The Mamas and the Papas
25. "One Mint Julep," Ray Charles

. . . but you didn't think we were gonna stop there, did you? Oh no . . .

26. "Rain," The Beatles
27. "She's the One," The Chartbusters
28. "Some Kind-A Earthquake," Duane Eddy
29. "Turn! Turn! Turn!," The Byrds
30. "The Twist," Chubby Checker (but he even ripped off *that* part from Hank Ballard and the Midnighters)

. . . not to mention Sandy Nelson's "Teen Beat."

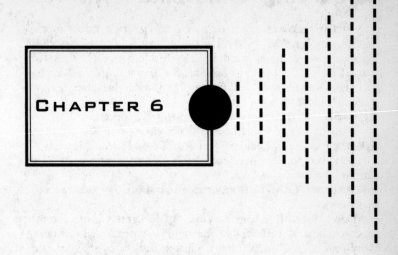

Awards

The Book of Rock Lists Dubious Recording Achievement Awards

1. MOST NEGATIVE SONG EVER TO HIT THE TOP FORTY

"Nobody But Me" by the Human Beinz uses the word *no* more than one hundred times in a mere 2:16. In addition, the word *nobody* is used forty-six times. For balance, the Beinz throw in the word *yeah* once. Runner-up: "Tell Her No" by the Zombies uses *no* sixty-three times in 2:08.

2. MOST OBNOXIOUS SONG TO HIT A JUKEBOX

"Aaah-Ah, Yawa Em Ekat Ot Gnimoc Er'yeht," by Napoleon XIV, the B-side of "They're Coming to Take Me Away, Ha-Haaa!" The song is reputed to have completely cleared a restaurant of forty patrons in two minutes flat.

3. RECORD LEAST LIKELY TO ACCOMPLISH ITS STATED PURPOSE

"Don't Worry, Be Happy" by Bobby McFerrin. Cloying the first time you hear it, insufferable the third, maddening and irritating every time thereafter. Naturally, George Bush used it as his campaign theme song. Naturally, McFerrin never had another hit, which is maybe what he gets for commercializing the most famous slogan of Indian guru Meher Baba.

4. MOST TASTELESS SONG TO HIT THE TOP ONE HUNDRED

Despite much competition, the victor remains "I Want My Baby Back" by Jimmy Cross. In the song, an auto accident splatters Jimmy's girlfriend all over the highway. Three months later, he decides he can't live without her, digs her up, and joins her in the pine box. Honorable mention (well, OK, "honorable" has nothing to do with it—let's just say "direct descendant"): Warren Zevon's "Excitable Boy."

5. MOST POLITICALLY INCORRECT RECORD EVER MADE

"Rodney K" by Willie D of the Geto Boys, in which Willie and company mock Rodney King's pleas for peace, rhyme "nonviolence" with "a nigger can't even shit in silence," ridicule "We Shall Overcome," and at the conclusion, execute a simpering King in a hail of automatic weapons fire.

6. SHORTEST RECORD TO MAKE THE TOP FORTY

"Some Kind-a Earthquake," a 1959 Duane Eddy instrumental, clocked in at 1:17. Several artists have cut flip sides just as short: for instance, the Beach Boys, "You're Welcome" (the flip side of "Heroes and Villains"). "John's Music Box," the flip side of "Dancing Bear," by the Mamas and Papas, was timed at one minute flat. (But flip sides aren't eligible for this award because they aren't listed on the Top Forty.)

7. BEST ACT OF SELF-PLAGIARISM

John Fogerty's "The Old Man Down the Road" sounds so much like his Creedence Clearwater Revival hit "Run Through the Jungle" that he was sued for copyright infringement by CCR's label, Fantasy Records.

8. MOST BLASPHEMOUS RECORD

Even if you suspected Madonna as the recipient of this truly dubious achievement trophy, you probably didn't get the record right. "Act of Contrition," the B-side of "Like a Prayer," features Madonna reciting the Catholic prayer called the Act of Contrition, then deteriorates into a hysterical monologue in which Madonna grows increasingly obstreperous over being denied a restaurant reservation. The track remains obscure, primarily because Southern Baptists do not recite the Act of Contrition.

9. THE "THROW-IN-AN-EXTRA-PREPOSITION-AND-CALL-IT-ARTISTIC-LICENSE" AWARD

Moby Grape, for "Funky Tunk" (on the 1968 LP *Wow*): "How come you ain't got on your clothes on?"

Paul McCartney, for 1973's James Bond theme song, "Live and Let Die": "In this ever-changing world in which we live in."

10. MOST UNLIKELY SURFER

Bo Diddley, on his album *Surfin' with Bo Diddley*. (*Bo Diddley is a Gunslinger* at least had a basis in reality in downtown Chicago, but *surfer?* Where, on Lake Michigan?)

11. MOST UNLIKELY-BUT-INEVITABLE COLLABORATORS

Johnny Lydon (nee Rotten) and Arika Bambaataa in a 1989 one-off group called Time Zone, whose record perfectly summarized their joint ambitions: "World Destruction." Talk about your punk-funk!

12. LONGEST ALBUM VERSION OF A TOP FORTY HIT

At 22:30, Kraftwerk's *Autobahn* exceeds Rare Earth's runner-up "Get Ready" by exactly one minute. Even in the age of extended CD running times, these are unlikely ever to be exceeded.

13. WORST SONG ISSUED BY A MAJOR RECORD LABEL

Despite Michael Bolton, there's really one choice: "Paralyzed" and its B-side, a record by the Legendary Stardust Cowboy, a one-man band incapable of playing any instrument, singing in tune, or keeping in time even with himself. Rumors say that Mercury released an album by this guy, and that certain outlaw country fans consider this record a camp classic. The very thought's enough to break our achy hearts.

14. BEST UNCONSCIOUS SELF-PARODY

Pat "Hit Me with Your Best Shot" Benatar for releasing, on the very same album, "Hell Is for Children," a song opposing domestic violence. Uh-Huh.

Runner-up: Mick Jagger for 1986's "Ruthless People."

15. LONGEST PAUSE FOR BREATH IN A TOP FORTY RECORD

"Surfin' Bird" by the Trashmen. Was there ever a doubt?

16. LONGEST FINAL CHORD

At twenty-four seconds, the end to the Beatles' "A Day in the Life" gets a little flaky: The engineers turned the sound level so high, to capture those last few bits of aural decay, that the room's air-conditioners became audible.

17. MOST OFF-COLOR LINE IN THE LP VERSION OF A NUMBER-ONE HIT

Jefferson Starship's "Miracles" for the line, "I got a taste of the real world when I went down on you girl." Lou Reed's "Walk on the Wild Side" with, "She never lost her head even when she was giving head," and Blondie's "I'll give you some head—and shoulders to cry on" never made number one. Fortunately, Tipper Gore never bought any of these records or she might be First Lady today. Interesting, though, that no *rap* record of similar disposition has ever come close to enough air play to make this list.

18. MOST DISCREET USE OF "LOUIE LOUIE"

Boston, "More Than a Feeling." Check the chords in the chorus if you're doubtful.

19. BEST USE OF "FOUND" DIALOGUE

Mark Knopfler wrote "Money for Nothing" after hearing a New York City appliance store employee griping about how easy those guys on MTV had it: "You get your money for nothin' and your chicks for free." Sting added "I want my MTV," the asinine slogan he and other pop stars used to help hype the video channel in its inaugural season, to the final mix.

20. LONGEST NOTE HELD

Shortly after Jay and the Americans released "Cara Mia," WTRY in Troy, New York, aired a "special version" in which Jay held the long note near the end for just over a minute and then continued without missing a beat. The award goes jointly to the group and the WTRY production staff.

21. MOST UNLIKELY TRIBUTE TO A MUSIC INDUSTRY EXECUTIVE

"Whispering / Cherchez La Femme / Se Si Bon" by Dr. Buzzard's Original Savannah Band (the group that became Kid Creole and the Coconuts) paid tribute to its then-manager by including the line "Tommy Mottola lives on the road." Once Tommy settled down, he became president of Sony Music, in which capacity he saw to it that Kid Creole got its first major label release in the better part of a decade.

22. ARTIST WITH THE MOST RECORDS CONTAINING STUDIO TALK

The Beach Boys dwarf all competition. They made more than a dozen songs that contain extraneous talking in the background,

most of it easily audible, especially on recent high-tech CD reissues.

23. NASTIEST MANIFESTATION OF CONFLICT IN A BROTHER ACT

The Beach Boys' continued legal and personal agony with Brian
Wilson doesn't qualify, not even in the wake of Mike Love's multimillion-dollar plagiarism lawsuit against him, because it didn't appear on record (except in the track " 'Cassius' Love vs. 'Sonny'
Wilson" from *Shut Down Volume II*, where it's passed off as a joke).
Therefore, the choice must be Jermaine Jackson's 1991 anti-Michael
message disc, "Word to the Badd!!" which dissed Mike so badly
that Jermaine eventually had to renounce it, which halted its chart
climb at number seventy-eight. Not that it was likely to have entered the Top Ten on musical merit.

24. MOST DELICIOUS UNCAUGHT IRONY

Eric Clapton's 1978 Top Twenty hit, "Wonderful Tonight," so
delights loving couples that one often hears it butchered by wedding
bands. Little do they suspect that Clapton wrote it while waiting for
his wife, Patti Boyd (yes, the same one he wrote "Layla" about), to
finally finish getting dressed and made up for dinner. Clapton used
the dutiful husband's cry of long-suffering exasperation, "Yes, darling, you look wonderful tonight," and successfully contrived to turn
it into a love song. The couple divorced not long afterward.

25. WORST GUITAR SOLO ON A NUMBER-ONE RECORD

Scotty Moore on Elvis Presley's "Heartbreak Hotel." Stan Fre-
berg wasn't far off when he said, "That's close enough for jazz."

26. WORST USE OF SCRATCHING

"Jam On It" by Newcleus. An emergent art form reduced to
rubble. "Wicki-wicki" indeed!

27. MOST OVERELABORATED ALBUM VERSION OF A HIT SINGLE

Jan and Dean's "Dead Man's Curve" which, on 1972's *Legendary
Master Series* LP, becomes a macabre ten-minute skit. What's more
amazing is that this act of brutal but brilliant self-parody ever saw
official release, considering that Jan Berry lived out the most gruesome aspects of this particular hit when he was brain-damaged in a
1965 auto accident.

28. MOST INTERESTING ACT OF SELF-CENSORSHIP

In 1980, the Cure's "Killing an Arab" was used by a nitwit University of Michigan college radio deejay as an opportunity to issue a
call for hatred and violence against all Arabs. Coming at a time when
the FBI's William Webster had declared all Arab-Americans "in a
zone of danger," and in the community that has the largest Arab-
American population in the United States, this naturally excited
some comment. The Arab-American Anti-Discrimination Committee (ADC) complained and the Cure agreed to withdraw the song—
a rewrite of Camus's *The Stranger*. It never did so—in fact, the song

still appears on *Standing on a Beach*, its 1986 singles compilation. But nobody's complained since the fuss died down.

29.   SONG GUARANTEED TO REIGNITE THE GENERATION GAP

Billy Joel's 1989 number-one single, "We Didn't Start the Fire," a numbingly didactic and superficial rampage through U.S. and world history. Parents and teachers loved its evocation of the nostalgic America-that-never-was. Kids, therefore, got saddled with it in the car on family outings *and* at school, where it was actually used to "teach" them factoids. Could there have been a better reason for the punk-funk-rap-grunge revolt?

30.   THE "WHO CARES WHAT THE ALBUM SOUNDS LIKE —DID YOU SEE THE COVER?" AWARD

Mom's Apple wins for its first album, or to be more exact, the jacket thereof. The original cover featured "mom" holding a pie with one slice removed. Hidden among the apples was a drawing of a vagina. After retailers protested, subsequent copies of the album had the slice bricked up, with barbed wire around it, and tears in "mom's" eyes. (It is just *barely* possible that the group and its management had been prepared for this reaction.) Has anyone ever bothered to listen to this album? Why?

Three Lashes with a Wet Noodle
The Wimp-Rock Top 40

This category may have been more competitive in the first edition, when we were just coming out of the seventies, an age in which wimps abounded. Blessedly, however, many of the names on the original list, though perhaps wimpier than some of those listed here by objective standards, have been deleted from most memory banks (though not ours, needless to add). Ranking on this list then, has to do with degree of wimpiness balanced by the degree to which such insufferables have been in our ears (and faces) of late.

1. Michael Bolton
2. Wilson Philips
3. The Osmonds
4. Air Supply
5. Pauly Shore
6. Kansas
7. Seals and Crofts
8. Suede[1]
9. Duran Duran
10. Freddie and the Dreamers
11. The Cowsills
12. Art Garfunkel
13. 10,000 Maniacs
14. It's A Beautiful Day
15. Richard Marx
16. The Moody Blues
17. Tesla
18. Morrissey[1]
19. Billy J. Kramer and the Dakotas
20. Hot Tuna
21. Jonathan Richman and the Modern Lovers[1]
22. The Chordettes

23. Spin Doctors
24. Billy Ray Cyrus
25. Fresh Prince
26. Extreme
27. Bon Jovi
28. Mr. Big
29. Loggins and Messina
30. The Duprees
31. Donovan [1]

32. Amy Grant
33. Nicolette Larsen
34. Sade
35. John Denver
36. Elvis Costello
37. The Royal Guardsmen
38. The Association
39. Crosby, Stills and Nash
40. The Grateful Dead

---

[1] Demoted several spaces for being proud of it.

The 10 Worst Performers of All Time

1. Michael Bolton
2. Pat Boone
3. Emerson, Lake & Palmer
4. Fabian
5. Grateful Dead

6. Richard Marx
7. The Osmonds
8. Linda Ronstadt
9. Vanilla Ice
10. Paul Williams

The First 10 Rock Records to Win Gold Discs

1. "Hard Headed Woman," Elvis Presley, 1958
2. *Pat's Greatest Hits*, Pat Boone, 1960
3. *Elvis*, Elvis Presley, 1960
4. *Elvis' Golden Records*, Elvis Presley, 1961
5. *Encore—Golden Hits*, The Platters, 1961
6. *Blue Hawaii*, Elvis Presley, 1961
7. "Can't Help Falling in Love," Elvis Presley, 1962
8. "I Can't Stop Loving You," Ray Charles, 1962
9. *Modern Sounds in Country and Western Music*, Ray Charles
10. "Hey Paula," Paul and Paula, 1963

Perry Como received the Recording Industry Association of America's (RIAA) first gold record, for "Catch a Falling Star," on March 14, 1958. Gordon McRae's Oklahoma LP and Laurie London's "He's Got the Whole World in His Hands" also scored gold awards before "Hard Headed Woman."

The initial criterion for receiving a gold award was $1 million in sales, at retail list price. For singles, which then listed for about one dollar each, *this represented an equivalent number of units sold. For LPs, the criterion was based on wholesale price, which initially made sales of about 400,000 albums equivalent to gold status. But as LP list prices rose, the quantity of sales necessary to receive the award continually shrank, necessitating revision in the mid-seventies, when today's standard of 500,000 albums sold was set.*

The First 10 Platinum Records

1. "Disco Lady," Johnnie Taylor, 1976
2. "Kiss and Say Goodbye," The Manhattans, 1976
3. "Play That Funky Music," Wild Cherry, 1976
4. "Disco Duck," Rick Dees and His Cast of Idiots, 1976
5. "Car Wash," Rose Royce, 1977
6. "You Light Up My Life," Debby Boone, 1977
7. "Boogie Nights," Heatwave, 1977
8. "Stayin' Alive," The Bee Gees, 1978
9. "Emotion," Samantha Sang, 1978
10. "We Are the Champions," Queen, 1978

Platinum singles were not officially issued by the RIAA until 1965. Sales of 2 million units merit the award, making it by far the rarest of all the gold and platinum awards the RIAA confers, since the prime function of a single in today's market is to spur album sales.

Rock and Blues Musicians in the Playboy Music Hall of Fame

1. Ray Charles, 1968
2. Bob Dylan, 1970
3. Paul McCartney, 1970
4. Jimi Hendrix, 1971
5. Janis Joplin, 1971
6. Elvis Presley, 1971
7. Mick Jagger, 1972
8. Jim Morrison, 1972
9. George Harrison, 1972
10. Eric Clapton, 1973
11. Duane Allman, 1974
12. Elton John, 1975
13. Stevie Wonder, 1976
14. Ringo Starr, 1977
15. Linda Ronstadt, 1978
16. Keith Moon, 1979
17. Bruce Springsteen, 1980
18. John Bonham, 1981
19. Pete Townshend, 1982
20. Willie Nelson, 1983
21. David Bowie, 1984
22. Michael Jackson, 1985
23. Phil Collins, 1986
24. Tina Turner, 1987
25. Madonna, 1988
26. Edward Van Halen, 1989
27. Roy Orbison, 1990
28. B. B. King, 1992
29. Frank Zappa, 1993

Rock and R&B Performers Who Won the Most Grammys (Through 1993)

1. Quincy Jones (artist and producer) — 26
2. Stevie Wonder — 17
3. Aretha Franklin — 15
4. Michael Jackson — 12
5. Ray Charles — 12
6. Miles Davis — 9
7. Anita Baker — 8
8. George Benson — 8
9. Eric Clapton — 8
10. Chick Corea — 8
11. David Foster (producer) — 8
12. Al Green — 8
13. Linda Ronstadt — 8
14. Paul Simon — 8[1]
15. Johnny Cash — 7
16. Natalie Cole — 7
17. Bonnie Raitt — 7
18. Phil Ramone (producer) — 7
19. Sting — 7[3]
20. Tina Turner — 7
21. The Bee Gees — 6
22. Phil Collins — 6
23. Earth, Wind and Fire — 6
24. The 5th Dimension — 6
25. Chaka Khan — 6
26. B.B. King — 6
27. U2 — 6
28. Stevie Ray Vaughan — 6
29. Muddy Waters — 6
30. The Beatles — 5[2]
31. Billy Joel — 5
32. Roy Orbison — 5
33. The Police — 5[3]
34. B. J. Thomas — 5
35. Toto — 5
36. Dionne Warwick — 5

---

[1] Simon also won four Grammys with Simon and Garfunkel. The total places him tied for fourth all time.

[2] Paul McCartney won four Grammys as a solo artist. The total places him sixth all time.

[3] Combining the Police and Sting's Grammys—all of which are presumably sitting on Sting's various mantel pieces—places him tied for fourth all time.

The all-time Grammy leaders, regardless of musical category, are: Sir Georg Solti, thirty; Jones, twenty-six; Vladimir Horowitz, twenty-five; Henry Mancini, twenty.

30 Artists Who've Never Won a Grammy (Through 1993)

1. AC/DC
2. The Beach Boys
3. Chuck Berry
4. Jackson Browne
5. The Byrds
6. Sam Cooke
7. Elvis Costello
8. Creedence Clearwater Revival
9. Cream
10. Fats Domino[1]
11. The Four Tops
12. Funkadelic
13. Jimi Hendrix
14. The Jackson 5
15. Led Zeppelin
16. Little Richard[1]
17. Curtis Mayfield and the Impressions[1]
18. Van Morrison
19. Buck Owens
20. Parliament
21. Public Enemy
22. The Rolling Stones[1]
23. Run-D.M.C.
24. Diana Ross
25. Sly and the Family Stone
26. Phil Spector
27. The Supremes
28. Talking Heads
29. The Who
30. Neil Young

[1] Winners of Grammy Lifetime Achievement Award (not selected by the voters).

Does Anybody Here Remember Milli Vanilli?
The Most Pathetic Grammys

1. ELVIS PRESLEY'S BING CROSBY AWARD, 1971

The Crosby award is a special Grammy presented to "members of the recording industry who, during their lifetimes, have made creative contributions of outstanding artistic or scientific significance." Elvis apparently won for science, since he never won a Grammy for the artistry of his pop recordings. He did win—in 1967, 1972, and 1974—for his gospel recordings, *How Great Thou Art* (which won in both '67 and '72 for some reason), and *He Touched Me*. Those are fine records but . . . *c'mon.*

2. BEST RHYTHM AND BLUES PERFORMANCE, 1958

In the first year of the Grammys—which was also the year that Jerry Butler and the Impressions recorded "For Your Precious Love," the Elegants graced us with "Little Star," and Chuck Berry created "Johnny B. Goode"—the Best Rhythm and Blues Grammy went to the Champs' instrumental, "Tequila." The Grammys were off to an atrocious start. And it got worse . . .

3. BEST ROCK AND ROLL RECORDING, 1962 AND 1963

The winners: Ben Fabric's "Alley Cat," a tame piano instrumental, and Nino Tempo and April Stevens's hardly rockin' ballad, "Deep Purple." This in the years that gave us "The Loco-Motion," "Up on the Roof," "Twist and Shout," "The Duke of Earl," "Louie Louie," "Heat Wave," James Brown's "Prisoner of Love" (if they *had* to choose a corny ballad), and the first amazing hits by Nino's mentor, Phil Spector.

4. RECORD OF THE YEAR, 1964

In the year of the Beatles, the Grammy voters, in all their wisdom, selected Stan Getz and Astrud Gilberto's "Girl from Ipanema" as Record of the Year. More outrageous, the Best Rock and Roll Recording award went to Petula Clark's quickie "Downtown." The Beatles did win for Best New Artist and for Best Performance by a Vocal Group, not bad compared to Elvis. (But then, the music industry slicksters who do the Grammy voting have always been sucker Anglophiles.) Ironically, the Best Vocal Grammy went to "A Hard Day's Night," even though the Best Motion Picture Score was . . . *Mary Poppins.*

5. BEST ROCK AND ROLL, 1966

Just as rock got rolling again, the Grammys dropped the rock and roll category—although the travesties picked from 1962 to 1966, when "Winchester Cathedral" was one of the victors, made it obvious that the Best Rock and Roll slot was a fraud from the start. There was no rock and roll category again until 1979, when Bob Dylan collected his first Grammy for the gospel song "Gotta Serve Somebody." Other winners that year: Best Rock Vocal Performance by a Duo or Group, the Eagles; Best Rock Instrumental Performance, Wings.

6. BEST ALBUM NOTES, 1975

Pete Hamill won for his fawning essay that appeared on the back cover of Dylan's *Blood on the Tracks*, a screed so patently asskissing that it was deleted from the album after the first pressing.

7. SONG OF THE YEAR, 1982

Won by "Always on My Mind," not a bad tune in Willie Nelson's version—but he got the idea from an Elvis record made just after the song was written, in *1971*. Never inclined to bow to the mere dictates of logic, the Grammys didn't change the rule to make only recent songs eligible for another decade.

8. BEST HARD ROCK/METAL PERFORMANCE, 1988

So the Grammys finally agree to recognize a twenty-year-old genre that's also the most commercially popular form of rock. And the award goes to . . . Jethro Tull?! A bunch of arty English has-beens, Tull didn't play metal and its rock, prominently featuring Ian Anderson's flute, has never been especially hard. Shunned nominees: AC/DC, Metallica, Iggy Pop, Jane's Addiction. *(Jane's Addiction?)* This is about the only thing that makes the year's other important new award, for Best Rap Performance, palatable: It went to the lame DJ Jazzy Jeff and the Fresh Prince, rather than such worthier contenders as L.L. Cool J, Salt-N-Pepa, Kool Moe Doe, or even the lightweight but not *that* flimsy J.J. Fad. The big dis here was that Public Enemy didn't even earn a nomination despite releasing one of the most ground-breaking albums of the decade, *It Takes a Nation of Millions to Hold Us Back*, and two of rap's greatest hits, "Bring the Noise" and "Don't Believe the Hype." On the other hand, to compare to Tull, the Grammy would have had to go to, say, Lou Rawls.

9. Best New Artist, 1989

It's hard to say which was more pathetic: the award to Milli Vanilli, over Neneh Cherry, Tone Loc, the Indigo Girls, and Soul II Soul, or the hysterical overreaction by both the Grammy bureaucracy and the press to the "revelation" that Milli Vanilli's records had been sung by others. The press reaction had every element of a tabloid scare classic, right down to the undercurrents of racism and homophobia, and the Grammys played along by withdrawing the award. Like it makes a difference *how the record sounds* depending on who sang on it? As George Clinton, among others, pointed out, there was no way that performers who danced as hard as M.V.'s Rob and Fab *could* be doing their own singing onstage, and that's why there is a long tradition of using ringers in pop, particularly black pop. The Milli Vanilli flap climaxed three decades of Grammy idiocy with a situation whose multiple stupidities (even if their practices are defensible, nobody—except the Grammy voters—would argue that the music was anything but worthless) are hard to fully measure.

10. Best Pop Vocal Performance, Male, 1991

Just to show that the nineties won't be all that different, the new decade kicked off with this humdinger—Michael Bolton given an award for absolutely butchering the Percy Sledge classic "When a Man Loves a Woman." Taste is taste, however, and this award wouldn't make the list if knucklehead Bolton hadn't added insult to injury by failing to number Sledge (who both cowrote and defined the song) among those he thanked, then arrogantly refusing to apologize for the gaffe backstage.

Performers with Stars on the Hollywood Walk of Fame

1. Paula Abdul, 1991
2. The Andrews Sisters, 1987
3. Paul Anka, 1984
4. Pearl Bailey, 1993
5. Count Basie, 1982
6. The Beach Boys, 1980
7. The Beatles, 1993
8. Tex Beneke, 1991
9. Chuck Berry, 1987
10. Sammy Cahn, 1990
11. The Carpenters, 1983
12. Diahann Carroll, 1990
13. Ray Charles, 1981
14. Chicago, 1992
15. Rev. James Cleveland, 1981
16. Sam Cooke, 1993
17. Celia Cruz, 1987
18. Bobby Darin, 1982
19. Rick Dees, 1984
20. Buddy DeSylva, 1992
21. Gloria Estefan, 1993
22. The Everly Brothers, 1986
23. The 5th Dimension (the original group), 1991
24. Marvin Gaye, 1990
25. Mickey Gilley, 1984
26. Lionel Hampton, 1982
27. Jimi Hendrix, 1991
28. Billie Holliday, 1986
29. Englebert Humperdinck, 1989
30. Julio Iglesias, 1985
31. Janet Jackson, 1990
32. Mahalia Jackson, 1988
33. Michael Jackson, 1984
34. Jimmy Jam and Terry Lewis, 1993
35. Jack Jones, 1989
36. Tom Jones, 1989
37. Casey Kasem, 1981
38. B. B. King, 1990
39. Jerry Lee Lewis, 1989
40. Little Richard, 1990
41. Frankie Lymon, 1993
42. Bette Midler, 1986
43. Thelonious Monk, 1993
44. The Monkees, 1989
45. Olivia Newton-John, 1981
46. Tony Orlando, 1990
47. Dolly Parton, 1984
48. Lou Rawls, 1982
49. Smokey Robinson, 1983
50. Diana Ross, 1982
51. Bob Seger and the Silver Bullet Band, 1987
52. The Steve Miller Band, 1987
53. Donna Summer, 1992
54. Tina Turner, 1986
55. Ritchie Valens, 1990
56. Sarah Vaughn, 1985
57. Billy Vera, 1988
58. Dionne Warwick, 1985
59. Andy Williams, 1982
60. Joe Williams, 1983
61. Paul Williams, 1983
62. Mary Wilson, 1990
63. Stevie Wonder, 1993

100 Artists and Their Years of Eligibility for the Rock and Roll Hall of Fame

1. Aerosmith — 1997
2. G.G. Allin — 2005
3. B-52s — 2004
4. Barney — 2018[1]
5. Beastie Boys — 2007
6. Biz Markie — 2013
7. Black Crowes — 2015
8. Bono — 2010[2]
9. Bootsy's Rubber Band — 2001
10. Garth Brooks — 2015
11. Jackson Browne — 1997
12. J. J. Cale — 1997
13. Cheech and Chong — 1996
14. Cypress Hill — 2017
15. Terence Trent D'Arby — 2012
16. Def Leppard — 2005
17. De La Soul — 2014
18. Depeche Mode — 2006
19. The Eagles — 1997
20. Eazy E — 2013
21. The Edge — 2022[2]
22. El Chicano — 1995
23. E.L.O. — 1997
24. Brian Eno — 1999
25. EnVogue — 2015
26. Eric B. & Rakim — 2012
27. Eurythmics — 2018
28. Bryan Ferry — 1999
29. Fishbone — 2010
30. Lita Ford — 2009
31. Peter Gabriel — 2002
32. Geto Boys — 2015
33. The Go-Go's — 2006
34. Grandmaster Flash and the Furious Five — 2007
35. Guns N' Roses — 2011
36. Guy — 2013
37. Sammy Hagar — 2002
38. M. C. Hammer — 2013
39. Don Henley — 2007
40. Hüsker Dü — 2006
41. Ice Cube — 2015
42. Ice-T — 2008
43. Billy Idol — 2006
44. Indigo Girls — 2014
45. INXS — 2008
46. Janet Jackson — 2007
47. Michael Jackson — 1997
48. Mick Jagger — 2010
49. Jesus Jones — 2016
50. Joan Jett — 2006
51. Jordy — 2018[3]
52. Journey — 2000
53. Big Daddy Kane — 2013
54. Chaka Khan — 2003
55. Lenny Kravitz — 2014
56. Living Colour — 2013
57. L.L. Cool J — 2011
58. Madonna — 2008
59. Teena Marie — 2004
60. Metallica — 2009
61. George Michael — 2012[4]
62. Morrissey — 2013[5]
63. The New York Dolls — 1998
64. Nirvana — 2013
65. N.W.A — 2014
66. The Ohio Players — 1997
67. Ozzy Osbourne — 2006[6]
68. Pearl Jam — 2017
69. Tom Petty and the Heartbreakers — 2001
70. Pretenders — 2005
71. Prince — 2003[7]
72. Public Enemy — 2013[8]
73. Public Image Ltd. — 2003

74. Queen	1998	87. Soul Asylum	2009
75. Queen Latifah	2014	88. Spinal Tap	2009
76. Bonnie Raitt	1996	89. Bruce Springsteen	1997
77. R.E.M.	2007	90. Steely Dan	1997
78. Keith Richards	2013	91. Talking Heads	2002
79. David Lee Roth	2010	92. 10,000 Maniacs	2007
80. Roxy Music	1997	93. The Time	2006
81. Todd Rundgren	1995	94. Tone Loc	2014
82. Run-D.M.C.	2009	95. 2 Live Crew	2012[9]
83. Sex Pistols	2002	96. U2	2005
84. Slick Rick	2014	97. Van Halen	2003
85. Patti Smith	2000	98. Vanilla Ice	2015
86. Snoop Doggy		99. Stevie Ray Vaughan	2008
Dogg	2017	100. ZZ Top	1997

Artists become eligible for the Rock and Roll Hall of Fame twenty-five years after the release of their first recording. There is no other overt qualification. However, this list may nevertheless be misleading because young artists often make obscure records that do not surface until sometime after they become famous.

---

[1] In 2018, Barney will be 88,002,018 years old.
[2] We estimate that The Edge will make his first solo album (whether or not U2 break up) about 1997. Bono will follow suit in 1998, but his date of eligibility for the Hall will not be 2023 but 2010, based on his contribution of "Silver and Gold" to the *Sun City* antiapartheid album in 1985.
[3] In 2018, Jordy will be thirty years old.
[4] Wham! is eligible in 2008.
[5] The Smiths are eligible in 2009.
[6] Black Sabbath is eligible in 1995.
[7] Christopher is not eligible.
[8] Professor Griff would be eligible in 2015, if anybody had the balls to vote for him.
[9] Hey, Hank Ballard made it.

Winners of the *Village Voice* Critics' Polls

1971: *Who's Next*, The Who
1974: *Court and Spark*, Joni Mitchell
1975: *The Basement Tapes*, Bob Dylan
1976: *Songs in the Key of Life*, Stevie Wonder
1977: *Never Mind the Bullocks . . .* , The Sex Pistols
1978: *My Aim Is True*, Elvis Costello

1979: *Squeezing Out Sparks*, Graham Parker
1980: *London Calling*, The Clash
1981: *Sandinista!*, The Clash
1982: *Imperial Bedroom*, Elvis Costello
1983: *Thriller*, Michael Jackson
1984: *Born in the U.S.A.*, Bruce Springsteen
1985: *Little Creatures*, Talking Heads
1986: *Graceland*, Paul Simon
1987: *Sign 'o' the Times*, Prince
1988: *It Takes a Nation of Millions to Hold Us Back*, Public Enemy
1989: *3 Feet High and Rising*, De La Soul
1990: *Ragged Glory*, Neil Young
1991: *Nevermind*, Nirvana
1992: *3 Years, 5 Months, and 2 Days . . .*, Arrested Development
1993: *Exile in Guyville*, Liz Phair

The 1971 poll was unofficially conducted on a much smaller scale than those from 1974 through the present. Thus, the Voice *refers to each annual poll as being one of two numbers. Hence, the 1993 poll was either the twentieth or twenty-first poll.*

Performers with the Most MTV Music Awards (Through 1993)

1. Madonna	12	6. Herbie Hancock	5
2. Peter Gabriel	11	7. Don Henley	5
3. a-ha	8	8. U2	5
4. R.E.M.	7	9. INXS	5
5. Michael Jackson	5		

Honorable mention (performers with four): Prince, Janet Jackson, Paula Abdul, Guns N' Roses, Aerosmith, En Vogue, Pearl Jam.

CHAPTER 7

Firsts and Debuts

What Was the First Rock 'n' Roll Record?

It's a controversy as old as rock 'n' roll itself—What was the very first, the original record that kicked off the rock 'n' roll craze? You could argue for no record at all, because rock 'n' roll was born of a long historical process that involved all sorts of music and the people who made it entering the mainstream of American life as geography, transportation, and recording and broadcasting technology allowed them to do so. But it's more fun to make a list, as Jim Dawson and Steve Propes did for their 1992 book What Was the First Rock 'n' Roll Record? *(Faber and Faber). These are their top fifty candidates, in the chronological order in which they presented them in their book.*

1. "Blues, Part 2," Jazz at the Philharmonic, 1944
2. "The Honeydripper," Joe Liggins and His Honeydrippers, 1945
3. "Be-Baba-Leba," Helen Humes with the Bill Doggett Octet, 1945
4. "House of Blue Lights," Freddie Slack and His Orchestra, with Ella Mae Morse, 1946
5. "That's All Right," Big Boy Crudup, 1946
6. "Open the Door, Richard," Jack McVea and His All Stars, 1946
7. "Tomorrow Night," Lonnie Johnson, 1948
8. "Good Rockin' Tonight," Wynonie Harris and His All Stars, 1948
9. "We're Gonna Rock, We're Gonna Roll," Wild Bill Moore, 1948
10. "It's Too Soon to Know," The Orioles, 1948
11. "Boogie Chillen," John Lee Hooker, 1948
12. "Guitar Boogie," Arthur Smith and the Crackerjacks, 1948
13. "Drinkin' Wine Spo-Dee-O-Dee," Stick McGhee and His Buddies, 1949
14. "Rock the Joint," Jimmy Preston and His Prestonians, 1949
15. "Saturday Night Fish Fry," Louis Jordan and His Tympany Five, 1949
16. "Mardi Gras in New Orleans," Professor Longhair, 1949
17. "The Fat Man," Fats Domino, 1950
18. "Rollin' and Tumblin'," Muddy Waters, 1950
19. "Birmingham Bounce," Hardrock Gunter and the Pebbles, 1950
20. "I'm Movin' On," Hank Snow and His Rainbow Ranch Boys, 1950
21. "Teardrops from My Eyes," Ruth Brown with Budd Johnson's Orchestra, 1950

22. "Hot Rod Race," Arkie Shibley and His Mountain Dew Boys, 1950
23. "How High the Moon," Les Paul and Mary Ford, 1951
24. "Rocket 88," Jackie Brenston with His Delta Cats, 1951
25. "Sixty Minute Man," The Dominoes, 1951
26. "Cry," Johnnie Ray with the Four Lads, 1951
27. "One Mint Julep," The Clovers, 1952
28. "Rock the Joint," Bill Haley and the Saddlemen, 1952
29. "Have Mercy Baby," The Dominoes, 1952
30. "Lawdy Miss Clawdy," Lloyd Price, 1952
31. "Kaw-Liga," Hank Williams and the Drifting Cowboys, 1953
32. "Hound Dog," Willie Mae "Big Mama" Thornton with Kansas City Bill, 1953
33. "Honey Hush," Big Joe Turner, 1953
34. "Money Honey," Clyde McPhatter and the Drifters, 1953
35. "Gee," The Crows, 1953
36. "Shake, Rattle, and Roll," Big Joe Turner, 1954
37. "Work with Me, Annie," The Royals / The Midnighters, 1954
38. "Sh-Boom," The Chords, 1954
39. "(We're Gonna) Rock Around the Clock," Bill Haley and His Comets, 1954
40. "Riot in Cell Block #9," The Robins, 1954
41. "That's All Right," Elvis Presley, Scotty and Bill, 1954
42. "Earth Angel (Will You Be Mine)," The Penguins, 1954
43. "Tweedle Dee," LaVern Baker and the Gliders, 1954
44. "Pledging My Love," Johnny Ace with the Johnny Otis Orchestra, 1954
45. "I've Got a Woman," Ray Charles, 1954
46. "Bo Diddley," Bo Diddley, 1955
47. "Maybellene," Chuck Berry, 1955
48. "Tutti Frutti," Little Richard, 1955
49. "Blue Suede Shoes," Carl Perkins, 1955
50. "Heartbreak Hotel," Elvis Presley, 1956

Beatles Firsts

1. First appearance at Liverpool's Cavern Club: March 21, 1961
2. First appearance on *The Ed Sullivan Show:* February 9, 1964
3. First record to use reverse tapes: "Rain," June 10, 1966
4. First record on Apple label: "Hey Jude," August 30, 1968
5. First outside album by a Beatle: *Unfinished Music No. 1: Two Virgins*, John Lennon and Yoko Ono, 1968
6. First solo single by a Beatle: "Give Peace a Chance," John Lennon, 1969
7. First solo album by a Beatle: *McCartney*, Paul McCartney, 1969

8. First rumor that "Paul is dead": *Northern Star* headline "Clues Hint at Beatle Death," September 23, 1969
9. First official release in U.S.S.R.: "Let It Be," 1972
10. First song sold for advertisement: "Revolution," 1987

The 20 Best Debut Albums

1. *Are You Experienced*, The Jimi Hendrix Experience, 1967
2. *With the Beatles*, 1963
3. *Elvis Presley*, 1956
4. *Here's Little Richard*, 1956
5. *Appetite for Destruction*, Guns N' Roses, 1987
6. *John Lennon / Plastic Ono Band*, 1970
7. *The Clash*, 1977
8. *AmeriKKKa's Most Wanted*, Ice Cube, 1990
9. *The Chronic*, Dr. Dre, 1992
10. *Music from Big Pink*, The Band, 1968
11. *Introducing the Hard Line According to Terence Trent D'Arby*, 1987
12. *Bob Dylan*, 1962
13. *The Rolling Stones*, 1964
14. *Of the Heart, Of the Soul, Of the Cross: The Utopian Experience*, PM Dawn, 1991
15. *Pronounced Leh-Nerd Skin-Nerd*, Lynyrd Skynrd, 1973
16. *Seal*, 1991
17. *My Aim Is True*, Elvis Costello, 1977
18. *Jerry Lee Lewis*, 1958
19. *Pretenders*, 1980
20. *Murmur*, R.E.M., 1983

The 20 Best Debut Singles

1. "I Want You Back," The Jackson 5, 1969
2. "That's All Right," Elvis Presley, 1954
3. "Anarchy in the UK," The Sex Pistols, 1976
4. "I Can't Live Without My Radio," L.L. Cool J, 1985
5. "Smells Like Teen Spirit," Nirvana, 1992 (their major label debut)
6. "Maybellene," Chuck Berry, 1955
7. "Lawdy Miss Clawdy," Lloyd Price, 1952
8. "These Arms of Mine," Otis Redding, 1963
9. "Mr. Tambourine Man," The Byrds, 1965
10. "Welcome to the Jungle," Guns N' Roses, 1987
11. "Reet Petite (The Finest Girl You Ever Want to Meet)," Jackie Wilson, 1957

12. "Fast Car," Tracy Chapman, 1988
13. "Holiday," Madonna, 1983
14. "I Can't Explain," The Who, 1956
15. "Roxanne," The Police, 1979
16. "Be-Bop-a-Lula," Gene Vincent and His Blue Caps, 1956
17. "Jump," Kriss Kross, 1992
18. "Ooby Dooby," Roy Orbison, 1956
19. "Let's Go Trippin'," Dick Dale and His Del-Tones, 1961
20. "I'm a Man" / "Bo Diddley," Bo Diddley, 1955

The 10 Most Ridiculous Debut Singles

1. "Baby Kittens," Carole King, 1959
2. "A Teenager's Romance," Ricky Nelson, 1957
3. "Baby Talk," Jan and Dean, 1959
4. "Long Tall Sally," The Kinks, 1964
5. "Movie Magg," Carl Perkins, 1955
6. "My Bonnie," The Beatles, 1961
7. "Love to Love You Baby," Donna Summer, 1976
8. "Stormy Weather," The Five Sharps, 1954
9. "Suzie-Q," Creedence Clearwater Revival, 1968
10. "Taxi Blues," Little Richard, 1951

The 10 Most Disappointing Debut Albums

1. BLIND FAITH, 1969
Supposed to be the ultimate in supergroups, sporting a lineup that included Eric Clapton and Ginger Baker fresh from Cream, and Steve Winwood just departed from Traffic. Imagine the world's surprise when the music turned out to be tepid, uninspired, and uninspiring.

2. THE GRATEFUL DEAD, 1967
Heralded as the grandaddy of all psychedelia, the Dead debuted as a pretentious fourth-rate blues band.

3. CROSBY, STILLS, AND NASH, 1969
Another supergroup fiasco. Combine members of the Byrds, the Hollies, and Buffalo Springfield and you get . . . the folkie equivalent of barber-shop harmony?!

4. *McCARTNEY*, PAUL McCARTNEY, 1970

How could the first pop-oriented, nonexperimental solo album by a Beatle fail? Easy, McCartney played all the music himself, and wrote about one and a half good songs. This banal, dumb album revealed the extent to which the Beatles were a group effort—and it also showed that the idea of John Lennon as the group's intellectual leader was more than an illusion.

5. *WILSON PHILLIPS*, 1991

Two daughters of Beach Boy Brian Wilson meet one offspring of the Mamas and the Papas' John Phillips. Result: Harmonies so lightweight they almost float off into the distance. Having redefined wimp for the nineties, they sold a ton, then disappeared off the face of the charts. Good riddance.

6. *I GOT DEM OL' KOZMIC BLUES AGAIN, MAMA*, JANIS JOPLIN, 1969

The album where Janis split from the supposedly amateurish Big Brother and the Holding Company and hired herself a band made up of solid professionals. But the leather-lunged belter's own technical limitations became glaring in that context, and the pros never reached anything like the energy level of Big Brother's semichaos. The resulting sterile drool belied all the vitality of Joplin's performance persona.

7. *WHITNEY HOUSTON*, 1985

As highly touted as any vocalist since Aretha Franklin, and with the pedigree (mom Cissy Houston; aunt Dionne Warwick) to encourage every shred of your belief. But Houston's career track was set by the same middle-brow tastes that brought us Barry Manilow, a commercial triumph amidst an artistic catastrophe. Executive producer Clive Davis prides himself on his taste in songs, but for saddling such a great voice with such unremitting banality he ought to hang his head in shame.

8. *SONG CYCLE*, VAN DYKE PARKS, 1968

For months, the West Coast hipster intelligentsia wrote about the brilliance of Parks, a former collaborator on some Brian Wilson lyrics, none of which had (of course) yet been heard. Turned out that his forte was pretentious movie music. Get that dog outta the house.

9. *WEDNESDAY MORNING, 3 AM*, SIMON AND GARFUNKEL, 1965

Those who loved "The Sound of Silence" for its electric folk-rock listened in sad surprise as they spun a first album of straight, often cloying folk, all high-pitched harmonies and overwrought wimp prosody.

10. *NEVER MIND THE BOLLOCKS, HERE'S THE SEX PISTOLS*, 1977

After their revolutionary hit singles, imagine the amazement when the singles turned out to be the only part of their album that transcended the pedestrian. How could such successful revolutionaries flop so badly? Call 'em a singles band, and remember that legendary bassist Sid Vicious couldn't write, while nonlegendary bassist Glen Matlock (whom Sid replaced) could.

Famous Turn-Downs

1. Elvis Presley was tossed out of the *Grand Ole Opry* in 1954 after a show. One of the Opry honchos reportedly suggested he go back to driving a truck. Elvis was also turned down by Arthur Godfrey's *Talent Scouts*.
2. Decca Records rejected the Beatles, as did several other labels, before producer George Martin finally saw some potential in them.
3. Stephen Stills flunked an audition to be in the Monkees; he joined Buffalo Springfield instead.
4. The Who were turned down by EMI Records. Later, American Decca would refuse the initial master of "My Generation" because it thought the feedback solo at the end was unplanned distortion.
5. Godfrey's *Talent Scouts* also spurned Sonny Til and the Orioles, who went on to hit with "Crying in the Chapel" and kick off the early-1950s bird-group craze.
6. The Sex Pistols were dropped by A&M Records without ever releasing a record. Actually, it was behavior at the band's signing party in the label offices that caused the dismissal, which cost A&M a pile of dough and enhanced the Pistols' outlaw imagery.
7. Boston's first demo tape, which was cut in Tom Scholz's basement but otherwise is almost identical to the group's first album, was turned down by virtually every major label in America. Finally, the tape returned for a second chance to Epic Records, which, on further listening, decided to sign them. The almost-identical album sold 8 million copies, the most commercially successful debut LP by a rock band in recording history.
8. When Andre Harrell approached his then-boss at Rush Management, Russell Simmons, about an artist, a heavyset, light-skinned Jamaican-American who claimed to be the "Overweight Lover," Simmons waved Harrell off with a curt "Nigga, don't no girl wanna give Heavy D. no pussy." This comment precipitated Harrell's exit from Rush to form Uptown Records, where Heavy D. has enjoyed platinum-level success.

Performers Discovered by John Hammond

John Hammond was a legendary talent scout for a variety of record companies, most notably Columbia, beginning in the 1930s and continuing virtually uninterrupted until his death in 1989. In 1938, he organized the now-legendary From Spirituals to Swing *concert at Carnegie Hall, which first brought the full scope of black American musical achievement to a sophisticated white audience. He always nurtured a wide range of performers, making him the most important nonperformer in the history of American music. This grouping represents only the cream of the crop among Hammond's discoveries (mainly people he was first to record—several already had found reputations but no Big Chance); he also nurtured, economically and with loving support, a host of others, in jazz, gospel, blues, rock, and classical music, including Bessie Smith, Mahalia Jackson, and Pete Seeger.*

1. Billie Holiday, 1933
2. Benny Goodman, 1934
3. Count Basie, 1935
4. Lester Young, 1936
5. Charlie Christian, 1939
6. Mitch Miller, 1952
7. Aretha Franklin, 1960
8. Bob Dylan, 1961
9. George Benson, 1965
10. Leonard Cohen, 1968
11. Bruce Springsteen, 1972
12. Stevie Ray Vaughan, 1980

Performers Discovered by Sam Phillips

Sam Phillips is the godfather of rock and roll, not only because he shepherded Elvis Presley, Scotty Moore, and Bill Black through their incredible early records for his Sun label, but also because of the performers he discovered and nurtured before and after that period. This list includes those he was first to record or nurtured early in their careers.

1. B. B. King, 1950[1]
2. Ike Turner[2]
3. Howlin' Wolf, 1951[1]
4. Walter Horton, 1951
5. Junior Parker, 1951
6. Rufus Thomas, 1953
7. Elvis Presley, 1954
8. Johnny Cash, 1955
9. Carl Perkins, 1955
10. Roy Orbison, 1956
11. Jerry Lee Lewis, 1957
12. Charlie Rich, 1958

[1] Never released recordings on Sun; masters leased to Modern/RPM Records in Los Angeles (King) or Chess in Chicago (Wolf).
[2] Turner functioned as a talent scout, band leader, songwriter, and all 'round musical genius during the period when Phillips leased his re-

cordings to Modern and Chess. They made many classic recordings during this period, including Jackie Brenston's "Rocket 88" (which was all Ike except for the vocal), arguably "the first rock and roll record."

Run-D.M.C.'s Famous Firsts

1. First rappers to earn a gold album
2. First rappers to earn a platinum album
3. First rappers to earn a triple platinum award
4. First rappers to earn platinum awards for three consecutive albums
5. First rap video on MTV
6. First rappers on *American Bandstand*
7. First rappers on the cover of *Rolling Stone*
8. First rappers to receive a corporate endorsement deal (Adidas)
9. First rappers to star in their own film *(Krush Groove)*
10. First rock/rap crossover hit with Aerosmith on 1986's "Walk This Way"
11. First rappers to perform at the Grammy Awards show (1988)
12. The only rap act at Live Aid

Source: Break It Down, *by Michael Small.*

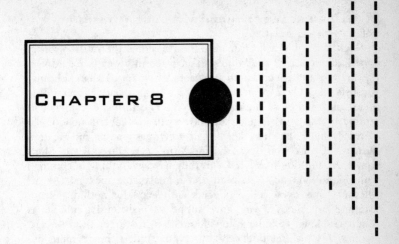

CHAPTER 8

Criticism

Discredited Rock Theories

1. ELVIS PRESLEY'S MUSIC WAS JUST IMITATION RHYTHM AND BLUES.

Rock and roll's worst canard—from it stems the music's gutter myths, about blacks and whites alike. Even in his early recordings, Presley was influenced as much by country singers, Italian bel canto vocalists like Dean Martin and Mario Lanza, and gospel music (black and white) as he was by R&B. The ultimate evidence is offered by the Sun singles themselves: All five contain nonoriginal material, and of the ten songs, half are from country and western sources. "I Love You Because" and "I'm Left, You're Right, She's Gone" are nothing like R&B, yet they have everything in common with country music. And both are unmistakable rockers. (As for whether Elvis ever said, "Niggers ain't good for nothing except to shine my shoes," you have to be as maliciously gullible as Albert Goldman to believe it. Throughout his career, Elvis *always* credited his black influences—surely, he did so much more explicitly than anybody who followed him, even the Rolling Stones.)

2. ROCK "DIED" BETWEEN 1959 AND 1964.

This is thought to be true because during that period Elvis was in the army, Buddy Holly died, Jerry Lee Lewis was banned, Chuck Berry went to prison, and Little Richard entered a seminary. Fact is, however, that from 1959 to 1964, the following not only had hits but had number-one hits: Lloyd Price ("Stagger Lee"), Wilbert Harrison ("Kansas City"), the Drifters ("Save the Last Dance for Me"), Del Shannon ("Running Scared"), Gary "U.S." Bonds ("Quarter to Three"), Dion ("Runaround Sue"), Little Eva ("The Loco-Motion"), the Four Seasons ("Sherry," "Walk Like a Man," "Big Girls Don't Cry"), the Crystals ("He's A Rebel"), the Chiffons ("He's So Fine"), Stevie Wonder ("Fingertips—Pt. 2")—not to mention a batch of other girl-group, Chicago soul, Motown, and surf hits. And if that ain't rock and roll . . .

3. PAUL IS DEAD.

A dead person would never have sued to dissolve the Beatles' partnership. However, it is true that when he reads his reviews, Paul sometimes *wishes* he were dead.

4. ALL ROCK CRITICS WEAR GLASSES.

Lester Bangs didn't.

5. ROCK LYRICS ARE POETRY.

Rock lyrics are verse and generally rhyme, but they aren't poetic, except in the rarest cases, and certainly, the best of them have little or no emotional impact when laid out on the page, unadorned by music. Rock lyrics are doggerel, maybe.

6. MTV CAN'T AIR VIDEOS BY BLACK ARTISTS.

When MTV began broadcasting in 1982, its chief programmers—Mississippi native Bob Pittman and his chum Les Garland, a pair of Top Forty radio strikeouts—insisted that the station must air videos only by white acts. MTV wasn't racist, they explained; the policy stemmed solely from the intolerance of the audience. Then Michael Jackson made videos for "Billie Jean," "Beat It," and "Thriller." MTV resisted the first but pressure from CBS Records got it on the air, where it was very enthusiastically received. "Beat It" transformed the channel from a joke to a central component of musical image making. And "Thriller," the first long-form video, created a sensation—a sensation that could only be seen in its entirety, with any regularity, on MTV. Still, MTV remained resistant to black videos, especially to the powerful new hybrid called hip-hop. Then Ted Demme, a young station exec, proposed filling the mostly ignored Saturday morning slot with a token rap show and new programmer Lee Michaels agreed. The result was *Yo! MTV Raps,* the most popular scheduled program in MTV history and both a rapper's and a rocker's delight. The MTV of the nineties not only has a fully integrated playlist but also makes documentaries preaching racial tolerance to its audience.

7. RAP ISN'T MUSIC.

Just because you don't understand it doesn't mean it's not music. There were people who thought that John Coltrane and Charlie Parker were idiots. Rap's musical innovations include the freshest approach to polyrhythms that popular music has ever seen, as well as the most daring use of voices as percussion devices ever placed on any electromagnetic device. The art of aural montage reached a pinnacle with rap's pioneering use of sampling and electronic percussion.

8. MIDDLE-CLASS PEOPLE MAKE THE BEST ROCK AND ROLL.

The long-standing confusion over this issue stems from the basic American denial of class issues in the first place. Was Elvis, born in a shotgun shack, living in a housing project, a son of the middle class? Were Chuck Berry, Little Richard, or Fats Domino? Were the MC5, even if their dads had steady factory jobs? But that doesn't mean that rock and roll can be attributed solely to the working class, either, unless you want to write Buddy Holly, Ricky Nelson, Bob Dylan, Phil Spector, Berry Gordy, the Beach Boys and Mick Jagger out of the picture. Class sympathy and class antagonism have a lot to do with rock and roll, but there *is* no prescription for who's going to make the best of it—people who grew up as impoverished as KRS-One, Patti Smith, Johnny Rotten, and Bruce Springsteen, and as dead-center middle class as Chuck D, Joe Strummer, Paul Westerberg, and Pete Townshend have all done just fine. We're not even sure that it's telling that nobody from the true upper class of England or America has ever made a good record; maybe it's just that no Kennedy or Windsor wants—or needs—to work that hard, though maybe it's something else too. Funk, after all, *might* be a class issue.

9. HEAVY METAL CONTAIN LYRICS SATANICALLY INSERTED BACKWARD THAT CAUSE SUICIDE.

Nonsense. Presuming that one verifiable suicide stemming from listening to *any* kind of music existed (none does), this would only mean that, as an inspiration, music had joined the ranks of the Bible (thank you, David Koresh). As to whether so-called backmasking even exists, the preachers, cops, and political spouses have yet to answer the basic questions posed by Robert D. Hicks in his book *The Pursuit of Satan: The Police and the Occult* (Prometheus Books, 1991): "How does your average consumer manage to play the messages backwards on a common record player or tape recorder? Assuming the messages are there, what mechanism allows a listener to perceive them, consciously or unconsciously, when the music is played forward at the correct speed? Even assuming that a listener somehow absorbs the messages subliminally, so what? What effects do such messages have?" For further debunking of the possibility of so-called subliminal messages having any effect—whether to make you stop smoking or to make you kill your grandma—see John R. Vokey and Don J. Read's 1985 study, "Subliminal Messages: Between the Devil and the Media," in *American Psychologist*, Vol. 40, No 11 (1985).

10. RAP KILLS COPS.

Beloved of Beverly Sills, Charlton Heston, other rank assholes, and Time/Warner board members as this saga may be, the facts don't hold up to the barest scrutiny. In 1992, the year of the great outcry over Ice-T's "Cop Killer" and several other antipolice message songs, the number of police killed by civilians went *down* across the United States, from a little more than sixty to fewer than fifty. Statistics on the number of civilians that the police murder—or let's be polite and say execute without benefit of trial—each year are not available because the only people who could tally them are the cops and they refuse to do so (source: FBI Uniform Crime Statistics). It is true that several criminals who have been apprehended after murdering cops *claim* to have been inspired by rap records, but observers other than propagandists and the totally buffaloed might notice that these criminals are in dire need of an alibi. In fact, if these criminals said that they'd shot the cops because of something they'd read in the Bible, nobody would take them seriously even though there is as much murder, rape, and mayhem in the book of Genesis alone as on any rap record.

11. GIRLS CAN'T PLAY ROCK 'N' ROLL.

Even it if were true that girls couldn't, grrrls (as in the "riot grrrls" of the early nineties) surely can. Anyway, despite the way that men have told the story, women have been involved in rock and roll from the very beginning, and not only as subjects: Ruth Brown became the queen of rock with her early fifties R&B hits well before anyone nominated a king; Deborah Chesler's songs provided the basis for the first great rock 'n' roll harmony group, Sonny Til and the Orioles; Elvis was first heard by Marion Keisker, general manager of Sun Records, and it was Keisker who prodded Sam Phillips to sign him. Without women like Darlene Love, Carole King, Wanda Jackson, Arlene Smith and the Chantels, and Martha and the Vandellas—to skim the surface of a very deep pool—rock wouldn't have lasted long enough to get to Janis Joplin, let alone Joan Jett.

12. ALL GANGSTA RAPPERS ARE SPOILED KIDS PLAYING OUT MIDDLE-CLASS FANTASIES.

Ice Cube didn't invent the deaths of his homies lost to street violence. DJ Quik really is a Piru Blood, and the "LBC" on Snoop Doggy Dogg's sweatshirt in Dr. Dre's "Ain't Nothin' but a 'G' Thang" video advertises the name of his real-life set, the Long Beach Crips. If you ask any gangsta rapper, he'd probably wish that he had made the shit up, but while many exaggerate, none of it is science fiction. *That* idea is just the middle-class fantasy of pundits who don't want to face facts.

13. "LOUIE LOUIE" HAS DIRTY LYRICS.

A trick question, in a sense, since various people *have* made up dirty lyrics to "Louie Louie" 's immortal *duh duh duh, duh duh duh* rhythm over the years and a couple of them have even landed on records, notably on Iggy Pop's *Metallic KO*. On the other hand, the original "Louie Louie," as famously recorded by the Kingsmen in 1963, never deserved to be banned in Indiana, much less investigated by the FBI for thirty months. What L.A. R&B great Richard Berry wrote, and the Kingsmen's Jack Ely sang, was a sea chanty about a homesick Jamaican sailor trying to get home to his girl— Louie being the bartender he's spieling to.

14. CLAPTON IS GOD.

Naw. Ask Bono.

15. MICHAEL JACKSON BLEACHES HIS SKIN.

He has vitiglio, a rare disease that's doing it for him. Do we believe him? Well, he said so to Oprah. And Janet swears it's the truth.

16. ALBUMS SOUND BETTER THAN CDs.

Actually, this one might be true—if you're willing to spend more than $10,000 on your album playback equipment. If you're more mortally endowed with cash, however (or if you'd simply rather spend your bucks on music than machines), then CDs are an unparalleled improvement on LPs. As for this wild concept that they're gonna self-destruct—try just leaving an old-fashioned vinyl record alone for a couple of years. Dust, dirt, the paper or plastic it's wrapped up in—any of these can cause near-fatal deterioration. Anybody who doesn't know this owns too few records and too many anti-CD audiophile magazines.

17. MADONNA SUCKS.

If you believe what she says in *Truth or Dare*, she refuses to.

18. PUBLIC ENEMY IS ANTI-SEMITIC.

Militant, yes. Hateful, no. Public Enemy Minister of Information Professor Griff did make anti-Semitic statements in 1989. He was almost immediately expelled from the group. The press proceeded to interview PE leader Chuck D endlessly about the subject, as if *he* had made those statements. (Griff was never even offered an interview by papers like *The New York Times* and *Village Voice*.) Chuck D has spoken on the subject many times. No one has ever accused him—or any other member of the group—of making anti-Semitic statements, except by taking one line ("So called chosen, frozen") from "Welcome to the Terrordome," the band's comment on the Griff incident, wildly out of context.

19. YOU CAN'T TRUST ANYONE OVER THIRTY.

If you believe that today, you can't even watch MTV, much less listen to the radio.

20. THE WORDS TO "SMELLS LIKE TEEN SPIRIT" ARE UNINTELLIGIBLE.

Just 'cause *you* can't understand 'em . . .

Frank Zappa's Favorite Rock Critics

1.
2.
3.
4.
5.

The Least Promising Interview Openers Cameron Crowe Has Encountered

1. "The gun is loaded."—Buddy Miles
2. "Let's do it in the bar."—Stephen Stills
3. "Hold on, aren't you the one who called me the Liberace of Rock?"—Elton John
4. "You're too young to grasp my complete musical scope."—Steve Miller

5. "I changed my mind."—Pete Townshend
6. "We don't believe in tape recorders."—ZZ Top
7. "There's nobody here except a few ghosts and I don't care. Let's rap."—Bob Weir
8. "I think I just saw a body drop right outside that window. Did you just see a body drop? Let's go outside and see. I know I saw a body drop."—David Bowie

Cameron Crowe began contributing to national magazines like Rolling Stone *and* Creem *while still attending junior high school in San Diego. Despite the unpromising beginnings listed above, most of Crowe's interviews and profiles turned out swell, but then he had the bright idea of going back to high school for a year. The result was* Fast Times at Ridgemont High, *and a career in films that includes, most recently, the Crowe-directed* Singles, *the acclaimed portrait of Seattle's postmodern rock and coffee bar culture.*

From the Page to the Stage— and Back
Performers and Producers Who Have Also Been Critics and Journalists

1. Lauren Agnelli (aka Trixie A. Balm)
2. Lester Bangs
3. Roy Blount, Jr.[1]
4. Robert Fripp
5. Bob Geldof
6. Kim Gordon
7. Matt Groening[1]
8. Steve Harley
9. Chrissie Hynde
10. Ira Kaplan (Yo La Tengo)
11. Lenny Kaye
12. Cub Koda
13. Al Kooper
14. Jon Landau
15. Greil Marcus[1]
16. Dave Marsh[1]
17. R. Meltzer
18. Robert Palmer (not *that* one)
19. Sandy Pearlman
20. Vernon Reid
21. Joel Selvin[1]
22. Davitt Sigerson
23. Patti Smith
24. Speech (Arrested Development)
25. Bill Stephney
26. Greg Tate
27. Neil Tennant (Pet Shop Boys)
28. Pete Townshend

---

[1] Members of the Critics Chorus of the Rock Bottom Remainders, an all-author band of the early nineties that also featured Stephen King, Dave Barry, Al Kooper, Ridley Pearson, Barbara Kingsolver, Amy Tan, and Tad Bartimus—but those guys actually played instruments and sang on key and stuff.

"When I Get My Picture on the Cover of the *Rolling Stone*"
Most Frequent Appearances on the Magazine's Cover (Through 1993)

NUMBER OF APPEARANCES	ARTIST
12	John Lennon
11	Bob Dylan
10	Mick Jagger
9	Bruce Springsteen
9	Bono/U2/The Edge
8	Paul McCartney
7	Madonna
6	Jackson Browne
6	Janis Joplin
6	The Rolling Stones
6	Linda Ronstadt
6	James Taylor
5	G n' R/Axl/Slash
5	The Beatles
5	Fleetwood Mac
5	Jimi Hendrix
5	Carly Simon
5	Rod Stewart
5	Pete Townshend
5	Prince
5	Sting
5	Tom Cruise
4	Elton John
4	Michael Jackson
4	Billy Joel

Most Appearances on the Cover of *16 Magazine*

From the heyday of Elvis through the late seventies power pop era, 16 Magazine *defined rock 'n' roll style for a generation of teenagers—mostly girls but a healthy smattering of boys included.* 16 *wasn't for sixteen-year-olds, you understand. It was aimed at even younger girls who dreamed of being sixteen, and whose fantasy mates were just that innocent. Of all the teendream books on the newsstands, which were in its era quite crowded with them, 16 became the most important because of its editor, Gloria Stavers. Stavers, who dated everyone from Mickey Mantle to Lenny Bruce to Jim Morrison, grew up in North Carolina as a prototype of the kids she wrote about, and she never lost sight of their desires—or their needs. So at the same time that she promoted the most white-bread teen exploitation stars, she also worked to turn her audience on to key bohemian figures. Her support led to the Doors becoming teen idols, her plug for Rolling Stone kept the magazine in business with quarters sent in for sample issues, and her obituary for Lenny Bruce remains justifiably famous. The following list expresses both the parameters of Gloria Stavers's taste and the impact of her personality on the teen starmaking process.*

1. The Beatles
2. The Monkees
3. The Bay City Rollers
4. Kiss
5. David Cassidy
6. Donny Osmond
7. Bobby Sherman
8. Sajid Khan
9. Elvis Presley
10. Rick Nelson

Note: We don't really know who Sajid Kahn was, either.

28 Songs About the Beatles

1. "ALL I WANT FOR CHRISTMAS IS A BEATLE," DORA BRYAN
Amazingly enough, the surge of Beatlemania that erupted on their arrival in the United States in February 1964 lasted long enough to produce this Christmas disc the next winter.

2. "THE BEATLES' BARBER," SCOTT DOUGLAS
A real weeper.

3. "BEATLE BEAT," ELLA FITZGERALD
An old-timer tries to catch up.

4. "BEATLE FLYING SAUCER," ED SOLOMON
This punch-in pastiche takes up where Buchanan and Goodman's original "Flying Saucer" left off. Buchanan had his own say. (See number 18.)

5. "A BEATLE I WANT TO BE," SONNY CURTIS
A tribute from one of Buddy Holly's Crickets, after whom the Fab Four had named themselves.

6. "BRING BACK THE BEATLES," DAVID PEEL
The weird denizen of New York's Lower East Side recorded this after his short-lived association with John Lennon (which resulted in one album by Peel for Apple Records).

7. "CRAZY JOHN," TOM PAXTON
Unsurprisingly sour take on Lennon's radicalism by rad-lib folk

singer who wears his resentment at never having found a mass audience on his sleeve, in his voice, just about everywhere.

8. "EARLY 1970," RINGO STARR

The B-side to "It Don't Come Easy" is Ringo's tribute to his mates, in which he describes his relationship to each of the others in musical terms. It's lovingly mournful and the one disc here that can in no way be termed exploitative.

9. "FRANKENSTEIN MEETS THE BEATLES," JEKYLL AND HYDE

Another "Flying Saucer"–style parody disc.

10. "GOD PART TWO," U2

Bono's snarling attack on Lennon ficto-biographer Albert Goldman.

11. "THE GUY WITH THE LONG LIVERPOOL HAIR," THE OUTSIDERS

A tribute from a frat-rock band the British Invasion soon made outmoded.

12. "I HATE THE BEATLES," ALLAN SHERMAN

The most famous of the antilonghair songs. History has told the story: Paul McCartney got a bigger obituary than Allan Sherman without even having to go to the trouble of dying.

13. "I LOVE YOU RINGO," BONNIE JO MASON

Mason became as famous as Cher, the only vaguely interesting thing about this record.

14. "I WANNA BE A BEATLE," GENE CORNISH AND THE UNBEATABLES

Cornish and friends made it, too. Within a year, they changed their name to the Young Rascals and reached major stardom.

15. "I WANT TO KISS RINGO GOODBYE," PENNY VALENTINE

Valentine was and is a British pop journalist, the most obvious explanation for why this record's so shameless.

16. "I'LL LET YOU HOLD MY HAND," THE BOOTLES

Answer song to a question never asked.

17. "I'M BETTER THAN THE BEATLES," BRAD BERWICK AND THE BUGS

A rare example of megalomania in its pure form.

18. "THE INVASION," BUCHANAN AND GREENFIELD

Dickie Goodman, the original "Flying Saucer" man, strikes again with a punch-in record mocking the rise of Beatlemania with artfully arranged song snippets and news clips.

19. "THE LATE GREAT JOHNNY ACE," PAUL SIMON

A tribute to John Lennon that compares his life to that of Ace, the great fifties R&B singer who died in a game of Russian roulette.

20. "A LETTER FROM ELAINA," CASEY KASEM

Unctuous sentimentality from one of the world's lamest Top Forty DJs.

21. "LITTLE BEATLE BOY," THE ANGELS

Beatles tribute from the "My Boyfriend's Back" bunch.

22. "MY BOYFRIEND GOT A BEATLE HAIRCUT," DONNA LYNN

Arguably the best of the Beatles fan songs, because Lynn could sing a little bit. Also a prime example of the way show biz devours its own. This exploitation effort came out on Capitol Records, the Beatles' own label.

23. "MY GIRLFRIEND WROTE A LETTER TO THE BEATLES," THE FOUR PREPS

This pop singing group, its career about to be destroyed by the British Invasion, probably wished that were the full extent of its problem.

24. "SAGA OF THE BEATLES," JOHNNY AND THE HURRICANES

Tribute from the famous instrumental group.

25. "TREAT HIM TENDER, MAUREEN," ANGIE AND THE CHICLETTES

Premature bubblegum group mourns Ringo's (first) marriage.

26. "WE LOVE THE BEATLES," THE VERNON GIRLS

Inferior attempt at saying what number 27 says much more eloquently.

27. "WE LOVE YOU BEATLES," THE CAREFREES

The only about-the-Beatles disc to make the Top Forty, it hit number thirty-nine in April 1964. The record consisted of the chant Beatlemaniacs spontaneously sent up outside the Plaza Hotel, where the group stayed on its first New York visit.

28. "YES, YOU CAN HOLD MY HAND," THE BEATLETTES

Another unasked question. But mainly, further evidence that the music business needed an awkward period of adjustment before the true impact of those four lovable moptops could be absorbed.

We Can Work It Out
Musical Comments on the Beatles' Breakup

1. "EARLY 1970," RINGO STARR, 1971

The B-side of "It Don't Come Easy" describes the band members' willingness to play music with Ringo when he sees them. He seems most distanced from Paul, closest to John, miserable about the entire situation.

2. "TOO MANY PEOPLE," PAUL McCARTNEY, 1971

John Lennon, at least, interpreted these lyrics, from the album *Ram*, as a subtle attack on him and as McCartney's way of shifting the blame for the breakup onto John's shoulder's.

3. "HOW DO YOU SLEEP?" JOHN LENNON, 1971

A direct hit on McCartney from *Imagine*. That album featured a freebie postcard that pictured John pulling a pig's ears, an apparent reference to McCartney's photo on the cover of *Ram*. Not exactly subtle, and neither's the song.

4. "BACK OFF BOOGALOO," RINGO STARR, 1972

This single was taken by many to be Ringo's attempt at conciliating the Lennon-McCartney feud. It didn't help much.

5. "SUE ME, SUE YOU BLUES," GEORGE HARRISON, 1973

George, of all people, has the last word on the breakup with this song about legal entanglements and resulting bad vibes. He'd later remember his bandmates more fondly in 1987's "When We Was Fab," but that was about the marriage, not the divorce.

Bob Dylan's 25 Greatest Hits

1. "Like a Rolling Stone"
2. "Visions of Johanna"
3. "Just Like Tom Thumb's Blues" (live version—B-side of "I Want You")
4. "All Along the Watchtower"
5. "When the Ship Comes In"
6. "I Want You"
7. "The Lonesome Death of Hattie Carroll"
8. "Stuck Inside of Mobile with the Memphis Blues Again"
9. "A Hard Rain's A-Gonna Fall"
10. "Subterranean Homesick Blues"
11. "Mr. Tambourine Man"
12. "I Shall Be Free #10"
13. "I Don't Believe You" (live version—electric)
14. "Every Grain of Sand"
15. "I Shall Be Released"
16. "Ballad of a Thin Man"
17. "Tangled Up in Blue"
18. "Knockin' On Heaven's Door"
19. "Most Likely You Go Your Way"
20. "If You Gotta Go, Go Now"
21. "Blind Willie McTell"
22. "She's Your Lover Now"
23. "When I Paint My Masterpiece"
24. "Please Mrs. Henry"
25. "You Ain't Goin' Nowhere"

Reginald C. Dennis's Favorite Songs of All Time

1. "La-Di-Da-Di," Doug E. Fresh & MC Ricky D (aka Slick Rick)
2. "Eric B. Is President," Eric B. & Rakim
3. "Rebel Without a Pause," Public Enemy
4. "The Message," Grandmaster Flash & the Furious Five
5. "8th Wonder," Sugarhill Gang
6. "Sucker MCs," Run-D.M.C.
7. "Peter Piper," Run-D.M.C.
8. "Straight Outta Compton," N.W.A
9. "So What'Cha Sayin," EPMD

Critics' Pets
Artists Critics Believe Can Do No Wrong

1. Arrested Development
2. The Beatles
3. James Brown
4. Butthole Surfers
5. The Clash
6. Elvis Costello
7. Cypress Hill
8. De La Soul
9. Peter Gabriel
10. The Disposable Heroes of Hiphoprisy
11. Gang of Four
12. George Jones
13. Wynonna Judd
14. Jungle Brothers
15. The Kinks
16. KRS-One
17. Lyle Lovett
18. Nick Lowe
19. Lynyrd Skynyrd
20. Madonna
21. Biz Markie
22. Van Morrison
23. PM Dawn
24. The Pixies
25. The Posies
26. Public Enemy
27. Queen Latifah
28. Bonnie Raitt
29. R.E.M.
30. The Replacements
31. The Rolling Stones
32. The Smiths
33. Sonic Youth
34. Bruce Springsteen (ret.)
35. Talking Heads
36. U2
37. X
38. XTC
39. Yo La Tengo
40. Neil Young

Sez Who? Bands and Singers Critics Love to Hate

1. Toto
2. 2 Live Crew
3. Michael Bolton
4. Supertramp
5. Rush
6. Pink Floyd
7. Styx
8. Foreigner
9. Yes
10. Emerson, Lake and Palmer
11. The Grateful Dead
12. Led Zeppelin
13. Kiss
14. Aerosmith
15. Linda Ronstadt
16. The Eagles
17. M. C. Hammer
18. Queen
19. Chicago
20. Genesis
21. Journey
22. Sting
23. Motley Crue
24. Too Short
25. Slick Rick
26. Kenny G
27. Billy Ray Cyrus
28. Duran Duran
29. Lenny Kravitz
30. Vanilla Ice
31. Madonna
32. Pat Benatar
33. Billy Idol
34. Kansas
35. Bee Gees
36. New Kids on the Block
37. Big Daddy Kane
38. Bobby Brown
39. Richard Marx
40. Marky Mark

What About Us? Musicmakers Critics Mistakenly Ignore

1. AC/DC
2. Alabama
3. Jeff Beck
4. Bobby Bland
5. Cameo
6. Luther Campbell
7. The Crass
8. Rodney Crowell
9. D.J. Magic Mike
10. Bob Dylan
11. Earth, Wind and Fire
12. Everybody in gospel music
13. Everybody in Latin music except Ruben Blades
14. Janet Jackson
15. The Jesus and Mary Chain
16. Joan Jett
17. B. B. King
18. Kool and the Gang
19. Patty Loveless
20. Madonna
21. Maze featuring Frankie Beverly
22. Metallica
23. Midnight Oil
24. The O'Jays
25. Alexander O'Neal
26. K. T. Oslin
27. Professor Griff
28. Brenda Russell
29. Santana
30. Sir Mix-A-Lot

31. Social Distortion
32. Donna Summer
33. Sylvester
34. James Taylor (these days)
35. UB40

36. Luther Vandross
37. War
38. Kelly Willis
39. Stevie Wonder
40. Frank Zappa

CHAPTER 9

Art

Most Beautiful Record Labels

1. Apple (red label)
2. Checker
3. Def American
4. Def Jam
5. Duke
6. End
7. Fire
8. J.O.B.
9. Motown (the original label with map)
10. Old Town
11. Rama
12. RCA (with Nipper the Dog)
13. Roulette (original)
14. States
15. Sun

75 Great Album Cover Designs

1. *EFIL4ZAGGIN*, N.W.A*
2. *Sgt. Pepper's Lonely Hearts Club Band*, The Beatles
3. *Their Satanic Majesties Request*, The Rolling Stones
4. *London Calling*, The Clash
5. *Elvis Presley*
6. *Two Sides of the Moon*, Keith Moon
7. *. . . And Justice For All*, Metallica*
8. *We're Only in It for the Money*, The Mothers of Invention
9. *Goo*, Sonic Youth*
10. *Yesterday . . . and Today* (butcher-block version), The Beatles
11. *Death Certificate*, Ice Cube*
12. *Born to Run*, Bruce Springsteen
13. *50,000,000 Elvis Fans Can't Be Wrong—Elvis' Gold Records, Volume 2*, Elvis Presley
14. *Nothing's Shocking*, Jane's Addiction
15. *The Who Sell Out*
16. *The Velvet Underground and Nico*
17. *Los Angeles*, X
18. *By All Means Necessary*, Boogie Down Productions
19. *Weasels Ripped My Flesh*, The Mothers of Invention
20. *Feats Don't Fail Me Now*, Little Feat
21. *Siren*, Roxy Music
22. *Ghost in the Machine*, The Police
23. *Houses of the Holy*, Led Zeppelin
24. *1999*, Prince
25. *Happy Trails*, Quicksilver Messenger Service
26. *Who's Next*, The Who
27. *Are You Experienced?* The Jimi Hendrix Experience
28. *Mama Said Knock You Out*, L.L. Cool J*
29. *Maggot Brain*, Funkadelic
30. *Lotus*, Santana
31. *Axis: Bold As Love*, The Jimi Hendrix Experience

32. *More Songs About Buildings and Food*, Talking Heads
33. *Beggars Banquet* (original men's room version), The Rolling Stones
34. *Ogden's Nut Gone Flake*, The Small Faces
35. *Daydream Nation*, Sonic Youth
36. *Dark Side of the Moon*, Pink Floyd
37. *A Nice Pair*, Pink Floyd
38. *Fire*, Ohio Players
39. *Aoxomoxoa*, The Grateful Dead
40. *Tommy*, The Who
41. *Caravanserai*, Santana
42. *We Can't Be Stoppped*, The Geto Boys*
43. *Mysterious Traveler*, Weather Report
44. *Cheap Thrills*, Big Brother
45. *Fair Warning*, Van Halen
46. *Gene Vincent and the Blue Caps*
47. *De La Soul Is Dead*, De La Soul*
48. *Presence*, Led Zeppelin
49. *Dinosaur Swamps*, The Flock
50. *King of the Delta Blues Singers*, Robert Johnson
51. *Lumpy Gravy*, The Mothers of Invention
52. *Wish You Were Here*, Pink Floyd
53. *I Wish It Would Rain*, The Temptations
54. *Two Steps from the Blues*, Bobby "Blue" Bland
55. *Bo Diddley is a Gunslinger*
56. *Seal**
57. *Never Mind The Bollocks, Here's the Sex Pistols*
58. *The Kids Are Alright*, The Who
59. *Zooropa*, U2*
60. *Back in Black*, AC/DC
61. *Nevermind*, Nirvana*
62. *Dirt*, Alice in Chains*
63. *A Wolf in Sheep's Clothing*, Black Sheep*
64. *Licensed to Ill*, Beastie Boys*
65. *The Bliss Album*, PM Dawn*
66. *East Side Story*, Kid Frost*
67. *Bringing It All Back Home*, Bob Dylan
68. *Dirty Mind*, Prince
69. *Off the Wall*, Michael Jackson
70. *Keep On Movin'*, Soul II Soul*
71. *Madonna*
72. *Some Girls*, The Rolling Stones
73. *Freedom of Choice*, Devo
74. *As Nasty As They Wanna Be*, 2 Live Crew
75. *The Teenagers Featuring Frankie Lymon*

---

* CD-era designs.

You Can't Judge a Record By Its Cover
10 Great Sleeves You Wouldn't Want to Open

1. *Climax*, The Ohio Players
2. *Ceremony*, The Cult
3. *Workingman's Dead*, The Grateful Dead
4. *The Stranger*, Billy Joel
5. *Sports Weekend*, 2 Live Crew
6. *Journey Through the Past*, Neil Young
7. *Dr. Feelgood*, Motley Crue
8. *5150* (EP), Eazy E
9. *Love Gun*, Kiss
10. *All Samples Cleared*, Biz Markie

Note: the word "record" refers to any LP, tape, or CD. People may only buy tapes and CDs these days, but they still call releases "records." Or we do, anyway.

Pedro Bell's Favorite Album Covers of All Time
(in Alphabetical Order)

1. *Abraxas*, Santana
2. *Brain Salad Surgery*, Emerson, Lake and Palmer
3. *Chief*, Dewey Terry
4. *Come Go With Us*, Pockets
5. *Cross-Collateral*, Passport
6. *Doremi Fasol Latido*, Hawkwind
7. *Evolution*, Malo
8. *Fiddler on the Rock*, Sugarcane Harris
9. *Hardcore Jollies*, Funkadelic
10. *Heartbeat City*, The Cars
11. *Honey*, Ohio Players
12. *Hustlers' Convention*, Lightning Rod
13. *Live*, The World of Ike & Tina
14. *New Hope for the Wretched*, Plasmatics
15. *Nightmares*, J. Geils Band
16. *Nuggets—Original Artyfacts of the Psychedelic Era*
17. *Rock and Roll Queen*, Mott the Hoople
18. *School's Out*, Alice Cooper
19. *Stepping*, Pointer Sisters
20. *Tales of Topographic Oceans*, Yes
21. *Technical Ecstasy*, Black Sabbath
22. *The Clones of Dr. Funkenstein*, Parliament
23. *The Electric Spanking of War Babies*, Funkadelic

24. *They Say I'm Different*, Betty Davis

25. *We're Only In It for the Money*, The Mothers of Invention

Pedro Bell—aka Captain Draw—composed the intricate, urban sci-fi-flavored covers for eight Funkadelic albums as well as all of George Clinton's solo albums. Yo! MTV Raps! has aired some of his Lasernet Intergalactic Home Shopping Service *cartoon shorts and he is currently designing a series of computer games.*

Lester Bangs Selects the Worst LP Covers of All Time by Major Rock Artists

1. *Blank Generation*, Richard Hell and the Voidoids
2. *Growing Up in Public*, Lou Reed
3. *Saved*, Bob Dylan
4. *Never Mind the Bollocks, Here's the Sex Pistols*
5. *Let It Bleed*, The Rolling Stones
6. *Hard Nose the Highway*, Van Morrison
7. Any Journey cover
8. *On the Corner; In Concert; Big Fun; Water Babies*, Miles Davis
9. Any Cher cover, but most especially that album she made with Gregg Allman, *Allman and Woman*
10. *Lust for Life*, Iggy Pop

Lester Bangs became America's preeminent rock critic through his work at Creem *and* Rolling Stone *in the seventies. He helped found and avidly championed punk, metal, and all manner of belligerent noise until his premature death in 1982.* Psychotic Reactions and Carburetor Dung *(Knopf, 1987) collects his essential writings.*

Arty Rockers

1. Laurie Anderson: Studied art history at Barnard College and sculpture at Columbia University.
2. Boy George: Before forming Culture Club, was a well-known drag artist.
3. David Bowie: Paints in his spare time.
4. Commander Cody: Studied painting at the University of Michigan and the University of Wisconsin.

5. Chuck D: Drew cartoon, *Tales of the Skind*, for the Adelphi University newspaper; created the Public Enemy logo.
6. Bob Dylan: Painted the *Self-Portrait* and *Music from Big Pink* covers.
7. John Entwistle: Did the sleeve for *The Who by Numbers* as a connect-the-dots puzzle drawing.
8. Perry Farrell: Designed the cover art for Jane's Addiction's *Nothing Shocking* and *Ritual de lo Habitual*.
9. Fab Five Freddy: Before becoming a television personality, was a prominent grafitti artist; directs music videos.
10. John Lennon: Did numerous line drawings, including some erotic ones published in *Rolling Stone* in the early 1970s.
11. John Cougar Mellencamp: Paints; you can see some of his work on the album cover for his *Whenever We Wanted*.
12. Masta Ace: Graffiti artist.
13. Joni Mitchell: Paints album covers, notably her own *Court and Spark* and the Crosby, Stills, Nash, and Young collection, *So Far*.
14. Gene Simmons: Serious amateur photographer, specializing in human subjects.
15. Jon Spencer (Pussy Galore, The Jon Spencer Blues Explosion): Before dropping out of Brown, was an Art/Semiotics major and made an infamous student film that depicted him, among other things, taking a shit and masturbating with a cow's head.
16. Ringo Starr: Designs furniture.
17. Chris Stein: Studied at the School of Visual Arts in New York and was an established photographer before playing guitar for Blondie.
18. Cat Stevens: Painted his own *Teaser and the Firecat* cover; since becoming a Muslim, has renounced all of his previous artwork.
19. Michael Stipe: Studied art at the University of Georgia (Athens).
20. Dean Torrance (of Jan and Dean): Through his Kittyhawk Graphics, designed *Will the Circle Be Unbroken?* album cover for The Nitty Gritty Dirt Band.
21. Don Van Vliet (Captain Beefheart): Sculpts, and has painted covers for several of his own LPs.
22. Klaus Voorman: Painted The Beatles' *Revolver* sleeve.
23. Charlie Watts: Does cartoonlike drawings, the most public being the back cover of *Between the Buttons* and his book about Charlie Parker, *Ode to a High-Flying Bird*.
24. Ronnie Wood: Paints and draws.
25. Nick Seymour (bassist, Crowded House): Painted the cover for the band's album, *Woodface*.
26. Chris Mars (former Replacements drummer): Painted album cover for his solo debut, *Horseshoes & Hand Grenades*, and for the followup album, *75% Less Fat*.

Faces on the Cover of
Sgt. Pepper's Lonely Hearts Club Band

1. American Legionnaire
2. Fred Astaire
3. Aubrey Beardsley
4. The Beatles in wax
5. Larry Bell
6. Wallace Berman
7. Issy Bonn
8. Marlon Brando
9. Bobby Breen
10. Lenny Bruce
11. William Burroughs
12. Lewis Carroll
13. Stephen Crane
14. Aleister Crowley
15. Tony Curtis
16. Marlene Dietrich
17. Dion
18. Diana Dors
19. Bob Dylan
20. Albert Einstein
21. W. C. Fields
22. Huntz Hall
23. Tommy Handley
24. Oliver Hardy
25. Aldous Huxley
26. C. G. Jung
27. Stan Laurel
28. T. E. Lawrence
29. Richard Lindner
30. Sonny Liston
31. Dr. Livingstone
32. Karl Marx
33. Merkin
34. Max Miller
35. Tom Mix
36. Marilyn Monroe
37. Sir Robert Peel
38. Edgar Allan Poe
39. Tyrone Power
40. Simon Rodia
41. George Bernard Shaw
42. Terry Southern
43. Karlheinz Stockhausen
44. Albert Stubbins
45. Stuart Sutcliffe
46. Shirley Temple
47. Dylan Thomas
48. Johnny Weismuller
49. H. G. Wells
50. Mae West
51. Oscar Wilde
52. Three drawings of unidentified women
53. Five unidentified gurus

Peter Wolf Lists His Favorite Rock and Roll Artists

1. George Grosz
2. Max Beckmann
3. Chaim Soutine
4. Edvard Munch
5. Elizabeth Shreve
6. Henri Rousseau
7. Edouard Vuillard
8. Marcel Duchamp
9. Albert Ryder
10. John Sloan
11. Henri Matisse
12. Pierre Bonnard
13. Franz Kline

Peter Wolf grew up in the Bronx and moved to Boston after high school to study painting. Somewhere down the line, his priorities changed, and he became the lead vocalist of the J. Geils Band, before embarking on a solo career. Wolf's greatest hits include "Must of Got Lost," "Give It to Me," "One Last Kiss," and his anthem, "Love Stinks."

Famous Musicians Who Have Appeared on U.S. Postage Stamps

1. Elvis Presley
2. Bill Haley
3. Buddy Holly
4. Clyde McPhatter
5. Otis Redding
6. Dinah Washington
7. Hank Williams

"Hey, Mate, Pass Me the Brush"
The Dreaded British Art School Connection

1. Adam Ant
2. Jeff Beck
3. Ray Davies
4. Ian Dury
5. Brian Eno
6. Brian Ferry
7. John Lennon
8. Lene Lovich
9. Malcolm McLaren
10. Freddie Mercury
11. Jimmy Page
12. Keith Richards
13. Sade
14. Pete Townshend

Art School Groups

1. Bauhaus
2. The Clash
3. Gang of Four
4. The Mekons
5. Pink Floyd
6. Soft Cell
7. The Specials
8. Talking Heads
9. Ultravox
10. The Who

Who Made Who?
Artists and the Bands that Helped to Make Their Names

1. David Bailey: The Rolling Stones
2. Pedro Bell: Funkadelic
3. Roger Dean: Yes
4. Jean-Paul Goude: Grace Jones
5. Rick Griffin and Stanley Mouse: The Grateful Dead
6. Robert Mapplethorpe: Patti Smith
7. Russell Mills: Brian Eno
8. Jamie Reid: The Sex Pistols
9. Gerald Scarfe: Pink Floyd
10. Andy Warhol: The Velvet Underground and The Rolling Stones

15 Great Psychedelic Poster Artists

Rock posters emerged as an art form in San Francisco during the mid-1960s. Originally, they served as announcements for the concerts held at early psychedelic ballrooms like the Fillmore Auditorium and the Avalon Ballroom. Their creators were primarily painters and fine artists who developed a style of graphic and commercial art that stands with the great European poster art of the nineteenth century. By the 1980s, posters from this era had become quite valuable. A complete set of Avalon Ballroom posters was auctioned in 1980 by Phillips in New York for thousands of dollars.

1. Stanley Mouse and Alton Kelly
2. Rick Griffin
3. Satty
4. John Van Hamersveld
5. Victor Moscosco
6. Wes Wilson
7. Bob Fried
8. Randy Tuten
9. Singer
10. Bob Smith
11. Danny Bread
12. Greg Irons
13. Tadanori Yokoo
14. Stanley Miller
15. Gary Grimshaw

Devo's Favorite Modern Conveniences

1. Voice stress analyzers
2. Chemotherapy
3. Recombinant DNA parlors
4. Taser guns
5. Aerosol air
6. Ankle grabbers
7. Short microwave heating units
8. Microwave food blenders

Devo, best known for their 1980 hit, "Whip It," are pioneers of techno-rock, as befits their philosophy of the regression (de-evolution) of humanity. The above list may be considered a representative sampling of the instruments of that decline.

Best Rock Photographers

1. Dezo Hoffman
2. Michael Cooper
3. David Gahr
4. Bob Gruen
5. Annie Leibovitz
6. Neal Preston
7. Timothy White
8. Peter Cunningham
9. Mick Rock
10. Ethan Russell
11. Gerard Mankowitz
12. Jim Marshall
13. Anton Corbijn
14. Barry Wentzell
15. Bob Moreland[1]

---

[1] Included for the awesome photos he took of Elvis before there ever was such a thing as rock photography.

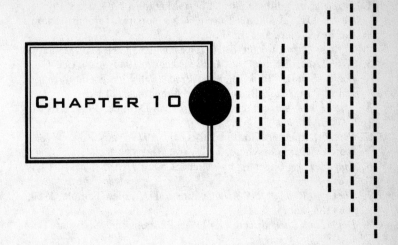

CHAPTER 10

Film

Best Rock and Rap Movies

1. *Purple Rain*, directed by Albert Magnoli, 1984; stars Prince, Morris Day, Apollonia Kotero, Olga Karlatos, Jerome Benton, the Revolution, and the Time
2. *Truth or Dare*, directed by Alek Keshishian, 1991; stars Madonna
3. *Wild Style*, directed by Charlie Ahearn, 1982; stars Lee Quinones, Sandra "Pink" Fabara, Fred "Fab Five Freddy" Brathwaite, Patti Astor, Busy Bee, and Grandmaster Flash
4. *Stop Making Sense*, directed by Jonathan Demme, 1984; stars the Talking Heads
5. *Superfly*, directed Gordon Parks, Jr., 1972; stars Ron O'Neal; score by Curtis Mayfield
6. *King Creole*, directed by Michael Curtiz, 1958; stars Elvis Presley
7. *The Great Rock'n' Roll Swindle*, directed by Julien Temple, 1980; stars the Sex Pistols
8. *Don't Look Back*, directed by D. A. Pennebaker, 1967; stars Bob Dylan
9. *A Hard Day's Night*, directed by Richard Lester, 1964; stars the Beatles
10. *The T. A. M. I. Show*, directed by Steve Binder, 1965; stars James Brown, the Rolling Stones, Jan and Dean, the Supremes, Marvin Gaye, Chuck Berry, and others
11. *The Girl Can't Help It*, directed by Frank Tashlin, 1956; features Little Richard, Gene Vincent, Eddie Cochran, and others
12. *The Harder They Come*, directed by Perry Henzell, 1972; stars Jimmy Cliff
13. *Monterey Pop*, directed by D. A. Pennebaker, 1968; stars Jimi Hendrix, Otis Redding, the Who, and others
14. *Privilege*, directed by Peter Watkins, 1967; stars Paul Jones and Jean Shrimpton
15. *O Lucky Man*, directed Lindsay Anderson, 1973; stars Malcolm McDowell; score by Alan Price
16. *The Buddy Holly Story*, directed by Steve Rash, 1978; stars Gary Busey
17. *Performance*, directed by Nicholas Roeg and Donald Cammell, 1970; stars Mick Jagger
18. *Krush Groove*, directed by Michael Schultz, 1985; stars L.L. Cool J, Run-D.M.C., The Fat Boys, Kurtis Blow, Blair Underwood, and Sheila E.
19. *Beyond the Valley of the Dolls*, directed by Russ Meyer, 1970; stars Dolly Read, Edy Williams, and other forty-plus-inch busts; features the Strawberry Alarm Clock
20. *Wild in the Streets*, directed by Barry Shear, 1968; stars Shelley Winters, Christopher Jones, and Richard Pryor

21. *The Kids Are Alright,* directed by Jeff Stein, 1979; stars the Who
22. *The Decline of Western Civilization Part II: The Metal Years,* directed by Penelope Spheeris, 1988; stars Joe Perry, Steven Tyler, Gene Simmons, Paul Stanley, Chris Holmes, Lemmy, Ozzy Osbourne, Faster Pussycat, Lizzy Borden, London, Odin, Seduce, and Megadeth
23. *Saturday Night Fever,* directed by John Badham, 1977; stars John Travolta, Karen Lynn Gorney, Barry Miller, Joseph Cali, Paul Pape, Donna Pescow, and Julie Bovasso
24. *Woodstock,* directed by Michael Wadleigh, 1970; stars a buncha bands and half a million hippies
25. *The Last Waltz,* directed by Martin Scorsese, 1978; stars the Band, upstaged by Muddy Waters and Van Morrison
26. *Jailhouse Rock,* directed by Richard Thorpe, 1957; stars Elvis Presley
27. *American Hot Wax,* directed by Floyd Mutrux, 1978; stars Tim McIntire as Alan Freed
28. *Mister Rock and Roll,* directed by Charles Dubin, 1957; stars Alan Freed and friends
29. *Having a Wild Weekend,* directed by John Boorman, 1965; stars the Dave Clark Five
30. *Shake, Rattle and R-O-C-K,* directed by Edward L. Cahn, 1956; stars Mike "Touch" Connors, Joe Turner, and Fats Domino
31. *That'll Be the Day,* directed by Claude Whatham, 1974; stars David Essex, Ringo Starr, Billy Fury, and Keith Moon
32. *The Decline of Western Civilization,* directed by Penelope Spheeris, 1981; stars Black Flag, Circle Jerks, Fear, Germs, X and the Alice Bag Band
33. *Yellow Submarine,* directed by George Dunning, 1968; stars the Beatles
34. *Tapeheads,* directed by Bill Fishman, 1988; stars John Cusack, Tim Robbins, Doug McClure, Connie Stevens, Clu Gulager, Mary Crosby, Katy Boyer, Lyle Alzado, Jessica Walter, Susan Tyrrell, Junior Walker, and Sam Moore
35. *Wayne's World,* directed by Penelope Spheeris, 1992; stars Mike Myers, Dana Carvey, Rob Lowe, Tia Carrere, Donna Dixon, Meat Loaf, and Ed O'Neill

Worst Rock and Rap Movies

1. *Lambada,* directed by Joel Silberg, 1990; stars J. Eddie Peck, Melora Hardin, Shabba-Doo, Ricky Paull Goldin, Basil Hoffman, Dennis Burkley
2. *Sgt. Pepper's Lonely Hearts Club Band,* directed by Michael Schultz, 1978; stars the Bee Gees, Peter Frampton, Billy Pres-

ton, Steve Martin, Aerosmith, Earth, Wind and Fire, and George Burns

3. *Disorderlies*, directed by Michael Schultz, 1987; stars the Fat Boys, Ralph Bellamy, Tony Plana, Anthony Geary, Marco Rodriguez, Troy Beyer

4. *The Horror of Party Beach*, directed by Del Tenney, 1964; stars John Scott, Alice Lyon, Allen Laurel, Eulabelle Moore, and Marilyn Clark

5. *Renaldo and Clara*, directed by Bob Dylan and Howard Alk, 1978; stars Bob Dylan, Joan Baez, Allen Ginsberg, Ronee Blakely, Sara Dylan, and the Rolling Thunder Revue

6. *The Song Remains the Same*, directed by Peter Clifton and Joe Massot, 1976; stars Led Zeppelin

7. *This Is Spinal Tap*, directed by Rob Reiner, 1984; stars Michael McKean, Christopher Guest, Harry Shearer, Rob Reiner, Tony Hendra, June Chadwick, R. J. Parnell, David Kaff

8. *Celebration at Big Sur*, directed by Baird Bryant and Johanna Demetrakas, 1971; stars Joan Baez, Crosby, Stills, Nash and Young, Joni Mitchell, John Sebastian, and Mimi Fariña

9. *Breakin' 2: Electric Boogaloo*, directed by Sam Firstenberg, 1984; stars Lucinda Dickey, Adolfo "Shabba-Doo" Quinones, Michael "Boogaloo Shrimp" Chambers, Susie Bono

10. *Xanadu*, directed by Robert Greenwald, 1980; stars Olivia Newton-John, Gene Kelly, and Michael Beck; music by the Electric Light Orchestra

11. *Can't Stop the Music*, directed by Nancy Walker, 1980; stars the Village People, Valerie Perrine, and Bruce Jenner

12. *Bye Bye Birdie*, directed by George Sidney, 1963; stars Janet Leigh, Dick Van Dyke, Ann-Margaret, Paul Lynde, and Ed Sullivan; score by Charles Strouse and Lee Adams

13. *Who's the Man?* directed by Ted Demme, 1993; stars Ed Lover and Dr. Dre

14. *A Star is Born*, directed by Frank Pierson, 1976; stars Barbra Streisand, Kris Kristofferson, and Gary Busey

15. *The Rose*, directed by Mark Rydell, 1979; stars Bette Midler, Alan Bates, and Frederic Forrest

16. *Riot on Sunset Strip*, directed by Arthur Dreifuss, 1967; stars Aldo Ray, Mimsy Farmer, Michael Evans, and Laurie Mock

17. *House Party 2*, directed by Doug McHenry and George Jackson, 1991; stars Kid N Play, Eugene Allen, George Anthony Bell, Tisha Campbell, Iman, Kamron, Queen Latifah, Helen Martin, and Martin Lawrence

18. *Roadie*, directed by Alan Rudolph, 1980; stars Blondie, Meat Loaf, and Alice Cooper

19. *Journey Through the Past*, directed by Neil Young, 1973; stars Neil Young, Crazy Horse, and Buffalo Springfield

20. *Sympathy for the Devil (One Plus One)*, directed by Jean-Luc Godard, 1970; features the Rolling Stones
21. *Thank God It's Friday*, directed by Robert Klane, 1978; stars Donna Ṣummer and Jeff Goldblum
22. *The Doors*, directed by Oliver Stone, 1991; stars Val Kilmer, Frank Whaley, Kevin Dillon, Meg Ryan, Kyle MacLachlan, and Billy Idol
23. *Tommy*, directed by Ken Russell, 1975; stars Roger Daltrey, Ann-Margret, Oliver Reed, Jack Nicholson, Eric Clapton, Tina Turner, Elton John, Robert Powell, and the Who
24. *Americathon*, directed by Neil Israel, 1979; stars John Ritter, Harvey Korman, and Zane Buzby; features Elvis Costello and the Beach Boys
25. *It's Trad, Dad*, directed by Richard Lester, 1962; stars Chubby Checker and Dusty Springfield
26. *Rude Boy*, directed by Jack Hazann, 1980; stars Roy Gange and the Clash
27. *Ladies and Gentlemen, the Rolling Stones*, directed by Richard Binzer, 1975; stars the Rolling Stones, oddly enough
28. *FM*, directed by John A. Alonzo, 1978; stars Martin Mull, Alex Karras, Cleavon Little, Michael Brandon; concert appearances by Linda Ronstadt and Jimmy Buffett
29. *Rust Never Sleeps*, directed by Bernard Shakey, aka Neil Young, 1979; stars Neil Young and Crazy Horse
30. *Sparkle*, directed by Sam O'Steen, 1976; stars Philip M. Thomas, Irene Cara, Lonette McKee, Mary Alice, and Dwan Smith; music by Curtis Mayfield
31. *The Blues Brothers*, directed by John Landis, 1980; stars Dan Aykroyd, John Belushi, and Aretha Franklin
32. *Under the Cherry Moon*, directed by Prince, 1986; stars Prince, Jerome Benton, and Kristin Scott-Thomas
33. *Beat Street*, directed by Stan Lathan, 1984; stars Rae Dawn Chong, Guy Davis, Kool Herc, Melle Mel, Afrika Bambaataa, and the Treacherous Three

Best Unreleased Rock Films

1. *Charlie Is My Darling*, stars The Rolling Stones, 1965
2. *Cocksucker Blues*, stars The Rolling Stones, 1972
3. *Something Is Happening*, stars Bob Dylan, 1966
4. *Eric Clapton—Train Tour of Europe*, 1974–1975
5. *Feast of Friends*, stars The Doors, 1969
6. *Weird Scenes Inside the Gold Mine*, stars The Doors, 1969
7. *Jimi Hendrix Live at Albert Hall*

8. *Sweet Toronto*, stars Jerry Lee Lewis, Little Richard, Bo Diddley, and Chuck Berry, 1971
9. *David Bowie and the Spiders from Mars Live at Hammersmith Odeon*, 1972
10. *Untitled film by Brian DePalma about The Animals, circa 1965*

Who Cares What Picture We See?
The 15 Best Songs About the Movies

1. "Act Naturally," The Beatles
2. "Action Not Words," Def Leppard
3. "Burn Hollywood Burn," Public Enemy featuring Ice Cube and Big Daddy Kane
4. "Celluloid Heroes," The Kinks
5. "Cool for Cats," Squeeze
6. "Dirty Movies," Van Halen
7. "Emma," Hot Chocolate
8. "Just Like in the Movies," The Upbeats
9. "Porno Star," Ultramagnetic MCs
10. "Sad Movies (Make Me Cry)," Sue Thompson
11. "Saturday Night at the Movies," The Drifters
12. "Sittin' in the Balcony," Eddie Cochran
13. "Spegetti [sic] Western," Primus
14. "35 Millimeter Dreams," Garland Jeffreys
15. "Western Movies," The Olympics

40 Songs Based on Film Titles

1. "A Night at the Opera/A Day at the Races," Queen
2. "A Soldier's Story," WC and the Maad Circle
3. "Anything Goes," Guns N' Roses
4. "Black Sabbath," Black Sabbath
5. "Blue Angel," Roy Orbison
6. "Body Snatchers," Scarface
7. "Chuckie," The Geto Boys
8. "Driveby Miss Daisy," Compton's Most Wanted
9. "Escape from the Killing Fields," Ice-T
10. "East Side Story," Kid Frost
11. "Ezy Ryder," Jimi Hendrix
12. "Gone with the Wind," The Duprees

13. "Goodbye Girl," Squeeze
14. "Johnny Come Home," Fine Young Cannibals
15. "Jools and Jim," Pete Townshend
16. "King Kong," The Jimmy Castor Bunch
17. "Lethal Weapon," Ice-T
18. "Li'l Boys in da Hood," Kriss Kross
19. "Many Rivers to Cross," Jimmy Cliff
20. "Night of the Living Baseheads," Public Enemy
21. "Night Moves," Bob Seger
22. "Pretty Baby," Sister Sledge
23. "Pride of Frankenstein," Too Much Joy
24. "Psycho Killer," Talking Heads
25. "Public Enemy #1," Public Enemy
    Honorable Mention: "Public Enemy Number One," Iron
    Maiden
26. "Romeo and Juliet," Biz Markie
27. "Scarface," The Geto Boys
28. "Schooldaze," Raheem
29. "Shaft's Big Score," X-Clan
30. "Shaft in Greenland," The Dead Milkmen
31. "Silence of the Lambs," Showbiz & A.G.
32. "The Thrill of It All," Roxy Music
33. "Thunder Road," Bruce Springsteen
34. "Torn Curtain," Television
35. "Toys in the Attic," Aerosmith
36. "Vertigo," Southside Johnny and the Asbury Jukes
37. "Walk on the Wild Side," Lou Reed
38. "Wanted: Dead or Alive," Kool G. Rap & D.J. Polo
39. "Who's the Mack?" Ice Cube
40. "Wild in the Streets," Garland Jeffreys

Beyond *The Big Chill*
The 25 Best Movie Soundtracks

1. *Purple Rain*, directed by Albert Magnoli, 1984; score by Prince
2. *Mean Streets*, directed by Martin Scorsese, 1973; score by various artists
3. *The Harder They Come*, directed by Perry Henzel, 1972; score by Jimmy Cliff and various artists
4. *Saturday Night Fever*, directed by John Badham, 1977; score by the Bee Gees and various artists
5. *Pat Garrett and Billy the Kid*, directed by Sam Peckinpah, 1973; score by Bob Dylan
6. *The Long Riders*, directed by Walter Hill, 1980; score by Ry Cooder

7. *Superfly*, directed by Gordon Parks, Jr., 1972; score by Curtis Mayfield

8. *American Graffiti*, directed by George Lucas, 1973; score by various artists

9. *O Lucky Man*, directed by Lindsay Anderson, 1973; score by Alan Price

10. *Performance*, directed by Nicholas Roeg and Donald Cammell, 1970; score by Jack Nitzsche, Randy Newman, and Mick Jagger

11. *Shaft*, directed by Gordon Parks, Jr., 1971; score by Isaac Hayes

12. *Menace II Society*, directed by the Hughes Brothers, 1993; score by various artists

13. *The Valley (Obscured by Clouds)*, directed by Barbet Schroeder, 1972; score by Pink Floyd

14. *Quadrophenia*, directed by Frank Roddam, 1979; score by the Who and various artists

15. *Car Wash*, directed by Michael Schultz, 1976; score by various artists

16. *Once Upon a Time in the West*, directed by Sergio Leone, 1969; score by Ennio Morricone

17. *Juice*, directed by Ernest Dickerson, 1992; score by various artists

18. *Sorcerer*, directed by William Friedkin, 1977; score by Tangerine Dream

19. *Maximum Overdrive*, directed by Stephen King, 1986; score by Angus Young

20. *Last Action Hero*, directed by John McTiernan, 1993; score by Alice in Chains and various artists

21. *American Me*, directed by Edward James Olmos, 1992; score by various artists

22. *Peter's Friends*, directed by Kenneth Branagh, 1993; score by various artists

23. *Boyz N the Hood*, directed by John Singleton, 1991; score by various artists

24. *Singles*, directed by Cameron Crowe, 1992; score by various artists

25. *Less Than Zero*, directed by Marek Kanievska, 1987; score by various artists

Best Film Appearances by Rock and Rap Performers

1. Ice Cube, *Boyz N The Hood*, 1991
2. Rick Nelson, *Rio Bravo*, 1959

3. Mick Jagger, *Performance*, 1968
4. Tupac, *Juice*, 1992
5. Gary Busey, *The Buddy Holly Story*, 1978
6. Grace Jones, *Boomerang*, 1992
7. Levon Helm, *Coal Miner's Daughter*, 1980
8. Ice-T, *New Jack City*, 1991
9. Kris Kristofferson, *Cisco Pike*, 1972
10. Adam Horovitz, *Lost Angels*, 1989
11. Ringo Starr, *Candy*, 1968
12. Roy Orbison, *The Fastest Guitar Alive*, 1968
13. Elvis Presley, *King Creole*, 1958
14. Joe Strummer, *Mystery Train*, 1989
15. Adam Faith, *Stardust*, 1975
16. David Essex, *That'll Be the Day*, 1974; *Stardust*, 1975
17. Diana Ross, *Lady Sings the Blues*, 1972
18. Lyle Lovett, *The Player*, 1992
19. Steve Jones, *The Great Rock 'n' Roll Swindle*, 1979
20. Art Garfunkel, *Carnal Knowledge*, 1971
21. Queen Latifah, *Jungle Fever*, 1991
22. L. L. Cool J, *Toys*, 1993
23. Sting, *Quadrophenia*, 1979

Worst Film Appearances by Rock and Rap Performers

1. Vanilla Ice, *Cool As Ice*, 1991
2. Elvis Presley, *It Happened at the World's Fair*, 1963
3. Neil Diamond, *The Jazz Singer*, 1980
4. Paul Williams, *Phantom of the Paradise*, 1975
5. Roger Daltrey, *Lisztomania*, 1975
6. Art Garfunkel, *Bad Timing/A Sensual Obsession*, 1980
7. Mick Jagger, *Ned Kelly*, 1970
8. Rita Coolidge, *Pat Garrett and Billy the Kid*, 1973
9. Barbra Streisand, *A Star Is Born*, 1976
10. The Village People, *Can't Stop the Music*, 1980
11. Frank Zappa, *Baby Snakes*, 1980
12. Adam Horovitz, *Roadside Prophets*, 1992
13. Ice Cube and Ice-T, *Trespass*, 1992
14. Janet Jackson, *Poetic Justice*, 1993
15. MC Shan, *L.A. Story*, 1991
16. Mick Jagger, *Freejack*, 1992
17. Sting, *Dune*, 1984
18. David Bowie, *The Linguini Incident*, 1992
19. Madonna, *Body of Evidence*, 1993

Performers Who Appeared at Woodstock But Not in the Movie

1. The Band
2. Blood, Sweat, and Tears
3. Paul Butterfield
4. Creedence Clearwater Revival
5. The Grateful Dead
6. Keef Hartley
7. The Incredible String Band
8. The Jefferson Airplane
9. Janis Joplin
10. Melanie
11. Mountain
12. Ravi Shankar
13. Bert Sommer
14. Johnny Winter

Rock Performers Who Appear in The Rolling Stones' "Rock and Roll Circus"

The Rolling Stones' "Rock and Roll Circus" was planned as a television special and filmed in December 1968 by Michael Lindsay-Hogg. Although it was never aired, various bootleg records of the musical performances have made it legendary.

1. Eric Clapton
2. Marianne Faithfull
3. John Lennon
4. Taj Mahal
5. Mitch Mitchell
6. Yoko Ono
7. The Rolling Stones
8. Jethro Tull
9. The Who

Performers also included a classical pianist and violinist and the Robert Fosset Circus with the Lovely Luna. Performers who were asked to appear but did not, include:

1. Johnny Cash
2. Dr. John
3. The Isley Brothers
4. Traffic

CHAPTER 11

Broadcasting

Can't Live Without It?
The Best Songs About Radio

1. "Border Radio," The Blasters
2. "Capitol Radio One," The Clash
3. "Caravan," Van Morrison
4. "FM (No Static at All)," Steely Dan
5. "Fuck Radio," Ultramagnetic MCs
6. "Heavy Music," Bob Seger
7. "How to Kill a Radio Consultant," Public Enemy
8. "I Can't Live Without My Radio," L.L. Cool J
9. "Mexican Radio," Wall of Voodoo
10. "Mohammed's Radio," Warren Zevon
11. "Mr. DJ (5 for the DJ)," Aretha Franklin
12. "On My Radio," The Selecter
13. "On the Radio," Donna Summer
14. "On Your Radio," Joe Jackson
15. "Radio," Eazy E
16. "Radio Free Europe," R.E.M.
17. "Radio Ga Ga," Queen
18. "Radio Lover," George Jones
19. "Radio Radio," Elvis Costello
20. "Radio Romance," Tiffany
21. "Radio Song," Joe Walsh
22. "Radio Song," R.E.M.
23. "Radio Wave," Roger Waters
24. "Raised on Radio," The Ravyns
25. "Road Runner," Jonathan Richman
26. "Rock and Roll," The Velvet Underground
27. "Turn Off the Radio," Ice Cube
28. "Who Listens to the Radio?" The Sports
29. "W*O*L*D," Harry Chapin
30. "You Can't Say Crap on the Radio," Stiff Little Fingers
31. "You Turn Me On (I'm a Radio)," Joni Mitchell

Radio DJs Who Became Performers

1. Chuck D and Flavor Flav, WBAU, Adelphi University
2. Doctor Dre (of *Yo! MTV Raps!*), WBAU, Adelphi University
3. Waylon Jennings, KLLL, Lubbock, Texas
4. B. B. King, WDIA, Memphis
5. Terry Knight, CKLW, Detroit

6. Jim Lowe, WNBC, New York
7. Marley Marl, WBLS, New York
8. Wink Martindale, WHBQ, Memphis[1]
9. Pete Nice, WKCR, New York
10. Soupy Sales, WJW, Cleveland[1]
11. Sly Stone, KSOL, San Francisco
12. Kim Weston, WCHB, Detroit

---

[1] *Although both Soupy Sales and Wink Martindale are best known as television personalities, they began their careers in rock and roll radio. In addition, both recorded minor hits: Sales had "Do the Mouse" in 1965 and Martindale made the Top Ten in 1959 with his cover of Tex Ritter's "Deck of Cards."*

Fabled British Pirate Radio Stations

Pirate radio was a phenomenon born of the British's government's broadcasting monopoly. As English rock became more and more outrageous, the conservative mentality of the BBC found it increasingly difficult to cope. The result was that several enterprising capitalists established ships, staffed with American-style Top Forty DJs, in the English Channel, just outside the three-and-a-half-mile limit, to blast the United Kingdom with high-powered transmitters and the latest pop music. The British government has since taken legal and bureaucratic measures against offshore broadcasting and made provisions for independent stations that can air the sort of music pirate stations were broadcasting. But in their mid-1960s heyday, pirate stations offered the best pop radio in Europe. About a dozen came and went. Among them:

1. Radio Caroline
2. Radio Atlanta
3. Radio Sutch
4. Radio City
5. Radio London
6. Radio Scotland
7. Radio 390

L.A.'s Top 100 Radio Hits, 1956–1979

Guy Zapoleon of KRTH, Los Angeles, compiled this list, which is based on sales reports from 1956 and 1957, KFWB surveys from 1958 through 1963, KRLA surveys from 1964 and 1965, KHJ surveys for 1966 through 1976, and sales reports from 1977 through 1979. Because of the rise of the consultant-dependent narrowcasting that dominates radio today, we couldn't find anyone who compiles this type of information anymore.

1. "The Twist," Chubby Checker, 1960 and 1961
2. "Mack the Knife," Bobby Darin, 1959
3. "Exodus," Ferrante and Teicher, 1961
4. "The Theme from *A Summer Place*," Percy Faith, 1960
5. "Love Will Keep Us Together," Captain and Tennille, 1975
6. "I'm a Believer," The Monkees, 1967
7. "Hey Jude," The Beatles, 1968
8. "You've Lost That Lovin' Feelin'," The Righteous Brothers, 1965
9. "Stayin' Alive," The Bee Gees, 1978
10. "I Can See Clearly Now," Johnny Nash, 1972
11. "Don't Be Cruel" / "Hound Dog," Elvis Presley, 1956
12. "Blue Bayou," Linda Ronstadt, 1977
13. "The Hawaiian Wedding Song," Andy Williams, 1959
14. "I Want to Hold Your Hand," The Beatles, 1964
15. "When Will I See You Again," The Three Degrees, 1974
16. "Joy to the World," Three Dog Night, 1971
17. "Let's Get It On," Marvin Gaye, 1973
18. "Limbo Rock," Chubby Checker, 1962
19. "My Sharona," The Knack, 1979
20. "We Can Work It Out" / "Day Tripper," The Beatles, 1966
21. "Seasons in the Sun," Terry Jacks, 1974
22. "Bridge Over Troubled Water," Simon and Garfunkel, 1970
23. "I'll Be There," The Jackson 5, 1970
24. "If You Leave Me Now," Chicago, 1976
25. "Bennie and the Jets," Elton John, 1974
26. "It's Too Late," Carole King, 1971
27. "Night Fever," The Bee Gees, 1978
28. "Love Rollercoster," Ohio Players, 1976
29. "Sugar, Sugar," The Archies, 1969
30. "Love Is Blue," Paul Mauriat, 1968
31. "Raindrops Keep Fallin' on My Head," B. J. Thomas, 1969
32. "Killing Me Softly with His Song," Roberta Flack, 1973
33. "Alone Again (Naturally)," Gilbert O'Sullivan, 1972
34. "Boogie Oogie Oogie," Taste of Honey, 1978
35. "Someday We'll Be Together," Diana Ross and the Supremes, 1969
36. "Handy Man," Jimmy Jones, 1960
37. "The Jerk," The Larks, 1964
38. "Be True to Your School," The Beach Boys, 1963
39. "The Battle of New Orleans," Johnny Horton, 1959
40. "Gloria," Them, 1966
41. "You're So Vain," Carly Simon, 1973
42. "All Shook Up," Elvis Presley, 1957

43. "Light My Fire," The Doors, 1967
44. "Round and Round," Perry Como, 1957
45. "(You're My) Soul and Inspiration," The Righteous Brothers, 1966
46. "I Just Want to Be Your Everything," Andy Gibb, 1977
47. "Blowin' in the Wind," Peter, Paul and Mary, 1963
48. "Me and Mrs. Jones," Billy Paul, 1972
49. "It's Now or Never," Elvis Presley, 1960
50. "Baby Love," Supremes, 1964
51. "Emotion," Samantha Sang, 1978
52. "Easy to Be Hard," Three Dog Night, 1969
53. "Big Girls Don't Cry," The Four Seasons, 1962
54. "Love Letters in the Sand," Pat Boone, 1957
55. "Don't Go Breaking My Heart," Elton John and Kiki Dee, 1976
56. "Kung Fu Fighting," Carl Douglas, 1974
57. "Wooly Bully," Sam the Sham and the Pharoahs, 1965
58. "Afternoon Delight," Starland Vocal Band, 1976
59. "I Can't Stop Loving You" / "Born to Lose," Ray Charles, 1962
60. "Mashed Potato Time," Dee Dee Sharp, 1962
61. "Rapper's Delight," The Sugarhill Gang, 1979
62. "Goodbye Cruel World," James Darren, 1961
63. "These Boots Are Made for Walkin'," Nancy Sinatra, 1966
64. "Please Mr. Postman," The Carpenters, 1975
65. "Just My Imagination (Running Away from Me)," The Temptations, 1971
66. "Surfer Girl," The Beach Boys, 1963
67. "Sugar Shack," Jimmy Gilmer and the Fireballs, 1963
68. "Hey Paula," Paul and Paula, 1963
69. "Jailhouse Rock," Elvis Presley, 1957
70. "Viva Tirado—Part 1," El Chicano, 1970
71. "Born to Be Wild," Steppenwolf, 1968
72. "Nel Blu Dipinto Di Blu (Volare)," Domenico Modugno, 1958
73. "How Deep Is Your Love," The Bee Gees, 1978
74. "Aquarius" / "Let the Sun Shine In," The 5th Dimension, 1969
75. "Without You," Harry Nilsson, 1972
76. "Play That Funky Music," Wild Cherry, 1976
77. "My Guy," Mary Wells, 1964
78. "Happy Together," The Turtles, 1967
79. "Moon River," Henry Mancini, 1961
80. "At the Hop," Danny and the Juniors, 1958
81. "My Girl," The Temptations, 1965
82. "Le Freak," Chic, 1979
83. "Ladies Night," Kool and the Gang, 1979
84. "All I Have to Do Is Dream," The Everly Brothers, 1958

85. "Cherish," The Association, 1966
86. "Winchester Cathedral," New Vaudeville Band, 1966
87. "Theme from *Shaft*," Isaac Hayes, 1971
88. "Crystal Blue Persuasion," Tommy James and the Shondells, 1969
89. "Lisbon Antigua," Nelson Riddle, 1956
90. "Get Down Tonight," KC and the Sunshine Band, 1975
91. "Johnny Angel," Shelley Fabares, 1962
92. "There's a Kind of Hush" / "No Milk Today," Herman's Hermits, 1967
93. "Spirit in the Sky," Norman Greenbaum, 1970
94. "Something" / "Come Together," The Beatles, 1969
95. "Chances Are," Johnny Mathis, 1957
96. "Love Me Tender," Elvis Presley, 1957
97. "Help!" The Beatles, 1965
98. "Donna," Ritchie Valens, 1959
99. "Half-Breed," Cher, 1973
100. "Oh, Pretty Woman," Roy Orbison, 1964

KNAC's Top 75 Songs

KNAC 105.5, L.A.'s premier metal station, compiled this list in 1993.

1. "One," Metallica
2. "Master of Puppets," Metallica
3. "Paranoid," Black Sabbath
4. "Welcome to the Jungle," Guns N' Roses
5. "Fade to Black," Metallica
6. "Run to the Hills," Iron Maiden
7. "Back in Black," AC/DC
8. "Crazy Train," Ozzy Osbourne
9. "Livin' After Midnight," Judas Priest
10. "Peace Sells," Megadeth
11. "Sweet Child O' Mine," Guns N' Roses
12. "Number of the Beast," Iron Maiden
13. "Enter Sandman," Metallica
14. "Anarchy X-Revolution Calling," Queensryche
15. "Symphony of Destruction," Megadeth
16. "Highway to Hell," AC/DC
17. "You've Got Another Thing Coming," Judas Priest
18. "Cowboys from Hell," Pantera
19. "Seek and Destroy," Metallica
20. "Rock and Roll All Nite," Kiss
21. "Heaven and Hell," Black Sabbath
22. "Paradise City," Guns N' Roses

23. "Runnin' with the Devil," Van Halen
24. "Go to Hell," Megadeth
25. "No One Like You," The Scorpions
26. "Welcome Home (Sanitarium)," Metallica
27. "Iron Man," Black Sabbath
28. "18 and Life," Skid Row
29. "Whole Lotta Love," Led Zeppelin
30. "Walk This Way," Aerosmith
31. "Shout at the Devil," Motley Crue
32. "You Shook Me All Night Long," AC/DC
33. "The Last in Line," Dio
34. "This Love," Pantera
35. "2 Minutes to Midnight," Iron Maiden
36. "Cat Scratch Fever," Ted Nugent
37. "For Those About to Rock," AC/DC
38. "Ain't Talkin' 'Bout Love," Van Halen
39. "Breadfan," Metallica
40. "South of Heaven," Slayer
41. "Looks that Kill," Motley Crue
42. "Empire," Queensryche
43. "Round and Round," Ratt
44. "Sweet Emotion," Aerosmith
45. "You Could Be Mine," Guns N' Roses
46. "Modern Day Cowboy," Tesla
47. "War Pigs," Black Sabbath
48. "Blitzkrieg," Metallica
49. "Live Wire," Motley Crue
50. "Ace of Spades," Motorhead
51. "Thunder Kiss '65," White Zombie
52. "The Zoo," The Scorpions
53. "Mr. Crowley," Ozzy Osbourne
54. "Lights Out," UFO
55. "Holy Wars . . . The Punishment Due," Megadeth
56. "Hell Bent for Leather," Judas Priest
57. "Photograph," Def Leppard
58. "For Whom the Bell Tolls," Metallica
59. "Queen of the Reich," Queensryche
60. "The Trooper," Iron Maiden
61. "Smoke on the Water," Deep Purple
62. "In My Darkest Hour," Megadeth
63. "Smells Like Teen Spirit," Nirvana
64. "Stone Cold Crazy," Metallica
65. "The Lady Wore Black," Queensryche
66. "Mr. Brownstone," Guns N' Roses
67. "Eruption/You Really Got Me," Van Halen
68. "Whole Lotta Rosie," AC/DC
69. "Would?" Alice in Chains

70. "Alive," Pearl Jam
71. "The Spirit of Radio," Rush
72. "Black Dog," Led Zeppelin
73. "Dirty Black Summer," Danzig
74. "Back in the Saddle," Aerosmith
75. "Love Gun," Kiss

Nothin' On?
20 Songs About TV

1. "Along Came Jones," The Coasters
2. "Channel Z," The B-52s
3. "57 Channels (and Nothin' On)," Bruce Springsteen
4. "Found a Job," The Talking Heads
5. "However Much I Booze," The Who
6. "Johnny Carson," The Beach Boys
7. "My TV," Vinx
8. "She Watch Channel Zero," Public Enemy
9. "Sleeping with the Television On," The Dictators
10. "Soap Commercial," The Psychedelic Furs
11. "Surrender," Cheap Trick
12. "Television (the Drug of the Nation)," The Beatnigs, later known as The Disposable Heroes of Hiphoprisy
13. "Televisionary," World Entertainment War
14. "The Revolution Will Not Be Televised," Gil Scott-Heron
15. "Top of the Pops," The Kinks
16. "TV Eye," The Stooges
17. "TV Mama," Joe Turner
18. "T.V.O.D.," The Norml
19. "Watching the Detectives," Elvis Costello
20. "Which Way to America?" Living Colour

20 Great TV Themes Based on
Rock, Country, and Soul

1. "The Associates," performed by B. B. King
2. "Ironside," composed by Quincy Jones
3. "Hawaii 5-0," performed by The Ventures
4. "The Jackie Thomas Show Theme," performed by Snuffy Walden

5. "Batman," performed by Neil Hefti
6. "Kids in the Hall," performed by Shadowy Men from a Shadowy Planet
7. "Martin," performed by cast, written by Kid of Kid N' Play
8. "Square Pegs," performed by The Waitresses
9. "In Living Color," performed by Heavy D
10. "Mystery Science Theater 3000," performed by the MST 3000 gang
11. "Baretta's Theme" (originally titled "Keep Your Eye on the Sparrow"), composed by Steve Barri and Michael Omartian
12. "Chico and the Man," performed by Jose Feliciano
13. "The Mary Tyler Moore Show" (originally titled "Love Is All Around"), composed by Sonny Curtis
14. "Maude," composed by Donny Hathaway
15. "Movin' On," composed by Merle Haggard
16. "Welcome Back Kotter" (originally titled "Welcome Back"), composed and performed by John Sebastian
17. "Zorro," performed by The Chordettes
18. "The Courtship of Eddie's Father," composed by Harry Nilsson and George Tiptas; performed by Harry Nilsson
19. "Prince of Bel Air," performed by DJ Jazzy Jeff and the Fresh Prince
20. "The Larry Sanders Show Theme," performed by Frank Fitzpatrick

The 20 Best Rock TV Shows

1. *Shindig* (ABC), mid-1960s
2. *Ready Steady Go!* (ITV), mid-1960s
3. *Hullabaloo* (NBC), mid-1960s
4. *Yo! MTV Raps* (MTV), contemporary
5. *Unplugged* (MTV), contemporary
6. *The Week in Rock* (MTV), contemporary
7. *Video Music Box*, contemporary
8. *Top of the Pops* (BBC), since the early 1960s
9. *The Old Grey Whistle Test* (BBC), since the early 1970s
10. *American Bandstand* (ABC), 1952–1985
11. *Soul Train* (syndicated), since the early 1970s
12. *The Smothers Brothers*, (CBS), in the late 1960s
13. *Hollywood a Go Go* (syndicated), in the mid-1960s
14. *Rock Palast* (West German), since the 1970s
15. *The Johnny Cash Show* (ABC), 1969–71
16. *Austin City Limits* (PBS), since the early 1980s
17. *Saturday Night Live* (NBC), since the late 1970s

18. *Beavis and Butthead* (MTV), contemporary
19. *Schoolhouse Rock* (ABC), mid-1970s
20. *Tomorrow* (NBC), mid-1970s to the early 1980s

The 10 Worst Rock TV Shows

1. *Cop Rock* (ABC), early 1990s
2. *Throb* (Fox), early 1990s
3. *Dance Fever* (syndicated), early 1980s
4. *Midnight Special* (NBC), from 1973 to 1981
5. *In Concert* (ABC), mid-1970s
6. *Where the Action Is* (ABC), mid-1960s
7. *The Ed Sullivan Show* (CBS), 1950s and 1960s
8. *Don Kirschner's Rock Concert* (syndicated), early 1980s
9. *Da Grind* (MTV), contemporary
10. *MTV Jams* (MTV), contemporary

Performers Who Made Their TV Debuts on *American Bandstand*

Dick Clark, the show's host from 1956 through its cancellation in 1985, tells us, "There have been more than nine thousand musical appearances made by various artists on American Bandstand *since its debut in 1952. Among those thousands of performers, hundreds made their first national appearance on the program." Here's a partial list.*

1. ABC
2. Bryan Adams
3. The Alarm
4. Paul Anka
5. Adam Ant
6. Frankie Avalon
7. Bananarama
8. Chuck Berry
9. Bon Jovi
10. Boomtown Rats
11. Bow Wow Wow
12. Laura Branigan
13. James Brown
14. Kim Carnes
15. Johnny Cash
16. Chubby Checker
17. The Coasters
18. Sam Cooke
19. Creedence Clearwater Revival
20. Marshall Crenshaw
21. Jim Croce
22. Bobby Darin
23. Neil Diamond
24. Dion and the Belmonts
25. Fats Domino
26. The Doors
27. The Drifters
28. Sheena Easton
29. The English Beat
30. The Everly Brothers
31. Flock of Seagulls
32. The Four Seasons
33. The Four Tops

34. Bill Haley and His Comets
35. Buddy Holly and the Crickets
36. Billy Idol
37. Janet Jackson
38. The Jackson 5
39. The Jefferson Airplane
40. The Jefferson Starship
41. Greg Kihn Band
42. Gladys Knight and the Pips
43. Cyndi Lauper
44. Brenda Lee
45. Huey Lewis and the News
46. Jerry Lee Lewis
47. Loverboy
48. Madonna
49. The Mamas and Papas
50. John Cougar Mellencamp
51. Men at Work
52. The Motels
53. Night Ranger
54. Billy Ocean
55. Oingo Boingo
56. The Platters
57. Prince
58. Public Image Ltd.
59. Quarterflash
60. Otis Redding
61. R.E.M.
62. Smokey Robinson and the Miracles
63. Romantics
64. Romeo Void
65. Linda Ronstadt
66. The Shirelles
67. Simon and Garfunkel
68. Stray Cats
69. The Supremes
70. The Temptations
71. The Thompson Twins
72. Three Dog Night
73. Conway Twitty
74. UB40
75. Wall of Voodoo
76. Wham!
77. Wire Train
78. Stevie Wonder
79. X
80. Paul Young

Eight Is Enough
Rock 'n Rap Cartoon Shows

1. *The Archies*
2. *The Bay City Rollers*
3. *The Beatles*
4. *Hammerman*
5. *The Jackson 5*
6. *Kid 'n Play*
7. *The Monkees*
8. *New Kids on the Block*

Alice Cooper's 10 Favorite TV Shows

1. *Monty Python's Flying Circus*
2. *Fawlty Towers*
3. *SC-TV*
4. *The Untouchables*
5. *The Twilight Zone*
6. *The Prisoner*
7. *I Spy*
8. *The Man from U.N.C.L.E.*
9. *Taxi*
10. *The Many Lives of Dobie Gillis*

Musical Guests on *Saturday Night Live*, 1976–92

1. ABBA
2. Bryan Adams
3. Aerosmith
4. Allman Brothers Band
5. The Amazing Rhythm Aces
6. Laurie Anderson
7. Adam Ant
8. Joan Armatrading
9. Ashford and Simpson
10. Anita Baker
11. Arrested Development
12. The Band
13. The Bangles
14. George Benson
15. Chuck Berry
16. The B-52s
17. Big Country
18. The Black Crowes
19. Mary J. Blige
20. Blondie
21. The Blues Brothers
22. Michael Bolton
23. Jon Bon Jovi
24. David Bowie
25. Laura Branigan
26. Edie Brickell and New Bohemians
27. Bobby Brown
28. James Brown
29. Jackson Browne
30. Jack Bruce and Friends
31. Lindsey Buckingham
32. Jimmy Buffet
33. The Bus Boys
34. Paul Butterfield
35. David Byrne
36. Captain Beefheart & Magic Band
37. Mariah Carey
38. Joe "King" Carrasco
39. The Cars
40. Johnny Cash
41. Rosanne Cash
42. Tracy Chapman
43. Ray Charles
44. Cheap Trick
45. Cher
46. Chicago
47. Desmond Child and Rouge
48. Eric Clapton
49. Stanley Clarke Trio
50. The Clash
51. Johnny Clegg and Savuka
52. Jimmy Cliff
53. George Clinton
54. Joe Cocker
55. Color Me Badd
56. The Commodores
57. Harry Connick, Jr.
58. Ry Cooder
59. Elvis Costello
60. Cowboy Junkies
61. Robert Cray Band
62. Andrae Crouch
63. Julee Cruise
64. The Cult
65. E. G. Dailey
66. Charlie Daniels Band
67. Terrence Trent D'Arby
68. Miles Davis
69. Dee-Lite
70. Mink Deville
71. Devo
72. Dexy's Midnight Runners
73. The Dirt Band
74. The Doobie Brothers
75. Dream Academy
76. Duran Duran
77. Bob Dylan
78. Sheila E.
79. En Vogue
80. Eurythmics

81. Faith No More
82. Marianne Faithfull
83. Fear
84. Bryan Ferry
85. Fine Young Cannibals
86. Fishbone
87. The Fixx
88. Mick Fleetwood's Zoo
89. 14 Karat Soul
90. Frankie Goes to Hollywood
91. Peter Gabriel
92. Art Garfunkel
93. The J. Geils Band
94. David Gilmore
95. Phillip Glass
96. The Go-Gos
97. Eddy Grant
98. The Grateful Dead
99. Al Green
100. Gypsy Kings
101. Daryl Hall and John Oates
102. Hammer
103. Herbie Hancock
104. George Harrison
105. Deborah Harry
106. Levon Helm
107. Don Henley
108. John Hiatt
109. Jennifer Holliday
110. Bruce Hornsby and the Range
111. Hothouse Flowers
112. Whitney Houston
113. Janis Ian
114. Billy Idol
115. INXS
116. Chris Isaak
117. Mick Jagger
118. Rick James
119. Al Jarreau
120. Billy Joel
121. Elton John
122. Quincy Jones
123. Ricki Lee Jones
124. Chaka Khan
125. Kid Creole and the Coconuts
126. Greg Kihn
127. The Kinks
128. Kool and the Gang
129. Lenny Kravitz
130. Kris Kristofferson and Rita Coolidge
131. K. D. Lang
132. Annie Lennox
133. Level 42
134. Huey Lewis and the News
135. Gordon Lightfoot
136. Little Feat
137. Living Color
138. L. L. Cool J
139. Meat Loaf
140. Kenny Loggins
141. Lone Justice
142. Los Lobos
143. Loverboy
144. Madness
145. Madonna
146. Taj Mahal
147. Wynton Marsalis
148. Paul and Linda McCartney
149. Delbert McClinton
150. Michael McDonald
151. Bobby McFerrin
152. The McGarrigle Sisters
153. John Cougar Mellencamp
154. Men at Work
155. The Meters
156. Bette Midler
157. Midnight Oil
158. Mr. Mister
159. Eddie Money
160. Van Morrison
161. Morrissey
162. The Motels
163. Musical Youth
164. Rick Nelson
165. Willie Nelson
166. The Nelsons
167. Aaron Neville

168. The Neville Brothers
169. Randy Newman
170. Olivia Newton-John
171. Stevie Nicks
172. Nirvana
173. The Notting Hillbillies
174. Gary Numan
175. Ric Ocasek
176. Billy Ocean
177. Sinead O'Connor
178. Roy Orbison
179. Dolly Parton
180. Pearl Jam
181. The Persuasions
182. Tom Petty and the Heartbreakers
183. Wintley Phipps
184. Pirates of Penzance
185. Robert Plant and the Honeydrippers
186. The Pogues
187. Buster Poindexter
188. Power Station
189. Billy Preston
190. The Pretenders
191. Prince
192. Public Enemy
193. The Pull
194. Queen
195. Queen Ida
196. Sun Ra
197. Bonnie Raitt
198. Eugene Record
199. Leon Redbone
200. Lou Reed
201. Martha Reeves
202. R.E.M.
203. The Replacements
204. Keith Richards
205. Lionel Richie
206. Robbie Robertson
207. The Roches
208. The Rolling Stones
209. Linda Ronstadt
210. Kevin Rowland
211. Todd Rundgren
212. Run-D.M.C.
213. Leon and Mary Russell
214. Sade
215. Sam and Dave
216. Santana
217. Leo Sayer
218. Boz Scaggs
219. Gil Scott-Heron
220. John Sebastian
221. Ellen Shipley
222. Carly Simon
223. Paul Simon
224. Simple Minds
225. Simply Red
226. Skid Row
227. Percy Sledge
228. Patti Smith
229. The Smithereens
230. Phoebe Snow
231. Soul Asylum
232. Spanic Boys
233. Sparks
234. The Specials
235. Spin Doctors
236. Spinal Tap
237. The Spinners
238. Bruce Springsteen
239. Squeeze
240. Billy Squier
241. Rod Stewart
242. Sting
243. Stray Cats
244. Stuff
245. The Stylistics
246. Sugarcubes
247. Keith Sykes
248. Talking Heads
249. James Taylor
250. Technotronic
251. 10,000 Maniacs
252. Thompson Twins
253. George Thorogood and the Destroyers
254. Timbuk 3
255. The Time
256. Tin Machine
257. Peter Tosh
258. Randy Travis

Doing the Bartman
A Dozen Rockers Do *The Simpsons*

1. MICHAEL JACKSON, "LISA, IT'S YOUR BIRTHDAY"

Having been thrown into a mental institution, Homer meets a fat, balding white guy who thinks he's Michael Jackson. The King of Pop provided the voice and sang a duet with Bart as a tribute to Lisa's b-day.

2. LINDA RONSTADT, "PLOW KING THEME"

After Homer starts a successful snowplowing business (Mr. Plow), Barney gets into the act and blows him away with a TV spot starring Ronstadt, who sings the jingle (sample lyric: "Mr. Plow is a loser and I think he is a boozer / So you'd better make that call to the Plow King").

3. SPINAL TAP, "BREAK LIKE THE WIND"

Bart catches his first concert, which ends in a riot as technical problems drive the band offstage in protest. Later, the Spinal Tap tour bus crashes into Bart's school bus.

4. STING, "WE'RE SENDING OUR LOVE DOWN THE WELL"

Bart throws a Superstar Celebrity Microphone down a well. By speaking into the remote microphone, he convinces the town that a little boy has fallen into the well. Krusty the Klown organizes a "We Are the World"–type charity for the boy with Sting leading it off: "There's a hole in my heart as deep as a well for that poor little boy who's stuck halfway to hell."

5. TOM JONES, "IT'S NOT UNUSUAL"

Homer's boss, Montgomery Burns, falls for Marge and tries to buy her love with a private concert by her favorite artist.

6. AEROSMITH, "WALK THIS WAY"

When Moe the bartender steals Homer's new idea for a drink, the "Flaming Moe," his bar becomes the hip place. So hip that Aerosmith is spotted one night and is coaxed into performing.

7. TONY BENNETT, "CAPITOL CITY"

Driving from Springfield to Capitol City because Homer has a gig as a mascot for the local major league baseball team, the Simpsons see Tony Bennett singing on the side of the road.

8. BETTE MIDLER, "WIND BENEATH MY WINGS"

Bart and Lisa convince Bette to appear on Krusty the Klown's Komeback special after he loses his show.

9. RED HOT CHILI PEPPERS, "GIVE IT AWAY"

After being tricked into playing Moe's bar—they were told that it held thirty thousand people—the fellas allow Bart to talk them into appearing on, yes, Krusty the Klown's Komeback special. Krusty asks the group if they'd change the lyrics "What I got, you gotta get and put it in you" to "What I'd like is, I'd like to hug and kiss you." The group readily agrees, exclaiming, "Wow, that's much better! Everyone can enjoy that."

10. RINGO STARR

Flashback to Marge's high school painting class. All of her paintings feature the Beatles drummer and her teacher is not impressed. She sends the pictures to Ringo and never receives a reply so she quits the arts. However, because Ringo likes to read all of his fan mail, he takes more than twenty years to read her letter. His enthusiastic response to the pictures convinces her to take up painting again.

11. BARRY WHITE, "CAN'T GET ENOUGH OF YOUR LOVE, BABY"

The thunder-voiced soulster is asked to be the keynote speaker at Springfield's annual "Whacking Day" ceremony, which turns out to be an excuse to beat up snakes with sticks.

12. "THEME FROM SHAFT"

No, Isaac Hayes didn't appear on the show, but seeing Bart and Lisa trading the lines of the ode to Shaft at a karaoke bar (Bart: "Who's the black private dick that's the sex machine to all the chicks?" Lisa: "Shaft") is too funny not to include here.

Reginald C. Dennis Selects the Harshest Disses on Video

1. "Dre Day" (Dr. Dre): Luther Campbell and Eazy E are parodied. Luke gets sodomized. Eazy is seen dancing on the side of a highway holding a sign that reads "Will rap for food."
2. "Cowards from Compton" (Luke): Luke responds to Dr. Dre. Dre wears a sequined suit.

3. "Rat Bastard" (Prime Minister Pete Nice & Daddy Rich): Pete Nice bashes in the skull of an MC Serch (his former 3rd Bass partner) lookalike, in a scene taken from *The Untouchables*.
4. "Be True to the Game" (Ice Cube): Ice Cube disses Hammer, portraying him as a dancing and grinning hip-hop Steppin' Fetchit.
5. "Pop Goes the Weasel" (3rd Bass): Pete Nice and MC Serch administer a ghetto-style ass whipping to a Vanilla Ice lookalike.

Reginald C. Dennis is the music editor of The Source.

10 Best Things About MTV

1. YO! MTV RAPS
Probably you could make a case that rap did more for MTV than MTV's ever done for rap. The fact remains that this is the most watched show on the channel because it's the most watchable music show on TV. After all these years, the format holds up and, of course, it has the advantage of showing the most exciting music on the air. It's too bad that MTV didn't see fit to remain loyal to the show.

2. 120 MINUTES
Indie rock's moments of triumph.

3. MTV NEWS
Not just a highlight of MTV, a highlight of TV news coverage, period. Under Kurt Loder, the News department has become the brains and guts of MTV, and during the Gulf War, for instance, the nightly news was literally the only place to receive information and see footage that had not been censored by the Pentagon. Ted Koppel wishes the *Nightline* staff had the ethical or the reportorial sense that MTV's news crews bring to their jobs. (Actually, they don't wish it; that's the problem.)

4. THE MTV AWARDS SHOW
The only annual awards show that's *likely* to produce an important performance—someone always outdoes themselves—or a memorable acceptance speech.

5. SPECIALS
Not all of them work, but nobody does the at-home-with-the-stars bit better and when they decide to focus on an issue—racism, or even the elections—you're almost always going to learn some perspectives that you hadn't imagined existed.

6. BEAVIS AND BUTT-HEAD
The channel's first worthwhile talking heads.

7.   THE TOP TEN COUNTDOWN
A concise convenience for finding out what's going on. You don't need to see it more than once a week, but you *do* need a dose at least that often.

8.   LOGOS AND BUMPERS
Generally, viewers see a lot more visual imagination on display on their way in and out of programming than they do during the music videos themselves.

9.   CREATING OPPORTUNITIES FOR OTHER VIDEO CHANNELS
Without MTV, the Box, with its vastly superior lineup of videos, would not exist. Which is reason enough for MTV to exist.

10.   ATTITUDE
Brings rock 'n' roll irreverence to just about everything it touches.

10 Worst Things About MTV

1.   HYPE
It's what MTV really broadcasts on a twenty-four-hour-a-day, seven-days-a-week basis: hype for rock stars, hype for movies, hype for models, and unceasing hype for itself. No wonder it has the best bumpers and logos in the business—they're its true *raison d'être*.

2.   CONSERVATIVE PROGRAMMING
Whole networks can be—and are—programmed with popular and/or high-quality videos that this citadel of narrowcasting won't touch. Much of the best rap and metal, in particular, is excluded, as well as an increasing amount of adult rock. If you're over thirty-five, you'd better be flat-out great on *Unplugged* or you're sure to be banished to the old fart sister channel, VH-1, which has few viewers and generates even fewer sales.

3.   CENSORING VIDEOS
From the beginning, MTV practiced a policy of appeasing the most reactionary critics of its content. As a result, it perpetually insists on slicing shots from even its most popular videos (viz, Aerosmith's "Love in an Elevator") or banning outright amusing and important pieces, especially if they deal frankly with sexuality.

4.   SEXISM
On the other hand, the most rancid sorts of sexism—jiggle moves that would make Charlie's Angels blush—slide right on by. MTV panders so relentlessly to the mainly male teenagers who constitute the main body of its viewership that it's actually reached the conclusion that Christie Brinkley and Cindy Crawford are ideal talking heads. In a word: *Not*.

5.   THE VEEJAYS
Has there ever been one with an IQ in triple digits?

6. PAULY SHORE

Even among moronic veejays, in a category all by himself. Butt-head without Beavis, to put it mildly. A walking slander on his generation.

7. CONTESTS

Ceaselessly hyped, usually to no particular purpose except greed and the most craven star worship. Who the fuck would *want* to paint their house pink? Or live in Jon Bon Jovi's?

8. TABITHA SOREN

The reduction of the political process to stargazing, rumor-mongering and demographic gladhanding does not represent a journalistic breakthrough, or a triumph for the youth electorate.

9. ATTEMPTING TO PREVENT VIDEOS FROM BEING SHOWN ON OTHER VIDEO CHANNELS

On MTV, having an "exclusive" mainly means denying the competition an equal chance to grab viewers. That's partly because MTV plays music industry politics extremely shrewdly, but it also compromises the channel's ability to critique such ridiculous music biz misadventures as the attempt to prevent the sale of used CDs. And it goes a long way toward ensuring that the channel faces no real threat of competition, which encourages the worst kinds of complacency and mediocrity—not to mention programming conservatism—at MTV itself.

10. ATTITUDE

Brings sophomoric disrespectfulness to just about everything it touches.

Millicent Shelton Picks the 12 Best Music Videos

1. "JANIE'S GOT A GUN," AEROSMITH, DIR. DAVID FINCHER

When I first saw this video, I thought it was a work of art. I hoped that I could one day create a piece that was visually stimulating while simultaneously making an important social comment. I really feel that this video incorporated what Music Video (caps intentional) is all about: vision, style, and a message.

2. "EXPRESS YOURSELF," MADONNA, DIR. DAVID FINCHER

A movie adapted into a music video successfully. I really loved the "look" of this clip. The colors, the motion, the art direction, and the styling all came together neatly into a well-conceived and -executed music video.

3. "OH, FATHER," MADONNA, DIR. DAVID FINCHER

This clip emotionally moved me. The black and white is beautifully shot with a clean, moody film noir vibe. I loved this complete vision of a child's memory. The video is filled with powerful images with religious symbolism and realism. The shot of the dead mother in the casket with her lips stitched together was shocking and moving.

4. "LOSING MY RELIGION," R.E.M., DIR. TARSEM

The colors are fabulous and the freedom of the image is great. This clip incorporated traditional museum art works into contemporary "pop" culture. I think the best clips add something to the musical lyrics. This clip definitely succeeded in doing that.

5. "RAIN," MADONNA, DIR. MARK ROMANEK

I really love this clip because the images are breathtakingly beautiful. The video confronts the issues of Japanese influences on contemporary art and style. In a medium that is visually oriented, this clip satisfied my needs. I love looking at it.

6. "JAM," MICHAEL JACKSON, DIR. DAVID KELLOGG

The editing of this clip is slamming. It has a feeling that is fun yet there's a spiritual wantonness in the images. It's the look in the kids' eyes, the emotion in the dance and the ball playing. The video made me love the song.

7. "NEVER GONNA GET IT," EN VOGUE, DIR. MATTHEW ROLSTON

Moving pictures. . . . The group looked great, the energy is on top. . . . This clip made En Vogue true divas. I loved the characters he pulled out of the group, giving them more dimensions than any of us imagined.

8. "JEREMY," PEARL JAM, DIR. MARK PELLINGTON

When I first saw this video, it disturbed me in a good way. It made me think about a serious issue, it looked great and hyped a song's beat. That's not an easy task in four minutes. I also liked the editing a lot.

9. "VOGUE," MADONNA, DIR. DAVID FINCHER

They adapted great photographs and films into an interesting clip. This video is film noir with a nineties edge. It captures Madonna and the spirit of those around her. Voguing is about style as well as dance. The clip created a world where the dance could be appreciated by Middle America without the social stigmas attached.

10. "FREE YOUR MIND," EN VOGUE, DIR. MARK ROMANEK

Wow! I loved the lighting and the fierce attitude.

11. "RHYTHM NATION," JANET JACKSON, DIR. DOMINIC SENA

Great dance editing. I watch this video whenever I have a dance clip to shoot.

12. "THRILLER," MICHAEL JACKSON, DIR. JON LANDIS

This is the music video of all time. Looking back at it now, it was truly inspirational and revolutionary for that period. It paved the way for others to open their minds and break boundaries in the world of music video images.

Millicent Shelton is a music video director whose credits include Salt-N-Pepa's "Let's Talk About Sex," CeCe Peniston's "Keep On Walkin'," Mary J. Blige's "Love No Limit," and Robin S.'s "Show Me Move."

Katherine Turman Picks the 10 Best Metal Videos

1. Tool, "Sober"
2. Nine Inch Nails, "Head Like A hole"
3. Guns N' Roses, "Paradise City"
4. Motley Crue, "Too Young to Fall in Love"
5. Van Halen, "Hot for Teacher"
6. Soundgarden, "Outshined"
7. Alice in Chains, "Man in a Box"
8. Metallica, "Enter Sandman"
9. Iron Maiden, "Run to the Hills"
10. Def Leppard, "Photograph"

Katherine Turman is the senior editor of RIP *magazine.*

MTV's First 5 Veejays

1. Nina Blackwood
2. Mark Goodman
3. Alan Hunter
4. J. J. Jackson
5. Martha Quinn

12 Key Figures in the Founding of MTV, 1981–82

1. JOHN LACK

Then executive vice-president of Warner-Amex, the cable television joint venture between Warner Communications and American Express. Lack approached his bosses for "20-some-odd million dollars" to start a twenty-four hour video music channel. He is the true father of MTV.

2. JAMES ROBINSON III

Chairman of American Express, and one of the most profligate executives in the history of corporate America (see *Barbarians at the Gate*). When Lack made his pitch, Robinson turned to his partner, Warner Comm's chairman Steve Ross, and said, "I don't know much about the music business, but it makes sense to me. I'll buy it if you buy it."

3. STEVE ROSS

Warner Communications chairman. Agreed to back the channel with Robinson.

4. MIKE NESMITH

Former member of the Monkees. Early believer in synthesis of music and video. Lack hired him to produce a half-hour program for MTV's older sister channel, Nickelodeon. *Pop Clips* had the MTV look and style from the start. Its thirteen episodes were rerun more than fifty times.

5. BOB PITTMAN

Lack's crucial error came from hiring this failed Top Forty radio programmer (he'd flopped bigtime at WNBC in New York) to develop MTV with him. Pittman formed an alliance with Ross, eventually took the entire credit for developing the channel himself, writing his original employer out of the story entirely. Credit Pittman, legitimately, with the slickness and highly research-oriented aspects of early MTV. Debit this native Mississippian and Gore-for-president enthusiast with the channel's imposition of an artist color line, which held back the development of the channel by denying the audience its preferences.

6. LEE GARLAND

Experienced AM radio exec and Pittman's right hand in early programming decisions. The decisive force in getting record company support for the channel, most crucially in persuading the labels that their videos should be given—not sold—to MTV.

7. MARSHALL COHEN

Early research chief. Defined profile of MTV listenership. "The twenty-three-, twenty-four-year-old educated, affluent, suburban viewer . . ."

8. JERRY McGEE

Pittman credits this Ogilvy and Mather advertising agency exec with coining the term "veejay."

9. PAT GORMAN

His Manhattan Designs staff, including Frank Olinsky and Patty Rogoff, came up with the unforgettable early MTV logos.

10. STING

His (and other rock stars', but mainly his) delivery of the smarmy, "I want my MTV" promo really put the idea on the viewers' minds.

11. WALTER YETNIKOFF

Chairman of CBS Records Group. Broke the MTV color line by threatening to withdraw all CBS Records videos from the channel unless they agreed to air Michael Jackson's "Billie Jean."

12. MICHAEL JACKSON

"Billie Jean" turned out to be a breakthrough concept video. Beautifully directed and with a magical Michael performance at its center. "Beat It" took the concept video to new heights and rocked the funk, as well, helping swing the door open for future dance-rock and black-rock material on the channel. Finally, the long-form "Thriller" made MTV must viewing in households of many kinds and nailed home the creative potential of the music video.

CHAPTER 12

Literature

Biblical Characters Who Appeared in Bob Dylan's Songs *Before* He Became a Christian

1. Abraham, "Highway 61 Revisited"
2. Adam and Eve, "Talking World War III Blues"
3. Cain and Abel, "Desolation Row"
4. David, "If I Could Do It All Over Again, I'd Do It All Over You"
5. Delilah, "Tombstone Blues"
6. Eli, "The Wicked Messenger"
7. Goliath, "When the Ship Comes In"
8. The Good Samaritan, "Desolation Row"
9. The Good Shepherd, "Changing of the Guard"
10. Jesus, "Masters of War"
11. Jezebel, "Tombstone Blues"
12. St John, "Where Are You Tonight (Journey Through Dark Heat)"
13. John the Baptist, "Tombstone Blues"
14. Judas (Iscariot), "Masters of War," "With God On Our Side," "The Ballad of Frankie Lee and Judas Priest"
15. The King of the Philistines, "Tombstone Blues"
16. Lucifer, "New Pony"
17. Noah, "Desolation Row"
18. Pharaoh, "When the Ship Comes In"
19. St. Peter, "I'd Hate to Be You on That Dreadful Day"
20. Samson, "If I Could Do It All Over Again, I'd Do It All Over You"

Note to Wise Guys: St. Augustine lived several hundred years after the Bible was written.

Rock and Rap Music Based on Literature, Fairy Tales, Nursery Rhymes, and Comix

1. "Absolute Beginners," David Bowie—The theme song from the film, which was based on the novel by Colin McInnes.
2. "Annie Fanny," The Kingsmen—Based on Harvey Kurtzman's long-running *Playboy* satire.

3. "Boats Against the Current," Eric Carmen—The title and chorus line are taken from the last line of F. Scott Fitzgerald's *The Great Gatsby*.
4. "Born in the U.S.A.," Bruce Springsteen—Inspired by Ron Kovic's Vietnam memoir, *Born on the 4th of July*.
5. "Darkness on the Edge of Town," Bruce Springsteen—Based on Tom Joad's last speech in John Steinbeck's *The Grapes of Wrath*.
6. "Dirty Nursery Rhymes," 2 Live Crew—As advertised.
7. "Frankenstein," The Edgar Winter Group—Based on the character created by Mary Wollstonecraft Shelley.
8. "Future Shock," Curtis Mayfield—Title and concept based on Alvin Toffler's best-seller about the impact of technological change on the quality of modern life.
9. "Games People Play," Joe South—Title and concept taken from Eric Berne's best-seller about transactional analysis.
10. "A Gangsta's Fairytale," Ice Cube—This track from *AmeriKKKa's Most Wanted*, his debut album, parodies Mother Goose and the Brothers Grimm.
11. *The Ghost in the Machine*, The Police—Inspired by Arthur Koestler's philosophical book about the spiritual impact of technology, which has the same title.
12. "Golden Slumber," The Beatles—Based on a sixteenth-century poem by Thomas Dekker.
13. "Gone with the Wind," The Duprees—From Margaret Mitchell's novel of the Civil War; this, of course, is *white* doo-wop.
14. "The House at Pooh Corner," The Nitty Gritty Dirt Band—Based on A. A. Milne's *Winnie the Pooh*.
15. "The House That Jack Built," Aretha Franklin—From the nursery rhyme by the same name, via R&B great Don Covay, who composed the tune.
16. "I Am the Walrus," The Beatles—The "Walrus" refers to Lewis Carroll's *Alice in Wonderland*. The "goo goo boo joob" in the chorus comes from Humpty Dumpty's last lines in James Joyce's *Finnegans Wake*.
17. "I Believe in Jesus," Donna Summer—Certain sections from "Mary Had a Little Lamb."
18. "I Feel Like Going Home," Charlie Rich—Based on the title of Peter Guralnick's book of profiles of American blues and country musicians (including Rich), which took its title from Muddy Waters's first Chess Records single in 1948.
19. *Iron Man*, Pete Townshend—Based on the children's story by British poet laureate, Ted Hughes.
20. "Jack and Jill," Raydio—Ray Parker, Jr.'s rewrite of the nursery rhyme.
21. *John Lennon/Plastic Ono Band*, John Lennon—Concept derived

from *The Primal Scream*, a book by Lennon's then-psychiatrist/ guru, Dr. Arthur Janov (see number 32).

22. *Journey Through the Secret Life of Plants*, Stevie Wonder—Soundtrack album for the film; both movie and music based upon the best-selling book on how plants sorta feel and think.

23. *The Juliet Letters*, Elvis Costello—Based on letters written by a Venetian professor, conceived as replies to letters to Shakespeare's Juliet character received by the Venice post office.

24. "Last Chance to Turn Around" Gene Pitney—The chorus ("Last exit to Brooklyn/Last chance to turn around") explicitly refers to Hubert Selby's sordid novel of urban life, *Last Exit to Brooklyn*.

25. "Liar, Liar," The Castaways—Based on the name-calling rhyme, "Liar liar pants on fire / Nose is longer than a telephone wire," which forms the chorus of the song.

26. "Li'l Red Riding Hood," Sam the Sham and the Pharoahs— Sam the Sham and the boys took a leering two-step version of the old fairy tale to number two on the charts.

27. "Little Miss Muffet," Leon T. Gross—Based on the nursery rhyme.

28. "Little Star," The Elegants—Based on the children's nursery rhyme and the melody created around it by the young Mozart.

29. "Mary Had a Little Lamb," Otis Redding; "Mary Had a Little Lamb," Paul McCartney—Otis's second single (as B-side), McCartney's fifth. Otis did the better rewrite of the traditional nursery rhyme, McCartney scored the bigger hit (although even his disc reached only number twenty-eight).

30. *Men Without Women*, Little Steven and the Disciples of Soul— Title and concept taken from Ernest Hemingway's first book of short stories.

31. "Mother Goose," Jethro Tull—Features a panoply of childhood familiars.

32. "My Mummy's Dead," John Lennon—Based on the melody to "Three Blind Mice" (see number 21).

33. "Puddin' N' Tain," The Alley Cats—Based on the children's rhyme.

34. "Richard Cory," Simon and Garfunkel—Taken from a poem in Edgar Lee Masters's *Spoon River Anthology*.

35. "Simon Says," The 1910 Fruitgum Co.—One of the all-time bubblegum favorites, based on the kids' game. (Other Fruitgum hits with reference to children's games or speech include "1,2,3, Red Light," "May I Take a Giant Step," "Goody Goody Gumdrops," and "Indian Giver.")

36. "Spy in the House of Love," The Doors—Taken from a novel of the same title by Anaïs Nin.

37. "Suddenly Last Summer," The Motels—Title and emotional

mood based on the Tennessee Williams play with the same title.

38. "Sugar and Spice," The Cryan Shames—From the rhyme about what little boys and little girls are made of.

39. *Tales of Mystery and Imagination*, The Alan Parsons Project—Art-rock adaptation of Edgar Allan Poe's great stories and poem; "The Raven" was a minor hit.

40. "Tender Is the Night," Jackson Browne—Title and concept derived from F. Scott Fitzgerald's novel of the same name.

41. "Tobacco Road," The Nashville Teens—Both the title and the spirit of the record taken from Erskine Caldwell's white-trash novel.

42. "Tom Sawyer," Rush—Based on Mark Twain's novel.

43. "Tomorrow Never Knows," The Beatles—Originally entitled "The Void," and inspired by LSD gurus Timothy Leary and Richard Alpert (Baba Ram Dass) and their book, *The Psychedelic Experience*, which is based on *The Tibetan Book of the Dead*.

44. "True Love Never Runs Smooth," Gene Pitney—Based on a line from Shakespeare.

45. "Turn! Turn! Turn!" The Byrds—Written by Pete Seeger as a very slight adaptation of verses from the biblical book of Ecclesiastes.

46. "White Rabbit," Jefferson Airplane—From Lewis Carroll's *Alice in Wonderland*.

47. "A Whiter Shade of Pale," Procol Harum—Based on an old English poem of the same name.

48. "Who's Been Sleeping Here," The Rolling Stones—From "Goldilocks and the Three Bears."

49. "Wuthering Heights," Kate Bush—Three-minute condensation of a Gothic Bronte novel could only have reached number one in Great Britain.

50. "You, Me and Pooneil," Jefferson Airplane—Another song based on A. A. Milne's sappy novel *Winnie the Pooh*.

Most Profound Rock Lyrics— Sorta . . .

1. "Surfin' Bird," The Trashmen
2. "Tutti Frutti," Little Richard
3. "Da Doo Ron Ron," The Crystals
4. "Get a Job," The Silhouettes
5. "De Do Do Do, De Da Da Da," The Police
6. "Smells Like Teen Spirit," Nirvana

7. "The Bird's the Word," The Rivingtons
8. "Rubber Biscuit," The Chips
9. "Word Up," Cameo
10. "Papa Oom Mow Mow," The Rivingtons
11. "In-a-Gadda-da-Vida," Iron Butterfly
12. "I Do," The Marvelows
13. "Jam on Revenge (Jam on It)," Newcleus
14. "Little Darlin'," The Diamonds
15. "The Oogum Boogum Song," Brenton Wood
16. "Ooby Dooby," Roy Orbison
17. "Wooly Bully," Sam the Sham and the Pharoahs
18. "Sh-Boom," The Chords
19. "Be Bop A Lula," Gene Vincent
20. "Ooh Poo Pah Doo, Part II," Jessie Hill

What You Talkin' 'Bout? Outrageous House Song Titles or Lyrics, Selected by Larry Flick

1. "I'll rip out her eyes and put 'em in the punch bowl"—"Get Her," Roxy & the Ride Committee
2. "Here she comes, li'l Susie ho-maker, thinks she'll get respect if she screws it"—"Thief of Hearts," Madonna
3. "I'll have a man who's a woman but no woman's man"—"You Make Me Feel (Mighty Fierce)," Jack & Jill
4. "Been tied up in bed, it's a strange way to get head"—"Had It, Done It, Been There, Did That," Mike Walsh
5. "Gagging on the Lovely Extravaganza," The Fabulous Pop Tarts
6. "I just want to cut up and bring it to the runway, and turn it, and be the fierce disco queen . . . ruling"—"One Woman's Insanity," Ultra Nate
7. "The Devil Made Me Buy This Dress," I. M. T.
8. "Work This Pussy," Sweet Pussy Pauline
9. "A Shade Shadey (Now Prance)," RuPaul
10. "Queens that read are the best"—"Queen's English," Jose & Luis RCD, Jr.

Harshest Disses on Wax, Selected by Reginald C. Dennis

1. Shanté, "Big Mamma." Topic, MC Lyte's sexual preferences: "Watch the bitch stagger/'Cause I don't dig the bull dagger."
2. Ice Cube, "No Vaseline." Topic, his old partner Eazy E: "Throw a little nigga in a ditch/Half-pint bitch."
3. L.L. Cool J, "Jack the Ripper." Topic, Kool Moe Dee's challenge: "How you like me now?/I'm gettin' busier/I'm double platinum/I'm watchin' you get dizzier."
4. L.L. Cool J, "To The Break of Dawn." Topic, Ice-T's wife (who often graces his record covers): "You're gonna hear a real ill paragraph soon/I took the cover right home to the bathroom."
5. Dr. Dre, "Dre Day." Topic, his feud with Luke: "If it ain't another ho that I gots ta get with/Gap teeth in your mouth so my dick's got to fit."

The Rock and Roll Library
Best Rock Books

BIOGRAPHIES

1. *Divided Soul: The Life of Marvin Gaye,* David Ritz
2. *Chuck Berry: The Autobiography,* Chuck Berry
3. *'Scuse Me While I Kiss the Sky: The Life of Jimi Hendrix,* by David Henderson
4. *Before I Get Old: The Story of the Who,* Dave Marsh
5. *Big Beat Heat: Alan Freed and the Early Years of Rock and Roll,* John Jackson
6. *Dance with the Devil: The Rolling Stones and Their Times,* Stanley Booth
7. *Standing in the Shadows of Motown: The Life and Music of Legendary Bassist James Jamerson,* Dr. Lix (Alan Slutsky)
8. *Brother Ray,* Ray Charles and David Ritz
9. *Elvis and Gladys,* Elaine Dundy
10. *As Nasty As They Wanna Be: The Uncensored Story of the 2 Live Crew,* Luther Campbell and John R. Miller
11. *Route 666: On the Road to Nirvana,* Gina Arnold
12. *James Brown,* James Brown and Bruce Tucker

HISTORY

1. *Deep Blues,* Robert Palmer
2. *The Rolling Stone Illustrated History of Rock and Roll* (2d ed.), Jim Miller, ed.

3. *Where Did Our Love Go?: The Rise and Fall of the Motown Sound*, Nelson George
4. *Crosstown Traffic: Jimi Hendrix and the Rock and Roll Revolution*, Charles Shaar Murray
5. *The Sound of the City: The Rise of Rock and Roll*, Charlie Gillett
6. *Girl Groups: The Story of a Sound*, Alan Betrock
7. *Honkers and Shouters: The Golden Years of Rhythm and Blues*, Arnold Shaw
8. *Like Punk Never Happened: Culture Club and the New Pop*, Dave Rimmer
9. *Nowhere to Run: The Story of Soul Music*, Gerri Hirshey
10. *Hip Hop: The Illustrated History of Break Dancing, Rap Music and Graffiti*, Steven Hagar
11. *England's Dreaming: Anarchy, Sex Pistols, Punk Rock and Beyond*, Jon Savage
12. *The Motown Story*, Don Waller

CRITICISM AND THEORY

1. *Psychotic Reactions and Carburetor Dung*, Lester Bangs
2. *The Death of Rhythm and Blues*, Nelson George
3. *Mystery Train: Images of America in Rock and Roll Music*, Greil Marcus
4. *Runnin' with the Devil: Power, Gender and Madness in Heavy Metal Music*, Robert Walser
5. *The Heart of Rock and Soul: The 1001 Greatest Singles Ever Made*, Dave Marsh
6. *The Rap Attack: African Jive to New York Hip Hop*, David Toop
7. *The Best of Country Music: A Critical and Historical Guide to the 750 Greatest Albums*, John Morthland
8. *Dead Elvis: A Chronicle of a Cultural Obsession*, Greil Marcus
9. *Feel Like Going Home: Portraits in Blues and Rock and Roll*, Peter Guralnick
10. *Written in My Soul: Conversations with Rock's Great Songwriters*, Bill Flanagan
11. *Flyboy in the Buttermilk: Essays on Contemporary America*, Greg Tate
12. *"Looking Up at Down": The Emergence of Blues Culture*, William Barlow

ART AND PHOTOGRAPHY

1. *Rock Dreams*, Guy Peelaert and Nik Cohn
2. *The Art of Rock Posters from Presley to Punk*, Paul D. Grushkin
3. *Private Elvis*, Diego Cortez
4. *The Rolling Stone Illustrated History of Rock & Roll* (1st ed.), Jim Miller, ed.
5. *Motown*, Berry Gordy, Elvis Mitchell, Ben Fong-Torres, Dave Marsh

6. *Country: The Music and the Musicians,* the Country Music Foundation
7. *Rock 'n' Roll Times,* Jurgen Vollmer
8. *The Face of Folk Music,* Dave Gahr and Robert Shelton
9. *Elvis Fifty-Six: In the Beginning,* Alfred Wertheimer
10. *The Complete Air Guitar Handbook,* John McKenna and Michael Moffit

REFERENCE

1. *The Billboard Book of Number One Hits,* Fred Bronson
2. *The Beatles: Recording Sessions,* Mark Lewisohn
3. *Joel Whitburn's Pop Memories 1890–1954: The History of American Popular Music,* Joel Whitburn, compiler
4. *The R&B Book: A Disc-History of Rhythm and Blues,* Big Al Pavlow
5. *The Illustrated Discography of Surf Music,* John Blair
6. *The Gospel Sound: Good News and Bad Times,* Tony Heilbut
7. *The Penguin Encyclopedia of Popular Music,* Donald Clarke, ed.
8. *Duke/Peacock Records: An Illustrated History with Discography,* Galen Gart and Roy C. Ames
9. *The Down Home Guide to the Blues,* Frank Scott and the staff of Down Home Music
10. *The Complete Beatles Chronicle,* Mark Lewisohn

Is There a CD in the Cliff's Notes?
Best Pop Music Fiction, Selected by Greil Marcus

1. KEITH ABBOTT, "SPANISH CASTLE," IN *THE FIRST THING COMING* (MINNEAPOLIS: COFFEE HOUSE PRESS, 1987)

The early sixties. A roadhouse between Tacoma and Seattle. Grudge match battle of the bands: Checkmates versus Wailers. "Losing band to have heads shaved on stage!" And the best teen sex scene ever written.

2. GORDON BURNS, *ALMA COGAN* (LONDON: SECKER & WARBURG, 1991)

A complex, probably deep meditation on fame, spectacle, and the dissolution of the entertainer's personality, but before and after any of that a hypnotic first-person narrative by Britain's dead, premier postwar, pre-Beatles pop singer on where she came from and why she hasn't left.

3. RODDY DOYLE, *THE COMMITMENTS* (NEW YORK: VINTAGE, 1989, ORIGINALLY PUBLISHED DUBLIN: KING FAROUK PUBLISHING, 1987)

Twenty-some years after Otis Redding's plane went down, a bunch of Dublin kids get together to form a soul band (the Irish are the blacks of Europe, right?). They rehearse. They argue. Then they break up: the end. Literary strategy: Doyle slams bits of lyrics and exhortation onto bits of dialogue and lets the songs blow up in the musicians' faces, and in yours.

4. HARLAN ELLISON, *SPIDER KISS* (NEW YORK: ARMCHAIR DETECTIVE LIBRARY, 1990; ORIGINALLY PUBLISHED NEW YORK: GOLD MEDAL BOOKS, 1961, AS *ROCKABILLY*)

Inspired by Jerry Lee Lewis and a story then fellow-soldier Buddy Knox told the author about a pop singer tossing a fan out of his thirtieth-story hotel window, this fast, cruel tale—not so far from a Jim Thompson thriller, really—reads like the inside dope on the young Elvis, except that in these pages everything comes crashing down. And the narrator, a flack, looks genius in the eyes and walks away.

5. ARTHUR FLOWERS, *ANOTHER GOOD LOVING BLUES* (NEW YORK: VIKING, 1993)

It's 1918 when Lucas Bodeen meets conjure woman Melvira Dupree—early enough in the century that Bodeen remembers "when there wasn't no such thing as blues" and Dupree remembers when her kind were respected and feared. Now her powers are slipping away—this is the hoodoo version of the death of god—and it seems possible that they may be slipping into the blues.

6. WILLIAM PRICE FOX, *RUBY RED* (PHILADELPHIA AND NEW YORK: LIPPINCOTT, 1971)

Two good gospel girls from Columbia, South Carolina (so good they call themselves the Rose of Sharon Girls), take the road to sin, success, and perdition in Nashville. The plot is fine, but the musical descriptions—a fiddle suddenly cutting away from its band, say—fly right off the page. They're so powerful, so emotionally specific, that for some time after reading this book nothing you hear will sound so alive.

7. KINKY FRIEDMAN, *ELVIS, JESUS & COCA-COLA* (NEW YORK: SIMON & SCHUSTER, 1993)

A New York murder mystery where "Meeting Elvis" translates as "Going to Jesus"—that is, turning up dead. Plus proof that the guy you meet when you do isn't—all wrapped up with a hard-boiled softie's regret and sorrow, a sense of loss that can break your heart.

8. DAVID HELTON, *KING JUDE* (NEW YORK: SIMON & SCHUSTER, 1969)

"A parable of our collapsing times" (*New York Times Book Review*) about the rock and roll money machine and the soulless masses it feeds, with post–Plaster Caster groupies who collect sperm samples like vintage wine. Pretentious trash—and creepier than Nik Cohn's *King Death*.

9. BRIAN MORTON, *THE DYLANIST* (NEW YORK: HARPERCOLLINS, 1991)

Here, in a young woman's world bordered by the left-wing politics of her parents and those of the man she's just met, "a Dylanist" means "You don't believe in causes. You only believe in feelings." It's also a world where the woman knows Dylan's unpublished Basement Tape recording "I'm Not There" may be "the greatest song ever written" (no one has ever been able to understand the words) and finally learns that being a Dylanist is not as simple as it once seemed. "She would never find a home, as they had, in the effort to transfigure the world. But in her belief that she lived in a world that needed to be transfigured, she'd probably always feel homeless."

10. ISHMAEL REED, *MUMBO JUMBO* (NEW YORK: DOUBLEDAY, 1972)

Set mostly in the 1920s, when the forces of Western civilization conspire to stamp out the dread plague of "Jes' grew"—a dance craze rooted in the African-American community—not understanding that without the plague civilization cannot survive. Of course, the question of who's really civilized comes up, too. This great book is a dream of revenge, finally opening up into a psychogeographical map on which anyone can find a place.

11. JOSEPH C. SMITH, *THE DAY THE MUSIC DIED* (NEW YORK: GROVE PRESS, 1981)

In this long, surging, thrillingly complex novel, Smith—aka Sonny Knight, pioneer of L.A. R&B with "Confidential" and later "If You Want This Love"—writes the history of rock 'n' roll as altogether a story of power, money, and racism. Some whites want to take over black music, in order to kill it, some to spread the good news—and a few black people want to keep what's theirs. To pull that off they create a field for a kind of laissez-faire capitalism that is almost indistinguishable from crime on the one hand and folk authenticity on the other, and while that field is open you can't tell the good guys from the bad guys and everything is up for grabs.

12. MICHAEL THELWELL, *THE HARDER THEY COME* (NEW YORK: GROVE PRESS, 1980)

Written well after Perry Henzell's film became an international hit, and self-described as "the book the movie would have been based on if it had been based on a book"—in other words, the Jamaican author imagines everything a movie would have left out, all the corners that would have been cut, every compromise, for example the budget bullshit that forced the director to dump that fabulous scene in the back country when the dancers call up the gods and the gods appear . . .

Greil Marcus has been book critic of Rolling Stone, California, *and other publications. He's the author, most recently, of* Dead Elvis *and* Ranters

& Crowd Pleasers (*known to Anglos and expatriates as* In the Fascist Bathroom*), each of which has its fictive elements.*

The *Real* Rock Bottom Remainders
Worst Rock Books

1. *ELVIS*, ALBERT GOLDMAN

Not so much a biography as a malignancy, characterized by an old fogey's sense of hipsterism, a middle-brow intellectual's parochial sense of what's important (not to mention self-important), an extraordinary writing style that manages to be both flaccid and overblown, Freudianism that unmasks its author (Goldman believes that Elvis was disgusted by the sight of his own penis because it was uncircumcised), and truly fetid racism, which the author generously extends to both blacks and all nonelite southerners, for each of whom he has an amazing series of half-witted epithets. Beyond the fag-baiting innuendo, the clusters of nonfact obscure the occasional research breakthroughs (which are more about Colonel Tom Parker than Elvis, anyway).

2. *NO ONE HERE GETS OUT ALIVE*, DANNY SUGERMANN AND JERRY HOPKINS

The rock bio for those who believe that what's truly cool and heroic in our time is making big poetic pronouncements and living up to them by the most ridiculous and pathetic sort of childish self-destructive behavior. Get a life.

3. *ROCK ON*, NORM N. NITE

An "encyclopedia" based on rewritten (or at least, retyped) press bios, reciting and spreading all manner of factual errors and observational clichés without offering a shred of insight. The hideous reality is that the original volume, which focused on pre-Beatles Music, sold well enough to get a Volume Two published that distorts and diminishes later music in the same fashion.

4. *ELVIS WORLD*, JANE AND MICHAEL STERN

These pop culture "lovers" have never found a subject to which they could not condescend. The problem here isn't that their Elvis exists amidst a mound of tacky trivia, it's that the authors are so goddamn smug about their superiority to the junk they've collected. Whatever the Sterns may feel about Elvis, their hatred of his audience runs rampant through these pages.

5. *THE LIVES OF JOHN LENNON*, ALBERT GOLDMAN

The bigotry—homophobia, anti-Asian racism, idle whacks at blacks—picks up where *Elvis* left off, as does the hysterical overwriting, the cultural myopia, and the unfactual research. Less horrid only in its effect—almost no one took this bullshit for anything but the desperate ravings of a hack with a "debunking" formula.

6. *RAISING PG KIDS IN AN X-RATED SOCIETY*, TIPPER GORE

Lies, damn lies, and statistics.

7. *ROCK STARS*, TIMOTHY WHITE

White, the only rock writer ever to be best-known for wearing a bowtie, picks out purple images and applies them almost at random to all manner of performers. His specialty is overblown "insight" into behavioral pecadilloes. His Bob Marley biography, *Catch a Fire*, possesses a certain utility, but as for the rest of his work, God! Keep this man away from a thesaurus.

8. *UNSUNG HEROES OF ROCK 'N' ROLL*, NICK TOSCHES

Who gave this man permission to call the great blues shouter Joe Turner "a big fat fuck"? Tosches can be a riotous read—for about five hundred words. Then his smug assurance that he's superior to his subject matter and his bizarre conviction that he's the true heir of beatnik prose upsets the picture, after which all that can be seen is somebody small assaulting something large.

9. *HIT MEN: POWER BROKERS AND FAST MONEY INSIDE THE MUSIC BUSINESS*, FREDERICK DANNEN

Dannen's theory is that bad men make an essentially honest system corrupt and that if you just got rid of a few moguls, power-brokers, and mob-connected businessmen, all would be hunky-dory in the world of popular music, or maybe just the world, period. A thesis so puerile it's no wonder it made the best-seller list.

10. *SIGNIFYING RAPPERS: RAP AND RACE IN THE URBAN PRESENT*, MARK COSTELLO AND DAVID FOSTER WALLACE

Even if it's not an (entirely) black thing, these white boys don't understand. Condescending and atrociously written postacademic pomp.

11. *THE POETRY OF ROCK*, RICHARD GOLDSTEIN

A bad idea poorly executed. Spawned many imitators, sad to say, from *The Poetry of Soul* to *Rap The Lyrics*. Do you think any of the editors of these projects spend much time considering the nature of rock, rap, and related music as matters of *aural* culture, and thus ill-suited to be abstracted to the page? They all say they do, but the evidence is otherwise.

12. *SOUND EFFECTS: YOUTH, LEISURE AND THE POLITICS OF ROCK 'N' ROLL*, SIMON FRITH

Taken for what it is—a parochial analysis of white-made popular music, in the declining market and production center that was Great Britain in the late seventies and early eighties—*Sound Effects* isn't so bad. It's even relatively free of sociological jargon, if not of sociological cant. But taken for gospel, as it has been by a generation of postpunk critics, it makes a massive muddle of analysis, particularly in the United States. Even on more narrow grounds, it is an extremely partial account of how the music industry works, and one that takes for granted that the function of popular culture cannot be any larger than the moment in which it offers pleasure.

And Then I Wrote . . . 25 Musicians Who Are Also Authors

1. CHUCK BERRY—What was unique about *The Autobiography* wasn't just that it revealed so much about the life and ambitions of one of music's most secretive geniuses, but that Berry actually wrote it himself.

2. PETE BEST—*Beatle*—the autobiography of rock's unluckiest man.

3. MICHAEL BLOOMFIELD—*Me and Big Joe* thinly fictionalizes an encounter between the budding white blues guitar wizard and one of his mentors, the great Delta-transplanted-to-Chicago bluesman Big Joe Williams

4. ERIC BURDON—*I Used to Be an Animal but I'm All Right Now*, his 1986 autobiography, had the distinction of being edited by Pete Townshend, when Pete moonlighted as an editor at Britain's prestigious Faber and Faber publishing company during the mid-eighties. Burdon's highly impressionistic account of his life and career unfortunately failed to make an impressive case for his most estimable talent.

5. LUTHER CAMPBELL—*As Nasty As They Wanna Be*, written with John R. Miller, recounts the history and sexual proclivities of the 2 Live Crew leader and his merry band with such alacrity and honesty that no American publisher would touch it. It had to be brought out in Jamaica and imported, instead.

6. EXENE CERVENKA AND LYDIA LUNCH—These postpunks (one a leading light of L.A.'s X, the other a No Wave heroine in New York) published their book of postmod poetry, *Adulterers Anonymous*, in 1982.

7. RAY CHARLES—*Brother Ray* is the first and best of David Ritz's ghostwritten tomes, precisely because its voice never ceases to belong to Charles himself. No matter how hard it may be to credit his account of his twenty-four hour release from heroin addiction, the rest of the book rings so true that you'll buy even its least plausible moments.

8. LEONARD COHEN—A dedicated poet and novelist long before he became a recording artist, Cohen has a whole shelf-full of titles available in Canada. Alfred A. Knopf published a large-scale anthology of his poetry in 1993.

9. BOB DYLAN—His 1970 volume, *tarantula*, called itself a novel, but only if you can figure out where Aretha Franklin fits into his plot.

10. MICK FLEETWOOD—Not the least interesting member of his band, but of *My Life and Adventures in Fleetwood Mac*, the only thing you—or anybody else—is likely to recall is that he screwed Stevie Nicks (or she him). Which, let's face it, could've been guessed.

11. BOB GELDOF—The cheeky Irish rocker's autobiography, *Is That It?* (1986) appeared in the wake of the Band Aid and Live-Aid events he spearheaded.

12. GEORGE HARRISON—The autobiographical *I Me Mine* came out in a 1979 limited edition costing several hundred dollars, then appeared in 1981 as a lower-cost, though still essentially worthless, reprint.

13. IAN HUNTER—His *Autobiography of a Rock Star*, probably the first book by a rock star about *being* a rock star (certainly the first such published), came out in England in 1974. It never found an American publisher, probably because Mott the Hoople, his band, never found much of a U.S. career.

14. MICHAEL JACKSON—*Moonwalk* is the least qualified tell-all show-biz book ever written. His corporate sponsor for this one should have been Crayola.

15. AL KOOPER—*Backstage Passes*, written with Ben Edmonds, may be the frankest, if certainly the funniest first-person account of rock in the sixties.

16. JOHN LENNON—The original rock 'n' roll author with his comedic prose fiction, *In His Own Write* (1964) and *A Spaniard in the Works* (1965). These may have been published solely because of Beatlemania but they're still read because they're hilarious, far more droll than most of the avant-gardism they mock. The posthumous *Skywriting by Word of Mouth* lacks the focus of the early material, though.

17. MADONNA—*Erotica* shocked the shockable, bored the borable, delighted the predisposed, made millions, fell apart in your hands. In short, not an autobiography but the plot's the same.

18. GLEN MATLOCK—*I Was a Teenage Sex Pistol* (1990) essentially his riposte to history as ventilated by Messrs. McLaren and Rotten-Lydon. As such, it's one of the most intimate accounts of punk.

19. JIM MORRISON—*The Lords* and *The New Creatures*, compilations of his jejune psychedelicized poetry, were completed in his lifetime and published in 1970. Posthumous volumes—such as *American Prayer*—are even weaker as Jimbo's essential conceit ages badly.

20. JOHNNY OTIS—In *Listen to the Lambs* (1970), he recounts his history as a white passing for black with careers as band-leader, preacher and politician.

21. PATTI SMITH—She's published five volumes of poetry, beginning with *Seventh Heaven*, which appeared in 1973, well before she and Lenny Kaye started a band. Her poetry remains the greatest rock poetry because not only its subject matter but its cadences and rhythmic nuances derive directly from the turntable in her head.

22. PETE TOWNSHEND—*Horse's Neck* includes any number of stories, of varying degrees of comprehensibility, some of which establish that Townshend really did pay attention in art school, others that his lack of narrative ability isn't confined to rock opera, yet all somehow fascinating in the way that his musical psychodramas can sometimes be. Also, all somehow embarrassing in precisely the same degree.

23. TINA TURNER—*I Tina*, written with Kurt Loder before he'd ever seen the inside of an MTV studio, constitutes its own genre: The superstar autobiography as Movie of the Week.

24. BILL WYMAN—*Stone Alone* gets you closer to the inside of the Rolling Stones than any other book ever penned. It's amazing how boring and unrevealing a place it turns out to be.

25. FRANK ZAPPA—Zappa finally found a rock critic he liked in Peter Occhiogrosso and settled in to write *The Real Frank Zappa Book*, an autobiography, with him. It sets many details straight, renders many great stories, several salient facts, and more than a few crusty opinions. Not at all unlike listening to a good Zappa album.

Author! Author!
Rockers Who Should Write Books

1. ELVIS PRESLEY—Earlier in his career, it would have been ruinously anticlimatic, but now. . . . Think of the headlines! (Besides, what else does a rock star living in Kalamazoo have to do with his time?)

2. ARETHA FRANKLIN—For one thing, she already had a deal for about $400,000 and spit the bit, reportedly because the money wasn't sufficient, possibly because the story's too sordid to contemplate for long. But if she doesn't sell it, somebody else will and that'll most likely make her even more miserable.

3. DAVID BYRNE—It'd shut him up for a while

4. AFRIKA BAMBAATAA—A book to set the ignorant straight on the history, purposes, and potential of hip-hop. It'd be dedicated to Wynton Marsalis and Stanley Crouch.

5. CHUCK D—To give his enemies more ammunition for their lies.

6. JOHN MELLENCAMP—He can always use another excuse not to paint.

7. DARLENE LOVE—A chance to get one of rock's greatest, and bitterest, untold stories off her chest. And to defend her cooking against the scripts of *Lethal Weapon II* and *III*.

8. MICK JAGGER—He got as much money as Aretha wanted—a cool million—but spit the bit anyway, probably because he shrinks so readily from revelation.

9. KEITH RICHARDS—Just to piss off Mick.

10. BOY GEORGE—With malice afterthought.

11. BONNIE RAITT—Because she could fund the Rhythm and Blues Foundation for a decade with the proceeds, since every publisher in New York would kill to publish her memoirs.

12. VAN MORRISON—In Gaelic.

Buckle Down!
Rockers Who Should *Read* Books

1. SAMMY HAGAR—And not Rush Limbaugh's.

2. RICHARD MARX—Anything that keeps him from singing.

3. SNOOP DOGGY DOGG—Just to prove he can.

4. EDDIE VEDDER—Pop psychology recommended—even pop star psychology.

5. ROD STEWART—It's be less destructive to his marriage than his other hobbies.

6. PAUL SIMON—Recommended: critical analyses of imperialism and neocolonialism.

7. LUTHER CAMPBELL—Knowing Luther, he'd probably come out of it with a comedy album based on Susan Faludi's *Backlash*.

8. MICHAEL BOLTON—We'd recommend books on magic paying special attention to chapters on how to disappear.

9. ERIC CLAPTON—Something's got to get his nose out of those fashion magazines.

10. MICHELLE SHOCKED—Volumes of black history, starting with W. E. B. DuBois's *The Souls of Black Folk*, to serve as a corrective to her very strange theories about African-American history and the roots and function of hip-hop.

Loosen Up!
Rockers Who Should Read Fewer Books

1. ELVIS COSTELLO—Who *cares* why people write letters to Shakespearean characters?

2. JACKSON BROWNE—Pulp fiction possibly acceptable but definitely no current events.

3. ANDY PARTRIDGE (XTC)—To take a break, and just to remind yourself that you're a real guy, not a fictional conceit. (You are, aren't you?)

4. TOM WAITS—Take the pledge on that beatnik stuff. No fair unloading all that used Kenneth Rexroth on poor Rickie Lee Jones, either.

5. KRS-ONE—More fresh beats, fewer stale facts.

6. BRUCE SPRINGSTEEN—Cut him off till his music catches up with his lyrics.

7. ROBERT FRIPP—And cancel his subscription to *Guitar Player* while you're at it.

8. BILLY JOEL—Those high-school textbooks always were a yawn for the rest of us. Setting them to music doesn't help.

9. RAY DAVIES (THE KINKS)—You're too old to be Bertie Wooster, anyhow.

10. VERNON REID—Spend that spare time learning how to make your band swing. (Hint: It starts with operating as a *unit*, not a collection of soloists.)

"We Play Music As Well As Metallica Writes Novels"
The Rock Bottom Remainders

In 1992, San Francisco media escort Kathi Goldmark, who drives around with authors on book promotion tours in that city, invited several of those she knew best to play a show with her at the American Booksellers Association convention in Anaheim. Those who agreed to join the band, dubbed the Rock Bottom Remainders in reference to books that don't sell, then hired Al Kooper, a rock veteran and author of Backstage Passes *(1976), to teach them how to put on a passable show. They enjoyed it so much that they did an entire tour the next year, traveling from Boston to Miami Beach, where that year's ABA convention was held. This threatens to become an annual event and, given the overall competence of the musicians, one of the most sordid chapters in rock and soul history. Or as Remainder emcee Roy*

Blount, Jr., put it each night when introducing the show, "Ladies and gentlemen, suspend your credibility for the Rock Bottom Remainders!"

1. Dave Barry
2. Tad Bartimus
3. Roy Blount, Jr.[1]
4. Michael Dorris[2]
5. Robert Fulghum
6. Kathi Goldmark
7. Matt Groening[1]
8. Josh Kelly[3]
9. Stephen King
10. Barbara Kingsolver
11. Al Kooper
12. Greil Marcus[1]
13. Dave Marsh[1]
14. Ridley Pearson
15. Jerry Peterson[1]
16. Joel Selvin[1]
17. Amy Tan

---

[1] Members of the Critics' Chorus (aka the Society for the Singing Impaired).
[2] Anaheim only.
[3] Ringer (pro musician, not a writer).

Truman Capote's 10 Favorite Rock Performers

1. Bruce Springsteen
2. The Who
3. The Rolling Stones
4. Rod Stewart
5. The Doobie Brothers
6. The Eagles
7. The Grateful Dead
8. Pat Benatar
9. The Cars
10. Blondie

Truman Capote was one of America's leading novelists and talk-show celebrities until his untimely death in 1984. Among his most important books were Breakfast at Tiffany's, *the "nonfiction novel"* In Cold Blood, *and* Answered Prayers.

Best Liner Notes

1. Nelson George, James Brown, Alan M. Leeds, Cliff White, and Harry Weinger, *Star Time*, James Brown (Polydor)
2. Robert Palmer, Bo Diddley, *Bo Diddley* (Chess/MCA box set)
3. Malcolm Jones and John Beecher, *The Complete Buddy Holly* (MCA box set)
4. Marty Ostrow, *I Want Candy*, The Strangeloves
5. Jim Dawson, *Hang Your Tears Out to Dry*, Jesse Belvin (Earth Angel/Sweden)

6. Greil Marcus, *The Basement Tapes*, Bob Dylan and the Band (Columbia)
7. Unsigned, *Elvis*, Elvis Presley (RCA, his second album)
8. Bruce Springsteen, *I Don't Want To Go Home*, Southside Johnny and the Asbury Jukes (Epic)
9. Bill Millar, *A Shot of Rhythm and Soul*, Arthur Alexander (Ace/UK)
10. Jerry Wexler, *The Ray Charles Story, Volumes 1 and 2* (Atlantic)
11. Lenny Kaye, Lester Bangs, Kosmo Vinyl, *The Clash on Broadway* (Epic)
12. John Swenson, Ron O'Brien, with Andy McKaie, *Lynyrd Skynyrd* (MCA box set)
13. John Sinclair, *Kick Out the Jams*, The MC5 (Elektra)
14. Peter Grendysa, *Let the Good Times Roll*, Louis Jordan (Bear Family/Germany)
15. Paul Ackerman, *History of Rhythm and Blues, Volumes 5 and 6* (Atlantic)
16. Jon Landau, *Tell the Truth*, Otis Redding (Atlantic)
17. William Ruhlmann, Paul Revere, Mark Lindsay, *The Legend of Paul Revere*, Paul Revere and the Raiders (featuring Mark Lindsay) (Columbia)
18. Andrew Loog Oldham, *The Rolling Stones, Now!* (London)
19. Dave Marsh, Dean Torrance, *Jan and Dean Legendary Masters Series* (United Artists)
20. Lester Bangs, *Them featuring Van Morrison* (London, anthology, not original Them album)
21. Peter Guralnick, *My Story*, Chuck Willis (Epic)
22. Bob Galgano, Sal Mandrone, Tom Luciani, *Echoes of a Rock Era, The Groups: The Heartbeats / Shep and the Limelites* (Roulette)
23. Peter Blecha, *The Best of the Kingsmen* (Rhino)
24. Donn Fileti, *The Five Royales Sing Laundromat Blues, The Five Royales Sing Baby Don't Do it* (Relic)
25. Phil Groia, Bob Hyde, *Frankie Lymon and the Teenagers* (Murray Hill box set)

Worst Liner Notes

1. Pete Hamill, *Blood on the Tracks*, Bob Dylan (Columbia)—So bad they were quickly deleted, although Hamill *did* win a Grammy for them, even after that.
2. Process Church of the Final Judgment, *America Eats Its Young*, Funkadelic (Westbound)—Truly scary stuff and George Clinton did not make it up.
3. John Bauldie, *The Bootleg Series Volumes 1–3*, Bob Dylan (Columbia)—Assiduously narrows the context of Dylan's music, with-

out understanding most of his references to folklore or folk music and with altogether too much emphasis on his "literary quality."

4. Full Force, *Smoove* (Columbia)—Eight full pages of notes, consisting entirely of thank yous and such side-of-the-mouth remarks as "My florist bill is higher than the cost of my house but I don't give a shit!" (Columbia).

5. (tie) Donovan, *Catch the Wind* (Hickory).

5. (tie) Andrew Loog Oldham, *December's Children (and Everybody's)*, The Rolling Stones (London)—If you're going to do a bad Bob Dylan imitation, it's his music you should copy, not his prose.

7. Janet Planet, *His Band and the Street Choir*, Van Morrison (Warner Bros.)—Some of the most banal hippie blather ever written.

8. John Mendelsohn, *Arthur (or the Decline and Fall of the British Empire)*, the Kinks (Reprise)—Overwrought, overripe, and half-baked.

9. Robert Fripp, *God Save the Queen/Under Heavy Manners*, Robert Fripp (Atlantic)—Makes Bono look humble.

10. Marvin Gaye, *Let's Get It On*, Marvin Gaye (Tamla)—Makes Madonna seem like a celibate.

Mike Callahan's "Rock and Roll Soap Opera"
20 Tragic Tales

1. "TEEN ANGEL," MARK DINNING

Mark's girlfriend is flattened by a train when she rushes back to the car, stalled on the tracks, to retrieve his high-school ring. (With the price of gold what it is today, I can see why.) Mark is left singing to the sky, asking that his Teen Angel answer him, please. Tune into number 4 for the next installment.

2. "TELL LAURA I LOVE HER," RAY PETERSON

Poor Tom can't support Laura in the way he'd like, but he sees a way to make a quick buck by entering the local stock car races. He flips his car in the heat of battle, killing himself. Heartbroken Laura later has a supernatural experience when she hears Tommy's voice in the chapel while she prays for his reckless soul.

3. "THE WATER WAS RED," JOHNNY CYMBAL

In this early *Jaws* thriller, Johnny and his true love enjoy a few lovely nights on the deserted beach, watching the last rays of the sun turn the water red. One day, however, while Johnny's girl is swimming, a shark rips her to shreds. Johnny wades through the bloody waves and hauls her remains to shore, then materializes a knife and swims out to kill the shark. As the song ends, Johnny is wading back to shore, once more through red waves, carrying the shark's fin. *Ole!*

4. "THE PICKUP," MARK DINNING

Mark simply doesn't have any luck with women. In this song, his friends dare him to date the town tramp, and after two years of singing to the sky, he figures he might as well. As luck would have it, Mark and the Pickup fall in love. Under normal circumstances, this would set the stage for a happy ending. But Mark can't stand the thought of telling his friends that he loves the Pickup, so instead, he dumps *her*. The poor Pickup is driven to leaping off a bridge and Mark is left to read about it in the paper the next day.

5. "PATCHES," DICKEY LEE

Another suicide, this one with a surprise ending. Patches, the poor girl from Shantytown, has her hopes inflated when she dates Dickey, but soon he's forbidden by his dad to see her again. Despairing, Patches drowns herself in the dirty old river that runs by the coal yard. When he hears of the tragedy, Dickey just can't go on, and as the story ends, he's preparing to commit suicide, too

6. "GIVE US YOUR BLESSING," THE SHANGRI-LAS

The kids were in love, but their folks laughed and told them they were too young. After one final attempt to get parental approval, the young couple drive off with tears in their eyes to elope, miss a detour sign, and total both the car and themselves. The next morning, in the rain, the parents kneel beside the bodies of their kids. From somewhere off in the great beyond, the kids are probably thinking, "Now I'll bet you're sorry."

7. "DEAD MAN'S CURVE," JAN AND DEAN

Our hot-rod hero is cruising in his Sting-Ray late one night when a guy driving an XKE challenges him to a drag. They agree to come off the line at Sunset and Vine and race all the way to Dead Man's Curve. When they get to the curve, the singer cracks up his car and is hospitalized. But he recovers sufficiently to make a million-seller telling his story. (Jan and Dean actually recorded a ten-minute version of the saga, a year or so before Jan Berry had a remarkably similar auto accident in 1965. It's included on the original LP version of United Artists' *Jan and Dean: Legendary Master Series*.)

8. "LAST KISS," J. FRANK WILSON AND THE CAVALIERS

Yet another car crash. J. Frank crashes his daddy's car into a stalled vehicle and manages to cancel his date, permanently. He makes it up to her by giving his baby one last kiss after she's checked out, holding out strong hopes for a reunion in the next world.

9. "THE LEADER OF THE PACK," THE SHANGRI-LAS

Jimmy, a leather-jacket biker, meets Betty at the candy store (an updated version would probably be set in a video game arcade).

Betty's parents forbid her to see her new, scruffy beau, and after a tearful breakup scene, Betty watches as Jimmy revs up and peels out, only to crash before her horrified eyes. Where is the Pack when you need it? This record spawned several takeoffs, including the Detergents' "Leader of the Laundromat," in which the heroine meets her untimely demise under the wheels of a garbage truck, and Jimmy Cross's "I Want My Baby Back," which is sick, sick, sick.

10. "I CAN NEVER GO HOME ANYMORE," THE SHANGRI-LAS

After her brief and unsuccessful fling with the Leader of the Pack, our heroine latches on to another boy, but once more, her mean, nasty parents demand a breakup. Not wanting another bike crash on her hands, the girl leaves home with her guy, only to find that life in the real world can get pretty hairy. Pride keeps her from going home, however, and she's doomed to drift aimlessly and alone for the rest of her life. Her mother, who took the departure (you could hardly call it an elopement) badly, finally dies of loneliness. As the episode ends, our heroine has become a counselor, devoting her life to preventing other young girls from repeating her errors.

11. "THE HERO," BERNADETTE CARROLL

Sue is pretty snooty about snaring the high-school football hero, and lets everybody know that they'll be married after graduation. As the story opens, Sue is sitting at home, wondering why Johnny isn't back from the game, which is only thirty miles away. The phone rings. Sue grabs it, and breathlessly answers, "Johnny? Johnny?" Alas, it's Patty, her girlfriend, who has just learned that the bus turned over and the entire team was killed. As the song ends, Sue has collapsed in a pool of self-pity, her dreams dashed to pieces. (Doesn't anybody here care about the rest of the team?)

12. "A YOUNG GIRL," NOEL HARRISON

A girl from a filthy-rich neighborhood runs off with a vagabond, who seduces her with words she's never heard (?!?) In the end, he dumps her, and she's found by the side of the road, a girl of sixteen, child of springtime so green, dead. Tsk, tsk.

13. "BILLY AND SUE," B. J. THOMAS

Everything was going fine for Billy and Sue when that evil Vietnam War cropped up and he got his ass drafted. He went off to war, Sue went off to party. For months, he wrote her religiously without receiving a reply. Finally, during an intense firefight (?), Billy gets a letter from Sue. It opens, "Dear John." Billy is so surprised that Sue has forgotten his name that he stands up in the trench and gets greased by Charlie. A likely story.

14. "NIGHTMARE," WHYTE BOOTS

Everyone likes to see a good cat fight, and when one of the girls in school steals Bobby from Lori, Lori's friends egg her on. Lori doesn't like the idea much, but she's swept up as her friends chant,

"Get her! Get her!" Lori kills her antagonist, and the police come to haul her off to jail. In the end, she proclaims: "I didn't want to fight, but what could I do? No boy is worth the trouble I'm in."

15. "ODE TO BILLIE JOE," BOBBIE GENTRY

Soap opera, down-home style, the pieces of a puzzle presented between snatches of dinner-table small talk. Bobbie and Billy Joe have evidently been having a secret affair, but it is only at dinner that Bobbie learns that Billy Joe has jumped off the Tallahatchee Bridge. This one is so complicated that they made a movie out of it; if you want to get all of the plot, see the flick.

16. "CONDITION RED," THE GOODIES

A story similar to "Leader of the Pack," but this time the parents disapprove because the boyfriend needs a haircut and a shave. Aside from being somewhat hilarious, this record is notable as the first tragedy song to feature the police "yelp" siren rather than the old "whine" variety.

17. "MR. TURNKEY," ZAGER AND EVANS

A sickie. Our boy is in prison for raping a woman who teased him in a Wichita Falls bar. After half a song of listening to him describe her beauty and how much he hates himself, we discover that he's nailed his left wrist to the cell wall and is hanging there bleeding to death. His last words are "Tell her I'm sorry." This was Zager and Evans's followup to the massive world hit "In the Year 2525."

18. "D.O.A." BLOODROCK

An unbelievably gruesome account of a plane crash victim's trip to the hospital in an ambulance. He describes, in graphic detail, seeing that his arm has been torn off, watching his girlfriend die next to him, hearing an attendant say he has no chance, the feeling of bleeding to death, and finally, death itself, This scandal sheet even hit the Top Forty.

19. "EMMA," HOT CHOCOLATE

Emma's childhood dream was to become a movie star. Her boyfriend, who'd been with her from age five until they were married at seventeen, shared her vision. But in her late teens, Emma finds the road to stardom too tough, and late one December, her husband finds her dead in their bedroom, love letter in her hand. Merry Christmas.

20. "POINT BLANK," BRUCE SPRINGSTEEN

Many of Springsteen's songs could fall into the soap-opera category, but in another way, his music is much more sophisticated and realistic than that of rock's earlier dabblers in melodrama. Looking over the list of tragedies from 1959 onward, there's an obvious progression from pure fantasy to more realistic events. "Point Blank" is perhaps the prototypical tragedy of the 1980s. We learn of a little girl saying her prayers at night, then follow her as she grows up, accepting what her elders teach, falling in Romeo-and-Juliet love, dancing at the clubs with her boyfriend. From there, in *Looking for*

Mr. Goodbar fashion, her life unravels. She starts walking the streets, and finally, she's dead, shot point blank. But her spirit was killed long before. There's probably some more existential degree to which rock soap opera could be taken (John Mellencamp's "Jackie Brown" tries), but why bother?

Mike Callahan has been a record collector since 1954, specializing in early stereo rock and roll and Top Forty music. He has been music director of WMOD-FM, an all-oldies station in Washington, D.C., where he also produced shows, a columnist for Goldmine *and* Classic Wax *magazines, and a contributor to Jerry Osborne and Bruce Hamilton's* Price Guide, *the bible of record collectors. He's also edited and published* Both Sides Now, *a newsletter for stereo collectors.*

Every Day I Sing the Book

1. "The Book I Read," The Talking Heads
2. "Book of Dreams," Suzanne Vega
3. "The Book of Love," The Monotones
4. "Buying a Book," Joe Tex
5. "Every Day I Write the Book," Elvis Costello
6. "I Could Write a Book," Jerry Butler
7. "If You Could Read My Mind," Gordon Lightfoot
8. "Life Is Just a Book," Ernest Lawlars
9. "My Back Pages," The Byrds
10. "My Little Red Book," Love
11. "Old Friends / Bookends," Simon and Garfunkel
12. "Paperback Writer," The Beatles
13. "The Snake and the Bookworm," The Coasters[1]
14. "You Can Make the Story Right," Chaka Khan[2]
15. "You Can't Judge a Book by Its Cover," Bo Diddley
16. "You're in My Book First," Jimmy McCracklin

---

[1] This song does *not* encapsulate the history of rock criticism. Only the idea of it.
[2] Editor's delight.

CHAPTER 13

Fashion

Stylin' and Profilin'
The Rock 'n' Rap Wardrobe

1. "The Angels Wanna Wear My Red Shoes," Elvis Costello
2. "Aphrodisiac Jacket," The Cult
3. "Back to My Roots," RuPaul
4. "Black Leatherette," The Sex Pistols
5. "Black Slacks," Joe Bennett and the Sparkletones
6. "Blue Jean Bop," Gene Vincent and the Blue Caps
7. "Blue Suede Shoes," Carl Perkins
8. "Blue Velvet," Bobby Vinton
9. "Boogie Shoes," KC and the Sunshine Band
10. "Boots of Spanish Leather," Bob Dylan
11. "Brown Shoes Don't Make It," The Mothers of Invention
12. "Chantilly Lace," The Big Bopper
13. "Cheap Sunglasses," ZZ Top
14. "Dawn of the Dreads," Arrested Development
15. "Devil With a Blue Dress On," Shorty Long
16. "Diamonds and Pearls," Prince
17. "Dying With Your Boots On," Scarface
18. "Gucci Time," Schoolly D
19. "Harborcoat," R.E.M.
20. "Hi-Heel Sneakers," Tommy Tucker
21. "Hot Pants," James Brown
22. "Itsy Bitsy Teenie Weenie Yellow Polkadot Bikini," Brian Hyland
23. "Leave My Curl Alone," Hi C
24. "Leopard-skin Pill-box Hat," Bob Dylan
25. "Lipstick," Buzzcocks
26. "Long Cool Woman (in a Black Dress)," The Hollies
27. "My Adidas," Run-D.M.C.
28. "My Drawers," The Time
29. "My Umbrella," Tripping Daisy
30. "No Nose Job," Digital Underground
31. "Patches," Clarence Carter
32. "Short Shorts," The Royal Teens
33. "Sad Dress," Belly
34. "Skintight," Ohio Players
35. "Spanish Boots," Jeff Beck
36. "Sucker in a 3 Piece Suit," Van Halen
37. "Sunglasses after Dark," The Cramps
38. "Thirsty Boots," Eric Andersen
39. "Venus in Blue Jeans," Jimmy Clanton
40. "Why Do I Wear My Fro," The Afros

The Source Magazine's Hip-Hop Fashion Do's and Don'ts

THE WACK LIST

1. "8-Ball Jackets"
2. Rainbrow Brite hair: Hair should be one color. One believable color. Unless, of course, you're George Clinton.
3. Shredded clothes: The recent wave of dancehall videos have shown us how wrong this look can be.
4. The copycat look: Kris Kross said "Jump!" not "Wear your clothes backward!" So if you're not thirteen, don't try it.
5. Truck jewelry: Don't OG (overgold) on multiple dookey ropes.
6. Barely there fashions: Don't go for the Soul Train Award. When too much of your stuff hangs out, you risk being picked up by Luke's video directors on a one-way to Miami.
7. Wack kicks: There are ample selections of the right brands and color combinations, so why mess around with a pair that your grandfather would wear with sky-blue socks?
8. Beeper-in-a-stupid-place/beeper accessories: Remove pagers from cap brims, ties, and sneakers. And we strongly suggest a move away from leather beeper cases.
9. Things that are too big: The oversized rule does not mean gear should make you look sloppy, fat, or unkempt.
10. Anything bootleg: Don't cheapen your look with peeling letters and crooked logos. If it ain't the real thing, leave it alone. That includes your Black Bart Simpson Tee's and "I Love Rap" hats.

THE DOPE LIST

1. Headgear: Fitted baseball caps are the best flavor. Skullies a la Das EFX. Tie tops are cool too.
2. Vests: The ever-popular vest, layered under a jacket or on its own over a T, always adds flavor. Down vests, plaid vests, denim vests—any vest.
3. Baseball-style jerseys: Not quite shirts, not exactly jackets— jerseys work over turtlenecks, over T's, or alone. Of course, the doper the logo, the fatter the jersey.
4. Negro League Wear: In remembrance of the brothers who played the game but never got paid. Imagine this, the original school, like the Cuban X Giants on a hat, jersey, or jacket.
5. Natural heads: Anything natural is so much better. Bald, blown-out, braids, or nappy. Just no Jheri curls.
6. Boots: Rude, rough boots. Jeans in or out, this is the rugged style that will last for years to come.
7. Colored denim: When you get tired of blue, try green or red or brown.

8. Top stitching: Not just fat on denim but even more flavor on leather and suede. Contrasting stitch like white on black, or red on blue is the new look.
9. Plaid shirts and jackets: Great in cotton, flannel, or wool—check for hooded ones.
10. Old-school flavor with a new-school twist: Especially sneaks.
11. Work wear: Once for construction workers and custodians but now for everybody. Detailing like snaps or toggles enhances the look. Rugged and durable is definitely in and won't break your pockets.

Originally published in The Source, *January 1993.*

Music Stars Who Have Made Mr. Blackwell's Worst-Dressed List

Since 1960, Mr. Blackwell has been America's fashion arbiter, a self-appointed watchdog of the garment trade who each year issues his lists of the best- and worst-dressed celebrities, together with pithy comments about the latter.

1. David Bowie, 1973—"A cross between Joan Crawford and Marlene Dietrich doing a glitter revival of New Faces!"
2. Cher, a five-time winner—1974: "Looks like a Hawaiian bar mitzvah!" 1984: "A plucked cockatoo setting femininity back twenty years!" 1986: "Popular Mechanics Playmate of the month. Someone must have thrown a monkey wrench into her fashion taste!" 1989: " 'If she could turn back time,' she'd still be a bag of tattooed bones in a sequined slingshot." (For her other award, keep reading.)
3. Deborah Harry, 1979—"Ten cents a dance, with a nickel change!"
4. Elton John, 1975—"Would be the campiest spectacle in the Rose Parade!"
5. Loretta Lynn, a two-timer—1976: "The right dress in the wrong century!" 1981: "Up the music charts, down the fashion charts!"
6. Bette Midler, a four-timer—1973: "Potluck in a laundromat." 1975: "Betsy Bloomer . . . didn't pantaloons go out with hoop skirts?" 1978: "She didn't go to a rummage sale, she wore it!" 1982: "Second-Hand Rose after a hurricane!"
7. Olivia Newton-John, a two-time winner—1978: "The right dress in the wrong century!" 1983: "From toes to nose, a shredded tragedy."

8. Yoko Ono, 1972—"A disaster in stereo . . . oh, no, Yoko!"
9. Dolly Parton, a quadruple-award winner—1977: "Scarlett O'Hara dressed like Mae West in *My Little Chickadee!*" 1978: "Too many yards of Dolly poured into too few yards of fabric!" 1979: "A ruffled bedspread covering king-sized pillows!" 1981: "An atomic jelly bean explosion!"
10. The Pointer Sisters, 1974—"Their fashion instinct is definitely *pointed* in the *wrong* direction!"
11. Helen Reddy, two-time award winner—1974: "Isn't ready!" 1975: "She spent the year proving I was right . . . should have saved her costumes for the Bicentennial!"
12. Linda Ronstadt, another two-time loser—1977: "Bought her entire wardrobe during a five-minute bus stop!" 1978: "Hits the high note in song, low note in fashion!"
13. Tammy Wynette and Donna Fargo, 1975—"Tied for yearly double . . . country magic dressed in circus tents!"
14. Marie Osmond, 1980—"Someone should unplug this Christmas tree!"
15. Barbara Mandrell, 1981—"Yukon Sally playing the Alamo!"
16. Sheena Easton, 1981—"A London roadrunner dressed for the fog!"
17. Barbra Streisand, a four-time winner—1983: "A boy version of Medusa!" 1984: "The Al Capone look with electrocuted hair!" 1986: "A shoddy Second-Hand Rose looking for a tour guide in Brooklyn!" 1990: "What can I say? Yentl's gone mental!"
18. Joan Jett, 1983—"A Bronx Pocahontas in black leather goes porn!"
19. Boy George, 1983—"Victor/Victoria in bad drag!"
20. Cyndi Lauper, 1984—"Looks like the aftermath of the San Francisco earthquake!"
21. Twisted Sister and Prince, 1984—Twisted Sister: "A Mardi Gras nightmare!" Prince: "A toothpick wrapped in a purple doilie!"
22. Tina Turner, 1985—"Some women dress for men . . . some dress for women . . . some dress for laughs!"
23. Apollonia, 1985—"Living proof that every prince needs his jester. Big Bird bites the dust!"
24. Cyndi Lauper (her second) and Cher (her fourth), 1987—"Minsky's rejects, still trying!"
25. Madonna, a three-time winner—1988: "Helpless, hopeless, and horrendous!" 1992: "The Bare-bottomed Bore of Babylon . . . looks like an over-the-hill Lolita, sinking in a sea of sleaze! A masochistic monstrosity!" (For her third, see below.)
26. LaToya Jackson, a two-timer—1989: "More fashion freak than biker chic. In leather and chains, she's Cher for the nineties." 1992: "This over-hyped horror . . . is a hymn to Halloween— 365 nightmares a year!"

27. Madonna (her second) and Sandra Bernhard (her first), 1989 —"The Mutt and Jeff of MTV: vampy, trampy, and cartoon campy."
28. Grace Jones, "Fashion Fiasco of the Year Award, 1989"— "Darth Vader's fantasy in a Martian bird cage."
29. Sinead O'Connor, her second—1990: "Nothing compares to the bald-headed banshee of MTV. A New Age nightmare!" 1992: "No tresses, no dresses—The High Priestess of Pretense down-right depresses!"
30. Wynonna Judd, 1991—"The shaggy songbird of country kitsch looks like Hulk Hogan—in sequins.
31. Carly Simon, 1991—"Little Orphan Annie meets Mr. Ed. A fright-wigged fiasco of the Carly kind."

Music Stars Who Have Made Mr. Blackwell's "Fabulous Fashion Independents" List

1. Diana Ross: 1979
2. Lena Horne: 1981, 1982
3. Liza Minnelli: 1988, 1989
4. Bette Midler: 1991
5. Barbra Streisand: 1991
6. Vanessa Williams: 1992

Rockers with Items in the Hard Rock Café

NEW YORK

1. Jimi Hendrix—Trademark felt hat with his scarf hatband; antique Civil War belt
2. Prince—*Purple Rain*–era costume, including his purple cotton and leather Edwardian-style jacket with chrome studs across one breast, his patterned velvet pants, gathered with white buttons up the sides
3. Joan Jett—Her Converse high-top sneakers
4. Chrissie Hynde—Warner Brothers wool-and-leather baseball jacket, autographed on the sleeve
5. Elvis Presley—Elaborately decorated stage costume from the Las Vegas period. Designed by Bill Belew, it features a one-piece jumpsuit, cape, and boots heavily bejeweled with a floral motif of colored glass and brass studs. Lined in red stain. The boots are monogrammed with the initials "EP" in brass studs.

6. Felix Pappalardi (late bassist, Mountain and Cream)—Blue embroidered jacket; reverse lambskin and leather vest; power amulet of braided feather trimmed with tufts of Jimi Hendrix's hair; intricately beaded belt in a flower motif; embroidered black velvet sash with astrological symbols; pair of buckskin bellbottoms with beaded inserts worn at Woodstock

7. Joe Walsh—two-piece black velvet, rhinestone, and cut glass stage costume worn in performance at Carnegie Hall with the James Gang, circa 1969

8. Muhammad Ali—Warmup robe given to him by Elvis Presley. Designed by Bill Belew, it is elaborately decorated with colored glass and brass studs. Says "People's Choice" on the back in blue metal studs.

9. The Ramones—Joey's black leather motorcycle jacket autographed by the band

10. Cub Koda (rock journalist; Brownsville Station; wrote and recorded "Smokin' in the Boys Room")—Trademark costume featuring a black-and-white-striped referee's shirt, Acme "Thunderer" referee's whistle, and "stylistically advanced" spectacles with case

11. John Lennon—Blue-tinted, gold-rimmed glasses worn while performing "Live In New York City"

12. The Sex Pistols—Promotional T-shirt for "Nevermind the Bollocks . . ." and clear vinyl schoolbag

13. The Blues Brothers—Jake and Elwood's original hats and sunglasses

LONDON

1. Jimi Hendrix—Buckskin tasseled jacket together with antique German canteen; hand-tooled silver concho belt adorned with turquoise, onyx, and semiprecious stones, probably of Zuni tribe origin

2. Little Richard—Black leather and snakeskin boots

3. Keith Moon—Harley Davidson leather motorcycle cap signed for the Hell's Angels by Keith and Pete Townshend

4. Iron Maiden—Bruce Dickinson's fake fur and leather stage pants, signed by Bruce

5. Cliff Richards (The Shadows)—Two sport coats, one seersucker and one red rayon

6. Ozzy Osbourne—Autographed, white leather stage shoes from 1984 World Tour

7. David Bowie—Levi's 501 blue jeans, autographed to the Hard Rock Café

8. Jeff Beck—White cotton and black velvet jacket worn while with the Yardbirds, autographed

9. Jimmy Page—White cotton and black velvet jacket worn as one of the Yardbirds

10. Eric Clapton—White cotton and black velvet jacket worn as one of the Yardbirds, autographed
11. The Beatles—Original Beatles wig in its original package
12. Elton John—A pair of sunglasses
13. John Lennon—Black worsted wool and velvet sports jacket by D. A. Millings and Son
14. Ringo Starr—Synthetic fur vest worn in his NBC-TV Special, "Ognir Rrats"

20 Groups Known for Their Costumes

1. The Beatles
2. The Blues Magoos
3. Boys II Men
4. The Dave Clark Five
5. The Commodores
6. Devo
7. Green Jelly
8. Hammer
9. The J.B.'s
10. Kiss
11. Kris Kross
12. Motley Crue (circa 1982)
13. Parliament-Funkadelic
14. Gary Puckett and the Union Gap
15. Grandmaster Flash and the Furious Five
16. The Residents
17. Paul Revere and the Raiders
18. The S1W's (of Public Enemy)
19. The Temptations
20. The Village People

Fashion Accessories for the Serious Funkadelic Clone

1. Diaper
2. Shoulder-length platinum wig
3. Copious face paint
4. Holiday Inn bedsheet with hole in the middle
5. Knee-high platform boots
6. Bat wings
7. Crotchless tie-dyed long johns
8. Fencing mask
9. Indian headdress
10. Birthday suit

25 Known for Their Hats

1. Clint Black
2. Garth Brooks
3. Chuck D
4. Clarence Clemons
5. Charlie Daniels
6. The Edge
7. Bob Dylan
8. Kinky Friedman
9. Jimi Hendrix
10. Humpty Hump
11. Janis Ian
12. Elton John
13. Janis Joplin
14. Little Steven
15. L.L. Cool J
16. The Ohio Players
17. Ray Sawyer, aka Dr. Hook
18. Run-D.M.C.
19. Slash
20. Sly Stone
21. Izzy Stradlin
22. Peter Tosh
23. Ronnie Van Zant
24. X-Clan
25. Dwight Yoakum

Back in Black

1. The Jesus and Mary Chain
2. N.W.A
3. Public Enemy
4. Run-D.M.C.
5. Metallica
6. Johnny Cash
7. The Cure
8. Joy Division
9. Joan Jett
10. Peter Wolf

Five with Famous Leather Jackets

1. Ramones
2. MC5
3. George Michael
4. Waylon Jennings
5. Seal

Did It Hurt? Cool Tattoos

1. The Red Hot Chili Peppers
2. Henry Rollins
3. Guru of Gang Starr
4. Cypress Hill
5. Guns N' Roses
6. Aaron Hall
7. Everlast
8. Cher
9. Social Distortion
10. John Cougar Mellencamp

Best Hair

1. The Afros
2. The B-52s
3. B-Real of Cypress Hill (his blow-out era)
4. The Beatles, circa 1964
5. David Bowie
6. James Brown, circa 1965
7. The Beach Boys, surfer look, 1963–65
8. Big Daddy Kane
9. Boy George *(Kissing to Be Clever* era)
10. Exene Cervenka
11. George Clinton
12. Kurt Cobain
13. Tracy Chapman
14. Das-EFX
15. Bob Dylan, circa 1965–66
16. A Flock of Seagulls
17. Haircut 100
18. Rick James (the feathered extensions featured on the cover for *Street Songs*)
19. The Jesus and Mary Chain
20. The Jimi Hendrix Experience
21. Ice-T
22. Brian Jones
23. Cyndi Lauper
24. Annie Lennox (circa *Touch*)
25. John Lydon
26. Bob Marley
27. Morrissey
28. Dave Mustaine
29. Henry Rollins
30. Seal
31. Robert Smith of the Cure
32. Snoop Doggy Dogg
33. Yo Yo

Known for Their Long Hair

1. Jane Child
2. Alice Cooper
3. Flavor Flav
4. Corey Glover (pre-1993)
5. Anthony Kiedis
6. Kid of Kid 'N Play (high top era)
7. Milli Vanilli
8. DJ Quik
9. Joey Ramone
10. Slash
11. ZZ Top

Bald (by Choice or by Nature)

1. Ian Astbury
2. Peter Garrett
3. Guru
4. Isaac Hayes
5. Scott Ian
6. Elton John
7. Sinead O'Connor
8. Onyx
9. Paul Simon
10. David Lee Roth

Four Eyes

1. Adam Clayton
2. Bootsy Collins
3. Elvis Costello
4. Bo Diddley
5. D.M.C.
6. Flavor Flav
7. Jerry Garcia
8. Grand Puba Maxwell
9. Heavy D.
10. Buddy Holly
11. Jazzy Jeff
12. Elton John
13. Left Eye (of TLC)
14. John Lennon
15. Curtis Mayfield
16. Roger McGuinn
17. Mike Mills
18. Dave Mustaine
19. Jason Newsted
20. Randy Newman
21. Sinead O'Connor
22. Roy Orbison
23. Posdnous
24. Prince
25. Joey Ramone
26. Lou Reed
27. David Ruffin
28. Leon Russell
29. Scarface
30. Serch
31. Speech
32. Sting
33. Sly Stone
34. John Sebastian
35. Warren Zevon

Best Groomed

1. Anita Baker
2. The Beach Boys, up to *Pet Sounds* or so
3. Big Daddy Kane
4. Black Sheep
5. Pat Boone
6. Boyz II Men
7. Harry Connick, Jr.
8. Morris Day
9. Terrence Trent D'Arby
10. En Vogue
11. The Everly Brothers
12. Hammer
13. Michael Jackson
14. Jan and Dean
15. Grace Jones
16. Kraftwerk
17. Prince
18. Jonathan Richman
19. RuPaul
20. The Talking Heads

15 Tall Ones

1. Clarence Clemons
2. John Entwistle
3. Bryan Ferry
4. Mick Fleetwood
5. Michael Franti
6. Peter Garrett
7. Randy Newman
8. Ric Ocasek
9. Shaquille O'Neil
10. Teddy Pendergrass

11. Kris Parker
12. Todd Rundgren
13. Gene Simmons
14. Carly Simon
15. Sly Stone

18 Short Ones

1. Ian Astbury
2. Bushwick Bill
3. Roger Daltrey
4. Das EFX
5. Jermaine Dupri
6. Eazy E
7. Janet Jackson
8. Van Morrison
9. John Oates
10. Graham Parker
11. Dolly Parton
12. Prince
13. Paul Simon
14. Phil Spector
15. Ronnie Spector
16. Dan Spitz
17. Angus Young
18. Malcolm Young

Best Rap Songs About Butts

1. "Rump Shaker," Wrecks-N-Effect
2. "Baby Got Back," Sir Mix-A-Lot
3. "Dazzey Dukes," Duice
4. "Big Ole Butt," L.L. Cool J

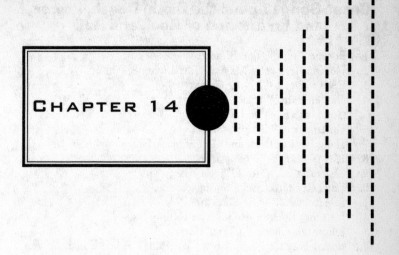

CHAPTER 14

History

Rock and Roll Celebrates Itself
Great Songs About the Birth, Death, Power, and Endurance of Rock and Roll

1. "Border Radio," The Blasters
2. "Do You Believe in Magic," The Lovin' Spoonful
3. "Elvis is Dead," Living Colour
4. "Garden Party," Rick Nelson
5. "God Gave Rock and Roll to You," Kiss
6. "Guitar Army," The Rationals
7. "Hang Up My Rock and Roll Shoes," Chuck Willis
8. "Hey Nineteen," Steely Dan
9. "I Love Rock 'n' Roll," Joan Jett
10. "I'm a Rocker," Bruce Springsteen
11. "It Will Stand," The Showmen
12. "It's Only Rock 'n' Roll," The Rolling Stones
13. "Johnny B. Goode," Chuck Berry
14. "Keep Playin' That Rock 'n' Roll," The Edgar Winter Group
15. "Kick Out the Jams," The MC5
16. "Long Live Rock," The Who
17. "Money for Nothing," Dire Straits
18. "Old Time Rock and Roll," Bob Seger
19. "Overnight Sensation (Hit Record)," The Raspberries
20. "Planet Rock," Afrika Bambaataa and Soulsonic Force
21. "Raised on the Radio," The Ravyns
22. "R.O.C.K. in the U.S.A. (A Salute to 60's Rock)," John Mellencamp
23. "Rock the Casbah," The Clash
24. "Rock Therapy," The Rock and Roll Trio
25. "Rock and Roll Music," Chuck Berry
26. "Rock and Roll," Led Zeppelin
27. "Rock and Roll," The Velvet Underground
28. "Rock and Roll Is Here to Stay," Danny and the Juniors
29. "Rock and Roll Never Forgets," Bob Seger
30. "Rock and Roll Part 2," Gary Glitter
31. "Rock 'n' Roll Fantasy," Bad Company
32. "Rockin' All Over the World," John Fogerty
33. "Rockin' in the Free World," Neil Young
34. "Rockin' Pneumonia and the Boogie Woogie Flu," Huey "Piano" Smith and the Clowns
35. "Roots Rock Reggae," Bob Marley and the Wailers
36. "So You Want to Be a Rock 'n' Roll Star," The Byrds
37. "Summer of '59," Bryan Adams
38. "That Is Rock 'n' Roll," The Coasters

39. "Those Oldies But Goodies (Reminds Me of You)," Little Caesar and the Romans
40. "Willie and the Hand Jive," Johnny Otis

Rappers Celebrate Themselves

1. "Da Rill Shit," Poor Righteous Teachers
2. "Eric B. Is President," Eric B. & Rakim
3. "I'm Bad," L.L. Cool J
4. "I'm Still # 1," Boogie Down Productions
5. "I'm the Man," Gang Starr
6. "It's Hard Being the Kane," Big Daddy Kane
7. "King of Rock," Run-D.M.C.
8. "Miuzi Weighs a Ton," Public Enemy
9. "Never Heard Nothin' Like This," MC Lyte
10. "Rap Like Me," Too Short
11. "The Shit's Real," Fat Joe
12. "That's How Smooth I Am," Lord Finesse

Broadway and Tin Pan Alley Standards that Have Been Converted to Rock and R&B

1. "Always" (Irving Berlin, 1925), Leonard Cohen
2. "Are You Lonesome Tonight" (Roy Turk, Lou Handman, Vaughn Deleath, 1926), Elvis Presley
3. "Baby Face" (Benny Davis, Harry Akst, 1926), Wing and a Prayer Fife and Drum Corps
4. "Besame Mucho, Parts 1 and 2" (Sunny Skylar, Consuelo Velazquez, 1944), The Coasters
5. "Bewildered" (Leonard Whitcup, Teddy Powell, 1938), James Brown
6. "Blueberry Hill" (Al Lewis, Larry Stock, Vincent Rose, 1940), Fats Domino
7. "Blue Moon" (Lorenz Hart, Richard Rodgers, 1934), The Marcels
8. "Blue Velvet" (Bernie Wayne, Lee Morris, 1951), The Clovers
9. "Cool Water" (Bob Nolan, 1948), Joni Mitchell
10. "Danny Boy" (Fred Weatherly, 1913), Jackie Wilson
11. "Deep Purple" (Mitchell Parish, Peter De Rose, 1934), Nino Tempo and April Stevens

12. "Don't Cry for Me Argentina" (Tim Rice, Andrew Lloyd Webber, 1976), Sinead O'Connor
13. "Ebb Tide" (Carl Sigman, Robert Maxwell, 1953), The Righteous Brothers
14. "Georgia on My Mind" (Hoagy Carmichael, Stuart Gorrell, 1930), Ray Charles
15. "Gloomy Sunday" (Sam M. Lewis, Rezso Seress, 1936), Sinead O'Connor
16. "Heart and Soul" (Hoagy Carmichael, Frank Loesser, 1938), The Cleftones
17. "I Only Have Eyes for You" (Harry Warren, 1934), The Flamingos
18. "I've Got You Under My Skin" (Cole Porter, 1932), The Four Seasons/Neneh Cherry
19. "It's All in the Game" (Carl Sigman, Charles Gale Dawes, 1951), Tommy Edwards / Van Morrison
20. "Just A Gigolo" (Irving Caesar, Leonello Casucci, Irene Bordoni), David Lee Roth
21. "Linda" (Jack Lawrence, 1947), Jan and Dean (written about the girl who would become Linda McCartney)
22. "My Way" (Paul Anka, Jacques Revaux, 1967), Sid Vicious
23. "Over the Rainbow" (E. Y. Harburg, Harold Arlen, 1939), Jimi Hendrix
24. "Prisoner of Love" (Leo Robin, Russ Columbo, Clarence Gaskill, 1931), James Brown
25. "Que Sera Sera (Whatever Will Be, Will Be)" (Jay Livingston, Ray Evans, 1935), Sly and the Family Stone
26. *Red Hot and Blue:* A collection of Cole Porter songs recorded as an AIDS benefit by, among others, U2, Sinead O'Connor, The Jungle Brothers, Annie Lennox, Aztec Camera, Neneh Cherry, Erasure, Tom Waits, k. d. lang, and David Byrne
27. "Scarlett Ribbons" (Jack Segal, Evelyn Danzig, 1949), Sinead O'Connor
28. "Singin' in the Rain" (Arthur Freed, Nacio Herb Brown, 1929), Just Water
29. "Smoke Gets in Your Eyes" (Otto Harbach, Jerome Kern, 1933), The Platters
30. "Summertime (George Gershwin, DuBose Heyward, 1935), Billy Stewart
31. "A Sunday Kind of Love" (Barbara Belle, Louis Prima, Anita Leonard, Stan Rhodes, 1946), The Harptones
32. "Till There Was You" (Meredith Willson, 1957), The Beatles
33. "Try a Little Tenderness" (Harry Woods, Jimmy Campbell, Reg Connelly, 1932), Otis Redding
34. "Unchained Melody" (Hy Zaret, Alex North, 1955), The Righteous Brothers
35. "Unforgettable" (Irving Gordon), Natalie Cole

36. "Where or When" (Lorenz Hart, Richard Rodgers, 1927), Dion and the Belmonts
37. "White Christmas" (Irving Berlin, 1942), The Drifters
38. "Yes, Sir, That's My Baby" (Gus Kahn, Walter Donaldson, 1925), The Clovers
39. "Zing Went the Strings of My Heart" (James Hanley, 1935), The Trammps
40. "Zip-A-Dee-Doo-Dah" (Ray Gilbert, Allie Wrubel, 1945), Bob B. Soxx and the Blue Jeans

Rick Whitesell's Prehistoric Rock and Roll
10 Records that Served As Important Stepping Stones

1. "Key to the Highway," Jazz Gillum, 1940
2. "Take Me Back to Tulsa," Bob Wills's Texas Playboys, 1941
3. "Choo Choo Ch'Boogie," Louis Jordan, 1946
4. "Good Rocking Tonight," Roy Brown, 1947
5. "Old Man River," The Ravens, 1947
6. "Move It On Over," Hank Williams, 1947
7. "The Great Medical Menagerist," Harmonica Frank, 1951
8. "Rockin' Chair Daddy," The Five Keys, 1951, 1953
9. "Rock the Joint," Bill Haley and the Saddlemen, 1952
10. "Feelin' Good," Little Junior Parker's Blue Flames, 1953

The late Rick Whitesell edited Goldmine, *the premier record collector's magazine, and was himself a consummate collector of vocal group, R&B, and rock and roll records. While serving as chief researcher on the first edition of this book, Whitesell selected these records to reflect his vision of how rock emerged from blues and country.*

The Father of Us All?

1. "Without Elvis, none of us could have made it."—Buddy Holly
2. "I didn't think he was as good as the Everly Brothers the first time I ever laid eyes on him."—Chuck Berry
3. "It took people like Elvis to open the door for this kind of music, and I thank God for Elvis Presley."—Little Richard
4. "Elvis was a hero to most / But he don't mean shit to me."—Chuck D, Public Enemy, "Fight the Power"
5. "Gosh, he's so great. You have no idea how great he is, really

you don't. You have no comprehension—it's absolutely impossible. I can't tell you why he's so great, but he is. He's sensational. He can do anything with his voice. He can sing anything you want him to, anyway you tell him. The unquestionable King of rock 'n' roll."—Phil Spector

6. "His kind of music is deplorable, a rancid smelling aphrodisiac."
—Frank Sinatra, 1956

7. "Hearing him for the first time was like busting out of jail."—
Bob Dylan

8. "It isn't enough to say that Elvis is kind to his parents, sends money home, and is the same unspoiled kid he was before all the commotion began. That still isn't a free ticket to behave like a sex maniac."—Eddie Condon

9. "Elvis had animal magnetism. He was even sexy to guys. I can't imagine what the chicks used to think."—Ian Hunter

10. "Elvis is my man."—Janis Joplin

11. "God, it was awful. He can sing, but he can't do much else."—
Natalie Wood after her first stay at Graceland.

12. "I don't think Elvis could have become the performer and man he was if that momma's boy thing were true."—Wayne Newton

13. "He was the greatest living pop idol in the whole world."—
Marc Bolan

14. "The King is gone but his look is not forgotten."—*Details*, 1990

15. "There have been many accolades uttered about his talent and performances through the years, all of which I agree with wholeheartedly."—Frank Sinatra, 1977

25 Elvis Songs and Where He Found Them

Elvis Presley is the only important rock and roll star who did not write any of his own songs. Instead, he made his mark as an interpreter—although he sometimes interpreted so drastically that he'd effectively rewritten the song (for example, "Milk Cow Blues," "Baby, Let's Play House"). This list shows the sources of some of the more interesting tunes Presley recorded, with the names of the original artists and the year that the first version appeared.

1. "Baby, Let's Play House," Arthur Gunter, 1955
2. "Big Boss Man," Jimmy Reed, 1961
3. "Blue Suede Shoes," Carl Perkins, 1956
4. "Bridge Over Troubled Water," Simon and Garfunkel, 1970
5. "Fever," Little Willie John, 1956
6. "Good Rockin' Tonight," Roy Brown, 1948
7. "Hi Heel Sneakers," Tommy Tucker, 1964

8. "I Feel So Bad," Chuck Willis, 1954
9. "I Need You So," Ivory Joe Hunter, 1950
10. "I Got a Thing About You Baby," Billy Lee Riley, 1972
11. "Lawdy Miss Clawdy," Lloyd Price, 1952
12. "Love Letters," Ketty Lester, 1962
13. "Love Me," Willie and Ruth, 1954
14. "Merry Christmas Baby," Johnny Moore's Three Blazers, 1949
15. "Milk Cow Blues," Kokomo Arnold, 1935
16. "My Baby Left Me," Arthur Crudup, 1950
17. "My Way," Frank Sinatra, 1969
18. "Mystery Train," Little Junior's Blue Flames, 1953
19. "One Night," Smiley Lewis, 1956
20. "Reconsider Baby," Lowell Fulsom, 1954
21. "Steamroller Blues," James Taylor, 1970
22. "Such a Night," The Drifters, 1954
23. "That's When Your Heartaches Begin," The Ink Spots, 1950
24. "Tomorrow Night," Lonnie Johnson, 1948
25. "Too Much," Bernard Hardison, 1954

Elvis's Mentors

1. The Blackwood Brothers
2. Arthur Crudup
3. The Golden Gate Quartet
4. The Inkspots
5. Dean Martin
6. Bill Monroe and His Bluegrass Boys
7. Little Junior Parker and His Blue Flames
8. Hank Snow
9. Sister Rosetta Tharpe
10. Rufus Thomas
11. Hank Williams
12. Bob Wills and the Texas Playboys

Elvis Presley's 20 Greatest Hits

1. "Mystery Train"
2. "Heartbreak Hotel"
3. "Good Rockin' Tonight"
4. "Jailhouse Rock"
5. "All Shook Up"
6. "Suspicious Minds"
7. "Hurt"

8. "Hound Dog"
9. "One Night" (from the NBC-TV special "Elvis," 1968)
10. "Milkcow Blues Boogie"
11. "How Great Thou Art"
12. "Viva Las Vegas"
13. "Are You Lonesome Tonight"
14. "Little Sister"
15. "Wear My Ring Around Your Neck"
16. "(You're So Square) Baby, I Don't Care"
17. "Blue Christmas"
18. "Blue Suede Shoes"
19 "Tryin' to Get to You"
20. "Bridge Over Troubled Water"

She's Your Lover Now
Best Non-Dylan Dylan Records

1. "All Along the Watchtower," Jimi Hendrix
2. "Mr. Tambourine Man," The Byrds
3. "The Mighty Quinn," Manfred Mann
4. "Tears of Rage," The Band
5. "It's All Over Now, Baby Blue," Them
6. "Percy's Song," Fairport Convention
7. "Emotionally Yours," The O'Jays
8. "Like a Rolling Stone," Jimi Hendrix
9. "Masters of War," Eddie Vedder / Mike McCready
10. "Blowin' in the Wind," Stevie Wonder
11. "A Hard Rain's A-Gonna Fall," Bryan Ferry
12. "Tomorrow Is a Long Time," Elvis Presley
13. "Foot of Pride," Lou Reed
14. "It Ain't Me Babe," The Turtles
15. "My Back Pages," The Byrds
16. "Sign on the Cross," Coulson, Dean, McGuinness, Flint
17. "Only a Hobo," Rod Stewart
18. "You Angel You," Manfred Mann's Earth Band
19. "When I Paint My Masterpiece," The Band
20. "Just Like a Woman," Joe Cocker

Mixed-Up Confusion
Bob Dylan on Other People's Records

1. Artist United Against Apartheid, "Sun City": Sings on this anti-apartheid recording produced by Little Steven Van Zandt and featuring everybody from Miles Davis to Run-D.M.C.
2. Harry Belafonte, *The Midnight Special:* Plays harmonica on the title track.
3. David Blue, *Com'n Back for More:* Plays harmonica on "Who Love."
4. *The Blues Project:* Appears on "Downtown Blues" as piano player Bob Landy.
5. Booker T. and Priscilla Jones, *Chronicles:* Plays harmonica on "Crippled Cow."
6. Eric Clapton, *No Reason to Cry:* Sings duet on "Sign Language," which Dylan wrote.
7. Leonard Cohen, *Death of a Ladies' Man:* Sings background vocals on two tracks.
8. *Disconnected: The Dial-a-Poem Poets Double:* Piano and backing vocals on "Jimmy Berman."
9. Ramblin' Jack Elliott, *Jack Elliott:* Plays harmonica on "Will the Circle Be Unbroken," under the name of Tedham Porterhouse.
10. Richard Fariña and Eric von Schmidt, *Dick Fariña and Eric von Schmidt:* Plays harmonica and sings backing vocals on four songs under the name Blind Boy Grunt.
11. Barry Goldberg, *Barry Goldberg:* Backup vocals and percussion (with his sense of time?!) on five tracks.
12. Steve Goodman, *The Essential Steve Goodman:* Plays piano and sings backup vocals on "Election Year Rag" and "Somebody Else's Troubles" (both title tracks of Goodman albums), with Dylan identified as Robert Milkwood Thomas.
13. George Harrison, "Miss O'Dell": Rumored to play harmonica; also did backing vocals on *All Things Must Pass*.
14. Carolyn Hester, *Carolyn Hester:* Plays harmonica on three tracks —his first recording.
15. Roger McGuinn, *Roger McGuinn:* Plays harp on "I'm So Restless."
16. Bette Midler, *Songs for the New Depression:* Does backing vocals on "Buckets of Rain."
17. Tom Rush, *Take a Little Walk with Me:* Rumored to play piano on three songs under the name Roosevelt Gook.
18. Doug Sahm, *Doug Sahm:* Plays harp, organ, and guitar as well as singing with Sahm on five tracks, including the single "San Antone."
19. Earl Scruggs, *Earl Scruggs: His Family and Friends:* Jams on "Nashville Skyline Rag."

20. U.S.A. for Africa, "We Are the World": Sings backup on the famous feed the world anthem.
21. Victoria Spivey, *Three Kings and the Queen:* Sings backup vocals and plays harp on "Sitting on Top of the World" and harp on "Wichita." On Spivey's *Two Kings and the Queen*, plays harp on "It's Dangerous," "Big Joe," and "Victoria."

The Beatles' Greatest Hits

WRITTEN BY THE BEATLES

1. "She Loves You"
2. "Ticket to Ride"
3. "I'm Down"
4. "Strawberry Fields Forever"
5. "I Saw Her Standing There"
6. "Don't Let Me Down"
7. "A Hard Day's Night"
8. "Revolution" (45 version)
9. "Helter Skelter"
10. *Abbey Road*, side two
11. "Help!"
12. "Back in the USSR"
13. "I Am the Walrus"
14. "We Can Work It Out"
15. "Norwegian Wood"
16. "Get Back"
17. "Slow Down"
18. "Dear Prudence"
19. "Day Tripper"
20. "You've Got to Hide Your Love Away"

WRITTEN BY OTHERS

1. "Money (That's What I Want)"
2. "Twist and Shout"
3. "Long Tall Sally"
4. "Boys"
5. "Words of Love"

New Facts on the Fab 4
From *Fabulous Magazine*, 1965

1. John flew to Hong Kong wearing pajamas
2. John is a cat lover.
3. Ringo spent much of his childhood in a Cheshire hospital.
4. John used to envy his cousin Stanley's Meccano set.[1]
5. Brian Epstein hesitated a long time before taking Ringo as a replacement for Pete Best.
6. George is afraid of flying.
7. George has bought a bow and arrow.
8. Patti Boyd didn't like the Beatles before she met them on the set of *A Hard Day's Night*.
9. John's father was a singer on prewar Atlantic liners.[2]

10. Ringo's stepfather, Harry Graves, sings Beatles songs at family parties.[3]
11. The Beatles never visit a barber.
12. Paul washes his hair every day.
13. The Beatles turned down the offer of an appearance on the 1964 *Royal Variety Show*.
14. Ringo cannot swim, except for a brief doggie paddle.
15. Brian Epstein made the Beatles have their hair cut short after he signed them in 1962.
16. They are never photographed with their hair "up."
17. Paul ate cornflakes and bacon and eggs at a champagne and caviar luncheon in London. Music publisher Dick James was host.[4]
18. The Beatles didn't want to go to Australia without Ringo when he was ill. But Brian Epstein persuaded them to change their minds.
19. Paul has a Mini as well as an Aston Martin DB 4.
20. George's personal Christmas card was a photograph of him scowling at a cameraman.
21. John never saw an audience properly until Dundee in Scotland. Then he wore contact lenses.
22. An American firm wrote to the Beatles asking if they could market the Beatles' bath water for a dollar a bottle.
23. They refused the offer.
24. Their road manager, Mal Evans, was once a bouncer at the Liverpool Cavern Club.
25. Neil Aspinall, their other road manager, was given a Jaguar last Christmas—a present from the Beatles.
26. Paul drinks coffee for breakfast. The other three drink tea—even in America.
27. Ringo had his new clothes designed by a woman, Caroline Charles.
28. Jane Asher bought Paul a record player for his Aston Martin.
29. Brian Epstein says, "America discovered Ringo."
30. Paul believes he is not a very good guitarist.[5]
31. None of the Beatles drinks Scotch and Coke. They now dilute the occasional spirit with lemonade.
32. John told an American journalist that U.S. fashions were five years behind the United Kingdom.
33. The Beatles never really liked jelly babies. They just said they did for a joke.[6]
34. They carry a crate of pop in the trunk of their Austin Princess.
35. Their new chauffeur, Alf Bicknell, used to drive for David Niven and Cary Grant.
36. Burt Lancaster has sent Ringo a set of pistols. They became friends in Hollywood.
37. Burt let them use his home for a showing of *A Shot in the Dark*.

38. Edward G. Robinson and his grandchild twice joined the queue to shake hands with the Beatles at their Hollywood garden party.[7]
39. So did Mrs. Dean Martin and her five children.[8]
40. The Beatles have no pockets in their trousers and only two side pockets in their jackets. Paul designed them.
41. All they carry on them in the way of money is a few banknotes.
42. John has bought his mother-in-law a house near his own in Surrey.
43. None of the Beatles wears undershirts.
44. Paul wants to buy a farm.[9]

---

[1] No, we don't know what a Meccano set is, either.
[2] Probably untrue.
[3] Sad but true.
[4] If Paul had known what James had in store for him and John (selling off their music publishing without giving them a chance to retain control), he'd have insisted on something pricier.
[5] Could this be why he played bass and keyboards?
[6] "Jelly babies" is English for jelly beans. They had to start saying they hated them because fans, believing they were the group's favorite confection (which they might at some point have been), threw them at the group onstage, and they hurt when they hit.
[7] Can you imagine today's trendiest rock band shaking hands in a queue, let alone hosting a Hollywood garden party?
[8] One of whom was soon imitating the Beatles in Dino, Desi and Billy.
[9] He did.

The 50 Greatest Rolling Stones Songs (with Commentary by Brian Keizer)

1. "Satisfaction": Because . . .
2. "Brown Sugar": Chuck Berry's body of work has been so completely apprehended by Keith that the signature riff here reads like a genetic alteration: Swing is to bop as "Johnny B. Goode" is to "Brown Sugar." Behind every great fortune is indeed a great crime and Jagger plays the villain and the bard so disarmingly that outrageous fortune becomes postmodern blues.
3. "Street Fightin' Man"
4. "Honky Tonk Women"
5. "Gimme Shelter": The harmonic elements of Chuck Berry's signature riff are decoded and modulated into a sinister and sublime loop of guitar menace.
6. "You Can't Always Get What You Want": The choirboy open-

ing through the melancholy of the instrumentation, through Jagger's romp amid the socio-cum-political-cum-sexual horseshit of the sixties in the opening verse up on to a new time party train ending perfectly traces the band's road from good English boys, "war babies," to Americanized Monkey Men.

7. "Sway": Charlie Watts's colloquium on how to swing in rock processed through Jagger and Richard's production skills on the verge of making the studio signify postmodern monkeyisms. Drug fiend existentialism and tax shelter blues.

8. "Monkey Man"

9. "Get Off My Cloud": Elvis in the studio at Sun was the greatest actor of the mass mind movie of the fifties. Jagger stakes his claim for that title in the sixties.

10. "Soul Survivor": Stones chain themselves like Sisyphus to the rock. "Wherever you are, I'll walk there/It's gonna be the death of me."

11. "Sympathy for the Devil": Comic autobiography Jagger took too seriously over time helped along by the Altamont body count and "American Pie." Rendered in original yet rightfully updated context live in 1989: Jagger as the coolest CEO of a multinational corporation.

12. "Tumbling Dice"

13. "Happy"

14. "Jumpin' Jack Flash": Born in the United Kingdom.

15. "Love in Vain": Yeah, it ain't theirs, but the transformation of Robert Johnson's gem into a modern country-blues-rock classic set Johnson and Gram Parsons free to float in the imagination and nightmares of Rock and Roll forevermore—post-post-post-modern ghosts.

16. "Torn and Frayed"

17. "19th Nervous Breakdown"

18. "Dead Flowers"

19. "Sister Morphine"

20. "Midnight Rambler"

21. "Shine the Light"

22. "As Tears Go By": Proto dream pop. Brian Jones as the archangel of eighties and nineties Brit rock.

23. "Time Waits for No One": Jagger, the great theoretician of time (as in how much time do I have to give this low-life fucker—to get my shit together to work another scam—to keep in shape to keep bringing in the dollars), in scary form as he serves up his most biting and sardonic couplet for the *Vanity Fair* set: "Time can tear down a building or destroy a woman's face/Hours are like diamonds, don't let 'em waste."

24. "Jigsaw Puzzle"

25. "Bitch"

26. "Can't You Hear Me Knocking"

27. "Memory Motel"
28. "Sweet Virginia"
29. "Salt of the Earth": Proves in spirit and shrewdness why they are the greatest white blues band—snot-nosed confrontationalism bleeding into postmodern populism. Jagger looks out over the crowd like every blues spirit has before him over Parchman or the Delta or the Sea and comes clean on how it looks, "so strange." The riff is so scientifically altered that Keith has to let you in on the joke—where they stole the soul from this time. Stole it so well you can't decipher it anymore, so Charlie downshifts and they romp: "Let us go to the Old Landmark (Campground, etc.)."
30. "I'm Free"
31. "Wild Horses"
32. "Start Me Up"
33. "Shattered": By *Exile*, they recognized they had to dive into the life of America to be what they had no choice but to be: the fetishized faces of the Rock and Roll Dream. Only in America could that predicament spell postmodern blues. This time they had to stop the exile and dive into the life of a city, so they chose an international island: Manhattan.
34. "All Down the Line"
35. "Slave"
36. "You Got the Silver"
37. "Let It Bleed"
38. "Waiting for a Friend"
39. "It's Only Rock and Roll"
40. "Winter"
41. "Coming Down Again"
42. "Star, Star"
43. "Sleep Tonight"
44. "Winning Ugly"
45. "Beast of Burden"
46. "Respectable"
47. "Before They Make Me Run"
48. "Angie"
49. "Cocksucker Blues"
50. Untitled: The piano loop at the end of *Dirty Work*. Ian Stewart, the sixth Stone, checks out so the soul survivors give him not the last word but a berth in the firmament of the eternal return.

Brian Keizer is a novelist, guitarist, and critic living in San Francisco, where he does not have a Rolling Stones altar in his bedroom.

The Best of Bruce Springsteen

ORIGINALS

1. "Born to Run"
2. "Thunder Road"
3. "Badlands"
4. "Incident on 57th Street"
5. "Darkness on the Edge of Town"
6. "Growin' Up"
7. "Reason to Believe"
8. "If I Should Fall Behind"
9. "Backstreets"
10. "The River"
11. "Tunnel of Love"
12. "Independence Day"
13. "For You"
14. "Dancing in the Dark"
15. "Nebraska"
16. "Glory Days"
17. "Fourth of July, Asbury Park (Sandy)"
18. "Because the Night"
19. "Rosalita"
20. "Soul Driver"

REMAKES (WITH ORIGINAL ARTIST)

1. "War," Edwin Starr
2. "Quarter to Three," Gary "U.S." Bonds
3. "Who'll Stop the Rain," Creedance Clearwater Revival
4. "Across the Borderline," Ry Cooder
5. "This Land Is Your Land," Woody Guthrie
6. "Jersey Girl," Tom Waits
7. "Devil with a Blue Dress"/"Good Golly Miss Molly," Mitch Ryder and the Detroit Wheels out of Shorty Long and Little Richard
8. "Trapped," Jimmy Cliff
9. "Gino Is a Coward," Gino Washington
10. "Chimes of Freedom," Bob Dylan

This Bus Does Not Stop at Eighty-second Street
10 Best Bruce Springsteen Songs that Do Not Mention Cars, Highways, or Other Modes of Transportation

1. "Badlands"
2. "Because the Night"
3. "Brilliant Disguise"
4. "Dancing in the Dark"[1]
5. "The Fever"[2]
6. "Janey, Don't You Lose Heart"
7. "Man's Job"
8. "No Surrender"
9. "Point Blank"
10. "Roll of the Dice"

---

[1] In the opinion of the authors, dancing does not constitute a mode of transportation. Walking, on the other hand, does, resulting in the

elimination not only of "Walk Like a Man" but "If I Should Fall Behind."

[2] OK, in two verses he talks about "coming home" and in the second, he also says they'll go "out." But he doesn't say *how* they'll get there.

Sting and the Boys
The Best of the Police

1. "Every Breath You Take"
2. "Bed's Too Big Without You"
3. "Every Little Thing She Does Is Magic"
4. "Spirits in the Material World"
5. "King of Pain"
6. "De Do Do Do, De Da Da Da"
7. "So Lonely"
8. "Wrapped Around Your Finger"
9. "Walking on the Moon"
10. "Don't Stand So Close to Me"

The Royal Court
The Best of Prince

1. "Adore"
2. "Another Lonely Christmas"
3. "She's Always in My Hair"
4. "Pop Life"
5. "When Doves Cry"
6. "Purple Rain"
7. "Head"
8. "I Wanna Be Your Lover"
9. "Starfish and Coffee"
10. "Soft and Wet"
11. "7"
12. "Controversy"
13. "Kiss"
14. "Delirious"
15. "Anotherloverholenyohead"
16. "Little Red Corvette"
17. "Take Me with You"
18. "Do Me, Baby"
19. "Sign O' the Times"
20. "Glam Slam"
21. "U Got the Look"
22. "1999"
23. "Joy in Repetition"
24. "If I Was Your Girlfriend"
25. "Sometimes It Snows in April"

The Purple Grail
Prince's B-Sides, Boots, and Rarities
(Compiled by Steve Perry)

B-SIDES AND RARITIES

THE BEST
1. "Erotic City" (B-side of "Let's Go Crazy," 1984)
2. "Good Love" (*Bright Lights, Big City* soundtrack, 1988)
3. "17 Days" (B-side of "When Doves Cry," 1984)
4. "Love or Money" (B-side of "Kiss," 1986)
5. "She's Always in My Hair" (B-side of "Raspberry Beret," 1985)

THE REST
6. "Gotta Stop (Messin' About)" ("Let's Work," 1981)
7. "How Come U Don't Call Me Anymore" ("1999," 1982)
8. "Horny Toad" ("Delirious," 1983)
9. "Irresistible Bitch" (Let's Pretend We're Married," 1983)
10. "Another Lonely Christmas" ("I Would Die 4 U," 1984)
11. "God" (Purple Rain," 1984)
12. "4 the Tears in Your Eyes" (*We Are The World*/U.S.A. for Africa album track, 1985)
13. "Hello" ("Pop Life," 1985)
14. "Girl" ("America," 1985)
15. "Alexa de Paris" ("Mountains," 1986)
16. "La, La, La, He, He, Hee" ("Sign O' the Times," 1987)
17. "Shockadelica" ("If I Was Your Girlfriend," 1987)
18. "Escape" ("Glam Slam," 1988)
19. "Scarlet Pussy" ("I Wish U Heaven," 1988)
20. "200 Balloons" ("Batdance," 1989)
21. "Feel U Up" ("Partyman," 1989)
22. "Sex" (extra track on "Scandalous Sex Suite" CD single, 1989)
23. "I Love U in Me" ("Arms of Orion," "Insatiable," 1989)

THE BOOTLEGGED TRACKS
1. "POWER FANTASTIC," CA. 1986

Actually, I'm cheating. This long-bootlegged track is now available in a legit version on the Hits/B-Sides collection. But that only sums up a truth about Prince that runs counter to the mythology: For all his fabled productivity (the vault containing three hundred, five hundred, seven hundred unreleased songs . . .) most of the studio recordings of any note that have come out on bootlegs have eventually come out on Prince records, too. The rest are often too incomplete to judge and largely forgettable. Not this one. "Power Fantastic," purportedly written by Wendy and Lisa, is one of the loveliest ballads he's ever recorded. And no, the horn's not Miles.

2. "NOON RENDEZVOUS," 1984

This isn't even a song, exactly; it's a lazy, sumptuous groove based on the melody from Leiber and Spector's "Spanish Harlem." Cooked up in rehearsal for the Purple Rain tour, it may or may not exist in a studio version—the bootlegged rendition is from a purloined rehearsal tape.

3. "CRYSTAL BALL," CA. 1986—87

When Prince delivered *Sign O' the Times* to Warners in 1987, it was three records' worth, not two, and according to some accounts it wasn't called *SOT*, the title was *Crystal Ball*. He was subsequently persuaded to pare it back to two records, and this bit of jazzy, minimalist funk was one of the casualties.

4. "CAN I PLAY WITH YOU," CA. 1985

Prince's rumored collaboration with Miles Davis stirred a lot of speculation, but according to former Paisley Park Records head Alan Leeds, this is the only track they finished. And they did it without ever entering a studio together. Prince sent the track to Miles for overdubbing. Available on a bootleg disc called *Crucial*, where it's listed as "Red Riding Hood." (Incidentally, Leeds points out this wasn't the last time the two ended up on the same record. Prince and Miles both appear on a Chaka Khan track called "Sticky Wicket"—though, once again, they weren't in the studio together.)

5. "CASE OF YOU," LIVE AT FIRST AVENUE, MINNEAPOLIS, 1983

Recorded at the same show that produced the version of "Purple Rain" eventually used in the film, this Joni Mitchell song represented the first time Prince ever performed anyone else's music publicly.

THE UNRELEASED ALBUM PROJECTS

Only the inner circle at Paisley Park has any idea how many Prince records have been conceived only to be scrapped part way to completion. Between *Parade* and *Sign O' the Times*, for instance, there were three different "albums" in the works: *Camille*, *Dream Factory*, and *Crystal Ball*—which eventually boiled down to the two-disc *SOT*. But at least two of his almost albums have been bootlegged. One you certainly know about, one you probably don't.

1. CAMILLE

Several months after a Minneapolis magazine piece about his *Parade* album (1986) suggested Prince's lyrics were becoming as overwrought as the death scene from *Camille*, he nearly released an album by that name. "Camille" was another in a long line of Prince's alter egos, the signature being a tweaked-up warbly vocal set against spare, playful—and deceptively complex—funk tracks. Funny and seemingly effortless, it would have made a great counterpoint to the adventurous but often ponderous *Parade*. Apparently Prince liked it, too, since most of the titles eventually got released. Tracks: "Re-

birth of the Flesh," "Housequake," "Strange Relationship," "Feel
U Up," "Shockadelica," "Good Love," "If I Was Your Girlfriend,"
"Rock Hard in a Funky Place."

2. THE BLACK ALBUM

Originally it was rumored to be due in the winter of 1987–88,
maybe before Christmas: a new Prince album, black cover, no type,
no graphics, no nothing—just a hot pink catalogue number on the
spine. It never arrived, of course. Broadly speaking, two rumors got
passed around to account for the record that never was. One held
that Warners refused to release it because it was just too offensive;
the other that Prince himself withdrew it because of a premonition.
The truth was that Prince pulled the album on the eve of its release,
causing Warners to eat the thousands of vinyl copies that were
pressed up and ready to go. He really did have a dream, or maybe a
vision, in which God let it be known he'd be very upset if Prince
unleashed this Dark Funk on the world. Some say he was doing a
lot of Ecstasy in those days. Prince, I mean. Tracks: "Le Grind,"
"Cindy C," "Dead on It," "When 2 R in Love," "Bob George,"
"Superfunkycalifragisexi," "2 Nigs United 4 West Compton,"
"Rock Hard in a Funky Place."

Steve Perry, in addition to freelance work as critic and journalist, edits
City Pages, *the stellar Minneapolis weekly.*

Reginald C. Dennis's 25 Musical Turning Points of Rap's Old School

1979

1. "RAPPER'S DELIGHT"—THE SUGAR HILL GANG (SUGAR HILL)

Although there is still some debate over who actually came first
(some people believe that "King Tim III" by the Fatback Band was
the first record to incorporate elements of rap), there is no doubt
in anyone's mind that this record singlehandedly ushered in the
commercial age of hip-hop and it is recognized as the focal point of
rap's entry into popular culture. Although the music had been secretly evolving for years, "Rapper's Delight" took rap out of the
parks and underground clubs of New York City and exposed it to
the world. Selling in excess of 10 million copies worldwide and
catapulting a small independent black-owned label called Sugar Hill
Records into rap's first dynasty, the efforts of Wonder Mike, Big
Bank Hank, and Master Gee opened the door for all that followed.

"Rapper's Delight," it is worth noting, caused more than its fair share of controversy upon its release fourteen years ago. The legal battle between the Sugar Hill label and the funk/disco group Chic —whose song "Good Times" was the musical basis of "Rapper's Delight"—foreshadowed today's arguments concerning sampling and publishing royalties by nearly a decade. Then there were the questions with regards to the group's authenticity. That the Sugar Hill Gang was a trio of nonrappers from New Jersey was not lost on hip-hop's pioneers, who immediately branded the record as a phony attempt to cash in on what was going on in the streets and clubs of NYC. "Rapper's Delight," they claimed, was a watered-down misrepresentation of rap. But all questions about its authenticity aside, the novelty record known as "Rapper's Delight" bears the burden of standing at ground zero for the greatest music and social revolution since rock 'n' roll.

2. "SUPER RAPPIN"—GRANDMASTER FLASH & THE FURIOUS FIVE (ENJOY)

Originally released on the Harlem-based Enjoy Records label, this record marked the first time that an authentic and respected rap crew from the streets, in this case, the boogie-down Bronx, had the opportunity to cut a record. Because this crew came from within the culture and had helped to pioneer and refine the sound of rap, "Super Rappin' " offered listeners a more authentic interpretation of rap's essence. Most important, however, this record introduced the world to six young men (Flash, Kid Creole, Cowboy, Rahiem, Scorpio, and Melle Mel) who in the coming years would be responsible for some of rap's greatest stylistic and technical innovations.

3. "FUNK YOU UP"—SEQUENCE (SUGAR HILL)

Until this point, on wax at least, rap had been solely a man's sport, but this early Sugar Hill release broke down walls and changed the game forever. The female trio known as Sequence (Blondie, Cheryl the Pearl, and Angie B) set the stage for rap's long-lasting female revolution. Often forgotten, these women deserve to be credited for the doors they opened.

1980

4. "RAPTURE"—BLONDIE (CHRYSALIS)

This crossover hit of the disco era marked the first time that a mainstream artist, in this case Debbie Harry and her new wave group Blondie, acknowledged the existence of and paid homage to the world of hip-hop. A song about what was going down in the streets of New York, "Rapture" featured a rap interlude by Harry in which she mentioned the name of a struggling hip-hop entrepreneur named Fab Five Freddy and remarked upon the swiftness of Grandmaster Flash's turntable abilities. The song's promotional video featured electric boogie dancing and an appearance by NYC graffiti legend Lee. This record solidified the relationship between the downtown New York artist crowd and the hip-hop underground and for a time Debbie Harry became a familiar icon in the world of hip-hop music and graffiti art.

5. "THE BREAKS"—KURTIS BLOW (MERCURY)

The first solo rapper to sign a long-term deal with a major record label, Blow had already tasted success both as a club MC and with a popular record called "Christmas Rappin'." A nationwide hit and anthem of countless backyard barbecues, "The Breaks," with its collection of humorous misfortunes was one of the first twelve-inch singles (a new format back then) to receive a gold certification. It should also be noted that the song's executive producer was none other than Russell Simmons, the man who would take rap to new heights with his Def Jam media empire.

6. "ADVENTURES OF SUPER RHYMES"—JIMMY SPICER (DAZZ RECORDS)

More than fifteen minutes long. The distinctively voiced Spicer helped pioneer the art of the extensive tale. With nonstop, humorous stories coupled with an exaggerated voice that hundreds would later imitate, this record became a textbook for some of hip-hop's greatest storytellers.

7. "RAPPER REPRISE"—THE SUGAR HILL GANG AND THE SEQUENCE (SUGAR HILL)

This followup to "Rapper's Delight" has the distinction of being the first record to combine two separate groups. With six people on the mike it was the precursor to today's posse cuts.

8. "RAPPIN' AND ROCKIN' THE HOUSE"—THE FUNKY FOUR + 1 (SUGAR HILL)

These accomplished and sought-after rappers added a new element to the hip-hop mix. Joining crew members Jazzy Jeff, Ronnie C, and KK Rockwell on the mike was the legendary Sha Rock, perhaps the greatest female MC of the day. As the first mixed-gender crew to grab the spotlight, they set an example of unity and influenced many of the male/female crews of today.

9. "THE BODY ROCK"—THE TREACHEROUS THREE (ENJOY)

Kool Moe Dee, Special K, and L.A. Sunshine specialized in lyrical innovation. With "Body Rock" they began to develop the quick-tongued, syncopated, super-fast delivery that would set them apart from the competition. Concentration on complex rhymes and experiments with creative delivery marked the beginnings of a departure from the popular "yes y'allin' " of the era. "Body Rock" was also the first song to use rock guitars in the music.

10. "LOVE RAP"—SPOONIE GEE (ENJOY)

A master wordsmith and self-proclaimed "metro-politician on the microphone," Spoonie Gee set the rap world on its ear with his confident butter-smooth delivery and his well-constructed and incredibly boastful rhymes regarding the dimensions of his sexual prowess. While he was not as explicit as rappers would later get, Spoonie got his message across: He was indeed a competent ladies' man. He pioneered what would be known as the "mack" or "player" flow, and his lyrics would influence a generation of rappers yet to come.

1981

11. "GRANDMASTER FLASH ON THE WHEELS OF STEEL"—GRANDMASTER FLASH & THE FURIOUS FIVE (SUGAR HILL)

This record for the first time on wax captured the excitement, complexity, and art of scratching and mixing. In this, the first and probably the best of its kind, Flash wove musical snippets and spoken phrases into an enduring tapestry of sonic art. This marked the birth of the "DJ cut." For many people outside New York, this was a formal introduction to scratching.

12. "SHOWDOWN"—GRANDMASTER FLASH & THE FURIOUS FIVE VS. THE SUGAR HILL GANG (SUGAR HILL)

This studio confrontation between rap's heaviest hitters was an attempt to make a record that would recreate a battle between two rival crews. While it didn't come off as a full-fledged battle (it ended in a draw), it was cool to hear your favorite groups collaborate on a record. It was a good try and the concept was historic, but then as now, real battles remain exclusively the domain of underground tapes.

13. "DISCO DREAM"—THE MEAN MACHINE (SUGAR HILL)

Because hip-hop has always brought together people of different nationalities, it should come as no surprise that this song by rappers Jimmy Mac, Julio, and Mr. Shick delved deep into the world of bilingual understanding. While essentially a party song (complemented by the bassline from Grace Jones's "Pull Up to the Bumper"), "Disco Dream" showed the universal appeal of rap as the lyrics went smoothly back and forth between English and Spanish before finally ending in a display of Spanish harmonizing.

1982

14. "FLASH TO THE BEAT"—GRANDMASTER FLASH & THE FURIOUS FIVE (SUGAR HILL)

In a nutshell, this record exposed many to a new dimension of rap—vocal routines and harmonizing. Essentially an extended a cappella routine, the song allowed the Furious Five to put some more elements of their live performances on wax. This track also introduced the world to the futuristic sounds of the electronic beatbox.

15. "PLANET ROCK"—AFRIKA BAMBAATAA AND THE SOUL SONIC FORCE (TOMMY BOY)

The undisputed anthem of the summer of '82, this composition took rap to the final frontier. With Afrika Bambaataa at the helm, the music of hip-hop took a twist, picking up where P-Funk and James Brown had left off. The futuristic synthesizer sounds and computer rhythms taken from European dance groups like Kraftwerk found a new audience—the street kids. The fallout from this historic record is still felt today. Not only did this release put a small label called Tommy Boy Records on the map, but the deep bass tones and quirky sound effects created by the Roland 808 drum machine helped to spawn a new division of hip-hop. Traveling from the Bronx to the South the technofunk sound slowly evolved into what is known today as the Miami Bass sound, where the legacy of Bam and his fellow funkateers (Mr. Biggs, Pow Wow, and MC G.L.O.B.E.) are felt by millions daily.

16. "THE MESSAGE"—GRANDMASTER FLASH & THE FURIOUS FIVE (SUGAR HILL)

A stark departure from the somewhat shallow party atmosphere that had come to symbolize rap, this record was the first to delve into social commentary and expose the problems of the inner city to the living rooms of middle America. From this point on it was clear that rap could be used as a powerful medium through which social concerns could be addressed. Melle Mel's impassioned, man-on-the-edge delivery heralded the political concerns of a new and no longer silent generation. A virtual laundry list of the problems plaguing the ghetto (apathy, despair, black-on-black violence, police harassment, unemployment), "The Message" served as a political blueprint for a Hip-Hop Nation just coming of age.

17. "BEAT BOP"—RAMMELLZEE VS. K-ROB (PROFILE)

Long before Cypress Hill, the Beasties or Hympty Hump, rapper's Rammellzee and K-Rob were searching for the lyrical outer limits. This nine-minute, back-and-forth, psychedelic freestyle featured abstract lyrical construction and nonlinear thought that seemed years ahead of its time. The seeds of rap's cerebral age were sown with this record. The equally surreal bass-driven track was produced and arranged by the late graffiti artist Jean Michel Basquiat.

18. "IT'S GOOD TO BE THE KING"—MEL BROOKS (WMOT RECORDS)

Even though it was generally regarded as a passing trend, rap music's increased commercial viability soon brought with it a host of outsiders eager to exploit the "fad" and make a quick buck. This record by comedian filmmaker Mel Brooks became an unlikely hit on the streets. In fact it was so popular that it prompted Sylvia Robinson, the president of Sugar Hill Records, to release her own version of the song: "It's Good to Be the Queen." While the MCing career of Mel Brooks (who has the distinction of being the first Jewish rapper to make it on wax) fell short, the record proved that rap was becoming a part of the nation's consciousness. It was only a matter of time before we were subject to hundreds of horrendous hip-hop-inspired novelty records.

1983

19. "BREAK DANCE ELECTRIC BOOGIE"—WEST STREET MOB (SUGAR HILL)

At the height of the breakdancing craze, this song, a collection of futuristic sounds strained through a synthesizer, could pack a dance floor on a moment's notice. The fast pace facilitated the rapid movements of breaking and complemented the freeze-frame rhythm of the electric boogie. The song's robotic voice commanded B-boys to "spin on your back, then freeze"—and crews of young dancers responded to every beat.

20. "ROCKIT"—HERBIE HANCOCK (CBS RECORDS)

This tune marked the first collaboration between hip-hop and jazz. Hancock's synthesized, "Planet Rock"–derived composition was enhanced only by the nimble scratching of the man called D.S.T. A massive crossover smash, "Rockit" made the sound of scratching an official part of popular culture. And the innovative video (which featured walking robotic mannequins and is regarded as one of the greatest videos of all time) matched the song's futuristic atmosphere perfectly.

21. "BUFFALO GALS"—MALCOLM MCLAREN (ISLAND)

"Buffalo Gals" mixed urban street culture with new-wave music and fringe white cultural rebellion. McLaren, who is best known for managing and promoting the premiere punk-rock group of the seventies, the Sex Pistols, turned his attention toward hip-hop and took it deeper into the seedy world of glamour and commercialized exploitation. A worldwide hit, "Buffalo Gals" took hip-hop to heights of exposure. The historic video featured live graffiti art as well as a B-boying performance by the internationally acclaimed Rock Steady Crew. This time capsule of hip-hop history was the first of many successful collaborations between McLaren and the World's Famous Supreme Team.

22. "PROBLEMS OF THE WORLD TODAY"—THE FEARLESS FOUR (ELEKTRA)

Although they had enjoyed years of success and had many hit records under their belts, it was still a historic occasion when DLB, Peso, Tito, Crazy Eddie, and O.C. became the first group to sign with a major label. And while the A-side, "Problems of the World," became an instant hit and spawned one of the first popular videos, it was the song's B-side, "Fearless Freestyle," that did the most damage on the underground. The go-for-broke microphone techniques employed by the crew can hold their own with much of the material out today. A testament to the Fearless Four's legendary abilities.

23. "WHITE LINES (DON'T DO IT)"—GRANDMASTER FLASH & THE FURIOUS FIVE (SUGAR HILL)

Once again, Flash and company were at the forefront when it came to matters of timely and topical social commentary. This look into the world of cocaine addiction foreshadowed the crack epidemic of the mid-eighties. The song itself attacked a variety of concerns head-on. The disparity of racial justice in America, the global ramifications of the drug trade, and the plight of auto-builder-turned-convicted-coke-dealer John DeLorean were just a few of the topics raised by the song. The rare video of the song was directed by a film student named Spike Lee and starred a young actor named Larry Fishburne.

24. "STREET JUSTICE"—THE RAKE (PROFILE)

It wasn't a smash hit by any stretch of the imagination, but this violent tale of bloody revenge seemed to mirror the graphic turns that our lives were beginning to take. Elements of what would be later called hard-core or gangsta rap can easily be traced to this song, the story of a desperate man who takes the law into his own hands, and seeks justice by any means necessary. The cheapness of life in the inner city and the increase in violent youth crime are but two of the topics that the Rake brought to the table.

25. "SUCKER MC'S"—RUN D.M.C. (PROFILE)

The catalyst for rap's present success. With the release of this twelve-inch, rap's long journey from the streets to full mainstream acceptance became inevitable. A trio from Hollis, Queens, Run-D.M.C. would start what is commonly referred to as rap's New School movement. This new generation of hip-hoppers waged a hard war against the old guard for the control of the culture, and when the smoke cleared the Hip-Hop Nation had no choice but to bow before its new rulers: DJ Run, D.M.C. and Jam Master Jay. A harsh synthesis of what rap had been and where it was now destined to go, the Kings from Queens became rap's original "niggas with attitudes." Their raw, stripped-down-to-the-beat music and defiant larger-than-life posturing sent a glaring message to anyone foolish enough to step to them: What, you want some of this? Suburban anger had arrived and hip-hop would never be the same again.

Reginald C. Dennis is the music editor of The Source. *This list was originally published in the magazine's November 1993 issue.*

10 Untouchable Rappers and Why They Fell Off (as Told by Reginald C. Dennis)

1. L.L. Cool J—Out of touch with the street.
2. Big Daddy Kane—Traded in his Timberlands and jeans for alligator shoes and silk suits. Participated in one too many Playgirl and Madonna sex book photo shoots.
3. Rakim—The fact that his musical tracks were not up to the level of his rapping ability finally sank in to the record buying public.
4. The D.O.C.—As a result of a tragic and freakish car accident his vocal chords were crushed and he now speaks in harsh rasps and whispers.
5. KRS-One—The post-1990 hip-hop audience decided it wanted style over substance. KRS refused to comply.
6. Chuck D—Terminally entangled in political dogma and a confused social agenda. Forgot that rapping is supposed to be fun.
7. Ice Cube—Paid too much attention to passing rap trends and not enough to his career. The quality of his studio work declined abominably.
8. MC Ren—After the breakup of N.W.A, he never quite adjusted to a solo career. Without the music of Dr. Dre to carry him it became apparent that he really didn't have much to talk about.
9. Heavy D.—Identity crisis. Mistakenly thought that pop acceptance meant that he wasn't respected on the street. In trying to appease the underground he lost both his crossover appeal and the street community.
10. Kool Moe Dee—The last holdover of the seventies Old School era, he stayed in the game too long. Carried his feud with L.L. Cool J one album too many. Went out on his shield.

Fab Five Freddy's 10 Favorite Hip-Hop Moments

1. May 1978: Hearing and receiving my first Flash tape, having been curious about where this new sound was coming from after having been exposed to it by top Brooklyn DJs like Grand Master Flowers, Pete DJ Jones, and Frankie D, who played the parks and colleges at that time.
2. June 1979: Seeing Flash and the Furious Five at the Alfred E. Smith housing project community center in the Lower East

Side. "What do you think about making a record out of this stuff?" I remember asking Melle Mel at the time. "I don't know," he replied. "Do you think anyone would buy it?"

3. After having developed an artist patron/cultural exchange type of relationship with Debbie Harry and Chris Stein of the then-mega-large new-wave pop group Blondie, I took them and several other Downtown art/music types to a slammin' hip-hop party at The Pal on 183 & Webster in the Bronx. The Cold Crush Brothers, the Mercedes Ladies, Spoonie Gee and Johnnie Wa, and Rayvon performed. I remember stunned fly girls and guys thinking Debbie Harry was maybe Patty Duke because that was the cool dance of the period.

4. October 1980: Chris and Debbie of Blondie call me over to their apartment to listen to their new album, *Autoamerican*. I remember I used to jokingly tell Debbie that they should make a song about me and that would help make me a legend. They played the song "Rapture" for me and when I heard my name, I thought, "How cute. They went to all that trouble to insert my name into this song." I really thought it was just a joke. About a month later I was in Paris and I heard the song on the radio. The rest is history.

5. Fall 1980: Meeting and collaborating with Charlie Ahearn on the making of the first and earliest record of hip-hop on film, *Wild Style*.

6. Among my many duties on the film *Wild Style*, which included starring as one of the leads ("Phade"), I produced all the original music in the form of a break beat record with twelve short instrumental tracks. For DJs like Grand Master Flash, Grand Wizard Theodore and Charlie Chase, the era of sampling was right around the corner, but Ahearn did not want to risk legal action from using other people's music. I remember the look on Flash's face when he finished slicing, dicing, and cutting my tracks down to the bone and he looked at me and said, "Damn, you made these songs?" I said, "Hell yeah."

7. 1982: The scene at the Roxy was the hottest thing in clubland because the synergy instigated by my ideas that rap, graffiti, and breakdancing were all the same culture were in full effect. Some friends of mine had the idea that I should make a rap record in French to be released by the Celluloid label. They were a culturally arty label known for the innovative jazz-funk band Material, which was led by Bill Laswell, who would also produce the record. The song was called "Change the Beat" and later inspired the greedy owner of the label, John Kurokos, to release a series of rap records by several other rising stars of that time like Phase 2, Grand Mixer DST, and Futura 2000. Trouble was, getting money from him was harder than imaginable. However, a song that I thought would only be heard in France came back

to the States as an import and became an underground hip-hop hit or maybe even a classic of sorts because of a strange sound on the end of side B, which was my voice having been run through a vocorder saying, "Ahhh, this stuff is really fresh." That part of the record, especially the word "fresh," became up until a point the single most used element on hip-hop records— every bonafide practitioner had to have a copy or two in his crate.

8. 1982: A tour of France was also part of the French connection of sorts that I helped set off. The tour was the first real hip-hop excursion to leave these shores and it included probably the truest representation of hip-hop culture of its kind to date because nobody was thinking about gold, platinum, or the mega-stardom that most artists dream of today. The lineup included myself on the mike solo along with Ramellzee to warm up the crowd and start the flow so the Rock Steady Crew could hit the floor with some breakdancing. There was also Futura 200 and Dondi spray painting a different slamming graffiti backdrop at every show, Grand Mixer DST and the Infinity Rappers, who had classic hip-hop rhymes and dope choreography, the McDon-alds Double Dutch girls, who were the top Double Dutch jump-ers in the city, and DJ Afrika Bambaataa of the Mighty Zulu Nation, the soul of the movement, who played dope music at every interval. We played all across France plus a gig in London as well as a grande finale in Paris. Now just about ten years later with hip-hop large all over Europe, the hip-hop community in France credits that tour as their movement's inspiration.

9. 1987: Sometime during that year I heard about a group named Public Enemy that was making a record that would change the face of the rap game. I heard some of the tracks and immediately realized I had discovered the next step after painting that I had been looking for: directing their first music video. I started a sort of lobbying campaign to get all involved to agree to let me direct. Chuck D, Russell Simmons, Rick Rubin, and Bill Stephney all seemed to think it was a great idea but the window for music video was a rather small one. As a matter of fact, it was barred and gated shut. With the exception of Ralph McDaniels's *Video Music Box* in the New York area or an occasional Run-D.M.C. video on MTV, it just wasn't happening.

The P.E. crew couldn't figure out what the second single would be after "Yo! Bum Rush the Show," so I had written concepts for half the songs on the album and spent many hours hanging out with the group but the video never happened. Chuck called me up and said he wanted to discuss videos for his forthcoming album, *It Takes a Nation of Millions to Hold Us Back*, so I started writing more concepts. Someone from Jive Records heard that I was supposed to direct the P.E. video and offered me the opportunity to do the first video for KRS-One, "My Philosophy." This led to my directing many music videos for the likes of EPMD, Queen Latifah, Shabba Ranks, and Snoop Doggy Dogg.

10. July 1988: I received a phone call from a good buddy of mine, Peter Daughtery, who had worked his way up through the ranks at MTV to become a producer. Peter was a music and pop culture fanatic who was knowledgeable about everything from hard-core punk to Parliament funk. He also knew and understood who I was and wasn't particularly happy about MTV's then extremely racist music programming policies. Peter told me about plans he had to try to launch a rap program on MTV and that he and a colleague, Ted Demme, had put my name down as their choice for host. I was, of course, flattered to be considered and never expected the end result, me hosting a nationally televised TV show, *Yo! MTV Raps*.

Fab Five Freddy really did all this shit—and still adds to his legend weekly on Yo! MTV Raps.

The 150 Essential Post-Punk Records (as Selected by Brian Keizer)

1980
1. *London Calling*, The Clash[1]
2. *Catholic Boy*, Jim Carroll Band
3. *Totale's Turns*, The Fall
4. *Unknown Pleasures*, Joy Division
5. *Dirty Mind*, Prince
6. *Metal Box*, Public Image Ltd.
7. *The River*, Bruce Springsteen
8. *Remain in Light*, Talking Heads
9. *Heart Attack and Vine*, Tom Waits
10. *Los Angeles*, X
11. *Black Sea*, XTC
12. *Greatest Hits*, Throbbing Gristle
13. *Queen of Siam*, Lydia Lunch
14. *Zenyatta Mondatta*, The Police
15. *Pretenders II*, The Pretenders

1981

16. *Damaged*, Black Flag
17. *Sandinista!*, The Clash
18. *Bad Reputation*, Joan Jett
19. *Closer*, Joy Division
20. *Minor Threat*
21. *Controversy*, Prince
22. *Wild Gift*, X
23. *Fresh Fruit for Rotting Vegetables*, Dead Kennedys
24. *The Blasters*
25. *Another Day/Another Dollar*, Gang of Four
26. *Solid Gold*, Gang of Four
27. *Talk Talk Talk*, The Psychedelic Furs
28. *Ghost in the Machine*, The Police

1982

29. *Back from Samoa*, The Angry Samoans
30. *Bad Brains*
31. *Imperial Bedroom*, Elvis Costello
32. *Milo Goes to College*, The Descendants
33. *The Generic Album*, Flipper
34. *1999*, Prince
35. *Chronic Town*, R.E.M.
36. *Stink*, The Replacements
37. *Singles—45's and Under*, Squeeze
38. *Nebraska*, Bruce Springsteen
39. *Songs of the Free*, Gang of Four
40. *Liliput*
41. *Vs*, Mission of Burma
42. *The Name of This Band Is Talking Heads*, Talking Heads
43. *Shoot Out the Lights*, Richard and Linda Thompson
44. *Story of the Mekons*, The Mekons

1983

45. *Butthole Surfers*
46. *Murmur*, R.E.M.
47. *Hootenanny*, The Replacements
48. *Tom Tom Club*
49. *Violent Femmes*
50. *Swordfishtrombones*, Tom Waits
51. *More Fun in the New World*, X
52. *Non Fiction*, The Blasters
53. *Synchronicity*, The Police
54. *War*, U2

1984
55. *Racer X*, Big Black
56. *Live '84*, Black Flag
57. *Zen Arcade*, Hüsker Dü
58. *Purple Rain*, Prince
59. *Double Nickels on the Dime*, The Minutemen
60. *Reckoning*, R.E.M.
61. *Let It Be*, The Replacements
62. *The Smiths*
63. *Sing No Evil*, Half Japanese
64. *Making History*, Linton Kwesi Johnson
65. *Repo Man* (movie soundtrack)
66. *Run-D.M.C.*

1985
67. *Bulldozer*, Big Black
68. *Rembrandt Pussyhorse*, The Butthole Surfers
69. *New Day Rising*, Hüsker Dü
70. *Fear and Whiskey*, The Mekons
71. *3-Way Tie for Last*, The Minutemen
72. *Rum, Sodomy and the Lash*, The Pogues
73. *Tim*, The Replacements
74. *Meat Is Murder*, The Smiths
75. *Rain Dogs*, Tom Waits
76. *Hounds of Love*, Kate Bush
77. *King of Rock*, Run-D.M.C.
78. *Radio*, L.L. Cool J
79. *Terminal Tower*, Pere Ubu

1986
80. *I Against I*, Bad Brains
81. *Liscenced To Ill*, The Beastie Boys
82. *Camper Van Beethoven*
83. *Psychocandy*, The Jesus and Mary Chain
84. *Pretty Little Baka Guy/Live in Rockville*, Shonen Knife
85. *Evol*, Sonic Youth
86. *Throwing Muses*
87. *The Whole Story*, Kate Bush
88. *King of America*, The Costello Show (Featuring Elvis Costello)
89. *Standing on a Beach: The Singles*, The Cure
90. *Raising Hell*, Run-D.M.C.

1987
91. *You're Living All Over Me*, Dinosaur Jr.
92. *The Lion and the Cobra*, Sinead O'Connor
93. *Sign O' the Times*, Prince
94. *Yo! Bum Rush the Show*, Public Enemy

95. *Document*, R.E.M.
96. *Pleased to Meet Me*, The Replacements
97. *Sister*, Sonic Youth
98. *While You Were Out*, Soul Asylum
99. *LSD C & W*, Eugene Chadbourne
100. *The Singles*, The Pretenders
101. *Joshua Tree*, U2

1988

102. *I'm Your Man*, Leonard Cohen
103. *I Am Kurious Oranj*, The Fall
104. *Nothing's Shocking*, Jane's Addiction
105. *Surfer Rosa*, The Pixies
106. *Superfuzz Bigmuff*, Mudhoney
107. *If I Should Fall from Grace with God*, The Pogues
108. *It Takes a Nation of Millions to Hold Us Back*, Public Enemy
109. *Daydream Nation*, Sonic Youth
110. *Straight Outta Compton*, N.W.A
111. *The Land of Rape and Honey*, Ministry
112. *The Tenement Year*, Pere Ubu
113. *Lucinda Williams*
114. *Strictly Business*, EPMD

1989

115. *Paul's Boutique*, The Beastie Boys
116. *Key Lime Pie*, Camper Van Beethoven
117. *Bleach*, Nirvana
118. *Doolittle*, The Pixies
119. *New York*, Lou Reed
120. *A Mind Is a Terrible Thing to Taste*, Ministry
121. *Cloudland*, Pere Ubu

1990

122. *Repeater*, Fugazi
123. *Rock 'n Roll*, The Mekons
124. *I Do Not Have What I Haven't Got*, Sinead O'Connor
125. *Songs for 'Drella*, Lou Reed and John Cale
126. *Giant*, Shonen Knife
127. *And the Horse They Rode in On*, Soul Asylum
128. *Ragged Glory*, Neil Young
129. *Harmony Corruption*, Napalm Death

1991

130. *Rosy Jack World*, The Blake Babies
131. *Pod*, The Breeders
132. *Nevermind*, Nirvana
133. *Gish*, Smashing Pumpkins

134. *Still Feel Gone*, Uncle Tupelo
135. *Loveless*, My Bloody Valentine
136. *Green Mind*, Dinosaur Jr.
137. *AmeriKKKa's Most Wanted*, Ice Cube

1992
138. *Check Your Head*, The Beastie Boys
139. *Bricks Are Heavy*, L7
140. *Slanted and Enchanted*, Pavement
141. *Dry*, P. J. Harvey
142. *Hey Babe*, Juliana Hatfield
143. *Bikini Kill*
144. *Death Certificate*, Ice Cube
145. *U2*, Negativland

1993
146. *Rid of Me*, P.J. Harvey
147. *In Utero*, Nirvana
148. *Live MCMXCIII*, The Velvet Underground
149. *Where You Been*, Dinosaur Jr.
150. *14 Songs*, Paul Westerberg

[1] *Actually, December 1979—as good a place as any to start post-punk. Brian Keizer is a novelist and music critic who lives in San Francisco.*

The Run at the Mouth Festival— 50 Great Multipart Songs: Songs Whose Hit Versions Were Only Half the Story
(Fact: All These Records Actually Charted)

1. "American Pie, Parts 1 and 2," Don McLean
2. "Another Brick in the Wall (Part II)," Pink Floyd
3. "Bad Luck (Part 1)," Harold Melvin and the Blue Notes
4. "Beat Street Breakdown—Part 1," Grandmaster Melle Mel and the Furious Five
5. "The Bottle—Part 1," Gil Scott Heron and Brian Jackson
6. "The Breaks (Part 1)," Kurtis Blow
7. "Bustin' Loose, Part 1," Chuck Brown and the Soul Searchers
8. "Cool (Part One)," The Time
9. "Dinner with Drac—Part 1," John Zacherle
10. "Fight the Power (Part 1)," The Isley Brothers
11. "Fingertips—Pt. 2," Stevie Wonder

12. "The Flying Saucer (Parts 1 and 2)," Buchanan and Goodman
13. "Funky Broadway, Part 1," Dyke and the Blazers
14. "Hip City—Pt. 2," Junior Walker and the All-Stars
15. "Honky Tonk (Parts 1 and 2)," Bill Doggett[1]
16. "I Don't Know What You've Got But It's Got Me—Part 1," Little Richard
17. "I Like It Like That, Part 1," Chris Kenner
18. "I Need Help (I Can't Do It Alone) Pt. 1," Bobby Byrd[2]
19. "I'll Always Love My Mama (Part 1)," The Intruders
20. "Jive Turkey (Part 1)," The Ohio Players
21. "Joy—Pt 1," Isaac Hayes
22. "Keep On Truckin' (Part 1)," Eddie Kendricks
23. "(Not Just) Knee Deep, Part 1," Funkadelic
24. "Let's Work Together (Part 1)," Wilbert Harrison
25. "Love In 'C' Minor—Pt. 1," Cerrone
26. "Love Is Better in the A.M. (Part 1)," Johnnie Taylor
27. "Mighty Love—Pt. 1," The Spinners
28. "More Bounce to the Ounce—Part 1," Zapp
29. "Oh Well—part one," Fleetwood Mac
30. "One Nation Under a Groove (Part 1)," Funkadelic
31. "Ooh Poo Pah Doo—Part II," Jessie Hill
32. "One Monkey Don't Stop No Show (Part I)," The Honey Cone
33. "Open Sesame—Part 1," Kool and the Gang
34. "Party Down—Part 1," Little Beaver
35. "Parrty—Part 1," Maceo and the Macks[2]
36. "Peppermint Twist—Part 1," Joey Dee and the Starliters
37. "The Player—Part 1," First Choice
38. "Rip Tips (Part 1)," Andre Williams
39. "Rock and Roll Part Two," Gary Glitter
40. "Rock & Roll Stew . . . Part 1," Traffic
41. "Rockhouse, Part 2," Ray Charles
42. "Romeo Part 1 & Part 2," The Real Roxanne with Hitman Howie Tee
43. "Shout—Part 1," The Isley Brothers
44. "Super Freak (Part 1)," Rick James[3]
45. "Synchronicity II," The Police
46. "There's Something on Your Mind, Part 2," Bobby Marchan
47. "Viva Tirado—Part 1," El Chicano
48. "What'd I Say (Part 1)," Ray Charles
49. "You Can't Win (Part 1)," Michael Jackson
50. "Your Love—Part 2," Keith Sweat

---

[1] "Honky Tonk, Part 2" was a hit twice.
[2] Produced by James Brown.
[3] Part Three *not* by M. C. Hammer—at least, not quite.

Hold It Right There!
The Most Unnecessary Multipart Records

1. "Baby Let's Rap Now," The Moments
2. "The Bertha Butt Boogie (Part 1)," The Jimmy Castor Bunch
3. "Disco Duck (Part 1)," Rick Dees and His Cast of Idiots
4. "Do the Funky Penguin (Part I)," Rufus Thomas
5. "Flapjacks—Part 1," Googie Rene Combo
6. "For You (A Disco Concerto) Part 1," Noel Pointer
7. "Get Off Your Aahh! And Dance (Part 1)," Foxy
8. "I Wanna Dance Wit' Choo (Doo Dat Dance), Part 1," Disco Tex and the Sex-O-Lettes
9. "MacArthur Park (Part II)," The Four Tops
10. "The Madison Time—Part 1," Ray Bryant Combo
11. "More More More (Pt. 1)," The Andrea True Connection
12. "Sadeness," Enigma
13. "Sho Nuff Boogie (Part I)," Sylvia and the Moments
14. "Sock It to Me, Part 1," The Deacons
15. "Soul Hootenanny (Pt. 1)," Gene Chandler
16. "Stars on 45 II" (let alone "Stars on 45 III"), Stars on 45
17. "The 2000 Pound Bee (Part 2)," The Ventures
18. "Uh! Oh! Part 2," The Nutty Squirrels
19. "Wide Receiver Part 1," Michael Henderson
20. "Your Thing Is Your Thing," New Horizons

Sad But True: All these records actually charted.

Origins of 40 Group Names

1. ALICE COOPER
Supposedly derived from a Ouija board reading that revealed that Vincent Furnier, the band's lead singer, was the reincarnation of Alice Cooper, a seventeenth-century witch. Furnier took Cooper's name, or so the story goes.

2. ANTHRAX
Anthrax is a bacterial infection, common among sheep and cattle but transmissible to people. It causes malignant ulcers, and the animals that get it usually are destroyed.

3. THE BEATLES
After the Crickets, because Buddy Holly influenced them so much.

4. THE B-52s
After their huge hairdos, which are known in Southern slang as B-52s in honor of the massive aircraft they resemble.

5. THE BOO-YAA T.R.I.B.E.

These Samoan-American brothers initially said their name derived from the sound of a shotgun blast—"*Boo*-yaa!" They later claimed that their audiences made the same noise.

6. BUFFALO SPRINGFIELD

From the brand name of a steamroller (not an airplane, as is commonly believed).

7. THE COASTERS

Rock's first great comedy group made its start in Los Angeles, as the Robins ("Riot in Cell Block #9," "Smokey Joe's Cafe"). When record producers Jerry Leiber and Mike Stoller moved to New York to work for Atlantic Records, they took the core of the group with them. The name change reflected their origins "on the Coast."

8. DEPECHE MODE

After a French fashion magazine.

9. THE DISPOSABLE HEROES OF HIPHOPRISY

Classic nineties name, selected to identify the band's musical genre (hip-hop) and its ideological attitude by ironically commenting on the false gods of both superstar heroism and the culture of planned obsolescence.

10. DURAN DURAN

Named after the villain in Roger Vadim's 1967 science fiction cartoon, *Barbarella*. It starred Jane Fonda as a brainless voluptuary plagued by Duran Duran, a perfectly appropriate allusion given this band's hedonist music and wear-your-model-on-your-sleeve lifestyle.

11. EMF

Every Mother Fucker, though their record label went to great pains to deny it.

12. EPMD

Erick Sermon and Parrish Smith picked a name that's an acronym of their ambition. It stands for "Erick and Parrish Making Dollars."

13. FLEETWOOD MAC

If you were told that this band's name came from the last names of its leaders, you'd get confused—unless you knew that Fleetwood Mac's founders weren't front-persons Lindsay Buckingham and Stevie Nicks but drummer Mick Fleetwood and bassist John McVie.

16. FRANKIE GOES TO HOLLYWOOD

Allegedly from a poster advertising Frank Sinatra's first film.

15. GUNS N' ROSES

Axl Rose and Izzy Stradlin joined their band, L. A. Guns, with Hollywood Rose, the group that featured Duff (Rose) McKagan, Slash, and Steven Adler. Thus, their name represents possibly the only compromise GN'R has ever voluntarily made.

16. HÜSKER DÜ

After a board game popular among snowbound Minnesotans.

17. IRON MAIDEN

A famous medieval torture device, the iron maiden consisted of a metal form with spikes on the inside. Those placed inside it would be pierced by the spikes, until they confessed (or until the innocent died).

18. JETHRO TULL

Tull was the eighteenth-century inventor of the seed drill.

19. KISS

Named after the pleasurable sociosexual activity. Does *not* stand for Kids in Satan's Service, no matter what the local preacher claims.

20. L7

Make an "L" with your left hand and a "7" with your right. Bring them together and they form a square. This is one of the mysteries cited in "Woolly Bully," to wit: "Let's don't be L7 / Come and join the dance." These riot grrrls chose the name to dare you to ask, which if you do proves your hipness might take that shape.

21. LED ZEPPELIN

The Who's John Entwistle (originally slated, along with drummer Keith Moon, to be a member of Jimmy Page's post-Yardbirds band) joshed that such a group would go over like the world's biggest lead balloon—a veritable Led Zeppelin.

22. LYNYRD SKYNRD

In honor of their high-school nemesis, gym teacher Leonard Skinner.

23. THE MOTHERS OF INVENTION

From necessity.

24. N.W.A

An acronym for Niggers with Attitude.

25. THE O'JAYS

Cleveland deejay Eddie O'Jay gave them their break, and they named themselves in his honor.

26. PERE UBU

From the demented king in Alfred Jarry's surrealist play *Ubu Roi.*

27. THE POGUES

Short for the Gaelic expression *pogue mo chone,* which means kiss my ass, a perfect rendition of the group's attitude.

28. PUBLIC ENEMY

During the Depression, F.B.I. director J. Edgar Hoover would refer to bank-robbing criminals like John Dillinger and Pretty Boy Floyd as "Public Enemy Number One," perhaps influenced by William Wellman's 1931 film, *The Public Enemy,* starring James Cagney. PE's Chuck D adopted the name to reflect today's perception of young black males as inherently criminal.

29. R.E.M.

The initials stand for Rapid Eye Movement, which is the stage of sleep in which the most intense dreams occur.

30. RUFUS

From the *Mechanics Illustrated* magazine column "Ask Rufus." *Ask Rufus* also became a Rufus album title. (This truth of this information bears no relationship to the sense it makes.)

31. STEELY DAN

The original Steely Dan appeared in William Burroughs's novel *Naked Lunch*. A milk-squirting dildo with which lesbians buggered males, its specific appeal to the young Donald Fagen and/or Walter Becker remains lost in the shrouds of time.

32. TALKING HEADS

According to drummer Chris Frantz (in the liner notes to the Heads' greatest hits album, *Sand in the Vaseline*), when the band got its first gig at CBGBs it didn't have a name. Instead, it used a series of temporary names—the Vogue Dots, the Tunnel Tones, the World of Love—that the group would paint on the bass drum head to try them out. Crony Wayne Zieve found Talking Heads (broadcasting jargon for an announcer who's always seen seated at a desk) in a copy of *T. V. Guide*. Frantz had a red and silver T-shirt saying "Talking Heads" made for him. The first person who saw him wearing it on Bleecker Street told him, "That's a terrible name." The music was good, though.

33. TEARS FOR FEARS / PRIMAL SCREAM

Both these eighties groups took their names from phrases used by controversial psychiatrist Arthur Janov, whose "primal scream" therapy came to prominence when John Lennon and Yoko Ono briefly adopted it in the early seventies.

34. 10cc / LOVIN' SPOONFUL

The British and American estimates, respectively, of the amount of ejaculate in the average man's come. "I gave my baby a lovin' spoonful" and similar phrases recur frequently in country blues songs. Kevin Godley and Lol Creme's name selection had no similar artistic references in U.K. culture.

35. THE TROGGS

Short for "troglodytes," who were prehistoric cave dwellers. Based on their playing style, the Troggs in question would have to be considered Neanderthals. Cro-Magnons had art.

36. UB40

Named after the form English workers have to fill out to receive unemployment benefits.

37. URIAH HEEP

The original Uriah Heep appears in Dickens as a paragon of false humility. The name fit since, like the band, this conniver had a great deal to be humble about.

38. THE VELVET UNDERGROUND

The Velvet Underground first appeared as a classic novel of sadomasochism. The first Velvet Underground lineup, with its links to the Warholian Manhattan demimonde, fit the moniker to a tee, even recording one song, "Venus in Furs," named after a novel of similar bent.

39. THE YARDBIRDS

Name chosen in honor of the great alto saxophonist Charlie "Yardbird" Parker.

40. THE WHO

Name selected to deliberately frustrate anyone who tried to get information about the band: "Who's playing tonight?" "Yep." "Who?" "That's what I said."

Origins of 10 Individual Names

1. AFRIKA BAMBAATAA

Name selected when he converted his faction of the Bronx gang the Black Spades, from mayhem to music, as the Zulu Nation. He went on to become a seminal club deejay and record-maker, among the first to electronify contemporary dance beats. Today, one of the Jungle Brothers, a significant hip-hop crew, sustains a tradition by identifying himself as Afrika Baby Bambaataa. Many in the Hip-Hop Nation could say the same.

2. BOY GEORGE

Just to make sure you were sure.

3. THOMAS DOLBY

In honor of the noise reduction device.

4. M. C. HAMMER

As a kid, he worked for the Oakland A's as clubhouse attendant, occasional broadcaster, and frequent spy for owner Charles O. Finley. Some of the players noted a facial resemblance to home run king Henry Aaron aka Hammerin' Hank. Thus, the Hammer was born. (It was A's players who gave Hammer his initial capital to become a rap entrepreneur.)

5. ICE-T

Picked in honor of the notorious pimp-novelist Iceberg Slim. Inspired hordes of imitators, headed by Ice Cube.

6. L.L. COOL J

Stands for Ladies Love Cool James.

7. MADONNA

It's her real name, stupid. No blasphemy involved.

8. MITCH RYDER

Selected by opening the New York City telephone book at random. "After that, naming the band the Detroit Wheels came pretty easily," said the former Billy Levise.

9. SLASH

Born Saul Hudson, the Guns N' Roses guitarist took his name from his playing style.

10. CONWAY TWITTY

Harold Jenkins took a gander at the map and selected two obscure cities, Conway, Arkansas, and Twitty, Texas, as a rockin' pseudonym before he headed out on the road. More surprisingly, the owner of such an unexceptionable real name kept the spurious one after he turned his talents to country.

Original Names of Famous Bands

1. Actress (The New York Dolls)
2. Al and the Silvertones (The Guess Who)
3. Bastard (Motorhead)
4. The Beefeaters (The Byrds)
5. The Canadian Squires, Levon and the Hawks (The Band)
6. The Detours, The High Numbers (The Who)
7. The Disco Three (The Fat Boys)
8. Earth (Black Sabbath)
9. The Farriss Brothers (INXS)
10. Tommy Fogerty and the Blue Velvets (Creedence Clearwater Revival)
11. The Hallucinations (The J. Geils Band)
12. Hotlegs (10cc)
13. The Hourglass (The Allman Brothers Band)
14. The Jazziacs (Kool and the Gang)
15. Johnny and the Self-Abusers (Simple Minds)
16. Joy Division (New Order)
17. London (Motley Crue)
18. Mammoth (Van Halen)
19. The Metropolitan Blues Quartet (The Yardbirds)
20. Mudcrutch (Tom Petty and the Heartbreakers)
21. Praise of Lemmings (Culture Club)
22. The Primes, The Primettes (The Temptations, The Supremes)
23. Pud (The Doobie Brothers)
24. The Quarrymen, The Silver Beatles (The Beatles)
25. Raw Soul (Maze featuring Frankie Beverly)
26. The Red Roosters (Spirit)
27. The Robins (The Coasters)
28. The Roundabouts (Deep Purple)
29. The Screaming Abdabs (Pink Floyd)
30. Smile (Queen)
31. Soft White Underbelly, The Stalk-Forrest Group (Blue Oyster Cult)
32. The Tangerine Puppets (The Ramones)

33. Tom and Jerry (Simon and Garfunkel)
34. The Tourists (Eurythmics)
35. VCL XI, Hitlers Underpantz, The Id (Orchestral Manoeuvres in the Dark)
36. The Warlocks (The Grateful Dead)

Expelled
25 People Who Quit or Were Fired Before Their Groups Became Famous

1. Signe Anderson, vocals, The Jefferson Airplane (quit)
2. Syd Barrett, vocals, guitar, songwriter, Pink Floyd (quit because of mental illness)
3. Jeff Beck, guitar, The Jeff Beck Group (quit—more than once, too)
4. Pete Best, drums, The Beatles (fired)
5. Arthur and Richard Brooks, singers, The Impressions (quit—because they didn't like Curtis Mayfield's songs)
6. Eric Clapton, guitar, The Yardbirds (quit—because band too pop)
7. Tory Crimes, drums, The Clash (fired)
8. Ian Curtis, singer, Joy Division (quit—via rope)
9. Peter Green, guitar, Fleetwood Mac (quit—joined religious cult)
10. Al Jardine, guitar, The Beach Boys (quit—temporarily)
11. Jarobi, A Tribe Called Quest (mode of departure uncertain)
12. Al Kooper, guitar, keyboards, vocals, Blood Sweat and Tears (quit)
13. Keith Levine, guitar, The Clash (mode of departure uncertain)
14. Vinnie Lopez, drums, E Street Band (fired)
15. Glen Matlock, bass, The Sex Pistols (fired)
16. Henri Padovani, guitar, The Police (quit)
17. Anthony Phillips, guitar, Genesis (quit)
18. Professor Griff, minister of information, Public Enemy (fired—the group had already had hits when he left but only came to full national prominence as a result of his expulsion)
19. John Rutsey, drums, Rush (quit)
20. David Sancious, keyboards, The E Street Band (quit)
21. Doug Sandom, drums, The Who (fired)
22. Jeremy Spencer, guitar, Fleetwood Mac (quit—joined religious cult)
23. Ian Stewart, piano, The Rolling Stones (fired, became road manager)
24. Stu Sutcliffe, bass, The Beatles (quit)
25. Pete Willis, guitar, Def Leppard (fired)

Previous Convictions
Former Occupations

1. Gregory Abbott, Wall Street broker
2. Chuck Berry, hairdresser
3. Marc Bolan (T. Rex), model
4. David Bowie, commercial artist for advertising agency
5. Joe Cocker, gas fitter (plumber)
6. Phil Collins, child actor *(Oliver!)*
7. Bo Diddley, construction worker
8. Elvis Costello, computer technician
9. Eazy E (N.W.A), entrepreneur ("The Gordon Gekko of Compton")
10. John Entwistle (The Who), tax clerk
11. Deborah Harry (Blondie), Playboy Club Bunny
12. Ice-T, jewel thief
13. Janet Jackson, TV actress
14. Scott La Rock (Boogie Down Productions), homeless shelter counselor
15. Van Morrison, window cleaner
16. Elvis Presley, truck driver
17. Paul Revere, barber
18. Grace Slick, model
19. Tom Scholz (Boston), computer designer
20. Sting, teacher

Most Important Women
Female Performers Who've Made the Greatest Impact

1. MADONNA
More than any other artist, Madonna deconstructed the roles that women play, not only in music but in all of popular culture. While it's true that her appeal came as much from playing into stereotypes as from exploding them, the combination remodeled expectations and for the first time placed female voices at the center of pop discourse, as actors rather than spectators. Plus the music's good, except when it's great.

2. ARETHA FRANKLIN
The single greatest female singer of the rock era—possibly the single greatest singer of this era, without regard to gender or genre. From her Atlantic Records debut in 1966 through the mid-seventies, every rock and R&B singer worked off models of gospel intensity

and pop craft that Aretha established. When the disco divas first developed a new standard, it can be credibly argued, they did so precisely in reaction to Aretha's dominance. But her importance can't be measured strictly in its effect on women; Aretha changed the way that everyone heard the spiritual potential of popular music. In Rock and Roll Hall of Fame.

3. DIANA ROSS AND THE SUPREMES

The transcendent girl group; the apotheosis of glitz. As both of these things, for a very long time, the polar (and virtually only) alternative to Aretha. Made some truly great records, and their stage shows were legendary. In Rock and Roll Hall of Fame, and on merit, too.

4. JANIS JOPLIN

Sweaty, brassy, uncontrolled, and maybe uncontrollable. Not a great blues singer but a magnificent symbol of femininity unleashed into something like protofeminism. Joplin established a model so powerful that for almost a decade, virtually nobody *could* follow her except as parody.

5. PATTI SMITH

Rock's truest poet, bar none; a charismatic performer, live and on record; and an artistic role model for every genuinely ambitious punk and postpunk.

6. TINA TURNER

The incarnation of rock 'n' roll energy. If she'd played piano, she'd rank with anarchists like Little Richard and Jerry Lee Lewis. As it is, she has to settle for being sexier than Elvis or Jagger or anybody else. In Rock and Roll Hall of Fame.

7. CHAKA KHAN (SOLO AND WITH RUFUS)

The voice of funk, one of the most fabulous rhythm singers ever, and as one of the world's great human special effects, a prime progenitor of hip-hop.

8. MAHALIA JACKSON

Gospel greatness incarnate, the power of holiness made flesh and slipped into a profound groove by the grace of God. In Rock and Roll Hall of Fame.

9. DONNA SUMMER

Queen of Disco. The original diva, never funky but always rocking.

10. RUTH BROWN

First Queen of Rock 'n' Roll, even though she was—and is—probably more comfortable with sinuous blues numbers than the driving rhythms now associated with "rocking." In Rock and Roll Hall of Fame.

11. JOAN JETT (SOLO AND WITH THE RUNAWAYS)

The present-day rocker refuses to die, no matter how much the beat changes. Her black leather contained far more vision than the Ramones ever imagined. And if she's something of a cartoon, she came complete with a great nemesis, in the (not really villainous) Lita Ford.

12. JONI MITCHELL

More than just Prince's favorite singer-songwriter—the one who figured out how to take those folky rhythms and make them groove, then blasted past all the clichés (that she helped establish) with jazz records that grow on you over time. Besides all that, a lyric writer of surpassing grace and insight.

13. MARION WILLIAMS (SOLO, WITH THE CLARA WARD SINGERS, AND WITH THE STARS OF FAITH)

She gave Little Richard his falsetto "whoo," which means she established one of the fundamental vocal platforms of rock 'n' roll. She also made some of the most stomping rhythm records of the Golden Age of Gospel, with the Ward Singers and up through her stellar series with the Stars of Faith. The only popular musician ever to receive a MacArthur Foundation "genius grant."

14. DARLENE LOVE (SOLO, WITH THE BLOSSOMS, AND STANDING IN FOR THE CRYSTALS)

Mainly went uncredited on all those Phil Spector (et al.) sides, but the ones where you know it's her—"He's a Rebel," "Today I Met the Boy I'm Gonna Marry," "A Fine Fine Boy"—stand as definitive.

15. CHRISSIE HYNDE (THE PRETENDERS)

That rare performer of whom it can truly be said, if she hadn't existed, we'd have had to invent her. What makes Hynde special is that, unlike most theoretically required stars, she brought great (if oft obnoxious) personality to the task.

16. JANET JACKSON

Closer to Queen of (current) Pop than most suspect. Her work with Jimmy Jam and Terry Lewis sounds like a true collaboration, and her records have grown denser, more ambitious each time out, never retreating to formula.

17. CAROLE KING

It may be that "Will You Still Love Me Tomorrow," or at least its melody, will outlast "It's Too Late" or "You've Got a Friend," but all that means is that she peaked early. That she sustained such creativity for so long (the span is roughly a decade) is what really counts. In Rock and Roll Hall of Fame (as writer).

18. ETTA JAMES

Original queen of L.A. R&B. "Roll with Me Henry" was first great dirty rock record by a woman. Sustained her career in the fifties (at Modern), the sixties (at Chess and Muscle Shoals), and on into the eighties and nineties when she made some strikingly mature R&B albums. In Rock and Roll Hall of Fame.

19. ANNE AND NANCY WILSON (HEART)

Established female hard rock credentials—not as punkish as the Runaways or Patti Smith, and too melodic to quite be metal, their distinction lies as much in Nancy's guitar heroics as in Anne's post–Rob Halford belting.

20. BONNIE RAITT

Sustainer of the blues tradition; best slide guitarist of her generation; late in career, found out she could also write songs; an immensely engaging live performer; darling of the Grammys (which translates as "beloved of her peers").

21. KIM GORDON (SONIC YOUTH)

In her own way, the most macho figure on this list. Gordon leads her noise-rock combo by the basic expedient of making the strongest noises.

22. LORETTA LYNN

Wisest, warmest voice in country music and to top it off, an incipient feminist (listen to "The Pill," "One's on the Way," "Trouble in Paradise").

23. LAVERN BAKER

A grand fifties rock 'n' roll shouter, Baker rode to stardom on the crest of great dance beats that she rode as if they were stallions, and some of the wildest lyric scenarios ever written, which she conveyed as if they simply recounted everyday love affairs. In Rock and Roll Hall of Fame.

24. JOAN BAEZ

Prime folkie icon. Her readings of contemporary material tend to be icily distant, maybe betraying an uncertain grasp of such songs' meaning (if not their worth or purpose), but for an entire generation or two, Baez created an image in sound and looks that dictated what serious music-making was all about. Without her, no Natalie Merchant, no Indigo Girls, no Joni Mitchell, and in an important sense, no Bob Dylan.

25. TAMMY WYNETTE

Prime country icon. Not exactly a victim, though she could play the part. Comfortable with slickly pop arrangements but never lost her fundamental twang. "Stand By Your Man" might not have been an anthem coming out of any other throat, but emerging from hers, it threatens to outlast feminism.

26. YOKO ONO

It took two decades but the effect of her avant-gardism finally reached the mainstream through such heirs as the B-52s. In between, Ono's calculated caterwauling helped generate punk staples from Siouxsie Sioux to Lora Logic to Lydia Lunch to Exene Cervenka.

27. TRACY CHAPMAN

Singlehandedly revived the idea of the solo singer-songwriter with "Fast Car" and her brilliant debut album. She remains one of today's most undervalued songwriters, and her subsequent records seem to suffer more for the musical subtlety both critics and audiences miss than from any lack of material or performance intensity.

In other words, commercially punished for refusing to recapitulate the formula of her hit, which suggests she will eventually undergo a strong revival of popularity. The quality won't dwindle, either way.

28. STEVIE NICKS (SOLO AND WITH FLEETWOOD MAC)

If you doubt she could rock, check out her live version of "Edge of Seventeen." An icon from the days when rock found itself enveloped in a coked-out haze, but an icon nonetheless.

29. DOLLY PARTON

Despite the caricature she's become, Dolly's early work revealed not only an excellent voice but a songwriting sensitivity ("Coat of Many Colors," "My Tennessee Mountain Home") rarely paralleled.

30. ROXANNE SHANTÉ

Demolished hip-hop as all-male preserve and in the process created one of the great spontaneous answer record cycles of contemporary times. Subsequent releases suggest she may rise again.

31. TINA WEYMOUTH (WITH TALKING HEADS AND TOM TOM CLUB, AND AS RECORD PRODUCER FOR ZIGGY MARLEY, AMONG OTHERS)

First prominent female instrumentalist in an otherwise male band. Strong bass player whose personality flavors all she touches. With Chris Frantz, created one of the most distinctive rhythm sections of their era in the Heads; as Tom Tom Club, unleashed wicked sense of humor built on dance grooves; as producer, showed she understood hits and propulsion.

32. BRENDA LEE

Lee stands in here for Janis Martin; Laurie Collins; Rose Maddox; Wanda Jackson—an entire generation of women who rocked when just about everybody claimed no woman could rock. Rockabilly may forever remain a male domain in image but it never was in fact.

33. MARIANNE FAITHFULL

Original sixties boy-toy (and semiproperty of Mick Jagger, at that) who became one of the most ravaged voices of the eighties. Since *Broken English*, her records have presented rock as a literal battleground of the sexes, with all the brutal beauty that implies.

34. QUEEN LATIFAH

One of the strongest images in hip-hop, and her raps lay claim to maternal and sisterly wisdom as something powerful and eternal.

35. SIOUXSIE SIOUX (SIOUXSIE AND THE BANSHEES)

The most potent, if not always poetic, yawp on early London punk scene. Later became postmod dance pop fixture.

36. KITTY WELLS

Country's first godmother.

37. EXENE CERVENKA (X)

The most potent poetic yawp in L.A.'s punk and postpunk scene.

38. DEBBIE HARRY (BLONDIE)

Pre-Madonna, she wreaked havoc on dumb blonde imagery, not so much by playing into it (though she did) as by dancing all over it.

39. LABELLE

Prototypical female rock group: one soul diva (Patti Labelle), one supper-club soul singer (Sarah Dash), one hard rock leather queen (Nona Hendryx). Added up to much, much more than "Lady Marmalade"—added up to an act tough enough to tour with the Who.

40. SINEAD O'CONNOR

Blabbermouth that she undoubtedly is, nobody in recent years has emerged as a more trenchant songwriter and speaker on issues, nor a more moving and mesmerizing performer. Sinead symbolizes all the damage that has been done to women in the past, and their indomitability in the face of it.

Great Girl Groups and the Hits that Made Them Famous

"Girl groups" refers not to just any rock group with female members, but to a specific aggregation of singing groups, composed exclusively of young women, operating primarily out of New York (but also Los Angeles, Detroit, and occasionally elsewhere) in the pre-Beatles sixties. Because the majority of the women involved were still in their teens, the term "girl groups" describes more than denigrates. Girl groups assume a special importance in rock history because, even though males dominated the record production and songwriting that established their musical architecture, these female combos represent the first important infusion of anything like a female perspective in rock. For further information, see Alan Betrock's excellent history, Groups: The Story of a Sound.

1. The Crystals, "Da Doo Ron Ron," "Then He Kissed Me"
2. The Ronettes, "Be My Baby," "Baby I Love You"
3. The Shirelles, "Will You Love Me Tomorrow," "Baby It's You"
4. The Shangri-Las, "The Leader of the Pack," "Give Him a Great Big Kiss"
5. Martha and the Vandellas, "Heatwave," "Dancing in the Street"
6. The Chiffons, "He's So Fine," "One Fine Day"
7. The Supremes, "Baby Love," "Stop! In the Name of Love"
8. The Chantels, "Maybe," "Look in My Eyes"
9. The Marvelettes, "Please Mr. Postman," "BEechwood 4-5789"
10. The Dixie Cups, "Iko Iko," "Chapel of Love"

11. The Orlons, "Don't Hang Up," "South Street"
12. The Cookies, "Don't Say Nothin' Bad (About My Baby)," "Chains"
13. The Velvelettes, "Needle in a Haystack," "He Was Really Sayin' Something"
14. The Three Degrees, "Gee Baby (I'm Sorry)," "When Will I See You Again"
15. The Angels, "My Boyfriend's Back," "Thank You and Goodnight"
16. The Jaynetts, "Sally, Go 'Round the Roses"
17. Reparata and the Delrons, "Whenever a Teenager Cries," "I'm Nobody's Baby Now"
18. Shirley Gunter and The Queens, "Oop Shoop"
19. The Murmaids, "Popsicles and Icicles"
20. The Chordettes, "Lollipop"
21. The Ad Libs, "The Boy from New York City"
22. The Jelly Beans, "I Wanna Love Him So Bad"
23. The Bobbettes, "Mr. Lee," "I Shot Mr. Lee"
24. The Qin-Tones, "Down the Aisle of Love"
25. The Teen Queens, "Eddie My Love"

Don't You Dare Call Them "Girl" Groups
It Ain't All Grunge, It Just Seems That Way

1. The Au Pairs
2. The Bangles
3. BWP (Bytches with Problems)
4. Fanny (See Indigo Girls)
5. The Go-Gos (See Indigo Girls)
6. H.W.A. (Hoes with Attitude)
7. Hole
8. The Indigo Girls (Let's not get too technical, OK?)
9. L7
10. Labelle
11. Lilliput
12. The Raincoats
13. The Runaways
14. Salt-N-Pepa
15. The Shaggs
16. The Slits

And Let's Not Hear Any Jokes About Molly Hatchet, Either
Women Who Rocked Before It Was Fashionable (or, In Many Quarters, Even Thought Possible)

1. Maggie Bell (Stone the Crows)
2. Pat Benatar
3. Big Maybelle
4. Lita Ford
5. Nona Hendryx
6. Wanda Jackson
7. Etta James
8. Joan Jett
9. Janis Joplin
10. Chaka Khan
11. Barbara Lynn
12. Joni Mitchell (Doubters, attend to "You Turn Me On I'm a Radio" and "Raised on Robbery")
13. Stevie Nicks (Doubters: check the live "Edge of 17")
14. Esther Phillips (aka Little Esther)
15. Suzi Quatro
16. Bonnie Raitt
17. Martha Reeves
18. Patti Smith
19. Donna Summer
20. Teena Marie
21. Big Mama Thornton
22. Tina Turner
23. Mary Wells
24. Ann Wilson (Heart)
25. Nancy Wilson (Heart)

Great Folk-Rock Hits

1. "Like a Rolling Stone," Bob Dylan
2. "Mr. Tambourine Man," The Byrds
3. "House of the Rising Sun," The Animals
4. "Hey Joe," The Jimi Hendrix Experience
5. "Norwegian Wood," The Beatles
6. "Free Fallin'," Tom Petty
7. "Do You Believe in Magic," The Lovin' Spoonful
8. "I Want You," Bob Dylan
9. "If I Were a Carpenter," Tim Hardin
10. "Runaway Train," Soul Asylum
11. "I Got You Babe," Sonny and Cher
12. "Catch the Wind," Donovan

Greatest Bands of the British Invasion

1. The Beatles
2. The Rolling Stones
3. The Who
4. The Animals
5. The Yardbirds
6. The Spencer Davis Group
7. Them
8. The Kinks
9. The Pretty Things
10. The Searchers
11. Manfred Mann
12. The Small Faces
13. The Dave Clark Five
14. John Mayall's Bluesbreakers
15. The Hollies
16. The Swinging Blue Jeans
17. Wayne Fontana and the Mindbenders
18. The Zombies
19. The Moody Blues
20. The Merseybeats

Colonies
The Places Where Music Was Made, Decade by Decade

THE FIFTIES

1. MEMPHIS

Key record label: Sun. Home to or destination of Elvis, B. B. King, Jerry Lee Lewis, Junior Parker, Bobby Bland, and a host of lesser but unforgettable artists. Its location at the top of the Mississippi Delta made it the first stop on the way out of the rural South for both black and white Americans engaged in one of history's great diasporas. Consequently, Memphis became the place where the white and the black versions of blues and gospel music mingled and merged most intensely.

2. NEW ORLEANS

Key record labels: Imperial, Specialty, Ace. Notably, none of these were actually based in New Orleans (the first two in L.A., Ace in Jackson, Mississippi) but all recorded their most important rock and rhythm and blues artists there. Those performers included Little Richard, Fats Domino, Professor Longhair, Huey "Piano" Smith, Lloyd Price, and Smiley Lewis. They were aided by the great bandleaders and songwriters Dave Bartholomew and Allen Toussaint, abetted by session musicians led by drummer Earl Palmer, who transformed the Hollywood recording scene when they relocated there as the New Orleans scene dwindled.

3. CHICAGO

Key record labels: Chess/Checker, VeeJay. Central outpost of blues and gospel music, notably Muddy Waters, Howlin' Wolf,

Mahalia Jackson, and Sam Cooke, but also the place where Chuck Berry and Bo Diddley defined central currents of rock and roll. VeeJay, one of the first important black-owned labels, added doo-wop and R&B crooning to the mix, with such artists as Gene Chandler, the Dells, and the Impressions featuring Jerry Butler and Curtis Mayfield.

4. NEW YORK

Key labels: Atlantic, End/Gone, Fire/Fury. But there were hordes of labels in New York, and several different kinds of R&B and rock 'n' roll found a home there, notably doo-wop led by Frankie Lymon and the Teenagers, a more adult black vocal harmony approach epitomized by the Drifters, the updated jump blues of Big Joe Turner and Ruth Brown, and the more down-home blues approach fostered by Fire/Fury's Bobby Robinson from his record shop on Harlem's 125th Street.

5. LOS ANGELES

Key labels: Modern/RPM, Specialty, Imperial. One of the most neglected R&B scenes, which featured some of the great doo-wop-pers, including the Robins (pre-Coasters), Penguins, Jesse Belvin, Richard Berry and the Pharoahs, Arthur Lee Maye and the Crowns and many more; proto-soul singers like Sam Cooke and Etta James; great songwriters and bandleaders like Percy Mayfield, Maxwell Davis, and Johnny Otis. For rock 'n' roll, L.A. served primarily as a destination, but Ricky Nelson, Eddie Cochran, and Johnny Burnette made most of their important records here.

6. PHILADELPHIA

The key institution here wasn't a record company but Dick Clark's *American Bandstand*. In one way or another, most of the city's record companies, music publishers, performers, and even pressing plants had economic ties to Clark, or at least they did until the payola scandals of 1959–60, which forced Clark to divest his music business interests to remain in broadcasting. Jamie Records (Duane Eddy et al.) and Cameo-Parkway Records (Bobby Rydell, the Dovells, et al.) recorded some important rock 'n' roll and even the odd piece of R&B but the city's real musical boom happened several years later, when Clark's influence had waned. Its importance as a music business center is belied by the Rydell-Fabian-Frankie Avalon fare that typified its fifties repertoire.

7. CINCINNATI

Key record label: King/Federal. In fact, Syd Nathan's record company was about all the city had going for it, musically, but that was more than plenty, given an artist roster that included such R&B greats as James Brown, Hank Ballard and the Midnighters, Little Willie John, Bill Doggett, and Earl Bostic plus a healthy complement of important country stars like Cowboy Copas, Hawkshaw Hawkins, and the Delmore Brothers.

8. DETROIT

The Motor City's biggest record label, at this point, was tiny Fortune, which hadn't much to boast about outside of the marvelous Nolan Strong and the Diablos ("The Wind"). Detroit's importance stemmed from being a major talent center, the place from which Jackie Wilson, Hank Ballard, Little Willie John, LaVern Baker, and Jack Scott, among many others, emerged. Wilson's songwriter, Berry Gordy, had bigger plans and by the end of the decade, he'd begun putting them into action. The city was also, with Houston, one of the two most important radio breakout points for rock and R&B material.

9. CLOVIS, NEW MEXICO

All that Clovis had going for it was Norman Petty and his studio. That was plenty, though, since Buddy Holly made his most important hits there, and fellow Texan rockabillies Roy Orbison, Jimmy Bowen, and Buddy Knox also cruised over to get their start in Petty's complex.

10. HOUSTON

Key record label: Duke/Peacock. Run by gangster-entrepreneur Don Robey, this black-owned label exploited its artists as badly as anything a white man ever ran. Its impressive talent pool included Bobby Bland, Little Junior Parker, Willie Mae "Big Mamma" Thornton, and a gaggle of gospel stars, including the 5 Blind Boys of Mississippi and the Dixie Hummingbirds. Also from Houston: blues great Lightning Hopkins.

THE SIXTIES

1. DETROIT

Key record label: Motown, its heady roster of performance, production, and songwriting stars too familiar to need recitation here. The Motor City also led the way in blue-eyed soul with Mitch Ryder and the Detroit Wheels and the Rationals, pioneered punk-rock with the MC5 and the Stooges, provided a home to the Grande, the psychedelic ballroom with the finest acoustics and most beautiful atmosphere, and churned out gobs of other soul and proto-funk from artists like Wilson Pickett, Deon Jackson, Barbara Lewis, the Dramatics, and a few dozen more.

2. LONDON

Expanding the rock and soul sensibility across the ocean suffices to measure the city's importance, but in addition, the Rolling Stones, the Who, the Kinks, the Yardbirds, and a few hundred more bands all hailed from London. Britain's most important provincial stars, including the Beatles, Eric Burdon and the Animals, and Van Morrison, soon relocated there. The British blues scene and its psychedelic successor both started here. And the revolution the Brits inaugurated had to do with substance every bit as much as with style.

3. MEMPHIS

Key record label: Stax/Volt. In addition to that label's formidable artist/producer/songwriter roster, highlighted by Otis Redding, Booker T. and the MGs, Sam and Dave, and Isaac Hayes and David Porter, Stax Studios and the MGs also hosted key sessions for Aretha Franklin and Wilson Pickett. Across town, Chips Moman's American Studios fostered a funky pop-rock sound with the Box Tops, among others, and brought Elvis back home for some of his crucial "comeback" sides late in the decade.

4. LIVERPOOL

Beyond the Beatles, Merseybeat didn't amount to much. Why would it need to?

5. MUSCLE SHOALS

Probably the smallest town anywhere on this list, certainly the only one where sale of liquor was illegal, this tiny Alabama burg featured not only Rick Hall's killer Fame studio but a legendary soul rhythm section highlighted by drummer Roger Hawkins, bassist David Hood, and keyboardist Barry Beckett. Pickett, Franklin, and Clarence Carter, among many others, made some of their best hits either in these precincts or with those musicians transplanted to other locations. As late as the late seventies, Bob Seger still used the town and its sound to great effect.

6. SAN FRANCISCO

Psychedelia, soul, and swamp rock. The Grateful Dead, Janis Joplin, the Jefferson Starship, and their cohorts got the ink for having a scene and a sound, as indeed they did, but across the Bay, even more enduring music got made by Sly and the Family Stone and John Fogerty's Creedence Clearwater Revival. With the exception of the Dead, not as musically indelible as it's made out to be. San Francisco nevertheless played a central role in creating both the image and the noise that identified the sixties as an era.

7. NEW YORK

Inevitably important, from the Brill Building uptown, the heartland of girl-group pop and the soul of slicksters like Dionne Warwick and Chuck Jackson, to the Greenwich Village clubs where Dylan's folk legacy played itself out and groups as diverse as the Velvet Underground, the Blues Project, the Lovin' Spoonful, and the Mamas and Papas got their start. New York became a major destination for everybody from Jimi Hendrix on down and turned out such unique individual talents as Laura Nyro and Simon and Garfunkel. Not to mention being home base for Miles Davis and the jazz-rock fusion that followed his *Bitches Brew*.

8. LOS ANGELES

The other inevitability, from the Beach Boys/Jan and Dean surf vocal scene to the psychedelia *plastique* of the Doors and Love, among many others. It's a pop town and groups like the Turtles, the Grassroots, and the Mamas and Papas abounded. But it's also the place that launched Leiber and Stoller and, even more important, Phil Spector, meaning its pop could have bite and power. Blue-eyed soul reached its pinnacle in Orange County, of all places, courtesy of the Righteous Brothers, and the recording studio scene remained both prolific and creative.

9. NEW ORLEANS

Now waning because the business side fell apart. A diaspora to Los Angeles couldn't stop such stalwarts as Allen Toussaint, Chris Kenner, Lee Dorsey, Aaron Neville, Dr. John the Nightripper, Irma Thomas, the Meters, and a whole crowd of lesser lights from turning out great discs in the Crescent City's distinctively slinky funk mode.

10. SEATTLE

Already grunge central, thanks to the Wailers, the Sonics, the Frantics, and, if you pick up nearby Portland, the Kingsmen and Paul Revere and the Raiders. Meantime, the Fleetwoods offered harmonies so slick and pale that they made the Beach Boys sound like the Rivingtons, while, for reasons still little understood, the likes of Loretta Lynn and Buck Owens cut some of their first important sides in local studios.

THE SEVENTIES

1. LOS ANGELES

Fleetwood Mac, the Eagles, Barry White, Linda Ronstadt, the remnants of Motown including the great work done by Stevie Wonder, Earth, Wind and Fire, Steely Dan, Jackson Browne, Crosby, Stills and Nash, the main stem of the singer-songwriter scene—like it or lump it, you've got to face facts and admit that the Hollywood recording scene of the seventies was the center of the popular music universe. Fortunately, there were many, many satellites.

2. LONDON

From Led Zeppelin to punk rock, the principal alternatives to being L.A. slick cropped up in British circles. The main themes were post-bluesy (led by Zep with zillions of lesser lights), avantgarde arty (Genesis, David Bowie, Yes, Roxy Music, a host of others), and finally punk—an explosion loud enough to be felt 'round the world and powerful enough that its fallout still determined not only much of the music that got made but many of the ways it was interpreted fifteen years later. From 1977 onward, in many ways, this *is* the story of Johnny Rotten.

3. NEW YORK

Center of the disco industry, home to much funk and hard rock, and thanks to the New York Dolls and Kiss, some excellent glamrock. Max's Kansas City became home to certain streams of the avant-garde (Lou Reed's post–John Cale Velvet Underground) and many singer-songwriters (including Bruce Springsteen, who first played there as second on the bill to Bob Marley and the Wailers).

But aside from the star-fucking at Studio 54 and elsewhere, the city's "scene" lacked a center. Until a Bowery Bar called CBGB (Country, Blue Grass, Blues) began allowing poetess Patti Smith and her nascent ensemble to play there a couple of nights a week, followed by some Rhode Island School of Design expatriates called Talking Heads, a band that sounded like the Grateful Dead intellectualized known as Television, a scruffy band of leather-jacketed outerborough punks named the Ramones . . . then the deluge, on a worldwide scale.

4. Philadelphia

Key record label: Philadelphia International. Primarily a producer's scene, led by label owners Kenneth Gamble and Leon Huff, starring Thom Bell, McFadden and Whitehead, and a handful of others, working with talented songwriters and, at Sigma Sound, one of the great studio bands of all time—call them the Trammps, and you connect to another of disco's highlights.

5. Jamaica

Reggae began (as ska and bluebeat and then the thing itself) in the sixties but it blossomed in the seventies, with the Wailers and Toots and the Maytals perfecting the classic style, then Bob Marley internationalizing the sound by making it more band-oriented, and the island's toasters, beginning with Big Youth, beginning to set their part of the stage for the emergence of rap.

6. Miami

Key record label: TK. In addition to funk- and disco-oriented TK, where K.C. and the Sunshine Band, Betty Wright, Little Beaver, the dirty-mouthed genius Blowfly (Clarence Reid), and Gordon and Gwen McRae reigned supreme, the city's Criteria studio played a central role in international pop-disco production (the Bee Gees made their hits here), and for several rock stars (notably Eric Clapton and Bob Seger).

7. Munich

From Kraftwerk to Donna Summer seems like not only a broad spread but a bit of a stretch. In fact, producer Giorgio Moroder and his associates Pete Bellote and Keith Forsey crafted the beginnings of Eurodisco there, while "Autobahn" and other Kraftwerk masterworks kicked off Europop. In short, nothing less than the seeds of all that made eighties facelessness so engaging and danceable took root here—as did the first reports that pop music again had a truly multinational basis, big news back in the day.

8. Austin, Texas

Although its aficionados can be as obsessive as Deadheads, that doesn't discredit Austin's credentials as having provided a *mise en scène* for rebel country (Willie Nelson, Jerry Jeff Walker, Joe Ely, Steve Earle, et al.), potent blues-rock (Stevie Ray Vaughan and the Fabulous Thunderbirds lead that pack), and the folkier side of the avant-garde, typified by the eccentricities of Townes Van Zandt.

The *Tejano* connection remains powerful in the work of Doug Sahm, Freddy Fender, Flaco Jiminez, Augie Meyers, and Hendrix-level accordion player Esteban (Steve) Jordan.

9. WASHINGTON, D.C.

Home to the world's first and only go-go scene and therefore a key generator of funk and progenitor of punk-funk. George Clinton dubbed it Chocolate City for good reason—like Frisco, Liverpool, and Detroit before it, D.C. has one of the world's great *audiences*.

10. DETROIT

Though its importance dwindled with the decade, the city's musical magnetism started off great, with Marvin Gaye leading the remnants of Motown, George Clinton forming the P-Funk mob and leading them to their world conquest, many marginal R&B acts, and more than a few rockers, including such expatriates as Alice Cooper. The Faces and J. Geils found their most important audiences here, and again in the first but not second half of the decade, Detroit radio led the way, with Top Forty reaching a musically integrated apotheosis of the form at just-across-the-border Windsor, Ontario's CKLW and free-form FM topping out at WABX.

THE EIGHTIES AND NINETIES

1. NEW YORK

Key record labels: Def Jam, Sugarhill, Tommy Boy, Profile. Home to the rap and hip-hop explosion. New York had declined as a mainstream music production center, but the new music—the most powerful rhythmic revolution since the rise of rock 'n' roll and be-bop—placed it once more in the middle of the action.

2. LOS ANGELES

Still the American production center, though its more interesting assets, early and late, included a properly festering punk scene, a web of big-haired, scuzzy-living, post-metal, punk-affected hard rockers (a range that extends from Guns N' Roses to Warrant, a far broader spectrum than most imagine), and the country's most important gangsta rap scene, featuring N.W.A, Ice-T, Ice Cube, and the phalanx coming out of East L.A. led by Kid Frost and Mellow Man Ace.

3. OAKLAND, CALIFORNIA

Though far less well known than New York's or L.A.'s, Oakland's hip-hop scene proved immensely fertile, featuring Digital Underground, Tupac, Too Short, Paris, Toni Tone Tony, and, for a time *über alles*, M. C. Hammer and his Oaktown posse. Plus the Bay Area has always been a center for boho developments in rock.

4. SEATTLE

Key record label: Sub-Pop. Nirvana, Pearl Jam, Soundgarden, and a horde of others, plus the jacked beats of Sir Mix-A-Lot offering the funniest hip-hop on the scene.

5. DUBLIN

The key players here were U2 and Sinead O'Connor, both internationalized and expatriated a good deal of the time. But interesting new bands regularly appeared from Ireland's capital and by mid-decade, even Jerry Lee Lewis had taken up residency here.

6. PARIS

Epicenter of world music, particularly Afropop, but also a center for bands who wanted to dabble in such sounds, for example, Talking Heads for *Remain in Light*. The city's influence seems likely to grow as the importance of world pop does.

7. CHICAGO

House music got its start in clubs here, making it also the center of the disco revival too. The Windy City possessed a healthy rap scene and its own brand of grunge—Smashing Pumpkins, Steve Albini.

8. DETROIT

Techno got its start in inner-city basements and garages even as the rest of the world wrote the town off as a complete burnout.

9. ATLANTA

Prime destination city of the period, attracting Teddy Riley and Elton John, Curtis Mayfield and Isaac Hayes, and providing a metropolitan center for bands like R.E.M. and the B-52s that emerged from the Athens, Georgia, new-wave scene.

10. MINNEAPOLIS

Prince, the Replacements, and production maestros Jimmy Jam and Terry Lewis centered a scene that also generated such hipster heroes as Soul Asylum, the Time, and Alexander O'Neal. The final proof that music production had become completely decentralized was that a definitive Southern California girl like Janet Jackson wound up traveling to the nation's snowiest metropolis to make her pop-funk LPs. Why do such financially enabled types as Prince, Paul Westerberg, and Jam and Lewis remain in their frigid hometown? Good question. Maybe someday somebody will come up with an answer to it.

The London R&B Scene and Its Mutations

1. CYRIL DAVIES ALL STARS

Davies, a remarkable harmonica player and one of the first Brits to make an effort to understand and play blues, died of leukemia in 1964, just before the scene broke wide open. Alexis Korner, one of his students and bandmates, took the mantle of blues leadership, soon passed along to John Mayall. But Davies himself trained some of the best British blues-rock players: Rolling Stone Charlie Watts, pianist Nicky Hopkins, Long John Baldry, Dick Heckstall-Smith.

2. ALEX KORNER'S BLUES INCORPORATED

The blues band leader as gentleman, beloved by all his many offspring, even after they'd moved on to greater, or at least more remunerative, things. The Rolling Stones, among many others, came together as part of Korner's band. (See "15 Veterans of Alexis Korner's Blues Incorporated," p. 284.)

3. JOHN MAYALL'S BLUESBREAKERS

The blues band leader as ideologue, unable in his purism to hold a band together long no matter how great. (See "Veterans of John Mayall's Bluesbreakers," p. 283.)

4. THE ROLLING STONES

Came together as a fill-in act for Korner. Drummer Watts played with Cyril Davies. Early member Dick Taylor went on to found the Pretty Things. Their residency at the Crawdaddy Club near Richmond Bridge kicked off the scene as something more than a fringe offshoot of the local jazz world.

5. THE YARDBIRDS

The great R&B guitar band produced Eric Clapton, Jeff Beck, and Jimmy Page (Led Zeppelin), as well as sending Keith Relf to Renaissance (if that's anything for an R&B group to boast about). It was the pop success of the Yardbirds, following in the wake of the Stones, that generated a London R&B craze out of the city's blues cult.

6. THE PRETTY THINGS

Phil May and ex–Rolling Stone Dick Taylor led the original band. Mitch Mitchell (Jimi Hendrix Experience) played drums briefly. Their big hit, "Don't Bring Me Down," got banned in the United States for reasons now obscure.

7. STEAMPACKET

Graduates: Long John Baldry, Brian Auger, Auger's singer Julie Driscoll, and drummer Mickey Waller (Jeff Beck, Rod Stewart).

8. THE ARTWOODS

Featured Art Wood, Ron Wood's brother and himself a good guitarist, singer Jon Lord of Deep Purple, and drummer Keef Hartley, later with Bluesbreakers and his own band.

9. GRAHAM BOND ORGANISATION

Graduates: Jack Bruce and Ginger Baker (Cream), Dick Heckstall-Smith, John Hiseman.

10. LONG JOHN BALDRY

Baldry himself served time with both Korner and Cyril Davies's bands, then had a couple of hits as a vocalist. His groups included the Steampacket and the Hoochie Coochie Men, which also included the young Rod Stewart.

11. THE CHEYNES

Graduates: Peter Bardens (Them, Camel) and Mick Fleetwood (Bluesbreakers, Fleetwood Mac).

12. BRIAN AUGER

Another member of Steampacket, Auger also led his own bands, Trinity and Oblivion Express.

13. GARY FARR AND THE T-BONES

Contributed Keith Emerson to the Nice and then to Emerson, Lake and Palmer.

14. MARK LEEMAN FIVE

Drummer Brian Davison went on to the Nice.

15. ZOOT MONEY BIG ROLL BAND

Money (later a member of Eric Burdon's New Animals) ran a group that produced Andy Somers, also of the New Animals, and Johnny Almond, a seventies hit with Mark-Almond.

16. JIMMY POWELL AND THE FIVE DIMENSIONS

Rod Stewart's first band.

17. SHOTGUN EXPRESS

Featured Rod Stewart, Peter Green (Fleetwood Mac), Peter Bardens (late Them), as well as Merseybeat singer Beryl Marsden.

18. THE BIRDS

First band for Ron Wood (later with Jeff Beck, the Faces, the Rolling Stones).

19. MANFRED MANN

Marginal to this scene because they played more pop-jazz than blues, at least until the Stones and Yardbirds showed Mann and company where the money was. On the other hand, lead singer Paul Jones (later star of *Privilege*, one of the definitive pop star movie vehicles) proved one of the best. Also included singer Mike D'Abo, Hughie Flint and Tom McGuinness, and Beatles associate (and *Revolver* cover illustrator) Klaus Voorman.

20. THE ZEPHYRS

They're best known for their version of Bo Diddley's "I Can Tell," as produced by Shel Talmy (the Who, the Kinks). Mick Jagger hated it, and said so a lot.

Veterans of John Mayall's Bluesbreakers

1. Colin Allen, drums (Stone the Crows)
2. Johnny Almond, sax (Mark-Almond)
3. Jack Bruce, bass (Manfred Mann, Graham Bond Organisation, Cream, Tony Williams Lifetime, West Bruce and Laing, B.L.T., solo)

4. Eric Clapton, guitar (Cream, Blind Faith, Delaney and Bonnie and Friends, Derek and the Dominoes, solo)
5. Roger Dean, guitar (album cover artist)
6. Aynsley Dunbar, drums (ubiquitous for twenty years, eventually sliding all the way to the West Coast of North America with Jefferson Starship)
7. Mick Fleetwood, drums (Fleetwood Mac)
8. Hughie Flint, drums (Manfred Man, McGuinness-Flint)
9. Andy Fraser, bass (Free)
10. Peter Green (Fleetwood Mac, solo)
11. Keef Hartley, drums (The Artwoods, The Keef Hartley Band)
12. Jon Hiseman, drums (Graham Bond Organisation, Colosseum)
13. Harvey Mandel, guitar (Canned Heat, sessions, solo)
14. Jon Mark, guitar (Mark-Almond)
15. John McVie, bass (Fleetwood Mac)
16. Chris Mercer, guitar, sax (Juicy Lucy)
17. Tony Reeves, bass (Colosseum)
18. Larry Taylor, bass (Canned Heat)
19. Mick Taylor, guitar (The Rolling Stones, solo)

15 Veterans of Alexis Korner's Blues Incorporated

1. Ginger Baker, drums (Graham Bond Organisation, Cream, Ginger Baker's Air Force)
2. Long John Baldry, vocals (Steampacket, solo)
3. Graham Bond, sax (Graham Bond Organisation)
4. Jack Bruce, bass (Manfred Mann, Graham Bond Organisation, Cream, Tony Williams Lifetime, West Bruce and Laing, B.L.T., solo)
5. Eric Burdon, vocals (The Animals, War, solo)
6. Terry Cox, drums (Pentangle)
7. Dick Heckstall-Smith, sax (John Mayall's Bluesbreakers, Colosseum, solo)
8. Lee Jackson, bass (The Nice, Jackson Heights)
9. Mick Jagger, occasional vocals, harp (The Rolling Stones, solo)
10. Brian Jones, guitar jams (The Rolling Stones)
11. Paul Jones, vocals (Manfred Mann, *Privilege*, *Evita*, The Blues Band, solo)
12. Robert Plant, vocals (Led Zeppelin)
13. Keith Richards, guitar jams (The Rolling Stones, solo)
14. Danny Thompson, bass (Pentangle)
15. Charlie Watts, drums (The Rolling Stones, solo)

You Can't Say We Didn't Warn You
25 of the Most Absurd Group Names of the Psychedelic Era

1. Autosalvage
2. Ball Point Banana
3. Bubble Puppy
4. The Charging Tyrannosaurus of Despair[1]
5. Chocolate Watchband
6. The Crab Cometh Forth
7. Daisy Overkill
8. The Electric Prunes
9. Everpresent Fullness
10. The Fifty Foot Hose
11. Frosted Suede
12. Frumious Bandersnatch
13. Hmmm
14. It's a Beautiful Day
15. The Jefferson Airplane
16. Jesus Christ and the Nailknockers
17. Lothar and the Hand People
18. The Only Alternative and His Other Possibilities
19. The Peanut Butter Conspiracy
20. Purple Earthquake
21. Strawberry Alarm Clock
22. 13th Floor Elevator
23. Transatlantic Chicken Wicken No. 5
24. Ultimate Spinach
25. Uncut Balloon

---

[1] Name later changed to Detroit Edison White Light Co., because the drummer refused to be associated with despair.

10 Songs Every Sixties Band Had to Know

1. "Foxy Lady," Jimi Hendrix
2. "Gloria," Them, The Shadows of Knight
3. "Hey Joe," The Leaves, Jimi Hendrix Experience, Love, The Byrds, et al.
4. "(I Can't Get No) Satisfaction," The Rolling Stones, Otis Redding
5. "I'm a Man," The Yardbirds (after Bo Diddley)
6. "In the Midnight Hour," Wilson Pickett
7. "Little Latin Lupe Lu," The Righteous Brothers, Mitch Ryder and the Detroit Wheels
8. "Louie Louie," The Kingsmen and a cast of millions
9. "Twist and Shout," The Isley Brothers, The Beatles
10. "Walking the Dog," Rufus Thomas, The Rolling Stones

Songs Every Eighties Band Had to Know
(Compiled by Stewart Francke)

In the '80s and '90s, the live music scene split, much as radio did. Pub or bar bands fell loosely into AOR; alternative was then called "new music" and had little radio and club exposure; and Top 40 was in every Sheraton lounge in America. The oldies rooms were the rage in the '80s but I've confined my list to songs released or successfully re-released in the decade. ("Old Time Rock and Roll" qualifies because of the film Risky Business.*) My choices are influenced by a certain empirical gristle that was in turn determined by where I live. I've played every song on the bar band list at least 300 times and there is still some regional sense of music around here, as you know. Of these songs, "Bad to the Bone" always elicited the most rabid response—it's a great mock-tough guy story with a primal E major blues riff. John Cafferty is Kmart Bruce, but people in bars (not clubs, as they're referred to today, but bars, like The Sawmill in Grayling, Michigan) love "On The Dark Side"—it's "Cherry Cherry" and a million other songs in the fast part. In fact, we would often go from "Bad to the Bone" to "Take Me to the River" to "Pink Cadillac" to "Lonely Ol' Night" to "Gloria" to "On the Dark Side" without a break, changing only the tempo. They're all in E. The band didn't like it much—you know, stump the band —but the world's in E.*

BAR BAND TOP TEN

1. "Bad to the Bone," George Thorogood
2. "Old Time Rock and Roll," Bob Seger
3. "Pink Cadillac," Bruce Springsteen
4. "Jump," Van Halen
5. "I Want a New Drug," Huey Lewis and the News
6. "867-5309/Jenny," Tommy Tutone
7. "On the Dark Side," John Cafferty and Beaver Brown
8. "Rock This Town," The Stray Cats
9. "Lonely Ol' Night," John Mellencamp
10. "Stand By Me," Ben E. King[1]

HONORABLE MENTION

11. "Give Me All Your Lovin'," ZZ Top
12. "Givin' It Up for Your Love," Delbert McClinton
13. "The Breakup Song," Greg Kihn
14. "Middle of the Road," Pretenders
15. "La Bamba," Los Lobos
16. "Start Me Up," The Rolling Stones

TOP 40 BAND TOP TEN

1. "Beat it," Michael Jackson
2. "Billie Jean," Michael Jackson
3. "Footloose," Kenny Loggins
4. "The Heat Is On," Glenn Frey
5. "Celebration," Kool and the Gang
6. "Lady in Red," Chris DeBurgh
7. "Maneater," Hall and Oates
8. "Eye of the Tiger," Survivor
9. "Mony Mony," Billy Idol
10. "Jessie's Girl," Rick Springfield

NEW MUSIC BAND TOP TEN

1. "I Melt with You," Modern English
2. "Who Can It Be Now?" Men at Work
3. "Our House," Madness
4. "Rock the Casbah," The Clash
5. "Walking on Sunshine," Katrina and the Waves
6. "The One I Love," R.E.M.
7. "De Doo Doo Doo, Da Da Da Da," The Police
8. "I Ran (So Far Away)," A Flock of Seagulls
9. "New Year's Day," U2
10. "Love Will Tear Us Apart," Joy Division

---

[1] "Stand By Me" reentered the *Billboard* chart (because of the movie of the same title) and reached number 67 in 1986.

Stewart Francke writes the "Sign Language" column for The Metro Times *in Detroit, where he is a contributing editor. Francke writes for* CD Review *and wrote liner notes for* Hitsville II, *a box-set of Motown singles. He is also a musician and songwriter with three independent releases,* Across Decker's Field; The Beautiful Go Blameless, *and* Turning in the Twilight, *available from 26034 Dundee, Huntington Woods, MI 48070.*

U.S. Rock Festivals with Attendance of 100,000 or More

The following information was gleaned from Robert Santelli's Aquarius Rising: The Rock Festival Years *and* The Rolling Stone Encyclopedia of Rock and Roll, *edited by Jon Pareles and Patricia Romanowski.*

FESTIVAL, SITE, DATE	ATTENDANCE
1. The US Festival, San Bernadino, California, May 28–30, June 4, 1983	725,000
2. Watkins Glen Summer Jam, Watkins Glen, New York, July 28, 1973	600,000
3. Woodstock Music and Art Fair, Bethel, New York, August 15–17, 1969	400,000
4. The US Festival, San Bernardino, California, September 3–5, 1982	400,000
5. Altamont, Livermore, California, December 6, 1969	300,000
6. California Jam II, Ontario, California, March 18, 1978	250,000
7. Mount Pocono Festival, Long Pond, Pennsylvania, July 18, 1972	200,000
8. Atlanta Pop Festival, July 3–5, 1970	200,000
9. California Jam I, Ontario, California, April 16, 1974	200,000
10. Newport '69, Northridge, California, June 20–22, 1969	150,000
11. Atlanta Pop Festival, July 4–5, 1969	140,000
12. Texas International Pop Festival, Lewisville, Texas, August 30–September 1, 1969	120,000
13. Atlantic City Pop Festival, August 1–3, 1969	110,000
14. Newport Pop Festival, Costa Mesa, California, August 4–5, 1968	100,000
15. Miami Pop Festival, Hallandale, Florida, December 18–30, 1968	100,000
16. Live Aid, Philadelphia, Pennsylvania, July 13, 1985	100,000

Performers at the Monterey International Pop Festival, June 16–18, 1967

1. The Association
2. Booker T. and the MGs
3. Buffalo Springfield
4. Eric Burdon and the Animals
5. The Paul Butterfield Blues Band
6. The Byrds
7. Canned Heat
8. Country Joe and the Fish
9. The Electric Flag
10. Aretha Franklin
11. The Grateful Dead

12. The Jimi Hendrix Experience
13. The Jefferson Airplane
14. Janis Joplin and Big Brother and the Holding Company
15. Al Kooper
16. The Mamas and the Papas
17. Hugh Masekela
18. The Steve Miller Band
19. Moby Grape
20. Laura Nyro
21. The Paupers
22. Quicksilver Messenger Service
23. Otis Redding
24. Johnny Rivers
25. Ravi Shankar
26. Simon and Garfunkel
27. The Who

Performers at Woodstock, August 15–17, 1969

1. Joan Baez
2. The Band
3. Blood, Sweat and Tears
4. The Paul Butterfield Band
5. Canned Heat
6. Joe Cocker
7. Country Joe and the Fish
8. Creedence Clearwater Revival
9. Crosby, Stills, Nash, and Young
10. The Grateful Dead
11. Arlo Guthrie
12. Tim Hardin
12. The Keef Hartley Band
14. Richie Havens
15. Jimi Hendrix
16. The Incredible String Band
17. The Jefferson Airplane
18. Janis Joplin
19. Melanie
20. Mountain
21. Quill
22. Santana
23. John Sebastian
24. Sha Na Na
25. Ravi Shankar
26. Sly and the Family Stone
27. Bert Sommer
28. Sweetwater
29. Ten Years After
30. The Who
31. Johnny Winter

Performers Who Sang on Band Aid's "Do They Know It's Christmas?"

"Do They Know It's Christmas?" by Band Aid, an ad hoc group assembled by Bob Geldof of the Boomtown Rats and Midge Ure of Ultravox, kicked off the mid-eighties boom in high-profile rock charity events. Recorded in London on Sunday, November 25, 1984, in support of those suffering from the famine then devastating Ethiopia, the record became for a time the

biggest-selling single in British history and was a hit all over the world. The song and its B-side, a series of recorded antifamine messages, featured the following:

1. Bob Geldof	11. The Human League
2. Midge Ure	12. Us
3. Sting	13. Eurythmics
4. Duran Duran	14. Bananarama
5. Spandau Ballet	15. Wham!
6. Kool and the Gang	16. Status Quo
7. Culture Club	17. Paul McCartney
8. Frankie Goes to Hollywood	18. David Bowie
9. Paul Young	19. Heaven 17
10. Style Council	20. Phil Collins

Note: The original British picture sleeve was done by the great British pop artist Peter Blake, who also did the covers for Sgt. Pepper's Lonely Hearts Club Band *and the Who's* Face Dances.

Performers at Live Aid, Wembley Stadium, London, and Kennedy Stadium, Philadelphia, July 13, 1985

Bob Geldof and his Band Aid organization staged the Live Aid concerts, and their international broadcast, as a benefit for relief of famine in Ethiopia. The events, together with the Band Aid record, "Do They Know It's Christmas?" and related efforts, raised more than $10 million for hunger relief. Yet the sub-Saharan region of Africa fell back into famine in less than a decade, suggesting that world hunger is a problem whose eradication requires more than public goodwill and the application of forces greater than rock and roll. But this isn't a book about geopolitics, so here's a list of those who tried to help.

LONDON
1. Status Quo
2. Style Council
3. Ultravox
4. Boomtown Rats and Adam Ant
5. Spandau Ballet
6. Elvis Costello

PHILADELPHIA
1. Tom Petty and the Heartbreakers
2. Kenny Loggins
3. The Cars
4. Neil Young
5. Power Station
6. Phil Collins, Robert Plant,

7. Nik Kershaw
8. Sade
9. Sting, Phil Collins, and Julian Lennon (Collins then jumped on the Concorde and raced to Philadelphia, appearing at both shows)
10. Howard Jones
11. Bryan Ferry
12. U2
13. Dire Straits
14. Queen
15. David Bowie
16. The Who
17. Elton John and Wham!
18. Wembley Finale: Freddie Mercury and Brian May (Queen), Paul McCartney, Tour Ensemble

John Paul Jones, and Jimmy Page (a version of Led Zeppelin)
7. Duran Duran
8. Madonna
9. Rod Stewart
10. Patti Labelle
11. Hall and Oates
12. The Temptations
13. Mick Jagger
14. The Beach Boys
15. Tina Turner
16. Judas Priest
17. Simple Minds
18. Pretenders
19. Santana and Pat Metheny
20. The Thompson Twins and Nile Rodgers
21. Teddy Pendergrass
22. Billy Ocean
23. Paul Young
24. Joan Baez
25. Run-D.M.C.
26. Bob Dylan
27. U.S. Ensemble Finale including Keith Richards

"Ain't Gonna Play Sun City"
Artists United Against Apartheid

In the summer of 1985, Little Steven Van Zandt (then running his own band, the Disciples of Soul, and late of Bruce Springsteen's E Street Band) and producer Arthur Baker (cocreator with Afrika Bambaataa of the seminal hip-hop classics "Planet Rock" and "Searching for the Perfect Beat") assembled a demo version of a Van Zandt–composed song called "Sun City," a protest against the resort that attempted to lure American and European artists to perform in apartheid-ridden South Africa by pretending to be located in one of the white-supremacist Pretoria government's "homelands." The demo was recorded by Will Downing. The artists who assembled to make the record and accompanying video over a period of several weeks that July and August included the most diverse lineup of popular musicians ever assembled for a single session—rappers, rockers, reggae, Latin, and jazz all together.

1. Tina B.
2. Arthur Baker

3. Afrika Bambaataa
4. Ray Barretto

5. Stiv Bators
6. Pat Benatar
7. Ruben Blades
8. Kurtis Blow
9. Bono
10. Duke Bootee
11. Jackson Browne
12. Ron Carter
13. Clarence Clemons
14. Jimmy Cliff
15. George Clinton
16. Miles Davis
17. Will Downing
18. Bob Dylan
19. The Fat Boys
20. Fats Comet
21. Peter Gabriel
22. Peter Garrett
23. Bob Geldof
24. Lottie Golden
25. Daryl Hall
26. Herbie Hancock
27. Nona Hendryx
28. Linton Kwesi Johnson
29. Stanley Jordan
30. Kashif
31. Eddie Kendrick
32. Keith LeBlanc
33. Darlene Love
34. Malopets
35. Melle Mel
36. Michael Monroe
37. B. J. Nelson
38. John Oates
39. Sonny Okosuns
40. Bonnie Raitt
41. Joey Ramone
42. Lou Reed
43. Keith Richards
44. David Ruffin
45. Run-D.M.C.
46. Scorpio
47. Gil Scott-Heron
48. Shankar
49. Bruce Springsteen
50. Zak Starkey
51. Ringo Starr
52. Peter Townshend
53. Little Steven Van Zandt
54. Via Afrika
55. Tony Williams
56. Charlie Wilson
57. Doug Wimbish
58. Peter Wolf
59. Bobby Womack
60. Ron Wood
61. Zoe Yanakis

Performers on "We Are the World" by U.S.A. for Africa, Recorded in 1985 as a Benefit for African Hunger Relief

1. Michael Boddicker
2. Lindsey Buckingham
3. Kim Carnes
4. Paulinho da Costa
5. Bob Dylan
6. Sheila E.
7. Bob Geldof
8. Hall and Oates
9. James Ingram
10. Jackie Jackson
11. LaToya Jackson
12. Marlon Jackson
13. Michael Jackson[1]
14. Randy Jackson

15. Tito Jackson
16. Al Jarreau
17. Waylon Jennings
18. Billy Joel
19. Louis Johnson
20. Quincy Jones[2]
21. Cyndi Lauper
22. Huey Lewis and the News
23. Kenny Loggins
24. Bette Midler
25. Willie Nelson
26. Michael Omartian
27. Jeffrey Osborne
28. Steve Perry
29. Greg Phillinganes
30. The Pointer Sisters
31. Lionel Richie[1]
32. John Robinson
33. Smokey Robinson
34. Kenny Rogers
35. Diana Ross
36. Paul Simon
37. Bruce Springsteen
38. Tina Turner
39. Dionne Warwick
40. Stevie Wonder

[1] Cowriters of the song.
[2] Producer of the record.

Performers at George Bush's 1988 Inaugural Concert for Young Americans

1. Lee Atwater, guitar
2. William Bell, singer
3. George Bush, fake guitar
4. Joe Cocker, singer
5. Albert Collins, guitar, singer
6. Steve Cropper, guitar
7. Bo Diddley, guitar and vocals
8. Willie Dixon, singer
9. Dr. John, keyboards and vocals
10. Donald "Duck" Dunn, bass
11. Anton Figg, drums
12. Eddie Floyd, singer
13. Chuck Jackson, singer
14. The Jersey Horns, horn section
15. Cheryl Ladd, speech on R&B history
16. Lafayette Leake, piano
17. Delbert McClinton, guitar, harmonica, and vocals
18. Sam Moore, singer
19. Chuck Norris, speech on the meaning of the blues
20. Billy Preston, keyboards and vocals
21. Red Hot and Blue Memphis All-Stars Band
22. Percy Sledge, singer
23. Koko Taylor, singer
24. Carla Thomas, singer
25. Jimmie Vaughan, guitar and vocals
26. Stevie Ray Vaughn and Double Trouble, guitar and vocals
27. Joe Louis Walker, guitar and vocals
28. Ronnie Wood, guitar and vocals
29. Betty Wright, singer

The 10 Most Obscure Rock Operas

1. "AN EXCERPT FROM A TEENAGE OPERA," KEITH WEST

West's single, released in 1967, well before the Who's *Tommy*, kicked off the pop-opera craze; the whole thing captured on a single.

2. S.F. SORROW, THE PRETTY THINGS

Another one released before *Tommy*, though this opera takes a full album to get across what isn't entirely clear once you've heard it, anyway.

3. THE GIANT CRAB COMETH FORTH

Mystical but dull.

4. THE GOLDEN SCARAB, RAY MANZAREK

Mystical, ambitious, and dull.

5. LOVE CHRONICLES, AL STEWART

Romantic rather than mystical, but not any less dull.

6. KEYNSHAM, BONZO DOG DOO DAH BAND

The great comic opera, rock or otherwise. Takes the hot air out of everything from *Tommy* to Gilbert and Sullivan, traditional England to the American space age.

7. 666, APHRODITE'S CHILD

Satanic, mischievous, and dull.

8. JOE'S GARAGE, ACT ONE AND ACT TWO, FRANK ZAPPA

The story of a rock musician in a world in which music has been declared illegal. Pete Townshend proposed the story long before (as one of his many concepts for the aborted *Lifehouse*), but it took Zappa (and the inspiration of Ayatollah Khomeini's ban on pop music in Iran) to bring this rancid version to fruition. Even though the storyline lacks charm or subtlety (the absence of these qualities being one of Zappa's lyrical hallmarks), *Joe's Garage* is on the mark often enough to be alternately whimsically hilarious and frightfully prophetic: The parallels with the Tipper Gore–led campaign against pop music in real-life America are many and scary.

9. "THE GIFT," THE VELVET UNDERGROUND

A macabre John Cale story from the *White Light, White Heat* album brings Edgar Allan Poe into the atomic age, with appropriate sound effects.

10. ROCK JUSTICE, MARTY BALIN

Balin presents the story of a rock singer on trial for not making hits. Allegorical, absurd, not terribly listenable, and a nice parable of Balin's problems with Jefferson Airplane/Starship.

15 Rock Songs Based on Classical Concepts

SONG	SOURCE
1. "Because," The Beatles	Beethoven's *Moonlight Sonata*, backward
2. "Beck's Bolero," The Jeff Beck Group	Ravel's "Bolero"
3. "Brown Shoes Don't Make It," The Mothers of Invention	Holst's "The Planets"
4. "Deserts," Frank Zappa	derived from Edgar Varese
5. "Farandole," Dave Edmunds and Love Sculpture	derived from a Bizet piece
6. "Forms and Feelings: Sabre Dance," Dave Edmunds and Love Sculpture	Khatchaturian's "Sabre Dance" and Holsts's "Mars"
7. "I'll Never Fall in Love Again," Eric Carmen	Rachmaninoff melody
8. "Joy," Apollo 100	Bach melody
9. "Little Star," The Elegants	Mozart's "Twinkle Twinkle Little Star"
10. "Lover's Concerto," The Toys	Bach's "Five Finger Concerto"
11. "Night," Jackie Wilson	Saint-Saëns's "My Heart at Thy Sweet Voice," from *Samson and Delilah*
12. "Nut Rocker," B. Bumble and the Stingers (later, Emerson, Lake and Palmer)	Tchaikovsky's "Nutcracker Suite"
13. "Ride of the Valkyries," Andy MacKay	Wagner melody
14. "Roll Over Beethoven," The Move	Fuses opening theme of Beethoven's Fifth Symphony with Chuck Berry's song
15. "A Whiter Shade of Pale," Procol Harum	Bach's cantata, "Sleepers Awake"

The 25 Best Rock and R&B Instrumentals

1. "Rumble," Link Wray and His Ray Men
2. "Pipeline," The Chantays
3. "Honky Tonk, parts 1 and 2," Bill Doggett
4. "Wild Weekend," The Rockin' Rebels
5. "Green Onions," Booker T. and the MGs
6. "Wipe Out," The Surfaris
7. "TSOP (The Sound of Philadelphia)," MFSB
8. "Night Train," Jimmy Forrest
9. "Shotgun," Jr. Walker and the All-Stars
10. "Rockit," Herbie Hancock
11. "Soul Finger," The Bar-Kays
12. "Soul Twist," King Curtis
13. "Hide Away," Freddie King
14. "The Lonely Surfer," Jack Nitzsche
15. "One Mint Julep," Ray Charles
16. "Last Night," The Mar-Keys
17. "Machine Gun," The Commodores
18. "Memphis," Lonnie Mack
19. "Let's Go Trippin'," Dick Dale and His Del-Tones
20. *Hot Rats*, Frank Zappa
21. "Love's Theme," Love Unlimited Orchestra
22. "Cissy Strut," The Meters
23. "Ain't It Funky Now," James Brown
24. "Via Tirado," El Chicano
25. "Apache," The Incredible Bongo Band

The Sons of Kenny G
The Dozen Worst Instrumentals

1. "Hocus Pocus," Focus (The definitive example of "progressive rock" as oxymoron.)
2. *Tubular Bells*, Mike Oldfield (Nearing the end of Western Civilization . . .)
3. "Star Wars Theme / Cantina Band," Meco (The DeFranco Family of instrumentals, truly transcendent hackwork—transcended to the point of maddening any music lover who hears it.)
4. *Death Wish II* (soundtrack), Jimmy Page (The true death wish must have belonged to Page, whose self-immolation of his career reached an apex here.)

5. "Classical Gas," Mason Williams (Bach did not survive several centuries for this.)
6. "A Fifth of Beethoven," Walter Murphy and His Big Apple Band (Neither did Beethoven.)
7. "Whole Lotta Love," C.C.S. (The blues may be the most beautiful creation of North American culture, but here all its splendor wafts away in a mere instant.)
8. "Autobahn," Kraftwerk (Heavily influential heavy metallic dance noise from heavy German combo weighs heavily on the modern postpunk mind. In English: Piffle.)
9. "Disco Lady (I Love Lucy Theme)," The Wilton Place Street Orchestra (Imagine doing an injustice to the composing skills of Desi Arnaz, Sr.)
10. "Morning Dance," Spyro Gyra (The nadir of jazz-rock.)
11. *Batman Original Motion Picture Score*, Danny Elfman (Wouldn't you love to drive a stake through the heart of the producers who prefer this to Prince?)
12. (tie) "Outa-Space," Billy Preston, and "Love Is Blue," Jeff Beck (Great musicians at their nadir. *Nobody* needs a hit this badly.)

Rick Whitesell Selects the 10 Best Cover Versions

"Cover versions" are remakes of a song by a performer other than the original artist. Originally applied only to contemporaneous, market-competitive versions, the term has since come to mean any new version that competes even aesthetically with the original.

This list stops where the first edition of The Book of Rock Lists *left off, because the person who compiled it has since died. Rick Whitesell provided much of the inspiration and even more of the research for that first volume, which was dedicated to him. Whitesell, a renowned record collector whose accumulated recordings now reside in the library of his alma mater, Marist College, edited* Goldmine, *when that magazine was the collector's (and particularly rockabilly, R&B, and soul fan's) American bible. He seemed to know everyone, no matter how obscure, who had contributed a portion of his or her heart and soul to rock 'n' roll, rockabilly, and R&B music. And he did all of this as an insomniac quadriplegic. His body failed him in January 1981. As his writing here suggests, his spirit never failed anyone.*

1. "ADORABLE," THE DRIFTERS, 1955

The West Coast–based Colts, managed by Buck Ram, did this medium-tempo ballad first, but the Drifters' version was infinitely superior. The Colts were forgotten, though Buck Ram got lucky and discovered the Platters.

2.   "CRYING IN THE CHAPEL," THE ORIOLES, 1963

This pop tune is a thinly veiled spiritual, originally written and recorded by Darrell Glenn, a country singer no one had heard of even then. Sonny Til, the Orioles' lead singer, was a friend of Glenn's, and his cover of the tune went right to the top. It's not known whether Glenn and Til remained friendly afterward.

3.   "LITTLE DARLIN'," THE DIAMONDS, 1957

R&B purists will scream in pain at this contention, but in 1957, the rhythm and blues record buyers bought more copies of this Maurice Williams composition in its version by the Diamonds, a white quartet from Canada, than the one by Williams's own Gladiolas, a black group that recorded for Excello. Why? Because the Diamonds did it better.

4.   "SUGAR, SUGAR," WILSON PICKETT, 1970

The Wicked Pickett displayed talent above and beyond the call of duty when he made this bubble-gum smash by the Archies sound like a real song. And he did a good job in 1968 on "Hey Jude," too.

5.   "GIRLS TALK," DAVE EDMUNDS, 1979

Elvis Costello wrote it but couldn't sing it worth a damn. Linda Ronstadt covered it, but of course she covers *everything*. Dave Edmunds clearly had the best and last word this time.

6.   "FIRE," THE POINTER SISTERS, 1978

Bruce Springsteen, the composer, gave this tune to Robert Gordon (Elvis had died, unfortunately) and it appeared on *Fresh Fish Special*, the LP Gordon recorded with guitar virtuoso Link Wray. But it was The Pointer Sisters' cover of "Fire" that burned up the hit parade and reminded AM radio listeners of what cruisin' around music once sounded like.

7.   "MY BACK PAGES," THE BYRDS, 1967

While the Byrds reinterpreted many of Bob Dylan's songs, this recording turned a nondescript acoustic tune into a rock gem.

8.   "BORN TO RUN," ALLAN CLARKE, 1975

The ex-Hollies lead singer did not top Springsteen, but Clarke did give us perspective on what "Born to Run" would have been like *without* Wall of Sound production. The only problem with Clarke's version is that it appeared only on a British eight-track tape.

9.   "GET A JOB," THE MILLS BROTHERS, 1958

After launching their careers in 1931 with a series of recordings on which they imitated musical instruments with voices and cupped hands, the Mills Brothers drifted into a pattern of dreary pop tunes rendered in such a manner that each disc sounded like the one before it. But they did a surprisingly fine cover of the Silhouettes' sole hit, "Get a Job." It really rocks!

10. "CHANGES," JIM AND JEAN, 1966

This duo did a fine, folk-rock cover of Phil Ochs's most sentimental composition, sparked by Al Kooper's accompaniment on harpsichord.

The Greatest Chuck Berry "Rewrites"

The following songs are modeled after the basic Chuck Berry guitar style.

1. "Surfin' U.S.A.," The Beach Boys
2. "Brown Sugar," The Rolling Stones
3. "Jumpin' Jack Flash," The Rolling Stones
4. "Get Out of Denver," Bob Seger
5. "Fun, Fun, Fun," The Beach Boys
6. "Rockin' All Over the World," John Fogerty
7. "Back in the U.S.S.R.," The Beatles
8. "Working on the Highway," Bruce Springsteen
9. "I Knew the Bride," Dave Edmunds
10. "Katmandu," Bob Seger
11. "Come Together," The Beatles
12. "Johnny 99," Bruce Springsteen

The Sincerest Form of Flattery
Songs You'd Swear Were by Someone Else

1. "American Girl," Tom Petty and the Heartbreakers (The Byrds)
2. "Black Is Black," Los Bravos (Gene Pitney)
3. "Child of the Novelty," Mahogany Rush (Jimi Hendrix) (similarly: Robin Trower's first three albums, everything else Mahogany Rush and its guitarist Frank Marino ever cut)
4. "Crazy on You," Heart (Jefferson Starship)
5. "The Fire Down Below," Bob Seger (Frankie Miller)
6. "Give Me All Your Love," Whitesnake (Led Zeppelin)
7. "Hang On in There Baby," Johnny Bristol (Barry White)
8. "Horse with No Name," America (Neil Young)
9. "In the Air Tonight," Phil Collins (Peter Gabriel)
10. "It's a Heartache," Bonnie Tyler (Rod Stewart)
11. "Jack and Jill," Raydio (Sly and the Family Stone)
12. "Jamie," Eddie Holland (Jackie Wilson)
13. "Let Me Roll It," Paul McCartney (John Lennon)

14. "Lies," The Knickerbockers (The Beatles) (similarly: "Sub Rosa Subway," Klaatu)
15. "The Look," Roxette (Prince)
16. "Love Will Tear Us Apart," Joy Division (The Doors)
17. "Mama Used to Say," Junior (Stevie Wonder) (similarly: "Competition Ain't Nothin'," Little Carl Carlton)
18. "My Sweet Lord," George Harrison (The Chiffons)
19. "Old Man Down the Road," John Fogerty (Creedence Clearwater Revival) (similarly: "Long Cool Woman [In a Black Dress]," The Hollies)
20. "On the Dark Side," John Cafferty and the Beaver Brown Band (Bruce Springsteen)
21. "One Bad Apple," The Osmonds (The Jackson 5)
22. "A Public Execution," Mouse and the Traps (Bob Dylan) (similarly: "Sultans of Swing," Dire Straits; "Stuck in the Middle with You," Stealer's Wheel)
23. "Straight Up," Paula Abdul (Janet Jackson)
24. "U Can't Touch This," M. C. Hammer (Rick James)
25. "You Shook Me," Led Zeppelin (The Jeff Beck Group)

Hit Me with Your Guest Shot
100 Notable Cameo Appearances

1. **DUANE ALLMAN**—Plays guitar on "Layla," Derek and the Dominoes; "Hey Jude," Wilson Pickett; "Loan Me a Dime," Boz Scaggs; John Hammond's *I Can Tell*; "The Weight," Aretha Franklin; "The Road of Life," Clarence Carter; *To Bonnie from Delaney* and *Motel Shot*, Delaney and Bonnie.

2. **AVERAGE WHITE BAND**—Back Chuck Berry on "My Ding-A-Ling."

3. **GINGER BAKER**—Drummed with Atomic Rooster and on Hawkwind's *Levitation*.

4. **AFRIKA BAMBAATAA**—Duets with James Brown on "Unity," and with John Lydon on "World Destruction" by Time Zone.

5. **JEFF BECK**—Plays guitar on Donovan's "Barabajagal," and Tina Turner's "Private Dancer" and "Steel Claw."

6. **BLUE MAGIC**—Vocal background on the Rolling Stones' "If You Really Want to Be My Friend."

7. **BONO (U2)**—Produced and plays guitar (?!) on Roy Orbison's "She's a Mystery to Me."

8. **JACKSON BROWNE**—Sings harmony on Warren Zevon's early albums, John Prine's "If You Don't Want My Love," and "Rockin' the Res" by John Trudell.

9. BUSHWICK BILL (THE GETO BOYS)—Vocals on Dr. Dre's *The Chronic*.

10. J. J. CALE—Plays the guitar solo on Bob Seger's "Midnight Rider."

11. THE CHIFFONS—Backing voices, "Rock and Roll Lullaby," B. J. Thomas

12. ERIC CLAPTON—Plays guitar "obbligato" on Aretha Franklin's "Good to Me as I Am to You." Also plays on *We're Only in It for the Money*, The Mothers of Invention; "While My Guitar Gently Weeps," the Beatles; Dr. John's *The Sun Moon and Herbs; The London Howlin' Wolf Sessions*. Appears as rhythm guitarist on *John Lennon/Plastic Ono Band—Live Peace in Toronto*. Plays on Paul Brady's *Songs & Crazy Dreams*, Buddy Guy and Junior Wells's *Buddy and Junior Sing the Blues*, Pete Townshend and Ronnie Lane's *Rough Mix*.

13. GEORGE CLINTON—Appears on Thomas Dolby's *Cube*.

14. RY COODER—Plays guitar on *Sticky Fingers* and *Let It Bleed*, The Rolling Stones; *12 Songs*, Randy Newman; *Safe as Milk*, Captain Beefheart and His Magic Band; *Ambush*, Marc Benno; *Midnight at the Oasis*, Maria Muldaur; *Duane Eddy* (1987 album); Aaron Neville's *Warm Your Heart*.

15. ELVIS COSTELLO—Sings on *Nothing But the Truth*, Ruben Blades. Produced the Pogues' *Rum, Sodomy and the Lash*.

16. THE CRICKETS—Backup singers on the Everly Brothers' " 'Til I Kissed You." Played and sang on *Bobby Vee Meets the Crickets*, a 1962 album of Buddy Holly songs.

17. CHUCK D (PUBLIC ENEMY)—Vocals on Janet Jackson's "New Agenda," Kool Moe Dee's "Rise 'N' Shine," and Ice Cube's "Endangered Species (Tales from the Darkside)."

18. DE LA SOUL—Appear on Queen Latifah's "Mama Gave Birth to the Soul Children."

19. BOB DYLAN—Sings backup on "Buckets of Rain," Bette Midler; on Leonard Cohen's "Don't Go Home with Your Hard-On," and on *Doug Sahm and Band*. Plays harmonica on Harry Belafonte's *Midnight Special*, also on *Carolyn Hester*, both 1962. Plays Hammond organ on U2's "Hawkmoon 269"; sings on their "Love Rescue Me."

20. MELISSA ETHERIDGE—Sings on Don Henley's "Gimme What You Got."

21. THE EVERLY BROTHERS—Sing on Paul Simon's "Graceland."

22. PHIL EVERLY—Sings on Warren Zevon's debut album. (Zevon used to be the Everly Brothers' bandleader.)

23. FLAVOR FLAV (PUBLIC ENEMY)—Vocals on Ice Cube's "I'm Only Out for One Thing."

24. FLEA (RED HOT CHILI PEPPERS)—Plays bass on Mick Jagger's *Wandering Spirit*.

25. FLO AND EDDIE (HOWARD VOLMAN AND MARK KAYLAN, AKA THE TURTLES)—Sang backup on Bruce Springsteen's "Hungry Heart" and on Frank Zappa's *200 Motels* soundtrack.

26. ROBERT FRIPP—Plays guitar on Talking Heads' *Fear of Music*, Blondie's *Parallel Lines*, Daryl Hall's *Sacred Songs*, and even *Desire* and *Prostitute*, by Toyah Wilcox, the English pop star he married.

27. JERRY GARCIA AND PHIL LESH (THE GRATEFUL DEAD)—Play on David Bromberg's *Demon in Disguise* and *Wanted Dead or Alive*. Garcia plays guitar on the Neville Brothers' "You're the One."

28. LOWELL GEORGE—Played guitar on Robert Palmer's *Sneaking Sally Through the Alley, Paris 1919* by John Cale, Jackson Browne's *The Pretender*, and Bonnie Raitt's *Taking My Time* and *Streetlights*. Produced the Grateful Dead's *Shakedown Street*.

29. HERBIE HANCOCK—Plays keyboards on Bonnie Raitt's *Nick of Time*, synthesizers on the Isley Brothers' *Tracks of Time*.

30. GEORGE HARRISON—Plays guitar on "Badge," Cream; *Desire*, Bob Dylan; *Straight Up*, Badfinger; *That's the Way God Planned It*, Billy Preston; *Duane Eddy* (1987); Roy Orbison's career-concluding *Mystery Girl*. Produced "Costafine Town" by Splinter, a U.K. hit. Plays guitar and sings on Tom Petty's "I Won't Back Down."

31. JERRY HARRISON (TALKING HEADS)—Plays on the Fine Young Cannibals' *The Raw and the Cooked*.

32. HEAVY D.—Raps on Michael Jackson's "Jam."

33. JIMI HENDRIX—Plays guitar on Timothy Leary's *You Can Be Anything This Time Around, Stephen Stills* (his first solo album) and Love's *False Start*.

34. DON HENLEY—Provides backing vocals (along with fellow Eagles Glenn Frey and Timothy B. Schmitt) on Bob Seger's "Fire Lake." Sang background vocals on *Christopher Cross* by the Grammy-laden one-hit wonder and on Jackson Browne's *The Pretender* and several Warren Zevon albums. Henley, Frey, and Randy Meisner, an early Eagle, played and sang on *Linda Ronstadt*, her second album. Duets with Stevie Nicks on "Leather and Lace."

35. BRUCE HORNSBY—Plays keyboards on Don Henley's "The End of the Innocence," and piano and accordion on Bob Seger's *The Fire Inside*. Lord only knows what he might have done while touring as pianist with the Grateful Dead.

36. WHITNEY HOUSTON—Sings on the Neville Brothers' *Fiyo on the Bayou*.

37. ICE CUBE—Appears on Public Enemy's *Fear of a Black Planet*.

38. MICK JAGGER—Sings backup on "You're So Vain," the Carly Simon record that may or may not be about him, Peter Frampton's *I'm in You*, Dr. John's *The Sun Moon and Herbs*, Peter Tosh's "Don't Look Back" from his album, *Bush Doctor*, Peter Wolf's *Lights Out* and the Jacksons' *Victory*. Duets with David Bowie on remake of "Dancing in the Street," which debuted on the Live Aid broadcast.

39. RICK JAMES—Plays drums, bass, rhythm guitar, and keyboards on *Too Sharp* by Process and the Doo Rags; sings on "Rick James Style," by the Lemonheads.

40. ELTON JOHN—Appears on Neil Sedaka's "Bad Blood," Rod Stewart's "Let Me Be Your Car" (which he and Bernie Taupin wrote), Rick Astley's *Free*. Sang with Stevie Wonder and Gladys Knight on Dionne Warwick's "That's What Friends Are For."

41. BOOKER T. JONES (BOOKER T. AND THE MGs)— Plays Hammond B3 organ on Soul Asylum's *Grave Dancer's Union*.

42. JOHN PAUL JONES (LED ZEPPELIN)—Plays surdu, bass, and keyboards on Peter Gabriel's "Fourteen Black Paintings."

43. STEVE JONES AND PAUL COOK (THE SEX PISTOLS)—Back Joan Jett on *Bad Reputation*.

44. BIG DADDY KANE—Appears on Public Enemy's *Fear of a Black Planet*.

45. CHAKA KHAN—Sings on *More Than Ever* by Blood, Sweat and Tears, Robert Palmer's "Addicted to Love," Stevie Winwood's "Higher Love," and duets with David Bowie on "Underground" from the movie *Labyrinth*.

46. B. B. KING—Vocal and guitar on U2's "When Love Comes to Town."

47. CAROLE KING—Plays piano on *Sweet Baby James*, James Taylor's breakthrough album. But she doesn't play on "You've Got a Friend," her song that Taylor made a hit.

48. KOOL AND THE GANG—Although rarely credited for it, they were the only American-based artists to appear on "Do They Know It's Christmas?" Bob Geldof's 1984 single that kicked off the mid-eighties charity-rock craze.

49. KRIS KRISTOFFERSON—Sings backup on John Trudell's *AKA Graffiti Man*.

50. JOHN LENNON—Sang backup on "We Love You," the Rolling Stones, with David Bowie on "Fame," and with Elton John on Elton's version of "I Saw Her Standing There." Produced and played on Harry Nilsson's *Pussy Cats*. Usually can be detected on Yoko Ono's albums, surprisingly enough.

51. LITTLE RICHARD—Sings on "Elvis Is Dead" from Living Colour's *Time's Up*, New Edition's "Tears on My Pillow," "900-Force Line" by Full Force, Philip Bailey on "Twins" from the movie of the same name, and the Beach Boys' "Happy Endings."

52. LOS LOBOS—Back Paul Simon on "All Around the World or the Myth of Fingerprints," from *Graceland*. Complained bitterly that they'd been done out of compositional credit.

53. MC LYTE—Appears with Sinead O'Connor on the "I Want Your (Hands On Me)" twelve-inch and video.

54. PAUL MCCARTNEY—Sang backup on Donovan's "Mellow Yellow" and "We Love You" by the Rolling Stones. Played on *EB '84* by the Everly Brothers and *Duane Eddy* (1987). Produced Bonzo Dog Doo Dah Band's "I'm the Urban Spaceman," under the pseudonym Apollo C. Vermouth.

55. ROGER MCGUINN (THE BYRDS)—Sings a medley of the Byrds' "Mr. Tambourine Man," "Eight Miles High," and "So You Want to Be a Rock 'N' Roll Star" with Crowded House on the CD single of their "I Feel Possessed."

56. BRANFORD MARSALIS—Played saxophone on Sting's *The Dream of the Blue Turtles* and *The Soul Cages*, and his brother stopped speaking to him. His punishment for appearing on James Taylor's *New Moon Shine* received no publicity. Playing on the Neville Brothers' *Uptown* was probably OK, the Nevilles being from New Orleans same as the Marsalis brothers and all.

57. CURTIS MAYFIELD—Plays guitar on Style Council's *The Cost of Loving*.

58. STEVE MILLER—Plays guitar on the Neville Brother's version of his "Fly Like an Eagle."

59. JONI MITCHELL—Sings on James Taylor's "You've Got a Friend."

60. KEITH MOON—Plays drums on "Ole Man River" with the Jeff Beck Group. Also appears on Harry Nilsson's *Flash Fearless* and *Pussy Cats; Sometime in New York City* by John Lennon; *The 20th Anniversary of Rock and Roll* by Bo Diddley; and the soundtrack to *All This and World War Two*.

61. VAN MORRISON—Sings "4 Percent Pantomime," from *Cahoots* by the Band. Sang duet with Cliff Richard on "Whenever God Shines His Light."

62. RANDY NEWMAN—Plays and arranges synthesizers on Don Henley's *Building the Perfect Beast*.

63. SINEAD O'CONNOR—Sings with Peter Gabriel on "Come Talk to Me."

64. JIMMY PAGE—Plays guitar on *The Kinks*, that group's first LP; "Bald Headed Woman," the B-side of the Who's first single; Van Morrison's debut album with Them; Donovan's "Hurdy Gurdy Man"; Joe Cocker's *With a Little Help from My Friends;* the Rolling Stones' *Dirty Work*.

65. ROBERT PALMER—Plays percussion (that's what it says) on the Talking Heads' *Remain in Light*.

66. PRINCE—Played guitar with 94 East, whose lead singer was Colonel Abrams. Probably plays several instruments on every record he ever produced, which are too numerous to enumerate here.

67. R.E.M.—Back Warren Zevon (though not as a single unit) on *Sentimental Hygiene*.

68. BONNIE RAITT—Duets with John Lee Hooker on "I'm in the Mood," from *The Healer;* sings on John Prine's *The Missing Years*. Sings on Jackson Browne's "The Times You've Come," Warren Zevon's "Join Me in L.A.," Allen Toussaint's *Motion*, and Bob Seger's "Makin' Thunderbirds." Sings and plays guitar on the live version of John Prine's "Angel from Montgomery." Plays guitar and sings on Marc Cohn's *The Rainy Season*.

69. RAKIM (ERIC B. AND RAKIM)—Raps on Jody Watley's "Friends."

70. LOU REED—Sings on *Nothing But the Truth*, Ruben Blades.

71. VERNON REID—Plays lead guitar with Public Enemy on "Sophisticated Bitch"—unexpectedly, since Reid, one of rock's more politically correct sorts, did not know the title during the session. Also plays guitar on Tracy Chapman's *Matters of the Heart*, which contains no known secret subtexts.

72. KEITH RICHARDS—Plays guitar on The Neville Brothers' "Midnight Key."

73. ROBBIE ROBERTSON (THE BAND)—Plays guitar on John Hammond's *I Can Tell*. (The Band's Rick Danko plays bass.) Also plays on Joni Mitchell's *Court and Spark*.

74. CHUBB ROCK—Appears on *Derelicts of Dialect* by 3rd Bass.

75. AXL ROSE (GUNS N' ROSES)—Sings on Don Henley's "I Will Not Go Quietly."

76. CARLOS SANTANA—Recorded *Love Devotion Surrender* with John McLaughlin; *Illuminations* with Alice Coltrane. Plays guitar on John Lee Hooker's *The Healer, Middle Man* by Boz Scaggs, and Bobby Womack's *Save the Children*.

77. PAUL SIMONON (THE CLASH)—Plays bass on Bob Dylan's *Down in the Groove*.

78. SLASH (GUNS N' ROSES)—Plays guitar on Michael Jackson's *Dangerous* and Iggy Pop's *Brick by Brick* (where he's joined by GNR bassist Duff McKagan).

79. PATTI SMITH—Guest vocals on Blue Oyster Cult's *Agents of Fortune* (for which she also wrote two songs). Also sang on Ray Manzarek's *The Whole Thing Started with Rock 'n' Roll*.

80. PHIL SPECTOR—Plays guitar on the Drifters' "On Broadway," and piano on *Out of Our Heads* by the Rolling Stones.

81. BRUCE SPRINGSTEEN—Sings backup on Nils Lofgren's "Valentine" and on "Take a Look at My Heart" from John Prine's *The Missing Years*. Plays guitar and sings on Southside Johnny's *Better Days* and on Gary Bonds's albums, *Dedication* and *On the Line;* wrote several songs for both Bonds albums and duets with

Bonds on "Jole Blon" from the latter. Plays guitar on two tracks from Patti Scialfa's *Rumble Doll*. Plays guitar on Donna Summer's "Protection," which he wrote. Sings on Little Steven's "Native American."

82. MAURICE STARR—The founder and producer of New Kids on the Block plays bass and sings backgrounds on Peter Wolf's *Lights Out*.

83. RINGO STARR—Sings backup on "Valentine," by Nils Lofgren.

84. STEVEN STILLS—Lead guitar, "Ain't No Sunshine," Bill Withers. Bass and guitar on Joni Mitchell's "Carey" and "Blonde in the Bleachers."

85. JAMES TAYLOR—Vocals on *Marc Cohn* (duets on "Perfect Love"); guitar on Joni Mitchell's *Blue*.

86. RICHARD THOMPSON—Guitar solo, "Sister Madly," Crowded House. Electric guitar and background vocals on Bonnie Raitt's *Luck of the Draw*.

87. PETE TOWNSHEND—Plays guitar on Eric Clapton's *Live at the Rainbow*, which he organized.

88. TREACH (NAUGHTY BY NATURE)—Vocals on Digital Underground's *Son's of the P*.

89. MIDGE URE (ULTRAVOX)—Backing vocals on Thin Lizzy's "Chinatown."

90. EDDIE VAN HALEN—Plays guitar on Michael Jackson's "Beat It."

91. KARL WALLINGER (WORLD PARTY)—Arranged Sinead O'Connor's "Black Boys on Mopeds."

92. JOE WALSH—Plays guitar on Emerson, Lake and Palmer's *Works Volume 1*, on the side devoted to the bright ideas of drummer Carl Palmer. Adds guitar to Bob Seger's "The Mountain," Warren Zevon's *Bad Luck Streak in Dancing School*.

93. WENDY AND LISA—Prince's celebrated sidemen back up Seal on his self-titled debut album.

94. PAUL WESTERBERG (THE REPLACEMENTS)—Plays guitar on Joan Jett's *Notorious*.

95. STEVIE WINWOOD—Keyboards on Joe Cocker's *With a Little Help from My Friends*, Jimi Hendrix's *Electric Ladyland*, *The London Howlin' Wolf Sessions*, *The London Muddy Waters Sessions*, and *Ginger Baker's Air Force*. Sings with James Brown on *Gravity*.

96. BOBBY WOMACK—Plays guitar on Tracy Chapman's *Matters of the Heart*. Appears on the Rolling Stones's *Dirty Work*.

97. STEVIE WONDER—Appears on Peter Frampton's *I'm In You*. Performed on gospel singer Andrae Crouch's "I'll Be Thinking of You." Sang with Elton John and Gladys Knight on Dionne Warwick's "That's What Friends Are For."

98. RON WOOD (THE ROLLING STONES, THE FACES,

THE JEFF BECK GROUP—Plays guitar on Izzy Stradlin's "Take a Look at the Guy," and all of Rod Stewart's early records.

99. BILL WYMAN (THE ROLLING STONES)—Plays bass on John Hammond's *I Can Tell* and *The London Howlin' Wolf Sessions* (where he's joined by Stones Charlie Watts and Ian Stewart).

100. NEIL YOUNG—Plays guitar on Warren Zevon's *Sentimental Hygiene*.

Heavy Metal Ore
The Records that Dug the Pit From Which Metal Was Mined

Note: All these records predate the first chart appearance of Black Sabbath, in August 1970.

1. "How Many More Years," Howlin' Wolf, 1951
2. "I'm a Man," Bo Diddley, 1955
3. "Rumble," Link Wray and His Ray Men, 1958
4. "Boom Boom," John Lee Hooker, 1962
5. "I Want Candy," The Strangeloves, 1965
6. "Psychotic Reaction," Count Five, 1966
7. "Mystic Eyes," Them, 1966
8. *Are You Experienced?* The Jimi Hendrix Experience, 1967
9. *Journey to the Center of Your Mind*, The Amboy Dukes (featured Ted Nugent), 1968
10. "Yer Blues," The Beatles, 1968
11. *Vincebus Eruptum*, Blue Cheer, 1968
12. *Wheels of Fire*, Cream, 1968
13. *In-A-Gadda-Da-Vida*, Iron Butterfly, 1968
14. *Led Zeppelin*, 1969 (equally, *Led Zeppelin II*, also 1969)
15. *Deep Purple*, 1969 (Deep Purple evolved into a true heavy metal act with such albums as *Deep Purple in Rock* and *Machine Head*)
16. *On Time*, Grand Funk Railroad, 1969
17. *Frijid Pink*, January 1970
18. "Mississippi Queen," Mountain, March 1970
19. *The Who Live at Leeds*, May 1970
20. *Cactus*, July 1970

Punk Roots
Records that Displayed the Punk Sound and Attitude Before the Sex Pistols

1. "Rumble," Link Wray and His Ray Men, 1958
2. "Louie Louie," The Kingsmen, 1963

3. "Surfin' Bird," The Trashmen, 1963
4. "Gloria," Them, 1965
5. "My Generation," The Who, 1965 (and many subsequent pre-operatic efforts)
6. "Wild Thing," The Troggs, 1966
7. *Freak Out*, The Mothers of Invention, 1967
8. *The Velvet Underground and Nico*, 1967 (also subsequent releases, particularly 1968's *White Light/White Heat*)
9. *Kick Out the Jams*, The MC5, 1968 *(Back in the USA* [1970] *also made its mark)*
10. *The Stooges*, 1969
11. "Bang a Gong (Get It On)," T. Rex (Marc Bolan), 1971
12. "School's Out," Alice Cooper, 1972
13. *America Eats Its Young*, Funkadelic, 1972
14. "All the Young Dudes," Mott the Hoople, 1972
15. *The New York Dolls*, 1973 (also, 1974's *In Too Much Too Soon)*
16. *Raw Power*, Iggy and the Stooges, 1973
17. *Rock N Roll Animal*, Lou Reed, 1974
18. *On the Beach*, Neil Young, 1974
19. *The Tubes*, 1975
20. *Horses*, The Patti Smith Group, 1975

10 Reasons Punk Had to Happen
Number One Albums of the Two Years Preceding "Anarchy in the U.K."

(In descending order of awfulness.)
1. *Frampton Comes Alive!*, Peter Frampton
2. *Chicago IX—Chicago's Greatest Hits*
3. *Between the Lines*, Janis Ian
4. *Windsong*, John Denver
5. *Captain Fantastic and the Brown Dirt Cowboy*, Elton John
6. *Venus and Mars*, Wings
7. *Red Octopus*, Jefferson Starship
8. *Eagles/Their Greatest Hits 1971–1975*
9. *Presence*, Led Zeppelin
10. *Black and Blue*, The Rolling Stones

Note: Don't be misled. Things did not *improve the deeper into the charts you went. In 1977, the year following the release of "Anarchy," America's number-one albums included Barbra Streisand's soundtrack to* A Star Is Born, *live albums by Wings and Barry Manilow, and Linda Ronstadt's* Simple Dreams.

Worst Career Moves

1. **MICHAEL JACKSON INVITES HIS PLAYMATES TO SPEND THE NIGHT.** Apparently, it never occurred to Jackson and his many renowned advisers that it's one thing for a thirty-four-year-old man to dote on preteen and adolescent boys, quite another to sleep in the same bed with them.

2. **MARVIN GAYE TELLS HIS FATHER WHAT HE *REALLY* THINKS.** On April 1, 1984, Marvin informed his dad that he'd had enough of his shit and that he planned to fuck him up. His father, Marvin Sr., replied by shooting him to death.

3. **BUDDY HOLLY CONVINCES RITCHIE VALENS AND THE BIG BOPPER TO FLY AHEAD TO FARGO, TO GET THEIR LAUNDRY DONE.** Actually, Buddy, Ritchie, and the Bopper had better reasons for trying to skip ahead of the rest of promoter Irving Feld's Winter Dance Party. For one thing, the heater on the tour bus didn't work; for another, they all needed some sleep. They found a lot more of it than they'd bargained for when their chartered prop plane smacked down in a cornfield just outside Clear Lake, Iowa, where they'd just played the Surf Ballroom. Others who've made similar errors include Lynyrd Skynyrd, whose plane crashed because it *ran out of gas;* Otis Redding, where bad weather may also have been the culprit; Stevie Ray Vaughan, who flew in a helicopter on a foggy night; Harry Chapin, who overestimated his own driving skills, despite a significant clue (his driver's license had been revoked); and Marc Bolan, who let his girlfriend drive.

4. **JOHN LENNON MAKES ALLEN KLEIN THE REPLACEMENT FOR BRIAN EPSTEIN; GEORGE HARRISON AND RINGO STARR AGREE.** Lennon once said that his pal Mick Jagger, who'd been involved with Klein for several years, told him "it's awfully hard to get your money." John took that to mean nothing more than that Klein kept his charges on a tight allowance. Eventually, even after Klein went to jail for selling copies of George Harrison's *Bangladesh* benefit album off the books, the Beatles regained control of their masters only after extensive, and expensive, litigation with Klein. The determination of Paul McCartney to avoid being represented by Klein (he favored his brother-in-law John Eastman) broke up the band, killing the goose and the golden eggs that came with it in one fell swoop.

5. **BILLY JOEL DIVORCES HIS WIFE-MANAGER, THEN DECIDES THE IDEAL REPLACEMENT WOULD BE HER BROTHER.** It's one thing when Pat Benatar demolishes her career by insisting on having her husband Neil Geraldo produce her records. It's another when Joel, having come out of a traumatizing divorce, decides the best possible choice to guide his career would

be his ex-brother-in-law, Frank Webber, whose principal previous experience had been selling real estate. When the dust finally cleared, Joel alleged he was out millions and Webber went bankrupt, making them noncollectable.

6. MICK TAYLOR QUITS THE ROLLING STONES. Taylor, the guitarist who replaced Brian Jones, apparently concluded he'd acquired enough profile for a solo career after a doing a couple of tours and playing on *Sticky Fingers* and *Exile on Main Street*. He should have thought again, because while he never disappeared, Taylor never again came close to claiming anybody's full attention, either.

7. THE CLASH FIRE MICK JONES. For some bizarre reason, almost as soon as the world's premier punk band made its U.S. commercial breakthrough with "Rock the Casbah," singer Joe Strummer and bassist Paul Simonon decided they'd be better off without guitarist Mick Jones. Jones went on to nothing more than the reggafied mediocrity of Big Audio Dynamite. Strummer and Simonon, on the other hand, have yet to accomplish that much, either on their own or as the Clash. Unless there's a late nineties reunion tour in the offing, this qualifies as one of the biggest wastes in rock history. The parallel case (it even took place around the same time) saw the J. Geils Band fire frontman Peter Wolf, just as their career arced to the top. It descended far more rapidly than it had arisen when keyboardist Seth Justman, the new lead singer, proved he couldn't sing, a process that took all of an album.

8. PROFESSOR GRIFF GIVES AN INTERVIEW TO *THE WASHINGTON TIMES*. The *Times*, a right-wing Washington, D.C., newspaper, sent David Mills, a young black reporter, to query Griff, then Public Enemy's Minister of Information, about P.E.'s politics. Mills had heard Griff make anti-Semitic remarks at earlier speaking appearances, and without much prompting, Griff repeated them. The ugly, indefensible comments kicked off a farcical set of PR maneuvers that found Griff first fired then rehired, then fired again by P.E. leader Chuck D, Chuck D blamed for what his side-kick said and for not getting rid of Griff quickly or decisively enough, Griff never invited to defend himself by the major media outlets that attacked him, and P.E.'s career virtually destroyed by the whole mess. At least it was a good career move for somebody: Mills wound up at *The Washington Post*, the respectable D.C. daily.

9. SLICK RICK DEALS WITH HIS COUSIN'S PERFIDY ALL BY HIMSELF. According to the story he told in court, Slick Rick found himself being exploited by his cousin, Mark Plummer. So Rick shot Plummer, then tried to elude the cops in a high-speed chase that wound up with him crashing his Jeep, badly injuring himself, then being found guilty of attempted murder and being given a long jail sentence. Though Def Jam's Russell Simmons shrewdly got him out on bail long enough to stockpile a few albums' worth of material, Slick Rick's career as one of the original street tough rappers closed out in consequence.

10. OZZY OSBOURNE BITES A BAT. Actually, Ozzy didn't *know* he was biting off the head of a bat. He thought he'd been thrown a fake and bit its head off as a gag in the heat of a gig. The joke went down badly: He had to go through an extremely painful series of rabies shots. Ozzy *did*, however, deliberately bite the head off a dove at an Epic Records staff meeting, in an effort to make some sort of point now lost to history. These legends pursue him to this day, rendering ridiculous the career of one of heavy metal's most interesting record-makers.

11. ELVIS COSTELLO DESCRIBES RAY CHARLES TO STEPHEN STILLS AND BONNIE BRAMLETT. In his cups in a Kentucky bar after a gig, wanting to needle old-fart rockers Stills and Bramlett and their cohorts, Costello chose to do so by insulting Ray Charles, whom he called "a blind ignorant nigger." He said the phrase just leaped out of him, that he couldn't possibly have meant it, and recorded a blue-eyed soul album for his next release to try to prove it. Many decided that even one sentence of nasty-mouthed racism constituted too much and never forgave him. His U.S. career went downhill from that point.

12. SINEAD O'CONNOR GETS PISSED AT THE POPE. Appearing on *Saturday Night Live*, she concluded her performance by tearing up Pope John Paul II's photograph and proclaiming "Fight the real enemy," rousing the wrath of every devout Catholic, many of the simply religious, and not a few hypocrites. Weeks later, at Bob Dylan's Thirtieth Anniversary Concert, a portion of the Madison Square Garden audience booed her, presumably because of her antipapist stance, and rather than replying with a snappy comeback or simply shrugging them off, Sinead lost it completely, jettisoning her planned performance of a Dylan song and singing Bob Marley's "War," a transcription of a speech by Rastafarian idol Emperor Haile Selassie of Ethiopia, instead. At worst, Sinead totally lost her mass audience with these actions; at best, she damaged her credibility as anything but a Grade A flake.

13. MILLI VANILLI RENEGOTIATES. Almost everyone forgets it, but Milli Vanilli's lipsynching became public knowledge only after Rob Pilatus and Fab Morvan tried to get producer Frank Farian to up their royalty rate on the second Milli Vanilli album. Farian undid their effort by publicly proclaiming that they hadn't sung on the debut album in the first place, resulting in a media snit that led to the rescinding of their Grammy Award as Best New Artists of 1989. Not that they were that in the first place.

14. WALTER YETNIKOFF INFORMS TOM SCHOLZ HE ISN'T WORKING FAST ENOUGH ON THE NEXT BOSTON ALBUM. Scholz, a craftsman as pokey as he was painstaking, told

THE NEW BOOK OF ROCK LISTS

CBS Records chief Yetnikoff he could only work at his own pace. Yetnikoff tried to stand on a contractual stipulation requiring timely delivery of his work. Scholz, a former Polaroid engineer with ample personal resources from both his multiplatinum debut LP and his invention of the Rockman amplifier, countersued to be released from his CBS contract. The court found in the artist's favor, and Yetnikoff's career began a downhill slide that culminated in his removal as CBS Records president not long after he'd arranged the sale of the division to Sony Corporation.

15. PRINCE CHANGES HIS NAME. The mere change might not have been so bad, but what he changed it to—that indecipherable hieroglyph that adorns the cover of his fourteenth album—annoyed everybody in the media and made him seem a pretentious laughingstock even to most of his audience. Within a few months, Prince compounded his problem by announcing that the indecipherable hieroglyph was pronounced "Christopher."

16. QUINCY JONES MAKES A SPEECH AT THE ROCK AND ROLL HALL OF FAME INDUCTION DINNER. Jones, record producer and sometime recording artist, had been personally selected by Hall honcho Ahmet Ertegun to make the speech inducting Ertegun's brother, Neshui, another record producer. Quincy's windy speech said little about Ertegun but a great deal about himself, most of the coherent parts concerning his own qualifications for the Hall. Those twenty minutes probably cost Quincy whatever chance he may have had for induction, at least during his lifetime, since all inductees give speeches and nobody's about to risk sitting through another one of his.

17. MARY WELLS LEAVES MOTOWN. Wells had been Motown's first big star. But by 1965, pissed off that Diana Ross got all the attention and promotion (a mood she shared with every other female performer at the label, including Martha Reeves), she wriggled loose from her Motown deal and signed with the fledgling Twentieth Century–Fox. Despite making some good records later on for Atlantic, she never had another hit.

18. THE TURTLES PLAY THE WHITE HOUSE. Before they accepted the invitation of Lyndon Johnson's daughters, the Turtles seemed like a fairly hip pop group. After all, they'd scored their first hit with "It Ain't Me Babe," a Bob Dylan song. But they played Lucy and Linda Bird's party at the height of the hip community's anti–Vietnam war sentiment, and their appearance seemed to indicate sympathy with LBJ's escalating prosecution of the war. (It probably signified nothing more than political naiveté or indifference.) In any event, the group's reputation never really recovered, even though it went on to make several fairly ambitious pop-rock albums before its breakup spawned Flo and Eddie.

19. DIRE STRAITS SPENDS SIX YEARS BETWEEN BROTHERS IN ARMS AND ON EVERY STREET. *Brothers* spent nine weeks at number one and sold six million copies in the United States alone. *Street* peaked at number twelve and barely went platinum in the States.

20. GRAHAM PARKER DECIDES HE'S IN A HURRY TO RELEASE HIS THIRD ALBUM. Somehow, though, the first version's tapes got destroyed. Rather than miss out on touring America with Thin Lizzy (now *there's* an irreplaceable opportunity), Parker, whom both radio and the press were poised to anoint the next singer-songwriter superhero, decided to go in and quickly rerecord the songs with everybody's favorite production slob, Nick Lowe, at the controls. Result: *Stick to Me*, a sloppy record that not even his fans in the media could salvage, and the end of one of the most promising commercial careers of the post-punk era.

21. TERRY KNIGHT PRESENTS HIS PROTÉGÉS, MOM'S APPLE PIE, WITH A GREAT NEW ALBUM COVER DESIGN. Knight, then the high-flying manager of Grand Funk Railroad, sold his new group (and Capitol Records) on releasing their debut disc with a cover featuring a wholesome-looking Mom, her hair in a bun, holding out a steaming pie with one slice missing. Rather than an apple filling, however, the missing slice revealed the lips of a vagina. *Mom's Apple Pie* soon disappeared from most retail shelves and even though Capitol reissued it with the vagina slice literally bricked up, that was the last that was heard from the group. The record didn't even make *Billboard's* Top Two Hundred album chart.

22. DAVID SANCIOUS QUITS THE E STREET BAND. Quitting might not have been a bad move: Sancious had ambitions to make his own music, which had much more to do with jazz and avant-rock than anything Bruce Springsteen wanted to do. What made it such a bad move was that Sancious quit just *before* Bruce began making his breakthrough album, *Born to Run.* Maybe it's just New Jersey luck, because Springsteen sidekick Little Steven Van Zandt did the same thing to himself by opting for a solo career just before the sessions for *Born in the U.S.A.* began. (Incidentally, this process works only one way: When Springsteen fired what was left of the E Street Band, his followup albums became the first flops of his career.)

23. MICK FLEETWOOD BEGINS MANAGING HIS OWN BAND. Fleetwood soon went bankrupt, the result of high living and bad investments. Given that the rest of the group had similar habits, Fleetwood Mac, which ranked with Led Zeppelin and the Eagles as the richest bands of the seventies, found itself under entirely unnecessary economic pressure, the torque of which forced the group to make albums and tours in which it had evidently small interest, and finally broke the band up.

24. AL KOOPER POSES AS THE STATUE OF LIBERTY FOR THE COVER OF HIS ALBUM, *I STAND ALONE.* A brilliant

visual conceit that in its own weird way reflected a sort of humility
—Kooper couldn't have put his music in perspective any more decisively—found a rather humorless reception among critics and, for
that matter, even casual onlookers. That the music failed and that
many had already become fed up with the "super session" craze
Kooper initiated hurt, too. But then, one definition of a bad career
move might be doing the right thing at the wrong time. After all, in
the postmodern nineties, making bad music while posing as the
Statue of Liberty would have been an MTV sensation. But in the
self-conscious seventies, Kooper never lived down the presumptive
egomania, even though he went on to discover Lynyrd Skynyrd,
among other more important matters.

**25. STEVIE WONDER WRITES THE LYRICS FOR HIS
SOUNDTRACK TO *JOURNEY THROUGH THE SECRET LIFE
OF PLANTS* FROM THE POINT OF VIEW OF THE PLANTS.**
Most people did not understand this. Many mocked him. Wonder,
who had never gotten bad reviews before, let alone lost his grip on
the popular audience, seemed crushed, and he's never really recovered the momentum he lost with this project, either commercially or
artistically. The saddest part is that Stevie's music on that album
ranks with the most ambitious he ever conceived or performed.

Your Generation
Star Kids of Today—OK! Everybody Out of the Gene Pool!

1. BLOODLINE—Band featuring Miles Davis's son, Erin, Allman Brothers Berry Oakley's son Berry Jr., and Waylon Kreiger,
fathered by Doors guitarist Robby Kreiger.

2. BONHAM—Ultrahard rock band led by Jason Bonham, son
of Led Zep's John Bonham. Jason's a drummer, too.

3. BECCA BRAMLETT—Daughter of Delaney and Bonnie,
has sung with Fleetwood Mac.

4. BILLY BURNETTE—Son of Dorsey Burnette of the Rock
and Roll Trio. Occasional member of Fleetwood Mac (apparently
rock's biggest believers in nepotism, though they've yet to recycle
any of their own kids). Cousin of Rocky Burnette, nephew of Johnny
Burnette.

5. ROCKY BURNETTE—Son of rockabilly great turned teen
idol Johnny Burnette. Cousin of Billy Burnette, nephew of Dorsey
Burnette.

6. CARLENE CARTER—Daughter of Johnny Cash and June
Carter, once boasted she'd "put the 'cunt' back in country," married
Nick Lowe, but when all the jiving was done made several terrific
country-rock albums, anyway.

7. ROSANNE CASH—Johnny's daughter from his first marriage has become the first country star to specialize in self-help songs.

8. CEREMONY—Band led by Chastity Bono, daughter of Sonny and Cher.

9. CHRISTOPHER—Son of Prince.

10. NONA GAYE—Daughter of Marvin Gaye made some noise with 1992 debut album, recently worked with Prince.

11. LOUISE GOFFIN—Daughter of Gerry Goffin and Carole King, displays some of Mom's singing ability, little of either parent's writing talents. One solo album.

12. WHITNEY HOUSTON—Daughter of soul singer and Elvis and Aretha backup Cissy Houston; niece of Dionne Warwick.

13. JULIAN LENNON—The unimaginative mediocrity of John Lennon's first son will make you hope that Sean takes up knitting. Real name: John Lennon.

14. LEVERT—Leader Gerald La Vert and his brother, Sean, are sons of Eddie Levert, who's long led the O'Jays. Gerald also has a solo career, discovered and produces Troop.

15. ZIGGY MARLEY—Son of Bob and Rita Marley made a big splash in the late eighties with reggae-rock albums.

16. MILLI VANILLI—Sons of the Monkees, though the white boy rock critics who slammed M.V. wouldn't want to admit it.

17. JENNIE MULDAUR—Daughter of Maria and Geoff Muldaur possesses spectacular voice, though she's yet to make the right record for it.

18. NELSON—Matthew and Gunnar Nelson, blonde wimps supreme, are the twin sons of Rick(y) Nelson.

19. PRETTY IN PINK—Features Millini Khan, daughter of Chaka.

20. THE REDDINGS—Dexter and Otis III, sons of Otis Redding, formed this middling black harmony group in the early eighties with cousin Mark Lockett.

21. ROCKWELL—Pseudonym of Kennedy Gordy, son of Berry Gordy, Jr., who hit with "Somebody's Watching Me," paranoid pop-funk—on Motown, of course.

22. ZAK STARKEY—Ringo's son, also a drummer, who's toured and recorded with his father, among others.

23. WILSON-PHILLIPS—Chynna Phillips is the daughter of John and Michelle Phillips of the Mamas and Papas; Carnie and Wendy Wilson are the daughters of Beach Boy *Maximus* Brian Wilson.

24. LINDA WOMACK—Female member of Womack and Womack is Sam Cooke's daughter, married to Cecil Womack, brother of her mother's second husband, Bobby (i.e., her uncle by marriage).

25. DWEEZIL ZAPPA—Sometime MTV veejay makes more impact as a guitarist, whose taste in noise and avant-gardism highly resembles that of his father, Mother Frank Zappa. He sometimes works with brother Ahmet, a singer. Their sister, Moon Unit, another TV miniceleb, appeared with Pop on his last hit, "Valley Girl."

The Jacksons
Members of the Family

1. JOSEPH JACKSON—Biggest bully on the block; they call him Pop.

2. KATHERINE JACKSON—Moms. A Jehovah's Witness, like Joe's mother (but not Joe).

3. REBBIE JACKSON—Eldest daughter. Least talented musically. Alleged target of dad's abuse.

4. JACKIE JACKSON—Eldest brother. Without discernible talent *or* ambition.

5. TITO JACKSON—Icon of all layabouts.

6. JERMAINE JACKSON—Most independent of Michael's brothers, with not only a separate solo career as soon as the Jackson 5 split with Motown, but eventually an entirely separate career on a separate record label (Arista), which none of his siblings pulled off until baby Janet.

7. LATOYA JACKSON—Publicity hound who makes Michael look a regular wallflower. Best tits, as far as we can see.

8. MARLON JACKSON—Prime distinction: As sixth-oldest child, the one born right before Michael. Actually charted a solo album once, but then, the group *was* a craze.

9. MICHAEL JACKSON—King of Pop, headline hunter, grown man who favors kids as sleeping partners. A man with an exceedingly strange future, whatever it may be.

10. RANDY JACKSON—Only briefly a member of the group, when he replaced Jermaine. Most arrested family member.

11. JANET JACKSON—Arguably the most musically talented, though certainly not the best singer. Could stand some additional acting lessons but has fared well in movies *(Poetic Justice)* and on TV *(Good Times, Dif'frent Strokes, Fame)*. Signed $32 million contract with Virgin Records, 1991; may earn it all back.

10 Best Comebacks

1. ELVIS PRESLEY
When Elvis returned from the Army in 1960, he hadn't appeared in civilian life since the death of his mother in 1958. Although RCA

Victor had stockpiled plenty of Presley hits, nobody believed that any pop singer—let alone someone who was essentially a teen idol —could recover more than a smidgen of his premilitary acclaim. Elvis, however, returned with a vengeance: His first post-Army album, *Elvis Is Back!* went only to number two, but *G.I. Blues* spent ten weeks at number one, and by the fall's *Blue Hawaii*, he was bigger than ever.

2. Tina Turner

Even if you don't credit every shred of her soap-opera-friendly account of her escape from a monstrous Ike Turner (and anybody who's ever gazed into Ike's eyes has to believe the bulk of it), you have to be heartened by Tina's return to glory after years of stomping the chitlin' circuit and a few seasons of display as a sexual caricature. Even though her recent music adds up to little more than fumbled attempts to repeat *Private Dancer* as formula, Tina's triumph at the very least represents the ascendance of heart and humanity over bitter realities.

3. Bonnie Raitt

Raitt bottomed out around 1987. She'd lost the Warner Brothers recording contract she'd had since 1971, not only because her records hadn't sold well (she'd only had one gold award), but because she was in terrible shape: alcoholic, drug-addicted, and overweight. Raitt faced down her terrors and returned with 1989's *Nick of Time*, which she made with producer Don Was steering her to fine material and with the additional assistance of the first songs she'd ever written herself. When *Nick* won four Grammys, including Record of the Year, Raitt went from being a much admired blues-rock performer to a true celebrity.

4. Aerosmith

Split up and virtually dropped out of sight after 1979's *Night in the Ruts*. Cleaned up their act, personally and professionally, regrouped, and beginning with 1987's *Permanent Vacation*, reascended the charts. Especially impressive because they did it in hard rock, the most fickle and youth-oriented genre.

5. John Lee Hooker

Hooker became a blues star with "Crawling King Snake" in 1949, and he scored R&B hits right up through "Boom Boom" in 1962. Like all surviving bluesmen, he underwent a revival of popularity in the late sixties and early seventies. In 1971, he scored a success with *Hooker 'N Heat* featuring the white blues band Canned Heat, and the next year with *Never Get Out of These Blues Alive*, which featured Van Morrison, among others. When he put *The Healer* on the charts in 1989, it had been seventeen years between chart appearances, and even though *The Healer* features its share of rock stars (Bonnie Raitt, Carlos Santana, Los Lobos), it's pure Hooker music. So was 1991's slightly less successful *Mr. Lucky*, which showcased Hooker with Morrison, Keith Richards, Santana, and more.

6. THE J. GEILS BAND

Peaking with the number-ten *Bloodshot* in 1973, Geils descended a few more steps down the chart ladder with each subsequent album, as the seventies saw bluesified boogie-rock dwindle. But in 1980, *Love Stinks* returned them to the Top Twenty, and the next year, *Freeze-Frame* brought them all the way to number one. After that, they soon disappeared for good, although ex-frontman Peter Wolf had a brief mid-eighties Top Forty fling.

7. ELTON JOHN

Presumed commercially and creatively dead after his 1985 *Rolling Stone* interview acknowledgment that he was "bisexual," Elton pulled both his private and public lives back together again so that by the early nineties, he appeared as the venerable prince of Anglopop. His renewal also presaged an era in which it was safe for established performers to emerge from the closet.

8. COUNTRY MUSIC

So dead that *The New York Times* (accurately) frontpaged the story in the mid-eighties, it had become bigger than ever by the early nineties, thanks to Garth Brooks and a passel of other cowboy-hatted neohonky-tonkers, as well as to a reactionary response to mainstream pop dominance by hip-hop and related black forms.

9. ERIC CLAPTON

Clapton went from 1983 through 1988 without so much as a Top Twenty album, but late in 1988, the box set *Crossroads* revived interest in him and gave him enough of a boost on radio—"Promises" from the box became a Top Ten hit—that 1989's *Journeyman* became his first multiplatinum new release. By 1992, with *Unplugged* and "Tears in Heaven," he'd become the leading light of the Grammies, the epitome of yuppie soul.

10. MARIANNE FAITHFULL

After her big sixties hits, "As Tears Go By" and "Come and Stay With Me," in which she featured as a Rolling Stones boy-toy, Faithfull dropped off the pop map for better than a decade. Then, in 1980, she returned with the ravaged and rocking *Broken English*, one of the first signals that the postpunk pop sensibility had room for some older voices, too. Since then, she's made a handful of brilliant albums that portray the battle of the sexes with ruthless skill.

CHAPTER 15

Who Put the Bomp
(The Writers)

The 100 Best Songwriters

THE FIFTIES

1. CHUCK BERRY—"Maybellene," "Roll Over Beethoven," "School Day," "Sweet Little Sixteen," "Johnny B. Goode," "Let It Rock," "Little Queenie," "Almost Grown," "Back in the U.S.A.," "You Never Can Tell." A basic rock library of brilliant lyrical narratives, blues-haunted melodies and driving guitar-based rhythms, all originally recorded by Berry, then reconceived by the Rolling Stones, the Beatles, the Beach Boys ("Surfin' U.S.A.," "Fun Fun Fun"), and dozens of others.

2. JERRY LEIBER AND MIKE STOLLER—"Jailhouse Rock," "Kansas City," "Hound Dog," "Riot In Cell Block #9," "Charlie Brown," "Yakety Yak," "On Broadway," "Love Potion Number Nine," "Searchin'," "Ruby Baby," "Poison Ivy," "Spanish Harlem," "Young Blood," "I (Who Have Nothing)," "I'm a Woman," numerous other hits for the Coasters, Elvis Presley, and others. Established rock's dramatic song form.

3. BUDDY HOLLY—"Peggy Sue," "Rave On," "That'll Be the Day," "Oh Boy," "Maybe Baby," "Not Fade Away," "True Love Ways," "Love's Made a Fool of You," "Well All Right," "Think It Over," "Fool's Paradise," "Every Day," "It's So Easy," "Words of Love," often with various collaborators. Holly's tunes have been indispensable to the Beatles, the Rolling Stones, and Linda Ronstadt, as well as post-Dylan (Springsteen, Seger, Petty, Mellencamp) "heartland rock."

4. DOC POMUS AND MORT SHUMAN—"Save the Last Dance for Me," "This Magic Moment," "I Count the Tears," "A Teenager in Love," "Seven Day Weekend," "Spanish Lace," "Hushabye," "Viva Las Vegas," "Little Sister," "Suspicion." Pomus also wrote "Jelly Jelly Jelly," "Lonely Avenue," "Boogie-Woogie Country Girl," "Young Blood," "His Latest Flame," and "There Must Be A Better World Somewhere." Shuman became Jacques Brel's translator, as well as penning hits like "Little Children," "Get It While You Can," "Look at Granny Run, Run."

5. JESSIE STONE (ALSO KNOWN AS CHARLES CALHOUN)—"Money Honey," "Shake Rattle and Roll," "Flip Flop and Fly," "Smack Dab in the Middle," "Don't Let Go," "Down in the Alley," "Cole Slaw," "Your Cash Ain't Nothin' But Trash," "It Should Have Been Me," "Bip Bam," "Losing Hand." A principal architect of 1950s R&B.

6. FELICE AND BOUDLEAUX BRYANT—Supplied the Everly Brothers with their biggest hits, from "Bye Bye Love" through "Wake Up Little Susie," "All I Have to Do Is Dream," and "Bird Dog." Gave Buddy Holly "Raining in My Heart," Roy Orbison

"Love Hurts." Also wrote country hits like "Hey Joe!" and "Rocky Top."

   7. BERRY GORDY—For Jackie Wilson, Gordy and Tyrone Carlo (Billy Davis) wrote "Lonely Teardrops," "Reet Petite," "To Be Beloved," and "I'll Be Satisfied," his biggest and best hits. At Motown, Gordy wrote, or cowrote, "Do You Love Me" and "Shake Sherry" for the Contours, Barret Strong's "Money," the Miracles' "Way Over There" and "Shop Around," Marvin Gaye's "Try It Baby," and Brenda Holloway's "You've Made Me So Very Happy."

   8. DAVE BARTHOLOMEW—"Ain't That a Shame," "Blue Monday," "The Fat Man," "I Hear You Knockin'," "I'm Gonna Be a Wheel Someday," "I'm in Love Again," "I'm Walkin'," "Let the Four Winds Blow," "One Night," "Walking to New Orleans," "Whole Lot of Loving," "Witchcraft." Usually with his artists.

   9. OTIS BLACKWELL (JOHN DAVENPORT)—"Don't Be Cruel," "All Shook Up," "Fever," "Great Balls of Fire," "Return to Sender," "Daddy Rolling Stone," "One Broken Heart for Sale," "Hey Little Girl," "Breathless," "Handy Man."

   10. ROY ORBISON—"Only the Lonely," "Crying," "Oh, Pretty Woman," "In Dreams," "Blue Bayou," "Blue Angel," "Ooby Dooby," "Running Scared," "Claudette," "Leah," "Dream Baby." All except "Claudette" were hits for Orbison; that one hit for the Everly Brothers. Later, they hit for Van Halen, Linda Ronstadt, k. d. lang, and others.

   11. SAM COOKE—"Bring It On Home to Me," "Another Saturday Night," "Cupid," "Having a Party," "Only Sixteen," "Shake," "Twistin' the Night Away," "Soothe Me."

   12. WILLIE DIXON—"Hoochie Coochie Man," "I Just Want to Make Love to You," "Little Red Rooster," "You Can't Judge a Book by Its Cover," "Wang Dang Doodle," "Seventh Son," "I'm Ready," "Mellow Down Easy," "Evil," "I Ain't Superstitious," "Pretty Thing," "I Can't Quit You Baby."

   13. PERCY MAYFIELD—"Please Send Me Someone to Love," "Hit the Road Jack," "The River's Invitation," "Hide Nor Hair," "At the Club," "But on the Other Hand," "I Don't Want to Be President," "Life Is Suicide," "Strange Things Happening," "My Heart," "I Ain't Gonna Cry No More," "Diggin' the Moonglow."

   14. LITTLE RICHARD (PENNIMAN)—"Tutti Frutti," "Long Tall Sally," "Lucille," "Slippin' and Slidin'," "Jenny Take a Ride," "Jenny Jenny," each a perfection of rhythmic and vocal control amidst an anarchic atmosphere. But these are solid songs, as Elvis, the Beatles, and Mitch Ryder and the Detroit Wheels could testify.

   15. HARVEY FUQUA—Fuqua worked with the Moonglows (a group he led), Bo Diddley, Marvin Gaye and Smokey Robinson, though his best collaborator was Johnny Bristol at Motown. "If I

Could Build My Whole World Around You," "Sincerely," "My Whole World Ended," "Someday We'll Be Together," "25 Miles," "What Does It Take to Win Your Love," "Most of All," "Diddley Daddy."

16. JOHN MARASCALCO AND BUMPS BLACKWELL—"Good Golly Miss Molly," "Ready Teddy," "Rip It Up," "Send Me Some Lovin' "—the other half of the Little Richard story.

17. LOWMAN PAULING—All the Five Royales hits including "Dedicated to the One I Love," "Think," and "Tell the Truth," which were later hits for the Shirelles, the Mamas and Papas, James Brown, Ray Charles, and Eric Clapton.

18. RICHARD BARRETT—Credits are slim because Barrett worked with George Goldner, a brilliant entrepreneur who unfortunately also mastered the art of the "cut-in" (placing a label owner or producer's name on songs that he has not written). But he definitely wrote "The ABCs of Love" and "I Want You to Be My Girl" for Frankie Lymon and the Teenagers, and "Maybe," "He's Gone," and "Look in My Eyes" for the Chantels, among the finest doo-wop records ever made.

19. FATS DOMINO—Usually with Dave Bartholomew. "Ain't That a Shame," "I Want to Walk You Home," "I'm Gonna Be a Wheel Someday," "I'm in Love Again," "I'm Ready," "I'm Walkin'," "Poor Me," "Whole Lot of Loving," "Walking to New Orleans."

20. BO DIDDLEY (ELIAS MCDANIEL)—"I'm a Man," "Bo Diddley," "Who Do You Love," "Mona," "Before You Accuse Me," "Say Man," "Love Is Strange" (as Ethel Smith), "Diddy Wah Diddy," "Crackin' Up," "Road Runner."

21. JESSE BELVIN—Belvin was notorious for selling songs outright to whatever Los Angeles record companies would have them. We know he wrote "Earth Angel" (he won a lawsuit over that one), "Goodnight My Love," "Hang Your Tears Out to Dry," "Beware," "Funny" and "Guess Who."

22. LLOYD PRICE—"Just Because," "Lawdy Miss Clawdy," "Personality," "I'm Gonna Get Married," and his version of "Stagger Lee," a classic blues changed so much that its new "author" earned acknowledgment.

23. HANK BALLARD—"The Twist," "Work with Me Annie" and its numerous sequels, "Finger Poppin' Time," "Let's Go Let's Go Let's Go."

24. RUDY TOOMBS—"One Mint Julep," "5-10-15 Hours," "Teardrops from My Eyes," "One Scotch, One Bourbon, One Beer," "In the Morning," "Nip Sip." Another whose credits may be in some disarray.

25. RAY CHARLES—"I Got a Woman," "Greenbacks," "Come Back Baby," "A Fool for You," "This Little Girl of Mine,"

"Hallelujah I Love Her So," "Talkin' 'Bout You," "What'd I Say," "I Believe to My Soul," "If You Were Mine," "Booty Butt."

THE SIXTIES

1. **BOB DYLAN**—"Like a Rolling Stone," "Don't Think Twice, It's All Right," "Mr. Tambourine Man," "A Hard Rain's A-Gonna Fall," "Quinn the Eskimo," "Girl from the North Country," "The Times They Are A-Changin'," "All Along the Watchtower," "My Back Pages," "The Lonesome Death of Hattie Carroll," plus such albums as *The Freewheelin' Bob Dylan, The Times They Are A-Changin', Another Side of Bob Dylan, Bringing It All Back Home, Highway 61 Revisited, Blonde on Blonde, John Wesley Harding* . . . The best credentials here *before* you start talking about influence.

2. **BRIAN HOLLAND, LAMONT DOZIER, AND EDDIE HOLLAND**—"Where Did Our Love Go," "Reach Out I'll Be There," "Stop! In the Name of Love," "Heat Wave," "Bernadette," "Standing in the Shadows of Love," "You Keep Me Hangin' On." "I Can't Help Myself," "Back in My Arms Again," "Nowhere to Run," "How Sweet It Is (To Be Loved by You)," "Please Mr. Postman," "You Can't Hurry Love," "Wonderful One." A deeper catalogue than Lennon and McCartney's and with an effect nearly as revolutionary as Dylan's.

3. **JOHN LENNON AND PAUL McCARTNEY**—"She Loves You," "I Want to Hold Your Hand," "Please Please Me," "Love Me Do," "A Hard Day's Night," "Help!," "Yesterday," and a couple dozen others—all *before* they created *Rubber Soul, Revolver, Sgt. Pepper's Lonely Hearts Club Band,* and *Abbey Road.* Their tandem supremacy works to the detriment of their solo work but *John Lennon/Plastic Ono Band, Imagine,* and *Band on the Run* are rife with songs for which other songwriters would sell their careers.

4. **MICK JAGGER AND KEITH RICHARDS**—"Satisfaction," "Get Off of My Cloud," "Jumping Jack Flash," "Street Fighting Man," "As Tears Go By," "Honky Tonk Woman," "Gimme Shelter," "You Can't Always Get What You Want," "Sympathy for the Devil," "Tumbling Dice," plus albums like *Aftermath, Between the Buttons, Beggars Banquet, Let It Bleed,* and *Exile on Main Street.*

5. **SMOKEY ROBINSON**—"My Girl," "My Guy," "The Tracks of My Tears," "Don't Look Back," "I Second That Emotion," "My Girl Has Gone," "I'll Be Doggone," "Ain't That Peculiar," "Get Ready," "Tears of a Clown," "Ooo Baby Baby," "The Way You Do the Things You Do," "Cruisin." Also the 1965 LP *The Temptations Sing Smokey.* That's why Bob Dylan called him "America's greatest living poet."

6. **CURTIS MAYFIELD**—"For Your Precious Love," "He

Will Break Your Heart," "Gypsy Woman," "It's All Right," "I'm So Proud," "Keep on Pushing," "People Get Ready," "Choice of Colors," "This Is My Country," "We the People Who Are Darker than Blue," "Monkey Time." Also composed the soundtracks to *Superfly* and Aretha Franklin's *Sparkle*, including "Something He Can Feel."

7. JEFF BARRY AND ELLIE GREENWICH—"Da Doo Ron Ron," "Then He Kissed Me," "Be My Baby," "Baby I Love You," "I Can Hear Music," "River Deep Mountain High," "Do Wah Diddy Diddy," "What A Guy," "Chapel of Love," "The Leader of the Pack," "Hanky Panky," "Why Do Lovers Break Each Other's Hearts."

8. ISAAC HAYES AND DAVID PORTER—All of Sam and Dave's hits, including "Hold On, I'm Comin'," "Soul Man," "When Something Is Wrong with My Baby," "I Thank You," "Wrap It Up." Also Carla Thomas's "B-A-B-Y" and Mabel John's "Your Good Thing (Is About to End)." On his own, Hayes created "Theme from *Shaft*," followed by excellent scores for *Truck Turner* and *Tough Guys*.

9. GERRY GOFFIN AND CAROLE KING—"Will You Love Me Tomorrow," "(You Make Me Feel Like) A Natural Woman," "Who Put the Bomp," "Take Good Care of My Baby," "The Loco-Motion," "Up on the Roof," "Chains," "One Fine Day," "I'm Into Something Good." King wrote some of the best singer-songwriter hits, notably on the massive *Tapestry*, which included "You've Got a Friend" and "It's Too Late." Goffin, the lyricist, cowrote Gladys Knight's "I've Got to Use My Imagination," Whitney Houston's "Saving All My Love for You," and more.

10. PETE TOWNSHEND—Adolescent anthems—"My Generation," "Substitute," "Pictures of Lily," "I'm a Boy," and other early Who singles—gave way to concept albums like *The Who Sell Out*, then "rock operas" *Tommy* and *Quadrophenia*. Also composed fine songs for his numerous solo albums.

11. BRIAN WILSON—"Shut Down," "Surfer Girl," "In My Room," "Don't Worry Baby," "I Get Around," "Wendy," "Help Me Rhonda," "California Girls," "Wouldn't It Be Nice," "God Only Knows," "Caroline No," "Good Vibrations," *Pet Sounds*, "Wild Honey," "Do It Again."

12. NICKOLAS ASHFORD AND VALERIE SIMPSON—"Ain't No Mountain High Enough," "Let's Go Get Stoned," "Solid," "I Don't Need No Doctor," "Ain't Nothing Like the Real Thing," "You're All I Need to Get By," "Reach Out and Touch (Somebody's Hand)," "Good Lovin' Ain't Easy to Come By," "Your Precious Love," "I'm Every Woman," "Who's Gonna Take the Blame," "Some Things You Never Get Used To."

13. BURT BACHARACH AND HAL DAVID—"Don't Make Me Over," "The Man Who Shot Liberty Valance," "Baby It's

You," "One Less Bell to Answer," "What the World Needs Now is Love," "Wishin' and Hopin'," "I Just Don't Know What to Do with Myself," "Anyone Who Had a Heart," "Only Love Can Break a Heart," "Walk On By," "Do You Know the Way to San Jose," "I Say a Little Prayer." Bacharach also wrote Chuck Jackson's "Any Day Now" and Gene McDaniels's "Tower of Strength"with Bob Hilliard.

14. SLY STONE (SYLVESTER STEWART)—"Dance to the Music," "Everyday People," "Hot Fun in the Summertime," "C'mon and Swim," "Family Affair," "I Want to Take You Higher," "Thank You (Falettin Me Be Mice Elf Again)," "Don't Call Me Nigger, Whitey," "You Can Make It If You Try," "Stand," "Everybody Is a Star." Sly wrote all the music on the Sly and the Family Stone albums, except for "Que Sera Sera."

15. JOHN FOGERTY—All Credence Clearwater Revival's hits, most of their albums. "Proud Mary," "Bad Moon Rising," "Fortunate Son," "Lodi," "Green River," "Who'll Stop the Rain," "Centerfield," "Run Through the Jungle," "The Old Man Down the Road," "Sweet Hitchhiker," "Travelin' Band," "Down on the Corner," "Rockin' All Over the World."

16. PAUL SIMON—"Bridge Over Troubled Water," "Graceland," "50 Ways to Leave Your Lover," "America," "Sounds of Silence," "My Little Town," "The Boxer," "Kodachrome," "American Tune," "Loves Me Like a Rock," "Mother and Child Reunion," "Mrs. Robinson."

17. ALLEN TOUSSAINT (NAOMI NEVILLE)—"Mother-in-Law," "Holy Cow," "I Like It Like That," "Java," "Southern Nights," "Working in the Coal Mine," "Yes We Can Can," "Ruler of My Heart" (melody became Otis Redding's "Pain in My Heart"), "Ride Your Pony," "Get Out of My Life, Woman," "It's Raining."

18. OTIS REDDING—Often with collaborators, notably Steve Cropper and Jerry Butler. "Dock of the Bay," "I've Been Loving You Too Long," "Respect," "Mr. Pitiful," "Sweet Soul Music," "These Arms of Mine," "I Can't Turn You Loose," "My Lover's Prayer," "Hard to Handle," "I've Got Dreams to Remember," "Direct Me," "Chained and Bound," "Love Man," "Fa-Fa-Fa-Fa-Fa (Sad Song)."

19. BERT BERNS (BERT RUSSELL)—Usually with collaborators, notably Jerry Ragavoy and Phil Medley. "Twist and Shout," "Piece of My Heart," "Hang On Sloopy," "Cry Baby," "Time Is on My Side," "Everybody Needs Somebody to Love," "Here Comes the Night," "I Want Candy," "Down in the Valley," "Cry to Me," "Goodbye Baby (Baby Goodbye)," "I'll Take Good Care of You"

20. ROBBIE ROBERTSON, RICK DANKO, RICHARD MANUEL (THE BAND)—Composed virtually all of the material, separately or in various collaborations (including some with Bob

Dylan) on the first Band album. After that, Robertson wrote almost everything. "Tears of Rage," "The Weight," "Chest Fever," "Up on Cripple Creek," "Rag Mama Rag," "The Night They Drove Old Dixie Down," "The Shape I'm In," "Stage Fright," "This Wheel's on Fire," "It Makes No Difference," "Life is a Carnival," "Get Up Jake."

21. NORMAN WHITFIELD AND BARRETT STRONG—"I Heard It Through the Grapevine," "Papa Was a Rolling Stone," "Just My Imagination," "War," "(I Know) I'm Losing You," "Ain't Too Proud to Beg," "I Can't Get Next to You," "Ball of Confusion," "Friendship Train," "Beauty's Only Skin Deep," "Psychedelic Shack," "I Wish It Would Rain."

22. RAY DAVIES—All the Kinks' various albums and singles. "You Really Got Me," "Waterloo Sunset," "All Day and All of the Night," "A Well Respected Man," "Rock and Roll Fantasy," "Dedicated Follower of Fashion," "Lola," "Come Dancing."

23. DON COVAY—"Chain of Fools," "See-saw," "Pony Time," "Lights Out," "Mercy Mercy," "Sookie Sookie," "Letter Full of Tears," "I'm Hanging Up My Heart for You," "I Don't Know What You've Got (But It's Got Me)," "I Was Checkin' Out, She Was Checkin' In."

24. JERRY RAGAVOY—Mainly with collaborators. "Time Is on My Side," "Cry Baby," "Stay with Me," "Mecca," "I'll Take Good Care of You," "Piece of My Heart," "What's It Gonna Be," "This Silver Ring," "A Wonderful Dream," "Tra La La."

25. JAMES BROWN—Remodeled the idea of a "song" almost as much as Dylan by virtually abolishing most components of the category. "Cold Sweat," "It's a Man's, Man's, Man's World," "Get on the Good Foot," "Licking Stick Licking Stick," "I Can't Stand Myself," "I Got You (I Feel Good)," "Papa's Got a Brand New Bag," "Sex Machine," "Say It Loud—I'm Black and I'm Proud."

THE SEVENTIES

1. STEVIE WONDER—The most important R&B artist to emerge in the decade and the best love songwriter, period. "Superstition," "Signed, Sealed, Delivered I'm Yours," "Higher Ground," "I Was Made to Love Her," "Uptight," "I Wish," "Living for the City," "Sir Duke," "Isn't She Lovely," "You Haven't Done Nothin'," "Don't You Worry 'bout a Thing," "You are the Sunshine of My Life."

2. BOB MARLEY—"I Shot the Sheriff," "Get Up Stand Up," "No Woman, No Cry," "Lively Up Yourself," "Stir It Up," "Trenchtown Rock," "Redemption Song," "One Love," "Bend Down Low," "Could You Be Loved," "Duppy Conqueror," "Small Axe," "Guava Jelly," "Jammin'," "Waiting in Vain."

3. BRUCE SPRINGSTEEN—The bridge between Dylanesque singer-songwriters and Stones/Byrds-influenced heartland rockers. "Born to Run," "Born in the U.S.A.," "Badlands," "Darkness on the Edge of Town," "The River," "Hungry Heart," "Because the Night," "Prove It All Night," "Dancing in the Dark," "Brilliant Disguise," "Glory Days," "Fire," "Cover Me," "Spirit in the Night," "Thunder Road."

4. JONI MITCHELL—Prince's favorite songwriter. "You Turn Me On, I'm a Radio," "Blue," "Woodstock," "Both Sides Now (Clouds)," "Carey," "A Free Man in Paris," "Circle Game," "Big Yellow Taxi," "For the Roses," "Help Me," "Song to a Seagull," "Chelsea Morning," "Blonde in the Bleachers."

5. VAN MORRISON—"Gloria," "Domino," "Jackie Wilson Said (I'm in Heaven When You Smile)," "Brown Eyed Girl," "Wild Night," "Moondance," "Caravan," "Cypress Avenue," "Crazy Love," "Someone Like You," "Into the Mystic," and the most soulful, bluesy, occasionally even rocking series of New Age albums ever made, from *Astral Weeks* to whatever he's up to this year.

6. KENNETH GAMBLE AND LEON HUFF—Architects of The Sound of Philadelphia, Motown's first heir and disco's direct precursor. "Love Train," "Cowboys to Girls," "Don't Leave Me This Way," "Drowning in the Sea of Love," "Hey, Western Union Man," "Expressway to Your Heart," "For the Love of Money," "If You Don't Know Me by Now," "Me and Mrs. Jones," "Only the Strong Survive," "Use Ta Be My Girl," "When Will I See You Again."

7. GEORGE CLINTON—Composer of all the Parliament/Funkadelic albums. "One Nation Under a Groove," "Give Up the Funk (Tear the Roof Off the Sucker)," "Flash Light," "I Wanna Testify," "The Big Bang Theory," "Funkentelechy," "Mothership Connection," "Cosmic Slop," "Standing on the Verge of Getting It On," "Let's Take It to the Stage," "Up for the Down Stroke."

8. RONNIE VAN ZANT (LYNYRD SKYNYRD)—"Free Bird," "Sweet Home Alabama," "Gimme Three Steps," "Saturday Night Special," "Was I Right or Wrong," "Workin' for MCA," "Don't Ask Me No Questions," "The Ballad of Curtis Lowe," "The Needle and the Spoon," "What's Your Name," "That Smell," "You Got That Right."

9. LEONARD COHEN—The only song-poet worth the name. "Bird on the Wire," "Suzanne," "Sisters of Mercy," "Hey, That's No Way to Say Goodbye," "The Traitor," "Our Lady of Solitude," "Democracy," "First We Take Manhattan," "I'm Your Man," "Lady Midnight," "Famous Blue Raincoat," "Who By Fire."

10. NEIL YOUNG—Auteur of a series of artsy-electro-folk-rockabilly albums. "Helpless," "Hey Hey, My My (Out of the Blue and into the Black)," "Like a Hurricane," "Ohio," "Heart of Gold," "Only Love Can Break Your Heart," "Rockin' in the Free

World," "Cortez the Killer," "Powderfinger," "Tonight's the Night," "Cowgirl in the Sand," "Everybody Knows This is Nowhere," "Mr. Soul."

11. WALTER BECKER AND DONALD FAGEN (STEELY DAN)—Auteurs of a series of fussy-artsy, electro-jazzbo albums. "Bodhisattva," "Do It Again," "Hey Nineteen," "Bad Sneakers," "Josie," "Peg," "Reeling in the Years," "Rikki Don't Lose That Number," "Deacon Blues," "Chain Lightning," "Black Cow," "Black Friday."

12. THOM BELL AND LINDA CREED—"Betcha By Golly Wow," "Break Up to Make Up," "Rockin' Roll Baby," "Didn't I (Blow Your Mind This Time)," "Rubberband Man," "I'm Stone in Love with You," "You Are Everything," "You Make Me Feel Brand New," "La La (Means I Love You)."

13. RANDY NEWMAN—"I Love L.A.," "Sail Away," "Let's Burn Down the Cornfield," "Dayton, Ohio, 1903," "Burn On, Big River," "Baltimore," "Davey the Fat Boy," "Simon Smith and the Amazing Dancing Bear," "Mama Told Me Not to Come," "I Think It's Going to Rain Today," "Short People."

14. JOE STRUMMER AND MICK JONES (THE CLASH) —"Rock the Casbah," "Train in Vain," "Lost in the Supermarket," "White Riot," "1977," "Career Opportunities," "Garageland," "Complete Control," "I'm So Bored with the U.S.A.," "White Man in Hammersmith Palais," "London Calling," "Should I Stay or Should I Go."

15. MAURICE WHITE (EARTH, WIND AND FIRE)—"Serpentine Fire," "Shining Star," "Let's Groove," "Saturday Night," "Evil," "September," "That's the Way of the World," "Best of My Love," "Kalimba Story," "In the Stone," "Fall in Love with Me," "Reasons."

16. JACKSON BROWNE—Prince of Singer-Songwriters, Pacific Division. "Running on Empty," "The Pretender," "Lawyers in Love," "These Days," "Doctor My Eyes," "For a Dancer," "Take It Easy," "Before the Deluge," "The Load Out," "Somebody's Baby," "Redneck Friend," "Ready or Not."

17. JOHN PRINE—Prince of Singer-Songwriters, Appalachian Division. "Hello in There," "Sam Stone," "Jesus The Missing Years," "Unwed Fathers," "If You Don't Want My Love," "That's the Way That the World Goes 'Round," "Angel from Montgomery," "Illegal Smile," "Six O'Clock News," "Souvenirs," "Sabu Visits the Twin Cities Alone."

18. JAMES TAYLOR—Prince of Singer-Songwriters, Atlantic Division. "Fire and Rain," "Sweet Baby James," "Country Road," "Steamroller," "Don't Let Me Be Lonely Tonight," "Carolina in My Mind," "Something in the Way She Moves," "Frozen Man," "Copperline," "Hey Mister, That's Me Up on the Juke Box."

19. MARVIN GAYE—"What's Going On," "Inner City

Blues," "Let's Get It On," "Dancing in the Street," "Mercy Mercy Me (The Ecology)," "Sexual Healing," "Come Get to This," "Distant Lover," "Pride and Joy," "Trouble Man," "Baby, I'm for Real," "Beechwood 4-5789," "Bells."

20. PATTI SMITH—More than any great songwriter except Leonard Cohen, Smith's albums contain almost inseparable compositions. Best known for "Because the Night," "Horses," "Land" (a rewrite of "Land of a Thousand Dances"), "Free Money," "Piss Factory," "Frederick," "Hymn," "People Have the Power," "Pissing in a River," "Radio Ethiopia."

21. ELVIS COSTELLO—"Less Than Zero," "Alison," "The Angels Wanna Wear My Red Shoes," "Everyday I Write the Book," "Watching the Detectives," "Pump It Up," "Accidents Will Happen," "Oliver's Army," "Clowntime is Over," "Peace in Our Time," "Shipbuilding," "Pills and Soap."

22. BOB SEGER—"Night Moves," "Ramblin' Gamblin' Man," "Get Out of Denver," "Katmandu," "Roll Me Away," "Still the Same," "We've Got Tonight," "Beautiful Loser," "Back in '72," "Turn the Page," "Rock and Roll Never Forgets," "Heartache Tonight," "Sock It To Me Santa," "Lookin' Back."

23. CHRISTINE MCVIE (FLEETWOOD MAC)—Gems buried amidst semisoft-rock claptrap. "You Make Loving Fun," "Don't Stop," "Little Lies," "Over My Head," "Hold Me," "Say You Love Me," "Got a Hold On Me."

24. LOU REED (VELVET UNDERGROUND)—Master of psycho-song cycles; laconic poet of decadence. "Sweet Jane," "Rock and Roll," "Heroin," "I'm Waiting for the Man," "Walk on the Wild Side," "Pale Blue Eyes," "Coney Island Baby," "Street Hassle," "I Love You Suzanne," "Venus in Furs," "Sister Ray."

25. THE SEX PISTOLS (WITH GLEN MATLOCK)—"Anarchy in the U.K.," "God Save the Queen," "Holidays in the Sun," "Pretty Vacant," "Bodies." Slim pickings but revolutionary ones.

THE EIGHTIES AND NINETIES

1. PRINCE—"When Doves Cry," "1999," "Little Red Corvette," "Delirious," "Kiss," "Let's Go Crazy," "When You Were Mine," "U Got the Look," "Manic Monday," "Sign O' the Times," "Raspberry Beret," "Controversy," "Sugar Walls," "I Wanna Be Your Lover," "If I Was Your Girlfriend."

2. CHUCK D (PUBLIC ENEMY)—"Bring the Noise," "Don't Believe the Hype," "Welcome to the Terrordome," "She Watch Channel Zero?!," "By the Time I Get to Arizona," "How to Kill a Radio Consultant," "Black Steel in the Hour of Chaos," "Rebel Without a Pause," "Sophisticated Bitch," "Cold Lampin' with Flavor," "Yo! Bum Rush the Show," "Can't Truss It."

3. STING (THE POLICE)—"Every Breath You Take," "Every Little Thing She Does Is Magic," "Wrapped Around Your

Finger," "Don't Stand So Close to Me," "King of Pain," "Fortress Around Your Heart," "If You Love Somebody Set Them Free," "All This Time," "Do Do Do Do, De Da Da Da," "Money for Nothing," "Russians."

4. DON HENLEY—Ex-Eagle; always with collaborators. "The Boys of Summer," "The Heart of the Matter," "The End of the Innocence," "The Last Worthless Evening," "Dirty Laundry," "All She Wants to Do Is Dance," "Desperado," "Hotel California," "Heartache Tonight," "Life in the Fast Lane," "New Kid in Town," "I Will Not Go Quietly."

5. RUN-D.M.C. (RUN, D.M.C., JAM MASTER JAY)— "It's Like That," "Sucker M.C.'s (Krush Groove 1)," "You Be Illin'," "King of Rock," "Rock Box," "Jam-Master Jammin'," "It's Tricky," "Jam-Master Jay," "My Adidas," "Can You Rock It Like This," "Roots, Rap, Reggae," "Run's House," "Christmas in Hollis."

6. PETER GABRIEL—"Sledgehammer," "Biko," "Shock the Monkey," "Big Time," "Don't Give Up," "Red Rain," "Solsbury Hill," "Games Without Frontiers," "In Your Eyes." His solo albums have musical, not necessarily thematic, links. Earlier works with Genesis were more conceptual.

7. L.A. AND BABYFACE (ANTONIO "L.A." REID AND KENNETH "BABYFACE" EDMONDS)—Revivers of R&B on hip-hop's terms. "Girlfriend," "It's No Crime," "Tender Lover," "My Kinda Girl," "Whip Appeal," "Superwoman," "Rock Witcha," "Don't Be Cruel," "Humpin' Around," "Body Talk," "I'm Your Baby Tonight," "Miracle," "Every Little Step," "Dial My Heart."

8. DAVID BYRNE—"Life During Wartime," "Burning Down the House," "Once in a Lifetime," "Road to Nowhere," "And She Was," "Wild Wild Life," "Psychokiller," "Love > Building On Fire," "Don't Worry About the Government," "The Big Country," "Stay Up Late."

9. CHRISSIE HYNDE (PRETENDERS)—"Brass in Pocket," "Back on the Chain Gang," "Middle of the Road," "Talk of the Town," "Message of Love," "Kid," "Precious," "2000 Miles," "My City Was Gone," "Don't Get Me Wrong," "Hymn to Her," "Up the Neck."

10. GUNS N' ROSES (IZZY STRADLIN, AXL ROSE, DUFF MCKAGAN, SLASH)—"Welcome to the Jungle," "Sweet Child O' Mine," "Don't Cry," "Mr. Brownstone," "Paradise City," "Civil War," "November Rain," "Get in the Ring," "Nighttrain," "Coma."

11. ICE CUBE—"F—— Tha Police," "Dead Homiez," "The Drive-By," "It Was a Good Day," "Jackin' for Beats," "Wrong Nigga to Fuck Wit'," "Steady Mobbin'," "Gangsta's Fairytale," "AmeriKKKa's Most Wanted," "Gangsta Gangsta," "Endangered Species (Tales from the Darkside)," "Dopeman."

12. PAUL WESTERBERG (THE REPLACEMENTS)—"Left of the Dial," "Bastards of Young," "Can't Hardly Wait," "Here Comes a Regular," "Achin' to Be," "I'll Be You," "All Shook Down," "Swingin' Party," "Alex Chilton," "Waitress in the Sky."

13. RICHARD THOMPSON—"Shoot Out the Lights," "Wall of Death," "Back Street Slide," "Tear Stained Letter," "Calvary Cross," "Twisted," "Waltzing's for Dreamers," "Walking on a Wire," "Small Town Romance," "Jet Plane in a Rocking Chair," "Hokey Pokey (The Ice Cream Song)," "Hand of Kindness."

14. TRACY CHAPMAN—"Fast Car," "Talkin' 'Bout a Revolution," "Bang Bang Bang," "Baby Can I Hold You," "For My Lover," "I Used to Be a Sailor," "Matters of the Heart," "Crossroads," "All that You Have Is Your Soul," "Dreaming on a World," "This Time," "If Not Now . . ."

15. SIR MIX-A-LOT—"Baby Got Back," "My Hooptie," "National Anthem," "Beepers," "One Time's Got No Case," "Swap Meet Louie," "Posse on Broadway," "Gortex," "Mack Daddy," "Seminar," "Something About My Benzo," "Hip Hop Soldier."

16. JOHN HIATT—"Thing Called Love," "Sure As I'm Sittin' Here," "She Loves the Jerk," "The Way We Make a Broken Heart," "It Hasn't Happened Yet," "Alone in the Dark," "Feels Like Rain," "Tip of My Tongue," "Have a Little Faith in Me," "Memphis in the Meantime," "Tennessee Plates."

17. MARSHALL CRENSHAW—"Someday, Someway," "Cynical Girl," "Rockin' Around in N.Y.C.," "The Usual Thing," "Brand New Lover," "She Can't Dance," "There She Goes Again," "Something's Gonna Happen," "Our Town," "Someplace Where Love Can't Find Me," "Whenever You're On My Mind."

18. U2 (BONO AND THE EDGE)—"I Still Haven't Found What I'm Looking For," "One," "With or Without You," "Silver and Gold," "I Will Follow," "All I Want Is You," "New Year's Day," "Sunday Bloody Sunday," "Pride (In the Name of Love)," "Eleven O'Clock Tick Tock," "When Love Comes to Town," "Gloria."

19. TERENCE TRENT D'ARBY—*Introducing the Hardline According to Terence Trent D'Arby, Terence Trent D'Arby's Neither Fish nor Flesh,* and *Terence Trent D'Arby's Symphony or Damn.*

20. DAVID BAERWALD—Most politically (and perhaps rhythmically) sophisticated of nineties singer-songwriters. With David and David (Ricketts): *Welcome to the Boomtown.* On his own, *Bedtime Stories* and *Triage.*

21. MICHAEL STIPE (R.E.M.)—"Radio Free Europe," "Fall on Me," "It's the End of the World As We Know It (And I

Feel Fine)," "Losing My Religion," "so. Central Rain (I'm Sorry),"
"Man on the Moon," "The One I Love," "Maps and Legends,"
"Ages of You," "Burning Down," "Shiny Happy People."

22. STEVIE NICKS (FLEETWOOD MAC)—"Edge of Seventeen," "Rhiannon," "Stand Back," "Sara," "Rooms on Fire,"
"Dreams," "If Anyone Falls," "Whole Lotta Trouble," "Beauty
and the Beast," "I Can't Wait."

23. CULTURE CLUB (BOY GEORGE AND JON MOSS)—
"Do You Really Want to Hurt Me," "Church of the Poison Mind,"
"Kharma Chameleon," "Miss Me Blind," "Time (Clock of the
Heart)," "War Song," "Mistake No. 3," "I'll Tumble 4 Ya."

24. MADONNA—Almost always with collaborators. "Live to
Tell," "Like a Prayer," "True Blue," "Express Yourself," "Open
Your Heart," "Cherish," "Lucky Star," "Into the Groove,"
"Vogue."

25. ROSANNE CASH—"Seven Year Ache," "Hold On,"
"Blue Moon with Heartache," "I Don't Know Why You Don't Want
Me," "If There's a God on My Side," "Seventh Avenue," "The
Real Me."

Songwriters Who Never Wrote a Song

1. ALAN FREED—Freed's credits for writing Chuck Berry's
"Maybellene" and the Moonglows' "Sincerely" represent the purest
examples of the deejay "cut-in," in which an influential radio programmer was (is?) given credit for writing a song with which he had
nothing to do. Why? Because composers' credits generate income
from both record sales and air play. One way or another, this information suffices to explain the motivation behind just about everybody on this list.

2. MORRIS LEVY—Although Levy once testified in court,
"You couldn't exactly say I ever wrote any music," his credits used
to include the Teenagers' "Why Do Fools Fall in Love," until the
group members sued and won. Any number of other Roulette Records classics also bear his stinkin' name.

3. DEADRIC MALONE—The name under which Duke Records' gangster-entrepreneur Don Robey scarfed up the songwriting
credits actually belonging to his blues superstar, Bobby Bland, and
Bland's arranger, Joe Scott, and others associated with them. Among
the numbers Malone "wrote": "Ain't Nothing You Can Do," "Ain't
That Loving You," "Call on Me," and "Share Your Love with Me."

4. ELVIS PRESLEY—Elvis would have told you that he'd
never written a song. But Hill and Range Music and his manager

Colonel Tom Parker often made it a condition of writing for him in the fifties that Elvis get a "cut-in" on the songwriting royalties. Among Elvis's noncompositions: "All Shook Up," "Don't Be Cruel," "Heartbreak Hotel," "Love Me Tender."

5. EDYTHE WAYNE—When Holland-Dozier-Holland's production contracts with Motown ran out, their songwriting contracts with Jobete, Motown's publishing arm, hadn't. So when they started their own Invictus Records they invented the fictitious Ms. Wayne, who's credited with writing such hits as "Band of Gold," "Give Me Just a Little More Time," and "You've Got Me Dangling on a String."

6. JOSEA, LING, AND TAUB—The Bihari brothers of Modern/RPM/Flair Records used these names to cut-in on songs by B. B. King ("Rock Me Baby," etc.) and others. Richard Berry (author of "Louie Louie") quit working for them over such practices.

7. JOHN DAVENPORT—The name under which Otis Blackwell wrote "The Fever," a huge hit for Little Willie John and Miss Peggy Lee. Why Blackwell chose to write pseudonymously isn't clear; perhaps he was seeking to work outside an exclusive publishing contract, or maybe he wanted to work with an ASCAP writer, which ASCAP would not permit a BMI composer to do.

8. NANKER-PHELGE—The name under which Mick Jagger and Keith Richards wrote several minor Rolling Stones' songs, notably the instrumental "2120 South Michigan Avenue."

9. EDWARD ANDERSON—The name under which Chuck Berry wrote his hit, "Let It Rock," for reasons that remain muddy as hell. But since when did anybody ever understand Chuck's motivation for anything? At least we know where we got the pseudonym: His legal name is Edward Anderson Berry.

10. GEORGE GOLDNER—Unlike his sometime-partner Levy, Goldner may have had the talent to write a song. But he did not write such rock and roll classics as "I Want You to Be My Girl," "Maybe," and "Why Do Fools Fall in Love," even though he has been credited with doing so.

11. ETHEL SMITH—Bo Diddley was so fed up with Chess Records that when he wrote "Love Is Strange," he didn't want to record it. And with his exclusive "work-for-hire" (i.e., no royalty) song-publishing deal with Chess, he *certainly* didn't want to let the owners know he'd written it. So he gave the tune to Mickey and Sylvia and copyrighted it under his wife's name.

12. CHARLES CALHOUN—The name Jesse Stone adopted when Ahmet Ertegun told him he needed separate monickers for ASCAP and BMI.

Greil Marcus Lists 100 New Dylans

At least since Bob Dylan's breakthrough Freewheelin' *album in 1963, the music industry has felt itself obliged to produce at least one new Dylan every year or so. In certain periods, when the Minnesota Kid's most easily absorbed tendencies come to the fore—eras when protest, folk-rock, or singer-songwriter records sell a lot—Dylans sprout like mushrooms. Many of them have been included here. (Various incarnations of Bob Dylan himself have not been included in order to make room for other people.) Within the strictly preset boundaries of this accounting—established solely for purposes of elegance—room has also been made for those figures who, at one time or another, perhaps only for a moment, have truly or madly or bravely embodied Dylanism perhaps even more fully than Bob Dylan. Like Dylan, these people took big chances, betting they could do anything with music—change the world, save it, destroy it—even if it meant they'd end up looking like fools. Or getting shot. Or bursting into flames.*

1. Steve Albini
2. Eric Anderson
3. David Baerwald
4. Joan Baez
5. Lester Bangs
6. Big Youth
7. Ruben Blades
8. David Blue
9. Bono
10. David Bowie
11. Billy Bragg
12. David Bromberg
13. Tim Buckley
14. Kate Bush
15. The Byrds
16. Jim Carroll
17. Jimmy Carter
18. Nick Cave
19. Tracy Chapman
20. John Cooper Clarke
21. Leonard Cohen
22. Sam Cooke
23. Elvis Costello
24. Chuck D.
25. Terence Trent D'Arby
26. Sandy Denny
27. John Denver
28. Dion
29. Donovan
30. Jacob Dylan
31. Marianne Faithfull
32. Richard Fariña
33. Firesign Theatre
34. John Fogerty
35. Steve Forbert
36. Peter Garrett
37. Marvin Gaye
38. Bob Geldof
39. Allen Ginsberg
40. Albert Grossman
41. Kathleen Hanna
42. Richie Havens
43. Jimi Hendrix
44. Ian Hunter
45. Hüsker Dü
46. Chrissie Hynde
47. Janis Ian
48. Ice Cube
49. Tonio K
50. Garland Jeffreys
51. Robert F. Kennedy
52. David Koresh
53. Kris Kristofferson
54. Peter Laughner

55. John Lennon
56. Bob Lind
57. John Lydon
58. Madonna
59. Charles Manson
60. Bob Marley
61. Don McLean
62. The Mekons
63. Melanie
64. The Minutemen
65. Joni Mitchell
66. Elliot Murphy
67. Bob Neuwirth
68. Jack Nicholson
69. Nico
70. Mojo Nixon
71. Sinead O'Connor
72. Peter, Paul, and Mary
73. Prince
74. John Prine
75. Lou Reed
76. Robbie Robertson
77. Tom Rush
78. Doug Sahm
79. Sky Saxon
80. Michele Shocked
81. Patti Smith
82. Sonny and Cher
83. Bruce Springsteen
84. Harry Dean Stanton
85. Steely Dan
86. Sly Stone
87. Joe Strummer
88. Levi Stubbs
89. Tanita Tikaram
90. Richard Thompson
91. Sal Valentino
92. Eddie Vedder
93. Robert Thomas Veline
94. Loudon Wainwright III
95. Sammy Walker
96. A. J. Weberman
97. Stevie Wonder
98. Neil Young
99. Your Name Here
100. Warren Zevon

Greil Marcus, author of Mystery Train *and* Lipstick Traces, *is currently working on a book about Dylan's Basement Tapes.*

Songs Bob Dylan Wrote but Never Recorded

This list includes only songs Bob Dylan has never performed—or at least, of which no version has ever turned up. It does not *include any songs that appear on bootlegs. Interestingly, even though Dylan has released two boxed sets,* Biograph *and* The Bootleg Series, Vol. 1–3, *since the first edition of* The Book of Rock Lists, *only seven of the eighteen songs we originally listed appear on them (all on* Bootleg, *except "Up to Me" and "Long Distance Operator," the latter of which is on* The Basement Tapes, *and can still be most accurately described as by the Band, not Dylan, though that album is officially "his" in its entirety). Perhaps in another ten years, all of the remainder will have surfaced in Dylan's own voice, too.*

1. "Ballad of Easy Rider"—Allegedly written with Roger Mc-Guinn for the film *Easy Rider,* but for one reason or another, Dylan left his name off the composing credit. The song has

been recorded by the Byrds and by Fairport Convention with Richard Thompson singing lead.

2. "Champaign Illinois"—Recorded by Carl Perkins.
3. "Coming from the Heart"—Written with and recorded by the Searchers.
4. "I'd Have You Any Time"—Written with George Harrison, and released on Harrison's *All Things Must Pass*.
5. "If I Don't Be There By Morning"—Written with Helena Springs, recorded by Eric Clapton.
6. "Jack of Diamonds"—This is the poem that serves as liner notes to *Another Side of Bob Dylan*. Set to music by Ben Carruthers, it was recorded with his band, the Deep, and later by the original Fairport Convention.
7. "Love Is Just a Four Letter Word"—Recorded by Joan Baez.
8. "Sign Language"—Another recorded by Clapton; Dylan sang lead with Clapton, which makes its inclusion here somewhat marginal.
9. "Troubled and I Don't Know Why"—Sung by Joan Baez in concert, though never released by her.
10. "Walk Out in the Rain"—Another written with Helena Springs and recorded by Clapton.
11. "Wanted Man"—Recorded by Johnny Cash for the movie *Little Faus and Big Halsey*. Dylan *has* sung this song onstage.

25 Songs that the Beatles Recorded but Did Not Compose (with Original Artists)

1. "Act Naturally," Buck Owens, 1963
2. "Ain't She Sweet," Paul Ash and His Orchestra, 1927
3. "Anna (Go to Him)," Arthur Alexander, 1962
4. "Baby It's You," The Shirelles, 1961
5. "Bad Boy," Larry Williams, 1959
6. "Boys," The Shirelles, 1960
7. "Chains," The Cookies, 1962
8. "Devil in Her Heart," The Donays, 1962
9. "Dizzy Miss Lizzie," Larry Williams, 1958
10. "Everybody's Trying to Be My Baby," Carl Perkins, 1958
11. "Honey Don't," Carl Perkins, 1956
12. "Kansas City," Little Willie Littlefield, 1952[1]
13. "Long Tall Sally," Little Richard, 1956
14. "Matchbox," Carl Perkins, 1957
15. "Mr. Moonlight," Dr. Feelgood and the Interns, 1962
16. "Money (That's What I Want)," Barrett Strong, 1959

17. "Please Mr. Postman," The Marvelettes, 1961
18. "Rock and Roll Music," Chuck Berry, 1957
19. "Roll Over Beethoven," Chuck Berry, 1956
20. "Slow Down," Larry Williams, 1958
21. "A Taste of Honey," Bobby Scott and Combo, 1960[2]
22. "Till There Was You," Robert Preston and Barbara Cook, 1958[3]
23. "Twist and Shout," The Isley Brothers, 1962
24. "Words of Love," Buddy Holly, 1957
25. "You Really Got a Hold on Me," The Miracles, 1962

The Beatles also recorded several other cover versions in their role as backing band for British singer Tony Sheridan. Those numbers include "My Bonnie," "Nobody's Child," "Sweet Georgia Brown," "Take Out Some Insurance, Baby," and "Why (Can't You Love Me Again)."

---

[1] The Beatles' arrangement seems to be based on Little Richard's "Hey Hey Hey," released in 1958. Of course, Wilbert Harrison's 1959 version of "Kansas City" eclipsed Littlefield's in chart success and popular memory.
[2] From the soundtrack of the movie of the same name.
[3] From the play *The Music Man*, 1957.

10 Songs Michael Jackson Wishes He Had Written

1. "Respect"
2. "Bridge over Troubled Water"
3. "Walk on the Wild Side"
4. "Moon River"
5. "For the Good Times"
6. "Living in the City"
7. "You Send Me"
8. "Yesterday"
9. "Fool on the Hill"
10. "Eleanor Rigby

Michael submitted this list for the first edition of this book. We saw no reason to ask him to change it, just because he's become the King of Pop.

Greg Tate's 10 Favorite Song Lyrics

1. "I'm the man you think you are." (Malcolm X)
2. "I am human and I need to be loved. Just like anybody else does." (The Smiths, "How Soon Is Now?")
3. "I make love to you in your sleep and you feel no pain. Because

I'm a million miles away and at the same time I'm right here in your picture frame." (Jimi Hendrix, "Voodoo Chile")

4. "Southern trees bear a strange fruit. Blood on the leaves and blood at the root." (Billie Holiday, "Strange Fruit")

5. "Money won't change you, but time will take you out." (James Brown, "Money Won't Change You")

6. "When you base your love on credit and your loving days are done, checks you signed with love and kisses later come back signed 'insufficient funds.' " (George Clinton, "Can You Get to That")

7. "You singers are spineless as you sing your songs to the mindless. Your general subject, love, is minimal. It's sex for profit." (Public Enemy)

8. "Calvin Klein is no friend of mine. Don't want nobody's name on my behind." (Run-D.M.C., "Rock Box")

9. "Fame makes a man loose and hard to swallow." (David Bowie, "Fame")

10. "Could you be loved?" (Bob Marley)

A longtime writer for The Village Voice, *Greg Tate has written several articles that, in many ways, have inspired an entire generation of young artists and critics whose work is only starting to come to fruition. These pieces were collected in his first book,* Flyboy in the Buttermilk. *A guitarist, Tate is a founder of the band Women in Love.*

20 Answer Songs
Songs Written in Response to Other Songs

1. **"ANNIE'S ANSWER," HAZEL MCCOLLUM AND THE EL DORADOS, 1955**—A retort to the Midnighters' successful mid-fifties string of allegations about Annie ("Work with Me Annie," "Annie Had a Baby," etc.).

2. **"ANNIE PULLED A HUMBUG," THE MIDNIGHTS, 1955**—Obscure but blunt reply to "Annie Had a Baby," by a West Coast group in which the lead singer asserts that Annie's baby looks nothing like *him*, concluding, "That's not my kid!" (Shades of "Billie Jean"!)

3. **"ARETHA, SING ONE FOR ME," GEORGE JACKSON, 1971**—Memphis writer-singer Jackson's lovely reply to Aretha's hit, "Don't Play That Song."

4. **"BALLAD OF THE YELLOW BERETS," BOB SEGER, 1966**—A hilarious spoof of "Ballad of the Green Berets," in which Seger sings a tale of draft-dodger woe.

5. "CAN'T DO SIXTY NO MORE," THE DU-DROPPERS, 1951—A response to the Dominoes' 1951 R&B smash, "Sixty Minute Man."

6. "COME BACK, MAYBELLENE," BIG JOHN GREER, 1955—The one-time Lucky Millinder Band vocalist responds to Chuck Berry's 1955 hit.

7. "COPY CAT," GARY "U.S." BONDS, 1962—In which the Outer Space Echo King severely chastises any number of competitors, not least Chubby Checker, for "trying to copy my groove." Gary is quite agitated about the injustice, although he assures himself in the last verse that copycats don't last long.

8. "THE DAWN OF CORRECTION," THE SPOKESMEN, 1965—Middle America's answer to the rad-lib sentiments of "Eve of Destruction."

9. "DEAR MICHAEL," KIM FIELDS, 1984—Released at the height of Michaelmania, this minor hit responds to the lonely, dancing boy of "Thriller" by offering faithful love and companionship. Despite this exploitation move, in real life, Fields (who starred in TV's *Facts of Life*) was close friends with Janet Jackson, Mike's favorite sister.

10. "DEATH BLOW," KOOL MOE DEE, 1990—Kool Moe Dee answers nemesis L.L. Cool J's "Mama Said Knock You Out" by promising to blast Cool J out of the ring if he gets his hands on him. The latest in a long series of feuding answer raps.

11. "GOT A JOB," THE MIRACLES, 1959—The Miracles' Motown career began with this reply to the Silhouettes' "Get a Job," although Smokey and friends failed to achieve the originals' marvelous incoherence.

12. "HEY MEMPHIS," LAVERN BAKER, 1961—Reply to Elvis Presley's "Little Sister," written by the same composing team, Doc Pomus and Mort Shuman.

13. "I'LL BRING IT ON HOME TO YOU," CARLA THOMAS, 1962—Queen of Memphis soul replies to Sam Cooke's "Bring It On Home to Me."

14. "I'M JUST A DOWN HOME GIRL," THE AD LIBS, 1963—Response to Alvin Robinson's "Down Home Girl" by the girl group that had a hit with "The Boy from New York City."

15. "IT WOULDN'T HAPPEN WITH ME," JERRY LEE LEWIS, 1961—In which the Killer warns fans with roving eyes that neither Ricky Nelson nor Elvis deserves their adoration as much as he does. A monumental act of humility, and a perfect testament to why Jerry Lee's popularity is enduring: If you don't pay attention, he'll beat you up.

16. "MY GIRL," THE TEMPTATIONS, 1965—Smokey Robinson's answer to the charms proposed by his own "My Guy," a hit for Mary Wells. If anything, "My Girl" had bigger, more enduring impact.

17. "RAPPIN' ABOUT RAPPIN' (UH-UH-UH)," JUNIE, 1981—Reply to earliest rappers, by Junie Morrison, former member of the Ohio Players and sometime P-Funkateer.

18. "ROCK THE BELLS," L.L. COOL J—Comeback to Madonna's "Material Girl" and Bruce Springsteen's "Born in the U.S.A." (most prominently), in which Cool J reigns supreme.

19. "ROLL WITH ME HENRY," ETTA JAMES, 1954—The great soul singer had her first hit with this response to the Midnighters' original "Annie" hit, "Work with Me Annie." The male role, by the way, is played by Richard Berry, who wrote "Louie Louie."

20. "ROXANNE'S REVENGE," ROXANNE SHANTÉ—First and best answer record to UTFO's "Roxanne, Roxanne." Produced by Marley Marl.

21. "SON-IN-LAW," THE BLOSSOMS, 1961—Riposte to Ernie K-Doe's "Mother-in-Law," a significant 1961 hit. The lead singer is ultimate Phil Spector chanteuse Darlene Love.

22. "SWEET HOME ALABAMA," LYNYRD SKYNYRD, 1974—Ronnie Van Zant's brilliant retort to the undigested anti-southern bile of Neil Young's "Southern Man" (Young reportedly loved it). Maybe the greatest answer record of all time.

23. "TELL TOMMY I MISS HIM," MARILYN MICHAELS, 1960—Ghostly reply to Ray Peterson's "Tell Laura I Love Her." Thus, an answer record from beyond the grave.

24. "YOUR BOYFRIEND'S BACK," BOBBY COMSTOCK AND THE COUNTS, 1963—Tough reply to the Angels' "My Boyfriend's Back," in which the hero's return is to little or no avail.

25. "YOUR GENERATION," GENERATION X, 1978—Punk reply to the Who's mod anthem, "My Generation," doesn't hold a candle to the original but serves as a great example of punk's rejectionist rebellion anyhow. Also kicked off the career of lead vocalist Billy Idol.

The Staff of *Uncut Funk* Picks the Heaviest P-Funk Lyrics for the Head

1. "With the rhythm it takes to dance to what we have to live through, you can dance underwater, and not get wet."
2. "Free your mind and your ass will follow. The kingdom of heaven is within."
3. "If you don't like the effects, don't produce the cause."
4. "When getting over is the high above your head, and getting high can get you dead, what are you supposed to do?"

5. "Why must I feel like that? Why must I chase the cat? Nothing but the dog in me."
6. "It's good to be hard, but it's hard to be good when there's nothing before you but thang."
7. "Mind your wants, 'cause someone wants your mind."
8. "Feeling good is the bait Satan uses to fish for you and me. Comfort is the poison when it's the spirit he want to kill."

CHAPTER 16

Musicians and Their Instruments

Best Guitarists

1. Jimi Hendrix
2. Chuck Berry
3. Peter Townshend (The Who)
4. Eddie Van Halen (Van Halen)
5. Mickey "Guitar" Baker (Mickey and Sylvia, sessions)
6. Steve Cropper (Booker T and the MGs)
7. Eric Clapton (The Yardbirds, John Mayall's Bluesbreakers, Cream, Derek and the Dominoes, Delaney and Bonnie and Friends, solo)
8. Eddie Hazel (Parliament/Funkadelic)
9. Jimmy Page (The Yardbirds, Led Zeppelin, solo)
10. James Burton (Elvis Presley, Ricky Nelson)
11. Keith Richards (The Rolling Stones)
12. Ernie Isley (Isley Brothers, Isley-Jasper-Isley, solo)
13. Scotty Moore (Elvis Presley)
14. Michael Bloomfield (The Paul Butterfield Blues Band, Bob Dylan, The Electric Flag, solo)
15. Robert White, Joe Messina (The Funk Brothers—Motown session band)
16. Richard Thompson
17. Stevie Ray Vaughan
18. Curtis Mayfield
19. Carlos Santana
20. Link Wray
21. Jeff Beck (The Yardbirds, The Jeff Beck Group, Beck Bogert and Appice, The Big Town Playboys, solo)
22. Prince
23. The Edge (U2)
24. Duane Allman
25. Jesse Johnson
26. Ry Cooder
27. Bob Marley
28. Bobby Womack
29. Joe Walsh (The James Gang, The Eagles, Ringo Starr, solo)
30. Slash (Guns N' Roses)
31. Robbie Roberston (Bob Dylan, The Band, solo)
32. Dick Dale (King of the Surf Guitar)
33. Joe Satriani
34. Steve Jones (The Sex Pistols)
35. Bo Diddley
36. Peter Green (John Mayall's Bluesbreakers, Fleetwood Mac, solo)
37. Nils Lofgren (Neil Young, Crazy Horse, Bruce Springsteen, Ringo Starr, solo)

38. Steve Gains (Lynyrd Skynyrd)
39. Jimmy Nolen (James Brown)
40. Randy Rhoads (Ozzy Osbourne, solo)
41. Joe Perry (Aerosmith, The Joe Perry Project)
42. Thurston Moore, Lee Renaldo (Sonic Youth)
43. Vernon Reid (Living Colour, Defunkt)
44. Ted Nugent
45. Roy Buchanan
46. Kirk Hammett (Metallica)
47. Stone Gossard (Mother Love Bone, Pearl Jam)
48. Johnny Thunders (N.Y. Dolls, The Heartbreakers, solo)
49. Wayne Kramer (MC5)
50. Kim Thayil (Soundgarden)

Great Slide Guitarists—Rock and Roll Style

1. Elmore James
2. Mick Taylor (The Rolling Stones)
3. Hound Dog Taylor
4. Ry Cooder
5. Bonnie Raitt
6. Mike Bloomfield (*Highway 61 Revisited*)
7. Eric Clapton
8. Jeremy Spencer (Fleetwood Mac)
9. Ron Wood (The Faces)

Vernon Reid's Favorite Guitarists of All Time

1. Chuck Berry
2. Robert Fripp
3. Jimi Hendrix
4. Allan Holdsworth
5. Bruce Johnson
6. Robert Johnson
7. The 3 Kings (Freddie, Albert, and B.B.)
8. Pat Martino
9. John McLaughlin
10. Arthur Rhames
11. Carlos Santana
12. James Blood Ulmer

Joe Goldmark Picks 35 Notable Steel Guitarists

1. MAURICE ANDERSON—Pop and jazz player from Dallas who popularized the "universal" tuning that continues to gain popularity.

2. BOBBY BLACK—A major figure in country rock, Bobby brought respectability to the Commander Cody band in the early seventies. He is equally adept at C&W and country jazz.

3. NOEL BOGGS—Solid western swing player from the forties and fifties. He played with Spade Cooley and Bob Wills. Known for his full chordal voicings and bass string work.

4. TOM BRUMLEY—Expressive player who worked with Buck Owens, Rick Nelson, and Dwight Yoakum. His back-up on Owens's "Together Again" was a turning point in modern playing.

5. JERRY BYRD—"The Master of Touch and Tone." The best nonpedal player ever. He left Nashville after many years and sessions to live the good life playing Hawaiian music in Hawaii.

6. CURLY CHALKER—A true master of the instrument. Tremendous pop and jazz player with unique style and amazing technique. Great full chordal voicings.

7. BUDDY CHARLETON—Terrific feeling combined with awesome chops. Buddy played equal amounts of gorgeous country corn and hip country jazz. Made his mark playing with Ernest Tubb's Texas Troubadours.

8. JIMMY CRAWFORD—Monster picker who often takes banjo runs and adapts them to the steel. He also builds steel guitars and is a major influence in Nashville.

9. TERRY CRISP—Extremely fast and gifted player, very underrated. Currently with the Reba McEntire band.

10. JIMMY DAY—In the late fifties, Jimmy and Buddy Emmons played together in Ray Price's Cherokee Cowboys. They went on to modernize the steel and still define the way it's played. Very expressive player, said to have his volume pedal connected directly to his heart.

11. BOB DUNN—First electric steel man, from the early thirties. His jazzy western swing stylings are still admired.

12. BUDDY EMMONS—The best ever. Equally proficient at country or jazz. Draws so much feeling out of the instrument. His 1963 LP, *Steel Guitar Jazz*, wrote the book for steel guitar as a jazz instrument.

13. SANTO FARINA—One half of brother act Santo and Johnny. Only player since the thirties to have a number-one hit with a steel instrumental ("Sleepwalk," 1959). Santo and Johnny went on to record numerous albums and become pop stars in Europe.

14. PAUL FRANKLIN—The heir apparent to Emmons. Tremendous technique and talent. Currently rules the Nashville studio scene, when not being paid prodigious amounts of money to tour with Dire Straits.

15. BOBBY GARRETT—Underrated Texas player who adapted "Travis" picking for the steel. He wrote "Rose City Chimes," later recorded by Buddy Emmons.

16. SONNY GARRISH—Made his reputation with Bill Anderson's Po' Boys, then became the number-one session man in Nashville in the late seventies and early eighties. Known for his quick arrangements and lick ideas.

17. LLOYD GREEN—Revolutionized the concept of hot steel picking with his late sixties albums and continued to make lush, brilliant albums through the eighties. Has been a Nashville studio ace for twenty-five years, heard on many hit records.

18. SOL HOOPII—The finest early Hawaiian player. Great single line improviser. Played pop, religious, and Hawaiian music with feeling and creativity.

19. JOHN HUGHEY—One of the most soulful players around. Helped define Conway Twitty's sound and is finally getting major recognition playing with Vince Gill.

20. BUD ISAACS—Invented the E9 "Nashville tuning" in the mid-fifties, when he was a studio ace. Recorded some great sides with Chet Atkins.

21. DOUG JERNIGAN—Extremely fast player who uses his enormous chops to go between jazz and bluegrass with equal skill. Has made many fine albums.

22. DAVID KELII—Virtuoso Hawaiian player who was the original "Hawaii Calls" steel man from 1935 to 1952. Said to have the best technique and tonal quality ever.

23. "SNEAKY PETE" KLEINOW—Played and recorded with all the L.A. country rock artists. A mainstay of the Flying Burrito Brothers. Has a unique "phased" sound and an original tuning. Always an innovator.

24. DAVID LINDLEY—The number-one R&R slide style steel player. Made his reputation with Jackson Browne, and also fronted his own band, El Rayo-X.

25. J. D. MANESS—Probably the best player on the West Coast for the past twenty years. Super clean and quick and always interesting. Recently in the Desert Rose Band. A fixture in the house band at the Palomino in North Hollywood.

26. LEON McAULIFFE—The father of the steel guitar. Featured in Bob Willis's bands of the thirties. Had hits with "Steel Guitar Rag" and "Panhandle Rag."

27. RALPH MOONEY—Defined the sound of every band he played with, including Buck Owens, Merle Haggard, and Waylon Jennings. A totally original and much-imitated player. Credited with creating the "West Coast sound."

28. JIMMY MURPHY—Would play hot licks on the steel, then grab his sax and play hip be-bop riffs. Underrated player who recorded with Carl Smith and Johnny Paycheck.

29. JOAQUIN MURPHY—Brilliant improviser from the forties and fifties, during the heyday of western swing. He played with Spade Cooley and was the most influential player of that era.

30. WELDON MYRICK—Very clean, soulful player who's been a mainstay of Nashville studios for the past thirty years. Member of Area Code 615.

31. JEFF NEWMAN—Master instructor and player. Has done more than anyone to teach and promote the instrument.

32. HERB REMINGTON—Terrific western swing player featured with Bob Wills and Hank Penny. Wrote many great instrumentals, including "Remington Ride." Still recording and playing beautifully.

33. HAL RUGG—A wonderful and versatile player who has been a leading Nashville session player for a quarter century. Featured on all the Loretta Lynn albums. Has now branched out to play very original country/jazz fusion.

34. SPEEDY WEST—In the fifties, Speedy ruled the L.A. Capitol Records session scene. He had a unique style and recorded a number of very hot albums with guitar great Jimmy Bryant.

35. BOB WHITE—His great style helped to create a unique variety of western swing in the late fifties, when he starred with Hank Thompson and His Brazos Valley Boys.

Joe Goldmark is a San Francisco pedal steel guitarist, record collector, and pizzeria owner. He has recorded three instrumental albums and publishes The International Steel Guitar Discography, *a booklet listing every known steel guitar and Dobro instrumental.*

Les Paul's 12 Favorite Guitarists

1. George Benson
2. Pat Martino
3. Al DiMeola
4. Jeff Beck
5. James Burton
6. Andres Segovia
7. Django Reinhardt
8. Jimi Hendrix
9. George Barnes
10. Eddie Lang
11. Snoozer Quinn
12. Wes Montgomery

Les Paul still stands as one of the greatest guitarists in American music. He was a pioneer in electrifying the guitar, creating multitrack recordings, and using a wide variety of studio effects. The guitar he designed for Gibson in the 1950s remains one of the quintessential rock and blues instruments.

John Cipollina's Guitar Influences

1. **SCOTTY MOORE**—The original pioneer rock guitar player.

2. **CHET ATKINS**—Truly the "Country Gentleman." I met him when I knew three chords. He said, "You look like a guitar player. Do you play?" I said, "No." I learned precision and finger work from him.

3. **JAMES BURTON**—Palming and cupping technique, especially for Dale Hawkins's "Suzie-Q."

4. **MICKEY BAKER**—Primal influence; electric guitar as an entity. When I heard Mickey and Sylvia's "Love Is Strange," I asked my mother what that sound was. She told me it was an electric guitar.

5. **MERLE TRAVIS**—He got me into the image of the guitar. I liked the pearl work on his, so when everybody else was putting lake pipes into their '57 Chevys, I was customizing my guitars.

6. **LINK WRAY**—He convinced me that you could swear without using words.

7. **MONTOYA**—Classical flamenco.

8. **SABICAS**

9. **PACO**

10. **MANITAS DE PLATA**—The punk of flamenco.

11. **JIMI HENDRIX**—He taught me how to resonate and carry tones. I still play the guitar he broke.

12. **LEADBELLY**—I still can't figure out what he was doing.

13. **DJANGO REINHARDT**—Guitar as violin.

The late John Cipollina was the guitarist with Quicksilver Messenger Service and one of the hottest, hardest rockers in the legendary San Francisco scene. He made this list for the first edition.

Danny Kortchmar's 10 Favorite Guitar Players

1. Django Reinhardt
2. Jimi Hendrix
3. Joseph Spence
4. Steve Cropper
5. Leadbelly
6. Keith Richards
7. Paul Burlison
8. Johnny Moore
9. Chuck Berry
10. Lightnin' Hopkins

Danny Kortchmar, "Kootch" to his friends, has played guitar with everyone from the Fugs to Jackson Browne and was one of the key members of Jo Mama and the Section. He's also recorded several solo albums, and produced hits for Don Henley, Bon Jovi, and Billy Joel, among others.

30 Outstanding Country Guitar Pickers
Joe Goldmark's Humble Opinions

1. PETE ANDERSON—Dwight Yoakum's producer and guitar man. Obviously influenced by Don Rich, his classic picking helped roots country music make its comeback.

2. CHET ATKINS—The master who's recorded more than one hundred guitar albums. As a producer for RCA, he was credited, for better or worse, with taking the "corn" out of country in the seventies.

3. PHIL BAUGH—Legendary picker from Texas who recorded some great guitar albums. He became a Nashville studio man in the eighties.

4. HAROLD BRADLEY—Guitarist on thousands of sessions; the brother of producer Owen Bradley.

5. JIMMY BRYANT—Brilliant picker with chops for days. Recorded memorable albums with steeler Speedy West. A major West Coast session man in the fifties and sixties.

6. JAMES BURTON—Starred with Ricky Nelson, Elvis, and Emmylou. Heard on thousands of L.A. sessions. Very influential Telecaster picker.

7. BOBBY CALDWELL—St. Louis picker who can play it all. With Dewitt Scott, helps organizes and plays at the annual Steel Guitar Convention.

8. GLEN CAMPBELL—Was L.A. session cat long before becoming pop star.

9. THUMBS CARLISLE—Got his nickname from playing the

guitar with it situated face up on his lap. Great player featured with Roger Miller.

10. Roy Clark—Parlayed his picking and personality into superstardom.

11. Ray Flacke—Got national recognition playing hot Telecaster with Ricky Skaggs's first band.

12. Hank Garland—Legendary country jazz cat whose career got short-circuited by an auto accident. Wrote "Sugarfoot Rag."

13. Danny Gatton—Can play in any style; has made many fine albums. Was in Red Neck Jazz, a hot band with Buddy Emmons.

14. Vince Gill—Has finally become a major star. He could always pick.

15. John Jorgenson—Multistyled guitarist who starred in the Desert Rose Band.

16. Albert Lee—Amazing British picker who has left his mark on L.A. and Nashville. Played with rockers Heads Hands and Feet, and with Emmylou Harris.

17. Joe Maphis—"King of the Strings." Terrific multi-instrumentalist who was a West Coast star in the fifties. Played a double-neck Mosrite.

18. Grady Martin—Nashville session man who garnered recognition for his playing on Marty Robbins's "El Paso."

19. Scotty Moore—He was basically a country picker who hooked up with Elvis to create history.

20. Roy Nichols—Played the hot licks with Merle Haggard and His Strangers. Widely imitated and influential.

21. Jerry Reed—One of Chet Atkins's favorite pickers. Jerry went on to become a major star with his novelty songs and outlandish guitar accompaniment.

22. Andy Reiss—Versatile player fluent in all styles of pop music. He is currently playing with Reba McEntire's band.

23. Leon Rhodes—Featured soloist with Ernest Tubb and His Texas Troubadours during the sixties. One of the hottest country/swing players ever.

24. Don Rich—Very influential and oft-imitated Telecaster player. His twangy picking helped define the Buck Owens sound.

25. Steuart Smith—Nashville session man made his rep on Rodney Crowell's *Diamonds and Dirt*.

26. Marty Stuart—An outstanding player, Marty has become a star by singing and playing roots-influenced country.

27. Merle Travis—Totally innovative. His "Travis picking" (the style in which the thumb plays bass notes while the fingers pick chordal riffs or the melody) is one of the fundamentals of modern playing.

28. Buck Trent—Unique five-string banjo player who used

"Scruggs Pegs" to bend notes to chicken-pick and play funkier than most guitarists. Featured with Porter Wagoner and Roy Clark.

29. CLARENCE WHITE—Originally a great flattop bluegrass player with the Kentucky Colonels. White and Gene Parsons developed a string-bender device that Clarence used while playing with the Byrds and other L.A. acts.

30. REGGIE YOUNG—Great soulful picker originally from Memphis. Heard on many hit records, notably Dobie Gray's "Drift Away."

Joe Goldmark is well-known in San Francisco as a pedal steel guitarist who's made three albums, a record collector, and the owner of Escape from New York Pizza. He publishes The International Steel Guitar Discography, *a booklet listing every known steel guitar and Dobro instrumental.*

45 Greatest Keyboardists

1. Jerry Lee Lewis/Little Richard (tie)
2. Professor Longhair
3. Johnnie Johnson (with Chuck Berry)
4. Booker T. Jones
5. Ray Charles
6. Billy Preston
7. Prince
8. Jimmy Jam
9. Nicky Hopkins (sessions)
10. Steve Winwood (Traffic, The Spencer Davis Group, solo)
11. Fats Domino
12. Stevie Wonder
13. Roy Bittan
14. Garth Hudson
15. Jack Nitzsche
16. Bill Payne (Little Feat, etc.)
17. Bernie Worrell
18. Huey "Piano" Smith
19. Benmont Tench
20. Barry Beckett (The Muscle Shoals Rhythm Section)
21. Teddy Riley
22. Bill Doggett
23. David Sancious
24. Richard Tee (sessions)
25. Paul McCartney (The Beatles, Wings)
26. Keith Emerson (The Nice, Emerson, Lake and Palmer)
27. Seth Justman
28. Ian Stewart (The Rolling Stones)
29. Ian MacLaglan (The Faces, The Rolling Stones)
30. Danny Federici (The E Street Band)
31. Brian Eno (with Talking Heads, U2)
32. Richard Manuel
33. Sly Stone
34. Craig Doerge (sessions)
35. Leon Russell (sessions)
36. Art Neville
37. Gregg Allman
38. Al Kooper
39. Steve Nieve
40. Mike Stoller
41. Aretha Franklin

42. Jerry Harrison (The
    Modern Lovers, Talking
    Heads)

43. Babyface
44. Doctor Fink
45. Ray Manzarek

10 Great New Orleans Pianists

1. PROFESSOR LONGHAIR—The indisputable king of Mardi Gras rhythm from whom all the rest stole their licks.

2. ARCHIBALD, AKA LEON GROSS—Longhair's predecessor.

3. FATS DOMINO—The greatest New Orleans recording artist and Longhair's most adept student.

4. HUEY "PIANO" SMITH—Celebrated for his work with the Clowns—"Rockin' Pneumonia" and so forth—but a considerable player in his own right.

5. EDWARD FRANK—With the all-star band, Royal Dukes of Rhythm, and many sessions.

6. JAMES BOOKER—More strictly a jazz player, and more schooled than the rest, but a genius R&B figure for one record, the immortal "Gonzo," and as a member of Dave Bartholomew's sixties group.

7. ART NEVILLE—The Meters leader began as a session pianist, though he has since devoted more attention to playing organ.

8. ALLEN TOUSSAINT—Best known as songwriter and producer, but the mainstay of sixties New Orleans sessions with his keyboard playing.

9. SALVADOR DOUCETTE—Pianist with Dave Bartholomew's fifties band.

10. TOMMY RIDGLEY—On his own and in sessions.

Ray Manzarek's Keyboard Influences

1. Albert Ammons, boogie-woogie
2. Lafayette Leake, Chuck Berry's one-time pianist
3. Glenn Gould, classical
4. Horace Silver, funk jazz
5. Joe Zawinul, electric jazz
6. Bill Evans, Debussy jazz
7. Jerry Lee Lewis, rockabilly

Ray Manzarek was the keyboard player for the Doors. He still lives in Los Angeles, where he is involved in record and film production.

Al Kooper's Greatest Projects

1. PLAYED ORGAN ON BOB DYLAN'S "LIKE A ROLLING STONE." He'd never played organ before. All he did was come up with the most distinctive instrumental sound on one of rock's most distinctive records. Kooper went on to collaborate with Dylan on such albums as *Blonde on Blonde* and *New Morning*, as well as supporting him on keyboards at his 30th Anniversary pay-per-view show in 1992.

2. DISCOVERED LYNYRD SKYNYRD. He did this by being the first prominent musician to relocate from New York to Atlanta—or for that matter, to the Deep South—in American history. Skynyrd only turned out to be the best American rock group of the seventies and early eighties. (This compensates for Kooper producing the first Tubes album.)

3. PLAYED FRENCH HORN ON THE ROLLING STONES' "YOU CAN'T ALWAYS GET WHAT YOU WANT." A much more impressive feat than, say, playing rhythm guitar on *Electric Ladyland*, which he also did. Or for that matter, playing piano and organ on "You Can't Always Get What You Want," which he also did.

4. WROTE *BACKSTAGE PASSES*, THE BEST ACCOUNT OF THE SIXTIES WRITTEN BY A MUSICIAN. Well, all right, he had a collaborator, but Ben Edmonds did more straightening out the narrative than ghosting. *Backstage Passes* remains the only book to capture the essential flavor of the sex, drugs, and rock 'n' roll era in all its seduction and silliness. And the only one that really understands the glory of Gene Pitney.

5. FOUNDED BLOOD, SWEAT AND TEARS, AND HAD THE GOOD TASTE TO QUIT BEFORE THOSE CLOWNS HIRED DAVID CLAYTON-THOMAS AND BEGAN CREATING THE LOUNGE ROCK OF THE FUTURE. Much more impressive than founding the Blues Project. Although the electric flute thing probably can't be blamed on Koop, either. (Although there *was* that French horn . . .) If *Child Is Father to the Man*, his BS&T LP, had set the pace, jazz-rock might be something better than a dead letter today.

6. NEVER APOLOGIZED FOR WRITING "THIS DIAMOND RING." And rarely denies being in the Royal Teens when they did "Short Shorts," even though he didn't join until after the record was cut.

7. CREATED SOME OF THE MOST MEMORABLE ALBUM COVER ART IN HISTORY, MOST NOTABLY *I STAND ALONE*, ON WHICH HE APPEARS DRESSED IN DRAG AS THE STATUE OF LIBERTY. A picture is worth a thousand words.

8. SERVED AS MUSICAL COORDINATOR FOR THE ROCK BOTTOM REMAINDERS, THE ALL-AUTHOR ROCK

BAND. It takes a brave man, indeed, to essay such a task. Sorta makes up for *Super Session*, we'd say.

Michael Azerrad Picks the 50 Greatest Rock and Roll Drummers

1. Keith Moon (The Who)
2. John Bonham (Led Zepplin)
3. Earl Palmer (Little Richard, etc.)
4. Ginger Baker (Cream, Blind Faith, Air Force, etc.)
5. Al Jackson (Stax house band, Al Green)
6. Hal Blaine (sessions)
7. Benny Benjamin (Motown house drummer)
8. Ringo Starr (The Beatles)
9. Charlie Watts (The Rolling Stones)
10. D. J. Fontana (Elvis Presley)
11. Mick Waller (Jeff Beck, Rod Stewart)
12. Clyde Stubblefield (James Brown)
13. John "Jabbo" Starks (James Brown)
14. Mitch Mitchell (Jimi Hendrix)
15. Bill Bruford (King Crimson)
16. Sly Dunbar (Bob Marley, Toots and the Maytals, etc.)
17. Roger Hawkins (Aretha Franklin, Wilson Pickett, etc.)
18. Ziggy Modeliste (Meters, New Barbarians, etc.)
19. Jim Keltner (sessions)
20. Andy Newmark (Sly and the Family Stone, Roxy Music, etc.)
21. Stewart Copeland (The Police)
22. Pete Thomas (Elvis Costello)
23. Budgie (Siouxsie and the Banshees)
24. Larry Mullen, Jr. (U2)
25. Jerome "Bigfoot" Brailey (P-Funk)
26. Dave Garibaldi (Tower of Power)
27. Martin Chambers (Pretenders)
28. Mike Bordin (Faith No More)
29. Stephen Perkins (Jane's Addiction, Porno for Pyros)
30. Prairie Prince (Tubes, XTC)
31. Manu Katche (Paul Simon, etc.)
32. Jerry Allison (Buddy Holly)
33. Simon Kirke (Free)
34. Tommy Ramone (Ramones)
35. Richie Hayward (Little Feat, Robert Plant)
36. Dale Crover (Melvins, Nirvana)
37. Rob Hirst (Midnight Oil)

38. Drumbo (Captain Beefheart)
39. Dave Grohl (Nirvana)
40. Bernard "Pretty" Purdie (sessions)
41. Kenny Aronoff (John Cougar Mellencamp)
42. Tony Thompson (Chic, Bowie, Madonna, etc.)
43. Maureen Tucker (Velvet Underground)
44. Carlton Barrett (sessions)
45. Pete DeFreitas (Echo and the Bunnymen)
46. Hugo Burnham (Gang of Four)
47. Chris Sharrock (World Party)
48. Yogi Horton (David Byrne, etc.)
49. Stanley Demeski (Feelies)
50. Jimmy Bralower (sessions)

Michael Azerrad is a contributing editor of Rolling Stone. *He is also the author of* Come As You Are: The Story of Nirvana, *as well as being the drummer in the semilegendary New Wave cover band Utensil.*

5 Great New Orleans Drummers

1. EARL PALMER—A mainstay of the fifties scene down home, Palmer has since become a major sessionman in Hollywood and is widely regarded as the definitive New Orleans percussionist.

2. CHARLES "HUNGRY" WILLIAMS—Palmer's successor, at least in the esteem of his fellow New Orleans sessionmen, Williams had stopped recording by the mid-1960s and moved to New York. He worked with Huey Smith and the Clowns.

3. ZIGGY MODELISTE—The drummer with the Meters (and the New Barbarians), Modeliste is possibly the most brilliant American funk percussionist of the contemporary era.

4. JOHN BOUDREAUX—Boudreaux drummed for Professor Longhair and Dr. John.

5. JOE "SMOKEY" JOHNSON—Johnson was the drummer with the Royal Dukes of Rhythm and Alvin "Red" Tyler.

Max Weinberg's Favorite Drummers in Bands

1. RINGO STARR—Most everything he did, but especially "Anytime at All," "Please Please Me," "I Want to Hold Your Hand," "She Loves You," "Dizzy Miss Lizzie," "Rock and Roll Music," "Slow Down" (great bass drum line), "Long Tall Sally" (especially the long fill in the guitar solo), "I Should Have Known Better," and "Tell Me Why."

2. JOHN BADANJEK—With Mitch Ryder and the Detroit Wheels on "Jenny Take a Ride," "Devil with the Blue Dress On," "Good Golly Miss Molly," and "Little Latin Lupe Lu." With Edgar Winter on "Free Ride" and live with Dr. John.

3. DAVE CLARK—On "Can't You See that She's Mine," "Anyway You Want It," "Because," "Glad All Over," "Bits and Pieces," and "Do You Love Me." His whole style of playing was built up from his snare drum.

4. MIKE HUGG—With Manfred Mann on "Sha La La," "Do Wah Diddy Diddy," "When You Walk in the Room," and "You Got to Take It."

5. KEITH MOON—When do I stop? "The Kids Are Alright," "Out in the Street," "I Can See for Miles," "Happy Jack," "My Generation" (from *Live at Leeds*), "Young Man Blues," "Baba O'Reilley," "Won't Get Fooled Again," and "Pictures of Lily."

6. BOBBY ELLIOTT—With The Hollies on "Look Through Any Window," "On a Carousel," and "Don't Run and Hide."

7. CHARLIE WATTS—With the Rolling Stones on "19th Nervous Breakdown," "(I Can't Get No) Satisfaction," "Tumbling Dice," "Rip This Joint," "Jumpin' Jack Flash," "Around and Around," "Street Fighting Man," "Brown Sugar" and "Sway."

8. LEVON HELM AND DOUG CLIFFORD—Classic American rockers. Especially Levon on the Band's "Up On Cripple Creek," "Don't Do It," "Rag Mama Rag," "The Night They Drove Old Dixie Down," "Chest Fever," and "Life Is a Carnival." Doug sounded great on Creedence Clearwater Revival's "Lodi," "Proud Mary," "Travelin' Band," "Who'll Stop The Rain," and "Green River."

9. D. J. FONTANA—On all of Elvis's fifties material, but especially "Heartbreak Hotel," "Jailhouse Rock," "Don't Be Cruel," "Hound Dog," and "Wear My Ring (Around Your Neck)."

10. DINO DANELLI—With the Rascals on "Good Lovin'," "People Got to Be Free," "I Ain't Gonna Eat My Heart Out Anymore," "Groovin'," and "A Beautiful Morning."

11. KENNEY JONES—With Rod Stewart on "Maggie May" and with the Faces on "Stay With Me."

12. JIM McCARTY—With the Yardbirds on "Heart Full of Soul" and "Over Under Sideways Down."

Max Weinberg was the drummer with Bruce Springsteen's E Street Band. He is musical director of NBC's Late Night with Conan O'Brien.

Max Weinberg's Favorite Freelance Drummers

1. BERNARD "PRETTY" PURDIE—With Aretha Franklin on "Rock Steady," "Since You've Been Gone," "Respect," "(You Make Me Feel Like a) Natural Woman," "Day Dreaming," "Until You Come Back to Me," and on almost everything from his Atlantic Records dates in the fifties and sixties. Purdie invented hi-hat "kicks."

2. HAL BLAINE—With the Byrds, the Beach Boys, and on so much sixties Los Angeles stuff, especially Phil Spector's "Baby, I Love You" and "Then He Kissed Me." Also with Simon and Garfunkel on "The Boxer" and "Bridge Over Troubled Water."

3. JIM KELTNER—With Joe Cocker's Mad Dogs and Englishmen. On John Lennon's *Rock 'n' Roll* album, and his double drumming with Ringo Starr in the mid-1970s. Also with Phil Spector and Gary Lewis and the Playboys in the 1960s. Very tasteful drumming.

4. RUSS KUNKEL AND RICK MAROTTA—Studio dates with Linda Ronstadt, Carole King, and Steely Dan. They epitomize L.A. rock drumming.

5. BOBBY GREGG—With Bob Dylan, especially on "Like a Rolling Stone," and many of his other mid-sixties recordings.

6. ROGER HAWKINS—On his Memphis and Muscle Shoals sessions particularly. Also on Percy Sledge's hits and misses, notably "Dark End of the Street," "Out of Left Field," and "When a Man Loves a Woman." Unbelievable feel and time.

7. AL JACKSON—With Booker T. and the MGs on "Born Under a Bad Sign" (from the LP *Soul Limbo*) and on all Sam and Dave, Otis Redding, and other Stax hits.

8. BENNY BENJAMIN AND URIEL JONES—Any and all drumming by these two at Motown. They patented the intro pickup (for example, on "Tears of a Clown") that I use on "Hungry Heart." Their singles are simply too numerous to mention.

9. GARY CHESTER—On all Coasters records, especially "Little Egypt (Ying Yang)" and "Yakety Yak."

10. BUDDY SALTZMAN—With the Four Seasons on their Crewe-Gaudio productions and on some Spector records and sessions with Charlie Callelo.

11. EARL PALMER—On "You've Lost That Lovin' Feelin' " by the Righteous Brothers and on a dozen other Los Angeles and New Orleans classics.

Max Weinberg's List of 10 Great Anonymous Drummers— *Whoever played on . . .*

1. "Louie Louie," The Kingsmen
2. "Stay Awhile," Dusty Springfield
3. "Here Comes My Baby," The Tremeloes
4. "Maybellene," "You Never Can Tell," "School Days," "Around and Around," Chuck Berry
5. "Lucille," Little Richard
6. "Red River Rock," Johnny and the Hurricanes
7. "Denise," Randy and the Rainbows
8. "The Wanderer," Dion
9. "You Can't Sit Down," The Dovells
10. "The Twist," Hank Ballard and Chubby Checker

J.D. Considine Picks the Top 50 Bass Players

1. James Jamerson (Motown sessions)
2. Paul McCartney (Beatles, etc.)
3. Chuck Rainey (King Curtis All-Stars, Aretha Franklin)
4. Larry Graham (Sly & the Family Stone)
5. Bill Black (Elvis Presley)
6. Aston "Family Man" Barrett (The Wailers)
7. Duck Dunn (Booker T. and the MGs)
8. Jaco Pastorius (Weather Report, Joni Mitchell)
9. John Entwistle (The Who)
10. Bernard Edwards (Chic)
11. Bill Wyman (Rolling Stones)
12. Tommy Cogbill (Muscle Shoals Rhythm Section)
13. Jack Bruce (Cream)
14. Robbie Shakespeare (Sly & Robbie)
15. Bootsy Collins (James Brown, Parliament-Funkadelic)
16. Doug Wimbush (Sugar Hill Band, Tackhead, Living Colour)
17. Tony Levin (Peter Gabriel, King Crimson)
18. Pino Palladino (Paul Young)
19. Sting (The Police)
20. Francis Rocco Prestia (Tower of Power)
21. Verdine White (Earth, Wind and Fire)
22. Willie Dixon (Chess sessions)
23. Les Claypool (Primus)

24. Louis Johnson (Brothers Johnson)
25. Noel Redding (Jimi Hendrix Experience)
26. Willie Weeks (Donny Hathaway, Aretha Franklin)
27. Billy Sheehan (Mr. Big)
28. Jimmy Williams (Philadelphia International Rhythm Section)
29. Michael Henderson (Stevie Wonder, Miles Davis)
30. Flea (Red Hot Chili Peppers)
31. Leland Sklar (James Taylor, Phil Collins, etc.)
32. Billy "Bass" Nelson (Parliament-Funkadelic)
33. John McVie (Fleetwood Mac)
34. Robert "Kool" Bell (Kool and the Gang)
35. T-Bone Wolk (Hall and Oates)
36. Rick Danko (The Band)
37. "Sweet Charles" Sherrell (James Brown, JBs)
38. Bruce Thomas (The Attractions)
39. John Paul Jones (Led Zeppelin)
40. Peter Hook (New Order)
41. Ready Freddy Washington (Al Jarreau, sessions)
42. Adam Clayton (U2)
43. Stuart Hamm (Joe Satriani)
44. Nick Lowe (Rockpile, Little Village)
45. Jimmy Haslip (Yellow Jackets, Bruce Hornsby)
46. Anthony Jackson (O'Jays, sessions)
47. Marcus Miller (Luther Vandross)
48. Kenny Aaronson (Billy Idol, Sammy Hagar)
49. Geddy Lee (Rush)
50. Nathan East (Eric Clapton, Phil Collins)

J. D. Considine Picks 15 Great Bass Solos

1. "Another Man's Woman," Atlanta Rhythm Section (Paul Goddard)
2. "Astral Weeks," Van Morrison (Richard Davis)
3. "Dark Star," The Grateful Dead (Phil Lesh)
4. "Dreaming From the Waist," The Who (John Entwistle)
5. "Everything Is Everything," Donny Hathaway (Willie Weeks)
6. "Fat Angel," Jefferson Airplane (Jack Casady)
7. "Le Freak," Chic (Bernard Edwards)
8. "Gotta Love It," Aerosmith (Tom Hamilton)
9. "Mountain Jam," The Allman Brothers (Berry Oakley)
10. "Moon in June," Soft Machine (Hugh Hopper)
11. "1983 . . . (A Merman I Should Turn to Be)," Jimi Hendrix (Noel Redding)

12. "The Ol' Diamond Back Sturgeon," Primus (Les Claypool)
13. "Refugee of the Road," Joni Mitchell (Jaco Pastorius)
14. "Scorpio," Dennis Coffey and the Detroit Guitar Band (Bob Babbitt)
15. "Spoonful," Cream (Jack Bruce)

J. D. Considine is a bassist and critic whose work has appeared in Rolling Stone, Musician, Request, Playboy, The Washington Post *and a host of now-defunct music magazines. He is currently pop music critic at the* Baltimore Sun.

The 20 Best Harmonica Players

1. Sonny Boy Williamson
2. Little Walter
3. Big Walter Horton
4. Charlie McCoy
5. Tony Glover
6. Jazz Gillum
7. Magic Dick
8. P.T. Gazell
9. Jimmy Riddle
10. James Cotton
11. Southside Johnny Lyon
12. Jimmy Reed
13. Sonny Terry
14. Paul Butterfield
15. Don Van Vliet, aka Captain Beefheart
16. Lee Oskar
17. John Sebastian
18. Delbert McClinton
19. Neil Young
20. Bob Dylan

The 17 Best Screams

1. "The Beautiful Ones," Prince and the Revolution (Prince)
2. "Beck's Bolero," The Jeff Beck Group (Keith Moon)
3. "Civil War," Guns N' Roses (Axl Rose)
4. "The End," The Doors (Jim Morrison)
5. "Fire," Arthur Brown
6. "Gimme Danger," Iggy and the Stooges (Iggy Pop)
7. "Helter Skelter," The Beatles (John Lennon)
8. "Hey Jude," Wilson Pickett
9. "I Feel Good," James Brown
10. "Jump," Van Halen (David Lee Roth)
11. "Let It Loose," The Rolling Stones (Mick Jagger)
12. "Mildred Pierce," Sonic Youth (Thurston Moore)
13. "Scentless Apprentice," Nirvana (Kurt Cobain)
14. "The Strain," Bonzo Do Doo Dah Band (Viv Stanshall)
15. "Twist and Shout," The Beatles (Paul McCartney)

16. "Why," Lonnie Mack
17. "Won't Get Fooled Again," The Who (Roger Daltrey)

Michael Jackson's 10 Favorite Vocalists

1. Diana Ross
2. Stevie Wonder
3. Barbra Streisand
4. Jermaine Jackson
5. Jackie Wilson
6. Aretha Franklin
7. Paul McCartney
8. Sam Cooke
9. Slim Whitman
10. Otis Redding

Liberace's 10 Favorite Rock Performers

1. Billy Joel
2. David Bowie
3. Boz Scaggs
4. The Doobie Brothers
5. Teddy Pendergrass
6. Blondie
7. The Eagles
8. Supertramp
9. Linda Ronstadt
10. Bob Seger

Before his death, Liberace had absolutely nothing to do with rock and roll, but he always did his best to keep up, anyway.

Gene Vincent's 5 Favorite Singers

Gene Vincent was one of early rock's grandest figures. Best known for "Be-Bop-a-Lula," Vincent continued to record prolifically in both rock and country styles until his death in 1972.

1. Brook Benton
2. Little Richard
3. Connie Francis
4. Johnny Cash
5. Cliff Richard

Source: "Wild Cat": A Tribute to Gene Vincent, edited by Eddie Muir.

Eddie Cochran's Favorite Singers and Instrumentalists

Eddie Cochran was one of the greatest of the fifties rock and roll singers before his tragic death in a car crash in 1960.

1. Ray Charles
2. Brenda Lee
3. Duane Eddy
4. Joe Brown

Source: Somethin' Else: A Tribute to Eddie Cochran *by Eddie Muir and Tony Scott.*

Reginald C. Dennis Picks the Best Rappers of All Time

1. Spoonie Gee
2. Melle Mel
3. Grandmaster Caz
4. Kool Moe Dee
5. L. L. Cool J
6. Rakim
7. Del the Funkee Homosapien
8. Big Daddy Kane
9. The D.O.C.
10. Ice Cube
11. MC Ren
12. Snoop Doggy Dogg
13. Treach
14. KRS-One

WORST RAPPER OF ALL TIME
Geraldo. Wack in two languages. English and Spanish.

Underrated Rap Artists

1. **MAGIC MIKE**—Even though it has made him a multimillionaire, the Orlando Bass sound has yet to catch on nationwide.

2. **MCI EIHT (COMPTON'S MOST WANTED)**—Has the misfortune to record for the worst label handling rap, Epic Records.

3. **COLD 187UM. (ABOVE THE LAW)**—Just when it was his turn to shine the whole N.W.A thing came apart at the seams.

4. **KOOL KEITH (ULTRAMAGNETIC MCS)**—Too far ahead of the competition. Commitment to art and innovation do not make for popularity or radio play.

Overrated Rappers

1. TREACH (NAUGHTY BY NATURE)—Take away his charisma, his muscles, his chainsaw, and his machete and what do you have left? Das-EFX.

2. DAS-EFX—Their stiggedey-wiggedy gets on your niggedy-nerves after a while.

3. CYPRESS HILL—You smoke pot. We get the joke already.

4. HOUSE OF PAIN—It's about time for these boys to shower, shave, and rejoin white society.

5. A TRIBE CALLED QUEST—Incredible musical arrangements that camouflage limited rapping skills. Where's the lyrical beef?

Writing My Rhymes Bobbito Garcia Picks the Greatest MCs (as told to Minya Oh)

1. THE TREACHEROUS THREE: SPECIAL K., KOOL MOE DEE, AND LA SUNSHINE—"The first group to really try to innovate and be different with their rhymes; like, while everybody else was saying party rockin' rhymes, The Treacherous Three were like the first group to focus, in my eyes, on having rhymes that were more geared to be on record, to be listened to over and over."

2. KOOL KEITH OF ULTRAMAGNETIC MCS—"Kool Keith is, fuckin', a lyrical genius. His shit is genius 'cause he took Treacherous to the next level. He started using big words, started putting science in his rhymes, started repeating certain words and phrases. His written rhymes are beautiful. Basically, the reason why he's one of the top ten lyricists is because he's capable of rhyming about a lot of surprise things, like while everybody was rhyming about shit around their way, about stories, and about how fresh they are, Kool Keith just brought it to another level and started rhyming with big words about science and other bugged shit."

3. RAKIM—"Rakim is just one of the deepest MCs ever. He can paint the mad, in depth. The rhymes that he writes are very in depth with his mind, you see this picture of his mind."

4. KOOL G RAP—"Metaphors ridiculous. You always look forward to hearing G Rap rhyme because you're always looking for that one line that's just gonna make you laugh, and you just hear that shit over and over 'cause you be like, 'How the fuck did he think of that?!' "

5. ORGANIZED KONFUSION: PRINCE POETRY AND MONCH—"They took off where Kool Keith left and brought that shit up another level in terms of being scientific, writing complex rhymes. They have double metaphors, hidden meanings, complex word usage. They didn't get the recognition they should have, but people will catch up."

6. THE RHYME INSPECTOR PERCEE-P—"Percee-P, fuckin', is just like a brilliant MC whose specialty is fitting a billion words within one line and having them rhyme one after the other and still make sense. That's a very hard thing to do."

7. NASTY NAS—"Nasty Nas is another mad deep MC, but don't compare him to Rakim, he's in his own right. He's really in touch with himself and capable of painting vivid pictures, and his mind is deep so there's depth in his lyrics."

8. O.CEE, FEATURED ON ORGANIZED KONFUSION'S "FUDGE PUDGE"—"O.Cee is another one who's highly capable of pulling together intricate rhyme schemes. He can make a story of something really abstract, but make you understand it perfectly. Other people may not know him but I've heard his demo and I've heard him perform live. Like, check this, he said, 'Give me some room to breathe / nigga / I'm claustro-phobic / gimme some space so I could do lyric aerobics.' That's dope. He talked about aerobic and claustrophobic but it made sense within his metaphor."

9. ACEY ALONE OF FREESTYLE FELLOWSHIP—"He's another MC who is able to use complex rhyme patterns and multiple words that rhyme with each other in one line. It's a gift to be able to do that and still make sense."

10. BIG DADDY KANE, ONLY FOR HIS FIRST TWO ALBUMS—"He's another punchline MC. He's just witty."

11. GODFATHER DON—"He's able to master many many styles. On one verse he could have punchlines, could have wit, could have depth, could be complex. He can be all that, and not a lot of MCs are that versatile."

Going Off the Top of the Dome
Bobbito Garcia Picks the 10 Greatest Freestyle MCs

1. SUPERNATURAL (WINNER OF THE '93 MC BATTLE FOR WORLD SUPREMACY)—"When it comes to battle rhymes, he's mad precise; like, he can pinpoint like any weakness in another MC and just exploit it."

2. CRAIG G, FORMERLY OF THE JUICE CREW—"He's ill 'cause he can just go on forever."

3. KURIOUS JORGE—"He's ill 'cause he'll come up with a

metaphor that he wouldn't even be able to think of if he was writing, like when he's freestyling. And that's a special skill: When people freestyle they're not usually metaphorical, they're more like, well . . . 'I freaked the flow, hit the ho . . .' but actually Kurious when he rhymes sometimes he's got substance in his flow and that's very unique. Like one time when Jorge was freestyling he said some shit like, 'I'm taking knocks / I get more puss than a litterbox.' He completely made that up right there. I know he's never written it before, and he just came up with that right there on the spot, and that's brilliant. Like who would think? And it just came out like that 'cause it just fit."

4. MICAH NINE OF FREESTYLE FELLOWSHIP—"Ridiculous! He's another one that comes off the top of his head. You never know where he's going next. When most people freestyle, they get predictable at times; for example, they might always rhyme in a certain cadence. The reason why Micah Nine is ill off the top of his head is 'cause his cadence always changes, he's like all over the place."

5. TAJAI OF SOULS OF MISCHIEF—"Tajai is ill 'cause he's just brilliant. He's just brilliant, like, he's brilliant in that he's another one along the lines of Kurious that can come up with a metaphor, just a line, that MCs wouldn't even be capable of writing if they spent hours at it."

6. KING SUN—"King Sun is ill just 'cause of his timing. The reason why he's ill is because he's just very steady, like, he'll just keep his cadence and he won't break it, like, he'll always say something that rhymes and he'll make it fit."

7. MC SERCH—"He's ill 'cause he's just a funny motherfucker. Not humorous all the time but he'll say like, 'I'll put ya in a bowl / like, bisque / Manhattan clam chowder.' You know? He'll just say bugged shit."

8. KOOL KEITH OF ULTRAMAGNETIC MCs—"Keith is just, like, in another world. I'm serious, like, I've seen Keith freestyle about food groups. But the thing about Keith is that he can pick any topic and still make it fly. He doesn't even rhyme sometimes but his flow and his voice and his delivery just makes it all work."

9. A-PLUS OF SOULS OF MISCHIEF—"A-Plus is just another one, like Tajai, he's just brilliant. Like one time they were up in the studio and he was like, 'Peace to Stretch, / and Bobbi too!' He rearranged my name . . . like, if you spell my name, it's spelled Bobbi-to . . . but instead of saying Bobbito, he split my name into Bobbi-to; to say my name but also to give it a double meaning. Him, Tajai, and [Kurious] Jorge have the ability to say things that afterward can be interpreted as brilliant."

10. KEIGE OF MUDBONES (FEATURED ON PETE NICE'S ALBUM)—"He's just ill. His voice and his delivery, it just sets him apart. He has a real unique voice and his topics are like on

that bugged sick shit, but the way he presents it is not typical at all. It's sick shit but again it's very atypical."

Bobbito Garcia is the host of Stretch Armstrong's weekly radio show on WKCR-FM (Columbia University radio), which the Gavin Report *named rap's college station of the year for both 1992 and 1993. A former Def Jam radio promoter, Garcia now runs Hoppoh Recordings and Hit-U-Off Management, both with partner Pete Nice.*

CHAPTER 17

Groups

Reincarnated Groups

1. THE ANIMALS

First formed in Newcastle around 1962 as the Alan Price Combo, the original Animals enjoyed their greatest success during the British Invasion from 1964 to 1966. After Price left in 1966, continued attrition eventually saw the act evolve into Eric Burdon and the Animals, with none of the originals save Burdon on the psychedelic hits "Monterey" and "When I Was Young." But in 1976, the original members gathered together once more for an album, appropriately entitled *Before We Were So Rudely Interrupted*. Although a longer tenure was reportedly considered, the group has not performed together since.

2. BAD BRAINS

In 1976, vocalist HR (real name: Paul Hudson), guitarist Dr. Know (Gary Miller), drummer Earl Hudson, and bassist Darryl Jenifer formed the Bad Brains, who immediately became the premier punk/reggae/rock/jazz band in the world. After eleven years on the club circuit and eight indie releases, the group splintered. By 1988, the Hudson brothers were touring with a reggae sextet, while Dr. Know and Jenifer recruited a new drummer and lead singer to tour under the Bad Brains banner. Luckily, the group's four original members buried the hatchet in 1989 long enough to record *Quickness* (Caroline) and hop on the road for a well-received reunion tour. But this was shortlived and the Hudson brothers left for good by the end of the year. Three years later, the Bad Brains were up and running again with their first major label deal (with Epic), a new drummer (Mackie), a new vocalist (Israel Joseph-I) and a new album, *RISE*.

3. BIG BROTHER AND THE HOLDING COMPANY

Originally, of course, Big Brother was Janis Joplin's group. After some scathing reviews focusing on Big Brother's reputed musical ineptitude, Joplin dumped the band, and at that point (circa 1969), it looked like the end of the road for Big Brother. But in the early seventies, the band did re-form for two decent last-gasp Columbia LPs and a tour, with Los Angeles session vocalist Kathi McDonald.

4. BLOOD, SWEAT AND TEARS

This horn-based group was meant to be Al Kooper's ultimate expression of his art-pop ambitions. But after only one album in that vein, *Child Is Father to the Man*, Kooper was sacked, and David Clayton-Thomas was brought in for the succeeding albums, which fostered the band's popularity within diluted big-band-rock circles. After the third album, *Three*, personnel changes became so frequent that at various points in the seventies, the current version of Blood,

Sweat and Tears had none of the original members on hand. Thus, this is perhaps not so much a tale of rock reincarnation as of parthenogenesis.

5. THE BYRDS

The original group, the pioneers of folk-rock, lasted for three albums, before Gene Clark left during the recording of the fourth LP, *Fifth Dimension*. This left the band a quartet. Two years later, in 1968, it became a trio when David Crosby absented himself. Leader Roger McGuinn added Gram Parsons and continued the group with ever-shifting personnel. The Byrds folded for good in 1972. In 1973, the original band was reincarnated for a disastrous one-shot album, *The Byrds*, on Asylum Records.

6. CRAZY HORSE

Neil Young found this band in the southern California boondocks. They hung in for a few albums of their own before guitarist-writer Danny Whitten split in 1972. The group disbanded after releasing *Crazy Horse at Crooked Lake* later that year. But in 1975, with Whitten dead of a drug overdose, Young re-formed the band as his backing group, this time with Frank Sampedro on guitar.

7. CROSBY, STILLS, NASH AND YOUNG

It was C, S & N, until the trio got ex–Buffalo Springfield guitarist Neil Young to join in 1970. By the next year, the group folded. Even though Crosby, Stills and Nash did some work with one another, the entire group did not re-form until 1988, when Young briefly rejoined them.

8. THE DRIFTERS

There are at least three distinct incarnations of the Drifters. The first began in 1953—with Clyde McPhatter as lead vocalist—and pioneered the merger of gospel and rhythm and blues with such hits as "Money Honey" and "White Christmas." When McPhatter left for a solo career in 1956, manager George Treadwell (who owned the rights to the group's name) selected Johnny Moore as his replacement. But Moore was drafted, and the group didn't develop a solid lineup until 1959, when Treadwell simply disposed of all the members and hired a group that had been performing in Harlem as the Five Crowns. The lead vocalist was Ben E. King, and their first recording, "There Goes My Baby," was an important, innovative hit that incorporated strings with R&B for the first time, thereby inaugurating one of the key changes that led to soul. But in 1961, King went solo, and Treadwell created a third version of the group, this time to support lead singer Rudy Lewis, who sang on the Drifters' best-known hits, including "On Broadway" and "Up on the Roof." When Lewis died in 1964, Moore returned, for "Under the Boardwalk" and a string of other hits. Managed by Fay Treadwell, George's widow, the Drifters are still active today and are especially popular in Europe, where *another* incarnation recut many of the old hits in 1972 with surprising success. Ironically, Johnny Moore is the oldest surviving member.

9. THE ELECTRIC FLAG

Mike Bloomfield was thinking along the same lines as his friend Al Kooper in 1967, and the Electric Flag became his version of a big rock band. The Flag debuted at the Monterey Pop Festival, but made only two albums before splitting up. In 1974, however, Bloomfield and several other original band members, including Buddy Miles, Barry Goldberg, and Nick Gravenites, reunited to cut one album for Atlantic. Its lack of success prevented them from continuing.

10. FAIRPORT CONVENTION

Fairport has made more than a dozen albums, but hardly any have featured the same lineup. Judy Dyble was lead vocalist on the band's first album, in 1967, but was replaced by Sandy Denny for the second. Denny left in 1969 for a solo career and the band carried on without a lead singer, which led to a series of departures that found the group, in 1973, with no original members. Denny returned in 1974 but left in 1976. The group struggled onward until very late in the decade.

11. FLEETWOOD MAC

The group was originally formed in 1967 by Peter Green, John McVie, and Mick Fleetwood—all alumni of John Mayall's Bluesbreakers. But in 1970, Green, the acknowledged leader, retired, and a year later, so did second guitarist Jeremy Spencer (for religious reasons). Having added guitarists Danny Kirwan and Bob Welch (an American), and keyboardist Christine McVie, the group carried on, until Kirwan was fired in 1972. Various replacements occurred until 1975, when the addition of Californians Lindsey Buckingham and Stevie Nicks completely transformed the original blues-based sound into romantic folk-rock. Thus, this is more a musical reincarnation than one involving personnel changes or breakups and regroupings. (Although in the dark days of 1973, when the group *did* consider disbanding, former manager Clifford Davis formed a group on his own—a la Treadwell's many Drifters—for a short period.)

12. THE GUESS WHO

Formed in Winnipeg in 1959, the original Guess Who didn't have a hit until 1965 with "Shakin' All Over." Leader Chad Allan then left to go to college, and guitarist Randy Bachman took over, with Burton Cummings as lead vocalist. They developed an altogether different pop-rock sound that led to many hits in the ensuing years, until Bachman quit after the band recorded "American Woman," in 1970. Bachman went on to more success with Bachman-Turner Overdrive. Cummings carried on with various replacements until 1975, when the group finally disbanded, no original players having been in the group for several years.

13. THE HOLY MODAL ROUNDERS

Peter Stampfel and Steve Weber formed this acid-folk group in the early sixties and have disbanded and re-formed it on a frequent basis. It best recent incarnations have featured the redoubtable Michael Hurley.

14. JEFFERSON AIRPLANE

After the group came together in 1965, with the intention of injecting some rock 'n' roll into the folksy San Francisco coffeehouse scene, Jefferson Airplane survived several early personnel changes, the most notable of which was the replacement of original vocalist Signe Anderson with Grace Slick. By 1972, the band had disintegrated into a Paul Kantner and Grace Slick partnership with famous session musicians like Jerry Garcia, David Crosby, and Graham Nash filling out their sound. With little fanfare, the group officially disbanded. In 1974, Kantner and Slick re-formed the band under the name Jefferson Starship. They held on (not incidentally, with the help of founding member Marty Balin, who briefly returned to the fold) until 1985 when Kantner and Slick's personal relationship splintered. (Lawsuits with an old manager had forced Slick and company to shorten the band's name to Starship.) Later that year, they had a number one single, "We Built This City," but 1989 saw Slick reunite with four of the band's founding members (Kantner, Balin, bassist Jack Casady, and guitarist Jorma Kaukonen). Lawsuit settled, they were once again called Jefferson Airplane, while Starship plodded along sans Slick—until neither band could plod no more.

15. JOY DIVISION

Ian Curtis, Bernard Albrecht, Stephen Morris, and later, Peter Hook formed a band called Warsaw in 1977, soon changing its name to Joy Division. Contrary to its moniker, the band's music was depressing and dirgelike. After vocalist Curtis's 1980 suicide, the remaining members became New Order. They learned to dance and smile and scored with a string of dance-oriented singles throughout the eighties.

16. LOVE

This legendary L.A. band formed in 1964. By the next year, they had recorded their first album and had a minor hit, "My Little Red Book" that led to a certain cult notoriety on the psychedelic fringe. Personnel shifts were near constant—two members added after the first album, two subtracted after the second, and so on. The only constant was guitarist-vocalist-writer Arthur Lee. By the end of 1967, Lee had gotten rid of all the other original members. The lineup thereafter lasted, more or less intact, through 1971. In 1974, Lee resurfaced with another incarnation of the group, for one album and a tour, as he did again in 1993–94. But the original had all the magic.

17. LYNYRD SKYNYRD

When guitarist Steve Gaines and singer-writer Ronnie van Zant died in a plane crash in 1977, the group was about to reach its commercial zenith. In 1979, the remaining members of the group formed the Rossington Collins Band with a new vocalist, Dale Krantz, as well as guitarist Barry Harwood and drummer Dell Hess. This collective cut two albums before splitting. In 1987, the band reformed under its original name with Van Zant's brother Johnny of .38 Special fronting the group.

18. MANFRED MANN

The group was named after one of its members, so personnel changes shouldn't matter much. But Mann is a keyboard player, not a lead vocalist, and it was the signing of Paul Jones that gave the band its British Invasion hits ("Do Wah Diddy Diddy," "5-4-3-2-1," etc.). The group first splintered in 1966, with Jones replaced by Mike D'Abo, who sang lead on "The Mighty Quinn." In 1969, Mann broke up the band altogether to form Manfred Mann Chapter Three (a jazz-rock-oriented outfit), and then Manfred Mann's Earth Band.

19. THE MOODY BLUES

Formed in Birmingham, England, in 1964, the Moody Blues had a major international hit the next year with their second single, "Go Now." They promptly disappeared from the public eye until 1968, when they recorded *Days of Future Passed*, establishing a mock-orchestral style in which the group continued, prosperously, until well into the seventies. However, in the interim, two key members, Denny Laine (later of Wings) and Clint Warwick, left, to be replaced respectively by Justin Hayward and John Lodge, who were effectively the leaders of the band thereafter.

20. THE MOTHERS OF INVENTION

Frank Zappa enjoyed posturing as a misanthrope, and maybe there was a reality behind the pose. In any event, there have been at least as many editions of the Mothers of Invention as there have been Mothers albums, with Zappa the *only* constant.

21. MOTT THE HOOPLE

Formed in Herefordshire, England, the core of Mott moved to London in 1968 and cut its debut album in 1969. Three more followed, but none had any chart success. In March 1972, the group formally disbanded, but within a few weeks, Mott re-formed after David Bowie encouraged them to do so. The band went on to its successful *All the Young Dudes*, written and produced by Bowie. Although they continued to make some fine music, their commercial successes were limited. When vocalist Ian Hunter split in 1974 to go solo, the band was, for all practical purposes, finished, although some of the original members carried on for a time as Mott.

22. THE MOVE

Formed in 1965 in Birmingham, and almost instantly successful in Britain, the Move never had a hit in America. By 1968, two original members had left, and so had the direction of the band, which became increasingly arty and conservative. By 1970, when vocalist Carl Wayne was replaced by Jeff Lynne, the Move was virtually a new group, symbolized by a name change in 1972 to the Electric Light Orchestra.

23. THE PRETTY THINGS

The Pretty Things were formed in 1963 by Phil May and Dick Taylor as a Stones-style R&B band, only dirtier. By the time they completed the rock opera *S. F. Sorrow* in 1968, May was the only original member left in the band; he finally left in 1976. The Prettys continued, feebly.

24. THE SMALL FACES

Archetypal sixties mods, the Small Faces had a rip-roaring heyday from 1965 until 1968. In 1969, leader Steve Marriott left to form Humble Pie, which was presumably the end of the tale. But shortly after, the other members found two Jeff Beck Group alumni, Ron Wood and Rod Stewart, to take his place. As the Faces, they went on to greater glories through the mid-70s. In 1977, with Stewart gone solo and Wood a Rolling Stone, the group tried it again with the original membership minus bassist Ronnie Lane, who was replaced by Rick Wills. However, this version lasted for only one LP.

25. THE SONS OF CHAMPLIN

This second-rank San Francisco band was formed in 1965 by Bill Champlin. Despite a name change in the late sixties (to the Sons), and various hirings and firings, the band never had any real commercial success. They first broke up in early 1970, re-formed later that year and changed their name to Yogi Phlegm, a Mahavishnu Orchestra–style outfit. This incarnation lasted only six months. With an expanded lineup, the band reverted to the Sons name and early funk sound, which they kept until 1977, when they finally disbanded. Bill Champlin went on to form a completely new band, Full Moon, in 1978.

26. SPINAL TAP

Originally formed on April 1, 1967, Spinal Tap came to national attention with their 1984 album *Smell The Glove* and a Rob Reiner–directed rockumentary, which ended with their break-up at the end of their 1983 Japan tour. Their keyboardist, Viv Savage, was dead, a victim of his own "have a good time all the time" philosophy. Their manager, Ian Faith, "ran out of blood vessels to burst in his forehead," and was buried with his beeper and cellular phone. And their drummer, Mick Shrimpton, had spontaneously combusted behind his drumkit. The band re-formed (with Mick's younger brother Rick on drums) to play the 1991 MTV Music Awards and released a new album, *Break Like The Wind*, the next year.

27. THE WHO

After Keith Moon died in 1978, the band considered disbanding but didn't. With Kenney Jones behind the kit, the Who released two albums and survived further tragedy in Cincinnati where eleven fans were crushed to death at a December 1979 concert. In 1982, the band finally called it quits, only to re-form seven years later, in 1989, for a lucrative American tour.

28. YES

Formed in 1968 out of the remnants of founders Jon Anderson and Chris Squire's old bands, Yes immediately set about trying to fuse classical musical structure with rock instrumentation and energy. The original lineup, in addition to Anderson and Squire, included Peter Banks, Tony Kaye, and Bill Bruford. By their third album, *The Yes Album*, Banks had left and had been replaced by Steve Howe. By their fourth album, *Fragile*, Kaye had been replaced by Rick Wakeman. After this album, Bruford left to play drums for King Crimson and Alan White took over percussion in 1972. By 1980, Wakeman had quit twice and Anderson had left to do solo work. The band hung on to record *Drama* with ex-Buggles Trevor Horn (who later produced *Seal*) and Geoff Downes, but disbanded in 1980. The next year, Howe and Downes formed Asia. The band rejoined in 1983 to record *91025*. At this time, Yes consisted of Anderson, Squire, White, Kaye, and Trevor Rabin. In 1987, they released *Big Generator*. Anderson did a couple of solo records and then quit the band again, recruiting Bruford, Wakeman, and Howe for a reunion. They toured together in 1989 but for legal reasons couldn't call themselves Yes. By 1991, Yes had once again officially re-formed with a band consisting of Anderson, Squire, Wakeman, Kaye, White, and Howe. This band released *The New Union* in 1991.

Bands that Died Before Their Time

1. THE BONZO DOG DOO DAH BAND

Although they had some success in England (the Paul McCartney–produced "I'm the Urban Spaceman" was a Top Ten hit there), the Bonzos, with their mix of parodistic rock and surrealistic comedy, might have hit it really big worldwide if they had lasted past 1969. (After all, it's listening to the Bonzos that makes it easy to understand how puerile such "satiric" successors as Sparks and the Ramones ultimately are.)

2. BRINSLEY SCHWARZ

Schwarz was simply the best of the pub-rock bands. But disastrous hype for their first LP—and a public apathetic to all but boogie and bombast—doomed the band to a mid-seventies breakup. Its version of country was very like what became known as new wave, partly because new wave was inaugurated by producer-bassist Nick

Lowe and guitarist Brinsley himself (as a member of Graham Parker's Rumour).

3. BUFFALO SPRINGFIELD
Nothing more clearly demonstrates that this group broke up too soon than the massive success of members Neil Young, Stephen Stills, Richie Furay, and Jim Messina both as solo artists and as members of such groups as Poco (which Furay joined); Crosby, Stills, Nash and Young; and Loggins and Messina.

4. DUCKS DELUXE
This was another of the pub-rock bands that could not continue against the trend. Guitarist Martin Belmont later joined the Rumour.

5. THE ELECTRIC FLAG
The original version of this group never quite got its bearings. But the blues-band-with-a-horn-section concept it helped pioneer quickly became big business with such inferior groups as Blood, Sweat and Tears and Chicago.

6. THE MC5
They pioneered what would later become known as punk rock with a political ferocity equalled only by the Clash. But because of drug problems and managerial contretemps, the group simply couldn't hold together long enough for its turn in the limelight.

7. MOBY GRAPE
A disastrous CBS Records hype for its first album, and the fact that the group played deceptively simple and straightforward rock and roll songs, obscured the genuine virtues of the one nonpsychedelic band to emerge from mid-sixties San Francisco. Like Brinsley Schwarz in England, Moby Grape would have seemed a natural in the new-wave context of the seventies.

8. THE NEW YORK DOLLS
Their semitransvestite appearance was so offputting in the halcyon days of the early seventies that the Dolls never quite found an audience. But, like the MC5, this band was a progenitor of punk. The early Sex Pistols singles, for one thing, sounded like Dolls remakes. Had they lasted into the punk moment, they might have been viewed as the semigeniuses they were.

9. BARRY AND THE REMAINS
Lead singer Barry Tashian had the fire and fervor of the classic rockers, to hear people in New England tell the tale. But their one album didn't reveal much of that, and they never got the chance to make another. Chances are, they're the great lost band of the sixties.

10. THE CLASH
The story is well-known. Joe Strummer, who'd been chasing R&B into harder post-mod terrain with the 101ers, joined forces with Mick Jones and an unskilled bass player, Paul Simonon, and then drummer Tory Crimes (later to be replaced by Topper Headon) as foils of the Sex Pistols. One of the greatest punk bands, they birthed post-punk with *London Calling* and went further out without

flaking out on *Sandinista!* Manchester, Seattle, the lionization of U2, all would be altered by the continuance of the only band that ever broke up while they were "The Greatest Rock and Roll Band in the World."

11. MOTHER LOVE BONE

Born from the embers of seminal grunge fathers, Green River, the Seattleites of Mother Love Bone did some time in San Francisco, too. Their career was iced by the heroin-induced death of lead singer Andrew Wood. They had more to say. The embers of this unit gave us two-fifths of Pearl Jam.

12. THE MINUTEMEN

No band did as much to establish punk as a folk music in the basement bohemias of America, the places that sprung the alternative nation on the world in the nineties. Formed in San Pedro, California, in the early 1980s by singer-guitarist D. Boon, bassist Mike Watt, and drummer George Hurley, they were the first band to make effortless sense out of the connection between be-bop and punk, poetry and dinosaur rock. Politically (with a small *p* and a large *P*) trenchant, they were also the great historiographers of the Unheard Music (see "History Lesson Part II"). Their career was cut short by the automobile death of D. Boon in 1985. Watt and Hurley formed Firehose in 1986.

13. N.W.A

Think about it in an artistic way, since none of their postbreakup careers (except for Yella's, of course) could be deemed failures. But imagine the possibilities if *Niggaz4Life* had the benefit of Ice Cube's level(er) head. Or if Ice Cube's post–Bomb Squad albums (or any of Ren's solo joints) were Dre-constructed sonic onslaughts instead of the stop-and-start confusion we actually got. Or if Eazy still had Cube and Ren to write rhymes for him. None of them can do alone what they could all do together.

14. THE BEATNIGS

If Michael Franti and Rono Tse had held this loopy Bay Area Afro-percussion-industrial dance crew together instead of breaking off to form the terminally unfun Disposable Heroes of Hiphoprisy, they might have made it to Lollapalooza. And then, who knows? What's Ministry, after all, but the white Beatnigs?

Greatest Duos

1. Marvin Gaye and Tammi Terrell
2. Sam and Dave
3. The Righteous Brothers
4. The original Boogie Down Productions, KRS-One and Scott LaRock
5. The Everly Brothers
6. Simon and Garfunkel
7. Mel and Tim

8. Ike and Tina Turner
9. Marvin Gaye and Kim Weston
10. Steely Dan
11. Jan and Dean
12. Ashford and Simpson
13. Eric B. & Rakim
14. Peaches and Herb (seventies incarnation)
15. James and Bobby Purify
16. The Communards
17. Erasure
18. Eurythmics
19. Pet Shop Boys
20. Daryl Hall and John Oates

Greatest Trios

1. The Beastie Boys
2. Cream
3. The Crickets
4. Cypress Hill
5. De La Soul
6. Elvis, Scotty and Bill
7. The Impressions
8. The Isley Brothers
9. The Jam
10. The Jimi Hendrix Experience
11. The Minutemen
12. Nirvana
13. The Police
14. The Ramones
15. The Rock and Roll Trio
16. Run-D.M.C.
17. Shalamar
18. The Supremes
19. Third Bass
20. A Tribe Called Quest
21. ZZ Top

The Jordanaires' 15 Favorite Recordings

1. "Sugaree," The Jordanaires
2. "Battle of New Orleans," Johnny Horton
3. "Big John," Jimmy Dean
4. "Gone," Ferlin Husky
5. "Paper Roses," Marie Osmond
6. "Poor Little Fool," Ricky Nelson
7. "Lonesome Town," Ricky Nelson
8. "The Gambler," Kenny Rogers
9. "I Can't Stop Loving You," Don Gibson
10. "Four Walls," Jim Reeves
11. "Crazy," Patsy Cline
12. "Coal Miner's Daughter," Loretta Lynn
13. "Don't Be Cruel," Elvis Presley
14. "All Shook Up," Elvis Presley
15. "Young Love," Sonny James

The Jordanaires, who helped to arrange or sang on the above records, are best known for providing harmonies for all of Elvis Presley's recordings from the time he joined RCA Records in 1956 until the end of the 1960s.

The Greatest Quartets

1. B-52s
2. The Beatles
3. Boyz II Men
4. The Clash
5. Creedence Clearwater Revival
6. En Vogue
7. The Four Seasons
8. The Four Tops
9. The Kinks
10. Led Zeppelin
11. Living Colour
12. Metallica
13. The Ravens
14. R.E.M.
15. The Replacements
16. The Sex Pistols
17. Talking Heads
18. U2
19. Van Halen
20. The Who

Gene Simmons Rates the Kiss LPs

In its October 15, 1993, issue, Goldmine *magazine had writer Ken Sharp ask the members of Kiss to rate their own records on a one-star to five-star scale. Here are Kiss leader and notorious critic-hater Gene Simmons's ratings of his own work, compared with the ratings from* The Rolling Stone Record Guide *(second edition), which were written by Kissaholic David McGee.*

ALBUM TITLE	SIMMONS RATING	RECORD GUIDE RATING
1. *Kiss*	★★★	★
2. *Hotter Than Hell*	★★★	★
3. *Dressed to Kill*	★★ ½★	★
4. *Alive*	★★★★	★★★
5. *Destroyer*	★★★★ ½★	★★★★
6. *The Originals*	not rated	★
7. *Rock and Roll Over*	★★★	★★★
8. *Love Gun*	★★★	★★
9. *Alive II*	★★★	★★
10. *Gene Simmons* (solo)	★	★★
11. *Paul Stanley* (solo)	★★	★★

12.	*Ace Frehley* (solo)	★★★	★★
13.	*Peter Criss* (solo)	zero	★★
14.	*Double Platinum*	not rated	★★★
15.	*Dynasty*	★★	★★★
16.	*Unmasked*	★	★★
17.	*Music From "The Elder"*	zero[1]	★★★
18.	*Killers*	★	not rated
19.	*Creatures of the Night*	★★★★ ½★	★★
20.	*Lick It Up*	★★	not rated
21.	*Animalize*	★★	not rated
22.	*Asylum*	★★	not rated
23.	*Crazy Nights*	★★	not rated
24.	*Smashes, Thrashes and Hits*	★★★ / ★★ / ★[2]	not rated
25.	*Hot in the Shade*	★★	not rated
26.	*Revenge*	★★★★ ½★	not rated

---

[1] "As a Kiss record I'd give it a zero. As a bad Genesis record I'd give it a two." Paul Stanley gave it a question mark.

[2] "For a new fan I'd probably give it a higher rating. For the new fan three stars. For the old fan, one or two."

James Bernard Lists 10 Reasons to Love Kiss

1. Because the kids at school believed that Gene Simmons actually was a demon.
2. Because there was always some bass player in the school orchestra who would figure out the bass solo in "She."
3. Because they were fun to draw in seventh-grade art class (before they were unmasked, of course).
4. Because their live albums were so much better than their studio albums.
5. Because you could actually dance to "Firehouse" or "Christine Sixteen."
6. Because they were the P-Funk of white rock.
7. Because in Queens in the late seventies, fights would break out between the Kiss fans and the Led Zeppelin fans over who was a better guitarist, Ace Frehley or Jimmy Page. Nobody in school got into fights over Jeff Beck.
8. Because even though he is an ex-teacher like Sting, Gene Simmons never became an overwrought, tortured intellectual.
9. Because "Beth" was the original power ballad, before such songs became de rigueur.

10. Because, at twentysomething, it's fun to rub the fact that you still like them in the faces of all those people who, for fifteen years, told you that you'd outgrow them.

The Greatest Quintets

1. AC/DC
2. Aerosmith
3. The Animals
4. Anthrax
5. The Band
6. The Beach Boys
7. Buffalo Springfield
8. The Byrds
9. The Dave Clark Five
10. Def Leppard
11. The Dells
12. The Drifters (the Ben E. King and Clyde McPhatter editions)
13. The Eagles
14. Guns N' Roses
15. The Jackson 5
16. New Edition
17. N.W.A (pre–Ice Cube's departure)
18. The Rolling Stones
19. The Temptations
20. The Yardbirds

Great Backup Bands

1. THE ATTRACTIONS—Elvis Costello's New Wave partners in crime.

2. BIG BROTHER AND THE HOLDING COMPANY—Unless you think that Joplin was Big Brother herself, or that the band was something more than support . . .

3. THE BLUE CAPS—Gene Vincent's great band.

4. BODY COUNT—Behind Ice-T, they consummated the marriage between metal and rap.

5. CRAZY HORSE—Neil Young found them playing in bars in rural California and put them together with arranger Jack Nitzsche in 1969. Thereafter, Young had one of the greatest supporting bands ever (at least until Danny Whitten died). No wonder he keeps returning to them even after trying other solo and group projects, as he did in 1979 and then again in 1990.

6. THE CRICKETS—This floating assortment of West Texas hotshots backed Buddy Holly, and once even included Waylon Jennings. But mostly it was Jerry Allison, Sonny Curtis, Niki Sullivan, and Buddy himself.

7. ELEPHANT'S MEMORY—True enough, it recorded on its own, but this group of New York politico-rockers made a name for itself only when backing up John Lennon on *Some Time in New York City*.

8. THE E STREET BAND—Bruce Springsteen's crew of cosmic East Coast hoodlums.

9. THE FAMOUS FLAMES—James Brown's original collection of soul masters featured keyboardist Bobby Byrd and saxman Maceo Parker.

10. THE GREASE BAND—After starting out with Joe Cocker, pre–Mad Dogs and Englishmen, they turned to a freelance career backing various artists.

11. GUAM—Bob Dylan's combo for the Rolling Thunder Revue.

12. THE HAWKS—You know them as the Band, but when they backed Ronnie Hawkins and then Bob Dylan, they were Levon and the Hawks—even made a couple of rare singles that way.

13. THE HEARTBREAKERS—Tom Petty's, of course, not Johnny Thunders's.

14. THE JB'S—James Brown's later assemblage of soul masters were led by the redoubtable Fred Wesley, who eventually took them solo as the Horny Horns, part of George Clinton's Parliafunkadelicment.

15. THE KINGPINS—King Curtis's crew of ace New York session pros had one of the all-time steamiest sounds on record. They featured guitarist Cornell Dupree and the fabled drummer Bernard Purdie.

16. MAD DOGS AND ENGLISHMEN—This massive rock and roll orchestra made up of Los Angeles heavyweights and relative unknowns was put together by Leon Russell for Joe Cocker.

17. THE NOBLE KNIGHTS—King Curtis's original band of funk innovators.

18. THE PIRATES—They made their reputation backing early British rocker Johnny Kidd, and are most famous for the original version of "Shakin' All Over." But Kidd was never much of a singer: The real thrill was guitarist Mick Green's fretboard wizardry.

19. THE REVOLUTION—This *Purple Rain*-era band was tight enough to convince Prince to let them play on his records. They gave his music a fullness that the earlier solo joints didn't have and a precision that the later New Power Generation–backed albums lost.

20. THE RHYTHM ROCKERS—Ike Turner used this band when he was a touring R&B showman (pre-Tina) and talent scout in the fifties.

21. ROCKPILE—Sometimes this group was led by Dave Edmunds, sometimes by Nick Lowe. Either way, it was the greatest oldies-influenced rock and roll band in history.

22. RUFUS—Their upscale funk made Chaka Khan shake her big hair and provided a context for her sometimes-silly outfits. That is, until she became a bigger star than the band and went solo in 1978.

23. THE RUMOUR—Graham Parker's backing band was formed from the splinters of two great pub-rock combos, Brinsley Schwarz and Ducks Deluxe.

24. THE SILVER BULLET BAND—Maybe they'd have been nothing without Bob Seger, but these journeymen Detroit rockers outlasted everything else in Motown through sheer tenacity and ferocity.

25. SILVERTONE—Originally a quartet with a deal on Warner Brothers, but quickly turned into a backing trio when frontman Chris Isaak got a solo deal and became a star.

26. THE WAILERS—Maybe anyone would seem great if they got to stand behind Bob Marley, but in reality these musicians had to be great just to keep up. Otherwise, they would have looked like bozos.

27. WAR—Before they scored with "The World Is a Ghetto" and "Slippin' into Darkness," War was Eric Burdon's supporting cast for a couple of notable years, connecting with "Spill the Wine" and "They Can't Take Away Our Music," the funkiest Burdon ever got.

28. WONDERLOVE—Stevie Wonder's free-floating assemblage of modern funksters.

Beyond Plutonium
24 Great Bands with the Heavy Metal Crunch

1. AC/DC
2. Aerosmith
3. Black Sabbath
4. Blue Oyster Cult
5. Led Zeppelin
6. Van Halen
7. Thin Lizzy
8. Motorhead
9. Deep Purple
10. Ted Nugent and the (latter-day) Amboy Dukes
11. Grand Funk Railroad
12. Judas Priest
13. Guns N' Roses
14. Sepultura
15. Iron Butterfly
16. Alice in Chains
17. Uriah Heep
18. Metallica
19. Megadeth
20. Anthrax
21. Kiss
22. Iron Maiden
23. The Butthole Surfers
24. Urge Overkill

The term heavy metal *comes from a phrase coined by William Burroughs in his novel,* The Soft Machine.

Katherine Turman Picks 30 Essential Metal Albums

1. *Ace of Spades*, Motorhead
2. *Agents of Fortune*, Blue Oyster Cult
3. *Alive 1*, Kiss
4. *Appetite for Destruction*, Guns N' Roses
5. *Back in Black*, AC/DC
6. *Badmotorfinger*, Soundgarden
7. *Balls to the Walls*, Accept
8. *Black Sabbath*
9. *Body Count*
10. *British Steel*, Judas Priest
11. *Chaos A.D.*, Sepultura
12. *Diary of a Madman*, Ozzy Osbourne
13. *Go Girl Crazy*, Ministry
14. *Highway To Hell*, AC/DC
15. *Inna-Gadda-da-Vida*, Iron Butterfly
16. *Iron Maiden*
17. *Kick Out the Jams*, MC5
18. *Machine Head*, Deep Purple
19. *Master of Puppets*, Metallica
20. *Montrose*
21. *Persistence of Time*, Anthrax
22. *Psalm 69*, Ministry
23. *Reign in Blood*, Slayer
24. *Scarred for Life*, Rose Tattoo
25. *Smell the Glove*, Spinal Tap
26. *Stay Hungry*, Twisted Sister
27. *Too Fast for Love*, Motley Crue
28. *Toys in the Attic*, Aerosmith
29. *Van Halen*
30. *A Vulgar Display of Power*, Pantera

Honorable Mention: Any Led Zeppelin, any Jimi Hendrix, any Alice Cooper.

Katherine Turman is the senior editor of RIP *magazine.*

Scarface's Favorite Hard Rock Albums

1. *The Dark Side of the Moon*, Pink Floyd
2. *The Wall*, Pink Floyd
3. *The Final Cut*, Pink Floyd
4. *Down to the Moon*, Andreas Vollenweider
5. *Shooting Rubberbands at the Stars*, Edie Brickell & New Bohemians
6. *Are You Experienced?* Jimi Hendrix
7. *Funkentelechy vs. the Placebo Syndrome*, Parliament
8. *Computer Games*, George Clinton
9. *EFIL4ZAGGIN*, N.W.A
10. *Ignorance*, Sacred Reich
11. *Melissa*, Mercyful Fate
12. Everything from *Destroyer* to *Unmasked*, Kiss

Before pursuing a solo career, Scarface was a member of the Geto Boys. He was born in and still lives in Houston's Fifth Ward.

10 Great Surf Bands
Not Including the Beach Boys, Jan and Dean, or Even Jack Nitzsche

1. The Chantays, "Pipeline"
2. Dick Dale and the Del-Tones, "Misirlou," "Let's Go Trippin' "
3. The Surfaris, "Wipe Out," "Surfer Joe"
4. The Trashmen,[1] "Surfin' Bird"
5. The Pyramids, "Penetration"
6. The Wailers, "Tall Cool One"
7. The Sentinals, "Latina"
8. The Marketts, "Surfer's Stomp"
9. The Trade Winds,[2] "New York's a Lonely Town"
10. The Revels, "Church Key"

---

[1] Okay, so they were from Minnesota. They still played real surf music, reverb guitars and all.

[2] Okay, so they were from Providence, Rhode Island, and mostly a vocal group, when the great surf bands were all-instrumental. But Narragansett Beach is the hottest surf spot on the East Coast, so at least they knew what they were talking about. And every landlocked midwesterner who heard "New York's a Lonely Town" finally knew the truth about the music and himself. So how could we omit 'em?

Rich Whitesell's Greatest Doo-Wop Groups

BLACK GROUPS

1. The Cadillacs
2. The Dells
3. The Drifters
4. The Five Keys
5. The Flamingos
6. The Harptones
7. Frankie Lymon and the Teenagers
8. The Midnighters
9. The Moonglows
10. The Orioles
11. The Penguins
12. The Platters
13. The Ravens
14. The Robins

WHITE GROUPS

1. Danny and the Juniors
2. Dion and the Belmonts
3. The Duprees
4. The Earls
5. The Elegants
6. The Four Lovers, aka The Four Seasons
7. Jay and the Americans
8. The Mystics
9. The Regents
10. The Rivieras
11. The Skyliners
12. Vito and the Salutations

Rick Whitesell was editor of Goldmine *and* Classic Wax *and one of America's best-known historians and researchers on rock, rhythm and blues, and related music. His special interest was in harmony-group music. Whitesell, one of the chief researchers of the original version of this book, died in January 1981.*

Ebony and Ivory?
25 Notable Multiracial Groups

1. The Allman Brothers Band
2. The Average White Band
3. The Bus Boys
4. Culture Club
5. Cypress Hill
6. The Disposable Heroes of Hiphoprisy
7. The Doobie Brothers
8. The Electric Flag
9. The Foundations
10. Guns N' Roses
11. The Jimi Hendrix Experience
12. K. C. and the Sunshine Band
13. The Paul Butterfield Blues Band
14. Prince and the New Power Generation
15. Prince and the Revolution
16. Rufus
17. The Selecter
18. Sly and the Family Stone
19. The Specials
20. The Spin Doctors

21. Bruce Springsteen and the E Street Band
22. Third Bass
23. Tower of Power
24. UB40
25. The Village People

Comedy Nonstop

1. 2 Live Crew
2. Blow Fly (aka Clarence Reid)
3. Bobby Jimmy and the Critters
4. The Bonzo Dog Doo Dah Band
5. Buchanan and Goodman
6. Cheech and Chong
7. Doug Clark and His Hot Nuts
8. Devo
9. Digital Underground
10. Flo and Eddie
11. Frut
12. The Fugs
13. Green Jelly
14. DJ Jazzy Jeff & the Fresh Prince
15. Biz Markie
16. Monty Python
17. The Mothers of Invention
18. National Lampoon's Lemmings
19. Mojo Nixon
20. Nervous Norvus
21. The Plasmatics
22. Buster Poindexter
23. The Residents
24. The Rutles
25. The Sensational Alex Harvey Band
26. Sha Na Na
27. Spinal Tap
28. The Tubes
29. Weird Al Yankovic
30. Zacherle

Boring

1. Rhinoceros
2. The Grateful Dead
3. Electric Light Orchestra
4. Genesis
5. Rush
6. Kraftwerk
7. R.E.M. (*Out of Time* and afterward)
8. The Police (*Synchronicity*-era)
9. Whitney Houston
10. Pablo Cruise
11. The Eagles
12. Poco
13. Steely Dan
14. Uriah Heep
15. Queen
16. Pere Ubu
17. The Jesus and Mary Chain
18. Robert Cray Band
19. EMF
20. Paul Simon
21. Bryan Adams
22. Jesus Jones
23. Richard Marx
24. Boston
25. Michael Bolton (OK, OK, that's too easy)

CHAPTER 18

On the Road

"I'm on the Guest List"
Shelly Lazar Lists Excuses People Use to Try to Get Backstage at Rock Concerts

1. I just flew in from L.A.
2. I work for the record company.
3. ——— is my brother (or cousin, sister-in-law, aunt, uncle, etc.).
4. I'm a songwriter.
5. ——— lives next door to me.
6. I'm a good friend of Ron Delsener's.
7. I'm a good friend of Ahmet Ertegun's and he said I could use his pass.
8. I'm Shelly Lazar's cousin.
9. I'm Shelly Lazar.
10. I'm Bruce Springsteen's hairdresser.
11. I design Rod Stewart's clothing.
12. I tune Billy Joel's piano.
13. I'm Barry Manilow's dance instructor.
14. I'm Freddie Mercury's wife.
15. I hitchhiked from Cleveland.
16. I'm just in the United States for a few days (delivered with an accent).

As the coordinator of backstage security for Ron Delsener Productions in New York, Shelly Lazar heard lame excuses everywhere from the Palladium to Madison Square Garden. More recently, she's worked for the Rolling Stones, Bruce Springsteen, Barbra Streisand, and Bill Graham Presents.

The Greatest Live Albums

1. LIVE AT THE APOLLO, JAMES BROWN
Soul dementia. If you could see Brown dancing, this one would be perfect. Structured as an emotionally compelling concept piece. Actually, the recording quality isn't so hot (although it's improved on Solid Smoke's 1980 reissue and even more so on Polydor's CD reissue). Nonetheless, this is as hot and danceable as it gets.

2. LIVE IN EUROPE, OTIS REDDING
While it may be disputed that the live album is a good idea in the first place—since manipulating recording technology and working an audience are often mutually exclusive propositions—here's a good example of a moment when everything clicks. The definitive soul music show.

3.   LIVE 1975–1985, BRUCE SPRINGSTEEN AND THE E STREET BAND

Except for Brown's *Live at the Apollo*, no live album has ever spoken with such conscious thematic force, and what you're hearing isn't just the compelling "Growin' Up" of one man's vision, but the creation of a great rock 'n' roll from the scrapheap of the music's own history, the arrival of a great band through the strivings of mundane musicians.

4.   LIVE HARDCORE WORLDWIDE, BOOGIE DOWN PRODUCTIONS

There are no mediocre live rap concerts. Either you end up watching someone recite rhymes while walking back and forth holding his dick or you are treated to a rare transcendent experience. This disc captures the latter, capturing the collective rapture of a great hip-hop show. KRS-One exercises so much control over the (four) crowds represented here that they sound as if they were on payroll: They chant along with the lyrics, greeting each couplet enthusiastically. Not only does BDP do the greatest-hits thing, but they also kick in a heavy dose of its spontaneous call-and-response and reggae-flavored freestyle.

5.   IT'S TOO LATE TO STOP NOW, VAN MORRISON

In which everybody's favorite Irish blues singer rips through a fine selection of his standard repertoire, demolishing the best of it with a surgeon's skill and a zealot's relish.

6.   LIVE AT LEEDS, THE WHO

Paved the way for Led Zeppelin and the heavy-metal hordes. Hardly the best night the Who ever had, but it's an influential and gut-crunching document just the same.

7.   UNDER A BLOOD RED SKY, U2

Sure, it's drenched in we-are-an-important-band supersincerity, but anyone who peeped this short (eight-track) collection when it first came out in 1983 couldn't have been surprised when, by the end of the decade, this new-wave act became the biggest arena rock band on the planet.

8.   KICK OUT THE JAMS, THE MC5

Hard rock at its most trebly, interstellar, and punkesque. If this wasn't where the New York Dolls and the Sex Pistols got half their sonic ideas, it should have been.

9.   "GET YER YA-YA'S OUT!" THE ROLLING STONES

Recorded on a night when they really might have been the greatest rock band in the world.

10.   BAND OF GYPSYS, JIMI HENDRIX

This is prophetic funk with a band that included Billy Cox and Buddy Miles. It's not Hendrix at his happiest, but it represents a breakthrough toward the kind of funk/rock fusion he might have explored had he lived. George Clinton has spent much of his career trying to catch up with it.

11. *LIVE AT THE REGAL*, B. B. KING

With the exception of James Brown's *Live at the Apollo*, this is the definitive document of soul music on the chitlin' circuit.

12. *THE STAX/VOLT REVUE LIVE IN EUROPE*, VARIOUS ARTISTS

Lesser lights from the same tour on which Otis Redding made his album—but when the cast includes Sam and Dave, *lesser lights* becomes a highly relative term.

13. *LIVE! AT THE STAR CLUB, HAMBURG, GERMANY, 1962*, THE BEATLES

George Harrison says that the Beatles were never better than during their Reeperbahn tenure, and while there's much dross amid the nuggets here ("Red Sails in the Sunset"?), there's enough hot stuff to convince you that Harrison might be right.

14. *HENDRIX/REDDING AT MONTEREY*, JIMI HENDRIX AND OTIS REDDING

The first official LP released from the first and putatively greatest rock festival ever, this includes Hendrix's debut as an American star, with grand—no, majestic—versions of "Like a Rolling Stone" and "Wild Thing," and with Otis singing his heart out to what he called "the love crowd" on the other side. A rare coupling of both sides of the R&B's legacy: rock at its hardest, soul at its deepest.

15. *FIVE LIVE YARDBIRDS*

This is the only really great recording of the Yardbirds with Eric Clapton ("Slowhand" of the intros) on lead guitar. They're at their most blues-wailing, with a genius version of "Too Much Monkey Business."

16. *LIVE AT MADISON SQUARE GARDEN*, JAMES BROWN

Deeper into a groove already so deep that neither you nor he nor the rest of the human race will ever climb out—or want to.

17. *LIVE AT NEWPORT*, RAY CHARLES

The genius in full swing.

18. *LIVE*, BOB MARLEY AND THE WAILERS

Short, but sweetly mournful, melodic, and determined. Marley captured at his best before white American audiences "discovered" him.

19. *LIVE AT ROYAL ALBERT HALL 1965*, BOB DYLAN AND THE HAWKS

Not an official release (although easily available on bootleg) and not recorded at Royal Albert Hall (they actually made it in Birmingham), the pinnacle of Dylan as cosmic blues singer and the Band as psychotropic accompanists.

20. *ALIVE*, KISS

It's great. Fuck you.

21. *WOODSTOCK*, VARIOUS ARTISTS

Spotty, but the best performances—the Who, Joe Cocker, Jimi Hendrix, Sly Stone—are truly monumental.

22. ONE MORE FROM THE ROAD, LYNYRD SKYNYRD

They could've been the Rolling Stones, or the world's greatest bar band, or America's best answer to the Who, or the South's one great crop of singer-songwriters. This night, they were all that and more.

23. RUNNING ON EMPTY, JACKSON BROWNE

It's more audacious in concept than execution, but what a concept: a song cycle about life on the road, recorded in concert, and with a title track that's easily the greatest thing Browne has ever done.

24. LIVE RUST, NEIL YOUNG

When it was recorded in 1980, little did we know that this old horse was just crazy enough to be catching his second (or was it third?) wind.

25. LIVE AT THE APOLLO VOLUME 2, JAMES BROWN

Pure funk personified.

26. AC/DC LIVE

Clean and crisp, this two-disc, twenty-three song slab captures what should be an aging hard rock dinosaur pounding through its most celebrated tunes with precision and power.

27. THE GREATEST LIVE SHOW ON EARTH, JERRY LEE LEWIS

Recorded in July 1964 in Birmingham, Alabama—a time and place of great significance—this is one given-up-for-dead redneck's assertion of the greatness of his music and himself. The power and the energy of rockabilly has never been more alive.

28. THAT'S THE WAY IT IS, ELVIS PRESLEY

This is definitive spectacle, from the opening "Also Sprach Zarathustra" to the concluding "Bridge Over Troubled Water" (which was probably recorded in the studio, and the applause overdubbed, but that's appropriate, too).

29. MADE IN JAPAN, DEEP PURPLE

Greatest live heavy-metal record ever made.

30. THE NAME OF THIS BAND IS TALKING HEADS, TALKING HEADS

Disc one proves that the Heads, at one time in the late 1970s, were as tight and jangly and quirky as they come, even by today's Alternative Nation standards. Disc two showcases sprawling funk so rich and infectious that you'll wonder if disc one and disc two were packaged together by mistake.

31. MAD DOGS AND ENGLISHMEN, JOE COCKER

The only big-band rock album that really works.

32. THE ALLMAN BROTHERS BAND AT FILLMORE EAST

The pinnacle of southern rock and roll.

33. LIVE AT PACOIMA JR. HIGH SCHOOL, RITCHIE VALENS

Tinny sound, and a heart as big as all outdoors.

34. *LIVE SHOTS*, JOE ELY
Outlaw honky tonk personified.

35. *ROCK OF AGES*, THE BAND
The greatest example of the group's tension-and-release inter-play, with the additional fillip of horn charts by Allen Toussaint.

36. *BLOW YOUR FACE OUT*, THE J. GEILS BAND
The purity of the blues as pure energy music, with a comic touch.

37. *LIVE AT THE ANN ARBOR BLUES FESTIVAL*, MAGIC SAM
The purest energy music in the blues, with a tragic touch.

38. *LIVE AT CARNEGIE HALL*, BUCK OWENS
Now *that's* kulcher!

39. *WAR LIVE*
No deeper funk alive.

40. *LIVE AT ROYAL ALBERT HALL*, CREEDENCE CLEARWATER REVIVAL
Like hell they weren't a great live band. This rocks so hard it choogles, and there wasn't another band in the San Francisco Bay Area—'cept Sly—that could do that.

The Worst Live Albums

Choosing the worst live albums is actually more difficult than picking the best. After all, really inept pop bands usually make concert recordings no better than their usual junk, while better performers may simply have been captured on the wrong night (or in the wrong era). This list attempts to represent both.

1. *CHICAGO IV—LIVE AT CARNEGIE HALL*
A four-record boxed set by the blandest of the supergroup horn bands. The shrink wrap is as interesting as the music.

2. *EXTREMELY LIVE*, VANILLA ICE
Extremely rhythmless.

3. *LIVE AT BUDOKAN*, BOB DYLAN
From his Vegas-style "and then I wrote . . ." period, this is as soulless as any music he's ever made.

4. *DYLAN AND THE DEAD*
More dead than Dylan.

5. *ELVIS IN CONCERT*, ELVIS PRESLEY
Presley was at his most bored, had no interesting new material, and the sound quality suggests that the discs were recorded from a transistor radio a couple of rooms away from the mikes.

6. *EUROPE '72*, THE GRATEFUL DEAD
Dead fans consider this one of their definitive LPS, which en-sures its stature here.

7. *LIVE: RIGHT HERE, RIGHT NOW*, VAN HALEN

If you buy that there's only one way to rock (which you shouldn't), somebody oughta tell them that it sure ain't this one.

8. *FOUR-WAY STREET*, CROSBY, STILLS, NASH AND YOUNG

This is the personification of wimp, presumably offered as a method of fulfilling a contractual obligation.

9. *FLASHPOINT*, THE ROLLING STONES

Dull, dull, dull. Except, interestingly enough, "Highwire," one of the two new (studio) tracks.

10. *WOODSTOCK II*, VARIOUS ARTISTS

Leftovers from volume one, this features some of the lamest bands to play for the mudpie crowd: for serious Cactus fans only.

11. *LIVE IN CONCERT*, 2 LIVE CREW

The sound of one hand wacking.

12. *MILES OF AISLES*, JONI MITCHELL

Mitchell isn't particularly comfortable performing in public in the first place, and she can't conceal her loathing of the hockey arenas she played on the tour caught here. The sound of no hands clapping.

13. *LOVE YOU LIVE*, THE ROLLING STONES

In which the World's Greatest Rock Band reveals itself as the Over the Hill Gang. If the title is true, better hope your insurance is paid up.

14. *WHEELS OF FIRE (LIVE DISC)*, CREAM

After Ginger Baker's drum-solo workout on "Toad," there weren't any question that this kind of power trio was dead. Not that the band's breakup after this metallic slop was released stopped the genre from proliferating.

15. *LIVE ALBUM*, GRAND FUNK RAILROAD

See what we mean?

16. *YESSHOWS*, YES

Just say no to stick-up-the-ass bombast.

17. *WELCOME BACK, MY FRIENDS, TO THE SHOW THAT NEVER ENDS*, EMERSON, LAKE AND PALMER

Lives up to the title

18. *LIVE BOOTLEG*, AEROSMITH

If drugs are so good for rock 'n' roll, then why does this collection of live performances by such a hard-rockin', hard-livin' band sound so dull and uninspired? Just say no.

19. *LIVE AT THE COPA*, THE SUPREMES

Supper-club soul, the aural equivalent of DiGel.

20. *11/7/70*, ELTON JOHN

He may be Mr. Personality, but listening to him prove it with an overwhelming overlay of smugness and smarmy humor isn't exactly a privilege.

21. *ALIVE 3*, KISS

Three is most definitely a crowd.

22. LIVE WITH THE EDMONTON SYMPHONY ORCHESTRA, PROCOL HARUM

This did more for Edmonton than it did for Procol Harum. Middlebrow classicism gone berserk.

23. ERIC CLAPTON'S RAINBOW CONCERT

A superstar gala falls flat on its face.

24. COAST TO COAST: OVERTURE AND BEGINNERS, THE FACES

A splendid opportunity to witness the deterioration of a once-splendid rock band.

25. GOT LIVE IF YOU WANT IT, THE ROLLING STONES

Very muddy tapes of teenagers screaming.

Items Thrown Onstage at Bruce Springsteen's Madison Square Garden Concert, December 18, 1980

Jim McDuffie, Springsteen's righthand security man and Clown Prince, informs us that this night was not particularly notable, except for its array of Christmas-related items. "In Pittsburgh," he says, "we must have gotten a dozen pair of women's underpants."

1. One bedsheet painted with the words *Merry Christmas, Bruce Springsteen*
2. One stuffed dog
3. Five Santa Claus hats, three of them stenciled *Bruce*
4. One box of one dozen Twinkies
5. One box of one dozen Hostess Cupcakes
6. Three two-foot Christmas stockings stenciled *Bruce Springsteen and the E Street Band*
7. One eighteen-inch Christmas card with four rubber gnome musicians taped onto it
8. Two ordinary Christmas cards
9. One gift-wrapped package the size and shape of a shoebox
10. One rubber duck

Taking It to the Stage in Chocolate City
Memorable P-Funk Moments Onstage

1. Capital Centre, 1977: George Clinton asks the people for a joint. A blizzard of reefers falls upon the stage.
2. Capital Centre, 1981: George emerges naked from the Mothership.
3. Robert F. Kennedy Stadium: 1971: Funkadelic members reveal bare asses during "Loose Booty"; the band gets tear-gassed.
4. Capital Centre, 1981: Sly Stone sings a simple song with the Funk Mob.
5. Capital Centre, 1979: Phillipe Wynne, former Spinner, appears in white tie and tails to sing "Sadie" and "A Change Is Gonna Come."

15 Famous Psychedelic Ballrooms

1. The Aragon, Chicago
2. The Avalon, San Francisco
3. California Hall, San Francisco
4. The Carousel, San Francisco: most famous site of the Fillmore West
5. Cheetah, Los Angeles
6. The Electric Circus, New York City
7. The Electric Factory, Philadelphia
8. Family Dog on the Great Highway, San Francisco
9. Fillmore Auditorium, San Francisco: original site of the Fillmore, before Fillmore West
10. Fillmore East, New York City
11. The Grande Ballroom, Detroit
12. Longshoreman's Hall, San Francisco: site of Bill Graham's first rock concert promotion
13. Shrine Auditorium, San Francisco
14. The Tea Party, Boston
15. Winterland, San Francisco

Bill Graham's Most Memorable Concerts of the Sixties and Seventies

1. All the early Jefferson Airplane and Grateful Dead concerts
2. Otis Redding at the Fillmore Auditorium, San Francisco, December 20–22, 1966
3. Lenny Bruce/The Mothers of Invention at the Fillmore Auditorium, June 24, 25, 1966
4. Jimi Hendrix/John Mayall/Albert King at the Fillmore Auditorium and Winterland, February 1–4, 1968
5. The Matrix Benefit (Janis Joplin with Big Brother and the Holding Company/The Steve Miller Blues Band/Sandy Bull/Dan Hicks/Santana) at the Fillmore Auditorium, June 16, 1968
6. Aretha Franklin/King Curtis and the Kingpins/Tower of Power at the Fillmore West, San Francisco, March 5–7, 1971
7. The Watkins Glen Festival (The Grateful Dead/The Band/The Allman Brothers) in Watkins Glen, New York, July 28, 1973
8. S.N.A.C.K. Benefit (Students Need Activities, Culture, and Kicks) (Eddie Palmieri/Tower of Power/Santana/Joan Baez/The Grateful Dead/Neil Young/Bob Dylan/Jefferson Starship/Willie Mays/Marlon Brando, etc.) at Kezar Stadium, San Francisco, March 23, 1975
9. The Last Waltz (The Band/Bob Dylan/Van Morrison/Neil Young/Joni Mitchell/Neil Diamond/Muddy Waters/Ronnie Hawkins, etc.) at Winterland, November 25, 1976
10. Bruce Springsteen at Winterland, December 15, 16, 1978
11. The Grateful Dead at the Warfield Theatre, San Francisco, September 25–October 4, 1980

Until his untimely death in 1991, Bill Graham was the most celebrated concert promoter in rock. He earned his reputation with the greatest of the sixties ballrooms, the Fillmores East and West, and sustained it with frequent productions around his home base in the San Francisco Bay Area, as well as his national packages, the biggest of which was with the Rolling Stones. Graham also managed such artists as Santana and Eddie Money.

10 Bands that Opened for J. Geils

1. The Cars
2. The Eagles
3. Earth, Wind and Fire
4. Peter Frampton
5. Billy Joel
6. Little Feat
7. Tom Petty and the Heartbreakers
8. Bob Seger
9. Van Halen
10. Yes

Ray Manzarek's Most Memorable Doors Concerts

1. WHISKEY A GO-GO, LOS ANGELES—When Jim first did "Father, I want to kill you, Mother, I want to fuck you!" We were fired that night.

2. FILLMORE WEST, SAN FRANCISCO—The weekend of the Human Be-In, the world's first love-in ever. We were the opening act. The first number was "When the Music's Over." We'd never opened with it before, or since.

3. SINGER BOWL, NEW YORK—What a show! The Doors and the Who. And what a riot! One of the best riots I've ever been in.

4. THE ROUNDHOUSE, LONDON—The Doors and the Jefferson Airplane: Psychedelic West Coast comes to England

5. MIAMI—I think we all know what happened there. Or do we? Did he really do it? If he did it, how long was it?

6. DES MOINES—Thirty-four people in the audience. One of the last college gigs before "Light My Fire" hit the top of the charts. We were a little early for Des Moines. The promoters told us that the week before, more than five thousand people had come to the same auditorium to see the Association.

Ray Manzarek was the keyboard player for the Doors. He still lives in Los Angeles, where he is involved in record and film production.

Noel Redding Lists His 10 Most Memorable Concerts with the Jimi Hendrix Experience

1. **PARIS OLYMPIA, PARIS, OCTOBER 18, 1966**—We supported French pop singer Johnny Halliday and really enjoyed playing those early gigs.

2. **BAG O'NAILS, LONDON, NOVEMBER 25, 1966**—Our launching pad. I was awed by the star-filled audience.

3. **KIEL, WEST GERMANY, MAY 27, 1967**—Jimi was so stoned that I had to tune his guitar for him.

4. **MONTEREY INTERNATIONAL POP FESTIVAL, CALIFORNIA, JUNE 18, 1967**—My all-time favorite. Our first U.S. appearance, tension-filled as a result of following both the Who and a Brian Jones introduction.

5. **MINNEAPOLIS, NOVEMBER 2, 1968**—I was so stoned I fell off the stage, knocking over the right PA stack; I cut my leg but kept on playing.

6. **LULU SHOW, BBC-TV, JANUARY 3, 1969**—Hilarious! A tribute to Cream with powerless TV directors going insane.

7. **BERLIN, JANUARY 23, 1969**—A highly political atmosphere complete with a riot in a packed hall.

8. **ROYAL ALBERT HALL, LONDON, FEBRUARY 18, 24, 1969**—A rare onstage jam with Traffic on the eighteenth. Everyone knew the group had really broken up and this would be the last English appearance, which made the shows exceptionally emotional. A good part of the audience ended up onstage. The Fat Mattress [Noel's solo group] backed the Experience for the first time.

9. **DEVONSHIRE DOWNS, LOS ANGELES, JUNE 20, 1969**—For the sheer heaviness of the vibes and persons who surrounded us.

10. **DENVER, JUNE 29, 1969**—The last show of the Experience—and nearly the last of us. I suddenly realized there were three of us and forty thousand of them as the audience and the tear gas started coming.

Noel Redding was the bassist in the Jimi Hendrix Experience. Since then, he has played in a number of groups and published a book about his experience in the Experience.

Farewell Concerts

1. **THE BEATLES, CANDLESTICK PARK, SAN FRANCISCO, AUGUST 29, 1966**—The band, of course, didn't know this was its last show. Nor did the crowd. But the next time a Beatle set foot on a concert stage with his own group was in 1969, when John Lennon appeared with Plastic Ono Band at the Toronto Pop Festival.

2. **THE BAND, WINTERLAND, SAN FRANCISCO, THANKSGIVING 1976**—A gala farewell performance, with guest appearances by everyone from Bob Dylan, Ronnie Hawkins, and Muddy Waters to Eric Clapton, Neil Young, and Joni Mitchell. The concert was filmed by Martin Scorsese and released as *The Last Waltz*, with additional studio music and footage. Various configurations of the Band have since worked together, but this *was* the last show for guitarist-songwriter Robbie Robertson.

3. **DAVID BOWIE, HAMMERSMITH ODEON, LONDON, JULY 3, 1973**—Bowie announced his retirement after this show but has since had several relapses.

4. **CREAM, ROYAL ALBERT HALL, LONDON, NOVEMBER 26, 1969**—Filmed and recorded as *Goodbye Cream*.

5. **GUNS N' ROSES, LOS ANGELES COLISEUM, OCTOBER 19, 1989**—Axl came out hoppin' mad, ranting about recent negative press coverage in the wake of the "One in a Million" spat and threatening to disband the group if some of its members didn't stop "dancing with Mr. Brownstone." The next night, Slash made an attempt at an antidrug statement. The band didn't break up, at least not at that time.

6. **LED ZEPPLIN, BERLIN, GERMANY, EISSPORTHALLE, JULY 7, 1980**—John Bonham's last show. Set ended with "Whole Lotta Love." The European tour was such a success that plans went immediately into effect for an American tour to start October 17. But Bonham was dead on September 25 and the grief-stricken band decided that "we could not continue as we were."

7. **JONI MITCHELL, ROYAL ALBERT HALL, LONDON, FEBRUARY 17, 1970**—Mitchell announced her retirement, but like Bowie's, it didn't stick.

8. **THE ROLLING STONES, THE ROUNDHOUSE, LONDON, MARCH 14, 1971**—Their final U.K. show before moving to France, a move at least partially prompted by England's excessive tax rates.

9. **THE SEX PISTOLS, WINTERLAND, SAN FRANCISCO, JANUARY 14, 1978**—Immediately after this gig, the last of their U.S. tour, Johnny Rotten announced that, due to a dispute with manager Malcolm Mclaren, he was leaving the group.

This effectively ended the Sex Pistols' career as enfants terribles, a.k.a. the world's greatest punk-rock band.

10. STEVIE RAY VAUGHAN, ALPINE VALLEY, WISCONSIN, AUGUST 26, 1990—Stevie Ray Vaughan's last concert took place at Alpine Valley, a southern Wisconsin ski resort about eighty miles from Chicago, which ended in a jam with his brother Jimmie Vaughan, Eric Clapton, Buddy Guy, and Robert Cray. They played "Sweet Home Chicago," and by all accounts, Stevie blew the others off the stage. Later that night, the helicopter that Stevie had chartered back to Chicago crashed into a three-hundred-foot hill, killing Stevie along with three members of Clapton's entourage.

11. THE WHO, TORONTO, 1982—The band had decided to end their career with a final U.S. Farewell Tour, which sold out in venue after venue, grossing over $40 million. But they regrouped to play Live Aid in 1985 and a smattering of special occasions. In 1989, the smell of fresh green dollars waved in their faces brought them out on another sold-out U.S. tour. And that's the end; they swear . . .

Rock's Most Ill-Fated Tour
The Winter Dance Party, January 23–February 3, 1959

The tour played its final engagement at the Surf Ballroom, in Clear Lake, Iowa, on February 2. Later that evening, Buddy Holly, Ritchie Valens, and J. P. Richardson (the Big Bopper) chartered a plane to take them to the next stop, so they would have some extra time to get shirts cleaned and could pick up their mail. The plane crashed, killing its passengers. The musicians on the tour were:

1. Buddy Holly and the Crickets
2. Dion and the Belmonts
3. Ritchie Valens
4. The Big Bopper
5. Frankie Sardo

Complete Itinerary for the Winter Dance Party

1. January 23, George Devine's Ballroom, Milwaukee
2. January 24, Kenosha, Wisconsin
3. January 25, Kato Ballroom, Kankato, Minnesota
4. January 26, Eau Claire, Wisconsin

5. January 27, Fiesta Ballroom, Montevideo, Minnesota
6. January 28, Prom Ballroom, St. Paul
7. January 29, Capitol Theatre, Davenport, Iowa
8. January 30, Laramar Ballroom, Fort Dodge, Iowa
9. January 31, Armory, Duluth, Minnesota
10. February 1, Cinderella Ballroom, Appleton, Wisconsin (afternoon); Riverside Ballroom, Green Bay, Wisconsin (evening)
11. February 2, Surf Ballroom, Clear Lake, Iowa
12. February 3, Armory, Moorhead, Minnesota
13. February 4, Shore Acres, Sioux City, Iowa
14. February 5, Val Air Ballroom, Des Moines
15. February 6, Danceland Ballroom, Cedar Rapids, Iowa
16. February 7, Les Buzz Ballroom, Spring Valley, Illinois
17. February 8, Aragon Ballroom, Chicago
18. February 9, Hippodrome Auditorium, Waterloo, Iowa
19. February 10, Melody Hill, Dubuque, Iowa
20. February 11, Memorial Auditorium, Louisville, Kentucky
21. February 12, Memorial Auditorium, Canton, Ohio
22. February 13, Stanbaugh Auditorium, Youngstown, Ohio
23. February 14, Peoria, Illinois
24. February 15, Springfield, Illinois

Katherine Turman Picks the 10 Best Live Rock Shows

1. **Guns N' Roses, Tribute to Todd Crew at the Coconut Teaser, Hollywood, July 21, 1987**—An impromptu show at a tiny club before the band (in its original lineup) became really huge. As a tribute to a member of their road crew who'd OD'd the week before, lead singer Axl Rose sang a tear-jerking version of Dylan's "Knocking on Heaven's Door" for his late comrade.

2. **Pink Floyd, The Wall Tour, Los Angeles Forum, 1981**—One of the select cities in which the band managed to create the massive set necessary to fully realize the amazing conceptual album *The Wall*. Pigs flying overhead . . . and a lot of illegal substances in the audience that night.

3. **Soul Asylum, the Whisky, November 15, 1990**—Before becoming the major MTV hunk, Dave Pirner and his dirty hair still had a packed house mesmerized for such pop-punk ditties as "Gullible's Travels." Minneapolis's finest, bar none (even Prince).

4. **Iggy Pop, Iguana's, Tijuana, Mexico, 1990**—The Ig-meister south of the border—viva rock. Despite the fact that

he was touring behind the rather too-slick *Brick by Brick*, the legendary Detroit madman had them jumping from the rafters, literally. Not bad for an old guy.

5. NIRVANA, THE ROXY, HOLLYWOOD, 1992—Right before "Smells Like Teen Spirit" made the unlikely Seattle trio an alternative poster band, Nirvana played a sold-out, sweaty mosh pit of a show for a couple hundred lucky industryites.

6. ANY AC/DC SHOW, 1980—1992—Even though some are diehard fans of the Aussie group's original lead singer, the late great Bon Scott, Brian Johnson is no slouch. Winners not only of the decibel award, but the consistency award. You can count on death, taxes, and AC/DC concerts.

7. PANTERA, THE PARAMOUNT THEATRE, NEW YORK CITY, APRIL 22, 1992—These Texas terrors possess such unbelievable, primal power that it's truly frightening. The song "Cowboys from Hell" doesn't even come close to describing the headbanging heaviness of Phil Anselmo and his cohorts.

8. MINISTRY, LOLLAPALOOZA, IRVINE MEADOWS AMPITHEATRE, IRVINE, CALIFORNIA, 1992—They evolved from dance band to scary industrial heavyweights and, at this show, an onslaught of lights and sound, Ministry easily stole the evening from the "headliner," the Red Hot Chili Peppers.

9. RAGE AGAINST THE MACHINE, THE WHISKEY, MAY 28, 1992—Quite possibly the most energetic and inspiring live band ever; the audience looked as if they were on pogo sticks for this one. With politics as hard-core as their musicality and amazing guitar noodlings from Tom Morello, Rage indeed raged.

10. BOOMTOWN RATS, THE COUNTRY CLUB, RESEDA, CALIFORNIA, 1981—Led ably by the prototype cute-smart-alternative-hunk, Bob Geldof, this was the height of the band's sadly meager U.S. success. Hot off his success starring in the Pink Floyd movie *The Wall* and with the Rats' breakthrough single, the true tale of "I Don't Like Mondays," Geldof and his quirky Irish band were at their engaging best.

Honorable Mention—Lynyrd Skynyrd, any show, any lineup: "Freebird." Need I say more? If you grew up in the seventies, this was de rigueur party music. Guitars for miles. Get out your lighters and keep on trucking.

Katherine Turman is the senior editor of RIP *magazine.*

CHAPTER 19

Dancing

Larry Flick Picks the 50 Greatest Dance Hits

1. "Last Dance," Donna Summer
2. "Vogue," Madonna
3. "Rock Lobster," The B-52s
4. "Into the Groove," Madonna
5. "Disco Inferno," The Trammps
6. "Land of 1000 Dances," Chris Kenner
7. "Le Freak," Chic
8. "The Stroll," The Diamonds
9. "Turn the Beat Around," Vicki Sue Robinson
10. "He's the Greatest Dancer," Sister Sledge
11. "One Nation Under a Groove," Funkadelic
12. "The Loco-Motion," Little Eva
13. "Dance With Me," Peter Brown
14. "Conga," Miami Sound Machine
15. "Work Your Body," Taana Gardner
16. "Whole Lotta Shakin' Goin' On," Jerry Lee Lewis
17. "Get Down Tonight," K.C. & the Sunshine Band
18. "Cool Jerk," The Capitols
19. "(Dance) Disco Heat," Sylvester
20. "Workin' Day & Night," Michael Jackson
21. "Rock with You," Michael Jackson
22. "Goin' to A Go-Go," The Miracles
23. "I've Got the Next Dance," Deniece Williams
24. "You Make Me Feel Like Dancin'," Leo Sayer
25. "You Should Be Dancin'," The Bee Gees
26. "Shadow Dancin'," Andy Gibb
27. "Dancin' Queen," Abba
28. "Dancing in the Sheets," Shalamar
29. "The Twist," Chubby Checker
30. "No Parking on the Dancefloor," Midnight Starr
31. "Le Spank," Le Pampelmoose
32. "Do You Love Me," The Contours
33. "At the Hop," Danny & the Juniors
34. "Mashed Potato Time," Dee Dee Sharp
35. "Blame It on the Boogie," The Jacksons
36. "Disco Nights (Rock, Freak)," G.Q.
37. "Night Fever," The Bee Gees
38. "Keep On Dancin'," Gary's Gang
39. "The Hustle," Van McCoy & the Soul City Symphony
40. "Get Off," Foxy
41. "Party Lights," Natalie Cole
42. "Sidewalk Talk," Jellybean

43. "Jingo," Candido
44. "Tighten Up," Archie Bell and the Drells
45. "Shake It Up Tonight," Cheryl Lynn
46. "Do Ya Wanna Funk," Sylvester
47. "Ain't That a Groove," James Brown
48. "Everybody Dance," Chic
49. "Rock Around the Clock," Bill Haley and the Comets
50. "Save the Last Dance for Me," The Drifters

Larry Flick is the dance music editor at Billboard.

The Top 40 Dance Steps

1. Vogue
2. Hustle
3. Electric Slide
4. Bus Stop
5. Bump
6. Locomotion
7. Grind
8. Watusi
9. Stroll
10. Runway
11. L.A. Hustle
12. Latin Hustle
13. Jerk
14. Frug
15. Swim
16. Moonwalk
17. Shimmy
18. Hand-Jive
19. Lindy
20. Limbo
21. Pony
22. Pogo
23. Bristol Stomp
24. Mashed Potato
25. Hully Gully
26. Hucklebuck
27. Skank
28. Suzie-Q
29. Freestyle
30. Freak
31. 81
32. Monkey
33. Pop-Eye
34. Philly Freeze
35. Sissy Strut
36. Shake
37. Popcorn
38. Boogaloo
39. Slop
40. Twist

20 Twist Records
The Wildest and the Weirdest

1. "Slow Twistin'," Chubby Checker and Dee Dee Sharp
2. "Twist and Shout," The Isley Brothers
3. "Let's Twist Again," Chubby Checker
4. "Twistin' the Night Away," Sam Cooke
5. "Dear Lady Twist," Gary "U.S." Bonds
6. "Peppermint Twist—Part One," Joey Dee and the Starliters

7. "Soul Twist," King Curtis and the Noble Knights
8. "The Twist," Hank Ballard and the Midnighters, Chubby Checker
9. "Twistin' Postman," The Marvelettes
10. "Bristol Twistin' Annie," The Dovells
11. "Twist, Twist Senora," Gary "U.S." Bonds
12. "Patricia Twist," Perez Prado
13. "The Basie Twist," Count Basie
14. "Tequila Twist," The Champs
15. "Twistin' Matilda," Jimmy Soul
16. "(Let's Do) the Hully Gully Twist," Bill Doggett
17. "Twistin' Bells," Santo and Johnny
18. "Twistin' With Linda," The Isley Brothers
19. "Twistin' U.S.A.," Danny and the Juniors
20. "Percolator (Twist)," Billy Joe and the Checkmates

10 Who Make Chubby Checker Dance

1. The Beatles, *Sgt. Pepper's Lonely Hearts Club Band*
2. Marvin Gaye, "Mercy Mercy Me (The Ecology)"
3. Elvis Presley, *G.I. Blues*
4. Nat King Cole
5. Steely Dan, *Katy Lied*
6. Stevie Wonder, *Innervisions*
7. Leon Russell at his 1974 Las Vegas concert with the Gap Band
8. Harry Belafonte
9. Crosby, Stills and Nash (without Neil Young)
10. Fats Domino

Chubby Checker is the auteur of dance music, especially through his "Twist" recordings, which created the greatest rock dance craze of all time. He continues to perform in nightclubs and on the oldies circuit.

The Greatest Dance Bands

1. The Trammps
2. Sly and the Family Stone
3. The Gap Band
4. Kool and the Gang
5. The Time
6. The J.B.'s
7. Chic
8. Parliament-Funkadelic
9. Jr. Walker and the All-Stars
10. Cameo
11. The Commodores
12. The Isley Brothers

13. Chuck Brown and the Soul Searchers
14. Brass Construction
15. War
16. Earth, Wind and Fire
17. Prince and the Revolution
18. Ohio Players
19. Toni Tone Tony
20. Rufus

Early Rumblings on the Dance Floor
The First Disco Records

1. "Theme from *Shaft*," Isaac Hayes, 1971
2. "Armed and Extremely Dangerous," First Choice, 1973
3. "Soul Makossa," Manu Dibango, 1973
4. "Under the Influence of Love," Love Unlimited, 1974
5. "The Player," First Choice
6. "Dreaming a Dream," Crown Heights Affair, 1975
7. "Foot-Stompin' Music," Bohannon, 1975
8. "Free Man," South Shore Commission, 1975
9. "Nice 'n' Nasty," Salsoul Orchestra, 1976
10. "Tangerine," Salsoul Orchestra, 1976
11. "We're on the Right Track," South Shore Commission, 1976
12. "Young Hearts Run Free," Candi Staton, 1976

Top 25 Disco Hits

1. "I Feel Love," Donna Summer
2. "At Midnight," T-Connection
3. "Let No Man Put Asunder," First Choice
4. "Relight My Fire," Dan Hartman
5. "Got to Be Real," Cheryl Lynn
6. "Turn the Beat Around," Vicki Sue Robinson
7. "MacArthur Park Suite," Donna Summer
8. "Brazil," The Ritchie Family
9. "Heart to Break the Heart," France Joli
10. "Love & Desire," Arpeggio
11. "There But for the Grace of God," Machine
12. "I'm Coming Out," Diana Ross
13. "It's Raining Men," The Weather Girls
14. "In the Name of Love," Sharon Redd
15. "More than a Woman," Tavares
16. "The Boss," Diana Ross
17. "Take Me Home," Cher

18. "Heaven Must Have Sent You," Bonnie Pointer
19. "Heaven Must Be Missing an Angel," Tavares
20. "I Will Survive," Gloria Gaynor
21. "Touch & Go," Ecstasy, Passion & Pain
22. "Love Sensation," Lolleata Holloway
23. "Doctor Love," First Choice
24. "Boogie Wonderland," Earth, Wind and Fire
25. "Love's Theme," The Love Unlimited Orchestra

The Sound of Philadelphia
Philadelphia's 20 Best Disco Records

1. "Ain't No Stoppin' Us Now," McFadden and Whitehead
2. "Ask Me," Ecstasy, Passion and Pain
3. "Bad Luck," Harold Melvin and the Blue Notes
4. "Dirty Ol' Man," The Three Degrees
5. "Disco Inferno," The Trammps
6. "Do It Anyway You Wanna," The People's Choice
7. "Doctor Love," First Choice
8. "For the Love of Money," The O'Jays
9. "I Love Music," The O'Jays
10. "I'll Always Love My Mama," The Intruders
11. "Livin' for the Weekend," The O'Jays
12. "Love Epidemic," The Trammps
13. "Love Train," The O'Jays
14. "Only You," Teddy Pendergrass
15. "That's Where the Happy People Go," The Trammps
16. "The Love I Lost," Harold Melvin and the Blue Notes
17. "TSOP (The Sound of Philadelphia)," MFSB
18. "Turn the Beat Around," Vicki Sue Robinson
19. "When Will I See You Again?" The Three Degrees
20. "Where Do We Go from Here," The Trammps

The Worst Disco Records

1. "D'Ya Think I'm Sexy," Rod Stewart
2. "Miss You," The Rolling Stones
3. "Disco Duck," Rick Dees & His Cast of Idiots
4. "Funky Town," Lipps Inc.
5. "Grease," Frankie Valli
6. "Lady Bump," Penny McClain
7. "Dance a Little Bit Closer," Charo
8. "Get Dancin'," Disco-Tek & The Sex-O-Lettes

9. "This Girl's Back in Town," Raquel Welch
10. "Love Rush," Ann-Margaret
11. "Shame, Shame, Shame," Shirley & Co.
12. "Ain't Gonna Bump No More (With No Big Fat Woman)," Joe Tex

The 15 Best Disco Albums

1. *Bad Girls*, Donna Summer
2. *Once upon a Time*, Donna Summer
3. *Saturday Night Fever* (original soundtrack)
4. *Dr. Buzzard's Original Savannah Band*
5. *Step Two*, Sylvester
6. *Chic*
7. *Diana*, Diana Ross
8. *The Village People*
9. *Never Gonna Let You Go*, Vicki Sue Robinson
10. *Four Seasons of Love*, Donna Summer
11. *Megatron Man*, Patrick Cowley
12. *We Are Family*, Sister Sledge
13. *Like an Eagle*, Dennis Parker
14. *Supernature*, Cerrone
15. *From Here to Eternity*, Giorgio

10 Greatest Acts from the Disco Era, as Compiled by Larry Flick

1. DONNA SUMMER—No other voice in the bottomless pit of divas could ever capture the genre's melodramatic intensity with such grace and depth. Summer deftly elevated an orgasm into revelatory theater, and turned a twirl on the dance floor into religion.

2. SLYVESTER—Once again, it was all in the voice. His rich, spine-tingling falsetto could draw tears and cheers within the space of eight musical bars. Flamboyant, and oh-so-glad to be gay, Sylvester took punters on a rollercoaster journey into defiant pride and unbridled sex.

3. THE VILLAGE PEOPLE—At first, they were a brash and ballsy queer statement in a sea of female-bearded gay producers and composers. Although they melted into a vat of goofy kitsch and camp, their statement remained crystal clear. And folks *still* love 'em!

4. CHIC—Oozing with sophistication and the exemplary musicianship of Nile Rodgers, and Bernard Edwards, Chic brought cool, soulful breezes—and a much-needed dose of credibility—to the critically damned disco genre.

5. CERRONE—A true musical genius. His creations had the flair and complexity of neoclassical compositions, splashed with raw heat and soothing sensuality. Climb into "Supernature" for a brief trip to heaven.

6. THE BEE GEES—Although "Saturday Night Fever" defined the impact disco had on Joe Q. Public, "Jive Talkin' " and "You Should Be Dancin' " better captured the genre's warped personality and live-for-the-moment mentality.

7. TAVARES—Easily the Temptations and the Four Tops of disco. Any questions?

8. FIRST CHOICE—Somewhere between being the Supremes and being the Martha and the Vandellas of disco.

9. SISTER SLEDGE—This sibling act would become the blueprint for En Vogue and a host of other nineties New Jill Swingers, but with a lot more charm and individual personality.

10. THE SALSOUL ORCHESTRA—Armed with winking tracks like "You're Just the Right Size" and "Nice & Nasty," this band deftly reflected the primal sexual freedom of discotheques, and the mating-dance ritual of the music. Their instrumental chops were pretty sharp, too.

Donna Summer's 10 Favorite Female Vocalists of the Sixties and Seventies

1. Irene Cara
2. Aretha Franklin
3. Chrissie Hynde
4. Bette Midler
5. Olivia Newton-John
6. Dolly Parton
7. Linda Ronstadt
8. Diana Ross
9. Barbra Streisand
10. Dionne Warwick

Macho Men
The Real Names of the Village People

1. Victor Willis (the cop, original)
2. Ray Simpson (the cop, replacement)
3. David "Scar" Hodo (the construction worker)
4. Glenn Hughes (the leatherman)

5. Alexander Briley (the GI)
6. Randy Jones (the cowboy)
7. Felipe Rose (the Indian)

Club Kids Gone Pop
Top Acts that Got Their Start in the Dance Club Scene

1. Madonna
2. Boy George
3. RuPaul
4. Pet Shop Boys
5. Lisa Stansfield
6. Abba
7. Gloria Estefan
8. Rick Astley
9. Expose
10. CeCe Peniston

Top Disco Producers

1. Nile Rodgers and Bernard Edwards (Chic)
2. Giorgio Moroder and Pete Bellotte (Donna Summer)
3. Jacques Morali and Henri Belolo (The Village People, The Ritchie Family)
4. Patrick Cowley (himself, Sylvester)
5. Cerrone (himself)
6. Dan Hartman (himself)
7. Vincent Montana, Jr. (Salsoul Orchestra)
8. Paul Jabara (himself, Donna Summer, Weather Girls)
9. Barry White (himself, Love Unlimited)
10. Karl Richardson and Albhy Galuten (The Bee Gees)

Best House Hits

1. "Love Can't Turn Around," JM Silk
2. "Move Your Body," Marshall Jefferson
3. "That's the Way Love Is," Ten City
4. "Jack Your Body," JM Silk
5. "The Whistle Song," Frankie Knuckles
6. "Gypsy Woman," Crystal Waters
7. "French Kiss," Li'l Louis & the World
8. "Baby Wants to Ride," Jamie Principle
9. "This Is Acid," Maurice
10. "Finally," CeCe Peniston
11. "Pride (A Deeper Love)," Clivilles & Cole

12. "Don't Lose the Magic," Shawn Christopher
13. "Where Love Lies," Allison Limerick
14. "Power of Love," Deee-Lite
15. "Another Sleepless Night," Shawn Christopher

Best House DJs

1. Frankie Knuckles
2. Ron Hardy
3. Larry Levan
4. David Morales
5. "Little" Louis Vega
6. Junior Vasquez
7. Tony Humphries
8. CJ MacIntosh
9. John "Jellybean" Benitez
10. Mike Pickering

Best House Producers

1. Steve "Silk" Hurley
2. David Morales
3. Marshall Jefferson
4. Frankie Knuckles
5. Maurice Joshua
6. "Little" Louie Vega and Kenny "Dope" Gonzalez
7. Roger Sanchez
8. Mood II Swing
9. Shep Pettibone
10. Robert Clivilles and David Cole
11. Brothers in Rhythm
12. Snack Productions
13. Tommy Musto
14. Kerri Chandler
15. The Basement Boys

Larry Flick Picks the Greatest Dance Clubs of All Time

1. PARADISE GARAGE, NEW YORK—Quite simply, it was the room where the late great Larry Levan played mama bird to a nest of underlings. He nurtured and educated them to the true art of turntable mixing and sent them off to spread the magic of dance music.

2. STUDIO 54, NEW YORK—The hall of excessive disco glamour and celebrities. The music was secondary to the fierceness of the folks allowed in. As people clamored for entrance, it was one of the first clubs to turn doormen and bouncers into stars.

3. THE WHEREHOUSE, CHICAGO—The room where the term "house music" was born. During the early eighties, in-house DJ Frankie Knuckles became one of the world's most important

(and gifted) turntable masters by dropping homemade grooves with familiar tunes.

4. SOUND FACTORY, NEW YORK—The world's most famous after-hours venue. DJ Junior Vasquez (and, for a hot second, Frankie Knuckles) gives house-starved partiers a place to go when everyone else has closed shop for the evening. You can work it from late Saturday evening until sometime Sunday afternoon.

5. THE SAINT, NEW YORK—During the eighties, this was the only gay club that mattered. On any given night, you could find a bevy of shirtless muscle men shaking to the hi-NRG anthem of the moment. It hung on to the decadence of the seventies disco era like few other venues.

6. THE TROCADERO, SAN FRANCISCO—One of the rooms where hi-NRG was born. The icy-cool electro grooves of the late Patrick Cowley ruled the roost, while poppers and Sylvester filled the air.

7. THE FUNHOUSE, NEW YORK—Best remembered as the birthplace of John "Jellybean" Benitez's career. Musically, this club deftly bridged the gap between pop music and disco, drawing industry folks to hear Jellybean's unique, homemade remixes of the hits of the day.

8. ODYSSEY: 2001, BROOKLYN—Famous for being the brilliant, light-filled dance floor in *Saturday Night Fever*. Currently named the Spectrum, it still draws oodles of nostalgic tourists for a twirl on the rotating floor where John Travolta shook his ass.

9. ZANZIBAR, NEW JERSEY—The place where the hard, underground New Jersey house sound was created. Then in-house jock Tony Humphries became a world-revered star by showcasing the raw demos of local talent, as well as his own spare, R&B-inflected compositions.

10. OSKO'S, LOS ANGELES—Another club immortalized on film. As the centerpiece of the disco epic *Thank God It's Friday*, Osko's was the epitome of over-the-top decor, glitzy lighting, and throbbing disco beats. It was like stepping into a scene from *Alice in Wonderland*.

Larry Flick is the dance music editor at Billboard.

Why the Lambada Flopped

1. Because this Spanish dance movement was born in France.
2. Because most Americans thought it was the name of a rare bird.
3. Because John Travolta was too old to make a movie about it.
4. Because only women with the flexibility of Marilyn Chambers could arch their backs that far.
5. Because it was a stupid dance.

Hits at the Wedding Dance
The 75 Songs Most Favored by Mobile DJs

1. "Old Time Rock 'n' Roll," Bob Seger
2. "Unchained Melody," Righteous Brothers
3. "Shout," Otis Day/Isley Brothers
4. "Mony, Mony," Billy Idol/Tommy James
5. "Electric Boogie (Slide)," Marcia Griffiths/G.M. Slice
6. "Achy Breaky Heart," Billy Ray Cyrus
7. "Love Shack," The B-52s
8. "Oh, Pretty Woman," Roy Orbison
9. "What I Like About You," The Romantics
10. "Gonna Make You Sweat (Everybody Dance Now)," C&C Music Factory
11. "Twist and Shout," The Beatles
12. "The Twist," Chubby Checker
13. "In the Mood," Glenn Miller
14. "Chicken Dance," Emeralds/Various
15. "Can't Help Falling in Love," Elvis Presley
16. "Hot, Hot, Hot," Arrows/Buster Poindexter
17. "Celebration," Kool and the Gang
18. "You Shook Me All Night Long," AC/DC
19. "Friends in Low Places," Garth Brooks
20. "Unforgettable," Nat King Cole and Natalie Cole
21. "I'm Too Sexy," Right Said Fred
22. "Everything I Do, I Do for You," Bryan Adams
23. "Vogue," Madonna
24. "New York, New York," Frank Sinatra
25. "Keep Your Hands to Yourself," Georgia Satellites
26. "Hurts So Good," John Cougar Mellencamp
27. "Do You Love Me," Contours
28. "Rock Around the Clock," Bill Haley and the Comets
29. "Locomotion," Minogue/Little Eva
30. "What a Wonderful World," Louis Armstrong
31. "Paradise by the Dashboard Lights," Meatloaf
32. "Lady in Red," Chris DeBurgh
33. "Can't Touch This," Hammer
34. "Wonderful Tonight," Eric Clapton
35. "Swing the Mood," Jive Bunny
36. "Don't Rock the Jukebox," Alan Jackson
37. "I've Had the Time of My Life," Medley/Kim Carnes
38. "YMCA," The Village People
39. "Conga," Miami Sound Machine
40. "Crazy," Patsy Cline
41. "Could I Have This Dance," Anne Murray
42. "Great Balls of Fire," Jerry Lee Lewis

43. "Boot Scootin' Boogie," Brooks and Dunn
44. "Just a Gigolo," Louie Prima/David Lee Roth
45. "Forever & Ever, Amen," Randy Travis
46. "Some Kind of Wonderful," Grand Funk Railroad
47. "Move This," Technotronic
48. "Hokey Pokey," Ray Anthony
49. "Everybody, Everybody," Black Box
50. "Bad Moon Risin'," Creedence Clearwater Revival
51. "The Wanderer," Dion
52. "Jump," Kris Kross
53. "Respect," Aretha Franklin
54. "I Got You (I Feel Good)," James Brown
55. "Baby Got Back," Sir Mix-A-Lot
56. "Rock Steady," The Whispers
57. "Push It," Salt-N-Pepa
58. "Thank God I'm a Country Boy," John Denver
59. "Louie, Louie," The Kingsmen
60. "Express Yourself," Madonna
61. "I Saw Her Standing There," The Beatles
62. "Wooly Bully," Sam the Sham and the Pharoahs
63. "Jump," The Pointer Sisters
64. "Brown-Eyed Girl," Van Morrison
65. "Jailhouse Rock," Elvis Presley
66. "Let's Twist Again," Chubby Checker
67. "Pink Cadillac," Bruce Springsteen
68. "La Bamba," Los Lobos/Richie Valens
69. "Tequila," The Champs
70. "Into the Groove," Madonna
71. "When a Man Loves a Woman," Percy Sledge/Michael Bolton
72. "Good Lovin'," The Rascals
73. "You're the Inspiration," Chicago
74. "Joy to the World," Three Dog Night
75. "Rock N' Roll Is King," Three Dog Night

Source: Mobile Beat, *1992 survey.*

DJ Mark the 45 King's 10 Records Guaranteed to Rock a Party

1. "Bra," Cymande
2. "Apache," Michael Veners and the Incredible Bongo Band
3. "Funky Drummer," James Brown

4. "Dance to the Drummer's Beat," Herman Kelley
5. "Catch a Groove," Juice
6. "Get Up and Dance," Freedom
7. "Scratchin'," The Magic Disco Machine
8. "I Just Wanna Do My Thing," Edwin Starr
9. "Seven Minutes of Funk," The Whole Damn Family
10. "Just Begun" The Jimmy Castor Bunch

Source: Source *magazine, June 1993.*

CHAPTER 20

Rhythm and Blues

100 Greatest Number One Rhythm and Blues Hits, 1950–1993

Guarantee: All records made number one on Billboard's *Rhythm and Blues (which have also been termed the Soul or Black) charts. There are no entries for 1964, because in that year,* Billboard *did not compile separate charts for black pop.*

1. "Please Send Me Someone to Love," Percy Mayfield, 1950
2. "Sixty Minute Man," The Dominoes, 1951
3. "Lawdy Miss Clawdy," Lloyd Price, 1952
4. "Juke," Little Walter, 1952
5. "(Mama) He Treats Your Daughter Mean," Ruth Brown, 1953
6. "Crying in the Chapel," Sonny Til and The Orioles, 1953
7. "Money Honey," The Drifters, 1953
8. "Work with Me Annie," The Midnighters, 1954
9. "Earth Angel," The Penguins, 1954
10. "Pledging My Love," Johnny Ace, 1955
11. "Ain't It a Shame," Fats Domino, 1955
12. "Maybellene," Chuck Berry, 1955
13. "The Great Pretender," The Platters, 1955
14. "Long Tall Sally"/"Slippin' and Slidin'," Little Richard, 1955
15. "Fever," Little Willie John, 1956
16. "Blue Monday," Fats Domino, 1957
17. "You Send Me," Sam Cooke, 1957
18. "It's All in the Game," Tommy Edwards, 1958
19. "Lonely Teardrops," Jackie Wilson, 1958
20. "Stagger Lee," Lloyd Price, 1959
21. "There Goes My Baby," The Drifters, 1959
22. "What'd I Say," Ray Charles, 1959
23. "Save the Last Dance for Me," The Drifters, 1960
24. "I Pity the Fool," Bobby Bland, 1961
25. "Mother-in-Law," Ernie K-Doe, 1961
26. "Stand By Me," Ben E. King, 1961
27. "You'll Lose a Good Thing," Barbara Lynn, 1962
28. "Do You Love Me," The Contours, 1962
29. "You've Really Got a Hold On Me," The Miracles, 1963
30. "Fingertips—Pt. 2," Little Stevie Wonder, 1963
31. "Heat Wave," Martha and the Vandellas, 1963
32. "It's All Right," The Impressions, 1963
33. "My Girl," The Temptations, 1965
34. "In the Midnight Hour," Wilson Pickett, 1965
35. "Papa's Got a Brand New Bag," James Brown, 1965
36. "Uptight (Everything's Alright)," Stevie Wonder, 1966

37. "When a Man Loves a Woman," Percy Sledge, 1966
38. "Hold On! I'm A-Comin'," Sam and Dave, 1966
39. "Reach Out I'll Be There," The Four Tops, 1966
40. "Knock on Wood," Eddie Floyd, 1966
41. "You Keep Me Hangin' On," The Supremes, 1966
42. "I Never Loved a Man (The Way I Love You)," Aretha Franklin, 1967
43. "Respect," Aretha Franklin, 1967
44. "Cold Sweat," James Brown, 1967
45. "Funky Broadway," Wilson Pickett, 1967
46. "(Your Love Keeps Lifting Me) Higher and Higher," Jackie Wilson, 1967
47. "Soul Man," Sam and Dave, 1967
48. "I Wish It Would Rain," The Temptations, 1968
49. "Ain't Nothing Like the Real Thing," Marvin Gaye and Tammi Terrell, 1968
50. "Stay in My Corner," The Dells, 1968
51. "Who's Making Love," Johnnie Taylor, 1968
52. "I Heard It Through the Grapevine," Marvin Gaye, 1968
53. "Everyday People," Sly and the Family Stone, 1969
54. "Only the Strong Survive," Jerry Butler, 1969
55. "I Want You Back," The Jackson 5, 1970
56. "Thank You (Falettinme Be Mice Elf Again)," Sly and the Family Stone, 1970
57. "Just My Imagination (Running Away with Me)," The Temptations, 1971
58. "What's Going On," Marvin Gaye, 1971
59. "Family Affair," Sly and the Family Stone, 1971
60. "Have You Seen Her," The Chi-Lites, 1971
61. "Let's Stay Together," Al Green, 1972
62. "(If Loving You Is Wrong) I Don't Want to Be Right," Luther Ingram, 1972
63. "Back Stabbers," The O'Jays, 1972
64. "I'm Still in Love with You," Al Green, 1972
65. "If You Don't Know Me By Now," Harold Melvin and the Bluenotes, 1972
66. "Superstition," Stevie Wonder, 1973
67. "Could It Be I'm Falling in Love," The Spinners, 1973
68. "Let's Get It On," Marvin Gaye, 1973
69. "Lookin' for a Love," Bobby Womack, 1974
70. "Shining Star," Earth, Wind and Fire, 1975
71. "Low Rider," War, 1975
72. "Wake Up Everybody," Harold Melvin and the Bluenotes, 1976
73. "Flash Light," Parliament, 1978
74. "One Nation Under a Groove," Funkadelic, 1978
75. "Le Freak," Chic, 1978

76. "Hot Stuff," Donna Summer, 1979
77. "Ain't No Stoppin' Us Now," McFadden and Whitehead, 1979
78. "(not just) Knee Deep," Parliament, 1979
79. "Rock with You," Michael Jackson, 1980
80. "Master Blaster (Jammin')," Stevie Wonder, 1980
81. "Burn Rubber (Why You Want to Hurt Me)," The Gap Band, 1981
82. "Sexual Healing," Marvin Gaye, 1982
83. "Billie Jean," Michael Jackson, 1983
84. "Atomic Dog," George Clinton, 1983
85. "Beat It," Michael Jackson, 1983
86. "When Doves Cry," Prince, 1984
87. "I Feel for You," Chaka Khan, 1984
88. "Nightshift," The Commodores, 1985
89. "What Have You Done for Me Lately," Janet Jackson, 1986
90. "Word Up," Cameo, 1986
91. "Fake," Alexander O'Neal, 1987
92. "Wishing Well," Terence Trent D'Arby, 1988
93. "Don't Be Cruel," Bobby Brown, 1988
94. "Me Myself and I," De La Soul, 1989
95. "Keep on Movin'," Soul II Soul, 1989
96. "Poison," Bell Biv Devoe, 1990
97. "Forever My Lady," Jodeci, 1991
98. "End of the Road," Boyz II Men, 1992
99. "My Lovin' (You're Never Gonna Get It)," En Vogue, 1992
100. "(Ain't Nuthin' But a) 'G' Thang," Dr. Dre, 1993

The Dictionary of Soul

The second edition of our dictionary is more comprehensive than the first, though both include only records that actually charted in the United States. The first edition's Dictionary of Soul, however, included just twenty-five records because at that time, we were unaware of any charted record whose title began with the letter X, except Blondie's "X-Offender," which hardly qualifies as soul, or even R&B. The editors would like to thank Joel Whitburn, whose Top R&B Singles now extends back to 1942, for resolving this problem. "X-Temporaneous Boogie," it turns out, was hidden from view because Whitburn's previous edition began in 1949, and it charted in 1948.

1. "Ace of Spades," O. V. Wright
2. "B-A-B-Y," Carla Thomas
3. "Can I Get a Witness," Marvin Gaye

4. "Doggin' Around," Jackie Wilson
5. "Everybody Needs Somebody to Love," Solomon Burke
6. "Fa-Fa-Fa-Fa-Fa (Sad Song)," Otis Redding
7. "Get Up, I Feel Like Being a Sex Machine," James Brown
8. "Hold On! I'm A-Comin'," Sam and Dave
9. "I (Who Have Nothing)," Ben E. King
10. "Jamie," Eddie Holland
11. "Knock on Wood," Eddie Floyd
12. "Love Makes a Woman," Barbara Acklin
13. "My Girl," The Temptations
14. "Need Your Love So Bad," Little Willie John
15. "Only the Strong Survive," Jerry Butler
16. "Precious, Precious," Jackie Moore
17. "Quicksand," Martha and the Vandellas
18. "Respect," Aretha Franklin
19. "S.Y.S.L.J.F.M. (The Letter Song)," Joe Tex
20. "Temptation 'Bout to Get Me," The Knight Brothers
21. "Um, Um, Um, Um, Um, Um," Major Lance
22. "Voice Your Choice," The Radiants
23. "We're Gonna Make It," Little Milton
24. "X-Temporaneous Boogie," Camille Howard Trio
25. "Yield Not to Temptation," Bobby "Blue" Bland
26. "Zing! Went the Strings of My Heart," The Trammps

Sonny Rollins Lists His 10 Favorite Records

1. *Amazing Grace*, Aretha Franklin
2. *Head Hunters*, Herbie Hancock
3. *Songs in the Key of Life*, Stevie Wonder
4. "Knock Me a Kiss," Louis Jordan and His Tympany Five
5. "Body and Soul," Coleman Hawkins
6. "Lover Man," Billie Holiday
7. "I Can't Get Started," Bunny Berrigan
8. "Ko-Ko," Charlie Parker
9. "I'm Gonna Sit Right Down and Write Myself a Letter," Fats Waller
10. "Afternoon of a Basie-ite," Lester Young

Sonny Rollins is one of the all-time greatest jazz saxophonists. In his forty-year career, he has worked with some of the top names in music, including the Rolling Stones, and recorded a series of brilliant albums. Most recently, he's recorded for Blue Note and literally dozens of his vintage LPs from the fifties and sixties have been reissued on CD.

John Lee Hooker's 10 Favorite Recording Artists

1. Muddy Waters
2. B. B. King
3. Albert Collins
4. Bobby Bland
5. Otis Spann
6. George Benson
7. Howlin' Wolf
8. Little Walter
9. Jimmy Reed
10. Lightnin' Hopkins

Sam Moore's Top 10 Soul Men and Soul Women

THE WOMEN

1. GERRI HIRSHEY, my friend, the journalist, author and Sammy Z's mommy
2. ARETHA FRANKLIN, when she's sitting at the 88s and singing
3. MARY WELLS, because of her courage and hope to have lived
4. ANNIE LENNOX, who almost blew me off the stage with my own song, "Wrap It Up"
5. BARBARA JORDAN, her essence
6. YMA SUMAC, just watch the movie
7. DINAH WASHINGTON, she was baaaaddd
8. MAVIS STAPLES, she'll get you there
9. SHIRLEY CAESAR, amen and hallelujah!
10. JOYCE MCRAE-MOORE, my wife and manager who I have finally realized must have soul to spare to put up with me

THE MEN

1. LEE ATWATER, Willie Horton aside, the man loved, knew, and felt the music
2. ISAAC HAYES AND DAVID PORTER, they wrote 'em, I sang 'em
3. RAY CHARLES, what can I say?
4. BILLY PRESTON, talent, talent, talent
5. LITTLE WILLIE JOHN, great singer, crazy human, what a toot, I mean, hot!
6. JACKIE WILSON, the essence, the reason I sing secular music
7. RICH PERLMAN, lawyer man par excellance
8. SAM COOKE, all I really have to say is "Sam"
9. DONALD "DUCK" DUNN, of Booker T. and the MG's fame, and the best bass player I know
10. BRUCE SPRINGSTEEN, if he was any better, they'd have named him Dave

Sam Moore, the world's greatest soul singer and Rock and Roll Hall of Famer, helped define "soul" with his great hits with Sam and Dave, whose stage show also packed an almighty atomic-scale wallop. He's currently recording as a solo artist and occasional Tapehead.

Most Unlikely Rhythm and Blues Hits

Guarantee: All these records made the Top Twenty of the Billboard *Rhythm and Blues, Soul, or Black charts.*

1. "Dede Dinah," Frankie Avalon
2. "Love Letters in the Sand," Pat Boone
3. "Sussudio," Phil Collins
4. "The Doo-Bop Song," Miles Davis
5. "Disco Duck," Rick Dees and His Cast of Idiots
6. "Soul Makossa," Manu Dibango
7. "The Humpty Dance," Digital Underground
8. "Teen Angel," Mark Dinning
9. "The Theme from *A Summer Place*," Percy Faith
10. "Rock Me Amadeus," Falco
11. "Exodus," Ferrante and Teicher
12. "It's My Party,"[1] Lesley Gore
13. "Ain't Got No Home," Clarence "Frogman" Henry
14. "I Found Out Too Late," Jackie and the Starlites
15. "Surf City," Jan and Dean
16. "If I Had a Hammer," Trini Lopez
17. "Jam On It," Newcleus
18. "Funky Worm," The Ohio Players
19. "Hey Paula," Paul and Paula
20. "Pink Shoe Laces," Dodie Stevens
21. "Banned in the U.S.A.," 2 Live Crew
22. "Ice Ice Baby,"[1] Vanilla Ice
23. "Calcutta," Lawrence Welk
24. "Bacon Fat," Andre Williams
25. "Respect Yourself," Bruce Willis

---

[1] Number-one record.

The 20 Most Influential Blues Performers

1. Robert Johnson
2. Muddy Waters
3. B. B. King
4. Howlin' Wolf
5. Bessie Smith
6. Little Walter
7. Son House
8. T-Bone Walker
9. John Lee Hooker
10. Jimmy Reed
11. Elmore James
12. Sonny Boy Williamson II (Rice Miller)
13. Bobby "Blue" Bland
14. Charley Patton
15. Otis Spann
16. Ma Rainey
17. Freddie King
18. Blind Lemon Jefferson
19. Big Bill Broonzy
20. Leadbelly

15 Great Electric Blues Guitarists

1. B. B. King
2. T-Bone Walker
3. Freddie King
4. Hubert Sumlin
5. Jimmy Rogers
6. Otis Rush
7. Ike Turner
8. Muddy Waters
9. Eric Clapton
10. Pat Hare
11. Son Seals
12. Hound Dog Taylor
13. Albert King
14. Lefty Bates
15. Chris Thomas

Muddy Waters's Dream Band

1. Otis Spann, piano
2. Little Walter, harmonica
3. Fred Below, drums
4. Big Crawford, bass
5. Willie Dixon, bass
6. Pat Hare, guitar
7. Jimmy Rogers, guitar

Muddy Waters took the Delta blues from Mississippi to Chicago, electrified it, and became a legend who lived his dream: Every one of the above musicians played in his bands, at one point or another, along with a host of others who form the cream of the crop among electric blues players. Waters inspired an incredible number of rock performers, including the Rolling Stones, who took their name from one of his first electric blues songs. He continued to record and tour until his death in 1983. His last public appearance came as special guest star at an Eric Clapton show.

Eddie Floyd's Favorite Soul Singers

1. Johnny Ace
2. William Bell
3. Jesse Belvin
4. Sam Cooke
5. Little Willie John
6. Otis Redding
7. Johnnie Taylor
8. Joe Tex
9. Chuck Willis
10. Jackie Wilson

Note: "Tell Wilson Pickett to forgive me," says Floyd.

Eddie Floyd wrote soul classics like "Knock on Wood," "634-5789," "Raise Your Hand," and "Ninety-Nine and a Half (Won't Do)," which have been hits for himself, Wilson Pickett, and other artists. He still actively tours and records.

Allen Ginsberg's Favorite Blues Records

1. "James Alley Blues," Richard "Rabbit" Brown
2. "Washington D.C. Hospital Center Blues," "Drunken Spree," Skip James
3. "Jim Crow Blues" (a rare, sublime political blues), "Birmingham Jail," "Irene," "Black Girl," etc., Leadbelly
4. "See See Rider Blues," "Jelly Bean Blues," Ma Rainey
5. "Baby Doll," Bessie Smith
6. "Don't Explain," "I Gotta Right to Sing the Blues," Billie Holiday
7. "Long Tall Sally," Little Richard
8. "Cannon Ball Blues," Frank Hutchinson
9. "Blueberry Hill," etc., Fats Domino
10. "I Got a Woman," "Georgia on My Mind," etc., Ray Charles
11. "Waiting for the Train," "Way Out on the Mountain," "Mule Skinner Blues," "T for Texas," "The Mystery of Number Five," Jimmie Rodgers
12. "Cold, Cold Heart," "Your Cheating Heart," Hank Williams
13. "Absolutely Sweet Marie," "It's all Over Now, Baby Blue," "Idiot Wind," "In the Garden," Bob Dylan

14. Oeuvre, John Lennon
15. Oeuvre, Mick Jagger
16. "Dildo Song," "Raspberry Song," "Keep It Clean in Between"
    (see *Asshole Poems and Smiling Vegetable Songs*, City Lights, 1978),
    Peter Orlovsky

Allen Ginsberg is America's leading bard. His interests have ranged from Tibetan Buddhism to singing the blues, which he's done on several albums. Many of the more obscure performers on this list, including Rabbit Brown, can be found on the Folkways Records American Folk Music Anthology.

The Pointer Sisters' 10 Favorite Harmony Groups

1. The Pointer Sisters
2. Seals and Crofts
3. The Temptations
4. The Jacksons
5. Sister Sledge
6. The O'Jays
7. Queen
8. Gladys Knight and the Pips
9. Earth, Wind and Fire
10. The Oak Ridge Boys

The Pointer Sisters are best known for their pop hits, "Jump (For My Love)," "Slow Hand," "Yes We Can Can Can," "Fire," and "He's So Shy," but the Oakland-based trio sings in a wide variety of styles from modern rhythm and blues to forties pop. This list remains unchanged from the first edition.

Carla Thomas's 5 Favorite Sweet-Soul Singers

1. Dinah Washington
2. Otis Redding
3. Larry Graham
4. Aaron Neville
5. Sam Cooke

Carla Thomas is best known for such hits as "B-A-B-Y" and "Gee Whiz," and for a series of duets with Otis Redding, especially "Tramp." The daughter of Rufus Thomas, Carla was one of the first acts signed to Stax Records. She remains active as a live performer.

The 10 Funkiest James Brown Song Titles

1. "I Don't Want Nobody to Give Me Nothing (Open Up the Door, I'll Get It Myself)"
2. "Hot Pants (She Got to Use What She Got to Get What She Wants)"
3. "Say It Loud, I'm Black and I'm Proud"
4. "Get Up, I Feel Like Being a Sex Machine"
5. "It's Too Funky in Here"
6. "Rapp Payback (Where Iz Moses)"
7. "Papa's Got a Brand New Bag"
8. "I Got Ants in My Pants and I Want to Dance"
9. "For Goodness Sakes, Look at Those Cakes"
10. "Let a Man Come In and Do the Popcorn"

Most Surprising Influences on George Clinton and P-Funk (Excluding James Brown, Jimi Hendrix, and Sly Stone)

1. Frankie Lymon and the Teenagers—Inspired a teenaged George to want to sing for a living.
2. The British Invasion—Before hitting it big, George produced soulful cover versions of a few Beatles songs; worked with British-born rocker Ruth Copeland.
3. Iggy and the Stooges, and the MC5—Their freaked-out stage shows in Detroit pointed the way for the early Funkadelic.
4. Frank Zappa—His approach to packaging influenced Funkadelic album-cover artist/conceptualist Pedro Bell.
5. Sun Ra—Let George know that space was the place.
6. Smokey Robinson—Taught George the importance of strong pop hooks.
7. Process Church of the Final Judgment—Quasi-satanic hippy cult's tracts published on first four Funkadelic LPs.

5 Greatest P-Funk Albums of All Time

1. *Let's Take It to the Stage*, Funkadelic (1975)—Track for track, the best rock album most rock fans never heard of
2. *Mothership Connection*, Parliament (1975)—Gave the people what they wanted when they wanted it and they wanted it all the time
3. *Standing on the Verge of Getting It On*, Funkadelic (1974)
4. *Funkentelechy vs. the Placebo Syndrome*, Parliament (1977)
5. *One Nation Under a Groove*, Funkadelic (1978)

P-Funk's 5 Most Transcendent Individual Instrumental Moments on Wax

1. Eddie Hazel's guitar solo throughout "Maggot Brain"—Technically extraordinary, emotionally serious. The greatest work by the least appreciated rock guitarist of all time.
2. Bernie Worrell's organ and synthesizer duet throughout "Atmosphere"—A slippery liturgy that displays what David Byrne, Jack Bruce, Bill Laswell, and not enough others saw in this classically trained virtuoso.
3. Bootsy Collins's bass playing in "Munchies for Your Love"—Definition of Space Bass; one of the very few things in music that can be called "new."
4. Tyrone Lampkin's drumming at the start of "Cosmic Slop"—Stunningly precise drumming that actually sets a mood.
5. The Horny Horns' blowing from start to finish in "Gamin' On Ya"—Fred Wesley, Maceo Parker, and company demonstrate their vital contribution to the P, with muscular yet melodic ensemble work.

10 Greatest P-Funk Songs of All Time

1. "One Nation Under a Groove" (1978)—A masterpiece of sonic texture
2. "Cosmic Slop" (1973)—Satanic gospel
3. "Maggot Brain" (1971)—A spiritual as sung by electric guitar

4. "P. Funk (Wants to Get Funked Up)" (1975)—Birth of a my-thology
5. "Funkentelechy" (1977)—Free speech is high finance
6. "The Goose" (1974)—Mind-expanding gutbucket groove
7. "Red-Hot Mama"/"Vital Juices" (1975)—A-side plus B-side equals Eddie Hazel's best up-tempo guitar solo
8. "Aqua Boogie" (1978)—Layer upon layer of Bernie Worrell keyboard wizardry
9. "(Not Just) Knee Deep" (1979)—Operatic party music
10. "I Wanna Know if It's Good to You" (1970)—Of course it is!

5 Classic P-Funk Party Chants

1. "Shit! God damn! Get off your ass and jam!"
2. "If you ain't gonna get it on, take you dead-ass home!"
3. "We want the funk! Give up the funk! Ow, we need the funk! Gotta have the funk!"
4. "Funk gettin' ready to go, funk gettin' ready to roll!"
5. "We be funkin' over here! Over there ain't shit!"

Most Obvious P-Funk Ripoffs to Hit *Billboard*'s R&B Singles Chart

1. "I Don't Believe You Want to Get Up and Dance (Oops, Upside Your Head)," The Gap Band (1980)
2. "For Those Who Like to Groove," Ray Parker, Jr. (1980)
3. "Wonder Worm," Captain Sky (1978)
4. "The Long Stroke," ADC Band (1978)
5. "Wide Receiver," Michael Henderson (1980)
6. "Ready or Not," Herbie Hancock (1979)
7. "Dukey Stick," George Duke (1978)

5 Best Uses of a P-Funk Sample or Hook in a Hip-Hop Song

1. "The Humpty-Dance," Digital Underground (Sample: Parlia-ment's "Let's Play House")

2. "Me, Myself, and I," De La Soul (Funkadelic's "Knee Deep")
3. "We Want Eazy," Eazy-E (Bootsy's Rubber Band's "We Want Bootsy")
4. "Everybody Get Up," Salt-N-Pepa (Parliament's "All Your Goodies Are Gone")
5. "Let Me Ride," Dr. Dre, featuring Snoop Doggy Dogg (Parliament's "Mothership Connection")

No Sell Out: 25 R&B, Soul, and Rap Stars Without Crossover Hits

None of these artists ever made the Top Forty of Billboard's *Hot 100, its pop single chart.*

ARTIST	(NUMBER OF R&B CHART SINGLES (THROUGH 1992)
1. Fatback[1]	31
2. Melba Moore	30
3. Al Hudson & the Soul Partners; One Way featuring Al Hudson	28
4. Maze featuring Frankie Beverly	26
5. Syl Johnson	19
6. Albert King	19
7. Phyllis Hyman[1]	18
8. Grandmaster Flash/Grandmaster Melle Mel & the Furious Five	17
9. Lakeside	17
10. O. V. Wright	17
11. Herbie Hancock	16
12. Michael Henderson	16
13. Z. Z. Hill	16
14. Muddy Waters[1]	16
15. Willie Hutch	15
16. Little Walter[1]	15
17. Angela Bofill[1]	12
18. Leroy Hutson[1]	12
19. Kleer[1]	12
20. Whodini	12
21. Me'lisa Morgan	11
22. Mtume	11
23. Zapp	11

24. George Clinton[1]   10
25. Public Enemy   9

Note: These are by no means ALL *the R&B, soul and rap artists of stature who haven't made the pop charts, just an outrageous sampling. Every such artist has his, her, or their pop chart stature diminished by broadcast/retail/audience racism.*

---

[1] Never had a single Hot 100 entry at all.

25 Great Blue-Eyed Soul Singers

1. The Righteous Brothers
2. Mitch Ryder
3. Eddie Hinton
4. Steve Winwood
5. Daryl Hall
6. The Rascals
7. Tony Joe White
8. Eric Burdon
9. Delaney and Bonnie
10. David Lasley
11. Mick Jagger
12. Michael McDonald
13. Lisa Stansfield
14. Roy Head
15. Peter Wolf
16. Boy George
17. Dr. John the Nighttripper
18. Lisa Keith
19. The Soul Survivors
20. Len Barry
21. Paul Carrack
22. George Michael
23. Willy Deville
24. The Rationals
25. Janis Joplin

It'll Never Fit if You Force It
The 10 Phoniest White Soulboys

1. Michael Bolton
2. David Clayton-Thomas
3. Billy Vera
4. Robert Palmer
5. George Thorogood
6. Marky Mark
7. Snow
8. Kevin Rowland (Dexy's Midnight Runners)
9. Glenn Frey
10. Vanilla Ice

Taking the A Train
Acceptable White Hip-Hoppers

1. MC Serch
2. Pete Nice
3. Everlast
4. DJ Muggs (Cypress Hill)
5. The Beastie Boys
6. DJ Fuze (Digital Underground)
7. Rick Rubin

Honorable mention: Blondie

Soul and R&B Veterans Who Made Comebacks in the Eighties and Nineties

1. TINA TURNER
The first true solo successes of her career came with *Private Dancer* (1984) and *Break Every Rule* (1986), both of which went Top Five pop, with *Private Dancer* a multiple Grammy winner, too. Her stage shows (which is to say, in part, her fabulous legs) once more stopped shows, and her voice rocked and rasped as beautifully, brilliantly, powerfully as ever. Though the commercial pace slacked with subsequent releases—and an injudicious four-year layoff—Tina's talents finally had the recognition they'd always deserved, and she seemed finally to have acquired a lifestyle of great ease, even if she had to overthrow Ike and Jesus for Europe and Buddha to gain it.

2. MARVIN GAYE
Hadn't had a hit since 1977 when 1982's "Sexual Healing" took him back to number one (pop *and* R&B). Gaye certainly would have had numerous followups, probably a full revival of his career, had he not gotten into a dispute with his father and been shot to death.

3. RUTH BROWN
Following three decades of neglect, Brown's career began to pick up when she landed the job of hosting National Public Radio's R&B radio programs, "Harlem Hit Parade" and "Blues Stage," then got a further lift from a starring role in John Waters's film *Hairspray*. She won a Tony for her appearance in the Broadway blues revue *Black and Blue*, and a Grammy for her series of fine, torchy albums on Fantasy. She also appeared frequently on TV, as both singer and actress, spoke before Congress on the ripoffs R&B artists of her generation suffered and suffer, led the forming of the Rhythm and Blues Foundation, saw her great Atlantic sides reissued, and generally made herself resplendent.

4. JAMES BROWN

His (highly unjust, non–drug related) prison term seemed to do his career more good than harm. But mainly it was hip-hop that elevated the Godfather's image from has-been to foundation stone. Sampled everywhere (there would literally *be* no rap industry without "Funky Drummer") and reissued almost fortnightly, including the majestic four-disc retrospective *Startime*, perhaps the greatest album ever assembled.

5. JOHN LEE HOOKER

After an eighteen-year absence from the charts, 1989's *The Healer*, made with such associates as Bonnie Raitt, Carlos Santana, and Los Lobos, brought him back with a roar. His televised and recorded duets with Raitt became legendary; his stage shows acquired renewed dynamism. By the mid-nineties Hooker stood alone as the last of the great first-generation bluesmen.

6. PATTI LaBELLE

Her career seemed hollowed out and discarded by 1980, but with 1981's *The Spirit's in It*, the ever-histrionic one began a new rise, abetted by Broadway and TV appearances. By 1986, she'd scored the first number-one album of her career with *Winner in You*, and though she surely could not sustain *that* pace, she's never been off the scene since.

7. ARETHA FRANKLIN

After a chart drought from 1977 through 1980, she hit with "United Together" and "Love All the Hurt Away" (with George Benson) and spent most of the mid-eighties at or near the top of the R&B charts, with occasional crossover forays like "Freeway of Love" and "Who's Zoomin' Who," and her duets with Annie Lennox and George Michael. Unfortunately, she's saddled with Arista Records president Clive Davis's velveteen schlock approach to material and arrangements, but Aretha remains possessed of popular music's finest voice, so it's only a matter of when, not if, she'll be back.

8. BOOKER T. AND THE MGs

Toured with Neil Young and recorded for Sony in 1993. Several years previously, began touring again with various drummers, notably Anton Figg of the World's Most Dangerous Band, filling in for the late Al Jackson, Jr. Booker T. recorded with Soul Asylum, among others; Steve Cropper became more ubiquitous than ever.

9. AL GREEN

Technically, Green never went away—he just turned to singing gospel. But nobody outside church paid much attention to his singing until he returned to pop in 1987 with "Everything's Gonna Be Alright," an immediate R&B hit. Although he never achieved his 1970s preeminence, he's had substantial pop success since then, including 1989's "As Long As We're Together," with Al B. Sure!

and as featured vocalist on several tracks made by producer Arthur Baker under Baker's own name.

10. CHARLES BROWN

The crown prince of forties blues balladry found himself in demand once more, not just to sing "Merry Christmas Baby" and "Please Come Home for Christmas" at Berkeley's New Year's Eve party at Chez Panisse, but to open a whole tour for Bonnie Raitt, to make a series of distinguished, dignified new albums for Rounder, and to play cozy, sensuous blues in clubs coast to coast.

11. NAT "KING" COLE

A quarter-century after his death, his songs, and even more crucially, his tape-recorded voice proved indispensable in reviving his daughter Natalie's flagging career.

12. CHUBBY CHECKER

Returned to the charts, 1988, with the Fat Boys revival of "The Twist."

apparent to the world's second-largest porn fortune to duke it any-time. It's unlikely either is capable of putting up a decent fight.

17. "HIV BLUES," DAVE RAY AND TONY GLOVER—Harrowing account of the death of one of Glover's old girlfriends, from AIDS.

18. "THE HUSTLER," ERIC ANDERSEN—A particularly jaundiced parable of the early Bob Dylan, by a folkie contemporary (one could hardly say "peer") who'd yet to go electric.

19. "I'M NOT BRUCE," RICK SPRINGFIELD—The Aussie soap opera/bubble-pop star's plaint re being mixed up with that guy from Jersey with a similar last name.

20. "JAN," MARVIN GAYE—About his second wife-to-be, Janis Hunter, then a California high-school student.

21. "JENNIE LEE," JAN AND DEAN—Ode to a stripper they'd seen work a club in downtown L.A.

22. "JOEY," BOB DYLAN—Homage to gangster Joey Gallo. Not the worst song he's written but close.

23. "JUST THE WAY YOU ARE," BILLY JOEL—Composed as a birthday present for his then-wife (and then-manager), Elizabeth. No one knows if Billy ever sang it to Christie Brinkley but as of 1993, he no longer sings it in concert.

24. "PRIDE (IN THE NAME OF LOVE)," U2—Concerning the life and times of Gandhian Baptist Dr. Martin Luther King. One suspects that not even that ultragenerous heart could bring itself to agree with the idea that his assassins "took his life / But they could not take his pride" somehow represents an actual *insight* about his achievement.

25. "KKK BITCH," BODY COUNT—Ice-T's fantasy about having group sex with Tipper Gore's nieces. Apparently, not even *his* stomach is strong enough to imagine having sex with Tipper herself.

26. "THE LATE, GREAT JOHNNY ACE," PAUL SIMON—Meditation upon the deaths of John Lennon and Johnny Ace, two great rock and rollers gone before their time.

27. "LAYLA," DEREK AND THE DOMINOES—Expression of Eric Clapton's frustrated love for Patti Boyd Harrison, then married to his friend, Beatle George. True love won out and Eric and Patti were joined, though not permanently. To hear the aggravating details of their actual wedded bliss, check out "Wonderful Tonight," Eric's deeply sarcastic song about the aggravations of waiting for her to finish getting dressed for dinner. (We're not making this up.)

28. "LESS THAN ZERO," ELVIS COSTELLO—A response to seeing Oswald Moseley, the British fascist leader of the thirties, rehabilitated in a mid-seventies television interview.

29. "LENNY BRUCE," BOB DYLAN—Homage to the world's greatest comedian. Worse than "Joey."

30. "LINDA," JAN AND DEAN—In 1947, Jack Lawrence visited his attorney, Lee Eastman, and was entranced by his four-year-old daughter, Linda. So he went home and wrote a song for her. Jan and Dean grew up to have a hit with a rock 'n' roll revamping of it. Linda grew up to become Mrs. Paul McCartney. Neither of the McCartneys have ever performed "Linda," at least publicly, though Linda might profitably add it to her rather limited musical repertoire.

31. "LONG TIME GONE," CROSBY, STILLS AND NASH—David Crosby's eulogy for Robert F. Kennedy.

32. "NEBRASKA," BRUCE SPRINGSTEEN—An account of Charles Starkweather and Carol Fugate, Lincoln's mass-murdering joyriders of the mid-fifties.

33. "NIGHTSHIFT," THE COMMODORES—Eulogy for Marvin Gaye and Jackie Wilson.

34. "NO VASELINE," ICE CUBE—About N.W.A, his former group, and their manager, Jerry Heller. The title is not a safe sex reference.

35. "OH, CAROL," NEIL SEDAKA—Written about Neil's high-school crush on Carole King.

36. "PEGGY SUE," BUDDY HOLLY—Buddy almost chickened out and called this one "Cindy Lou" but Jerry Allison prevailed upon him to name it after Jerry's girlfriend, Peggy Sue Gerrow. Allison and Peggy Sue later married.

37. "RODNEY K," WILLIE D—About Rodney King, centerpoint of 1992's Los Angeles urban insurrection. In an uncensored world, the title would conform to what Willie, a member of the Geto Boys, actually proclaims: "*Fuck* Rodney King."

38. "ROSANNA," TOTO—Written about actor Rosanna Arquette, then going out with Toto's guitarist, Steve Lukather.

39. "ROXANNE, ROXANNE," UTFO FEATURING FULL FORCE—Written for the finest girl on the block, who turned out to be *not* Roxanne Shanté but the Real Roxanne. We think.

40. "SAD-EYED LADY OF THE LOWLANDS," BOB DYLAN—Tribute to his future wife, Sara Lowndes.

41. "SHINE ON YOU CRAZY DIAMOND," PINK FLOYD—Mournful song about the group's original leader, Syd Barrett, whose nervous breakdown thrust the group into the hands of "Shine On" composer Roger Waters.

42. "SONG TO WOODY," BOB DYLAN—Homage to Woody Guthrie, Dylan's first folk music inspiration.

43. *SONGS FOR 'DRELLA*, LOU REED AND JOHN CALE—Opera about Andy Warhol, their old pal and putative manager from the Velvet Underground days.

44. *THE SOUL CAGES*, STING—Song cycle inspired by the death of his father.

45. "STAY FREE," THE CLASH—Written and sung by Mick Jones for an old friend who'd just returned from prison.

46. "TEARS IN HEAVEN," ERIC CLAPTON—Composed and performed by Eric Clapton about his grief and feelings of unworthiness after the death of his son, Connor.

47. "TONIGHT'S THE NIGHT," NEIL YOUNG—In memoriam roadie Bruce Berry and guitarist Danny Whitten of Crazy Horse, both of whom had recently overdosed and died.

48. "WENDY," THE BEACH BOYS—Brian Wilson wrote this fantasy of young love for his daughter, Wendy, who twenty years later wrecked it with the wimpiness of Wilson-Phillips.

49. "YOU GAVE ME THE ANSWER," PAUL McCARTNEY—Dedicated to Gene Kelly, Fred Astaire, and Lenny Bruce.

50. "YOU'RE SO VAIN," CARLY SIMON—Dozens of rumors about the subject of this vicious put-down, since writer-producer Simon had many affairs with famous (and famously vain) men. The consensus seems to be that the (deserving) victim is Warren Beatty, although Mick Jagger probably still thinks it's about him —he sings on it, after all.

Top 30 Songs About Elvis

1. "American Roulette," Robbie Robertson
2. "Big Train from Memphis," John Fogerty
3. "Black Velvet," Alannah Myles
4. "Bloc Bloc Bloc," Orchestral Manoeuvres in the Dark
5. "Blue Moon Revisited," Cowboy Junkies
6. "Bye Bye Johnny," Bruce Springsteen
7. "Calling Elvis," Dire Straits
8. "Elvis and Marilyn," Leon Russell
9. "Elvis and Me," Jimmy Webb
10. "Elvis Has Left the Building," Frank Zappa
11. "Elvis Is Dead," Living Colour
12. "Elvis Is Everywhere," Mojo Nixon
13. "Elvis on Velvet," The Stray Cats
14. "Elvis Presley and America," U2
15. "Elvis' Corvette," Didjits
16. "Elvis' Rolls Royce," Was Not Was (with Leonard Cohen)
17. "From Galway to Graceland," Richard Thompson
18. "Graceland," Paul Simon
19. "Happy Birthday Elvis," Loudon Wainwright III
20. "Hey Memphis," LaVern Baker
21. "Jesus Mentioned," Warren Zevon
22. "Man in the Moon," R.E.M.[1]
23. "Me and Elvis," Human Radio
24. "Moondog," Prefab Sprout
25. "My Boy Elvis," Janis Martin

26. "My My, Hey Hey (Out of the Blue)," Neil Young[1]
27. "Queen Elvis," Robin Hitchcock
28. "Riding with the King," John Hiatt
29. "Tupelo," Nick Cave
30. "What Would Elvis Do?" C. C. Chapman

---

[1] *This list was compiled by Peter Bochan, who collects Elvis junk when he is not producing* All Mixed Up *for New York's WBAI and* Short Cuts *for an assortment of stations, including National Public Radio each New Year. We mention this because the songs indicated may not seem to be about Elvis to ears less acutely tuned than his.*

5 Albums About Elvis

1. *The King and I*, The Residents
2. *The Last Temptation of Elvis*, Various Artists
3. *Elvis Mania*, Various Artists
4. *Honeymoon in Vegas*, Various Artists Soundtrack
5. *Un-Led-Ed*, Dread Zeppelin

Brian Keizer Picks 12 Songs About Mick and Keith (or the Whole Boys' Club en Masse)

1. "Live with Me," The Rolling Stones: "My best friend he shoots water rats and feeds 'em to his geese," a portrait of Keith at Redlands before the blaze.

2. "Jigsaw Puzzle," The Rolling Stones: "The singer he is angry 'bout being thrown to the lions/and the bass player looks nervous about the girls outside/the drummer he's so shattered from having to keep on time/and the guitar players they are damaged, they've been outcasts all their lives."

3. "Torn and Frayed," The Rolling Stones: Portrait of Keith through Jagger's cocaine keyhole.

4. "Loving Cup," The Rolling Stones: Mick is the sun. Keith is the moon. Mick is the dice. Keith is the card. Mick is up. Keith is down. The upstroke to the downstroke of "Torn and Frayed."

5. "Shine a Light," The Rolling Stones: Funeral for a certain friend that Mick wishes wouldn't check out so soon.

6. "Let It Loose," The Rolling Stones: Mick finds love. Wants Keith to find it before death finds him.

7. "Jail Guitar Doors," The Clash: Last verse is about Keith's bust and then-impending sentencing in Toronto.

8. "Keith Don't Go," Nils Lofgren: Nils warns Keith (after the fact) not to go to a town called Toronto.

9. "Monkey Man," The Rolling Stones: "All my friends are junkies, that ain't really true." Oh, really?

10. "Sleep Tonight," The Rolling Stones: Dirge for the band that Mick's disinterest is killing. Keith's first great love inspires one of the Stones' greatest ballads. Of what "they" have done to Mick: "They robbed you of your dignity, they even steal your heart from me."

11. "You Don't Move Me," Keith Richards: Keith's first solo outing and he pitches a bitch against "the bitch" like Dylan used to know how to.

12. "Mixed Emotions," The Rolling Stones: The band is back together and ready to reap the cash rewards of being one of the greatest intact social histories in the world as we know it. But first, Jagger has some things to get off of his chest. Keith says this one should be called "Mick's Emotions." Jagger says he wrote it about some woman he knows.

Do Ya Think I'm Sexy?
Rock Stars and Models, an Ongoing Saga

1. John Cougar Mellencamp and Elaine Irwin
2. Axl Rose and Stephanie Seymour
3. David Bowie and Iman
4. Billy Joel and Christie Brinkley
5. Adam Clayton and Naomi Campbell
6. Simon LeBon and Yasmin Parvaneh
7. Michael Jackson and Brooke Shields (admittedly a stretch)
8. Mick Jagger and Jerry Hall and Carla Bruni
9. Eric Clapton and Naomi Campbell, and Carla Bruni and Patti Boyd
10. Bobby Brown and Whitney Houston (a former fashion model)
12. Chris Isaak and Helena Christiansen
13. Bruce Springsteen and Julianne Phillips
14. Ric Ocasek and Pauline Porizkova
15. Rod Stewart and Rachel Hunter
16. Nick Kamen and Talia Soto
17. Keith Richards and Patty Hansen

Sam Moore's Top 10 Daves

1. DAVE MARSH, writer, author, journalist, and sometimes singer for a really weird band of his peers.

2. DAVID HINCKLEY, whom you would never call "Dave." He writes for the *New York Daily News*.

3. DAVE HOEKSTRA, writer for the *Chicago Sun-Times*.

4. DAVID STARK, another you'd never call "Dave." Publisher of *Songplugger*, a great British music industry resource.

5. DAVID SANBORN, sax man par excellence; not a guy you'd call "Dave," either.

6. DAVE STEWART, very, very eurythmic guy.

7. DAVID GILMOUR, amazing Pink axe man.

8. DAVID HIRSHEY, *Esquire* editor. He was married to Gerri and made her come to my concert to prove she was cool.

9. DAVID LETTERMAN, he's so David Lettermanish, don't you think? (Whatever that means.)

10. JAMES "DAVE" PRATER, the white drummer and producer who I took to Japan after the other Dave and I parted company.

11. DAVID PORTER, the man with the words to the songs.

12. DAVE PRATER, JR., my now-deceased partner.

OK, fine, so there's twelve Daves here. I never said I could count. I sing.

Sam Moore, star of a couple dozen great Sam and Dave duets, is the greatest living soul singer, and is featured as a soloist on many other artists' albums, notably Don Henley's Building the Perfect Beast *and Bruce Springsteen's* Human Touch. *He recently resumed his solo recording career by making an album with legendary producer Tom Dowd.*

Roxanne, Roxanne
An Epic

In New York City back in 1984, UTFO innocently triggered one of rap's biggest battles of all time when they released "Roxanne Roxanne" on Select Records, a song that got its initial airplay on Mr. Magic's WBLS radio show. Soon after this exposure, the record became a hit single and had everyone repeating its memorable lines (sample lyric: "She thought my name was Larry/I told her it was Gary/She said she didn't like it/So she chose to call me Barry").

However, when UTFO reportedly failed to live up to their promise to do a Christmas benefit to thank the radio crew for bumping their single, the battle erupted. "Roxanne's Revenge" was released under the moniker of the

East 42nd Street Crew, which was really the Juice Crew with Roxanne Shanté (the radio station's address was, yes, on East 42nd Street). When this response, which had Shanté rapping over UTFO's instrumental, started to create a buzz, Marley Marl laid down some new beats and the first commercially available Roxanne response was born.

After UTFO responded with "The Real Roxanne," introducing their own female rapper, also named Roxanne, the floodgates were opened and a slew of Roxanne response records popped up, culminating in a bootleg mix of all the best Roxanne records, Battle of the Roxannes. Here is a list of some of the more memorable Roxanne tracks.

1. "Roxanne, Roxanne," UTFO
2. "Roxanne's Revenge," The East 42nd Street Crew, featuring Roxanne Shanté
3. "Real Roxanne," UTFO
4. "Do It Ricardo (Roxanne's Man)," Ricardo & Chocolate Boogie
5. "Roxanne's Doctor," Doctor Fresh
6. "Roxanne Is a Man," Ralph Rolle
7. "The Parents of Roxanne," Gigolo Tony & Lace Lacy
8. "Do the Roxanne Dance," Doctor Rocx and Co.
9. "Sparky's Turn (Roxanne You're Through)," Sparky Dee
10. "Queen of Rock," Roxanne Shanté

Thanks to Billy Jam and Kut Masta Kurt.

L.L. Cool J vs. Kool Moe Dee
The Cutting Contest

1. HOW YA LIKE ME NOW, KOOL MOE DEE—The cover of this 1987 album kicked it off: It showed a Jeep running over L.L.'s famous red Kangol cap.

2. "JACK THE RIPPER," L.L. COOL J—Cool J's riposte came with this 1988 B-side, which termed Moe Dee nothing but an "old-school sucker punk." (Well, he *had* been in the Treacherous Three, so that definitely makes him "old-school.")

3. "LET'S GO," KOOL MOE DEE—Another 1988 reply, in which Moe Dee defines L.L. as standing for "lackluster, lower-level, last, least, limp lover."

4. "TO DA BREAK OF DAWN," L.L. COOL J—By 1989, they'd supposedly patched up the feud, but in 1990, Cool J rolled up on an unsuspecting Moe Dee with this dis.

5. "DEATH BLOW," KOOL MOE DEE—An actual answer record, in which Moe Dee takes on "Mama Said Knock You Out" and blasts it out of the ring, or at least tries to. Is this the end of the cycle or will their cutting contest continue for decades, for as long as bluesmen Muddy Waters and Howlin' Wolf maintained theirs? We'll see.

Reginald C. Dennis on Rap's Biggest Beefs

1. **BOOGIE DOWN PRODUCTIONS VS. MC SHAN**—Winner: BDP. Shan could not respond to the lyrical attack of KRS-One's "The Bridge is Over."
2. **L.L. COOL J VS. KOOL MOE DEE**—Winner: L.L. After L.L.'s decisive victories, Moe Dee found himself the laughing-stock of the hip-hop world.
3. **L.L. COOL J VS. ICE-T**—Winner: L.L. Called Ice-T a two-bit thief and threatened to cut his ponytail.
4. **ICE CUBE VS. ABOVE THE LAW**—Draw: Ice Cube is the clear winner in terms of career achievement. But in physical confrontation (backstage at an ATL show in Cali and the re-match in New York during the 1990 New Music Seminar) ATL has the advantage with two victories.
5. **TIM DOG VS. WEST COAST**—Winner: West Coast. Tim discovered that the rest of the country is a lot bigger than the Bronx.
6. **BOO-YAA TRIBE VS. TONE LOC**—Draw. No one got hurt in the gunfight between the two crews during a Leaders of the New School performance in L.A. They have since settled their differences in a rational manner.

Reginald C. Dennis is the music editor of The Source.

The Staff of *Uncut Funk* Picks 10 Probable Career Avenues for George Clinton if He'd Never Gone into Music

1. Hair stylist
2. Pimp
3. Voodoo priest
4. Pornographer
5. Semiotician
6. Boxing promoter
7. Pharmacist
8. Afronaut
9. Cult leader
10. Dog psychologist

Rockers and Rappers with Famous Parents

1. AD ROCK (THE BEASTIE BOYS)—Son of playwright Israel Horovitz.

2. FONTELLA BASS—Her mother is famed gospel singer Martha Bass, a former member of the Clara Ward Singers.

3. JASON BONHAM (BONHAM)—Young metaloid drummer is son of Led Zep's late John Bonham.

4. DEBBY BOONE—Daughter of chicken-rock hero Pat Boone; her maternal grandfather was Country Hall of Famer Red Foley.

5. BECCA BRAMLETT (FLEETWOOD MAC)—Late addition to Mac sings white soul much like her parents, Delaney and Bonnie.

6. EDIE BRICKELL—Her father is a professional bowler known as "The Fort Worth Southpaw."

7. ROCKY AND BILLY BURNETTE—These two began recording careers in the late seventies. Billy, another sometime member of Fleetwood Mac, is the son of Johnny Burnette. Johnny's brother, Dorsey, fathered Rocky. The Burnette brothers formed one of the first important rockabilly groups, the Rock and Roll Trio, in the fifties, each scored pop-rock hits after moving to Los Angeles a couple years later, and both died young. Neither of their offspring has so much distinction.

8. RANDY CALIFORNIA—Spirit's guitarist played with his stepfather, Ed Cassidy, who became that band's drummer, after spending time with Taj Mahal and Ry Cooder's Rising Sons.

9. CARLENE CARTER AND ROSANNE CASH—Daughters of Johnny Cash. Carlene uses the last name of her mother, June Carter, of The Carter Family.

10. SHAUN AND DAVID CASSIDY—Sons of late actor Jack Cassidy. Shaun's mother is actress Shirley Jones. She played David's mother in *The Partridge Family*, although in real life she was only his stepmother.

11. NENEH CHERRY—Stepdaughter of jazz trumpeter Don Cherry.

12. NATALIE COLE—Daughter of Nat "King" Cole, lately seen pilfering his musical grave.

13. HARRY CONNICK, JR.—The Frank Sinatra impersonator is the son of Harry Connick, Sr., the once-indicted district attorney of New Orleans.

14. ELVIS COSTELLO—Son of noted British bandleader Ross McManus.

15. DAVID CROSBY—Son of famed cinematographer Floyd Crosby.

16. QUINCY D III—Hot rap producer is son of Quincy Jones.

17. MARK DINNING—Son of one of the Dinning Sisters, famous singing group of the 1940s and 1950s. That means the others were, of course, the "Teen Angel" lad's aunts.

18. DINO, DESI, AND BILLY—The first two are sons of Dean Martin and Desi Arnaz, respectively. Billy Hinsche's brother-in-law is Carl Wilson. The group's manager, Bill Howard, is the son of Dorothy Lamour.

19. JACOB DYLAN (THE WALLFLOWERS)—Bob's son sounds quite a bit like him.

20. ED ECKSTINE—Mercury Records chief is the son of crooner Billy Eckstine.

21. THE EVERLY BROTHERS—Sons of Ike Everly, a major bluegrass instrumentalist.

22. KIM FOWLEY—Raunchy trashmeister and Svengali of the Runaways grew up the son of Douglas Fowley, the second person to play Doc Holliday on TV's *The Life and Legend of Wyatt Earp*.

23. ARETHA FRANKLIN—Daughter of famed Baptist preacher Reverend C. L. Franklin, who made more than thirty albums of his sermons for Chess Records and whose authority and power from the pulpit outstripped even his great ally, Dr. Martin Luther King, Jr.

24. ANDREW GOLD—Has-been pop rocker's father, Ernest, writes move scores. His mother's Marni Nixon, best-known for over-dubbing for famous voices in movies like *West Side Story*, *The King and I*, and *My Fair Lady*.

25. LOUISE GOFFIN—Daughter of famed songwriters Carole King and Gerry Goffin has never lived up to her gene pool.

26. JOHN PAUL HAMMOND—Blues-singing scion of John Hammond, Sr., the greatest talent scout in recording history.

27. PAUL KOSSOFF—The late guitarist's father, David, is a noted British actor.

28. JULIAN LENNON—John and Cynthia's kid. Sean, John and Yoko's kid, hasn't yet displayed any musical propensity but he'd have to be as worse as his mother to outstrip Julian for dullness.

29. LEVERT—Gerald and Sean Levert are the sons of the O'Jays' Eddie Levert.

30. GARY LEWIS—The perpetrator of Al Kooper's "This Diamond Ring" is the son of comedian/philanthropist Jerry Lewis.

31. PETER LEWIS—Moby Grape guitarist was son of actress Loretta Young.

32. ZIGGY MARLEY—Son of Bob Marley and his singing wife, Rita.

33. MAY MAY—Rapper is daughter of Muhammad Ali.

34. TERRY MELCHER—Producer of Paul Revere and the

Raiders, the Byrds, and many others is the son of Doris Day and her manager/husband, Martin Melcher.

35. JIM MORRISON—His father, Stephen, was an admiral in the United States Navy.

36. NELSON; RICK NELSON—Twins, Matthew and Gunnar, are the sons of Rick Nelson, whose parents were Ozzie and Harriet Nelson, of TV's *Ozzie and Harriet*. Musical talent may be genetic, but it doesn't necessarily increase with each new generation.

37. MICHAEL NESMITH—Son of the woman who invented liquid correction fluid.

38. SHUGGIE OTIS—Guitar-playing son of bandleader/deejay Johnny Otis.

39. MCKENZIE PHILLIPS—Formerly of the TV series *One Day at a Time*, she toured in a revamped Mamas and Papas with her father, John Phillips, an original member of that group along with her mother, Michelle (see Wilson-Phillips).

40. BILLY PRESTON—His mother, Ernesta Wade, played Saffire in both the radio and television versions of *Amos'n'Andy*.

41. PROFESSOR X (X CLAN)—Son of black nationalist political activist Sonny Carson.

42. BONNIE RAITT—Her father, John Raitt, played major roles in Broadway musicals, including *Pajama Game* and *Carousel*.

43. THE REDDINGS—Dexter and Otis III are the sons of the late King of 'Em All, Y'all. The group's other member, Mark Lockett, is their cousin, Otis's nephew.

44. HUNT AND TONY SALES—Soupy Sales's sons are best known for forming Tin Machine with David Bowie but have also played with Iggy Pop and Todd Rundgren.

45. CARLY SIMON—Her father, Richard, founded Simon and Schuster, the publishing house.

46. 2PAC—Tupac Shakur, solo rapper and member of Digital Underground, is the child of Afeni Shakur, one of the leaders of the New York City chapter of the Black Panther party.

47. KIM WILDE—Daughter of pre-Beatles British pop star Marty Wilde.

48. WILSON-PHILLIPS—Wendy and Carnie Wilson are the daughters of Beach-Boy-in-chief Brian Wilson; Chynna Phillips is the daughter of almost equally dysfunctional John and Michelle Phillips of the Mamas and Pappas (see McKenzie Phillips).

49. LINDA WOMACK (WOMACK AND WOMACK)—Daughter of Sam Cooke; stepdaughter of Bobby Womack, her husband Cecil's brother.

50. NEIL YOUNG—His father, Scott, was the best-known sportswriter in Canada while Neil was growing up. Since then, he's become an equally famous general interest columnist and author of several books, including one about Neil's early years.

25 Songs About Children, Childhood, and Parenting

1. "Another Brick in the Wall," Pink Floyd
2. "Baby Talk," Jan and Dean
3. "The Birth," Ice Cube
4. "First Born Son," The McGariggle Sisters
5. "Forever Young," Bob Dylan
6. "Growin' Up," Bruce Springsteen
7. "I Am a Child," Neil Young
8. "Little Children," Billy J. Kramer and the Dakotas
9. "Little Marie" Chuck Berry
10. "Living Proof," Bruce Springsteen
11. "Nick of Time," Bonnie Raitt
12. "Ob-La-Di, Ob-La-Da," The Beatles
13. "Our House," Crosby, Stills and Nash
14. "Penny Lane," The Beatles
15. "Ready or Not," Jackson Browne
16. "Rufus Is a Tit Man," Loudon Wainwright III
17. "Silver Thunderbird," Marc Cohn
18. "Someday Never Comes," Creedence Clearwater Revival
19. "Sweet Child of Mine," Guns N' Roses
20. "Tennessee," Arrested Development
21. "When I Grow Up to Be a Man," The Beach Boys
22. "Yellow Submarine," The Beatles
23. "You Angel You," Bob Dylan
24. "You Better Sit Down Kids," Sonny and Cher
25. "Younger Generation," The Lovin' Spoonful

The Kids Are Alright
50 Famous Siblings

1. **DUANE AND GREGG ALLMAN**—The late guitarist of the Allman Brothers Band and his kid brother, that group's keyboardist, sometime solo artist and ex-husband of Cher.

2. **PHIL AND DAVE ALVIN**—These Angeleno sibs led the Blasters until vocalist-songwriter Phil decided he'd rather go back to school and take a Ph.D. in math, leaving guitarist-songwriter Dave to pursue an artistically if not economically productive solo career.

3. **RON AND SCOTT ASHETON**—The original Stooges included older brother Ron on guitar and Scott on drums. As Rock Action, Scott went on to play with many other Motor City energy bands, most recently Scott Morgan's group.

4. RANDY AND ROBBIE BACHMAN—Randy led Bachman-Turner Overdrive as its guitarist, vocalist, and songwriter; Robbie played drums.

5. JOHNNY AND DORSEY BURNETTE—They started out in Memphis as the Rock and Roll Trio, helping pioneer rockabilly and (inadvertently through guitarist Paul Burlison) feedback on "Train Kept A-Rollin'," then went to L.A. where each saw a brief spell—Johnny's a bit longer—as a teen idol.

6. LESTER, GEORGE, AND JOE CHAMBERS—Aka the Chambers Brothers, folk-gospel trio turned psychedelicists on the periodically revived "Time Has Come Today."

7. HARRY, TOM, AND STEVE CHAPIN—All on the folkier side of singer-songwriters, these three brothers often worked together, usually on the impetus of Harry, the eldest and a true dynamo.

8. BOOTSY AND CATFISH COLLINS—Bassist and guitarist, respectively, first with James Brown's most celebrated unit of JB's, then with George Clinton's greatest P-Funk aggreggation. Bootsy, of course, made his mark as a solo artist, too.

9. BILL AND B. B. CUNNINGHAM—Memphis brothers met divergent success: Bill with Alex Chilton in the Box Tops ("The Letter"), B.B. with the Hombres, whose "Let It All Hang Out" marked a crazed point in the development of southern psychedelia.

10. RAY AND DAVE DAVIES—The core of the Kinks: Ray, the eldest, defines the band with his singing and writing, Dave adds punched-up counterpoint with lead guitar riffing.

11. RODNEY AND DOUG DILLARD—The Dillards, led by these brothers, were the most worthwhile of all the neo-bluegrass bands, featuring Rodney on guitar and Doug on banjo.

12. PHIL AND DON EVERLY—Vocalists extraordinaire and perhaps the single most important set of siblings in rock 'n' roll history.

13. ANDREW, JOHN, AND TIM FARRISS—INXS originally called itself the Farriss Brothers after these three.

14. JOHN AND TOM FOGERTY—Although John came to dominate Creedence Clearwater Revival with his writing, singing, and guitar playing, Tom's original role was defined in their first name: Tommy Fogerty and the Blue Velvets.

15. ARETHA, CAROLYN, AND ERMA FRANKLIN—Daughters of the Reverend C. L. Franklin. Aretha reigned as Queen of Soul, Carolyn became her most significant songwriting collaborator until her tragically early death, Erma came to fame primarily for providing Janis Joplin with the original model of "Piece of My Heart."

16. MARVIN AND FRANKIE GAYE—There are those at Motown who swear that soul master Marvin worked overtime to prevent Frankie from achieving the success his also-outstanding singing talent deserved. In any event, when Marvin sang about returning Vietnam vets, it was of Frankie that he spoke—ditto when he sang "brother, brother, brother," at the top of "What's Going On."

17. JIMMY, JACK, AND DONNA HALL—Sister Donna occasionally joined her brothers on backing vocals for Wet Willie, the great southern rock band Jimmy and Jack fronted.

18. RONALD, RUDOLPH, KELLY, ERNIE, AND MARVIN ISLEY—The original Isley Brothers were Ronald, Rudolph, and Kelly (actually O'Kelly). Ernie and Marvin were late babies and when they joined as backup instrumentalists—Ernie as mind-boggling guitarist, Marvin as rock-solid bassist, abetted by keyboardist/cousin Chris Jasper—the Isleys became a different unit, the one that gave birth to the nascent funk of "Fight the Power" and other mid-seventies greats.

19. MICHAEL, TITO, JACKIE, MARLON, JERMAINE, REBBIE, LaTOYA, RANDY, AND JANET JACKSON—At one time or another, all of these Gary, Indiana (and Beverly Hills, California), siblings participated in the act variously known as the Jackson 5 and the Jacksons. When the core of the group left Motown, only Jermaine stayed behind. Later, he, Michael, and Janet all had substantial solo success, Michael gave Rebbie a hit with "Centipede," and the others basically stayed out of any public activity between group tours, except for LaToya, whose career as *Playboy* model, sexless battered wife, and Michael impersonator needs no further elucidation here.

20. CHAKA KHAN AND TAKA BOOM—Imagine if Melle Mel had gone "Taka boom, taka boom, taka boom"?! And he could've because Chaka's little sister had a solo career as well as a brief stint in the Motown almost-supergroup Undisputed Truth ("Smiling Faces Sometime," the original "Papa Was a Rolling Stone").

21. ALVIN AND RIC LEE—Ten Years After, the best boogie band at Woodstock, featured guitar hero Alvin backed by brother Ric on drums.

22. SEAN AND JULIAN LENNON—Julian's career as the world's most uncanny, if not inspired, impersonator of father John has yet to be matched by his much younger half-brother, whose principal media forte has been being photographed with Mom and Michael Jackson.

23. GERALD AND SEAN LEVERT—The brothers who lead Levert are the sons of the O'Jays' Eddie Levert.

24. NILS AND TOM LOFGREN—Before Nils became a member of the E Street Band, or for that manner, a solo artist, he led a band called Grin that made a trio of fine albums, featuring his brother Tom on rhythm guitar.

25. DARLENE LOVE AND EDNA WRIGHT—Love

("Today I Met the Boy I'm Gonna Marry," ad infinitum for Phil
Spector, session vocalist supreme with the Blossoms) is the sister of
Wright, a member of Honey Cone ("Want Ads").

26. KATE AND ANNA McGARIGGLE—Canadian singer-
songwriter sisters

27. MARIA McKEE AND BRYAN McLEAN—McLean
first appeared as lead guitarist in Arthur Lee's Love, the best semi-
psychedelic band L.A. ever produced. Sister Maria, a good twenty
years younger, turned up first in the mid-eighties with Lone Justice,
then as an internationalized solo artist (she lived part of the time in
Dublin) during the nineties.

28. AARON, ART, CHARLES, AND CYRILLE NEVILLE
—The Neville Brothers are also the core of the Meters.

29. ANITA, BONNIE, JUNE, AND RUTH POINTER—
Originally, all four sisters constituted the Pointer Sisters. But Bonnie
later split for a solo career with Motown and the others continued as
a trio, the format in which they've had their biggest hits.

30. CHRIS AND RICH ROBINSON—Vocalist Chris and
guitarist Rich lead the Black Crowes, at one and the same time the
most mouthy and obnoxious and most rootsy and authentic new
blues-rock act of our era.

31. HUNT AND TONY SALES—Sons of Soupy Sales, they
got their start in big-time rock backing Iggy Pop, then Todd Rundgren. More recently, they've joined David Bowie as members of Tin
Machine.

32. SEN DOG AND MELLOW MAN ACE—Sen's crew is
Cypress Hill; Mellow Man Ace made his mark with "Mentirosa."

33. HANK AND KEITH SHOCKLEE—The one-time Boxley
brothers helped revolutionize modern music as members of Public
Enemy's production team, the Bomb Squad. Hank played the more
central, Keith the more peripheral, role.

34. RUSSELL SIMMONS AND RUN—Russell formed Def
Jam Records and Rush Management in part to exploit the talents of
his younger brother, Joseph (Run), of Run-D.M.C.

35. TOMMY AND BOBBY STINSON—Perhaps the true
heart of the Replacements were their guitarists: Stumbling drunk
Bob, who was eventually thrown out of the group because he hadn't
cleaned up his act, and younger brother Tommy, the bassist, who'd
barely passed puberty when they began but grew into one of the
most distinctive instrumentalists of the post-punk era.

36. SLY, FREDDIE, AND ROSE STONE—Sly and the
Family Stone was accurately named. In addition to Sly's guitarist
brother and pianist-vocalist sister, the group included bassist Larry
Graham, a cousin.

37. JOE AND LEVI STUBBS—Levi led the Four Tops; Joe
sang in both the Falcons (with Sir Mack Rice and Eddie Floyd) and
the Contours (though not on their biggest hits).

38. RALPH, POOCH, CHUBBY, BUTCH, AND TINY TAVARES—This all-brother band began performing around New England in the fifties, backing their father, but reached its chart success only in the seventies, with hits like "Check It Out," "She's Gone," and "It Only Takes a Minute."

39. JAMES, ALEX, LIVINGSTON, AND KATE TAYLOR—More singer-songwriter sibs: James, of course, had the most important career, followed by Liv, who still frequently records. Kate and the late Alex showed up a lot less often.

40. PETE AND SIMON TOWNSHEND—Pete's one of rock's greatest creators, as leader of the Who, composer of *Tommy* for stage and screen, and solo artist. Simon has recorded and performed very infrequently, and with much less success.

41. MARY AND BETTY WEISS; MARY ANN AND MARGE GANSER—Shangri-Las lead singer Mary and vocalist Betty are sisters; the Gansers, their partners in the 'Las, go them one better—they're twins.

42. ANN AND NANCY WILSON—Leaders of Heart, who would be the queens of heavy metal if heavy metal weren't ruled by male primogeniture.

43. BRIAN, CARL, AND DENNIS WILSON—Brian gets most of the credit for the Beach Boys and as main melodist, bassist, producer, co–lead singer, he deserves it, but guitarist-vocalist Carl and vocalist-drummer Dennis weren't just along for the ride. Mike Love, the other lead singer, is their cousin, though no one boasts about it, and the band was initially (and disastrously) managed by the Wilsons' father, Murry.

44. RICK AND CINDY WILSON—This brother-sister combo gave the B-52s two of their key members until Rick's death from cancer.

45. WENDY AND CARNIE WILSON—Brian Wilson's daughters made their public debut as Wilson-Phillips, with Chynna Phillips, daughter of John and Michelle Phillips of the Mamas and Papas. Chynna had a singing sister, too, though McKenzie is better known as a TV actress.

46. JOHNNY AND EDGAR WINTER—What could fool you about these albino Texas bluesmen is their birth order. Though Johnny came to fame first and remains the more respected in musical circles as one of the few really authentic-sounding white blues guitarists, Edgar, who had bigger pop hits ("Frankenstein"), is actually the elder.

47. STEVE AND MUFF WINWOOD—They called their first band the Spencer Davis Group but vocalist-multi-instrumentalist Stevie led it, even at age sixteen. Elder brother Muff played bass then, after Steve left for Traffic, Blind Faith, Traffic again, and finally a glitzy solo career, he became an A&R man in England.

48. BOBBY AND CECIL WOMACK—These Womacks

three of their other singing, guitar-playing brethren formed the Valentinos, whose "It's All Over Now" is one of the staples of the
R&B repertoire (covered by both the Stones and Ry Cooder, for
instance). Bobby had considerable success; Cecil and his wife, Linda
(daughter of Sam Cooke and Bobby's stepdaughter) still perform as
Womack and Womack.

49. ANGUS AND MALCOLM YOUNG—AC/DC's guitar heroes are the younger brothers of George Young, leader of the Easybeats and AC/DC's first producer.

50. DWEEZIL, MOON UNIT, AND AHMET ZAPPA—
Dweezil and Moon have been MTV veejays. Ahmet avoided that
fate but now joins Dweezil, an ace guitarist, as vocalist in a new
band. Moon's other big credit was doing the zoned-out mall chick's
voice on papa Frank's "Valley Girl."

Twins

1. Marge and Mary Ann Ganser, of The Shangri-Las
2. Maurice and Robin Gibb, of The Bee Gees
3. Mick and Keith Glimmer, of The Glimmer Twins
4. Scott and Thomas Herrick, of The Arbors
5. The Kalin Twins (their only hit: "When," 1958)
6. Gary and Martin Kemp, of Spandau Ballet
7. Matthew and Gunnar Nelson, of Nelson
8. John and Paul Nurk, of The Nurk Twins and George
9. Charles and John Panozzo, of Styx
10. Elvis Aron and Jesse Garon Presley (Jesse died at birth, altering
    history in unfathomable ways)

9 Distant Relations

1. JAMES BROWN—Barbra Marson ("Yes I'm Ready") is his
cousin.

2. SAM COOKE—R. B. Greaves ("Take a Letter Maria") is
his nephew.

3. HARVEY FUQUA—The lead singer of many Moonglows
hits and later a force at Motown, Harvey was the cousin of Charlie
Fuqua of the original Ink Spots. Harvey Fuqua later married Motown president Berry Gordy's sister, meaning his brothers-in-law
included Gordy and Marvin Gaye.

4. NONA GAYE—Besides Marvin Gaye being her father,
Slim Gaillard ("Flat Foot Floogie with the Floy Floy") was her
maternal grandfather.

5. ICE CUBE—Yo Yo and Del the Funkee Homosapien are his cousins.
6. JERRY LEE LEWIS—Country star Mickey Gilley is his cousin.
7. RANDY NEWMAN—His uncles, Alfred and Lionel, were famous composers of movie scores.
8. DIONNE WARWICK—Whitney Houston is her niece.
9. LINDA WOMACK—Bobby Womack is both her stepfather and her brother-in-law.

American Indian Performers

1. Jimmy Carl Black ("He's the Indian of the group," said the Mothers of Invention on their early album covers)
2. Johnny Cash (and thus, even more marginally, Rosanne Cash and Carlene Carter)
3. Jesse Ed Davis
4. Jimi Hendrix (one-quarter Cherokee)
5. Buffy Sainte-Marie
6. Robbie Robertson
7. Tom Petty
8. Patrick Sky
9. John Trudell
10. The Thunderbirds
11. Pat and Lolly Vegas (Redbone)
12. Link Wray

Italian-Americans

1. Anthrax (three of five members)
2. John Bon Jovi
3. Lou Christie
4. Jim Croce
5. Bobby Darin
6. Joey Dee
7. Chris DeGarmo (Queensryche)
8. Dion and the Belmonts
9. The Elegants
10. Madonna
11. Jerry Martini and Greg Errico (Sly and the Family Stone)
12. D. J. Muggs (Cypress Hill)
13. Maria Muldaur
14. Felix Pappalardi (Cream, Mountain)
15. Gene Pitney
16. The Rascals
17. Patti Scialfa
18. John Sebastian
19. Bruce Springsteen
20. Sal Valentino (Beau Brummels)
21. Frankie Valli and the Four seasons
22. Little Steven Van Zandt
23. Bobby Vee
24. Joe Vitale
25. Frank Zappa

Nice Jewish Boys

1. The Beastie Boys
2. Michael Bloomfield
3. Marc Bolan (T. Rex)
4. Leonard Cohen
5. Bob Dylan
6. Flo and Eddie (Howard Kaylan and Mark Volman —who were also the main guys in The Turtles)
7. Peter Green (Fleetwood Mac)
8. Billy Joel
9. Al Kooper
10. Lenny Kravitz
11. Manfred Mann
12. Phil Ochs
13. Joey Ramone (The Ramones)
14. David Lee Roth
15. Rick Rubin
16. M.C. Serch
17. Paul Simon (and Art Garfunkel, for that matter)
18. Gene Simmons and Paul Stanley (Kiss)
19. Phil Spector
20. Steely Dan (Walter Becker and Donald Fagen)
21. Chris Stein (Blondie)
22. Leslie West (Mountain)
23. Peter Wolf (J. Geils)
24. Zal Yanovsky (The Lovin' Spoonful)
25. Warren Zevon

Hispanics Causing Panic
Important Hispanic Musicians, from Rock 'n' Roll to Rap

1. Ruben Blades
2. The Blendells
3. Cannibal and the Headhunters
4. Cruzados
5. Fito de la Parra (Canned Heat)
6. El Chicano
7. Gloria Estefan
8. Freddy Fender
9. Kid Frost
10. Ruben Guevara (Ruben and the Jets; c/s; Zyanya Records)
11. Lisa Lisa
12. Los Illegals
13. Los Lobos
14. Malo
15. Mellow Man Ace
16. The Plugz
17. The Premiers
18. ? and the Mysterians
19. Chan Romero
20. Ronnie and the Pomona Casuals
21. Linda Ronstadt
22. Carlos Santana
23. Herman Santiago (Frankie Lymon and the Teenagers; cowriter of "Why Do Fools Fall in Love")
24. Sen Dog (Cypress Hill)
25. Tavares
26. Thee Midniters
27. Ritchie Valens
28. Suzanne Vega
29. War
30. Carlos Ward (B.T. Express)

Good Catholics

1. Black 47
2. Jon Bon Jovi
3. Elvis Costello
4. Dion DiMucci
5. Bob Geldof
6. Madonna
7. Natalie Merchant
8. Sinead O'Connor
9. The Pogues
10. The Rascals
11. Bruce Springsteen (*not* Patti Scialfa)
12. The Undertones (*not* U2)
13. Frankie Valli and the Four Seasons
14. Little Steven Van Zandt
15. Jah Wobble (Public Image Ltd.)

Jehovah's Witnesses

1. Lester Bangs
2. George Benson
3. Ornette Coleman
4. Larry Graham (Graham Central Station, Sly and the Family Stone)
5. Janet Jackson
6. Michael Jackson
7. Hank Marvin (The Shadows)
8. The Modern Jazz Quartet
9. Van Morrison
10. Huey "Piano" Smith
11. David Thomas (Pere Ubu)

Followers of Islam

1. Brand Nubian
2. Jimmy Cliff
3. Carter Cornelius (Cornelius Brothers and Sister Rose)
4. Professor Griff
5. Ice Cube
6. Big Daddy Kane
7. Poor Righteous Teachers
8. Rakim
9. Cat Stevens
10. Joe Tex
11. Richard Thompson
12. X-Clan

Preachers: Rock and Rollers Who Are Ordained Ministers

1. **SOLOMON BURKE**—Burke became a minister at age nine. Billed then as the "Wonder Boy Preacher," he returns to the cloth every now and then.

2. **LITTLE RICHARD**—He returns periodically to the church to cleanse his soul and denounce his decadent former lifestyle.

3. AL GREEN—Actually retired around 1976 to devote time to studying for the ministry, now divides his time in and out of the studio between secular and Christian pursuits.

4. FUZZY HASKINS—Former P-Funk genius now presides over Detroit congregation.

5. JOHNNY OTIS—After his musical career wound down, found himself a pulpit and settled in as a full-time parson, albeit one with political interests and an R&B radio show.

6. BARRY McGUIRE—"Eve of Destruction" protester now a contemporary Christian recording artist.

7. HANK MIZELL—Mizell, an obscure but great rockabilly, was ordained but never practiced.

8. JOHNNIE TAYLOR—Never preached, so far as we know.

9. JOE TEX—Ordained as a minister in the Nation of Islam.

Son of a Preacher Man—And His Daughter, Too

1. Sam Cooke
2. Rita and Priscilla Coolidge
3. Alice Cooper
4. Terence Trent D'Arby
5. Mark Dinning
6. Ernie K-Doe
7. Aretha, Carolyn, and Erma Franklin (they're all daughters of Reverend C. L. Franklin, himself a recording artist of note)
8. Marvin Gaye
9. Whitney Houston (her mother, Cissy Houston, had a music ministry, as well as a secular career)
10. Maria McKee
11. Clyde McPhatter
12. Curtis Mayfield (actually, his grandmother)
13. The Pointer Sisters (both parents preached)
14. Otis Redding
15. Bobby Womack
16. Link Wray (both parents preached)

I Dreamed I Saw St. Augustine
Most Unlikely Christians

1. Philip Bailey
2. Eric Clapton
3. Bob Dylan
4. Mark Farner (Grand Funk)
5. M. C. Hammer
6. Little Richard
7. Sinead O'Connor
8. Run-D.M.C.
9. Donna Summer
10. David Thomas (Pere Ubu)
11. U2 (except Adam Clayton)

If You All Get to Heaven
Preachiest Christians

1. Philip Bailey
2. Bono
3. Pat Boone
4. Solomon Burke
5. Richard "Dimples" Fields
6. Amy Grant
7. Boris Grebenshikov
8. Al Green
9. Kansas
10. Little Richard
11. Stryper
12. Deniece Williams

Dancin' With Mr. D
The Devil Music Top 40

1. "Angel of Death," Slayer
2. "Black Sabbath," Black Sabbath
3. "Bowels of the Devil," Body Count
4. "Children of the Grave," Ozzy Osbourne
5. "Demon's Eye," Deep Purple
6. "The Devil," Urban Dance Squad
7. "The Devil Came from Kansas," Procol Harum
8. "Devil Game," Kansas
9. "The Devil Inside," INXS
10. "The Devil Made Me Do It," Paris
11. "Devil Song," Camper Van Beethoven
12. "The Devil Went Down to Georgia," The Charlie Daniels Band
13. "The Devil's Been Busy," The Traveling Wilburys
14. "Devil's Hideaway," James Brown
15. "Devil's Workshop," B.T. Express
16. "Fallen Angels," Dinosaur Jr.
17. "Friend of the Devil," The Grateful Dead
18. "Gimme Hell," The Jesus and Mary Chain
19. "God Bless the Children of the Beast," Motley Crue
20. "The Great Deceiver," King Crimson
21. "Hell Awaits," Slayer
22. "Hell or High Water," Kiss
23. "Hellbound Train," Lita Ford/Foghat
24. "Highway to Hell," AC/DC
25. "Hot Rails to Hell," Blue Oyster Cult
26. "(Don't Worry) If There's a Hell Below, We're All Going to Go," Curtis Mayfield
27. "Into the Lungs of Hell," Megadeth
28. "King of Sodom and Gomorrah," W.A.S.P.
29. "Leper Messiah," Metallica

30. "Lil' Devil," The Cult
31. "Lord of the Flies," Lizzy Borden
32. "No Voices in the Sky," Motorhead
33. "Prince of Darkness," Alice Cooper
34. "Right Next Door to Hell," Guns N' Roses
35. "Runnin' with the Devil," Van Halen
36. "Satan," Teenage Fanclub
37. "Satan's Blues," Jr. Walker and the All Stars
38. "Straight to Hell," The Clash
39. "Sympathy for the Devil," The Rolling Stones
40. "Valley of Lost Souls," Poison

The Devil's Disciples
The 10 Most Dangerous Bands According to Jeff Godwin, Chick Ministries

Godwin presents this list in his book, The Devil's Disciples *(Chick Publications, 1985). The book could use a musical update, but not nearly so much as a theological overhaul.*

1. AC/DC—"This band has done more harm than almost any other group around today."

2. THE ROLLING STONES—These "miserable drug-eaten hedonists" "invented Diabolic Rock."

3. LED ZEPPELIN—A "jaded group of occult thrill seekers" with a "catalog of dismal, melancholy dirges and hyped up, Heavy Metal sex operas."

4. MOTLEY CRUE—"A ragtag gang of foul mouthed and vulgar fornicators who openly brag of their detestable lifestyles . . ."

5. KISS—"Not content with the millions of dollars already stolen from an innocent fandom consisting mainly of thirteen year old girls, KISS is still far from fading into the Rock & Roll trash heap."

6. TWISTED SISTER—"[B]latant ultra-macho, animalistic, 'I'll kick your teeth in' attitude combined with a sexual preference that is anybody's guess," "one of the weirdest, sickest, and most dangerous of the 80's Slime-Rock groups."

7. JUDAS PRIEST—"Flying saucers, Nazi biker glory, smash-em-up and spit out your teeth. Violence, violence, violence. The world is insane enough without this disgusting group of Rock & Roll fascists."

8. BLACK SABBATH—A "thudding, downer witch-Rock band of aging necrophiles."

9. OZZY OSBOURNE—Condemned for "repeated, disgusting, brainless acts of vulgar depravity." Geez, that's what we *like* about him.

    10. W.A.S.P.—"[U]nvarnished appeal to the basest and most perverse elements of today's Rock. Their name means '*We Are Sexual Perverts*' and their music proves it."

The Blackwood Brothers Choose 10 Pop Artists Who Can Sing the Gospel Well

1. Pat Boone
2. Johnny Cash
3. The Doobie Brothers, for "Jesus Is Just Alright with Me"
4. Larry Gatlin
5. Emmylou Harris
6. Marguerite Piazza
7. Billy Preston
8. The Rascals, for "People Got to Be Free"
9. The Statler Brothers
10. B. J. Thomas

The Blackwood Brothers have been leaders in the gospel field for five decades. Their harmonic blend inspired scores of rock, country, and pop artists. Elvis Presley himself auditioned for the Blackwoods in 1954: He was turned down.

"We Learned More from a Three-Minute Record than We Ever Learned in School"

1. "Another Brick in the Wall," Pink Floyd
2. "Be True to Your School," The Beach Boys
3. "Charlie Brown," The Coasters
4. "Class Is in Session," D.J. Magic Mike and M.C. Madness
5. "Class of '65," Joe Walsh
6. "Education," The Kinks
7. "Edutainment," Boogie Down Productions
8. "Hot for Teacher," Van Halen
9. "I Wish," Stevie Wonder
10. "My Old School," Steely Dan
11. "No Surrender," Bruce Springsteen
12. "Rock'n'Roll High School," The Ramones
13. "School Days," Chuck Berry/Loudon Wainwright III

14. "School's Out," Alice Cooper
15. "Smoking in the Boys' Room," Brownsville Station
16. "Teach the Children," Eric B. and Rakim
17. "Teach the Gifted Children," Lou Reed
18. "Teach Your Children," Crosby, Stills and Nash
19. "Teacher Teacher," Slick Rick/.38 Special
20. "Teachers, Don't Teach Us Nonsense!!" Leaders of the New School

The Nescafé Students' All-Time Top 20 Albums

The coffeemaker surveyed British students in 1987 to discover their favorite albums. And you thought the kids you went to school with in America had lousy, predictable tastes!

1. *Brothers in Arms*, Dire Straits
2. *The Joshua Tree*, U2
3. *The Wall*, Pink Floyd
4. *Rum, Sodomy and the Lash*, The Pogues
5. *So*, Peter Gabriel
6. *Bat Out of Hell*, Meat Loaf
7. *Suzanne Vega*
8. *Rumours*, Fleetwood Mac
9. *Graceland*, Paul Simon
10. *Misplaced Childhood*, Marillion
11. *Sgt. Pepper's Lonely Hearts Club Band*, The Beatles
12. *The Queen is Dead*, The Smiths
13. *Love Over Gold*, Dire Straits
14. *Invisible Touch*, Genesis
15. *Infected*, The The
16. *The Rise and Fall of Ziggy Stardust and the Spiders from Mars*, David Bowie
17. *Making Movies*, Dire Straits
18. *Led Zeppelin IV* (the one titled only with runes that has "Stairway to Heaven")
19. *Once Upon a Time*, Simple Minds
20. *Wish You Were Here*, Pink Floyd

Source: Vox *magazine (UK)*

Rock Performers Who Really Pumped Gas

1. Jeff Beck (still does)
2. Gene Clark (The Byrds)
3. Roger McGuinn (The Byrds)
4. Bob Mosley (Moby Grape)
5. Graham Parker
6. Bruce Springsteen
7. Tony Williams (The Platters)

Rockers Who Really Worked the Assembly Line

1. Chuck Berry
2. Sonny Bono
3. Johnny Cash
4. Berry Gordy, Jr.
5. Bob Marley
6. Jack Scott
7. The Spinners

10 Rockers You Wouldn't Want to Drive With

1. Jeff Beck
2. Eric Clapton
3. Flavor Flav
4. Peter Frampton
5. George Harrison
6. Vince Neil
7. Ted Nugent
8. John Oates
9. Bruce Springsteen
10. Luther Vandross

Jocks

1. **PAULA ABDUL**—Formerly head cheerleader for the NBA Los Angeles Lakers

2. **MUHAMMAD ALI**—In 1964, when his name was still Cassius Clay, he released "Stand By Me," the Ben E. King song, as a single. The followup album, *I Am the Greatest!*, reached *Billboard*'s album chart at number sixty-three.

3. **JEFF BECK**—Professedly cares far more about auto racing than about music making.

4. CHUCK BERRY—*Extremely* fond of water sports.

5. JAMES BROWN—Brown was a professional bantamweight fighter (sixteen wins, one defeat) before becoming a singer.

6. JOHNNY BURNETTE—Before becoming a Memphis Golden Gloves championship fighter, Burnette played on the football team at L. C. Humes High School in Memphis. Elvis Presley was a benchwarmer on the same team.

7. DAVE CLARK—The Dave Clark Five leader played soccer in his British youth.

8. ALICE COOPER—Became a fanatical amateur golfer after his first series of hit records.

9. TERENCE TRENT D'ARBY—It's hard to say which is stranger, the image of Terence as an Army private, or the thought of him as a company champion boxer during his hitch.

10. LEE DORSEY—Under the name Kid Chocolate, Dorsey was a light heavyweight championship contender.

11. THE EAGLES—Kicked ass on the staff of *Rolling Stone* in a 1978 softball game, winning $10,000 bet between *RS* editor/publisher Jann Wenner and their manager, Irving Azoff.

12. ART GARFUNKEL—Extremely devoted noncompetitive walker whose project over the past decade has been a (noncontinuous) walk across the continental United States.

13. MARVIN GAYE—Avid golfer, and such a fanatical football fan that he insisted on trying out for the Detroit Lions as a wide receiver, much to the bemusement of Mel Farr and Lem Barney, his All-Pro cronies on the team.

14. BERRY GORDY, JR.—From 1948 to 1951, he fought both as a Golden Gloves amateur and, briefly, as a professional boxer in Detroit.

15. SAMMY HAGAR—Hagar followed in his pro boxer father's footsteps for a while.

16. M. C. HAMMER—Grew up as Stanley Burrell, batboy for the Oakland A's (and frequent spy for their irascible owner, Charles O. Finley). Given the nickname "Hammer" by the team, because of his strong facial resemblance to home-run king "Hammerin' " Henry Aaron. Hammer and his father and brothers now run a highly successful racehorse business.

17. BOBBY HATFIELD—The Righteous Brother had enough baseball talent to earn a tryout with the Dodgers.

18. JOAN JETT—Diehard Baltimore Orioles fan and amateur ballplayer.

19. BILLY JOEL—Joel had twenty-two amateur boxing bouts, accounting for the somewhat disheveled state of his nose.

20. KRIS KRISTOFFERSON—Becoming a star football player in high school and at his small Texas college helped win him his Rhodes scholarship.

21. NILS LOFGREN—A trained gymnast, Lofgren sometimes uses a trampoline onstage; in fact, it made frequent appearances in the early stages of Bruce Springsteen's *Born in the U.S.A.* tour. (Under Nils's guidance, Springsteen learned to tumble, and during his *Tunnel of Love* tour sometimes took the stage with a running somersault.

22. BOB LUMAN—Turned down a Pittsburgh Pirates baseball contract to lead the rockabilly life.

23. JIMMY MCCRACKIN—Before hitting with "The Walk," McCrackin had twenty-two professional fights.

24. JACK MCDOWELL—The Chicago White Sox' ace pitcher spends a good deal of his multimillion-dollar annual salary on making demos with his various rock bands. Arrested in New Orleans with Pearl Jam's Eddie Vedder, November 1993.

25. LAMONT MCLEMOR—This member of the Fifth Dimension played for a Los Angeles Dodgers farm team.

26. BOB MARLEY—Unbridled soccer fan. He carried some Jamaican professional players in his entourage and was frequently photographed playing the game, often on beaches.

27. LEE MAYE—Undoubtedly the only singer of a classic doo-wop record ("Gloria," by Arthur Lee Maye [his real name] and the Crowns) to also appear in the World Series, as a member of the 1957 Milwaukee Braves. Maye had the most substantial sports/music career of any artist or athlete.

28. TED NUGENT—Avid bow-and-arrow hunter, runs a bow camp.

29. JOHN OATES—Grand Prix auto racing zealot.

30. SHAQUILLE O'NEAL—The NBA's most accomplished rookie since Michael Jordan also pursues a career as a hip-hopper.

31. OZZY OSBOURNE—Expert batsman.

32. IGGY POP—*Serious* amateur golfer.

33. ELVIS PRESLEY—A benchwarmer in high-school football but an inveterate backyard touch player, racquetballer, and alleged karate "master."

34. CHARLEY PRIDE—Country singer took up that profession only after being cut from a San Francisco (baseball) Giants farm team.

35. SMOKEY ROBINSON—Another of Motown's golf course fanatics.

36. DAVID LEE ROTH—Mountain climber, surfer, jungle explorer, and metal's onstage athlete par excellence.

37. BOB SEGER—Ran a 5:05 mile in high school, a most respectable time in the early sixties.

38. ROD STEWART—Seriously considered throwing over music for a career as a professional soccer player: Reportedly, Rod was good enough to have had a serious shot at U.K. football stardom. By 1993, he was forced to give up even kicking soccer balls into the

crowd during his concerts, owing to the many personal injury lawsuits that resulted.

39. GEORGE THOROGOOD—Relentless amateur baseball
player—dauntless and plays all the time but not very well, which
means his athletic skills perfectly match his musical ones.

40. CONWAY TWITTY—Pro baseball prospect who once
owned the Memphis minor league franchise.

Golden Gloves Champions

1. Willie Dixon
2. Johnny Burnette
3. Screamin' Jay Hawkins
4. Billy Ward
5. Jackie Wilson

OTHER GOLDEN GLOVES FIGHTERS

1. Berry Gordy, Jr.
2. Peter Criss (Kiss)
3. Kris Kristofferson
4. Tommy Tucker

Surfers

1. Jan Berry (Jan and Dean)
2. Eddie Bertrand (The Belairs, Eddie and the Showmen)
3. John Caffety (Beaver Brown)
4. Dick Dale (of course)
5. Dickey Dodd (The Belairs, Eddie and the Showmen, The Standells)
6. Jim Fuller (The Surfaris)
7. Russ Kunkel (Los Angeles session drummer)
8. Keith Moon (The Who—once, disastrously)
9. Bob Mosley (Moby Grape)
10. Elliott Murphy
11. Bob Spickard (The Chantays)
12. Bruce Springsteen
13. Dennis Wilson (The Beach Boys—Dennis was the only Beach Boy who actually surfed)
14. Ron Wilson (The Surfaris)
15. Eddie Vedder (Pearl Jam)

Gimme Back My Bullets
Marksmen

1. John Cipollina (Quicksilver Messenger Service)
2. John Entwistle (The Who)
3. Mark Farner (Grand Funk Railroad)
4. Ice-T

5. Terry Kath (Chicago)
6. Ted Nugent
7. Eazy E
8. Wilson Pickett
9. Elvis Presley
10. S1Ws
11. Sir Mix-A-Lot
12. Snoop Doggy Dogg
13. Tupac
14. Ronnie Van Zant (Lynyrd Skynyrd)
15. Kurt Cobain (R.I.P.)

Military Service

1. Johnny Ace (Navy)
2. Boyd Bennett (Navy)
3. The Big Bopper (Army)
4. Johnny Cash (Air Force)
5. Billy Cox (Band of Gypsies) (Army)
6. Terence Trent D'Arby (Army)[1]
7. The Del-Vikings (Air Force)[2]
8. The Essex (Marines)[3]
9. The Everly Brothers (Marines)[4]
10. John Fogerty (Army)
11. Jerry Garcia (Army)
12. Marvin Gaye (Air Force)
13. M.C. Hammer (Navy)
14. Tim Hardin (Marines)
15. Roy Harper (Air Force)[5]
16. Jimi Hendrix (Army)
17. Ice-T (Army)
18. Kris Kristofferson (Army)
19. Frankie Lymon (Army)
20. Clyde McPhatter (Air Force)
21. Bob Mosley (Moby Grape) (Marines)
22. Michael Nesmith (Air Force)
23. Fred Parris (The Five Satins) (Army)[6]
24. Elvis Presley (Army)
25. Lloyd Price (Army)
26. Del Shannon (Army)
27. Gene Vincent (Navy)
28. Bill Withers (Navy)
29. Link Wray (Army)
30. Bill Wyman (RAF)[5]

---

[1] Went AWOL from the U.S. Army while stationed in Germany in order to begin his music career.
[2] Entire group formed in the Air Force.
[3] Entire group served in the Marines around 1963, when they created their hit "Easier Said Than Done" while serving at a base in Okinawa. Their first album cover shows them in Marine uniform.
[4] Both Don and Phil Everly served in the Marine Corps.
[5] Served in the British Royal Air Force.
[6] Parris wrote the Five Satins' biggest and most beautiful song, "In the Still of the Night," while serving on guard duty late one night. This is perhaps the loveliest and certainly the most popular doo-wop ballad ever made.

Blind

1. Clarence Carter
2. Ray Charles
3. Jose Feliciano
4. The Five Blind Boys of Alabama
5. The Five Blind Boys of Mississippi
6. Jeff Healey
7. Blind Lemon Jefferson
8. Blind Willie Johnson
9. Ronnie Milsap
10. Sonny Terry
11. Edgar Winter (legally)
12. Johnny Winter (legally)
13. Stevie Wonder

David Bowie's 5 Favorite Unusual People

1. The Wild Boy of Aveyron, the French boy raised by wolves on whom François Truffaut based his film *The Wild Child*.
2. The Paw Paw Blowtorch, a 1930s Chicago black youth who set fire to his hospital sheets and pillow by breathing on them.
3. Sean Beany, a seventeenth-century Scottish highwayman and cannibal.
4. John Merrick, the Elephant Man.
5. The Farter of Moulin Rouge, a turn-of-the-century cabaret artist (Le Petomane: real name, Joseph Pujol) renowned for his melodious asshole and candle-extinguishing routine.

David Bowie has been a rock musician, a mime, and an actor on Broadway (in The Elephant Man*) and in films (in* The Man Who Fell to Earth, *among others). Bowie's hits include "Fame," "Young Americans" and "Space Oddity." He's also produced albums by Lou Reed, Iggy Pop, and Mott the Hoople, and led the bands the Spiders from Mars and Tin Machine.*

CHAPTER 22

Politics

Enemies List

1. THE PARENTS' MUSIC RESOURCE CENTER (PMRC); TIPPER GORE; SUSAN BAKER

This group presented itself as representative of "ordinary housewives." It turned out to consist of the wives of fifteen senators and congressmen, the secretary of the treasury (later, secretary of state), an influential Republican politician from the District of Columbia, and a major Beltway real estate developer—all connections kept concealed from press and public. After rock underwent a 1985 show trial by the Senate Commerce Committee—five of whose members secretly had wives in the PMRC—these "moralists" proceeded to cow the music industry into a series of disastrous "compromises," all supposedly voluntary, which resulted in the present ridiculous state of rap (and, occasionally, heavy metal) albums bearing Parental Warning Labels, which 1) do not warn parents but possibly do entice kids; 2) constructively censor this music by keeping the records out of the more than one thousand stores that will not sell labeled music; 3) provide a constructive guilty plea that leaves the music biz wide open for prosecution and persecution by every nitwit prosecutor and nutty preacher in the land; 4) provide some of the most direct connections the lunatic religious right (see below) has ever had to the upper echelons of government. For instance, Susan Baker, the wife of the Reagan-Bush treasury secretary/ secretary of state/campaign manager/chief of staff, sits on the board of directors of Dr. James Dobson's Focus on the Family, the cranks who stirred the war against N.W.A. Tipper Gore's book, *Raising PG Kids in an X-Rated Society*, recommends no prorock sources but *does* recommend the record-burners Dan and Steve Peters and the "cult/ metal deprogrammers" at Back in Control Center. For her efforts, Mrs. Gore now serves as President Clinton's special adviser on mental health, while her husband sits several heartbeats too close to the presidency itself. Meantime, the PMRC continues to send out its one-sided antimusic propaganda, referring inquiries on the "dangers" of rock 'n' rap from true housewives to Christian fanatics of the ugliest stripe.

2. THE FBI

Botched 1963 investigation of "Louie Louie" so badly that, to this day, no one knows where the folktale that that song had dirty lyrics originated—certainly, not the bureau, which actually took the story seriously and spent thirty months and uncounted tax dollars trying to find a way to incarcerate Richard Berry or the Kingsmen. Assisted in surveillance and persecution of John Lennon, among other radical sixties rockers. In 1989, issued "official position" against N.W.A's "F—— Tha Police," inciting multistate cop fax campaign that prevented the group from performing its best-loved tune on its national tour that summer. Promised not to take such an "official position"—which it never adopted against any other work of art—ever again but that doesn't mean it won't find other, perhaps more subterranean ways to meddle where the First Amendment says it doesn't belong.

3. ALBERT GOLDMAN

"Biographer" of Elvis, John Lennon, Lenny Bruce, Jim Morrison —all of whom are judged his inferiors in tomes empurpled by prose as gaseous as a week-old corpse, to put it in terms ol' weird Albert himself might prefer. Goldman's premise is that popular culture is not just juvenile but infantile; his loathing of other humans, especially blacks, Asians, women, and southerners, pervades books that, as *Rock and Rap Confidential*'s Lee Ballinger once remarked of *Elvis*, "would previously have been considered unpublishable outside of Nazi Germany." Goldman, a faded hepster and defrocked university professor, used one gimmick consistently: He entered a project with "respect" for his subject, lost it when he discovered excesses involving drugs or sex or both (usually—in Elvis's case, Goldman seems just to have learned that his subject was a poor white southerner at birth), then reconsidered the work in this light and devalued *that*. Died in early 1994 while preparing an assault on Jim Morrison.

4. THE PTA

The PMRC's most consistent comrade-in-arms, the PTA (yeah, the same thing your mom used to belong to) actually initiated the war against rock, after two Cincinnati parents brought Prince's *1999* to the attention of its 1983 national convention. Thus the PTA adopted a resolution opposing contemporary popular music several years before it finally adopted one against contemporary mass illiteracy. Its solo complaints to the major record companies were foolishly ignored—except in the case of Warner Brothers, which publicly scoffed at them—but once it formed an alliance with the Washington wives of the PMRC it became a major player in the music censorship field.

5. FOCUS ON THE FAMILY; DR. JAMES DOBSON; BOB DEMOSS

The Colorado-based group responsible for initiating the FBI witchhunt against N.W.A's highly constitutional "F—— Tha Police" in 1989 and for helping fan the flames against Body Count's censored "Cop Killer" in 1992 has deep ties to the PMRC through both its leader, Dr. James Dobson, a former USC pediatrician who believes wholeheartedly in spanking and other physical abuse (socalled "discipline") of children, and Bob DeMoss, its "youth minister" and editor of its rock 'n' rap blacklist sheet, *Parental Guidance*, Dobson maintained close ties to the Reagan-Bush administrations through Susan Baker, wife of James Baker, who sits on FOF's board. DeMoss put together the first version of *Rising to the Challenge*, the

PMRC's Reifenstahl-like antirock propaganda video, which had to be withdrawn because it included a bogus quotation from Bruce Springsteen. (The source of that quotation was an article in *Reader's Digest;* the person most prominently quoted in that article was De-Moss.) Through his daily radio show, which airs in hundreds of communities with religious stations, Dobson continues to poison parental minds about contemporary music, with DeMoss as his chief henchman in that aspect of his efforts. Which is hardly the worst of what the organization does: Abortion center terrorist Randall Terry, for instance, has long found much support from the group, and it was FOF, recently relocated to Colorado Springs in 1992, that spearheaded the successful drive in that state to pass an anti–gay rights amendment. Barry Lynn, head of Americans United for the Separation of Church and State (and formerly chief lobbyist for the American Civil Liberties Union) calls Dobson "the most dangerous censor in America," in part because he's the best-funded and most highly connected.

6. DONALD WILDMON; THE AMERICAN FAMILY ASSOCIATION

The hottest item to emerge from Tupelo, Mississippi, since Elvis himself, Methodist minister Donald Wildmon leads an organization whose active membership may number as many as fifty to one hundred thousand, but certainly fewer than the several hundred thousand he claims. (Wildmon includes as an AFA supporter everybody on his mailing list. But *we,* among others, get his mailings, too.) Absolutely crazed on every subject pertaining to media and sexuality, Wildmon likes to stage "consumer boycotts" of TV networks, their advertisers, hotel chains showing R-rated movies and the like. He also likes to take out ads thundering about mass hostility to sex 'n' violence in the media, and claiming that the First Amendment doesn't apply to . . . well, basically, all the stuff he dislikes. Neither approach has been especially effective, but he gets plenty of ink in the process and that keeps the checks coming in. His rock targets have been scattershot—MTV has always been a focus, because he's mainly TV-oriented, but he's also supported record-banning efforts by others.

7. THE AMERICAN MEDICAL ASSOCIATION

Adopted a paper condemning shock rock and rap at its 1992 annual convention. The "scientific report" on which the position was based consisted primarily of PMRC propaganda documents—no original research was done in order for the AMA to reach its conclusion. But then, despite what it pretends, the AMA speaks not for all American doctors but only for a thin, if well-heeled, conservative slice of them. What kind of justice would you expect from a group that finds denying treatment to millions of poor people ethically acceptable?

8. DARRYL GATES

Former head of LAPD may be the most attacked human being in rap history. Now runs right-wing radio talk show in L.A., where pop culture in general, rap in particular, receive frequent beatings.

9. WYNTON MARSALIS

Among other things, this trumpeter whose talents are as broad as his mind is narrow condemned Miles Davis for recording Cyndi Lauper's "Time After Time" and denounced his brother, saxophonist Branford, for playing in a band led by Sting. Less antirock than a fanatic be-bop ideologue but a bore and a boor nonetheless.

10. *THE NEW YORK TIMES*

The *Times* played up both the payola investigation of 1959–60 and the abortive one that lasted from 1972 to 1974. But the paper never mentioned the latter's lack of results or the inaccuracies of its own reporting on it. To this day, popular music may not be discussed in the Sunday edition on the page labeled Music; it has its own ghetto, Recordings. Day to day, the everyday coverage can be very good, although its censorship coverage has generally been miserable when not antipathetic. (When Professor Griff of Public Enemy was accused of making anti-Semitic statements, reporter Jon Pareles interviewed Chuck D several times, Griff not once.) But the paper's editorial position under Southern neopopulist Howell Raines remains unremittingly hostile, especially to rap, whose vulgarities and infelicities to milquetoast liberalism the old gray lady frequently inveighs against.

11. BOB LARSON

Radio evangelist who claims to be a "former rock band musician" (weren't any of these guys ever in a *choir?*), specializes in call-in bullying, which makes him a blowhard in the style of the more kindhearted Rush Limbaugh. Never met a disagreement he thought he had to tolerate.

12. DAN AND STEVE PETERS

Minnesota-based practitioners of a "youth ministry" that specializes in record (and tape and CD) burnings. Their most notorious book, *Why Knock Rock?*, contains a manual on how to conduct a burning; it is endorsed by Tipper Gore in *Raising PG Kids*, though she later claimed she doesn't recommend that part. She also doesn't steer anybody away from it. Amazingly, the chief impediment the Peters brothers now find to their public burnings comes from local environmental ordinances that prevent the burning of the plastics contained in music-carriers. They've been reduced to burning record covers, CD inserts, and tape J-cards. Frightening enough in any form.

13. REVEREND CALVIN BUTTS

Minister at Harlem's famous Abyssinian Baptist Church (the pulpit once helmed by Adam Clayton Powell), Butts decided in 1993 that he had no need to tolerate rap music that disdained Abyssinian Baptist values. So he gathered together a bunch of cassettes and hired a steamroller, setting out to do to these albums what the environmentalists will no longer allow Dan and Steve Peters to do. Rappers from the community stood in front of the steamroller and forced him to back down. But his verbal and written attacks continue.

14. JACK THOMPSON

South Florida Christian "profamily" attorney who stirred the campaign to jail 2 Live Crew. Thompson, a single practitioner, denies affiliation with any other group but he's been supported by both the Wildmon/AFA bunch and the Dobson/FOF crew, each of whose tactics and homiletics he adapts to his singular purpose. Thompson says the battle against 2 Live Crew began because he's seen so much suffering as the result of rape and domestic abuse among clients he's represented. Luther Campbell, 2 Live Crew's leader, believes it stems from Thompson's mid-eighties campaign for Dade County state's attorney, in which he ran against Janet Reno. (Thompson may have been the first to publicly accuse Reno of being a lesbian.) Campbell's Skyywalker Records released a record in support of the Reno campaign (ironically, it endorsed her for being tough on men who skip out on their child support payments), and in Luther's view, Thompson has never forgiven him for it. (The other key figure in the 2 Live Crew prosecution, Broward County [Fort Lauderdale] sheriff Nick Navarro, was tossed out of office by voters in 1992, on the heels of his failed pogrom against the Crew, revelations of corruption in the sheriff's department, and his stepdaughter's suicide note alleging that Navarro had sexually abused her. Thompson has mounted no prominent campaign to incarcerate Navarro.) In the sense that Luther Campbell and 2 Live Crew actually spent a night in jail thanks to his ministry, Thompson may be regarded as one of the more effective censors, though no one has paid much attention to his phone-and-fax operation lately.

15. REVEREND JIMMY SWAGGART

Before being functionally defrocked for his own sexual pecadilloes, Swaggart was known for hour-long exhortations on the demonic influence of rock, sermons of such fiery spirit that you'd have marked him as close kin to Jerry Lee Lewis even if he didn't frequently use the ill-fortune suffered by his illustrious cousin as a case-in-point. From the point of view of video entertainment (or for that matter, of the art of fundamentalist sermonizing), it's too bad the guy got nailed.

16. THE NATIONAL COALITION ON TELEVISION VIOLENCE

Astonishingly, people still pay attention to this crew of crackpots, frequent demonizers of music video, even though its original leader, Dr. Thomas Radecki, had his license to practice suspended by the state of Illinois in 1992 for reasons stemming from sexual exploitation of his patients.

17. ALLAN BLOOM

The late University of Chicago philosophy professor sold his *Closing of the American Mind,* a multimillion-copy bestseller, largely on the basis of its scabrous chapter fomenting against rock 'n' rap. Bloom unhesitatingly and without qualification compares rock stars to Hitler and considers it the central reason our contemporary civilization is approaching an end.

17. HARRY CONNICK, JR.

This Frank Sinatra impressionist gets PR mileage out of damning the low quality of rock songs. Yeah, so how does this son-of-an-indicted-politician feel about Ella Fitzgerald kicking off *her* career with "A Tisket, A Tasket"? Could rank higher given his ubiquitousness on late night TV if his minimal talent and outdated approach hadn't already rendered him fairly irrelevant.

19. STEVE ALLEN

First entered ranks of rock haters when he made Elvis Presley wear a white tie and tails and sing "Hound Dog" to a basset singing on a stool. Also did portentous poetry-style reading of Gene Vincent's "Be Bop A Lula," like the lyrics were the point. Since then, this celebrated video has-been, third-rate cocktail jazz pianist, owner of one of the world's worst toupees, and author of a ghostwritten book on ethics has rarely missed a chance to pillory the popular music people actually listen to.

20. BACK IN CONTROL CENTER

"Deprogramming" center run by two ex-cops in California. Promulgates scare stories, some of them with extremely dubious basis (for example, the Jewish star as Satanic device), designed to get parents to cough up dough to "cure" their kids, justify police activity against noncomformist metalheads.

Fake Friends

"You don't lose when you lose fake friends."—Joan Jett, 1983.

1. RUSS BACH

Head of CEMA, the Capitol-EMI Records distribution arm, encouraged record retailers in their campaign to create censorship labels (so-called "Tipper stickers"), encouraged the dropping of artists who didn't fit America's "increasingly conservative climate," and in 1993, launched the major labels' anti-used-CD spat, only to leave his own superstar, Garth Brooks, hung out to dry when Bach chose to back down rather than truly buck the big-time record sellers.

2. LEE ABRAMS AND RADIO PROGRAMMERS

Abrams pioneered the album-rock radio "Superstars" format, which mathematically justified FM rock radio's decline into a banal LP-track-oriented Top Twenty. He also presided over the formal, demographically rationalized splitting off of black pop from white. Meantime, Abrams plumped for the most bathetic sort of "progressive rock," actually going so far as to produce an album by Gentle Giant, one of the dullest of the lot. Abrams's fortunes waned as AOR died from the stagnant diet he devised, but the "narrowcasting" he, more than anyone, initiated remains the bane of the airwaves for music listeners, ensuring that you'll have to touch that dial at least once a quarter-hour unless your taste is as one-track as it is mundane. Label exciting pop music radio a suicide, broadcasters generally a sad, self-loathing bunch of advertising-fearing weasels, and the market-splintering radio consultants of which Abrams was a protoptype the vultures circling over the corpse.

3. CONCERT PROMOTERS

American concert promotion is controlled by a cartel that refuses to compete across markets, with several results, one of which is that several major markets—most notably New York—are not serviced by *anyone* competent to do anything more complex than pop a champagne cork. There is no more useless appendix in the music business than the contemporary concert promoter (who rarely has any say about who's on the bill, much less any concept of what to do if tickets don't sell, or, for that matter, who to book or what to pay them in the first place).

4. RUSS SOLOMON

With his long gray ponytail, the Tower Records chief looks far hipper than he is. Supports record labeling, even though he knows this means that many of his retail peers will simply not carry labeled music at all. Waged bitter campaign against the ecologically wasteful cardboard CD "longbox," during which he acted as if the cost of refixturing his record stores took precedence over the health of the environment. In the end, just another shopkeeper.

5. CAMELOT MUSIC AND OTHER CHAIN RETAILERS

Camelot, which led the battle to force record companies to label records (which artists allow about as voluntarily as any other act they might perform with a gun at their temple), is only the worst offender among many. Chain stores add their own labels to records whose artists manage to put out something with halfway "adult" content, refuse to sell records to minors, refuse to carry labeled records, or for that matter, anything they deem unfit (for example, Nirvana's *In Utero*), treat every customer as a potential felon with excessive "security" measures, and usually don't even sell used CDs, unlike the mom-and-pop stores they're continually trying to squeeze out of the action.

6. MAJOR RECORD LABELS

Gutless and greedy, disdainful of artistry in the face of the bottom line but not shrewd enough to defend their profits (if nothing else) against the depradations of cranks, politicians on the make, over-agitated schoolmarms, and tomfool preachers. Notorious for not pay-ing artists what they owe them, and yet never satisfied with what they're getting from their customers: They want a tax on home taping (and got one on DAT, killing a technologically superior form), have made record rentals illegal, and refuse to acknowledge that consumers own a record even after they get it home, by trying to stamp out the purchase of used CDs. They manufacture their tapes on third-rate cassettes, repackage music with little rhyme or reason, and promote new artists with the knowledge and sensitivity of the military in Kuwait. A pox.

7. *BILLBOARD* MAGAZINE

Always a friendly place for censors like the PMRC, but hospitable to those trying to fight for freedom of expression only under duress. Condemned Ice Cube for "No Vaseline," his song attacking former manager Jerry Heller that referred to Heller as a Jew. Has never said a word against the constant, unremitting exploitation of artists, and is particularly nonconfrontational about the racial basis of much of that exploitation. Its media critic Eric Boehlert has gone on record as agreeing with the fundamental premises of right-wing reverend Donald Wildmon's antimedia attack ads, including the idea that listening to the wrong music encourages young girls to get pregnant. Worse than useless.

8. LIBERALS

The crux of the problem. The main attacks on music—especially hip-hop and metal—have come from people who just can't compre-hend why blacks and poor whites don't behave with good manners and other impeccable social skills, and certainly have no intention of allowing dissenting voices to speak *crudely*. It was congressional lib-erals like Albert Gore who did the most to bring censorship into music; it's liberals in the media who did the least to report on the consequences of that censorship. And it's most often from the mildly left-of-center that the most divisive attacks on rap, metal, and other supposedly degenerate forms have emerged.

9. ELVIS PRESLEY

Tried to sign up with the FBI as an undercover agent for the express purpose of spying on contemporary rockers like the Stones and the Beatles.

10. MIKE CURB

Former California lieutenant governor and Ronald Reagan pro-tégé prospered surprisingly little from eighties political develop-ments, instead turned to churning out country albums, many by old veterans (generally with very stingy selection in terms of time and number of tracks), the most notable being several by honky-bluesman Delbert McClinton (a Lee Atwater crony, which explains a lot). Curb earned his fake friend stripes in the seventies, and not only by perpetrating some of the lamest excuses chicken rock has ever seen: He was the entrepreneur behind Debby Boone, the Osmond Family, Shaun Cassidy, and Leif Garrett, among others. In 1970, he took the helm of MGM Records and announced he was cutting from the label's roster all acts with "drug orientation"—a ploy designed to rid him of the company's many lame bands. The stratagem backfired, however, because Eric Brudon, then one of the few MGM Records stars, cheerfully admitted his drug use (he'd already been making records about it for three years) and petitioned Curb for his release. It wasn't forthcoming, which kinda made the exec look like a hypocrite, though not so much as MGM's concurrent release of an album of psychedelic Grateful Dead outtakes. Curb also handled the entertainment for the first inaugural ball of Richard Nixon and noted rockbasher Spiro Agnew.

11. MITCH MILLER

Chief A&R man for Columbia Records during the early rock era, Miller made many gutter-level attacks on rock, preferring to record his own cornball barbershop harmonies and refusing to record *any* rock. What little blues or rockabilly the CBS Records group did acquire appeared on its ghettoized Okeh subsidiary, although Miller frequently poached country, R&B, and rock 'n' roll songs for his label's stars to whitewash, even though he condemned the quality of this material in his public denunciations of its decadence. When rock did not disappear, Miller's career nosedived. These days, he says he was never against it but that's far from the truth.

12. LEE ATWATER

We can all agree that early death, especially from a hideous disease like brain cancer, is an awful thing. But a deathbed apology that reaches out to Michael Dukakis but not to Willie Horton, the man he *truly* vilified, hardly makes up for a lifetime spent in thrall to Strom Thurmond, Ronald Reagan, and other white supremacists, any more than giving B. B. King a gig at the inaugural ball amounts to a humanitarian gesture beyond what any Klan-related Mississippi fraternity would have done for its Saturday night beer bash when Atwater was growing up. Plus, he played shitty guitar on his one album, no matter how many R&B vets he inveigled into playing on it. (They're excused, since all of them desperately needed the gig, thanks to the policies Atwater spent the daylight hours fostering.)

Rap Haters

1. Black Crowes
2. Bob Dylan
3. David Geffen
4. George Harrison
5. James Hetfield (Metallica)

6. Wynton Marsalis
7. Prince (ret.)[1]
8. Michelle Shocked
9. Paul Simon
10. Phil Spector

---

[1] Did some righteous, wrongheaded rap-bashing on *Lovesexy*, then reversed course on subsequent albums, though he never did come up with an interesting hip-hop approach. If he's retired, you'd have to say he never truly got with the program. But then, if he's really retired maybe antipathy to rap is one of the reasons?

Tragedy, the Intelligent Hoodlum, Lists the 10 Best Rap Songs that Dis the Government and Politicians

Tragedy, whose "Arrest the President" highlighted our version of 1992's political campaign, comments: "These are factual songs and what I call words of creative courage. Many artists, as we know, are faced with the double standards of rights. This country prides itself on freedom and equality of all men. However, anyone with eyes to see and a brain to think with for themselves can see the everyday practice of Hypocrisy that reveals our America as the hell it truly is. I used to have hope for the people, but now I see more and more tricks to seduce our strong-minded people. People who once believed as I did now worship another cause. Realistically, what's the difference between J. Edgar Hoover and Bill Clinton or these so-called congressmen who are nothing more than Klansmen in three-piece suits? Nothing, only that Clinton gears you and I to believe that we can have some type of strong community with better living conditions, better education, and better health care for the so-called minorities. I assure you that it's all false. Take a trip to the ghetto. Find some strength in yourself and ride through the streets. Walk through the schools that stand in these neighborhoods. And you'll see that there has been no progress, only transgress. And like fire on a dry bush, it's spreading. If things keep going the way they are going, everyone is going to be in some deep shit. I hope that you're real, and if you're real, stay true to the game."

1. "Louder than a Bomb," Public Enemy
2. "Arrest the President," Intelligent Hoodlum (Tragedy)

3. "Bush Killa," Paris
4. "Paint the White House Black," George Clinton
5. "At Large," Intelligent Hoodlum
6. "America Eats the Young," Intelligent Hoodlum
7. "Black to the Future," Def Jeff
8. "Fight the Power," Public Enemy
9. "Black Steel in the Hour of Chaos," Public Enemy
10. "At War," Sister Souljah

Tragedy, the Intelligent Hoodlum, Lists the 10 Best Rap Songs that Dis the Police

1. "Deep Cover," Dr. Dre and Snoop Doggy Dogg
2. "F—— tha Police," N.W.A
3. "Get the Fuck Out of Dodge," Public Enemy
4. "Cop Killer," Ice-T
5. "Illegal Search," L.L. Cool J
6. "No Justice, No Peace," Intelligent Hoodlum
7. "Black Cop," KRS-1
8. "Killa Man," Cypress Hill
9. "Black and Blue," Brand Nubian
10. "Bullet," Intelligent Hoodlum

Shot Down in Flames
Reginald C. Dennis Lists Five Songs About Police that Never Came Out Due to the "Cop Killer" Controversy

1. "Bullet," The Intelligent Hoodlum
2. "Shoot 'Em Down," Boo-Yaa Tribe
3. "Justice for the Hood," Juvenile Committee
4. "Cop Hell," Mobb Deep
5. "Mr. Officer," Dr. Dre

Greatest Fifties Protest Songs

1. "Almost Grown," Chuck Berry
2. "Blue Suede Shoes," Elvis Presley

3. "Get a Job," The Silhouettes
4. "I've Had It," The Bell Notes
5. "Money (That's What I Want)," Barrett Strong
6. "Money Honey," The Drifters
7. "Riot in Cell Block # 9," The Robins
8. "School Days," Chuck Berry
9. "The Slummer the Slum," The 5 Royales
10. "Summertime Blues," Eddie Cochran
11. "Too Much Monkey Business," Chuck Berry
12. "Tutti Frutti," Little Richard
13. "Well All Right," Buddy Holly
14. "What About Us," The Coasters
15. "Yakety Yak," The Coasters

Greatest Sixties Protest Songs

1. "Abraham, Martin and John," Dion
2. "Alice's Restaurant," Arlo Guthrie
3. "Bad Moon Rising," Creedence Clearwater Revival
4. "Big Boss Man," Jimmy Reed
5. "Blowin' in the Wind," Stevie Wonder
6. "A Change Is Gonna Come," Sam Cooke
7. "Choice of Colors," The Impressions
8. "Don't Call Me Nigger, Whitey (Don't Call Me Whitey, Nigger)," Sly and the Family Stone
9. "Don't Look Now (It Ain't You or Me)," Creedence Clearwater Revival
10. "Everyday People," Sly and the Family Stone
11. "For What It's Worth," Buffalo Springfield
12. "Fortunate Son," Creedence Clearwater Revival
13. "Games People Play," Joe South
14. "Get Off of My Cloud," The Rolling Stones
15. "Get Together," The Youngbloods
16. "Give Peace a Chance," The Plastic Ono Band
17. "A Hard Rain's A-Gonna Fall," Bob Dylan
18. "I Ain't A-Marchin' Anymore," Phil Ochs
19. "I Don't Live Today," The Jimi Hendrix Experience
20. "If I Can Dream," Elvis Presley
21. "If 6 Was 9," Jimi Hendrix
22. "Is It Because I'm Black?" Syl Johnson
23. "Laugh At Me," Sonny
24. "The Lonesome Death of Hattie Carroll," Bob Dylan
25. "My Generation," The Who
26. "People Get Ready," The Impressions
27. "People Got to Be Free," The Rascals

28. "Pride of Man," Quicksilver Messenger Service
29. "Revolution," The Beatles
30. "Something in the Air," Thunderclap Newman
31. "Street Fighting Man," The Rolling Stones
32. "Thank You Falettinme Be Mice Elf Agin," Sly and the Family Stone
33. "This Is My Country," The Impressions
34. "The Under Assistant West Coast Promotion Man," The Rolling Stones
35. "Viet Nam," Jimmy Cliff
36. "We Gotta Get Out of This Place," The Animals
37. "We're a Winner," The Impressions
38. "Who'll Stop the Rain," Creedence Clearwater Revival
39. "With God on Our Side," Manfred Mann
40. "The Young Mod's Forgotten Story," The Impressions

Greatest Seventies Protest Songs

1. " 'A' Bomb in Wardour Street," The Jam
2. "America Eats Its Young," Funkadelic
3. "Anarchy in the U.K.," The Sex Pistols
4. "Badlands," Bruce Springsteen
5. "Before the Deluge," Jackson Browne
6. "Brother Louie," Stories
7. "Complete Control," The Clash
8. "Feel Like a Number," Bob Seger
9. "54-46," Toots and the Maytals
10. "George Jackson," Bob Dylan
11. "Gimme Some Truth," John Lennon
12. "Glad to Be Gay," The Tom Robinson Band
13. "God Save the Queen," The Sex Pistols
14. "Had Enough," The Who
15. "Holidays in the Sun," The Sex Pistols
16. "I Don't Like Mondays," The Boomtown Rats
17. "I Shot the Sheriff," Bob Marley and the Wailers
18. "I'm So Bored with the U.S.A.," The Clash
19. "Inner City Blues (Make Me Wanna Holler)," Marvin Gaye
20. "Less Than Zero," Elvis Costello
21. "Mercy, Mercy Me (The Ecology)," Marvin Gaye
22. "Miss-tra Know It All," Stevie Wonder
23. "Night Rally," Elvis Costello
24. "Ohio," Crosby, Stills, Nash and Young
25. "Respect Yourself," The Staple Singers

26. "Right to Work," Chelsea
27. "Southern Man," Neil Young
28. "Sweet Home Alabama," Lynyrd Skynyrd
29. "Thank You for Talkin' to Me, Africa," Sly and the Family Stone
30. "There but for the Grace of God Go I," Machine
31. "Waiting for the End of the World," Elvis Costello
32. "Wake Up Everybody," Harold Melvin and the Blue Notes
33. "War," Edwin Starr
34. "Welcome to the Working Week," Elvis Costello
35. "(What's So Funny 'Bout) Peace, Love and Understanding," Elvis Costello
36. "White Riot," The Clash
37. "Won't Get Fooled Again," The Who
38. "The World is a Ghetto," War
39. "You Haven't Done Nothin'," Stevie Wonder
40. "Your Generation," Generation X

Greatest Eighties Protest Songs

1. "Another Day in Paradise," Phil Collins
2. "Bad Reputation," Joan Jett
3. "Black Stations/White Stations," M + M
4. "Bring the Noise," Public Enemy
5. "The Call Up," The Clash
6. "Dirty Laundry," Don Henley
7. "Don't Believe the Hype," Public Enemy
8. "Don't Give Up," Peter Gabriel
9. "Eat the Rich," Krokus
10. "F—— Tha Police," N.W.A
11. "Fight for Your Right to Party," The Beastie Boys
12. "Five Minutes," Bonzo Goes to Washington
13. "Freedom of Speech," Ice-T
14. "Funny Vibe," Living Colour
15. "I Will Not Go Quietly," Don Henley
16. "If I Had a Rocket Launcher," Bruce Cockburn
17. "It's Like That," Run-D.M.C.
18. "Lawyers in Love," Jackson Browne
19. "London Calling," The Clash
20. "The Message," Grandmaster Flash and the Furious Five
21. "No Sell Out," Malcom X/Keith LeBlanc
22. "One," Metallica
23. "Papa Don't Preach," Madonna

24. "Party for Your Right to Fight," Public Enemy
25. "Pink Houses," John Mellencamp
26. "Rain on the Scarecrow," John Mellencamp
27. "Seeds," Bruce Springsteen
28. "Sign O' the Times," Prince
29. "Solidarity," Little Steven and the Disciples of Soul
30. "Still in Saigon," Charlie Daniels
31. "Stop the Violence," Boogie Down Productions
32. "Sun City," Artists United Against Apartheid
33. "This Is England," The Clash
34. "This Note's for You," Neil Young
35. "Two Tribes," Frankie Goes to Hollywood
36. "Watching the Wheels," John Lennon
37. "The Way It Is," Bruce Hornsby and the Range
38. "(We Don't Need This) Fascist Groove Thing," Heaven 17
39. "White Lines (Don't Do It)," Grandmaster Melle Mel
40. "Who Protects Us From You?" Boogie Down Productions

Greatest Nineties Protest Songs (So Far)

1. "Arrest the President," Intelligent Hoodlum
2. "Bang Bang Bang," Tracy Chapman
3. "Banned in the U.S.A.," 2 Live Crew
4. "Born to Lose," Social Distortion
5. "Bring the Noise," Public Enemy
6. "Bush Killa," Paris
7. "By the Time I Get to Arizona," Public Enemy
8. "Cop Killer," Body Count
9. "Countdown to Extinction," Megadeth
10. "Crooked Officer," The Geto Boys
11. "Dead Homiez," Ice Cube
12. "Elvis Is Dead," Living Colour
13. "Fight the Power," Public Enemy
14. "Freedom Got an A.K.," Da Lench Mob
15. "Fuck Compton," Tim Dogg
16. "Get in the Ring," Guns N' Roses
17. "Good Evening Mr. Waldheim," Lou Reed
18. "Home," Iggy Pop
19. "The Homeless," Boogie Down Productions
20. "How I Could Just Kill a Man," Cypress Hill
21. "I Wanna Kill Sam," Ice Cube
22. "Jeremy," Pearl Jam
23. "KKK Bitch," Body Count

24. "Letter from the KKK," Bushwick Bill
25. "Louie Louie," Iggy Pop
26. "Momma's Gotta Die Tonight," Body Count
27. "Money Don't Matter 2 Night," Prince
28. "National Anthem," Sir Mix-A-Lot
29. "One," U2
30. "100 Miles and Runnin'," N.W.A
31. "One Time's Got No Case," Sir Mix-A-Lot
32. "Rodney K," Willie D
33. "Size Ain't Shit," The Geto Boys
34. "Smells Like Teen Spirit," Nirvana
35. "Souls of the Departed," Bruce Springsteen
36. "Teachers, Don't Teach Us Nonsense," Leaders of the New School
37. "Tennessee," Arrested Development
38. "The Wrong Nigga to Fuck With," Ice Cube
39. "Young Black Male," 2 Pac
40. "Youth Against Fascism," Sonic Youth

Apocalypse Now
Songs of Nuclear Anxiety

1. " 'A' Bomb in Wardour Street," The Jam
2. "Armagideon Time," The Clash
3. "Atomic Dog," George Clinton
4. "Before the Deluge," Jackson Browne
5. "Eve of Destruction," Barry McGuire
6. "The Great American Eagle Tragedy," Earth Opera
7. "A Hard Rain's A-Gonna Fall," Bob Dylan
8. "I Come and Stand at Every Door," The Byrds
9. "It Came Out of the Sky," Creedence Clearwater Revival
10. "London Calling," The Clash
11. "Morning Dew," Tim Rose
12. "Mushroom Clouds," Love
13. "99 Red Balloons," Nena
14. "1983," Jimi Hendrix
15. "1999," Prince
16. "Nuclear Attack," Greg Lake
17. "Nuclear Burn," Brand X
18. "Plutonium Is Forever," John Hall
19. "Red Rain," Peter Gabriel
20. "Roulette," Bruce Springsteen
21. "Siberian Nights," Twilight 22
22. "Uranium Rock," Warren Smith
23. "Wars of Armageddon," Funkadelic

24. "We Almost Lost Detroit," Gil Scott-Heron
25. "Wooden Ships," Crosby, Stills, Nash and Young
26. "World Destruction," Afrika Bambaataa and Johnny Lydon

Musicians United for Safe Energy
Performers at the MUSE Concerts for a Non-Nuclear Future, Madison Square Garden, September 19–24, 1979

1. Jackson Browne
2. Ry Cooder
3. Crosby, Stills and Nash
4. The Doobie Brothers
5. John Hall
6. Chaka Khan
7. Graham Nash
8. Tom Petty and the Heartbreakers
9. Bonnie Raitt
10. Gil Scott-Heron
11. Carly Simon
12. Bruce Springsteen and the E Street Band
13. Sweet Honey in the Rock
14. James Taylor
15. Jesse Colin Young

The Antiwar Top 40

1. "Alice's Restaurant," Arlo Guthrie
2. "Architecture of Aggression," Megadeth
3. "Ball of Confusion," The Temptations
4. "Black Steel in the Hour of Chaos," Public Enemy
5. "Blackened," Metallica
6. "Blowin' in the Wind," Stevie Wonder
7. "Born in the U.S.A," Bruce Springsteen
8. "Bring the Boys Home," Freda Payne
9. "The Call Up," The Clash
10. "Casualties of War," Eric B and Rakim
11. "Civil War," Guns N' Roses
12. "Foxhole," Television
13. "Give Peace a Chance," The Plastic Ono Band
14. "Happy Xmas (War Is Over)," John Lennon and Yoko Ono
15. "A Hard Rain's A-Gonna Fall," Bob Dylan
16. "He Looks a Lot Like Me," Dion
17. "If I Had a Rocket Launcher," Bruce Cockburn
18. "Imagine," John Lennon

19. "Izabella," Jimi Hendrix
20. "Kill for Peace," The Fugs
21. "Life During Wartime," Talking Heads
22. "Lost in the Flood," Bruce Springsteen
23. "Machine Gun," The Jimi Hendrix Experience
24. "Masters of War," Eddie Vedder and Mike McCready
25. "Money Don't Matter Tonight," Prince
26. "Ohio," Crosby, Stills, Nash and Young
27. "Oliver's Army," Elvis Costello
28. "Peace Train," Cat Stevens
29. "Rompin' Through the Swamp," The Holy Modal Rounders
30. "Sam Stone," John Prine
31. "$2 + 2 = ?$" Bob Seger
32. "Universal Soldier," Buffy Sainte-Marie
33. "War," Edwin Starr
34. "War Pigs," Black Sabbath
35. "We've Got to Have Peace," Curtis Mayfield
36. "What's Going On," Marvin Gaye
37. "(What's So Funny 'Bout) Peace, Love and Understanding," Elvis Costello
38. "With God on Our Side," Bob Dylan
39. "Yes Sir, No Sir," The Kinks
40. "Your Flag Decal Won't Get You into Heaven Anymore," John Prine

Lee Ballinger Picks the 10 Best Antiwar Records

1. "Disorder," Slayer and Ice-T
2. "El Tiburon," Ruben Blades and Willie Colon
3. "Machine Gun," Jimi Hendrix
4. "Casualties of War," Eric B and Rakim
5. "Blackened," Metallica
6. "Money Don't Matter Tonight," Prince
7. "If I Had a Rocket Launcher," Bruce Cockburn
8. "Black Steel in the Hour of Chaos," Public Enemy
9. "Architecture of Aggression," Megadeth
10. "Viet Cong Blues," Junior Wells

Lee Ballinger, managing editor of Rock & Rap Confidential, *earned his antiwar credentials while in the Navy in Vietnam.*

Performers Whose Careers Were Damaged by Their Politics

1. JACKSON BROWNE

Browne supplanted his intense and revealing 1970s series of apocalyptic confessional albums with a series of increasingly doctrinaire, comparatively drab essays on human rights politics in the eighties. Combined with a virtually obsessive set of benefit concert appearances, this so alienated even the guy's core audience that when he emerged in 1993 with *I'm Alive*, a fine album of intimate songs, it received far less attention that it deserved. On the other hand, his political period produced one of the all-time great rock 'n' politics numbers, "Lawyers in Love." Which was, of course, a joke that pundits mainly missed. Aw shit . . . (See Steve Van Zandt.)

2. LUTHER CAMPBELL

You could argue that, without the politicized censorship prosecutions he suffered in 1990, 2 Live Crew leader Luther Campbell's Skyywalker/Luke Records would never have sold umpteen million records. But if those prosecutions hadn't happened, Campbell also wouldn't have 1) spent a night in jail (which seems like a harmless experience only if you've never done it); 2) spent millions of dollars in legal fees; 3) seen future 2 Live Crew releases banished from hundreds of stores without being given so much as a listen.

3. PROFESSOR GRIFF

Dumped from Public Enemy for his parroting of the Nation of Islam's anti-Semitic line, Griff then found his subsequent albums (made for Luke Records) utterly ignored, although they revealed a bright, intelligent hip-hop sensibility without any trace of inappropriate rancor whatsoever. But then, Griff's visit to a South Florida Holocaust memorial and his dialogue with the young Jewish student who brought him there also made no headlines.

4. WOODY GUTHRIE

After he and his cousin, Jack, hit with "Oklahoma Hills" in the late thirties, Woody had the same chance as any other "hillbilly" performer to go to Nashville and create a substantial career in what became the country music industry. He certainly had the lyrical aptitude, and perhaps the onstage charisma, for the task, although many would argue about his singing voice. In any event, Woody instead got political religion and turned his talents to entertaining, inspiring, and fund raising for a variety of radical causes. Not only were these tasks far less remunerative but they left his greatest songs in jeopardy. So, in the McCarthyite mid-fifties, when Guthrie came home from hospitalization as a result of the Huntington's Chorea that eventually killed him, he'd take his eldest son, Arlo, into the backyard and teach him the lyrics of "This Land Is Your Land" because he feared that otherwise even such great songs would be lost.

5. ICE-T

Speaking his mind on the proper reaction to police brutality cost Ice-T sleepless nights as the result of death threats from the hypocritically aggrieved cops and a commercial death sentence from the Time-Warner board of directors, thanks especially to opera pig Beverly Sills and such shareholders as the clenched-jaw ham Charlton Heston. Eventually, his political views cost him his Sire Records contract, meaning that his current opinions do not have the degree of circulation that a major recording company contract would afford him. *Ice-T did not sell out. He got fucked.*

6. EARTHA KITT

The sexiest black actress of her generation (she played the original Catwoman in the old *Batman* TV series) and a sultry singer, Kitt virtually disappeared from mainstream show business after daring to publicly criticize President Lyndon Johnson's handling of race relations and the war in Vietnam during a 1968 White House appearance.

7. JOHN LENNON

Virtually held hostage in the United States during his 1970s hassle with the Immigration and Naturalization Service, which turned down his residency application on the grounds that he was a dangerous subversive. Which he was but where would either America or art be without such subversion? Perhaps in the hands of racist reactionaries like Senator Strom Thurmond, main instigator of the INS's anti-Lennon crusade, and a man who preaches against media dissolution yet let his daughter audition as an MTV veejay. The battle affected Lennon's lifestyle, added to the tensions in his marriage, and contributed to the unfocused nature of his music during the period.

8. TOM ROBINSON

"2-4-6-8 Motorway" gave him a big hit right away, and "Glad to Be Gay" proved a powerful anthem for gay rockers years before opening closet doors acquired even the thinnest patina of chic. But Robinson never developed the at least journeyman mainstream rocker career he deserved precisely because he *did* speak so clearly about the subject that, apparently, still dare not sing its name, at least where males are concerned.

9. PETE SEEGER

Blacklisted as a member of the Weavers during the McCarthy period, Seeger found his way back to major label recordings through the intervention of John Hammond at Columbia Records. His recordings there in the early eighties sold better than any others in his long, storied solo career. But there was a distinct limit to his success. The early sixties urban folk scene TV show *Hootenanny*, on the ABC network, banned him (which actually caused the show significant problems, because so many other artists boycotted it to support Seeger). As late as 1968, when the Smothers Brothers invited him to sing "Waist Deep in the Big Muddy," a rather explicit anti–Vietnam War allegory, on their CBS TV show, Seeger still found himself and his left-wing point of view banned by network censors. (Next time you hear a complaint about the "liberal bias" of the news media, try to think of a parallel story involving a conservative performer.) (See the Weavers.)

10. BRUCE SPRINGSTEEN

The exception who proves the rule? On his 1984–85 *Born in the U.S.A.* tour, Springsteen involved himself with community groups working on such issues as labor, hunger, and homelessness. On his 1988 *Tunnel of Love* tour, he kept his commitments private. On his 1992–93 tour, they remained that way. Each step of the way, Springsteen found himself more and more alienated from his audience, whose raised expectations he wasn't (visibly) meeting. On the road in 1984, both Reagan and Mondale attempted to proclaim his endorsement of their policies. In 1992, when rockers became more involved with a political campaign than at any other time in history, no one mentioned his name. He returned to the Top 10 with "Philadelphia," a song about AIDS that could be construed as issue-oriented material.

11. STEVE VAN ZANDT

Bruce Springsteen's sidekick Miami Steve left his post as blue-eyed soul man for a solo career and became Little Steven, red-rimmed up-all-night activist. Unfortunately, his fine understanding of R&B and soul roots did not translate well into the hip-hop and metal contexts he tried to use for his solo records. Or, more likely, the problem was that his albums became more and more didactic and ideologically rigid with each release. Despite the brilliance of "Sun City," by far the most musically and politically articulate protest record of the eighties, his career almost totally foundered on the narrowness of his subject matter. (See Jackson Browne.)

12. THE WEAVERS

The first of the urban pop-folk groups grew directly out of a pre–World War II popular front combo, the Almanac Singers, which also featured Pete Seeger and Lee Hays. Decca Records scored significant hits with their "Tzena, Tzena, Tzena," "Goodnight Irene," "So Long (It's Been Good to Know Ya)," "On Top of Old Smokey," "Kisses Sweeter Than Wine," "Wimoweh," in 1950–52. But the McCarthy witch hunt simply wouldn't allow a major record label (Decca was among the top three in those days) to record a bunch of Reds and pinkos, let alone get airplay and sales with them. The Weavers were able to move to Vanguard, but even concert bookings had been affected by the blacklist and hard times engulfed them well into the sixties. Nevertheless, the Weavers deserve credit for kicking off the mid-fifties folk boom with their 1955 Carnegie Hall concert, and for introducing a generation to the songs of Woody Guthrie and Leadbelly, among others. (See Pete Seeger.)

The Staff of *Uncut Funk* Picks the Most Significant Overt Political Statements by the P-Funk Mob

1. "Chocolate City" (1975)—Reconstructs the Nation's Capital as the center of a cultural/political Afro-renaissance.
2. "March to the Witches Castle" (1973)—Acknowledges the humanity and the multifaceted victimization of the Vietnam veterans, ahead of its time.
3. "Biological Speculation" (1972)—Explores the karmic implication of Natural Law.
4. "Funky Dollar Bill" (1971)—Demonstrates that "funky" don't always mean good, with a condemnation of the capitalist ethic.
5. "Dope Dog" (1993)—Why do guns and drugs saturate the 'hood? Ask those who patrol the borders.
6. "Jimmy Got a Little Bit of Bitch in Him" (1974)—Offers acceptance and compassion (of a sort) for gays, contrary to long-established ghetto politics.

Right-Wingers

1. Lee Atwater
2. Richard Branson (Virgin Records)
3. James Brown
4. Belinda Carlisle (by marriage)
5. Ray Charles
6. Eric Clapton (on occasion)
7. Bob Dylan (sometimes)
8. Eazy-E
9. Ahmet Ertegun (Atlantic Records)
10. Sammy Hagar
11. Charles Koppelman (SBK/Capitol-EMI Records)
12. Stan Lee (Dickies)
13. Mike Love (Beach Boys)
14. Keith Morris (Circle Jerks)
15. Ted Nugent
16. Elvis Presley
17. Prince (in his Reagan period)
18. Skrewdriver
19. Neil Young (in his Reagan period)
20. Young M.C.

Riding a Stairway to Perdition
Records Accused of Satanic Backmasking

These examples come from the following books, all written by good Christians: Rock's Hidden Persuaders: The Truth About Backmasking *by Dan and Steve Peters;* The Devil's Disciples: The Truth About Rock *by Jeff Godwin; and* Backward Masking Unmasked *and* More Rock and Country Backward Masking Unmasked *by Jacob Aranza. (All of these books can be obtained at your local fundamentalist bookseller or other purveyor of fanatic wares, or get in touch with the Parents' Music Resource Center.) We have no idea whether any of this stuff can actually be heard because we own no machinery capable of playing music backward (nor do we possess any desire to hear it that way—what kinda perverts would that make us?). However, we* do *know that no credible academic study places any credence in the idea that passages recorded backward are somehow tumbled forward in the human brain and "subliminally" absorbed as commands to do certain things, whether worship the devil, buy more popcorn, or kill oneself.*

1. "ANOTHER ONE BITES THE DUST," QUEEN

Hidden Persuaders and *Backward Masking Unmasked* reveal that Freddie Mercury and crew concealed the phrase "Decide to smoke marijuana, it's fun to smoke marijuana, decide to smoke marijuana," though why you'd want to make such a mundane notion your big secret beats us. Godwin hears the simpler but probably more poignant "Start to smoke marijuana, start to smoke marijuana!"

2. "ANTHEM," RUSH

Goodwin hears these "communications with the Devil"—"Oh Satan, you, you are the one who is shining. Walls of Satan, Walls of Sacrifice. I know it's you are the one I love."

3. "A CHILD IS COMING," JEFFERSON STARSHIP

Dan and Steve Peters say that if you can spin this baby backward, you'll find that the child is named "Son of Satan."

4. "DARLING NIKKI," PRINCE

Tipper Gore's favorite passage here is the one where Nikki's found in a hotel lobby "masturbating with a magazine," but that is hardly obscenity enough for the Peters brothers, who turn the song around and hear "How R U? I am fine becos the Lord is coming soon." (The spelling approximates Prince.) This, the Peterses claim, is a Satanic reference, since Prince could not possibly be referring to anybody but Satan as "Lord." *"Huh!"* was our response too, until we read Aranza's comment that "if Prince knew the Lord was coming soon he wouldn't be doing what he's doing and singing what he's singing." *Oh!*

5. "THE DAY WHEN ELECTRICITY CAME TO ARKANSAS," BLACK OAK

If you can get this one to spin backward, you'll supposedly hear "Satan, Satan, Satan. He is god, he is god, he is god." (Godwin's description of how this sounds *forward* is one of the funniest passages in the history of rock criticism.)

6. *ELDORADO,* ELECTRIC LIGHT ORCHESTRA

Peters and Godwin both claim this album contains backmasked passages that say "Christ, you're the nasty one, you're infernal," and "He's there on the cross and dead." Godwin says it's the title song; the always less descriptive Peterses don't specify.

7. "EVIL GENIUS," PAT BENATAR

The Peterses hear "Oh-h, Satan, that's why I want you to hear my music. That voice that makes my money."

8. "FINAL SCREAM," GRIM REAPER

Godwin hears "very plainly" at the end "See you in hell." In reverse. Which might mean heaven to the rest of us.

9. "FIRE IS HIGH," ELECTRIC LIGHT ORCHESTRA

Everybody in the trade hears "The music reversible but time is not. Turn back . . . turn back . . . turn back" on this track from *Face the Music.*

10. "GONNA RAISE HELL," CHEAP TRICK

Rock detective Godwin discerns "Satan holds the keys" on his special backward-running machinery.

11. "GOODBYE BLUE SKY," PINK FLOYD

"Congratulations! You've just decoded the secret message. Please send your answer to 'Old Pink' in care of the Funny Farm" according to both *Devil's Disciples* and *Hidden Persuaders.*

12. "HELL'S BELLS," AC/DC

The verse beginning "I'll give you black sensations" (which is seven lines long) becomes "I will mesmerize you / But he is Satan / Let me out / Satan has me prisoner," according to the unmetrical Godwin.

13. "HELTER SKELTER," MOTLEY CRUE

Vince Neil sings "I'm still the Master," according to Godwin, who says this means that "Satan's shouting that after all these years he's STILL the master of Rock & Roll!" On the same *Shout at the Devil* album, Aranza discerns "Backward mask where you are, oh, lost in error, Satan," which would seem to us to be a jab at the Bad Guy but whadda we know?

14. "HOOKED ON A FEELING," BLUE SWEDE

The chorus "ooga-chooch-a ooga-chooch-a" has "obscenities embedded in the background," according to the Peterses.

15. "HOTEL CALIFORNIA," THE EAGLES

Godwin hears "Satan had help. He organized his own religion," while the Peterses hear the much more elaborate "Yes, Satan, he organized his own religion . . . it was delicious. He puts it in a vat and fixes it for his sons and gives it away." But they don't pin the *forward* lyric as replete with references to Anton LaVey and San

Francisco's First Church of Satan, as do Godwin and Aranza (who either are unaware that LaVey hates rock or consider that attitude a diabolical ruse). Aranza goes on and on about the Eagles and Satanism, even attacking them for an earlier song, "Good Day in Hell."

16. "HOUSES OF THE HOLY," LED ZEPPELIN

Everybody hears something diabolical in this one, mainly that the line "is the word that only leaves you guessing" becomes "Satan is really Lord."

17. "IN LEAGUE WITH SATAN," VENOM

You'd hardly think that a band that makes albums with titles like *Welcome to Hell* and *Black Metal* needed to conceal its messages with backmasking, but according to Godwin, reversing this song reveals "Satan! Raised in Hell. Raised in Hell. I'm gonna burn your soul. Crush your bones. I'm gonna make you bleed. You're gonna bleed for me." On the same album *(Welcome)*, Aranza hears "It's better to reign in hell than to serve in heaven," which is kinda literary considering the source.

18. "KISS, KISS, KISS," JOHN LENNON AND YOKO ONO

Talk about sick. Godwin claims that Yoko's voice is backmasked to say "Satan is coming . . . six six six. . . . We shot John Lennon," and that this "perfectly justifies" Mark David Chapman's claim that the devil made him do it.

19. "LOOKING FOR A STRANGER," PAT BENATAR

"I can almost hear you calling / I'm looking for a stranger in my life," the rest of us hear. But not Steve and Dan Peters. Their special backward turntable reveals: "And I love it . . . save us, please . . . help us, Satan . . . and I love it."

20. "MEAT CITY," JOHN LENNON

Godwin discovers "Can't let you shoot my kids" in this obscure track from *Mind Games*.

21. METAL HEALTH, QUIET RIOT

Aranza discerns "Serve beast for money" here.

22. "RAIN," THE BEATLES

Godwin calls this the earliest example of backmasking, in which the chorus "When the rain comes / they run and hide their heads" reverses as "They might as well be dead / Can you hear me / can you hear me." "This is only further proof that Lennon was the instigator of this whole backmasked mess we find ourselves in today," he continues.

23. "REVOLUTION #9," THE BEATLES

"Number nine, number nine," supposedly becomes "Turn me on dead man," a reference to the death of Paul McCartney, the Peters brothers and Aranza believe. (Does this mean they believe Paul is dead? They don't say.)

24. "Shooby Doo," The Cars
Godwin reverses the chorus to hear "voices chanting in unison, 'Satan, Satan, Satan, Satan.' " (At least now we know how Ric Ocasek got Paulina.)

25. "Snowblind," Styx
The Peters brothers think that "how did I ever get into this mess?" becomes "moves Satan in our voices." Godwin hears "Oh Satan, move in our voices," which at least makes a little more syntactical sense; Aranza eliminates the "Oh."

26. "Some Girls," The Rolling Stones
With a straight face, the Peters brothers deliver the horrifying news that when the Stones got threatened with censorship for the language in this 1978 hit, they backmasked the word "fucked" to become "humped." *Wow!*

27. "Stairway to Heaven," Led Zeppelin
The universality of the Christian condemnation of Led Zep may ultimately seem like one of their prime assets, especially in regard to their most famous record. "There's still time" supposedly becomes "Here's to my sweet Satan," while another passage unravels to reveal "There's no escaping it. . . . Here's to my sweet Satan. No other made a path, for it makes me sad, whose power is Satan." The Peters also quoted antirock crank David Noebel, who hears "There was a little child born naked. . . . Now I am Satan," and "I will sing because I live with Satan."

28. "Tops," The Rolling Stones
"I love you said the Devil" appears backmasked, per Godwin and Aranza (though the latter doesn't mention which song, perhaps to protect the innocent.)

29. *Young Americans*, David Bowie
According to Aranza's first book, Bowie told *Hit Parader* in 1975 that he'd purchased "a record player to play records backward because he believes songs on his *Young Americans* album resemble Tibetan spiritualistic chants." To which you may reply, "Huh?" Not for the first time, no doubt.

30. "You're Not the One," Blue Oyster Cult
This one's not backmasked, Godwin says, but just recorded at "high speed." Slowed down, this track from *Mirrors* supposedly yields "whole paragraphs of words and phrases" (what else can paragraphs be composed of?), the clearest stating, "Our father, who are in Heaven, Satan." Neither BOC nor Godwin explain how Satan could be in heaven.

The Most Diabolical Song of All Time
Great Versions of "Stagger Lee" (AKA Stackolee, Stack-A-Lee, etc.—The Bad-Man Ballad of the Century)

1. The Isley Brothers
2. Lloyd Price
3. Mississippi John Hurt
4. Frank Hutchinson
5. Dr. John
6. Archibald
7. James Brown
8. Bob Dylan
9. Wilbert Harrison
10. The Righteous Brothers

SONS OF "STAGGER LEE"—RECORDS THAT WOULD BE INCONCEIVABLE WITHOUT HIM

1. "The Nigga You Love to Hate," Ice Cube
2. "Cop Killer," Body Count
3. "Crawling Kingsnake," John Lee Hooker
4. "Gangster," Schooly D
5. "How I Could Just Kill a Man," Cypress Hill
6. "Living for the City," Stevie Wonder
7. "Midnight Rambler," The Rolling Stones
8. "Mind of a Lunatic," The Geto Boys
9. "My Mind Playing Tricks on Me," The Geto Boys
10. "Nebraska," Bruce Springsteen
11. "100 Miles and Runnin'," N.W.A
12. "Riot in Cell Block #9," The Robins
13. "Rodney K," Willie D
14. "Run Red Run," The Coasters
15. "Thank U for Talkin' to Me, Africa," Sly and the Family Stone

For further information on the legend of Stagger Lee (and some good additional connections), read Greil Marcus's Mystery Train. *There's useful, additional listening on the Rounder album* Get Your Ass in the Water and Swim Like Me, *an album of toasts—long rap-style stories recited by prison inmates, which is closer to the sourcepoint of rap than any other album ever released (and which somebody ought to put out on CD pronto).*

25 Famous Censorship Cases

1. AS NASTY AS THEY WANNA BE, 2 LIVE CREW, 1990

Their sex comedy rap albums began getting the Miami-based 2 Live Crew in trouble as soon as leader Luther Campbell's record label began issuing them, but it wasn't until this album, their third, that they actually got put in jail. The genesis of the story is long, complex, and somewhat bewildering but it involves a crazed fundamentalist porn-hunting attorney named Jack Thompson, Sheriff Nick Navarro of Broward County (Fort Lauderdale), Florida, Florida governor Robert Martinez (peripherally), future attorney general Janet Reno, and a host of others. In any event, the *Nasty* album got targeted for one of two reasons: 1) It spawned the first porn-rap radio hit, "Me So Horny," or 2) Thompson felt crossed because Campbell's label made a record supporting Reno for Dade County DA when Jack ran against her. Either way, Martinez sicced Navarro on the group, Navarro and the band sued each other, a federal judge ruled *Nasty* obscene, and when the Crew played a date at a Fort Lauderdale nightclub, Navarro threw them in jail overnight. The Crew won both cases on appeal, achieved national notoriety, and sold several million more records than they otherwise would have done, but future releases got banned in advance in many jurisdictions. A tragicomic mess.

2. THE BEACH BOYS AT THE WASHINGTON, D.C., MALL, FOURTH OF JULY, 1983.

For the previous several years, the Beach Boys had performed a nationally televised concert on the Mall to honor the nation's birthday. But in 1983, Ronald Reagan's secretary of the interior, an ultraconservative flake named James Watt, refused to issue a permit for the show, declaring that rock concerts drew "an undesirable element." The irony was that Beach Boys lead singer Mike Love himself had ultrarightist tendencies. Among those who spoke up on behalf of the Beach Boys or at least Love's rightness was Watergate spook G. Gordon Liddy. But the group did not get to play the Mall in 1983, and though the band was given a permit after Watt left office during Reagan's second term, by that time, the continuity had been broken and the custom withered away.

3. "BILLIE JEAN" AND "BEAT IT" VIDEOS, MICHAEL JACKSON, 1983

Initially, MTV refused to air Jackson's videos, claiming that its audience wasn't interested in seeing or hearing music made by black artists. Despite massive pressure from CBS Records, whose president, Walter Yetnikoff, allegedly threatened to pull white rock videos if Jackson didn't receive equal treatment, for months the visual and narrative breakthrough of "Billie Jean" could be seen only in the dead of night. "Beat It" finally made it into prime time after Jackson wowed the world with his climactic appearance on the NBC-TV special *Motown 25* in early 1984. Butter never did melt in MTV's mouth (it's axiomatic that no American censor ever admits to being one), but as "Beat It" director Bob Giraldi said at the time, "MTV can say all they want about over the line, under the line—they are obviously racist and there's nothing else to say about it." Since then, the channel has cleaned up its act considerably, though it continues to be wary of certain aspects of sex, gangsta rap, and metal's more impolite neighborhoods.

4. "BROWN EYED GIRL," VAN MORRISON, 1967

How could American radio programmers ever have broadcast such smut as "Making love in the green grass, behind the stadium"? To make matters worse, the second time Van meets her, he croons, "My, how you have grown." (Around the middle, perhaps?) Change that offensive line to "laughin' and a-runnin', behind the stadium." The uncensored version, which was the only one played on many stations, appeared on the stereo version of Van's *Blowin' Your Mind* LP, but both Sony Music's *T.B. Sheets* anthology and Mercury's *The Best of Van Morrison*, the two most widely available CD reissues, use the censored one.

5. "COP KILLER," BODY COUNT, 1992

Not (exactly) an Ice-T record, but one made by his other project, a satiric heavy-metal band. But in 1992, an election year crammed with low hustles, there were some things just not meant to be made fun of, and black rage against the police forces that prey upon minority communities led the list. Before long, a group of Texas cops calling themselves CLEAT (subtle, huh?) instigated a national boycott of all Time-Warner products (Ice-T had long been a Sire Records artist, and Sire is owned by Time-Warner), and the T-W board, led by piggish opera has-been Beverly Sills, demanded T's head. Which it finally got in August, after the Sire and Warner Brothers Records staffs had been subject to beaucoup death threats (from whom? cops or their fans?), but of course, it was "rap" (the record was metal, dummy) to blame for the "violence," even though cop killings were down 20 percent in 1992 (and there were never all that many to begin with), while the hundreds of civilians murdered by the police annually remain uncounted (because the cops would be the ones to do the counting, and they don't want you to know). If it had been such a dark day for music, you coulda choreographed it to that old Laurel and Hardy line: *"Another* fine mess you've gotten us into."

6. *DEATH CERTIFICATE,* ICE CUBE, 1992

Attacked by *Billboard* in an editorial condemning the record for violence, alleged anti-Asian racism, and alleged anti-Semitism, the editorial encouraged record stores not to carry the record, and many chains immediately took the industry's leading trade paper up on the idea. The state of Oregon made it illegal to display Ice Cube's image in a retail outlet; St. Ides Malt Liquor dropped him as advertising frontman. In England, Island Records released the album without the cuts "No Vaseline" and "Black Korea," the scissoring done without Ice Cube's knowledge. The record still came on the *Billboard* chart at number two and sold more than a million copies, as did its followup, *The Predator.*

7. "DOUBLE SHOT (OF MY BABY'S LOVE)," THE SWINGING MEDALLIONS, 1966

The original version of the frat-rock classic has the lyrics "the worst hangover I ever had" and "She loved me so long and she loved me so hard / I finally passed out in her front yard." Gasp! How immoral! To ensure air play, the lyric was changed to "the worst morning I ever had" and "She kissed me so long and she kissed me so hard . . ." The original version is on the mono LP, while the "cleaned-up" one is on the stereo LP. Most CDs and most reissued singles have the original lyrics.

8. "F—— THA POLICE," N.W.A, 1989

After Focus on the Family, the right-wing fundamentalist Christian pressure group, started a campaign against this song (in which "F——" stands for just what you think it does), a police fax campaign against the group (which included Ice Cube, Dr. Dre, and Eazy E) prevented N.W.A from ever doing their most popular song on their entire national tour that summer. Worse, on the last date, in Detroit, they tried and Motor City cops bumrushed them from the stage and chased them back to their hotel, where the group was illegally held incommunicado for several hours. Before the tour even started, the FBI wrote a letter to Priority Records, the group's label, stating that the bureau had taken "an official position against" "F—— Tha Police," the first time in its history that the home of the G-men had found it necessary to take an official stand against a work of art. The letter writer was chastised, the bureau promised it wouldn't do it again, and, well into the nineties, police harassment remains a constant factor for anybody wanting to sing about the brutal assaults of cops against civilians, particularly young black males.

9. *JAZZ FROM HELL,* FRANK ZAPPA, 1990

Given a warning sticker and thus, restricted access to minors by Meyer Music Markets, a retail chain in the Pacific Northwest.

The sticker warns of dirty lyrics. The album is entirely instrumental.

10. "KILLING AN ARAB," THE CURE, 1986

In 1979, this British fop-rock band's sophomoric rewrite of Albert Camus's *The Stranger* probably most appealed to young college kids who'd never read the book and could be wowed by its existentialist clichés. But it found a nastier audience in the United States, where Arabs had been dehumanized as all-'round cultural villains long before the Gulf War legitimized the prejudice. In 1986, "Killing an Arab" appeared as the lead track on the Cure's compilation album, *Standing on a Beach*. FBI director William Webster had recently declared that Arab-Americans lived in "a zone of danger." As if to verify that perception, several student deejays—including one in Princeton, New Jersey, and another at the University of Michigan in Ann Arbor—introduced the record by saying, "Here's a song about killing an A-rab." The Arab-American Anti-Discrimination Committee (ADC) protested (its West Coast director, Alex Odeh, had been murdered in a bombing of the group's office the year before), and the Cure responded by agreeing to sticker *Standing on a Beach* with the following statement: "The song 'Killing an Arab' has absolutely no racist overtones whatsoever. It is a song that decries the existence of all prejudice and consequent violence. The Cure condemns its use in furthering anti-Arab feeling." Songwriter/lead vocalist Robert Smith also requested that all radio stations cease to air the song. This may be the least coercive example of censorship on record; it certainly is the most voluntary act on this list.

11. "THE LEDGE" VIDEO, THE REPLACEMENTS, 1987

Banned by MTV because of its lyrics, in which Paul Westerberg portrays a kid on the verge of suicide, standing on a ledge. MTV said it believed that the video could or would encourage kids to commit suicide. Warner Brothers Records actually went so far as to produce a commercial defending the song, in which Westerberg outlined his intent, which was just to say "I know what it's like to feel that way." Warners never did those for, for instance, Ice-T and Body Count, but then five years later, repeated airings of Pearl Jam's "Jeremy" made a much more violent version of exactly the same idea one of the most popular videos in MTV history.

12. "LET'S PRETEND WE'RE MARRIED," PRINCE, 1984

Rick Alley and his wife liked Prince's "1999" so much that she went out and bought the album of the same title. As she and her husband listened to it in their Cincinnati home, they were ambushed by "Let's Pretend We're Married," and had to rush to the stereo controls to prevent their kids from hearing it. So they went to the Delshire Elementary PTA and proposed some type of warnings or ratings be placed on records. From such small seeds begin giant crises. At its June 1984 annual convention, the National PTA adopted a resolution calling for the record industry to rate and label material containing "profanity, sex, violence, or vulgarity." The record industry tried to laugh it off, with the only substantive public comment coming from a Warner Brothers spokesman who said, "The function of rock and roll is to annoy parents. This just proves that nothing changes." But the Alleys never stopped *liking* Prince, so that wasn't the issue, and things were about to change in a big way. By September 1985, the major record companies had agreed to the PMRC's demand to label their potentially "offensive" recordings, and three major record companies even agreed to sit down with the PTA itself. Five years later, after the PTA, in alliance with Tipper Gore and the phony housewives in the PMRC, had gotten its way, the same executive was announcing the bombing threats against "Cop Killer."

13. "LET'S TALK," ONE WAY FEATURING AL HUDSON, 1985

Possibly the first record to bear the now-standard parental warning label. MCA Records initially described it as "a pointed message song . . . over a pulsing, funky beat, the lyrics urge children and their parents to talk about sex and eliminate the number one cause of problems in the area, ignorance." Two weeks later, MCA sent a letter urging radio stations not to play the song, because it was allegedly obscene. Ever since, labeled records have received similar receptions—you're not censored but you can't get air play, distribution, or retail display.

14. "LIKE A PRAYER" PEPSI COMMERCIAL, MADONNA, 1989

On March 2, 1989, Pepsi debuted a commercial featuring Madonna and her new single, "Like a Prayer." It seemed like one of her more innocuous moves, the most memorable feature being a brief home movie of one of her childhood birthday parties. The next day, Madonna's own video presentation of the record debuted. It seemed like what it was: The most outrageous act of provocation in the career of popular music's most provocative performer of all time. The video featured Madonna saving a black man from being lynched and then making love to him. Some of this took place within a church, which made the subtext equating Christ's passion and crucifixion with Madonna's carnal passion and the oppression of black men plain as daylight. It's hard to say whether the religious figures who immediately attacked, who ranged from a conservative Catholic group in Italy to America's would-be censor-in-chief, Reverend Donald Wildmon of the American Family Association of Tupelo, Mississippi, were more outraged by the miscegenation or by what they called "blasphemy." In any event, the Pepsi commercial never again aired and the person making the official announcement that it would no longer be seen was none other than Wildmon, who had threatened a boycott of all PepsiCo products. (Pepsi allowed him to make his statement even though Wildmon had been condemned as an anti-Semite by, among others, Archbishop John L. May of St. Louis, Robert M. Overgaard, president of the Church of the Lutheran Brethren, and James M. Lapp, executive secretary of the Mennonite Church.) Madonna went on to better things: "Like a Prayer" became one of her biggest hits (it topped the Hot 100 for three weeks), and the video stayed on the MTV airwaves. Only the commercial got censored.

15. "LOCOMOTIVE BREATH," JETHRO TULL, 1971

Perhaps the ultimate censorship job. Not satisfied with the line "got him by the balls" from the LP, Chrysalis Records spliced in a word from another part of the song. Radio stations thus ended up with "got him by the fun." Do we detect a new euphemism being born here? A kick in the fun? That guy's got brass fun? I was out there freezing my fun off? Maybe someday radio stations and record companies will find the fun to play records as innocuous as this unedited.

16. "MONEY," PINK FLOYD, 1973

When Harvest Records sent out the original promo copies, they contained the line "Don't give me that do goody-good bullshit." But just in the nick of time, the morals of the country were saved when Harvest hurriedly issued a second DJ copy (the "bull-blank" version), with a desperate note instructing programmers to throw away the first one.

17. MOVE SOMETHIN', 2 LIVE CREW, 1988

Tommy Hammond, owner of Taking Home the Hits in Alexander City, Alabama, sold a copy of 2 Live Crew's sex-oriented comedy rap album to a regular customer, out of a special box he kept behind the counter, only to find himself arrested the next day for selling pornography. "Hey, the guy I sold it to was old enough to buy it," Hammond protested. "Not in this state," the cop told him. "Nobody's old enough in this state." The police seized all copies of 2 Live Crew's two albums, plus eleven other titles including Two $hort's *Born to Mack*, Ice-T, *Blowfly*, *Don't Be Bashful* by Byron Davis and the Fresh Krew, and *Lethal* by UTFO. Hammond lost his case and was fined, then won on appeal. A happy ending? The entire procedure cost him more than $100,000, he couldn't sell rap (25 percent of his integrated business) while stores just across town (in black neighborhoods) continued to do so, and 2 Live Crew became a target for the hard-core fundamentalist right wing (see *As Nasty as They Wanna Be*).

18. THE NATIONAL ASSOCIATION OF BROADCASTERS VS. THE RECORDING INDUSTRY, 1985

In June 1985, recording companies received a letter from NAB president Edward O. Fritts asking that they submit lyric sheets with all new releases sent to NAB stations. Fritts sent similar letters to 806 NAB radio and TV stations asking them to screen rock songs.

He was responding to pressure from the PTA and the newly formed Parents' Music Resource Center (PMRC), a front group for fifteen women who were not "ordinary housewives," but special ones, whose husbands were members of Congress.

19. *THE OFFICIAL RECORD ALBUM OF THE OLYMPICS*, 1984

Jingoism ran rampant in 1984, the year of Ronald Reagan's coronation-style reelection, "Born in the U.S.A," *Rambo*, and the most "patriotic" Olympics ever displayed. The Los Angeles sports orgy, in which the Soviet Union and other outposts of what Reagan called its "evil empire" declined to participate (in response to the U.S. refusal to attend the 1980 games in Moscow), typified the nationalist arrogance of the period, as well as the complete devotion to merchandising that typified the 1980s as a whole. To spoof the whole thing, Rhino Records, the L.A.-based reissue label, issued an album of old sides by the fifties–sixties doo-wop group the Olympics, and titled it *The Official Record Album of the Olympics*. The Los Angeles Olympic Organizing Committee, headed by baseball commissioner-to-be Peter Ueberroth, sued, claiming that the Rhino record would create confusion with the official musical products of the Olympic *Games*. Rhino won the case in court, but not before the company's Richard Foos got off a brilliant summary, not only of the "controversy" but of the era: "Anyone who could mix up an album cover of four pompadoured black men in 1950s gold rock 'n' roll suits singing songs with titles like 'My Baby Loves Western Movies' . . . with that of a nondescript package highlighted with roman numerals [and containing] such songs as 'Grace (the Gymnasts' Theme)' is probably in such wretched shape that we have serious doubts that they could even find their way into a record store."

20. "RHAPSODY IN THE RAIN," LOU CHRISTIE, 1966

Oh, the flak on this one! Such lyrics as "On our first date, we were makin' out in the rain" and "In this car, our love went way too far" became the subject of radio call-in shows. Christie pleaded innocent to writing a dirty song but agreed that maybe the lyrics could be open to misinterpretation. The remade version toned it down: "On our first date, we fell in love in the rain," Christie sang, and "In this car, love came like a falling star." It's hard to say which double entendres are more comic, but today, it's much easier to locate the original.

21. *RITUAL DE LOS HABITUAL*, JANE'S ADDICTION, 1989

Banned by many stores, and busted in Michigan, for its ménage à trois cover. The group's earlier album, *Nothing's Shocking* (1988), featured a naked woman on the cover and eight of twelve major record chains refused to carry it. But Warner Brothers held its ground and that album eventually got carried by all the chains.

22. SAN ANTONIO VS. HEAVY METAL, 1985

In the midst of 1985's PMRC/PTA-driven hysteria over "porn rock," the San Antonio city council passed a law that fined promoters two hundred dollars per underage fan at "obscene" concerts. It's unclear whether anyone ever paid such a fine—mainly, bands just shun playing in San Antonio—but that is one of the more peculiar forms censorship can take (if that seems exaggerated, you aren't a music fan living in a place where the sounds you love can't be heard). But mayor Henry Cisneros (later Bill Clinton's secretary of housing and urban development) made it clear that the law was anything but content-neutral when he commented, "Symphony musicians have nothing to fear from this ordinance but rock musicians do."

23. "STAGGER LEE," LLOYD PRICE, 1959

The original version of Price's rock 'n' roll reworking of the classic blues features a murder in which Stagger Lee shoots fellow gambler Billy Lyon. Bowing to antiviolence feelings (particularly the ones that could have kept the disc from being played on ABC-TV's *American Bandstand*—ABC happened to be Price's record company), Price recut the song in a nonviolent version, in which the boys essentially kiss and make up. The two are immediately distinguishable. In the original's opening line, Price says, "The night was Claire," while in the remake he says, "The night was clear." In both, the moon was yellow and the leaves came tumbling down.

24. "THERE AIN'T NOTHING LIKE SHAGGIN'," THE TAMS, 1987

Banned by the British Broadcasting Corporation (BBC) because, although in Virginia and the Carolinas the shag is a dance, in the United Kingdom the term is a euphemism for fucking.

25. TOO MUCH JOY CONCERT, HOLLYWOOD, FLORIDA, 1990

On August 11, 1990, about two months after 2 Live Crew had been busted for singing the songs from *As Nasty as They Wanna Be*, New York–based rock band Too Much Joy traveled to Fort Lauderdale and played a set at the same club the Crew had played, consisting entirely of Crew material. Sheriff Nick Navarro had them arrested, and they initially faced a year in prison, before the case was tossed out of court.

Phyllis Pollack Picks the 10 Best Songs that Dis Tipper Gore

Pollack writes: "The album burning bonfire guys, backwoods preachers, pissed-off Klansmen, uptight bitches and others who have wanted to control popular culture have been around since before the middle ages. However, here are the ten best tributes to the woman who brought rock and rap bashing from the backwoods into the Congress and the 'respectable' political realm. (All the way to the Naval Observatory if not quite—yet—the White House.) These songs are dedicated to Tipper, who set the stage for countless anti–free speech bills to be introduced on local and national levels.

1. "Porn Wars," Frank Zappa
2. "Freedom of Speech," Ice-T
3. "Hook in Mouth," Megadeth
4. "Jesse," Todd Rundgren
5. "Ode to Tipper Gore," Warrant
6. "Censorshit," The Ramones
7. "Pro-Me," B.W.P. (Bytches with Problems)
8. "KKK Bitch," Ice-T
9. "Washington Wives," Malcolm Tent
10. "Tipper Gore," Alice Donut

Phyllis Pollack earned her spurs as an anticensorship activist before forming Def Press, a public relations agency representing music artists, especially rappers.

Best Songs to Pass the Censor

1. "Blinded by the Light," Bruce Springsteen
2. "Do Me!" Bell Biv Devoe
3. "Don't Eat the Yellow Snow," Frank Zappa and the Mothers of Invention
4. "Feel Like Making Love," Bad Company/Roberta Flack
5. "Gloria," Them
6. "Good Golly Miss Molly," Little Richard
7. "Great Balls of Fire," Jerry Lee Lewis
8. "Hanky Panky," Tommy James and the Shondells
9. "Honky Tonk Woman," The Rolling Stones
10. "Humpin' Around," Bobby Brown
11. "I Shot the Sheriff," Bob Marley/Eric Clapton
12. "Imaginary Lover," The Atlanta Rhythm Section
13. "Juicy Fruit," Mtume
14. "Little Red Corvette," Prince
15. "Lola," The Kinks
16. "Louis Quatorze," Bow Wow Wow
17. "Love to Love You Baby," Donna Summer
18. "Me So Horny," 2 Live Crew[1]
19. "Miracles," Jefferson Starship
20. "Mr. Brownstone," Guns N' Roses

21. "Pictures of Lily," The Who
22. "Shake Rattle and Roll," Big Joe Turner
23. "She Bop," Cyndi Lauper
24. "Too Drunk to Fuck," The Dead Kennedys
25. "Walk on the Wild Side," Lou Reed

---

[1] Yeah, but it still made the Top Forty.

The Most Controversial Record Covers

1. *ACHTUNG BABY*, U2, 1992

The cover montage had to be replaced or covered up in some American stores because it showed bassist Adam Clayton in the altogether, a full frontal pose that settled for all time the question of his circumcision. (Answer: Albert Goldman would find Adam's organ ugly.) David Bowie's *Tin Machine II* had similar problems, although all he tried to show was an ancient priapic Etruscan statue. Appropriately, it's probably the hardest record of Bowie's career.

2. *BEGGARS BANQUET*, THE ROLLING STONES, 1968

The original outside sleeve of this foldout design featured a bathroom wall covered in mildly scatalogical graffiti. Decca Records, the Stones' staid English record label, and its American affiliate, London, both refused to release the cover in that fashion, and the altered version—looking like an invitation to a formal banquet—stayed on until the CD era, when the original artwork was restored. (The CD restoration probably happened because the original cover had been so often bootlegged.)

3. *BLIND FAITH*, BLIND FAITH, 1969

The Eric Clapton, Steve Winwood, Ginger Baker supergroup only made one album, and its cover got it jerked off the shelves almost as soon as it arrived there. The photograph featured a barechested pubescent girl holding a model airplane. Retailer resistance resulted in the creation of an alternative sleeve, featuring a photo of the band. Beginning in the late seventies, when RSO reissued the album on vinyl, only the original artwork has been used.

4. *BORN IN THE U.S.A.*, BRUCE SPRINGSTEEN, 1984

At first, pinheads accused Springsteen of jingoism, because of the title and the pose—Springsteen, back to the camera, face to a massive U.S. flag. Then, when the dimwits realized that the music contradicted that perspective, they came up with an alternative: Springsteen faced the flag because he was pissing on it. Lord! As Bruce himself put it, "It just turned out that the picture of my *butt* looked better than the picture of my *face*."

5. *DIRTY WORK*, THE ROLLING STONES, 1985

In the midst of the PMRC's early anti–porn rock hysteria, Columbia Records issued this album, with its "potentially controversial" title, in dull red shrink wrap that had the effect of canceling out the word "Dirty," leaving an album titled just *Work* so far as fundamentalist retailers would be concerned. Mick Jagger told *Musician* magazine that the group also was asked to delete certain words —he mentioned "cunt"—from the album's inner sleeve.

6. *ELECTRIC LADYLAND*, THE JIMI HENDRIX EXPERIENCE, 1968

The American cover, in this case, was Hendrix's original conception: a swirling montage of onstage action shots. Polydor in England, however, released a sleeve showing Hendrix surrounded by a dozen naked, voluptuous women. The sleeve remains a collector's item in America, although the *original* is the one that's always been available (until MCA reissued the album with a godawful "art" sleeve in 1993).

7. "GOD SAVE THE QUEEN," THE SEX PISTOLS, 1977

The Sex Pistols intended "God Save the Queen" as a blast at Queen Elizabeth's Silver Jubilee, and the 45 sleeve featured a defaced picture of HRH, engendering the usual protests from the guardians of taste and the usual banishments from shops of dignified mien.

8. *IN UTERO*, NIRVANA, 1993

This cover, which depicted cherubs and fetuses, got itself banned even while the music inside made *Billboard*'s number one on the album chart. The chains that banned it, Wal-Mart and Kmart, had gotten wise to anticensorship manuveurs by 1993, though, so they said, they weren't carrying the country's most popular album because *their* customers wouldn't be interested in that sort of music. Just before Kurt Cobain's suicide, the band agreed to modify its cover art (which featured winged fetuses) and change a song title in order to placate the chains.

9. *KILL AT WILL*, ICE CUBE, 1991

Features Ice Cube holding a gun by the barrel, as if handing it to a viewer/listener. Whether this was a gesture implying the risk of revolutionary suicide or encouraging violence never got discussed. Panicky moralists simply assumed the latter, even though the album's content made the former much more likely.

10. *LOVESEXY*, PRINCE, 1988

Showing Prince stretched out without clothing as a sort of flower, with a pistil where his pistol would be. More than one retail chain refused to openly display this masterpiece of unconscious comedy.

11. *MOBY GRAPE*, MOBY GRAPE, 1967

The San Francisco group's album featured drummer/cut-up Skip Spence holding his middle finger extended over a washboard, in the classic high school yearbook pose. Humorless Columbia Records soon reissued the sleeve with Skip's offending digit airbrush-amputated.

12. MOM'S APPLE PIE, MOM'S APPLE PIE, 1971

Grand Funk Railroad entrepreneur Terry Knight was responsible for this group and its unlistenable first album. The cover remains the only legendary or even memorable aspect of its existence, but it's a wowser: A drawing of an innocent-looking farmwife holding out a steaming pie with a single slice removed. The filling really caught your eye: Rather than apple or cherry, this mom served vagina (or as we used to know it, hair pie). After massive retailer protests, Capitol Records reissued the sleeve with the offending filling bricked up.

13. RITUAL DE LOS HABITUAL, JANE'S ADDICTION, 1990

Its ménage à trois album cover art got it banned from many stores and busted in Michigan. But no alternative was provided, and it still sold well, while leader Perry Farrell during the same period had a tremendous influence by inaugurating the Lollapalooza tours.

14. SOME GIRLS, THE ROLLING STONES, 1978

Designed in the form of a pulp magazine advertising column with die cuts through which peered famous faces (Lucille Ball, Brigette Bardot, Marilyn Monroe, Raquel Welch, Liza Minnelli), this one didn't last long in the stores. But not because retailers objected—several of the stars did, because they hadn't given permission to use their mugs. (The title track's lyrical content also came under attack, because of the racism of the line "Black girls like to fuck all night.")

15. TWO VIRGINS, JOHN LENNON AND YOKO ONO, 1968

Lennon and Ono posed in the buff, full frontal on the front cover and from the rear on the back. U.S. Customs sued to prevent any copies from being imported. Then, on domestic release, through tiny Tetragrammaton after Capitol, Apple's usual distributor, refused to handle it, the album sold in America in a brown paper bag in the few stores that carried it at all. With its departure from the clean-cut image of the Beatles, *Two Virgins* upset even rock fans, a portent of things to come. Which doesn't mean you'd want to listen to the music.

16. YESTERDAY . . . AND TODAY, THE BEATLES, 1966

Throughout the sixties, Capitol Records adopted the policy of leaving a British track or two off the Beatles' American albums. This meant they'd periodically be able to cannibalize the U.K. releases and compile an additional cash cow (e.g., *Something New* by the Beatles). By 1966, the Beatles were both bold enough and angry enough to take action against the policy (which had been designed not only for profit but to belittle a band that some key Capitol jazzbo staffers disdained). So when Capitol announced plans for an LP to fill the gap between *Revolver* and *Sgt. Pepper's*, the group delivered a cover featuring the boys draped in butcher's smocks, surrounded by raw meat and holding dismembered dolls. The cover was actually printed and a precious few were delivered to stores. But the satiric implications once more eluded the American merchant and moralizing classes, and Capitol had to (or chose to, let's face it) replace the cover with a much more conventional and entirely unironic one. In some cases, Capitol simply covered over the original cover with the new one, which can be steamed off, resulting in possession of what most estimate as the most valuable album in musical history.

Controversial Advertising Campaigns

1. BLACK AND BLUE, THE ROLLING STONES, 1976
First album to fall victim to political correctness? Rolling Stones Records bought the standard Sunset Strip billboard all superstar releases of the period got, and used it to display to all of Los Angeles an illustration of a woman bound and beaten, in "comic" reference to the album title. Soon, Women Against Violence Against Women (a predecessor of today's Dworkins and MacKinnons) defaced the billboard with the statement, "This is a crime against women!" They also attempted to institute a feminist boycott of all Warner Communications recordings (a predecessor of today's cops and Time-Warner board members). The boycott lasted for more than a year before Warners agreed to leave the sexism off the packaging and advertising. (In addition, the *Black and Blue* ad copy was rejected by a number of magazines.)

2. BLACK DEATH VODKA, SLASH (GUNS N' ROSES), 1990
The vodka itself played off the image of alcohol as poison. Choosing as its spokesman one of the most notoriously heroin-addicted humans in rock history conveyed the message with the same degree of subtlety. Both proved too controversial, and the product never made it to most shelves, while his endorsement subjected Slash to much media abuse.

3. FUCK HUDSON'S, THE MC5, 1968
Hudson's, the largest department store in Five's hometown, Detroit, refused to carry the group's debut album because of the line "Kick out the jams, motherfuckers." Incited by this banishment, the band took out its own ad in its affiliated underground newspaper, *The Sun*, using Elektra Records' standard ad with the additional line: "Fuck Hudson's." Hudson's responded by refusing to carry any albums by any Elektra artists, which led directly to Elektra dumping the MC5 from its artist roster. The Five went on to Atlantic Records

and the classic *Back in the U.S.A.;* Elektra became one of the major labels most notorious for repressing gangsta rap in the 1990s; Hudson's got bought out by the giant Dayton-Hudson chain in Minneapolis. Nobody lived happily ever after, except possibly Iggy and the Stooges, who managed to make two even more outrageous and certainly far more insulting records for the same label, without getting banned by hardly anybody.

4. HEAD GAMES, FOREIGNER, 1979

The ad for this album, like its cover, featured women emerging from men's toilets and inspired feminist protests similar to those surrounding *Black and Blue.*

5. THE HEARTBEAT OF AMERICA, CHRYSLER CORPORATION, 1985

Chrysler tried to buy Bruce Springsteen for a reported $10 million to do its ad jingles. Turned down, the company hired soundalikes (allegedly, Kenny Rogers and Kim Carnes) to do its "Heartbeat of America" ads, which came as close to "Born in the U.S.A." as copyright infringement restrictions would allow. Springsteen might have made a legal case against this studied ripoff—suits by Tom Waits, Bette Midler, and Tom Petty later established that a singer's voice is, if not his castle, at least the drawbridge—but chose not to.

6. "LIKE A PRAYER" PEPSI COMMERCIAL, MADONNA, 1989

On March 2, 1989, Pepsi debuted a commercial featuring Madonna and her new single, "Like a Prayer." It seemed like one of her more innocuous moves, its most memorable feature being a brief scene of one of her childhood birthday parties. The next day, Madonna's own video presentation of the record debuted. It seemed like what it was: The most outrageous act of provocation in the career of popular music's most provocative performer of all time. The video featured Madonna saving a black man from being lynched and then making love to him. Some of this took place within a church, which made the subtext equating Christ's passion and crucifixion with Madonna's carnal passion and the oppression of black men plain as daylight. It's hard to say whether the religious figures who immediately attacked, who ranged from a conservative Catholic group in Italy to America's would-be censor-in-chief, Reverend Donald Wildmon of the American Family Association of Tupelo, Mississippi, were more outraged by the miscegenation or by what they called "blasphemy." In any event, the Pepsi commercial never again aired and the person making the official announcement that it would no longer be seen was none other than Wildmon, who had threatened a boycott of all PepsiCo products. (Pepsi allowed him to make his statement even though Wildmon had been condemned as an anti-Semite by, among others, Archbishop John L. May of St. Louis, Robert M. Overgaard, president of the Church of the Lutheran Brethren, and James M. Lapp, executive secretary of the Mennonite Church.) Madonna went on to better things: "Like a Prayer" became one of her biggest hits (it topped the Hot 100 for three weeks), and the video stayed on the MTV airwaves. Only the commercial got censored.

7. "THE MAN CAN'T BUST OUR MUSIC"; "THE REVOLUTIONARIES ARE ON CBS," CBS RECORDS, 1968

CBS was a Johnny-come-lately to acid rock, thanks to the blind stewardship of Mitch Miller. The label's slogans (the second of which was composed by ad man turned gay activist/provocateur Jim Fouratt) attempted to improve its image among hipsters. They backfired miserably. Since CBS had about as much revolutionary potential as any other Fortune 500 corporation, its record division immediately got the reputation of being one of the all-time exploiters, trying to play the hip audience for a bunch of suburban dummies.

8. MILLER BEER AND THE WHO, 1982

The Who became one of the first bands to accept "corporate sponsorship" on one of their first "final tours" (it did turn out to be the last *with drummer Kenney Jones*), not only accepting several million dollars from one of America's largest breweries, but announcing the tour to its ad clients before it proclaimed the dates to the public. Monumental barely describes the degree of irony here, for a band whose drummer, Keith Moon, drank and doped himself to any early death, and whose guitarist, songwriter, and main moralist Pete Townshend had waged a long and storied (mainly by himself) battle against alcoholism which began when he served drinks to his *father's* bandmates as a child, did advertisements for beer (and for an American beer that any self-respecting Brit would tell you tasted worse than piss). Advertisements were, of course, prominently displayed on MTV despite the beer industry's solemn pledge not to advertise to kids under the legal drinking age. No short- or long-term damage was suffered by either the brand or the band (which found other beer sponsors for other "final" tours).

9. ST. IDES MALT LIQUOR, ICE CUBE AND CHUCK D (AGAINST THE LATTER'S WILL), 1991

Ice Cube quite willingly endorsed this brew, a street-corner favorite because of its extremely high alcohol content. But the brew came under severe criticism from more "respectable" elements in the black community, among them Public Enemy. Imagine P.E. leader Chuck D's amazement when he heard *his own voice* on a St. Ides commercial that summer. Chuck sued for several million dollars, calling as witnesses (during depositions) several dozen teenagers who talked about how disconcerted they were that he'd backed off from anti–malt liquor principles he'd rapped about. In 1993 the suit was settled, reportedly on terms very favorable to Chuck. Meantime, St. Ides dropped Ice Cube at the first sign of controversy when his uncompromising *Death Certificate* came out.

10. "YOU SAY YOU WANT A REVOLUTION" NIKE SPORTSWEAR, 1987

Extremely controversial because it involved the Beatles for the first time selling one of their most radical image-making songs to Madison Avenue interests. The "revolution" in question, far from Lennon's utopian anarchist vision, involved working out till you dropped. Not what most Beatle fans had in mind, it turned out, and Nike soon stopped using the TV spot, an indication that it backfired by alienating the very consumers it meant to persuade.

Tipper Gore's Favorite Records

1.
2.
3.
4.
5.
6.
7.
8.
9.
10.

Source: Her book, Raising PG Kids in an X-Rated Society. *There, she doesn't even acknowledge that she bought* Purple Rain *because she liked it herself but blames it on one of her kids. (For more on their habits, see* Spy *magazine.)*

CHAPTER 23

Drugs, Death, and Rock 'n' Rap

25 Pieces of Evidence Proving that Paul McCartney Is Dead

Twenty-odd years ago, the rumor that Paul McCartney had died and been secretly replaced with a lookalike Beatle stormed the rock world. It took months to get the story to subside, although its main promoter was nobody more well-connected than a minor Detroit acid-rock deejay. Apparently, people back then had some reason to believe that the Beatles communicated through secrecy and coded expression. Which is obviously something they did less and less of as time went by—"Norwegian Wood" and "Eleanor Rigby" are a lot more obtuse than, say, "Come Together" and "The Long and Winding Road." Anyway, nobody ever explained why, if the story was supposed to be true, the Beatles would have left clues around inviting a clever mind to (mis)interpret them. In the lingering aftermath of John Lennon's murder, maybe this isn't as funny as it used to be, but it remains just as strange, *and as telling of the Beatles supremacy in their era. (What would be today's equivalent—claiming that Kurt Cobain faked it?)*

1. On the cover of the Beatles album *Yesterday . . . and Today,* "Paul" sits in a trunk. Turn it sideways and he seems to be in a coffin.
2. On the cover of *Revolver,* "Paul" is turned to the side, as if he doesn't really fit in.
3. *Revolver* contains many references to death, such as "She Said She Said."
4. On the cover of *Sgt. Pepper's Lonely Hearts Club Band,* a hand is held directly over "Paul's" head. This is a symbol of death.
5. On the same cover, "Paul's" bass is laid on flowers atop a coffin.
6. "Paul" is also holding a black musical instrument.
7. On the inside of the *Sgt. Pepper's* cover, "Paul" wears a black armband with the letters *OPD,* which is a Canadian acronym for Officially Pronounced Dead. (Ed. note: Nobody thought of it at the time, but George Harrison's sister lived in Canada.)
8. On the back cover, "Paul's" back is turned to the camera.
9. Also on the back cover, the lyrics "Without You" (part of the title "Within You and Without You") bloom from "Paul's" head.
10. "A Day in the Life" contains the line, "He blew his mind out in a car"; this is supposedly the manner in which Paul died.
11. On "Revolution #9" from the White Album, there is a voice that repeats "number nine, number nine." If you play this segment backward, it becomes "turn me on, dead man." (John claimed that at the beginning of each take, an engineer would announce, "This is EMI Recording Studio Number 9." Lennon

said that he simply took the end of the phrase and added it in the final mix. According to him, the "turn me on, dead man" revelation was a coincidence.)

12. On Lennon's song "Glass Onion," he says, "And here's another clue for you all/The Walrus was Paul." In some societies, the walrus is an image of death, but this is most important as Lennon's acknowledgement of the rumor.

13. Between the end of "I'm So Tired" and the beginning of "Black Bird," Lennon utters some nonsense syllables. Played backward, they say (approximately), "Paul is dead, miss him, miss him."

14. While George is wailing away at the end of "While My Guitar Gently Weeps," he says, "Paul Paul."

15. "Don't Pass Me By" contains the line, "You were in a car crash."

16. The poster included with the White Album contains many references to McCartney's "death." For example, there is a picture of "Paul's" head lying back in a bathtub; this resembles what he may have looked like after "the car crash."

17. The pictures also show a scar on "Paul's" lip, which supposedly had never been there before.

18. At the end of "Strawberry Fields Forever," Lennon can be heard saying what sounds very much like "I buried Paul." (Lennon claimed that the Beatles would often say wild and crazy things while in the studio, and that what he was really saying was "cranberry sauce.")

19. On the cover of *Magical Mystery Tour*, the words of the title are written in stars. If you turn the album upside down, the letters reveal a phone number that some say you could dial to find out details of Paul's death. Some say this number belonged to Billy Shears.

20. Inside the booklet accompanying *Magical Mystery Tour*, there is a picture of "Paul" sitting at a desk on which there is a sign that reads, "I was you."

21. In the "Your Mother Should Know" sequence of the *Magical Mystery Tour* movie, "Paul" wears a black carnation; the others wear white ones. ("Paul" has explained that they ran out of white carnations.)

22. At the end of the *Magical Mystery Tour* photo book, there is a picture of the Beatles interspersed with shots of many other people. There is a hand directly over "Paul's" head.

23. On the cover of *Abbey Road*, "Paul" is barefoot (corpses are often buried without shoes) and out of step with the other Beatles. His eyes appear to be closed. He is also smoking. The other Beatles wear clothing contributing to the motif: John, all in white, is the preacher; Ringo, all in black, is the pallbearer;

George, all in denim, is the gravedigger. There is also a Volkswagen with the license number 28IF, symbolizing that McCartney would have been twenty-eight years old if he had lived.
24. On the back cover, immediately after the words *Abbey Road*, a skull-like drawing can be discerned.
25. In "Come Together," Lennon sings, "One and one and one is three." Three Beatles. What about Paul?

Note: We have used quotation marks to distinguish between the real Paul and the lookalike imposter who "replaced" him—Eds.

Death Songs

1. "All This Time," Sting
2. "Back on the Chain Gang," Pretenders
3. "Bang Bang Bang," Tracy Chapman
4. "The Bells," The Dominoes featuring Clyde McPhatter
5. "Bye Bye Johnny," Bruce Springsteen
6. "Cadillac Ranch," Bruce Springsteen
7. "Dead Homiez," Ice Cube
8. "Death Letter," Son House
9. "Death of a Clown," Dave Davies
10. "Enter Sandman," Metallica
11. "For a Dancer," Jackson Browne
12. "For You," Bruce Springsteen
13. "Freddie's Dead," Curtis Mayfield
14. "Frozen Man," James Taylor
15. "The Gift," The Velvet Underground
16. "Girlfriend in a Coma," The Smiths
17. "Give Us Your Blessing," The Shangri-Las
18. "Hand of Fate," The Rolling Stones
19. "Holidays in the Sun," The Sex Pistols
20. "Hunger Strike," Temple of the Dog
21. "I Am Stretched Out on Your Grave," Sinead O'Connor
22. "I Believe I'm Gonna Make It," Joe Tex
23. "I Don't Live Today," Jimi Hendrix
24. "I Shall Be Released," Bob Dylan
25. "I Will Not Go Quietly," Don Henley
26. "It Was a Good Day," Ice Cube
27. "Killer," Seal
28. "Last Night," Little Walter
29. "The Late Great Johnny Ace," Paul Simon
30. "Leader of the Pack," The Shangri-Las
31. "Leah," Roy Orbison
32. "Long Black Limousine," Elvis Presley

33. "Love Is Stronger than Death," The The
34. "Maria Novarro," Was (Not Was)
35. "Marie Provost," Nick Lowe
36. "Mother and Child Reunion," Paul Simon
37. "No Prayer for the Dying," Iron Maiden
38. "One," U2
39. "Papa Was a Rolling Stone," The Temptations
40. "People Who Died," The Jim Carroll Band
41. "Percy's Song," Fairport Convention
42. "Post Mortem," Slayer[1]
43. "Sign O' the Times," Prince
44. "Thank You (Falenttinme Be Mice Elf Agin)," Sly and the Family Stone
45. "That Smell," Lynyrd Skynyrd
46. "Tombstone Shadow,"Creedence Clearwater Revival
47. "Tonight's the Night," Neil Young
48. "Under the Bridge," The Red Hot Chili Peppers
49. "Wall of Death," Richard and Linda Thompson
50. "Wreck on the Highway," Bruce Springsteen

---

[1] The real challenge, of course, would be to come up with a list of three or more Slayer songs that don't involve death in some fashion.

Songs About Suicide

These songs do not "advocate" or "encourage" suicide; they discuss it, in every case, as the tragic mistake it is.

1. "Ball and Chain," Social Distortion
2. "The Ballad of Hollis Brown," Bob Dylan
3. "Blessed Death," Blue Oyster Cult[1]
4. "Choose Life," Debby Boone[2]
5. "Don't Fear the Reaper," Blue Oyster Cult[1]
6. "Endless Sleep," Jody Reynolds
7. "Ever So Clear," Bushwick Bill
8. "Goodbye Cruel World," Pink Floyd[1]
9. "Heroes End," Judas Priest[1]
10. "Is There Anybody Out There?" Pink Floyd[1]
11. "Jeremy," Pearl Jam
12. "Killing Yourself to Live," Black Sabbath[1]
13. "The Ledge," The Replacements
14. "Patches," Dickey Lee
15. "Ride the Lightning," Metallica[1]
16. "Shoot to Thrill," AC/DC[1]
17. "Suicide Solution," Ozzy Osbourne[1]

18. "Suicide's An Alternative/You'll Be Sorry," Suicidal Tendencies
19. "Waiting for the Worms," Pink Floyd[1]
20. "You're Only Human," Billy Joel[2]

---

[1] Songs accused by Tipper Gore of "promoting" suicide. These songs may or may not be about suicide in the minds of their composers or rational listeners. In any event, as we said, they are not "advocacy" or "encouragement."
[2] Songs identified by Tipper Gore as "deliver[ing] a strong antisuicide message."

Three Dozen Musical Murders

1. "Bo Bo Bo," Boogie Down Productions
2. "Coffee Donuts and Death," Paris
3. "The Crucifixion," Phil Ochs
4. "Dead Homiez," Ice Cube
5. "Did She Jump or Was She Pushed?" Richard and Linda Thompson
6. "Die," Willie D
7. "Don Henley Must Die," Mojo Nixon and Skid Roper
8. "Down by the River," Neil Young
9. "The End," The Doors
10. "Girl Tried to Kill Me," Ice-T
11. "Hey Joe," Jimi Hendrix
12. "Homicide," Kid Frost
13. "How I Could Just Kill a Man," Cypress Hill
14. "How to Kill a Radio Consultant," Public Enemy
15. "I Shot the Sheriff," The Wailers
16. "I'm Goin' Out Like a Soldier," Willie D
17. "I'm Gonna Murder My Baby," Pat Hare[1]
18. "Janie Got a Gun," Aerosmith
19. "July the 12th, 1939," Charlie Rich
20. "The Killing of Georgie," Rod Stewart
21. "Long Black Veil," The Band
22. "Meat Is Murder," The Smiths
23. "Midnight Rambler," The Rolling Stones
24. "A Minute to Pray, A Second to Die," Scarface
25. "Momma's Gotta Die Tonight," Body Count
26. "Money or Murder," Spice 1
27. "Murder in the First Degree," D.J. Magic Mike
28. "Murder in the Red Barn," Tom Waits
29. "99 to Life," Social Distortion
30. "Psycho Killer," Talking Heads
31. "Roland the Headless Thompson Gunner," Warren Zevon
32. "Sa Prize (Part 2)," N.W.A

33. "Soulja's Story," 2Pac
34. "Stagger Lee," Lloyd Price
35. "Trigga Happy Nigga," The Geto Boys
36. "2 + 2 = ?," The Bob Seger System

---

[1] The former Muddy Waters guitarist proved as good as his word, and served time for it, too.

10 Bob Dylan Songs About Death and Dying

1. "All Along the Watchtower"
2. "The Ballad of Hollis Brown"
3. "A Hard Rain's A-Gonna Fall"
4. "I Shall Be Released"
5. "Joey"
6. "Knockin' on Heaven's Door"
7. "The Lonesome Death of Hattie Carroll"
8. "Masters of War"
9. "See that My Grave Is Kept Clean"
10. "Tombstones Blues"

10 Bruce Springsteen Songs About Death and Dying

1. "Atlantic City"
2. "Bye Bye Johnny"
3. "Cadillac Ranch"
4. "For You"
5. "Nebraska"
6. "Point Blank"
7. "Reason to Believe"
8. "Souls of the Departed"
9. "Streets of Philadelphia"
10. "Wreck on the Highway"

The Johnny Ace Memorial Lists

SUICIDES
1. Johnny Ace, 1929–54[1,18]
2. Bobby Bloom, 1946–74
3. Roy Buchanan, 1940–88
4. Kurt Cobain (Nirvana), 1967–94
5. Ian Curtis (Joy Division), 1959–80

6. Don Drummond (Skatalites), 19??–71 [11]
7. Dickie Goodman (Buchanan and Goodman), 1915–87
8. Pete Ham (Badfinger), 1947–75
9. Donny Hathaway, 1945–79
10. Terry Kath (Chicago), 1946–78
11. Richard Manuel (The Band), 1944–86
12. Joe Meek (U.K. record producer), 1929–67 [16,26]
13. Phil Ochs, 1940–76
14. Danny Rapp (Danny and the Juniors), 1942–83
15. Del Shannon, 1940–90 [23]
16. Rory Storm, ca. 1941–74
17. Janet Vogel (The Skyliners), 1943–80
18. Paul Williams (The Temptations), 1939–73 [3,18,23]

AIRPLANE AND HELICOPTER CRASHES
1. The Bar-Kays (Ronnie Caldwell, Carl Cunningham, Phalon Jones, Jimmy King), 1967
2. Jim Croce, 1943–73
3. John Felton (The Diamonds), 19??–82
4. Cassie Gaines (Lynyrd Skynyrd), 1948–77
5. Steve Gaines (Lynyrd Skynyrd), 1949–77
6. Bill Graham, (concert promoter), 1931–91
7. Buddy Holly, 1936–59
8. Dean Martin, Jr. (Dino, Desi and Billy), 1952–87 [15]
9. Rick Nelson, 1940–85
10. Larry Palumbo (The Earls), 1941–59 [14]
11. Otis Redding, 1941–67
12. Randy Rhoads (Ozzy Osbourne), 1957–82
13. J. P. Richardson (The Big Bopper), 1953–59
14. Ritchie Valens, 1941–59
15. Ronnie Van Zant (Lynyrd Skynyrd), 1949–77
16. Stevie Ray Vaughan, 1955–90

AUTOMOBILE AND BUS CRASHES
1. Stiv Bators (The Dead Boys), 195?–90
2. Chris Bell (Big Star), 1951–78
3. Jessie Belvin, 1933–60
4. Marc Bolan (T. Rex), 1948–77
5. D. Boon, 1958–85
6. Chris Burton (Metallica), 1962–86
7. Tommy Caldwell (Marshall Tucker Band), 1951–80
8. Harry Chapin, 1943–81
9. Eddie Cochran, 1938–60
10. Allen Collins (Lynyrd Skynyrd), 1952–90
11. Keith Godchaux (The Grateful Dead), 1948–80
12. Earl Grant, 1931–70

13. Johnny Horton, 1927–60
14. Johnny Kidd, 1940–66
15. Rushton Moreve (Steppenwolf), 1948–83
16. Dave Prater (Sam and Dave), 1938–88
17. Razzle (Hanoi Rocks), 19??–84
18. Rockin' Robin Roberts (The Wailers), ca. 1943–67
19. Bessie Smith, 1894–1937
20. Billy Stewart, 1938–70
21. Ted Taylor, 1937–87
22. Thomas Wayne, 1940–70
23. Clarence White (The Byrds), 1944–73[4]

MOTORCYCLE CRASHES

1. Duane Allman, 1946–71[23]
2. Richard Fariña, 1937–66
3. Berry Oakley (The Allman Brothers Band), 1948–72[23]

DRUG OVERDOSES AND
RELATED CIRCUMSTANCES

1. G. G. Allin, ca, 1960–93
2. Lester Bangs (singer and critic), 1949–82[22]
3. John Belushi (The Blues Brothers), 1949–82
4. Michael Bloomfield (Paul Butterfield Blues Band, Electric Flag), 1945–81
5. Tommy Bolin (Deep Purple, James Gang), 1950–75
6. Tim Buckley, 1947–75
7. Paul Butterfield, 1943–87
8. Brian Cole (The Association), 1944–72
9. Darby Crash (The Germs), 1958–80
10. Nick Drake, 1948–74[21]
11. Brian Epstein (Beatles' manager), 1935–67
12. Pete Farndon (Pretenders), 1953–83
13. Marge Ganser (The Shangri-La's), ca. 1949–19??
14. Andy Gibb, 1958–88
15. Lowell George (Little Feat), 1945–79
16. Ric Grech (Family, Blind Faith), 1946–90
17. Tim Hardin, 1940–80
18. Jimi Hendrix, 1942–70[18]
19. James Honeyman-Scott (Pretenders), 1957–82
20. Janis Joplin, 1943–70
21. Frankie Lymon, 1942–68
22. Phil Lynott (Thin Lizzy), 1952–86
23. Jimmy McCulloch (Thunderclap Newman, Wings), 1953–79
24. Robbie MacIntosh (The Average White Band), 1944–74
25. Keith Moon, 1946–78[21,22,24]
26. Billy Murcia (N.Y. Dolls), 1951–72

27. Brent Mydland (The Grateful Dead), 1953–91
28. Gram Parsons (Byrds, Flying Burrito Brothers), 1946–73
29. Jeff Porcaro (Toto), 1954–92
30. Elvis Presley, 1935–77
31. Carl Radle (Derek and the Dominoes, Delaney and Bonnie and Friends), ca. 1945–80
32. David Ruffin (The Temptations), 1941–91
33. Stefanie Sargent (Seven Year Bitch), 1968–92
34. Hillel Slovak (Red Hot Chili Peppers), 1963–88
35. Johnny Thunders (N.Y. Dolls), 1953–91
36. Sid Vicious (Sex Pistols), 1958–79
37. Dinah Washington, 1924–63
38. Danny Whitten (Crazy Horse), 1945–72
39. Hank Williams, 1923–53
40. Alan Wilson (Canned Heat), 1943–70
41. Andrew Wood (Mother Love Bone), 1966–90

ALCOHOL AND RELATED ILLNESSES

1. Florence Ballard (The Supremes), 1943–76
2. John Bonham (Led Zeppelin), 1945–80
3. Gene Clark (The Byrds, Dillard and Clark), 1942–91
4. Steve Clark (Def Leppard), 1961–91
5. Alan Freed (pioneering AM disc jockey), 1923–65
6. Bill Haley, 1925–81
7. James Jamerson (Funk Brothers), 1938–85
8. Chris Kenner, 1929–76
9. Pvt. Cecil Gant, 1914–51
10. Eddie Hazel (P-Funk), 1950–92
11. Peter Laughner (Pere Ubu; rock critic), 1953–77
12. Little Walter, 1930–68
13. Ron "Pigpen" McKernan (the Grateful Dead), 1945–73
14. Clyde McPhatter, 1931–72
15. Amos Milburn, 1928–80
16. Gladys Presley, 1912–58
17. Jimmy Reed, 1926–76
18. Bon Scott (AC/DC), 1947–80
19. Chris Wood (Traffic), 1944–83

SHOOTINGS, STABBINGS, AND BEATINGS

1. Darrell Banks, 1938–70[19]
2. Carlton Barrett (Bob Marley and the Wailers), 1951–87
3. Shirley Brickley (Orlons), 1945–77[19]
4. Arlester "Dyke" Christian (Dyke and the Blazers), ca. 1945–71[19,25]
5. Sam Cooke, 1935–64[18]
6. King Curtis, 1934–71[18]

7. Mal Evans (The Beatles' road manager), 1936–76[8,18]
8. Charles Fizer (The Olympics), 1940–65[13]
9. Cornell Gunter (The Coasters), 1939–90[18]
10. Meredith Hunter, 1951–69[5,19,22]
11. Al Jackson (Booker T. and the MGs), 1935–75[19]
12. Scott LaRock (Boogie Down Productions), 1962–87
13. John Lennon, 1940–80[19]
14. Miami Show Band (Dublin pop trio—Fran O'Toole, Brian McCoy, Tomo Geraghty)[9,19]
15. Felix Pappalardi (Cream, Mountain), 1940–83[19,27]
16. Jaco Pastorius, 1952–87[17,19,22]
17. Bobby Ramirez (White Trash), 1947–70[10,19,22]
18. "Sir" Walter Scott (Bob Kuban and the In-Men), ca 1945–83[27]
19. James "Shep" Sheppard, ca. 1940–70[18]
20. Stacy Sutherland (13th Floor Elevators), 1947–78[18,27]
21. Peter Tosh (The Wailers), 1945–87
22. Larry Williams, 1936–80[18,21]
23. "Scarface" John Williams (Huey Smith and the Clowns), 19??–72[18]
24. Harris Womack (The Valentinos), ca. 1945–74[6,19,22]

POISONINGS
1. Bobby Fuller, 1942–66[12,21]
2. Robert Johnson, 1911–38[19]
3. Tommy Tucker, 1933–82[18]

ASPHYXIATIONS AND DROWNINGS
1. Johnny Burnette, 1934–64
2. Jimmy Hodder (Steely Dan), 1948–90
3. Brian Jones (The Rolling Stones), 1944–69[18,21,23]
4. Shorty Long, 1940–69
5. Robert Scholl (Mello-Kings), 1938–75
6. Dennis Wilson (Beach Boys), 1944–83

HEART ATTACKS AND STROKES
1. Jackie Brenston, 1930–79
2. Dorsey Burnette, 1933–69
3. Dee Clark, 1938–90
4. Bobby Darin, 1936–73
5. Mark Dinning, 1934–86
6. Tom Donahue (pioneer FM deejay), 1929–75[23]
7. Sherman Garnes (Frankie Lymon and the Teenagers), 1940–78
8. John Glascock (Jethro Tull), ca. 1947–79
9. Roy Hamilton, 1929–69
10. Martin Hannett (producer), ca. 1950–91
11. Slim Harpo, 1924–70

12. Alex Harvey, 1935–82
13. Bob Hite, 1945–81
14. O'Kelly Isley, 1938–86
15. Blind Lemon Jefferson, 1897–1930[12]
16. Louis Jordan, 1909–75
17. Leslie Kong (reggae producer), 1933–71
18. Van McCoy, 1941–79
19. Jim Morrison, 1943–71 [18,20,22,23]
20. Roy Orbison, 1936–88
21. Junior Parker, 1927–74
22. Ian Stewart (The Rolling Stones), 1938–85
23. Nolan Strong (The Diablos), 1934–77
24. Joe Tex, 1932–81
25. Sonny Til (The Orioles), 1925–81
26. Big Joe Turner, 1909–85
27. Rob Tyner (MC5), 1945–91
28. Muddy Waters, 1915–83
29. Howlin' Wolf, 1911–76
30. Jackie Wilson, 1935–84
31. Philippe Wynne (The Spinners, P-Funk), 1938–84

PNEUMONIA

1. Miles Davis, 1926–91
2. Guitar Slim, 1926–59[22]
3. Little Willie John, 1937–66[18,23]
4. Bob Luman, 1937–78
5. Jerry Nolan (N.Y. Dolls), 1947–92[23]
6. T-Bone Walker, 1911–75

CANCER

1. Bill Black (Elvis, Scotty and Bill; The Bill Black Combo), 1927–65
2. Neil Bogart (record executive), 1943–82
3. Eric Carr (Kiss), 1950–91
4. Linda Creed (songwriter), 1949–86
5. Bobby Day, 1932–90
6. Tom Fogerty (Creedence Clearwater Revival), 1942–90
7. Carolyn Franklin (songwriter), 1945–88
8. Wynonie Harris, 1915–69
9. Ivory Joe Hunter, 1911–74
10. Buddy Johnson, 1912–77
11. Eddie Kendricks (The Temptations), 1940–92
12. Smiley Lewis, 1920–66
13. George McRae, 1945–86
14. Ronnie Mack (songwriter), ca. 1938–63
15. Bob Marley, 1950–81
16. Joe Negroni (Frankie Lymon and the Teenagers), 1941–78

17. Junior Parker, 1932–71
18. Mike Patto (Spooky Tooth, Boxer, Patto), 1943–79
19. Doc Pomus (songwriter), 1926–91
20. William Powell (The O'Jays), 1942–77
21. Minnie Riperton (Rotary Connection), 1948–79
22. Earl Van Dyke (The Funk Brothers), 1930–92
23. Steve Wahrer (The Trashmen), 1942–89
24. Mary Wells, 1943–92

AIDS

1. Esquerita (Eskew Reeder), ca 1935–90
2. Freddie Mercury (Queen), 1946–91
3. Sylvester, 1947–88
4. Ricky Wilson (B-52s), 1953–85

OTHER DISEASES

1. Brook Benton, 1933–88; spinal meningitis
2. Big Maybelle, 1925–72; diabetic coma
3. Karen Carpenter, 1950–83; anorexia nervosa
4. Mary Ann Ganser (Shangri-Las), ca. 1949–71; encephalitis
5. Glenn Goines (P-Funk), 1950–78, "systemic disorder"[18]
6. Woody Guthrie, 1912–67; Huntington's Chorea
7. Freddie King, 1934–76; heart disease and hepatitis
8. Paul Kossoff (Free), 1950–76; heart attack and kidney failure
9. Leadbelly (Huddie Ledbetter), 1889–1949; ALS (Lou Gehrig's disease)
10. Angus McLise (Velvet Underground), ca 1945–ca. 1968); malnutrition
11. Donald McPherson (Main Ingredient), 1932–71; leukemia
12. George Smith (The Manhattans), ca. 1943–70; spinal meningitis
13. Stuart Sutcliffe (The Beatles), 1941–62; cerebral paralysis
14. Georgeanna Tillman (The Marvelettes), 1945–80; lupus
15. Chuck Willis, 1928–58, stomach disease[7]
16. Ron Wilson (the Surfaris), ca. 1945–89; brain aneurysm

ELECTROCUTIONS

1. Les Harvey (Stone the Crows), ca. 1947–72[25]
2. Keith Relf (Yardbirds, Renaissance), 1943–76
3. John Rostill (The Shadows), 1942–73[26]
4. Gary Thain (Uriah Heep), ca. 1947–76[23]

ACCIDENTS

1. Graham Bond, 1937–74; fell under subway train[21]
2. Sandy Denny (Fairport Conventions), 1941–78, fell down stairs[18]

3. Cass Elliott (Mamas and Papas), 1943–74; choked on ham sandwich[24]
4. Kit Lambert (Who manager), 1938–81; fell down stairs[23]
5. Stevie Marriot (Small Faces, Humble Pie), 1947–91; house fire
6. Nico (Velvet Underground), 1940–88; fell off bike, died of brain hemorrhage
7. Tammi Terrell, 1946–70; brain tumor resulting from contusion[18]
8. Trouble T-Roy (Heavy D and the Boyz), 1968–90; fell off balcony after show in Indianapolis
9. Steve Peregrine Took (T. Rex), 1949–80; choked
10. Gene Vincent, 1934–71; died of ulcerated wound suffered in car crash that killed Eddie Cochran, although Vincent survived fourteen years; alcohol also involved.[22]

---

[1] The official story has always been that Ace killed himself on Christmas Eve of 1954 by playing Russian roulette at a backstage gathering. But the only witnesses were record company owner (and gangster) Don Robey, with whom Ace had been trying to renegotiate, and singer Big Mama Thornton. Thornton and Robey went to their graves without ever changing the story, and without ever convincing many insiders that Ace hadn't been murdered.

[2] Storm, the Liverpool bandleader whose Hurricanes once featured Ringo (and who led the Beatles to Hamburg), died in a suicide pact with his mother. They took pills.

[3] Much speculation in soul circles that Williams was in fact murdered.

[4] Died of stomach hemorrhage after being hit by hit-and-run driver.

[5] Concertgoer stabbed to death at Altamont (December 1969) by Hell's Angels hired to provide "security" for the Rolling Stones.

[6] Inspired his brother, Bobby, to write and sing "Harry Hippie."

[7] Refused treatment until emergency surgery required; died during surgery.

[8] Shot by Los Angeles police when he refused to give up a gun; his gun was unloaded.

[9] Ambushed in van on way back from gig in Belfast.

[10] Beaten to death in Chicago bar for having long hair.

[11] Committed suicide after murdering lover.

[12] Heart attack occurred after he suffered exposure while sleeping in the streets of Chicago.

[13] Killed in Watts rioting, 1965.

[14] Killed during paratrooper training exercise; chute failed to open.

[15] Died while piloting National Guard jet.

[16] Shot himself while sitting at his studio console on Buddy Holly's birthday.

[17] Pastorius, who had become homeless as a result of a long history of mental illness and drug problems, was beaten to death by a nightclub bouncer in his hometown for trying to enter the club in a disheveled condition.

[18] Allegedly murdered.

[19] Definitely murdered.
[20] Allegedly overdosed.
[21] Allegedly a suicide.
[22] Alcohol-related (but nonalcoholic).
[23] Drug-related (nonoverdoses only).
[24] Moon and Elliott died in the same London flat.
[25] Died onstage or at a gig.
[26] Died in recording studio
[27] Shot to death by his wife.
[28] Died while imprisoned.

Most Spectacular Deaths

1. JOHNNY ACE—Died backstage on Christmas Eve 1954 at Houston City Auditorium, while playing Russian roulette.

2. JOHN BONHAM (LED ZEPPELIN)—The profoundly influential drummer found dead in his bed at Jimmy Page's house, of an overdose of alcohol. A prosaic death, except that it came not as the result of cumulative overexposure alone, but as the product of ingesting *forty shots* of vodka in a single day. *That* is a unique and impressive feat.

3. SAM COOKE—Shot to death under mysterious circumstances at a Los Angeles motel on December 10, 1964. The proprietor, who shot him, claimed Cooke appeared to be an intruder. (He was wearing only a shirt and his undershorts at the time.) A jury returned a verdict of justifiable homicide.

4. MAL EVANS—Beatles roadie cut down at his own home in 1976 by Los Angeles police because he was waving a pistol at them, after threatening his girlfriend with it. The gun was unloaded. No officers were ever charged in the case.

5. JIM GORDON—The only main entry on this list who is still living. Gordon, a great session drummer who heard psychotic voices, hacked up and killed his mother in 1985. He got sixteen to life.

6. BILL GRAHAM—Concert promoter died in a fireball explosion as his private helicopter hit high-tension electric wires while returning from a concert to Graham's Marin County home in 1991.

7. LES HARVEY (STONE THE CROWS)—Electrocuted onstage at Swansea University, Wales, in 1972 by touching a live microphone with wet feet.

8. BUDDY HOLLY, J. P. RICHARDSON, AND RITCHIE VALENS—Rock's first plane crash remains its most spectacular, not only because it bagged three stars at once, but because they were traveling by private plane from Clear Lake, Iowa, to Fargo, North Dakota, for such mundane reasons. They wanted to get some laundry done, to pick up mail that had been forwarded to Fargo, and to avoid riding all night on a bus with a defective heater.

9. AL JACKSON—Great soul drummer (Booker T. and the MGs) shot down on the sidewalk in front of his house as he came home at dawn, one day in 1975.

10. SCOTT LaROCK (BOOGIE DOWN PRODUCTIONS)—DJ and mixmaster, partner of KRS-One, whose homeless shelter supervisor he once was, got shot down outside a housing project in 1987. LaRock was sitting in his 4X4, purchased with proceeds from BDP's first album, preparing to enter a home to negotiate a truce in a feud in which he wasn't otherwise even involved.

11. JOHN LENNON—Shot to death outside his New York City apartment building on December 8, 1980, by a lone gunman, obsessed by the Bible and *The Catcher in the Rye*.

12. LYNYRD SKYNYRD—That their 1977 plane crash killed key members Ronnie Van Zant, Steve Gaines, and Cassie Gaines might not be so spectacular. That it crashed *because it ran out of gas* raises the story to the necessary improbable heights.

13. JAMES "SHEP" SHEPPARD—Leader of the Heartbeats and Shep and the Limelites found beaten to death in a car parked at the side of the Long Island Expressway, January 24, 1970.

14. RORY STORM—One-time Merseybeat bandleader (who contributed his drummer, Ringo Starr, to the Beatles after pioneering the Liverpool-to-Hamburg rock band caravan route) was found dead in 1974 from an overdose of pills. The body of his mother, with whom he'd had a suicide pact, was found nearby.

15. LARRY WILLIAMS—Early rock 'n' roll genius (gave the Beatles "Dizzy Miss Lizzy" and "Bad Boy," the world "Short Fat Fannie," and, with Johnny Watson, "Mercy Mercy") found by his mother in the garage of his million-dollar home, with a .38 caliber bullet through his brain, on New Year's Day, 1980. Williams made more money as a pimp and dope dealer than as a musician, so even though the police ruled it suicide, others have their doubts. Speculation about the perpetrators ranges from rival dealers to renegade cops.

Rock and Roll Heaven
A List of Probable Inductees

1. Master of ceremonies: Alan Freed
2. Promoter: Bill Graham[1]
3. Guitarists: Michael Bloomfield, Eddie Hazel, Jimi Hendrix, Buddy Holly, Bob Marley, Stevie Ray Vaughan
4. Bass: James Jamerson
5. Drums: Al Jackson

6. Horns: King Curtis with the Bar-Keys
7. Harp: Little Walker, Slim Harpo
8. Keyboards: John Lennon, Richard Manuel, Big Joe Turner
9. The choir: Jesse Belvin, Marvin Gaye, Little Willie John, Frankie Lymon, Clyde McPhatter, Roy Orbison, Bon Scott, Del Shannon, Sylvester, Tammi Terrell, Gene Vincent, Mary Wells, Chuck Willis
10. Choreography: Trouble T-Roy
11. Mixer: Scott LaRock
12. Roadies: Mal Evans, Ian Stewart
13. Stand-in for God: Elvis Presley (at least till James Brown arrives)

Rock and Roll Hell
A List of Probable Inductees

1. Master of ceremonies: Keith Moon
2. Promoter: Bill Graham[1]
3. Singers: Johnny Ace, David Ruffin, Ronnie Van Zant
4. Guitars: Duane Allman, D. Boon, Lowell George, Hillel Slovak, Johnny Thunders
5. Horns: Chris Wood
6. Drums: John Bonham, Jeff Porcaro
7. Keyboards: Assorted members of the Grateful Dead
8. Bass: Sid Vicious
9. Various stringed instruments: Brian Jones
10. Choir: G. G. Allin, Florence Ballard, John Belushi, Darby Crash, Janis Joplin, Freddie Mercury, Peter Tosh, Andrew Wood
11. Roadies: Bruce Barry, Meredith Hunter
12. Caterer: Karen Carpenter
13. Stand-in for Satan: Jim Morrison (at least till George Clinton arrives)

---

[1] At his own insistence, Graham controls both markets on an exclusive basis. Both God and Satan tried to talk him out of it, but failed to get him to budge, although there are no backstage basketball courts in Hell.

Ted Bundy's Top 5
Best Songs About Mass Murderers

1. "Mind of a Lunatic," The Geto Boys
2. "The Drifter," Green on Red

3. "Nebraska," Bruce Springsteen
4. "Psycho Killer," Talking Heads
5. "Whenever Kindness Fails," Robert Earle Keen, Jr./Joe Ely

King Heroin

1. "Before They Make Me Run," The Rolling Stones
2. "Berkshire Poppies," Traffic
3. "Carmelita's Way," Warren Zevon
4. "Chinese Rocks," The Ramones
5. "Cold Turkey," John Lennon
6. "Dancing with Mr. Brownstone," Guns N' Roses
7. "Drug Buddy," The Lemonheads
8. "Freddie's Dead," Curtis Mayfield
9. "Heroin," The Velvet Underground
10. "Jane Says," Jane's Addiction
11. "Junker's Blues," Michael Bloomfield
12. "Kid Charlemagne," Steely Dan
13. "King Heroin," James Brown
14. "Milk Me," Johnny Thunders
15. "The Needle and the Damage Done," Neil Young
16. "The Needle and the Spoon," Lynyrd Skynyrd
17. "The Pusher," Steppenwolf
18. "Sam Stone," John Prine
19. "Sister Morphine," The Rolling Stones
20. "Tonight's the Night," Neil Young
21. "Waiting for the Man," The Velvet Underground, Lou Reed
22. "White Light/White Heat," The Velvet Underground
23. "You Can't Always Get What You Want," The Rolling Stones

White-Line Fever

1. "A Blow for Me, a Toot for You," Fred Wesley and the Horny Horns
2. "Casey Jones," The Grateful Dead
3. "Cocaine," Jackson Browne
4. "Cocaine Charley," The Atlanta Rhythm Section
5. "Girl, That's Your Life," Too Short
6. "Life in the Fast Lane," The Eagles
7. "Memo from Turner," Mick Jagger
8. "Moonlight Mile," The Rolling Stones
9. "My Snowblind Friend," Hoyt Axton
10. "Night of the Living Bassheads," Public Enemy

11. "Pocket Full of Stones," U.G.K.
12. "Pop Life," Prince
13. "That Smell," Lynyrd Skynyrd
14. "White Lines," Melle Mel
15. "Witchy Woman," The Eagles

Reefer Madness

1. "Cheeba, Cheeba," Tone Loc
2. "Coming into Los Angeles," Arlo Guthrie
3. "Don't Step on the Grass, Sam," Steppenwolf
4. "Flying High," Country Joe and the Fish
5. "Hits from the Bong," Cypress Hill
6. "How to Roll a Blunt," Redman
7. "(I'm a Blunt Being Smoked and) I Can't Wake Up," KRS-One
8. "Indo Smoke," Mista Grimm
9. "Itchykoo Park," The Small Faces
10. "Let's Go Get Stoned," Ray Charles
11. "New Dope in Town," Spirit
12. "Okie from Muskogee," Merle Haggard
13. "One Toke over the Line," Brewer and Shipley
14. "Panama Red," The New Riders of the Purple Sage
15. "Rainy Day Woman #12 & 35," Bob Dylan
16. "Roll 'Em Phat," Ant Banks
17. "Stunts, Blunts and Hip-Hop," Diamond D
18. "Take Two and Pass," Gang Star
19. "Taxi," Harry Chapin
20. "Tha Bombudd," DJ Quik
21. "20 Sack," Yo Yo
22. "Wacky Tobaccy," NRBQ

Have a Drink On Us

1. "Alcohol,"The Kinks
2. "Brass Monkey," Beastie Boys
3. "Cold Gin," Kiss
4. "Cracklin' Rose," Neil Diamond
5. "Drinkin' Wine Spo-Dee-O-Dee," Stick McGhee
6. "Eight Ball," N.W.A
7. "Gin and Juice," Snoop Doggy Dogg
8. "Have a Drink On Me," AC/DC
9. "Letter to Johnny Walker Red," Asleep at the Wheel
10. "Nighttrain," Guns N' Roses

11. "One Bourbon, One Scotch, One Beer," Amos Milburn
12. "187 Proof," Spice 1
13. "Only when I'm Drunk," Tha Alkaholiks
14. "Pass the 40," Black Sheep
15. "Sitting and Thinking," Charlie Rich
16. "Take Your Whiskey Home," Van Halen
17. "Tequila Sunrise," The Eagles
18. "What's Made Milwaukee Famous (Has Made a Loser Out of Me), Jerry Lee Lewis
19. "White Port and Lemon Juice," The Four Deuces
20. "Wine," The Electric Flag

Antidrug Top 15

1. "Cold Turkey," John Lennon
2. "40 Million Bottlebags," Public Enemy
3. "Kicks," Paul Revere and the Raiders
4. "Straight Edge," Miner Threat
5. "Tonight's the Night," Neil Young
6. "Speed Kills," Steve Gibbons Band
7. "White Lines," Melle Mele
8. "Ever So Clear," Bushwick Bill
9. "Little Billy," The Who
10. "Chinese Rocks," The Ramones
11. "Let It Loose," The Rolling Stones
12. "The Pusher," Steppenwolf
13. "Sam Stone," John Prine
14. "The P Is Free," Boogie Down Productions
15. "Shut the Door," Fugazi

White Light, White Heat
Former Heroin Users

1. Gregg Allman
2. Tim Buckley
3. Ray Charles
4. Eric Clapton
5. Kurt Cobain
6. Marianne Faithfull
7. Perry Farrell
8. Anthony Kiedes
9. Courtney Love
10. Frankie Lyman
11. Jimmy Page
12. Lou Reed
13. Keith Richards
14. Axl Rose
15. Johnny Rotten
16. Slash
17. James Taylor
18. Johnny Thunders
19. Pete Townsend
20. Sid Vicious
21. Johnny Winter

Down on Drugs

1. Chubb Rock
2. Chuck D
3. Janet Jackson
4. Jonathan King
5. Little Richard[1]
6. Ian MacKaye
7. Madonna
8. Ted Nugent
9. Joe Perry[1]
10. Prince
11. Bruce Springsteen
12. Pete Townsend[1]
13. Steven Tyler[1]
14. Frank Zappa

---

[1] Reformed drug user.

Drugs Prescribed to Elvis by His Pal, Dr. Nick

In its malpractice charges against Dr. George Nichopoulos, known to Elvis's intimates as Dr. Nick, the Tennessee Medical Board used eight full-sized legal pages to list the prescriptions he had written. These are only some of them. In the eighteen months before he died, thousands of pills were prescribed to Presley, who did not suffer from any major illness (except drug dependency), an autopsy revealed.

1. Amytal
2. Biphetamine
3. Carbrital
4. Hydrochloride cocaine
5. Demerol
6. Dexamyl
7. Dexedrine
8. Dilaudid
9. Hycomine
10. Ionamin
11. Leritine
12. Lomotil
13. Parest
14. Percodan
15. Placidyl
16. Quaalude
17. Tuinal
18. Valium

Top Songs About Selling Crack

1. "Rox II Riches," P.K.O.
2. "Scarface," Geto Boys
3. "A Bird in the Hand," Ice Cube
4. "Dopeman" N.W.A
5. "Road to Riches," Kool G. Rap & DJ POLO
6. "Pocket Full of Stones," U.G.K.

CHAPTER 24

Born to Be Wild

Nik Cohn Picks Rock's "The Good, the Baaad and the Ugly" of the Fifties, Sixties, and Seventies

Nik Cohn says that his prime criterion was moral grace, rather than physical beauty or even musical talent.

THE GOOD

1. Elvis Presley
2. Smokey Robinson
3. Jimi Hendrix
4. Aretha Franklin
5. Arlene Smith (The Chantels)
6. John Lennon
7. Professor Longhair
8. Bob Marley
9. Roy Orbison
10. Billy Fury

THE BAAAD

1. Joe Tex
2. Jerry Lee Lewis
3. Johnny Rotten
4. P. J. Proby
5. Lou Reed
6. Millie Jackson
7. The Coasters
8. Gatemouth Brown
9. Chuck Berry
10. The Big Bopper

THE UGLY

1. Bob Dylan
2. Frank Zappa
3. Roger Daltrey
4. Leon Russell
5. Elvis Costello
6. The Village People
7. Tom Waits
8. Led Zeppelin
9. George Harrison
10. Peter Allen

An Irishman from Londonderry, Cohn has authored a number of novels and books on pop music, including his noted volume on rock history, Rock from the Beginning *(Stein and Day, 1969), but his most celebrated achievement was a* New York *magazine article, "Tribal Rites of the New Saturday Night," which became the film* Saturday Night Fever.

Paul Burlison Lists the 5 Wildest Rock and Roll Cats of the 1950s

1. Jerry Lee Lewis
2. Bobby Lee Trammell
3. The Judimars

4. Screamin' Jay Hawkins
5. Lonnie Donegan

Paul Burlison played an important part in the development of early rock as the lead guitarist in the Rock and Roll Trio, with Johnny and Dorsey Burnette. Burlison is responsible for creating fuzz tone, with his distorted solo on "Train Kept-a-Rollin'." He now lives in Memphis, where he has a record collection including more than one hundred thousand discs.

Jim Morrison's Arrest Record

1. NEW HAVEN, CONNECTICUT, DECEMBER 9, 1967

Morrison had turned twenty-four the day before. Prior to the Doors set, he was making out with a girl in a backstage shower room when they were rousted by a cop. Jim, of course, immediately harassed the cop, lipping off until he was maced. During the middle of "Back Door Man" in that night's show, Morrison launched into a tirade about the incident. The cops, retaliating, turned on the houselights, and Morrison was arrested onstage. He was charged with breach of peace and resisting arrest.

2. LAS VEGAS, EARLY 1968

Morrison was with writer Robert Gover (author of *The $100 Misunderstanding*) outside the Pussy Cat Au-Go-Go, a topless joint. The pair had made the mistake of starting a fight with a security guard in the parking lot. Both Gover and Morrison were charged with public drunkenness, Morrison also being hit with accusations of vagrancy and failure to identify himself.

3. MIAMI, MARCH 1, 1969

At Dinner Key Auditorium, Morrison was arrested for exposing his organ during a Doors performance that night. Morrison was not charged until some weeks later, when the incident had already become a media spat. He was charged with lewd and lascivious behavior (a felony carrying a maximum three-year sentence), indecent exposure, open profanity, and public drunkenness. After a lengthy trial, he was found guilty in 1970 of indecent exposure and profanity. He was sentenced to six months of hard labor with a five-hundred-dollar fine on the first charge, and sixty days hard labor on the second. The sentence was on appeal when Morrison died.

4. PHOENIX, NOVEMBER 11, 1969

On a Continental Airlines flight from Los Angeles, on their way to see a Rolling Stones concert in Phoenix, Morrison and friend Tom Baker were arrested by the FBI. They were charged with drunk and disorderly conduct and interfering with personnel aboard a commercial aircraft, the latter carrying a federal skyjacking penalty of a ten-thousand-dollar fine and ten years in prison. They were found innocent of the felony charge but guilty of "assaulting, threatening, intimidating and interfering with the performance of two stewardesses." However, the stewardess who made most of the accusations later changed her testimony, and the charges were dropped.

5. LOS ANGELES, AUGUST 4, 1970

Morrison was charged with public drunkenness after falling asleep on an old woman's porch in West L.A.; this occurred one day before the Miami trial began.

Slammer Blues

1. "Alice's Restaurant," Arlo Guthrie
2. "Belly of the Beast," The Lifers Group
3. "Black Steel in the Hour of Chaos," Public Enemy
4. "Call Tha Guardz," X-Raided
5. "Cell Number 7," John Entwistle
6. "Chain Gang," Sam Cooke
7. "Check Yo Self," Ice Cube
8. "Christmas in Prison," John Prine
9. "Country Bluz," South Central Cartel
10. "Electric Chair," Sleepy John Estes
11. "The First Day of School" (a skit), Ice Cube
12. "Folsom Prison Blues," Johnny Cash
13. "Friend of the Devil," The Grateful Dead
14. "Gas Chamber," Spice 1
15. "George Jackson," Bob Dylan
16. "Gonna Give Her All the Love I Got," Jimmy Ruffin
17. "Have Mercy Judge," Chuck Berry
18. "Hollaway Jail," The Kinks
20. "I Fought The Law," Bobby Fuller Four
21. "Jail," Big Mama Thornton
22. "Jailbreak," AC/DC
23. "Jail Guitar Doors," The Clash
24. "Jailhouse Rock," Elvis Presley
25. "Letter to the Pen," Yo Yo
26. "Liberation of Lonzo Williams," The Coup
27. "Lil' Ghetto Boy," Dr. Dre (featuring Snoop Doggy Dogg)

28. "Locked in Spofford," Mobb Deep
29. "Long Black Veil," The Band
30. "Lost in Da System," Da Lench Mob
31. "Mama Tried," Merle Haggard
32. "Me No Like Rikers Island," Cocoa-Tea and Nardo Ranks
33. "Out on a Furlough," WC and the Maad Circle
34. "Penitentiary," Kid Frost
35. "Penitentiary Blues," David Allan Coe
36. "Percy's Song," Bob Dylan
37. "Premonition of a Black Prisoner," K-Solo
38. "Rikers Island," Kool G. Rap and DJ Polo
39. "Sweet Lucy," Michael Hurley
40. "Take a Message to Mary," The Everly Brothers
41. "There's a Riot Jumpin' Off," UZI$BROS
42. "There's Gonna Be a Jailbreak," Thin Lizzy
43. "Thirty Days in the Hole," Humble Pie
44. "This Is for the Convicts," Convicts
45. "The Tower," Ice T
46. "Two to the Head," Kool G. Rap & DJ Polo (Ice Cube's lyrics)
47. "Up in the Mountains," 2 Black 2 Strong
48. "We Love You," The Rolling Stones
49. "Welcome Home (Sanitarium)," Metallica
50. "Wildside," Marky Mark and the Funky Bunch

In the County It's a Party 'Cause You Know Everybody
Artists Who've Done Time

1. CHUCK BERRY—He got put away twice, once in the late fifties on a Mann Act violation, and again in the late seventies for income-tax violation.

2. JOHNNY BRAGG—The leader of the Prisonaires, he served time first for rape, and later for parole violation. The parole violation apparently was a trumped-up charge for having sex with his wife in a car. While doing time, he and a group of inmates recorded "Just Walking in the Rain" and several other classics for Sun Records.

3. JAMES BROWN—As a kid, Brown spent three years in a Georgia reform school. As an adult, many decades later at the end of the eighties, he spent considerably more time behind bars (see "Famous Busts").

4. DAVID CROSBY—Spent five months behind bars on narcotics and weapons charges before being paroled in August of 1986.

5. FREDDY FENDER—Under his real name, Baldemar G. Huerta, Fender spent three years in a Louisiana prison on a marijuana-related conviction.

6. ICE CUBE—*Wall Street Journal:* "Have you ever been to prison?" Ice Cube: "Yeah, I been to jail." *WSJ:* "What for?" Ice Cube: "Something I don't want to put in the *Wall Street Journal.*"

7. J-DEE (OF DA LENCH MOB)—Arrested and charged with shooting and killing a twenty-three-year-old LA man, DeSean L. Cooper—known to music fans as J-Dee of Da Lench Mob—was held without bail in L.A. County Jail from his arrest on June 22, 1993, through his trial, which at press time was not yet completed.

8. KRS-ONE—Rapper Kris Parker told *The Source* magazine that he got caught with ten garbage bags filled with marijuana (indica, to be exact) and spent seven months in prison. After he was released, he went to the Franklin Men's Shelter where he met Scott La Rock, with whom he formed Boogie Down Productions.

9. LITTLE WILLIE JOHN—After a manslaughter conviction, he did time in Washington State Penitentiary, where he died of pneumonia.

10. MARKY MARK—On April 8, 1988, Mark Wahlberg and his friends spent the night smoking joints and sucking down beers until their supply ran out. They happened upon Thanh Lam, who was unloading two cases of beer, and Mark knocked him unconscious with a stick. He spent the night in jail and then forty-five days at the Deer Island House of Correction, with an additional two years on probation.

11. EUGENE MUMFORD—The leader of the Larks served a sentence for grass in 1949 and went on to write "When I Leave These Prison Walls."

12. PHIL OCHS—Ochs served a spell for vagrancy in Florida around 1960.

13. SNOW—This white reggae one-hit wonder has an annoying habit of waving his manslaughter conviction like a flag of authenticity.

14. RICK STEVENS—The Tower of Power lead vocalist did time in California on three counts of first-degree murder.

15. IKE TURNER—Convicted in 1989 for selling and possessing cocaine, he served eighteen months of a four-year sentence after violating the terms of his probation.

16. SID VICIOUS—After serving several weeks in New York City jails for the alleged murder of girlfriend Nancy Spungen, Vicious overdosed on heroin before the case came to trial.

Famous Busts

1. THE ROLLING STONES, MARCH 18, 1965
They were fined five pounds each for public urination at a gas station after a gig at the Romford ABC in Essex, United Kingdom.

2. KEITH RICHARDS, MICK JAGGER, AND MARIANNE FAITHFULL, FEBRUARY 12, 1967
At his home at Redlands, West Wittering, United Kingdom, Richards was busted with Jagger, Faithful, and art dealer Robert Fraser. The celebrated drug orgy raid.

3. MICK JAGGER AND KEITH RICHARDS, MAY 10, 1967
In Chichester, United Kingdom, they were arrested for drugs and sent to jail at West Sussex Quarter Session.

4. BRIAN JONES, MAY 10, 1967
After a bust for possession of marijuana in England, Jones was released on 250 pounds bail. He was sentenced to nine months in jail, which was later reduced to a one-thousand-pound fine and three years' probation.

5. THE GRATEFUL DEAD, OCTOBER 2, 1967
Narcotics agents raided their house at 710 Ashbury Street in San Francisco, and arrested Pigpen, Bob Weir, and nine others, although the bust was ultimately meaningless because the cops had failed to obtain warrants before breaking down the door.

6. MICK JAGGER AND MARIANNE FAITHFULL, MAY 24, 1968
At their home in Cheyne Walk, London, they were arrested for possession of pot and released on fifty-pound bail.

7. JOHN LENNON AND YOKO ONO, OCTOBER 18, 1968
At their flat in Montague Square, London. Lennon was fined 150 pounds and 21 pounds in court costs for possession of marijuana.

8. GEORGE AND PATTI HARRISON, MARCH 12, 1969
Their London home was raided and 120 joints found. Harrison claimed it was a frame-up, timed by police to coincide with the marriage of Paul McCartney.

9. PETE TOWNSEND AND ROGER DALTREY, MAY 16, 1969
They were charged with assault after Townsend kicked a cop offstage at New York's Fillmore East. The plainclothesman was trying to clear the hall because of a fire next door. Bill Graham bailed them out.

10. ARETHA FRANKLIN, JULY 22, 1969
In Detroit, Franklin was busted for causing a disturbance in a parking lot. Released on a fifty-dollar bond, she ran down a street sign as she left the police station.

11. JANIS JOPLIN, NOVEMBER 15, 1969

In Tampa, Florida, Joplin was accused of vulgar and indecent language and later released on a fifty-dollar bond.

12. THE GRATEFUL DEAD, JANUARY 31, 1970

They were busted for narcotics (LSD and barbiturates) in New Orleans, along with the celebrated LSD chemist Stanley Owsley.

13. PETER YARROW, MARCH 26, 1970

He pleaded guilty to charges of "taking immoral liberties" with a fourteen-year-old girl in Washington, D.C. Peter, Paul, and Mary had just won a Grammy for Best Children's Record.

14. PHIL LESH, JANUARY 14, 1973

The Grateful Dead bassist was busted for possession of drugs in Marin County, California.

15. PAUL McCARTNEY, MARCH 8, 1973

He was fined one hundred pounds for growing cannabis on his farm in Campbeltown, Scotland.

16. JERRY GARCIA, MARCH 27, 1973

After stopping him for speeding on Interstate 295 near Philadelphia, the cops found grass, acid, coke, and prescription pills in a suitcase.

17. KEITH RICHARDS, FEBRUARY 27, 1977

Richards was originally charged in Toronto, Canada, for possession of heroin for the purposes of trafficking, and for possession of cocaine. The cocaine charge was later dropped and Richards pleaded guilty to the possession of twenty-two grams of heroin. Despite official protests, Richards was given a suspended sentence. The only stipulation by the court was that he give a benefit concert for the Canadian Institute for the Blind, which he did give on April 22, 1979 and which included a guest appearance by Mick Jagger.

18. PAUL McCARTNEY, JANUARY 16, 1980

In Tokyo, customs inspectors discovered nearly half a pound of marijuana he had absentmindedly left in his suitcase. McCartney spent ten days in prison, had his Japanese tour canceled, and was forbidden from ever returning to that country. However, ten years later, he was allowed to return to perform six shows.

19. CHRISSIE HYNDE, MARCH 1980

The Pretenders' lead singer spent the night in a Memphis jail and was released the next day on $250 bond for drunken behavior, including kicking out a police car window outside a local bar.

20. WENDY O. WILLIAMS, JANUARY 18, 1981

The arrest, in Milwaukee, was initially for onstage obscenity, but after an officer allegedly made a sexual grab at her, a battle ensued. Williams was charged with resisting arrest and battery of a police officer. She was released on two thousand dollars' bond. The Plasmatics' lead singer had seven stitches above her eye and spent the night in jail, as did the band's manager.

21. BILLY IDOL, FEBRUARY 20, 1987

The singer was allegedly in possession of one hundred dollars' worth of crack in New York City's Greenwich Village. The young socialite he was with (who wasn't his girlfriend at the time, as he took great lengths to explain after the incident) was arraigned and released. Idol was not officially charged.

22. JAMES BROWN, SEPTEMBER 24, 1988

Brown entered an insurance office in Augusta, Georgia, waving a shotgun (according to authorities), upset that someone attending a seminar had used his private bathroom. This set into motion a high-speed chase that spilled over into South Carolina where police said that Brown tried to run over two officers setting up a roadblock, so they shot out the front tires of his truck. Brown said that he was in the process of surrendering to a black police officer at the site of the insurance office when a group of white officers approached and started breaking the windows of his vehicle. At that time, Brown claimed, he sped off, fearing for his life. At the trial, where he was charged with traffic violations, aggravated assault, carrying a pistol, and PCP possession, the black officer supported Brown's version of the events. Nevertheless, he was sentenced to six-and-a-half years in prison, of which he served approximately twenty-six months before being paroled on February 27, 1991.

23. BOBBY BROWN, JANUARY 1989

In Columbus, Georgia, Brown was cited for simulating sex during a concert. Under a local antilewdness statute, the cops arrested him for pulling a woman out of the audience, humping her, and "simulating sexual intercourse." Brown was arrested and taken to jail where he made six hundred dollars' bond before being allowed to return to the concert—where he was permitted to finish the show. On January 13, 1993, he was cited (but not arrested) again for a similar routine in Augusta, Georgia.

24. OZZY OSBOURNE, SEPTEMBER 2, 1989

Sharon, his manager-wife, had Ozzy arrested for threatening to kill her but later declined to press charges after he agreed to stay away from her.

25. TOMMY LEE, MARCH 25, 1990

During an Augusta, Georgia, concert, the Motley Crue drummer was arrested and charged with indecent exposure for mooning the crowd. The band was allowed to finish its show before he was booked and then freed on $1,680 bond.

26. 2 LIVE CREW, JUNE 10, 1990

After ruling *As Nasty as They Wanna Be* obscene, Fort Lauderdale, Florida, authorities arrested three members of the group after they performed at a nightclub. They were eventually acquitted on October 20.

27. SLICK RICK, JULY 3, 1990

Driving with his then-pregnant girlfriend, Rick spotted his cousin Mark Plummer—whom he had hired as a security guard but later suspected of conspiring to rip him off—walking down a street in the Bronx. Rick pulled over and took a shot at his cousin, hitting him in the leg and side and hitting an unrelated bystander in the foot. Shortly after driving away from the scene, Rick was pursued by the cops for two miles, a chase which involved much weaving in and out of traffic. Rick, whose given name is Ricky Walters, was indicted on seven charges, including two counts of attempted murder in the second degree. After Rick had spent eight months in prison, Russell Simmons, the CEO of Def Jam, bailed Rick out so that he could cut enough material for two albums in six weeks. (The songs from these sessions were never released.) By the summer of 1993, Rick had earned a slot on a work release program, which he used to hit the studio, and by Thanksgiving, he was released. Unfortunately, his freedom lasted less than a week. Rick was re-arrested on Thanksgiving Day and threatened with deportation to his native England, where he had not lived since he was a young child.

28. TWO MUCH JOY, AUGUST 10, 1990

Three members of the band were arrested after performing six songs from 2 Live Crew's *As Nasty as They Wanna Be*, which had been declared obscene in Fort Lauderdale, Florida, the site of the New York rock group's adults-only show. On January 18, 1991, it took jurors only thirteen minutes to acquit them.

29. AXL ROSE, OCTOBER 30, 1990

Allegedly, Rose hit a neighbor with an empty wine bottle during a dispute over the volume of his stereo. After spending several hours in jail, he posted five thousand dollars' bail. On November 29, Rose and his neighbor filed an agreement with the court, stating that they would try to avoid each other. The assault charges against Rose were dropped.

30. FLAVOR FLAV, FEBRUARY 10, 1991

The Public Enemy court jester spent twenty days in jail on charges of assaulting his girlfriend.

31. DONNIE WAHLBERG, MARCH 27, 1991

Police charged the New Kids on the Block singer with dumping vodka on a hotel carpet in Louisville, Kentucky, and setting it on fire. Nobody was hurt and there was no major damage, but Wahlberg turned himself in, pleaded innocent to an arson charge and was freed on five thousand dollars' bail. He was ordered to appear in court on April 11, but the authorities wanted to avoid a fan and media circus, so they held the hearing the night before. Wahlberg didn't enter a plea and agreed to make PSA's on such topics as fire safety and drugs in return for eventual dismissal of a reduced charge of misdemeanor criminal mischief.

32. CHRIS ROBINSON, MAY 29, 1991

After a Denver concert, the lead singer of the Black Crowes was in a 7-Eleven, where a clerk refused to sell them beer after midnight. He overheard somebody yell, "There's the lead singer of the Black Crowes!" and their companion answer, "Who are the Black Crowes?" Robinson, in the process of grabbing two cases of beer and heading for his car, spun around and said something like, "You'd know who we were if you didn't eat so many Twinkies!" A fight ensued, culminating in his spitting on her. Through his lawyer, he pleaded no contest to charges of disturbing the peace.

33. VANILLA ICE, JUNE 21, 1991

The alleged rapper was arrested, along with his bodyguard, for carrying concealed loaded weapons outside a Los Angeles supermarket.

34. AXL ROSE, JULY 4, 1991

Upset that a Kansas City, Missouri, concertgoer seemed to be videotaping his show, Rose was pissed off to see security "doing everything they can to let that guy go," so he jumped into the audience in an effort to grab him. When he returned to the stage, he lashed out at the security staff and stormed off. A riot ensured, resulting in over two hundred thousand dollars in damages and over sixty injuries. A warrant was issued for Rose's arrest but he had already skipped town. Guns N' Roses canceled three concerts in Chicago and Michigan—to the tune of $1.5 million in lost ticket sales—because St. Louis officials had made arrangements with local authorities to arrest the singer. Rose made arrangements to turn himself in by the next March but didn't show up. It wasn't until July 14, 1992, when he turned himself in to St. Louis officials two days after being arrested at JFK International Airport in New York City as a fugitive to face misdemeanor charges of assault and property damage. (They wanted to get him for inciting a riot but such a provision didn't exist in Missouri law.) The case was finally plea-bargained, with Rose essentially exonerated.

35. RICK JAMES, AUGUST 2, 1991

The King of Funk was arrested along with his twenty-one-year-old fiancée, Tanya Ann Hijazi, and charged with torturing a twenty-four-year-old woman. According to the alleged victim, James wanted to teach her a lesson because he suspected her of stealing less than an ounce of crack cocaine from him. She was burned on her legs and stomach with a hot crack pipe and forced to orally copulate Hijazi while James watched. The two were charged with assault with a deadly weapon, aggravated mayhem, torture, and forcible oral copulation. In addition, James was charged with making terrorist threats and furnishing cocaine. James was eventually convicted of only a misdemeanor and sentenced to a drug rehabilitation program.

36. FLAVOR FLAV, JANUARY 10, 1992

This time he was charged with two traffic violations and failure to pay child support.

37. HARRY CONNICK, JR., DECEMBER 27, 1992

The crooner was arrested at New York City's John F. Kennedy Airport for carrying a firearm, but the charges were eventually dismissed after he agreed to do a public service announcement warning folks not to carry unlicensed handguns in New York.

38. DAVID LEE ROTH, APRIL 16, 1993

The ex–Van Halen singer was busted for buying a dime bag of weed in New York City's Washington Square Park during a drug sweep. The charges were dropped when he agreed to behave himself for a year.

39. SNOOP DOGGY DOGG, SEPTEMBER 2, 1993

After acting as a presenter at the MTV Music Awards, Snoop turned himself over to police who sought him in the August 25 murder of a twenty-two-year old L.A. man. Allegedly, Snoop's bodyguard shot the man, who had made threats against the star. Snoop, the bodyguard, and another associate were charged with murder.

40. TUPAC SHAKUR, OCTOBER 31, 1993

Tupac was driving through downtown Atlanta when he allegedly came close to running over two off-duty cops who were out to dinner with their wives. The cops pulled their guns—without identifying themselves as police officers—and, according to authorities, Shakur shot one in the stomach and the other in the buttocks. Both were treated and released from the hospital. Shakur was charged with aggravated assault. Less than a month later, he was arrested for allegedly raping and sodomizing a woman in a New York hotel room.

41. FLAVOR FLAV, NOVEMBER 1, 1993

This time he was charged with attempted murder after an incident involving a neighbor. Supposedly paranoid from drug use, he thought that his girlfriend was having sex with a neighbor and he went next door demanding to search the apartment. After failing to find her, he chased the neighbor into the building's lobby, shooting at his feet. Flav was arrested and then checked into the Betty Ford Clinic.

Jailbait

1. "Bobby Sox to Stockings," Frankie Avalon
2. "Born Too Late," The Poni-Tails
3. "Brown Shoes Don't Make It," The Mothers of Invention
4. "Christine Sixteen," Kiss
5. "Come Up the Years," Jefferson Airplane

6. "Don't Stand So Close to Me," The Police
7. "I Saw Her Standing There," The Beatles
8. "I'm So Young," The Students
9. "It Hurts to Be Sixteen," Brenda Lee
10. "Jailbait," Andre Williams
11. "Little Queenie," Chuck Berry
12. "Only Sixteen," Sam Cooke
13. "Sent Up," The Falcons
14. "17," Rick James
15. "Sixteen Blue," The Replacements
16. "Sixteen Candles," The Crests
17. "Stray Cat Blues," The Rolling Stones
18. "Sweet Little Rock and Roller," Chuck Berry
19. "Sweet Little Sixteen," Chuck Berry
20. "Sweet Sixteen," The Colts
21. "Teenage Wildlife," David Bowie
22. "13 and Good," BDP
23. "What's Your Name," Lynyrd Skynyrd
24. "Young Blood," The Coasters
25. "You're Sixteen," Johnny Burnette

Performers Who Reached Stardom Before Turning 18

1. Another Bad Creation, "Lesha," 1990 (ages 8–12)
2. The Boys, "Dial My Heart," 1988 (ages 5–9)
3. Chi Ali, "Age Ain't Nothin' But A Number," 1992 (at age 15)
4. Fabian, "I'm a Man," 1959 (at age 16)
5. Debbie Gibson, "Shake Your Love," 1987 (at age 17)
6. Janis Ian," Society's Child (Baby I've Been Thinking)," 1967 (at age 15)
7. Janet Jackson, on the TV show *Good Times*, 1977 (at age 11)
8. Michael Jackson, "I Want You Back," 1970 (at age 11)[1]
9. Kris Kross, "Jump," 1991 (both Chris Kelly and Chris Smith were age 12)
10. Brenda Lee, "One Step at a Time," 1957 (at age 12)
11. Little Eva, "The Loco-Motion," 1962 (at age 16)
12. L.L. Cool J, "I Can't Live Without My Radio," 1985 (at age 16)
13. Frankie Lymon, "Why Do Fools Fall In Love," 1962 (at age 14)[2]
14. Menudo (all their members are always under 16 because they get booted out the group when their voices change)
15. Ricky Nelson, "A Teenager's Romance," 1957 (at age 17)

16. New Edition, "Candy Girl," 1983 (ages 13–15)
17. New Kids on the Block, "Be My Girl," 1986 (ages 14–17)
18. Little Esther Phillips, "Double Crossing Blues," 1950 (at age 15)
19. Roxanne Shanté, "Roxanne's Revenge," 1984 (at age 14)
20. The Schoolboys, "Please Say You Want Me," 1955[3]
21. Charlie Sexton, "Beat's So Lonely," 1985 (at age 16)
22. Raven Symone, "That's What Little Girls Are Made Of," 1993 (at age 7)[4]
23. Special Ed, "Youngest in Charge," 1989 (at age 16)
24. Rachel Sweet, "B-A-B-Y," 1979 (at age 16)
25. Tanya Tucker, "Would You Lay with Me (In a Field of Stone)," 1973 (at age 14)
26. Little Stevie Wonder, "Fingertips, Part 2," 1963 (at age 12)

---

[1] With the Jackson 5. Michael's brothers were also under 18.
[2] With the Teenagers.
[3] Ages unknown, but all attended Cooper Junior High School in Harlem.
[4] Was already a TV star on *The Cosby Show*.

10 Famous Bubblegum Groups

Buddah Records kicked off the bubblegum rock craze in 1968 with a batch of synthetic groups (floating collections of sessionmen). The result was some of the most ludicrous, if occasionally transcendent, trash produced in the rock and roll age. Kasenetz-Katz is the cream of the crop, but that doesn't mean a lot.

1. The Archies, "Sugar, Sugar"
2. The Banana Splits, "The Tra La La Song"
3. Crazy Elephant, "Gimme Gimme Good Lovin' "
4. Kasenetz-Katz Singing Orchestra Circus, "Quick Joey Small (Run Joey Run)"
5. The Lemon Pipers, "Green Tambourine"
6. The Music Explosion, "Little Bit of Soul"
7. The 1910 Fruitgum Company, "Simon Says"
8. The Ohio Express, "Yummy Yummy Yummy"
9. The Rock and Roll Dubble Bubble Trading Card Company of Philadelphia, 19141, "Bubble Gum Music"
10. Steam, "Na Na Hey Hey (Kiss Him Goodbye)"

Post-Punk Teendom's
Greatest Hits

1. "Smells Like Teen Spirit," Nirvana
2. "Nirvana," Juliana Hatfield
3. "Sixteen Blue," The Replacements
4. "Bastards of Young," The Replacements
5. "School," Nirvana
6. "Cherry Bomb," Joan Jett
7. "Cherry Bomb," Bratmobile
8. "Carnival," Bikini Kill
9. "Hate My Way," Throwing Muses
10. "Fight for Your Right to Party," The Beastie Boys

We Got the Beat
The Greatest Songs About Masturbation

1. "All I Have to Do Is Dream," The Everly Brothers
2. "Astral Plane," The Modern Lovers
3. "Back and Forth," Devo
4. "The Beat," Elvis Costello
5. "Better Off Without a Wife," Tom Waits
6. "Blinded by the Light," Bruce Springsteen
7. "Blue Moon," Elvis Presley
8. "Buttered Popcorn," The Supremes
9. "Captain Jack," Billy Joel
10. "Cool Jerk," The Capitols
11. "Dancing with Myself," Generation X
12. "Darling Nikki," Prince
13. "Don't Treat Me Bad," Michael Hurley
14. "Fiddle About," The Who
15. "Going Home," The Rolling Stones
16. "I Touch Myself," Divinyls
17. "Imaginary Lover," The Atlanta Rhythm Section
18. "In My Room," The Beach Boys
19. "Jamaica Jerk-Off," Elton John
20. "Just Out of Reach (Of My Two Empty Arms)," Percy Sledge
21. "Love or Confusion," Jimi Hendrix
22. "Move It On Over," Hank Williams
23. "Only the Lonely (Know How I Feel)," Roy Orbison
24. "Orgasm Addict," The Buzzcocks
25. "Pictures of Lily," The Who
26. "Pump It Up," Elvis Costello

27. "Rattlesnake Shake," Fleetwood Mac
28. "Rocks Off," The Rolling Stones
29. "Rosie," Jackson Browne
30. "Shake a Hand," Faye Adams
31. "She Bop," Cyndi Lauper
32. "Slippery Fingers," Grin
33. "Solo," Ellen Shipley
34. "Sonic Boom," The Gear Daddies
35. "The Stroke," Billy Squire
36. "Turning Japanese," The Vapors
37. "Walk the Dog," Aerosmith
38. "Walking the Dog," Rufus Thomas
39. "When Something Is Wrong with My Baby," Sam and Dave
40. "Whip It," Devo
41. "Whole Lotta Rosie," AC/DC
42. "Whole Lotta Shakin' Going On," Jerry Lee Lewis
43. "You'll Never Get Cheated by Your Hand," Stumblebum

20 Punk Groups of the 1960s

Between the British Invasion and the full onslaught of psychedelia two or three years later, it seemed as if virtually every American male with three friends and access to an electrical outlet formed a band. Playing in basements and garages, for beer blasts and sock hops, these bands were characterized by marginal competence, great naivete and a willingness to try anything. English accents, tough-guy looks, the longest hair in the neighborhood. These were the original punk rockers, from whom the more politicized and radical seventies version took its name and inspiration. These groups are best memorialized on Nuggets, *an album by Lenny Kaye for Elektra Records (and later reissued on Sire).*

1. The Amboy Dukes, "Baby Please Don't Go"
2. The Barbarians, "Are You a Boy or Are You a Girl?"
3. The Blendells, "La La La La La"
4. The Blues Magoos, "(We Ain't Got) Nuthin' Yet"
5. Cannibal and the Headhunters, "Land of 1000 Dances"
6. The Castaways, "Liar Liar"
7. The Count Five, "Psychotic Reaction"
8. The Cryin Shames, "Sugar and Spice"
9. The Gants, "Road Runner"
10. The Kingsmen, "Louie Louie"
11. The McCoys, "Hang on Sloopy"
12. The MC5, "Kick Out the Jams"
13. Mouse and the Traps, "Public Execution"
14. The Music Machine, "Talk Talk"

15. The Outsiders, "Respectable"
16. The Premiers, "Farmer John"
17. ? and the Mysterians, "96 Tears"
18. The Seeds, "Pushin' Too Hard"
19. The Shadows of Knight, "Gloria"
20. The Standells, "Dirty Water"

Punk Rock Records that Made the British Top Twenty Before It Was Fashionable

The maximum chart position for each single follows the date on which it first hit that slot.

1. "God Save the Queen," The Sex Pistols, June 44, 1977 (4)
2. "Pretty Vacant," The Sex Pistols, July 9, 1977 (6)
3. "Do Anything You Wanna Do," Eddie and the Hot Rods, August 13, 1977 (9)
4. "Gary Gilmore's Eyes," The Adverbs, September 27, 1977 (18)
5. "Holidays in the Sun," The Sex Pistols, October 22, 1977 (8)
6. "Angels with Dirty Faces," Sham 69, May 13, 1978 (19)
7. "My Way" / "No One Is Innocent," The Sex Pistols with Ronald Biggs, July 8, 1978 (7)
8. "If the Kids Are United," Sham 69, July 29, 1978 (9)
9. "Top of the Pops," The Rezillos, August 12, 1978 (17)
10. "Hong Kong Garden," Siouxsie and the Banshees, August 26, 1978 (7)
11. "Ever Fallen in Love," The Buzzcocks, September 23, 1978 (12)
12. "Hurry Up Harry," Sham 69, October 14, 1978 (10)
13. "Public Image," Public Image Ltd., October 21, 1979 (9)
14. "Germ Free Adolescence," X-Ray Spex, November 4, 1978 (19)
15. "Tommy Gun," The Clash, December 2, 1978 (20)

Lenny Kaye Chooses the Most Insane Novelty Records

1. "The Spider and the Fly," Bobby Christian and the Allen Sisters—Caught in the web, emphasis on the B.

2. "Delicious," Jim Backus and Friend—Post-Magoo and pre–*Gilligan's Island*. One of the many contagious laughter records to have dotted the landscape of recorded sound (see Large Larry's "Are You Ticklish?") and the theme song of Village Oldies.

3. "The Out Crowd," The Squares—"Horace, are you going out with Freda the Librarian? I hear she's brilliant." "Oh, Melvin, she's brilliant but she's not a genius!" A is for Artie Resnick.

4. "Stickball," P. Vert—Nostalgia of our time. Like stickball, and basketball, and playing in the streets. And you had a little girl, and she was your love. Because love between two people. . . . Mrs. Bruno, can Tony come out and play?

5. "Flying Saucer," Buchanan and Goodman—This is Cameron-Cameron at the scene of the first (and still best) break-in record. The outer space disc jockey cues up . . . the Clatters! A fairly accurate representation of what Top Forty radio was like in the flush opening years of rock and roll.

6. "Ambrose (Part Five)," Linda Laurie—A boy, a girl, a subway tunnel. Just keep walkin'.

7. "Oliver Cool," Oliver Cool—The swingingest superego in school, the role he was born to play. And with some lovely gooping.

8. "Transfusion," Nervous Norvus—So this twin-pipe papa goes out for a cruise and he's tooling down the highway doing ninety-five and the road skids to the sound of epic crash. Mr. Norvus was also known as DJ Jimmy Drake.

9. "Roaches," The Court Jesters—Doo-wop takes on a very real urban problem, offering advice ("Don't leave your food on the table!") and wry observation ("Crawling up the wall").

10. "Fluffy," Gloria Balsam—Who among us could resist a wet nose? The aural equivalent of *Come Back, Little Sheba* includes some notes only dogs can hear.

11. "Psycho," Jack Kittel—*La luna* beckons. Napoleon XIV is taken away, Fred Blassie ("Pencil Neck Geek") is a pro wrestler, but Jack Kittell simply *is*, peeling the layers of madness like an onion, garnishing the hamburger of his mind. Pass the fries.

Lenny Kaye is best known as the guitarist of the Patti Smith group, but he has also been a rock critic for Rolling Stone *and other publications, a record producer, and a solo artist. Kaye is a record collector with omnivorous rock and roll tastes but with a special passion for a cappella and novelty sides.*

Bobby Pickett's Favorite Novelty Records

1. "The Monster Mash"
2. "Deteriorata"
3. "Ahab, the Arab"
4. "Purple People Eater"
5. "Shaving Cream"
6. "Star Drek"
7. "Silly Drug Songs"
8. "Dragnet" (The first all-talk novelty song I remember hearing)
9. "Banana Boat Song"
10. "Flying Saucer"
11. "I Love Your Toes"
12. "Junkfood Junkie"

Bobby "Boris" Pickett had a trend-setting hit in the summer of 1962 with "The Monster Mash" but is best known as a television and film actor. He now lives in New York City.

Post-Punk's Greatest Hipster Bitch Sessions

1. "I Must Not Think Bad Thoughts," X
2. "Hate Your Friends," Lemonheads
3. "Left of the Dial," The Replacements
4. "Treatment Bound," The Replacements
5. "Banned in D.C.," Bad Brains
6. "Professor Booty," The Beastie Boys
7. Mark E. Smith's (the Fall) entire public discourse, 1980–present
8. "Thurston Hearts the Who," Bikini Kill
9. "Welcome to the Terrordome," Public Enemy
10. "Kill Yr Idols," Sonic Youth
11. "Youth Against Facism," Sonic Youth
12. Mark E. Robinson's collected work, aka Unrest, from whenever to now

Yuk-Yuk: Good for a Laugh

1. "Wipe Out," The Surfaris
2. "I Put a Spell on You," Screamin' Jay Hawkins
3. "Bob Dylan's 115th Dream," Bob Dylan
4. "Cold Lampin' with Flavor," Public Enemy (featuring Flavor Flav)

5. "Rip Van Winkle," The Devotions
6. "These Boots are Made for Walkin'," Nancy Sinatra
7. "Big Yellow Taxi," Joni Mitchell
8. "Baby Got Back," Sir Mix-A-Lot
9. "Do the Freddie," Freddie and the Dreamers
10. "Motorpsycho Nightmare," Bob Dylan
11. "Picking Boogers," Biz Markie
12. "Sister Mary Elephant (Shudd-Up)," Cheech & Chong
13. "Centerfold," J. Geils Band
14. "Come Sail Away," Styx
15. "Wait Until Tomorrow," Jimi Hendrix
16. "Little Girl," The Syndicate of Sound
17. "Me So Horny," 2 Live Crew
18. "Ob-La-Di, Ob-La-Da," The Beatles
19. "Wild Thing," Tone Loc
20. "Freaky Tales," Too Short

The Rap 'n' Roll Lifestyle

1. "Red Red Wine," UB40
2. "Street Fighting Man," The Rolling Stones
3. "Pretty Tied Up," Guns N' Roses
4. "Cocaine," Eric Clapton
5. "White Lines," Grandmaster Melle Mel
6. "Lord of the Thighs," Aerosmith
7. "Cold Gin," Kiss
8. "Spanked," Van Halen
9. "(Night Time Is) The Right Time," Ray Charles
10. "Tonite," DJ Quick
11. "Saturday Nite," Scholly D
12. "Nasty Girls," Venus 6
13. "King Heroin," James Brown
14. "The Card Cheat," The Clash
15. "Rock and Roll All Nite," Kiss
16. "Dancing with Mr. D," The Rolling Stones
17. "Pass Da Piote," Willie D
18. "Boyz N the Hood," Eazy E
19. "Cheeba Cheeba," Tone Loc
20. "You Don't Work, You Don't Eat," WC and the Maad Circle
21. "From the Back," Bell Biv Devoe
22. "Only When I'm Drunk," Tha Alkaholiks
23. "Millionaires Against Hunger," The Red Hot Chili Peppers
24. "Stunts, Blunts & Hip-Hop," Diamond D
25. "Super-Hoe," BDP

CHAPTER 25

Hits and Flops

Most Number-One Singles (Through 1992)

1.	The Beatles	21	16. Daryl Hall and	
2.	Elvis Presley	18	John Oates	6
3.	Michael Jackson	12	17. George Michael[2]	6
4.	The Supremes	12	18. Diana Ross	6
5.	Madonna	11	19. Paula Abdul	5
6.	Whitney Houston	10	20. The Eagles	5
7.	The Bee Gees	9	21. The Four Seasons	5
8.	Paul McCartney	9	22. Janet Jackson	5
9.	Stevie Wonder	9	23. K.C. and the Sunshine	
10.	The Rolling Stones	8	Band	5
11.	Phil Collins	7	24. Olivia Newton-John	5
12.	Elton John[1]	7	25. Prince	5
13.	Bon Jovi	6	26. Lionel Richie	5
14.	Pat Boone	6	27. Barbra Streisand	5
15.	Mariah Carey	6		

Source: Joel Whitburn's Record Research: Top Pop Singles 1955–1986 *and annual supplements, 1987 through 1992.*

[1] Includes one duet record with George Michael.
[2] Includes one duet record with Elton John.

Most Consecutive Number-One Singles (Through 1992)

   1. WHITNEY HOUSTON, 7 (1985—88)—"Saving All My Love for You," "How Will I Love You," "The Greatest Love of All," "I Wanna Dance with Somebody (Who Loves Me)," "Didn't We Almost Have It All," "So Emotional," "Where Do Broken Hearts Go"
   2. THE BEATLES, 6 (1964—65)—"I Feel Fine," "Eight Days a Week," Ticket to Ride," "Help!" "Yesterday," "We Can Work It Out"
   3. THE SUPREMES, 6 (1964—65)—"Where Did Our Love Go," "Baby Love," "Come See About Me," "Stop! In the Name of Love,""Back in My Arms Again," "I Hear a Symphony"
   4. THE JACKSON 5, 5 (1969—70)—"I Want You Back," "ABC," "The Love You Save," "I Found That Girl," "I'll Be There"

5. Michael Jackson, 5 (1987—88)—"I Just Can't Stop Loving You," "Bad," "The Way You Make Me Feel," "Man in the Mirror," 'Dirty Diana"

6. Elvis Presley, 5 (1959—61)—"A Big Hunk O' Love," "Stuck on You," "It's Now or Never," "Are You Lonesome Tonight," "Surrender"

7. George Michael, 4 (1987—88)—"Faith," "Father Figure," "One More Try," "Monkey"

8. Elvis Presley, 4 (1957)—"All Shook Up," "Let Me Be Your Teddy Bear," "Jailhouse Rock," "Don't"

9. The Supremes, 4, (1966—67)—"You Can't Hurry Love, "You Keep Me Hangin' On," "Love Is Here and Now You're Gone," "The Happening"

10. The Beatles, 3 (1964)—"I Want to Hold Your Hand," "Can't Buy Me Love," "She Loves You"

11. The Beatles, 3 (1969—70)—"Come Together"/"Something," "Let It Be," "The Long and Winding Road"

12. Phil Collins, 3 (1989—90)—"Groovy Kind of Love," "Two Hearts," "Another Day in Paradise"

Source: Joel Whitburn's Record Research: Top Pop Singles, 1955–1986 *and annual supplements, 1987 through 1992.*

The 50 Greatest Number-One Hits (Through 1992)

1. "The Great Pretender," The Platters, 1955
2. "Don't Be Cruel"/"Hound Dog," Elvis Presley, 1956
3. "Jailhouse Rock," Elvis Presley, 1957
4. "You Send Me," Sam Cooke, 1957
5. "Yakety Yak," The Coasters, 1958
6. "Kansas City," Wilbert Harrison, 1959
7. "Save the Last Dance for Me," The Drifters, 1960
8. "Quarter to Three," Gary "U.S." Bonds, 1961
9. "Duke of Earl," Gene Chandler, 1962
10. "He's So Fine," The Chiffons, 1963
11. "Fingertips, Part 2," Little Stevie Wonder, 1963
12. "She Loves You," The Beatles, 1964
13. "Oh Pretty Woman," Roy Orbison, 1964
14. "You've Lost That Lovin' Feeling," The Righteous Brothers, 1965
15. "My Girl," The Temptations, 1965
16. "Ticket to Ride," The Beatles, 1965
17. "(I Can't Get No) Satisfaction," The Rolling Stones, 1965

18. "When a Man Loves a Woman," Percy Sledge, 1966
19. "Reach Out, I'll Be There," The Four Tops, 1966
20. "You Keep Me Hangin' On," The Supremes, 1966
21. "Respect," Aretha Franklin, 1967
22. "(Sittin' On) The Dock of the Bay," Otis Redding, 1968
23. "People Got to Be Free," The Rascals, 1968
24. "I Heard It Through the Grapevine," Marvin Gaye, 1968
25. "Everyday People," Sly and the Family Stone
26. "I Want You Back," The Jackson 5, 1970
27. "Bridge Over Troubled Water," Simon and Garfunkel, 1970
28. "War," Edwin Starr, 1970
29. "Maggie May," Rod Stewart, 1971
30. "Oh Girl," The Chi-Lites, 1972
31. "Papa Was a Rolling Stone," The Temptations, 1973
32. "Superstition," Stevie Wonder, 1973
33. "Let's Get It On," Marvin Gaye, 1973
34. "Hotel California," The Eagles, 1977
35. "Hot Stuff," Donna Summer, 1979
36. "Good Times," Chic, 1979
37. "I Love Rock'n'Roll," Joan Jett and the Blackhearts, 1982
38. "Billie Jean," Michael Jackson, 1983
39. "Every Breath You Take," The Police, 1983
40. "Jump," Van Halen, 1984
41. "Time After Time," Cyndi Lauper, 1984
42. "When Doves Cry," Prince, 1984
43. "Let's Go Crazy," Prince, 1984
44. "West End Girls," The Pet Shop Boys, 1986
45. "Live to Tell," Madonna, 1986
46. "Sweet Child O'Mine," Guns N' Roses, 1988
47. "Wishing Well," Terence Trent D'Arby, 1988
48. "Nothing Compares 2U," Sinead O'Connor, 1990
49. "Set Adrift on Memory Bliss," PM Dawn, 1991
50. "Baby Got Back," Sir Mix-A-Lot, 1992

Source: Joel Whitburn's Record Research: Top Pop Singles, 1955–1986 *and annual supplements, 1987 through 1992.*

The 40 Worst Number-One Hits (Through 1993)

1. "Tammy," Debbie Reynolds, 1957
2. "Honeycomb," Jimmie Rodgers, 1957
3. "Why," Frankie Avalon, 1960
4. "Hey Paula," Paul and Paula, 1963

5. "Mrs. Brown You've Got a Lovely Daughter," Herman's Hermits, 1965
6. "Eve of Destruction," Barry McGuire, 1965
7. "Cherish," The Association, 1966
8. "The Happening," The Supremes, 1967
9. "Honey," Bobby Goldsboro
10. "Song Sung Blue," Neil Diamond, 1972
11. "I Am Woman," Helen Reddy, 1972
12. "Top of the World," The Carpenters, 1973
13. "The Loco-Motion," Grand Funk Railroad, 1974
14. "The Night Chicago Died," Paper Lace, 1974
15. "My Eyes Adored You," Frankie Valli, 1975
16. "Disco Lady," Johnnie Taylor, 1976
17. "Disco Duck, Part 1," Rick Dees and His Cast of Idiots, 1976
18. "Blinded by the Light," Manfred Mann's Earth Band, 1977
19. "Escape (The Piña Colada Song)," Rupert Holmes, 1979
20. "Do That to Me One More Time," The Captain and Tenille, 1980
21. "Sailing," Christopher Cross
22. "Stars on 45," Stars on 45
23. "Maniac," Michael Sembello, 1983
24. "Can't Fight This Feeling," REO Speedwagon, 1985
25. "Sussudio," Phil Collins, 1985
26. "A View to a Kill," Duran Duran, 1985
27. "Kyrie," Mr. Mister, 1986
28. "Rock Me Amadeus," Falco, 1986
29. "Addicted to Love," Robert Palmer, 1986
30. "Glory of Love," Peter Cetera, 1986
31. "At This Moment," Billy Vera and the Beaters, 1987
32. "Don't Worry Be Happy," Bobby McFerrin, 1988
33. "Baby, I Love Your Way/Free Bird Medley (Free Baby)," Will to Power, 1988
34. "Kokomo," The Beach Boys, 1988
35. "Satisfied," Richard Marx, 1989
36. "Ice Ice Baby," Vanilla Ice, 1990
37. "Baby Baby," Amy Grant, 1991
38. "When a Man Loves a Woman," Michael Bolton, 1991
39. "I'm Too Sexy," Right Said Fred, 1992
40. "I'd Do Anything for Love," Meat Loaf, 1993

Source: Joel Whitburn's Record Research: Top Pop Singles, 1955–1986, *and annual supplements, 1987 through 1992.*

15 Performers Who Never Had a Number-One Single

1. AEROSMITH—They made the Top Ten six times in a twenty-year period, both of which are astonishing for a hard rock band, but never got closer to the top spot than "Angel" in 1987. But then, "Dude (Looks Like a Lady)" didn't even make Top Ten, so go figure.

2. JAMES BROWN—Soul Brother Number One he may be, but the closest the Black Godfather ever came to making number one on the pop chart was with "I Got You (I Feel Good)" *(Awww-wow!)* in 1965, which stalled at number three. Six other times, Brown hit the Top Ten, from "Papa's Got a Brand New Bag" in 1965 (number eight) to "Living in America" in 1985 (number four), but like Moses and the Promised Land, he never quite got there.

3. CREEDENCE CLEARWATER REVIVAL—Creedence had no fewer than *nine* Top Ten singles. Between the spring of 1969 and the end of 1970, five of them spent a total of eight weeks at number two. In this period, while "Proud Mary," "Bad Moon Rising," and "Green River" were shut out of the gloryland, such momentous discs as Henry Mancini's "Love Theme from *Romeo and Juliet*," "In the Year 2525" by Zager and Evans, and, of course, "I Think I Love You" by the immortal Partridge Family, held sway at the top.

4. FATS DOMINO—Although only "Blueberry Hill" and "I'm In Love Again" made the Top Three, Fats scored ten Top Tens. Actually, though, his frustration level is probably lower than Brown's or CCR's, because in the fifties, rock and R&B had trouble gaining a chart foothold at any level.

5. BOB DYLAN—Dylan hit the Top Ten only four times, with his greatest success coming in 1965 and 1966, when both "Like a Rolling Stone" and "Rainy Day Woman #12 & 35" ("Everybody must get stoned . . .") hit number two.

6. THE GRATEFUL DEAD—In fact, these old album rockers ("hippies" hardly says it anymore) have only scored one Top Ten, with 1987's "Touch of Grey," and have reached the Hot 100 just six times in a recording career that started in 1967. Some people may even consider this an injustice.

7. THE HOLLIES—The Anglo-harmonizers hit the Top Ten six times in the sixties and seventies without ever passing number two—and the only disc that got that far was their virtual swan song, "Long Cool Woman (In a Black Dress)," in 1972.

8. MARTHA AND THE VANDELLAS—The only major Motown act never to top *Billboard*'s weekly listings, although, of their six Top Tens, "Dancing in the Street" did spend two weeks at number two back in 1964.

9.   STEVIE NICKS—She clocked four Top Tens, including a number-three collaboration with Tom Petty and the Heartbreakers on her solo debut, "Stop Draggin' My Heart Around," but never came closer to the top spot than that. Even Fleetwood Mac only scored one number one, despite nine Top Ten entries.

10.   TOM PETTY—With and without the Heartbreakers, Petty scored four Top Ten singles, most recently with the number-seven "Freefallin'," without ever getting to wear the crown. His closest brush with ultimate glory came with Stevie Nicks on "Stop Draggin' My Heart Around," which clawed its way to number three.

11.   BRUCE SPRINGSTEEN—He's hit the Top Ten eleven times, including six times with singles from *Born in the U.S.A.* alone, but only "Dancing in the Dark" made it as far as number two, and that one had the bad luck to be released the same week as "When Doves Cry." The Creedence of his era.

12.   STING—The Police did make number one with Sting's "Every Breath You Take" (although the fact that they only topped the chart *once* is already weird). Sting had hit the Top Ten four times as a solo artist through 1992 without coming any closer than he did with his first solo hit, "If You Love Somebody Set Them Free," which peaked at number three.

13.   THE STYLISTICS—Russell Thompkins, Jr., may have been the last of the great falsetto soul singers, but even though he led the Stylistics to the Top Ten five times, only "You Make Me Feel Brand New," in 1974, made it as far as number two.

14.   WAR—The lowrider heroes who helped pioneer funk spent two weeks at number two with "The Cisco Kid" in 1973, but the group never got that far afterward, despite six other Top Ten discs.

15.   THE WHO—Pete Townshend's prowess as a rock songwriter is widely and justifiably celebrated, but the Who still scored just one American Top Ten single: "I Can See for Miles," which reached number nine in 1967. Just another reason to bash your guitar? They never even made number eleven, although "See Me, Feel Me" clocked in at twelve.

Retread Rock
5 Songs that Have Been Number-One Hits More than Once

1. "The Twist"—Chubby Checker reached the top spot not only with the same song, but with the same *record*, in 1960 and 1961, the only time that particular feat has been pulled off.

2. "Go Away Little Girl"—Number one with an anchor for Steve Lawrence in 1963 and for Donny Osmond in 1971. Carole King and

Gerry Goffin wrote this awful fluff and may *perhaps* be forgiven only because they also penned both "The Loco-Motion" and "Will You Still Love Me Tomorrow."

3. "The Loco-Motion"—Goffin-King's song made number one for Little Eva in 1962 and, all-but-unrecognizably metallized, for Grand Funk Railroad in 1974

4. "Please Mr. Postman"—Motown's marvelous Marvelettes took this ditty to the top in 1961. The Carpenters recreated it as California corn and reached number one in 1974.

5. "When a Man Loves a Woman"—Percy Sledge's 1966 original provided the tragedy, Michael Bolton's 1991 retread dispensed the farce.

Most Number-One Albums (1955–1992)

1. The Beatles	15	9. Herb Alpert and the	
2. Elvis Presley	9	Tijuana Brass	5
3. The Rolling Stones	9	10. Chicago	5
4. Elton John	7	11. Frank Sinatra	4
5. Paul McCartney/Wings[1]	7	12. The Monkees	4
6. Barbra Streisand	6	13. Bruce Springsteen	4
7. Led Zeppelin	6	14. The Eagles	4
8. The Kingston Trio	5		

Source: Joel Whitburn's Record Research: Top Pop Albums, 1955–1992.

[1] Since McCartney was also in the Beatles, he has appeared on twenty-two number-one albums altogether, far more than anyone else.

The 50 Best Number-One Albums (1955–1993)

1. *Elvis Presley*, Elvis Presley, 1956
2. *Elvis*, Elvis Presley, 1956
3. *Modern Sounds in Country and Western Music*, Ray Charles, 1962
4. *Meet the Beatles*, The Beatles, 1964
5. *The Beatles Second Album*, The Beatles, 1964
6. *Out of Our Heads*, The Rolling Stones, 1965
7. *Rubber Soul*, The Beatles, 1966

8. *Revolver*, The Beatles, 1966
9. *Sgt. Pepper's Lonely Hearts Club Band*, The Beatles, 1967
10. *Electric Ladyland*, The Jimi Hendrix Experience, 1968
11. *The Beatles*, The Beatles, 1968
12. *Green River*, Creedence Clearwater Revival, 1969
13. *Abbey Road*, The Beatles, 1969
14. *Led Zeppelin II*, Led Zeppelin, 1969
15. *Cosmo's Factory*, Creedence Clearwater Revival, 1970
16. *Sticky Fingers*, The Rolling Stones, 1971
17. *Every Picture Tells a Story*, Rod Stewart, 1971
18. *Imagine*, John Lennon, 1971
19. *There's a Riot Goin' On*, Sly and the Family Stone, 1971
20. *Exile on Main Street*, The Rolling Stones, 1972
21. *Harvest*, Neil Young, 1972
22. *Superfly*, Curtis Mayfield, 1972
23. *The World Is a Ghetto*, War, 1973
24. *461 Ocean Boulevard*, Eric Clapton, 1974
25. *Fire*, The Ohio Players, 1975
26. *Blood on the Tracks*, Bob Dylan, 1975
27. *Still Crazy After All These Years*, Paul Simon, 1975
28. *Gratitude*, Earth, Wind and Fire, 1976
29. *Songs in the Key of Life*, Stevie Wonder, 1976
30. *Saturday Night Fever*, Various Artists, 1978
31. *The River*, Bruce Springsteen, 1980
32. *Thriller*, Michael Jackson, 1983
33. *Born in the U.S.A.*, Bruce Springsteen, 1984
34. *Purple Rain*, Prince, 1984
35. *Control*, Janet Jackson, 1986
36. *True Blue*, Madonna, 1986
37. *Licensed to Ill*, The Beastie Boys, 1987
38. *The Joshua Tree*, U2, 1987
39. *Tunnel of Love*, Bruce Springsteen, 1987
40. *Hysteria*, Def Leppard, 1988
41. *Appetite for Destruction*, Guns N' Roses, 1988
42. *Tracy Chapman*, 1988
43. *Janet Jackson's Rhythm Nation 1814*, Janet Jackson, 1989
44. *Out of Time*, R.E.M., 1991
45. *EFIL4ZAGGIN*, N.W.A, 1991
46. *Metallica*, Metallica, 1991
47. *Use Your Illusion II*, Guns N' Roses, 1991
48. *Nevermind*, Nirvana, 1992
49. *The Predator*, Ice Cube, 1992
50. *The Chronic*, Dr. Dre, 1993

The 40 Worst Number-One Albums (1955—93)

1. *Ballad of the Green Berets*, S/Sgt. Barry Sadler, 1966
2. *Waiting for the Sun*, The Doors, 1968
3. *Blood Sweat and Tears*, Blood, Sweat and Tears, 1969
4. *Hair*, Original Cast, 1969
5. *Led Zeppelin III*, Led Zeppelin, 1970
6. *Blood Sweat and Tears III*, Blood Sweat and Tears, 1970
7. *Jesus Christ Superstar*, Various Artists, 1971
8. *America*, America, 1972
9. *American Pie*, Don McLean, 1972
10. *Thick as a Brick*, Jethro Tull, 1972
11. *Chicago V*, Chicago, 1972
12. *Seventh Sojourn*, The Moody Blues, 1972
13. *Living in the Material World*, George Harrison, 1973
14. *Chicago VI*, Chicago, 1973
15. *A Passion Play*, Jethro Tull, 1973
16. *Chicago VII*, Chicago 1974
17. *Have You Never Been Mellow*, Olivia Newton-John, 1975
18. *Chicago VIII*, Chicago, 1975
19. *Windsong*, John Denver, 1975
20. *Barry Manilow/Live*, Barry Manilow, 1971
21. *Grease*, soundtrack, 1978
22. *Living in the U.S.A.*, Linda Ronstadt, 1978
23. *Briefcase Full of Blues*, The Blues Brothers, 1979
24. *Breakfast in America*, Supertramp, 1979
25. *Get the Knack*, The Knack, 1970
26. *Hi Infidelity*, REO Speedwagon, 1980
27. *Escape*, Journey, 1981
28. *Long Distance Voyager*, The Moody Blues, 1981
29. *Asia*, Asia, 1982
30. *Welcome to the Real World*, Mr. Mister, 1980
31. *Slippery When Wet*, Bon Jovi, 1986
32. *Tiffany*, Tiffany, 1988
33. *Electric Youth*, Debbie Gibson, 1989
34. *Repeat Offender*, Richard Marx, 1989
35. *Girl You Know It's True*, Milli Vanilli, 1989
36. *To the Extreme*, Vanilla Ice, 1990
37. *True Love and Tenderness*, Michael Bolton, 1991
38. *Slave to the Grind*, Skid Row, 1991
39. *Timeless (The Classics)*, Michael Bolton, 1992
40. *Some Gave All*, Billy Ray Cyrus, 1992

Solo Albums, Indeed
Artists Who Charted Eight or More Albums Without Ever Reaching the Hot 100 Singles Chart

1. Paul Butterfield
2. Ry Cooder
3. Rory Gallagher
4. Hot Tuna
5. Iron Maiden
6. Little Feat
7. Nils Lofgren
8. Mahogany Rush
9. John Prine
10. UFO
11. Tom Waits
12. Wishbone Ash

Source: Joel Whitburn's Top Pop Albums 1955–1992, *based on* Billboard *Album Charts.*

It's the Same Old Song
27 Hit Songs Intended for Others

1. "At the Hop"—A number-one hit for Danny and the Juniors, the first to record it was John Madara, a real Philly teen idol. Madara's version never got released.

2. "Birds and the Bees"—The Jewel Akens hit had been meant for the Four Tunes.

3. "Bye Bye Baby"—This Mary Wells hit was written for Jackie Wilson.

4. "California Dreamin' "—The Mamas and Papas made their breakthrough with a song first recorded by Barry McGuire; in fact, they used the exact same backing track as McGuire, just erasing his vocals and adding their own.

5. "The Diary"—Neil Sedaka wrote the song for Little Anthony and the Imperials but they recorded it too late—his had already hit.

6. "Don't Forbid Me"—Pat Boone made do with an Elvis Presley leftover in material as well as style.

7. "A Fool in Love"—Ike Turner planned to record this song with Art Lassiter, but he failed to show for the session. It became Ike and Tina's first big hit.

8. "Hello Mary Lou"—Gene Pitney originally meant Ricky Nelson's big hit to be recorded by East Coast lightweight Ray Peterson.

9. "Knock on Wood"—Floyd wrote this for his old Falcons mate, Wilson Pickett, but wound up cutting it himself.

10. "The Loco-Motion"—Gerry Coffin and Carole King never intended to use Little Eva, their babysitter, as anything but a demo singer for Dee Dee Sharp. But Eva's demo came out so well, they issued it and it went to number one.

11. "Lonely Blue Boy"—As "Danny," this Conway Twitty hit had been written for Elvis Presley (who was probably meant to use it as the theme song for *King Creole*, which is based on Harold Robbins's novel *A Stone for Danny Fisher*).

12. "Mr. Blue"—The Fleetwoods hit with a song meant for the Platters.

13. "One Fine Day"—The Chiffons hit with a tune meant for Little Eva, whose hit had been meant for Dee Dee Sharp.

14. "Only in America"—A mild hit for Jay and the Americans after the Drifters' original lead vocals had been erased from Leiber/Stoller's track. The song had been deemed too controversial for a black group.

15. "Only the Lonely"—Roy Orbison wrote his biggest hit with the Everly Brothers in mind.

16. "Palisades Park"—Freddy Cannon's smash was intended to be cut by Dion.

17. "Precious and Few"—This oddball one-shot by Alive and Kicking had been meant by Tommy James for himself. Instead he found a lead singer like Janis Joplin on her best day ever, and cut a smash with her.

18. "Sea Cruise"—First recorded by Huey "Piano" Smith and the Clowns. Frankie Ford, who sometimes appeared with Smith, used their track with his own vocal.

19. "Stormy Weather"—The immortal Ethel Walters side had been meant for Cab Calloway.

20. "Superstition"—Stevie Wonder wrote this song for Jeff Beck, when Beck conducted an abortive session at Motown in 1970. Beck later recorded it with Beck, Bogert, and Appice.

21. "A Teenager in Love"—Doc Pomus and Mort Shuman wrote this song for the Mystics but when Dion, a much bigger star, wanted it, they gave it to him. The Mystics got the marvelous "Hushabye" as a consolation prize.

22. "Tennessee"—First offered to the Ducanes, who were a doo-wop group (not a country group, despite Mark Ribowsky's claim in his Phil Spector biography). The Ducanes recorded the now-forgotten original of the Beatles' "Devil in Her Heart."

23. "This Old Heart of Mine"—Holland-Dozier-Holland intended the Isley Brothers' biggest Motown hit for the Supremes. Which is probably one reason why it *was* such a big hit—you could make a fortune from the Supremes' (or HDH's) leftovers in those days.

24. "Tramp"—A hit for both Lowell Fulson and the Otis Redding and Carla Thomas duo, but originally intended for its cowriter, Jimmy McCracklin.

25. "Travelin' Man"—Ricky Nelson got this one when Sam Cooke passed.

26. "Venus"—Frankie Avalon's postnasal immortality came with a song written for Al Martino.

27. "Where Did Our Love Go"—The Marvelettes passed on this Holland-Dozier-Holland masterpiece. All the tune did for the Supremes was kick off the longest string of number ones and Top Tens in chart history.

"Let's Give It to 'Em, Right Now!"
The Best of "Louie Louie"

1. The Kingsmen (1963 hit single)
2. Paul Revere and the Raiders (1963 runner-up single)
3. The Wailers (1960 Seattle hit)
4. Iggy Pop (1993 album track)
5. The Stooges (from *Metallic KO*; the one version with truly dirty lyrics)
6. The Fat Boys (1988 near-hit single; best video version)
7. Richard Berry and the Pharoahs (original version)
8. Otis Redding (from *Pain in My Heart*, his 1964 debut album)
9. Toots and the Maytals (1975 album track)
10. Wilbert Harrison (1969 album track)

Note: Rhino Records has two volumes of The Best of "Louie Louie," *though these records, while containing many fine versions, including the Rice University marching band renditions, contain very few of what's truly best about rock's most famous, or at least ridiculous song.*

Chuck D Picks 11 Hip-Hop Albums that No One Can Do Without

1. *Raising Hell*, Run-D.M.C. (1986)
2. *Death Certificate*, Ice Cube (1991)
3. *The Message*, Grandmaster Flash & the Furious Five (1982)
4. *Mama Said Knock You Out*, L.L. Cool J (1990)
5. *Criminal Minded*, Boogie Down Productions (1987)
6. *Paid in Full*, Eric B & Rakim (1987)
7. *Naughty by Nature*, Naughty by Nature (1991)
8. *Straight Outta Compton*, N.W.A (1989)
9. *Back in Black*, Whodini (1986)
10. *Looks like a Job for . . .* , Big Daddy Kane (1993)
11. *Power*, Ice-T (1988)

One-Shots
Top Ten Records by Artists Who Never Again Made the Charts

In the beginning, rock and roll was the music of one-shots, inspired 45s by people who almost deterministically were never heard from again (except, as it turns out, by the extremely devoted fanatics known as doo-wop and rockabilly collectors). Perhaps it was better that way. By the seventies, even the former porno starlet Andrea True could sustain a small "career," with three charted followups to her fluke Top Ten hit, while the typical one-shot was a novelty, such as "Rubber Duckie," by Ernie, the Sesame Street Muppet, or Elmo and Patsy's quintessential Christmas satire, "Grandma Got Run Over by a Reindeer." Still, one could fill a good-sized jukebox with one-shot rock and R&B hits made in the seventies and eighties. (It's still too early in the nineties to be certain that Martika will never be heard from again.) The following is an honor roll of heroic examples.

1. **"ALLEY-OOP," THE HOLLYWOOD ARGYLES, 1960 (#1)**—Like so many one-shots, the Hollywood Argyles contained within themselves the seeds of something quite long-lived—in this case, Kim Fowley, a writer/producer/hustler who went on to perpetrate the Runaways and many less successful scams. In a way, Fowley's entire career can be construed as a thirty-year attempt to follow up this takeoff on the comic strip caveman, although besides the Runaways, the closest he ever came was "Bumble Boogie" by B. Bumble and the Stingers—but alas, even that had its dreary successors.

2. **"AXL F," HAROLD FALTERMEYER, 1985 (#3)**—A high point of German industrial pop. We suppose.

3. **"BLACK DENIM TROUSERS," THE CHEERS, 1955 (#6)**—Give or take "Rocket 88," the original hot rod song—and the Cheers, vocally and productionwise, had a lot more in common with the Beach Boys than Jackie Brenston's Ike Turner–led R&B did. In fact, this is a Leiber and Stoller production and a good one, if a little on the theatrical side.

4. **"THE BOOK OF LOVE," THE MONOTONES, 1958 (#5)**—One supposes they never found out who wrote it—pity, because if they had, perhaps they'd have found it in them to repeat their success. (In truth, those who track down the Murray Hill Records album *Who Wrote the Book of Love* will be amply rewarded by fourteen tracks that represent a five-year career trying to climb back to where their debut disc put them, including the bittersweet "What Would You Do If There Wasn't Any Rock'N'Roll?")

5. **"DON'T DISTURB THIS GROOVE," THE SYSTEM, 1987 (#4)**—Atmospherically, almost a techno precursor. Condemned to one-shothood by being too far ahead of its time, then?

6. "EARTH ANGEL (WILL YOU BE MINE)," THE PENGUINS, 1955 (#8)—As with the Chords' "Sh-Boom," the surprise here isn't that such a fine doo-wop ballad found an audience but that the pop audience found it: a release by a black group (initially) on an out-of-the-way, R&B-specialist record label, and one based in Los Angeles, which inevitably meant that its distribution east of the Rockies stank. All this before Bill Haley, Elvis, et al. loosened the floodgates for rhythm records.

7. "FIRE," THE CRAZY WORLD OF ARTHUR BROWN, 1968 (#2)—This eccentric Englishman, one of the more byzantine products of psychedelia, actually set himself aflame during his stage shows. Brown later lapsed into art-rock of the most excruciating sort. "Fire" matters mostly as the most successful stateside single the Who's Peter Townshend ever appeared on. (The Who's "I Can See for Miles," their only Top Ten, made it only to number nine, while Townshend's other great one-shot production job, "Something in the Air" by Thunderclap Newman, peaked at number thirty-seven.)

8. "GET A JOB," THE SILHOUETTES, 1958 (#1)—The original "shadada-da" disc, a nonsense lyric with a protest message similar to the Coasters' "Yakety Yak."

9. "HAPPY, HAPPY BIRTHDAY BABY," THE TUNE WEAVERS, 1957 (#5)—Until Lesley Gore's, easily the most miserable birthday in rock and roll (or maybe even human) history. But where Lesley plays the spoiled brat, the Tune Weavers' Margo Sylvia acts out the tragedy through a letter that's both succinct and desperate.

10. "HOLD YOUR HEAD UP," ARGENT, 1972 (#5)—Although Rod Argent's group, which featured former Zombie Russ Ballard on lead vocals, went on to LP chart success, the band never again hit the Hot 100, predictably enough, since "Hold Your Head Up" doesn't exactly represent heavy metal at its most scintillating, and for all his talent, Ballard never again got much of a song to wrap his tonsils around.

11. "IN THE SUMMERTIME," MUNGO JERRY, 1970 (#3)—A horrible revival of the British skiffle (jugband) craze. One might have known then that the seventies wasn't going to be any match for the decade that preceded it.

12. "ISRAELITES," DESMOND DEKKER AND THE ACES, 1969 (#9)—The first reggae hit in the United States, and for many years, the only one by a Jamaican (well, Anglo-Jamaican) artist. What few North American ears could decipher any of the lyrics at all came to a too-hasty conclusion that it might harbor anti-Semitic sentiments. In fact, "the Israelites" seems to refer to Rastafarians, members of Jamaica's back-to-Africa/back-to-nature religious group.

13. "JUNGLE FEVER," CHAKACHAS, 1972 (#8)—

Protodisco novelty with a "Stranded in the Jungle" soul—wacky, like little one-shots were once meant to be.

14. "JUST ONE LOOK," DORIS TROY, 1963 (#10) —In this context, the title seems to say it all. Troy later recorded for the Beatles at Apple, and as a gospel singer.

15. "LITTLE STAR," THE ELEGANTS, 1958 (#2)— One of the most haunting vocal group singles ever made, maybe the most haunting by any white group. But only collectors know the followups, one of which even made *Billboard*'s rhythm and blues chart. A dozen Elegants sides are collected on the Murray Hill records compilation *Little Star—The Elegants*, and can still sometimes be tracked down.

16. "LOVE YOU SO," RON HOLDEN AND THE THUNDERBIRDS, 1960 (#7)—Written in a Tacoma jail (where Holden had been sent for contributing to the delinquency of the minors in his band, by sharing a bottle with them) as a love letter to his girlfriend. So *profoundly* crude that finding out that Holden is the man who brought "Louie Louie" to the Pacific Northwest (and eventually, to the Kingsmen) comes as little surprise. It would take a scientific expedition to reproduce the engaging primitivism of this sound, so it's no surprise that Holden, for all his instinctive genius, never scored another chart side.

17. "MULE SKINNER BLUES," THE FENDERMEN, 1960 (#5)—Pure silliness, a whoop and a crash, and maniacal laughter that stops just short of becoming a yodel. We probably couldn't have taken any more like this.

18. "99 LUFTBALLOONS," NENA, 1983 (#2)—Early MTV-driven Europop hit, distinguished by an English translation ("99 Red Balloons") and an antinuke theme, coinciding with European protests over U.S. missiles on their turf. Having done her bit for peace, Nena lapsed into welcome silence. (We don't say willingly.)

19. "ONE SUMMER NIGHT," THE DANLEERS, 1958 (#7)—Yet one more grand doo-wop ballad.

20. "PARTY LIGHTS," CLAUDINE CLARK, 1962 (#5) —Claudine's utter anguish that her mother won't let her cross the street to go to that party makes you suspect suicide as the reason this classic was never pursued. So drop-dead cool and beautiful that it justifies one-shot respectability all by itself.

21. "PIPELINE," THE CHANTAYS, 1963 (#4)—The great surf instrumental comes closer to capturing the awesome power of the ocean than any of its brethren, even Dick Dale's mighty "Misirlou." That bass line sucks you in like undertow, and then the guitar tosses you up like sitting on top of a wave—or the world.

22. "POP MUZIK," M, 1979 (#1)—U.K. popster Robin Scott practically perfected Europop as trash, creating an antirock, postdisco anthem whose attitude was so complete there was just nowhere further to go with it.

23. "POPSICLES, ICICLES," THE MURMAIDS, 1963 (#3)—Shimmering girl-group silliness.

24. "PSYCHOTIC REACTION," COUNT FIVE, 1966 (#5)—From the heyday of Yardbirds ripoffs and garage band groove, this is the heavyweight champion, the original punk-rock classic. Good-bad, but far from boring. Played a crucial role in the history of rock criticism thanks to Lester Bang's extended essay and curiously prophetic fictionalized history.

25. "THE RAIN," ORAN "JUICE" JONES, 1986 (#9) —Hip-hop's first great ballad—as lowering and threatening as a storm. Def Jam probably failed to get Jones a followup because his music, while ultimately a clear product of hip-hop sensibility and production technique, was just too far from what the company usually proferred.

26. "ROCKIN' CHAIR," GWEN McRAE, 1975 (#9)— McRae—whose husband, George, turned in a great one in 1974 with "Rock Your Baby" and had some followups—scored three other R&B chart hits, but this Miami-bred predisco dance number remains her sole excursion on the Hot 100.

27. "RUMORS," TIMEX SOCIAL CLUB, 1986 (#8)— Lyric-driven novelty may also have been the Bay Area's first successful hip-hop venture but even in that case, it was so far ahead of its time that the failure to follow up seems predictable in retrospect.

28. "SALLY, GO 'ROUND THE ROSES," THE JAYNETTS, 1963 (#2)—The most ominous of all girl-group records. Theories about its meaning abound, but the true story remains forever shrouded in the murk of history and failed careers.

29. "SEA OF LOVE," PHIL PHILLIPS, 1959 (#2)—A tragicomic love lyric set against one of the most absurd crooning choruses in rock and roll history, plus former bellhop Phillip's bizarrely bel canto vocal. A followup would have been inconceivable.

30. "SH-BOOM," THE CHORDS, 1954 (#5)—Crossed over even earlier than "Earth Angel," so the miracle isn't that it was a one-shot but that the pop audience found a way to get hold of this doo-wop release at all. It's not a weeper, but a rocker, which makes the feat all the more impressive.

31. "SHOUT! SHOUT! (KNOCK YOURSELF OUT)," **ERNIE MARESCA, 1962 (#6)**—Dion's bandleader buddy concocts a track that rocks so hard that repeating it might have gotten him indicted under the "cruel and unusual punishment" clause of the Constitution.

32. "SMOKE FROM A DISTANT FIRE," SANFORD-TOWNSHEND BAND, 1977 (#9)—Nice piece of soft southern rock, probably most notable as producer Jerry Wexler's last grasp on a top rung of the charts.

33. "SUNSHINE," JONATHAN EDWARDS, 1972 (#4)
—The absolute nadir of singer-songwriter pastoralism. Still, you'd think that anyone who could have come up with such a nauseatingly perfected treacle once could have repeated the feat. No way—which lends credence to the idea that God is just, or at least merciful.

34. "TAINTED LOVE," SOFT CELL, 1982 (#8)—Nice reworking of the Gloria Jones R&B nonhit as trashy Europop. Lead vocalist Marc Almond *did* score another hit—just one—and the group got lots of club play on their equally moody followups. But none hit the pop lists.

35. "TIRED OF TOEIN' THE LINE," ROCKY BURNETTE, 1982 (#9)—Johnny Burnette's son made a nice neorockabilly move with his debut but never managed to turn it into a career.

36. "TUBULAR BELLS," MIKE OLDFIELD, 1974 (#7)
—A pure fluke. The pop success of this electro-art-rock has more to do with its appearance in the film *The Exorcist* than anything else. Oldfield had about as much interest in making hit singles as he did in spitting pea soup all over the screen, so this may be one of the few one-shots whose lack of a followup could be construed as deliberate. More or less.

37. "YOU'VE GOT TO HIDE YOUR LOVE AWAY," THE SILKIE, 1965 (#10)—Perhaps the greatest British folk-rock record, give or take John Lennon's other genre effort, "Norwegian Wood." The Silkie, poor folks, had no more Lennon exclusives, and therefore no further hits.

Postpunk's Greatest One-Shot Hits that Never Really Were Hits or One-Shots

1. "Slack Motherfucker," Superchunk
2. "Unsatisfied," The Replacements
3. "Sex Bomb," Flipper
4. "Expressway to Yr. Skull," Sonic Youth
5. "Never Really Been," Soul Asylum

The 40 Most Boring "Classic" Albums

1. *Abacab*, Genesis
2. *Another Ticket*, Eric Clapton

3. *Around the World in a Day*, Prince
4. *Blondes Have More Fun*, Rod Stewart
5. *Breakfast in America*, Supertramp
6. *Crosby, Stills and Nash*
7. *Days of Future Passed*, The Moody Blues
8. *Diamond Dogs*, David Bowie
9. *Diver Down*, Van Halen
10. *Down with the King*, Run-D.M.C.
11. *Edutainment*, Boogie Down Productions
12. *Escape*, Journey
13. *Faces*, Earth, Wind and Fire
14. *The Hissing of Summer Lawns*, Joni Mitchell
15. *Hotter than Hell*, Kiss
16. *In the Court of the Crimson King: An Observation by King Crimson*
17. *It's Hard*, The Who
18. *The Juliet Letters*, Elvis Costello
19. *Kilroy Was Here*, Styx
20. *Let It Be*, The Beatles
21. *The Long Run*, The Eagles
22. *. . . Nothing Like the Sun*, Sting
23. *People's Instinctive Travels and the Paths of Rhythm*, A Tribe Called Quest
24. *Physical Graffiti*, Led Zeppelin
25. *Pictures at an Exhibition*, Emerson, Lake and Palmer
26. *Planet Waves*, Bob Dylan
27. *Point of Know Return*, Kansas
28. *Red Rose Speedway*, Paul McCartney
29. *Ritual to Habitual*, Jane's Addiction
30. *Sister*, Sonic Youth
31. *Storm Front*, Billy Joel
32. *Terence Trent D'Arby's Neither Fish nor Flesh*
33. *Their Satanic Majesties Request*, The Rolling Stones
34. *Thick as a Brick*, Jethro Tull
35. *trans*, Neil Young
36. *True Stories*, Talking Heads
37. *The Wall*, Pink Floyd
38. *Wheels of Fire*, Cream
39. *The Woman in Red*, Stevie Wonder
40. *Yessongs*, Yes

Note: The Grateful Dead do not appear on this list because they have, instead, been awarded a special citation by the authors for their entire ouevre, all of which is pretty near terminally boring.

CHAPTER 26

The Name Game

What's Your Name?

1. **JESSE BELVIN**—Belvin recorded "So Fine" in 1955 as the Sheiks, doing all the voices himself. He was also responsible for all the voices on the Cliques' 1956 hit, "Girl of My Dreams."

2. **CHER**—Cher recorded "I Love You Ringo," a Beatlemania disc, as Bonnie Jo Mason, for Phil Spector.

3. **AHMET ERTEGUN**—As one of the most important rhythm and blues writers of all time, he used the pseudonym A. Nugetre, a palindrome of his real name. (It's on "Mess Around" by Ray Charles, "Ting-a-Ling" by the Clovers, and "Whatcha Gonna Do" by the Drifters, among others.)

4. **BILL GRAHAM**—A World War II refugee named Wolfgang Wolodia Grajonka, the future promoter picked his new moniker out of the Bronx telephone book.

5. **JAMES BROWN AND HIS FAMOUS FLAMES**—King Records owner Syd Nathan didn't want "Mashed Potatoes" on his label, so they went to Atlantic and cut their hit as Nat Kendricks and the Swans.

6. **JERRY LEIBER AND MIKE STOLLER**—These great songwriters used Elmo Glick as a pseudonym. Similarly, Bert Berns often wrote as Bert Russell.

7. **JEREMY SPENCER**—Then guitarist with Fleetwood Mac, Spencer recorded the rockabilly-based "Somebody's Gonna Get Their Head Kicked in Tonight" as Earl Vance and the Valiants.

8. **THE BEACH BOYS**—They recorded "Barbee" as Kenny and the Cadets.

9. **THE VIBRATIONS**—The Vibrations, of "The Watusi" fame, had a hit with "Peanut Butter" (later covered by J. Geils) as the Marathons.

10. **RITCHIE VALENS**—He recorded "Fast Freight" in 1959 as Arvee Allens.

11. **CHUCK D**—As a member of the Bomb Squad, the infamous production team, the Public Enemy rapper is listed as "Carl Ryder" in album credits for PE's own work as well as Terminator X's solo outings.

12. **MARTHA WASH**—Her voice is all over the debut albums by both Black Box and the C & C Music Factory, but her name must be written in the credits in invisible ink.

13. **PRINCE**—The early Time albums were produced by one Jamie Starr, and the key female vocalist on Sign O' the Times is someone named Camille. Guess who?

14. **PAUL WESTERBERG**—Westerberg teamed up with Todd Newman, a veteran of the Lawrence, Kansas, music scene, to form the Leatherwoods in Minneapolis. The resulting album, *Topeka Oratorio* (Medium Cool/Twin Tone), had Westerberg's name

listed in the credits as Pablo Louseorama. Supposedly, Newman and Westerberg had a falling-out, and Westerberg refused to let his name be used in connection with the project, so Newman took a swipe back with the unflattering nom de plume.

15. THE TRAVELING WILBURYS—Old geezers Roy Orbison, Bob Dylan, Tom Petty, Jeff Lynne, and George Harrison hit the road (and the studio) camouflaged as a family of wandering musicians, all with the same last name . . . are you bored yet?

Famous Pseudonyms of the 1950s

1. Johnny Ace (John Marshall Alexander, Jr.)
2. The Big Bopper (Jiles Perry Richardson)
3. Freddy Cannon (Fredrick Anthony Picariello)
4. Dave "Baby" Cortez (David Clowney)
5. King Curtis (Curtis Ousley)
6. Bobby Darin (Walden Robert Cassotto)
7. Bo Diddley (Elias McDaniel)
8. Adam Faith (Terrence Nelhams)
9. Connie Francis (Constance Franconero)
10. Guitar Slim (Eddie Jones)
11. Slim Harpo (James Moore)
12. Peppermint Harris (Harrison Nelson)
13. Little Willie John (William J. Woods)
14. Ernie K-Doe (Ernest Kador)
15. Ben E. King (Benjamin Nelson)
16. Smiley Lewis (Overton Amos Lemmons)
17. Professor Longhair (Roy Byrd)
18. Nervous Norvus (Jimmy Drake)
19. Johnny Otis (John Veliotes)
20. Les Paul (Lester Polfus II)
21. Jack Scott (Jack Scafone, Jr.)
22. Dee Dee Sharp (Dione La Rue)
23. Conway Twitty (Harold Lloyd Jenkins)
24. Ritchie Valens (Richard Valenzuela)
25. Gene Vincent (Vincent Eugene Craddock)
26. Little Walter (Marion Walter Jacobs)
27. Muddy Waters (McKinley Morganfield)
28. Howlin' Wolf (Chester Burnett)

Famous Pseudonyms of the 1960s

1. Marty Balin (Martin Buchwald)
2. Captain Beefheart (Don Van Vliet)
3. Gene Chandler (Eugene Dixon)
4. Chubby Checker (Ernest Evans)
5. Cher (Cherilyn Sarkisian La Pierre)
6. Derek (Johnny Cymbal)
7. Bob Dylan (Robert Allan Zimmerman)
8. Cass Elliott (Ellen Naomi Cohan)
9. Georgie Fame (Clive Powell)
10. Wayne Fontana (Glyn Geoffrey Ellis)
11. Dobie Gray (Leonard Victor Ainsworth III)
12. Tommy James (Thomas Gregory Jackson)
13. Little Eva (Eva Narcissus Boyd)
14. Lulu (Marie McDonald McLaughlin Laurie)
15. Taj Mahal (Henry Saint-Claire Fredricks Williams)
16. Manfred Mann (Mike Liebowitz)
17. Ed Marimba (Artie Tripp III)
18. Van Morrison (George Ivan)
19. Mickie Most (Michael Peter Hayes)
20. P. J. Proby (James Marcus Smith)
21. ? of the Mysterians (Rudy Martinez)
22. Genya Ravan (Goldie Zelkowitz)
23. Johnny Rivers (John Ramistella)[1]
24. Bobby Rydell (Robert Lewis Ridarelli)
25. Mitch Ryder (Billy Levise)
26. Sam the Sham (Sam Samudio)
27. Del Shannon (Charles Westover)
28. Dusty Springfield (Mary Isobel Catherine O'Brien)
29. Ringo Starr (Richard Starkey)
30. Cat Stevens (Steven Demetri Georgiou)[2]
31. Dino Valenti (Chester Powers)
32. Frankie Valli (Francis Castelluccio)
33. Jr. Walker (Autry DeWalt, Jr.)
34. Wolfman Jack (Bob Smith)
35. Stevie Wonder (Steveland Judkins Morris)
36. Tammy Wynette (Wynette Pugh)
37. Jesse Colin Young (Perry Miller)

---

[1] Changed at the suggestion of Alan Freed.
[2] At present, his legal name is Yusef Islam.

Famous Pseudonyms of the 1970s

1. Marc Bolan (Marc Feld)
2. David Bowie (David Robert Hayward-Jones)
3. Jimmy Cliff (James Chambers)
4. Commander Cody (George Frayne)
5. Jessi Colter (Miriam Johnson Jennings)
6. Alice Cooper (Vincent Furnier)
7. Elvis Costello (Declan Patrick MacManus)
8. Kiki Dee (Pauline Mathews)
9. John Denver (John Deutschendorf)
10. Rick Derringer (Rick Zehringer)
11. Buck Dharma (Donald Roeser)
12. Dr. John the Night Tripper (Malcolm John Creaux Rebennack, Jr.)
13. Freddy Fender (Baldermar G. Huerta)
14. Gary Glitter (Paul Gadd)
15. Elton John (Reginald Dwight)
16. Chaka Khan (Yvette Marie Holland)
17. Denny Laine (Brian Arthur Haynes)
18. Magic Dick (Richard Salwitz)
19. Meat Loaf (Marvin Lee Aday)
20. Freddie Mercury (Frederick Bulsara)
21. Iggy Pop (James Jewell Osterburg)
22. Lou Reed (Louis "Butch" Firbank)
23. Johnny Rotten (John Lydon)
24. Leon Russell (Russell Bridges)
25. Southside Johnny (John Lyon)
26. Joe Strummer (John Mellor)
27. Steve Tyler (Steven Tallarico)
28. Sid Vicious (John Simon Ritchie)
29. Jerry Jeff Walker (Ronald Crosby)
30. Peter Wolf (Peter Blankenfield)

Famous Pseudonyms of the 1980s and 1990s

1. AMG (Jason Lewis)
2. Babyface (Kenny Edmonds)
3. Pat Benatar (Pat Andrejewski)
4. Big Daddy Kane (Antonio Hardy)
5. Boy George (George Alan O'Dowd)

6. Chuck D (Carlton Douglas Ridenhour)
7. Elvis Costello (Declan McManus)
8. DJ Quik (David Blake)
9. D.M.C. (Darryl McDaniels)
10. Dr. Dre (Andre Young)
11. Dres and Mista Lawnge of Black Sheep (Andres Titus and William McLean)
12. Sheila E. (Sheila Escovedo)
13. The Edge (David Evans)
14. Flavor Flav (William Drayton)
15. Flea (Michael Balzary)
16. John Foxx of Ultravox (Dennis Leigh)
17. Fresh Prince (Will Smith)
18. Hammer (Stanley Kirk Burrell)*
19. Heavy D. (Dwight Myers)
20. Ice Cube (O'Shea Jackson)
21. Ice-T (Tracy Marrow)
22. Jimmy Jam (James Harris III)
23. Jam Master Jay (Jason Mizell)
24. Jon Bon Jovi (John Bongiovi)
25. Kid Creole (August Darnell)
26. Kool Moe Dee (Mohandas Dewese)
27. KRS-One (Laurence Krisna Parker)
28. Huey Lewis (Hugh Cregg)
29. L.L. Cool J (James Todd Smith)
30. Ed Lover (Ed Roberts)
31. Madonna (Madonna Louise Veronica Ciccone)
32. Biz Markie (Marcell Hall)
33. George Michael (Georgious Panayatiou)
34. Gary Numan (Gary Anthony James Webb)
35. Ozzy Osbourne (John Osbourne)
36. Posdnous (Kelvin Mercer)
37. Prince (Prince Rogers Nelson)
38. Prince Be and DJ Minutemix of PM Dawn (Attrett and Jarrett Cordes)
39. Prince Paul (Paul E. Huston)
40. Queen Latifah (Dana Owens)
41. Q-Tip (Jonathan Davis)
42. Rakim (William Griffin)
43. Roxanne Shanté (Lolita Shanté Gooden)
44. Axl Rose (William Bailey)
45. Run (Joe Simmons)
46. Salt-N-Pepa (Cheryl James and Sandy Denton)
47. Shakin' Stevens (Michael Barratt)
48. Slash (Saul Hudson)
49. Slick Rick (Ricky Walters)
50. Snoop Doggy Dogg (Calvin Broadus)

51. Spinderella (Dee Dee Roper)
52. Sting (Gordon Sumner)
53. Izzy Stradlin (Jeffrey Isabelle)
54. Suggs, the frontman for Madness (Graham McPherson)
55. Treach (Anthony Criss)
56. Trugoy the Dove (David Jolicoeur)
57. Vanilla Ice (Robert Van Winkle)
58. Bono Vox (Paul Hewson)
59. Kim Wilde (Kim Smith)
60. Yo Yo (Yolanda Whitaker)

---

* Previously known as M. C. Hammer

Rappers Who Use Their Given Names

1. Erick Sermon
2. Parrish Smith
3. Keith Murray
4. Justin Warfield
5. Ali Shaheed Muhammad
6. Kenny Parker

The Ramones' Real Names

1. Jeffrey Hyman (Joey Ramone)
2. Thomas Erdelyi (Tommy Ramone)[1]
3. Douglas Coldin (Dee Dee Ramone)[1]
4. Mark Bell (Marky Ramone)
5. John Cummings (Johnny Ramone)
6. Richard Beau (Ricky Ramone)[1]
7. Christopher Joseph Ward (CJ Ramone)

---

[1] Retired.

The Real Names of the Original Kiss Lineup

1. Peter Crisscola (Peter Criss)
2. Paul Frehley (Ace Frehley)
3. Gene Klein (Gene Simmons)
4. Stanley Eisen (Paul Stanley)

The Real Names of Digital Underground[1]

1. Greg Jacobs (Shock G)
2. Ron Brooks (Money B)
3. Ramone Valentine (Pee Wee)
4. Edward Earl Cook (Schmoovy Schmoov)
5. Odis Valentine (Big Money Odis)
6. Tupac Shakur (2Pac)
7. David Elliot (DJ Fuze)
8. Jimi Dright (Chopmaster J)

---

[1] Beware: Lineup changes constantly.

Great Nicknames

1. Bad Boy (Clarence Palmer)
2. The Big Man (Clarence Clemons)
3. The Big O (Roy Orbison)
4. Bonzo (John Bonham)
5. The Boss (Bruce Springsteen)
6. The Clown Prince of Rap (Biz Markie)
7. The Duke of Earl (Gene Chandler)
8. Mr. Excitement (Jackie Wilson)
9. The Fab Four (The Beatles)
10. The Fat Man (Fats Domino)
11. The Genius (Ray Charles)
12. The Glimmer Twins (Mick Jagger and Keith Richards)
13. The Gloved One (Michael Jackson)
14. The Godfather of Grunge (Neil Young)
15. The Godfather of Punk (Lou Reed)
16. The Godfather of Soul (James Brown)
17. The Hawk (Ronnie Hawkins)
18. His Royal Badness (Prince)
19. The Ice Man (Jerry Butler)
20. The Killer (Jerry Lee Lewis)
21. The King (Elvis Presley)
22. The King of Pop (Michael Jackson)[1]
23. The King of Rock (DMC)
24. The King of Soul (Otis Redding, James Brown)
25. The Kings from Queens (Run-D.M.C.)
26. Little Miss Sharecropper (LaVern Baker)
27. Lizard King (Jim Morrison)
28. Material Girl (Madonna)

29. The Mats (the Replacements)
30. The Motor City Madman (Ted Nugent)
31. Mr. Blues (Wynonie Harris)
32. Mr. Personality (Lloyd Price)
33. Mr. Soul (Sam Cooke)
34. The Nurk Twins (John Lennon and Paul McCartney)
35. The Only Band that Matters (the Clash)
36. The Overweight Lover (Heavy D)
37. Pearl (Janis Joplin)
38. Pigpen (Ron McKernan)
39. Plonk (Ronnie Lane)
40. The Prince of Wails (Johnnie Ray)
41. The Queen of Disco (Donna Summer)
42. The Queen of Soul (Aretha Franklin, also Carla Thomas)
43. The Red Rocker (Sammy Hagar)
44. The Ruler (Slick Rick)
45. Slowhand (Eric Clapton)
46. Soul Brother Number One, Mr. Dynamite, the Hardest-Working Man in Show Business (James Brown, who else?)
47. The Teacher (KRS-One)
48. Towser (Pete Townshend)
49. The Toxic Twins (Joe Perry and Steven Tyler)
50. The Wicked Pickett (Wilson Pickett)

---

[1] Actually, the greatest thing about this nickname is that Michael himself successfully wheedled everyone into bestowing this accolade on him.

Pseudonyms, Titles, Alter Egos, and Fictive Personae for George Clinton

1. Dr. Funkenstein
2. Starchild
3. Supreme Maggot Overlord
4. Uncle Jam
5. Mr. Wiggles
6. Ultimate Liberator of Constipated Notions
7. Dome-headed Interstellar Cosmic Funkfather
8. The Nasty & Complete Minister of All Funkadelia

The Best Punk Names (of Individuals—Bands Too Numerous to Mention)

1. Stiv Bators (The Dead Boys)
2. Laura Logic (Essential Logic)
3. Tory Crimes (The Clash)
4. Siouxsie Sioux
5. Lux Interior (The Cramps)
6. Johnny Rotten (The Sex Pistols)
7. Rat Scabies (The Damned)
8. Joe Strummer (The Clash)
9. Dr. Know (Bad Brains)
10. Poly-Styrene (X-Ray Spex)
11. Ari Up (The Slits)
12. Sid Vicious (The Sex Pistols)
13. Johnny Gestapo (Murphy's Law)
14. Billy Zoom (X)
15. Rockets Red Glare (Sex Pistol friend and Jarmusch-directed actor)
16. DJ Bonebrake (X)
17. Lisa Suckdog (Roller Derby)
18. Flea (Red Hot Chili Peppers)
19. Butterfly Fairweather (The Dead Milkmen)
20. Pat Smear (The Germs)

Real Guitar Men

1. Mickey "Guitar" Baker
2. Guitar Crusher
3. Jorgen "Mr. Guitar" Ingmann
4. Guitar Nubbitt
5. Guitar Slim
6. Johnny "Guitar" Watson

A Dozen Cool Rock and Roll Johnnys

1. Johnny B. Goode
2. Johnny Too Bad
3. Johnny Rotten
4. Johnny Angel

5. Johnny Burnette
6. Johnny and the Moondogs
7. Johnny Ramone
8. Johnny Melody
9. Johnny and the Hurricanes

10. Johnny Thunder(s)
11. Johnny Kidd
12. Johnny Cash/Johnny Paycheck

This list was compiled by Andy Edelstein of Relix *magazine.*

Want Your Body?

1. "Ashtray Heart," Captain Beefheart
2. "Atak of Da Bal-Hedz," Onyx
3. "Baby Got Back," Sir Mix-A-Lot
4. "Babyface," U2
5. "Back in My Arms Again," The Supremes
6. "Back to My Roots," RuPaul
7. "Barefootin'," Robert Parker
8. "Big Booty," Ultramagnetic MCs
9. "Big Butt," Bobby Jimmy and the Critters
10. "Big Leg Emma," Frank Zappa
11. "Big Ole Butt," L.L. Cool J
12. "Blac Vagina Finda," Onyx
13. "Black Hand Side," Queen Latifah
14. "Boobs a Lot," The Holy Modal Rounders
15. "Brown-Eyed Girl," Van Morrison
16. "Butt Naked Booty Bless," Poor Righteous Teachers
17. "Eatin' Pussy," Pooh-Man
18. "Ebony Eyes," Stevie Wonder
19. "Eyes," Michael Hurley
20. "Faraway Eyes," The Rolling Stones
21. "Fingertips—Pt. 2," Stevie Wonder
22. "Greasy Heart," Jefferson Airplane
23. "Green Eyed Lady," Sugarloaf
24. "Hair," The Cowsills
25. "Hand of Fate," The Rolling Stones
26. "Hand to Mouth," George Michael
27. "Heart," Pet Shop Boys
28. "Hearts of Stone," Otis Williams and the Charms
29. "Hot Head," Captain Beefheart
30. "I Want to Hold Your Hand," The Beatles
31. "Insane in the Brain," Cypress Hill
32. "Jimmy," Boogie Down Productions
33. "King of Hands," Argent
34. "Knee Deep," Funkadelic
35. "Lord of the Thighs," Aerosmith

36. "Maggot Brain," Funkadelic
37. "Mo' Pussy," DJ Quik
38. "Mr. Moustache," Nirvana
39. "Mystic Eyes," Them
40. "Noises for the Leg," The Bonzo Dog Band
41. "Penis Dimension," The Mothers of Invention with the Royal Philharmonic Orchestra
42. "Pretty Little Angel Eyes," Curtis Lee
43. "Rumpshaker," Wreckx-N-Effect
44. "Shorty Gotta Fat Ass," Fat Joe
45. "Smash Your Head Against the Wall," John Entwistle
46. "Stink-Foot," Frank Zappa
47. "Stone Cold Bush," Red Hot Chili Peppers
48. "This Old Heart of Mine," The Isley Brothers
49. "Wounded Knee," Primus
50. "Your Feets Too Big," The Beatles

Your Highness . . .

1. Arabian Prince
2. Elvin Bishop
3. Joe "King" Carrasco
4. The Del-Lords
5. Duke and the Drivers
6. The Earls
7. The "5" Royales
8. Fresh Prince
9. Funky Kings
10. The Gentrys
11. Shirley Gunther and the Queens
12. Iron Maiden
13. The Jacks
14. Kingdom Come
15. Albert King
16. B. B. King
17. Ben E. King
18. Carole King
19. Earl King
20. Eddie King and Roomful of Blues
21. Freddie King
22. King Adrock
23. King Crimson
24. King Curtis
25. King Floyd
26. King Harvest
27. King Missle
28. King Pins
29. King Solomon
30. King Sun
31. King Sunny Ade
32. King Tech
33. King Tee
34. King's X
35. Kingfish
36. The Kingsmen
37. Gladys Knight and the Pips
38. Noble Knights
39. Lord Finesse
40. Lord Jamar
41. Mark the 45 King
42. Brian McKnight
43. Nefertiti
44. The Nobles
45. Prince
46. Prince Akeem
47. Prince Buster
48. Prince Markie Dee
49. Prince Paul
50. Prince Poetry

51. Queen
52. Queen Latifah
53. Queensryche
54. Redhead Kingpin
55. Royal Crescent Mob
56. The Royal Teens
57. The Royaltones
58. Sam the Sham and the Pharaohs
59. Screaming Lord Sutch
60. The Shadows of Knight
61. The Sir Douglas Quintet
62. Sir Jinx
63. Sir Mix-a-Lot
64. The Sultan of Hip-Hop
65. Teen Queens

Hungry?

1. The Sugarcubes
2. Smashing Pumpkins
3. The Juice Crew
4. Wild Cherry
5. The Cucumbers
6. Salt 'N Pepa
7. Kid Creole and the Coconuts
8. T-Bone Burnett
9. Vanilla Fudge
10. Hot Chocolate
11. Moby Grape
12. Jelly
13. Humble Pie
14. Sugar
15. Tangerine Dream
16. Prefab Sprout
17. The Equals
18. Eddie Rabbit
19. Cracker
20. Meat Loaf
21. Blue Oyster Cult
22. MC Peaches
23. Trugoy (of De La Soul; read it backward, dummy)
24. Red Hot Chili Peppers
25. Mark Chesnutt

NO THANKS, NOT HUNGRY
1. Anthrax
2. Fine Young Cannibals
4. Slaughter
5. Boomtown Rats

. . . AND NOW SERVING
1. The Waitresses
2. The Busboys
3. Sam Cooke
4. The Platters

Is There a Doctor in da House?

1. Dr. William Abruzzi, the doctor at Woodstock
2. "Doc" Berger, of Southside Johnny and the Asbury Jukes
3. Dr. Dre
4. Doctor Dre
5. Dr. Demento, disc jockey
6. Doctor Ice (of UTFO)

7. Dr. Feelgood
8. The Four Interns, gospel quartet
9. Dr. Hook and the Medicine Show
10. Dr. John the Night Tripper
11. Doc Pomus, songwriter
12. Dr. Robert, of the Beatles song
13. Dr. Love, of the Kiss song
14. Dr. Ross, blues singer
15. Dr. West's Medicine Show and Junk Band
16. The Force MD's

Katherine Turman Picks the 10 Most Innovative Band Names

1. Moby Grape
2. 7 Year Bitch
3. Severed Head in a Bag
4. Roger Roid and the Whirling Butt Cherries
5. Raging Slab
6. The Voluptuous Horror of Karen Black
7. Armageddon Dildos
8. Sandy Duncan's Eye
9. Jodie Foster's Army
10. Revolting Cocks

Honorable mention: Eve's Plum

Katherine Turman is the senior editor of RIP *magazine.*

The 50 Best Group Names

1. Niggas with Attitudes (N.W.A)
2. The Rolling Stones
3. Public Enemy
4. Funkadelic
5. U2
6. The Who
7. Guns N' Roses
8. The Geto Boys
9. AC/DC
10. Earth, Wind and Fire
11. Boo-Yaa TRIBE
12. The Grateful Dead
13. Arrested Development
14. The Miracles
15. Led Zeppelin
16. Dire Straits
17. Living Colour
18. The Band
19. The Temptations
20. A Tribe Called Quest
21. Them
22. Talking Heads
23. The Clash

24. R.E.M.
25. Nirvana
26. The Gang of Four
27. De La Soul
28. The Smithereens
29. The Velvet Underground
30. Soul Asylum
31. The Stooges
32. The Famous Flames
33. The Pretenders
34. Fugazi
35. Fishbone
36. The Fugs
37. The Mothers of Invention
38. Da Lench Mob
39. Fine Young Cannibals
40. The Beatles
41. The Crickets
42. The Yardbirds
43. Digital Underground
44. War
45. Urban Dance Squad
46. The Police
47. The Rascals
48. Megadeth
49. L7
50. Johnny and the Hurricanes

The 40 Worst Group Names

1. Was (Not Was)
2. It's a Beautiful Day
3. Wham!
4. New Kids on the Block
5. Edie Brickell and New Bohemians
6. Porno for Pyros
7. Disposable Heroes of Hiphoprisy
8. Boffalongo
9. Oingo Boingo
10. Toad the Wet Sprocket
11. The Slits
12. Vanilla Fudge
13. The Hooters
14. Def Leppard
15. Bananarama
16. Ultimate Spinach
17. The Pork Dukes
18. Wiggy Bits
19. Jo Mama
20. Jethro Tull
21. The Jungle Brothers
22. Styx
23. Journey
24. Moby Grape
25. Mashmakhan
26. Klaatu
27. Funkdoobiest
28. Air Supply
29. Tony Toni Toné
30. Thin Lizzy
31. Strawberry Alarm Clock
32. Digable Planets
33. Supertramp
34. New York Rock and Roll Ensemble
35. Brand New Heavies
36. 10,000 Maniacs
37. Lynyrd Skynyrd
38. Eurythmics
39. Divinyls
40. En Vogue

Real Dog Acts

1. Bonzo Dog (Doo Dah) Band
2. Bow Wow Wow
3. Bulldog
4. The Dingoes
5. Ed O.G. & the B.U.L.L.D.O.G.S.
6. The Fabulous Poodles
7. Hot Dog
8. Hound Dog Taylor and the House Rockers
9. The Hounds
10. John "Mutt" Lange
11. The Laughing Dogs
12. Pavlov's Dog
13. Phife Dog
14. The Pointer Sisters
15. Ray Dog
16. Sen Dog
17. Snoop Doggy Dogg
18. The Spaniels
19. Spot 1019
20. Swamp Dog
21. Three Dog Night
22. Tim Dog

Bands Named After Songs

1. Jo Jo Gunne, after a song written by Chuck Berry
2. Follow 4 Now, after Chuck D's lyrics in Public Enemy's "Bring the Noise"
3. The Stone Poneys, from Charley Patton's "Stone Poney Blues"
4. The McCoys, from the Ventures' instrumental, "McCoy"
5. The Lovin' Spoonful, from the lyrics of Mississippi John Hurt's "Coffee Blues"
6. The Skyliners, from the Charlie Barnett song
7. The Pretty Things, from the Bo Diddley song, which they perform on their first LP
8. The Rolling Stones, after Muddy Waters's great blues song
9. Deep Purple, from the classic Bing Crosby song
10. The Cocteau Twins, from a Simple Minds song
11. Shakin' Street, from the MC5 song
12. Raw Power, from the Stooges album of the same name
13. Sister Ray, from the Velvet Underground's "Sister Ray"
14. Kiss the Sky, from Jimi Hendrix's "Purple Haze"
15. Wednesday Week, from the Elvis Costello B-side

Bands Named After Places

1. Alabama
2. America
3. Asia
4. The Atlanta Rhythm Section
5. Atlantis

12. Booker T. and the MGs
13. Thin Lizzy

Oh, Jesus

1. Jesus Jones
2. Jesus Lizard
3. Liquid Jesus
4. MC 900 Ft. Jesus
5. Jesus and Mary Chain
6. Teenage Jesus and the Jerks
7. New Christs
8. Screaming Blue Messiahs

Long Dongs

1. The Buzzcocks
2. The Sex Pistols
3. 10cc
4. The Tubes
5. The Vibrators
6. Steely Dan
7. Whitesnake
8. The Cucumbers
9. Love Tractor
10. Revolting Cocks
11. Big Richard
12. Enormous Richard
13. Tower of Power
14. Helmet
15. Meatloaf
16. Wet Willie
17. Pole
18. Tool
19. Stick
20. Prong
21. King Missile

Freud Was Wrong
Bands with No Penis Envy

1. Snatch
2. Hole
3. Pussy Galore
4. Vertical Slits
5. Slits
6. L'Trimm

The Song Remains the Same
20 Songs Whose Titles Don't Appear in Their Lyrics (Compiled by Steve Propes)

1. "THE BALLAD OF JOHN AND YOKO," THE BEATLES —A/K/A "Christ you know it ain't easy"

2. "THE CHIPMUNK SONG," THE CHIPMUNKS—A/K/A "Alvin!"

3. "THE CHRISTMAS SONG," NAT "KING" COLE—A/K/A "Chestnuts roasting on an open fire"

4. "COME SOFTLY TO ME," THE FLEETWOODS—They do sing "Come softly" but that phrase by itself was considered too risqué

5. "EBB TIDE," ROY HAMILTON

6. "EL WATUSI," RAY BARRETTO

7. "FINGERTIPS," LITTLE STEVIE WONDER—A/K/A "Everybody say *yeah!*"

8. "FOR WHAT IT'S WORTH," BUFFALO SPRINGFIELD—A/K/A "Somethin's happenin' here . . ."

9. "GIMME LITTLE SIGN," BRENTON WOOD—Wood actually sings "Gimme some kinda sign"

10. "LAND OF 1000 DANCES," CHRIS KENNER—Doesn't appear in the versions by Cannibal and the Headhunters, Wilson Pickett, and Patti Smith, either

11. "MORSE CODE OF LOVE," THE CAPRIS—A/K/A "Baby come back to me," which is what Manhattan Transfer called their later version, which charted (while the original did not), so maybe it helped

12. "MULESKINNER BLUES," THE FENDERMEN—A/K/A "A-ha,ha,ha,ha,ha,ha"

13. "MY GIRL SLOOPY," THE VIBRATIONS—More accurately titled "Hang on Sloopy" when re-recorded by the McCoys

14. "MY TRUE STORY," THE JIVE FIVE—A/K/A "Cry, cry, cry"

15. "PSYCHO," BOBBY HENDRICKS

16. "RAINY DAY WOMEN #12 AND 35," BOB DYLAN—A/K/A "Everybody must get stoned"

17. "SUNSHINE SUPERMAN," DONOVAN

18. "UNCHAINED MELODY," ANY KNOWN VERSION FROM THE RIGHTEOUS BROTHERS TO ROY HAMILTON—The song came from the movie *Unchained*, about the minimum-security prison at Chino, California, where the prisoners never wore chains

19. "WILLIE AND THE HAND JIVE," JOHNNY OTIS—A/K/A "Doin' that crazy hand jive"

20. "WOO WOO TRAIN," THE VALENTINES

Steve Propes, the most famous disc jockey, record collector, and author in Long Beach, California, serves as this book's resident doo-wop and oldies freak.

The All-Time Best Album Titles

1. *AmeriKKKa's Most Wanted*, Ice Cube
2. *Bringing It All Back Home*, Bob Dylan
3. *Exile on Main Street*, The Rolling Stones
4. *Appetite for Destruction*, Guns N' Roses
5. *Darkness on the Edge of Town*, Bruce Springsteen
6. *Back in Black*, AC/DC
7. *Standing on the Verge of Getting It On*, Funkadelic
8. *The Young Mod's Forgotten Story*, The Impressions
9. *Licensed to Ill*, The Beastie Boys
10. *Rubber Soul*, The Beatles
11. *Guitar Town*, Steve Earle
12. *The Otis Redding Dictionary of Soul*
13. *Glamorous Results of a Misspent Youth*, Joan Jett
14. *Are You Experienced?* The Jimi Hendrix Experience
15. *It Takes a Nation of Millions to Hold Us Back*, Public Enemy
16. *Guerillas in the Mist*, Da Lench Mob
17. *A Whole New Thing*, Sly and the Family Stone
18. *Over Under Sideways Down*, The Yardbirds
19. *Too Much Too Soon*, The New York Dolls
20. *Shoot Out the Lights*, Richard and Linda Thompson
21. *Promised Land*, Elvis Presley
22. *Pretzel Logic*, Steely Dan
23. *Vs*, Pearl Jam
24. *Thriller*, Michael Jackson

The All-Time Worst Album Titles

1. *Aoxmoxoa*, The Grateful Dead
2. *Chicago XIV*
3. *A Salt with a Deadly Pepa*, Salt 'N Pepa
4. *Sloppy Seconds*, Dr. Hook and the Medicine Show
5. *Q: Are We Not Men? A: We Are Devo*
6. *3 Years 5 Months & 2 Days in the Life of . . .* , Arrested Development
7. *The Hissing of Summer Lawns*, Joni Mitchell
8. *Trombulation*, Parliament
9. *Neither Fish nor Flesh*, Terence Trent D'Arby
10. *Sir Army Suit*, Klaatu
11. *The Bliss Album*, PM Dawn
12. *Fulfillingness' First Finale*, Stevie Wonder
13. *The Raw and the Cooked*, Fine Young Cannibals
14. *A Gift from a Flower to a Garden*, Donovan

15. *Which Doobie U Be?* Funkdoobiest
16. *Tormato*, Yes
17. *Buddah and the Chocolate Box*, Cat Stevens
18. *Zenyatta Mondatta*, The Police
19. *Lovesexy*, Prince and the Revolution
20. *The Chronic*, Dr. Dre

Simon Sez . . .

1. "Stomp," The Brothers Johnson
2. "Shout," Joey Dee and the Starlighters
3. "Jump," Van Halen
4. "Sing," The Carpenters
5. "Be," Neil Diamond
6. "Jump," Kris Kross
7. "Stomp," K-Yze
8. "Chill," EPMD
9. "Flex," Mad Cobra
10. "Gett Off," Prince
11. "Push It," Salt 'N Pepa
12. "Wake Up," Brand Nubian
13. "Think," The "5" Royales (and Aretha Franklin and James Brown)
14. "Criticize," Alexander O'Neal
15. "May I," Maurice Williams & the Zodiacs

!!

1. "Betcha By Golly Wow," The Stylistics
2. "Great Balls of Fire," Jerry Lee Lewis
3. "Good Golly Miss Molly," Little Richard
4. "Holy Cow," Lee Dorsey
5. "Hot Diggity (Dog Ziggity Boom)," Perry Como
6. "Goody Goody," Frankie Lymon
7. "Goody Goody," 1910 Fruitgum Co.
8. "Zip-A-Dee-Doo-Dah," Bob B. Soxx and the Blue Jeans
9. "Dance, Dance, Dance (Yowsah, Yowsah, Yowsah)," Chic

CHAPTER 27

Sealed with a Kiss

"The Ten Commandments of Love"
The Moonglows, 1958

1. "Thou shall never love another"
2. "Stand by me all the while"
3. "Take happiness with the heartaches"
4. "Go through life wearing a smile"
5. "Thou shall always have faith in me in everything I say and do"
6. "Love me with all your heart and soul until our life on earth is through"
7. "Come to me when I am lonely"
8. "Kiss me when you hold me tight"
9. "Treat me sweet and gentle"
10. . . .[1]

---

[1] There is no tenth commandment of love.

About the Authors

DAVE MARSH started writing rock criticism at *Creem* in 1969, when he was just nineteen years old. He has never had a real job, unless you count working at *Newsday* and *Rolling Stone*. *The New Book of Rock Lists* makes seventeen books he's made dance on the pinhead of popular music.

JAMES BERNARD is a cofounder and editor of *The Source*, the magazine of hip-hop music, culture, and politics.